CONFESSIONS
OF AN
ILLUMINATI

AUTHOR:

❧ LEO LYON ZAGAMI ☙

VOLUME III

CCC PUBLISHING
SAN FRANCISCO, CALIFORNIA

Reviews for

Confessions of an Illuminati (Vol. II):

*The Time of Revelation and Tribulation
Leading up to 2020*

The agenda for a New World Order is real and it includes a plan to implement a World War III scenario by 2020, according to former Illuminati member Leo Lyon Zagami in volume two of his Confessions series. Zagami has a pedigree with roots in Italian/Sicilian nobility with Freemasonic heritage as well as in Scottish nobility, again with Freemasonic links (Lyon is his middle name). His bloodline and high-level Freemasonic initiation created unusual connections, but his "seeing the light" and "spilling the beans" landed him in prison. Undeterred, he continues to expose undercurrents at play in many countries.

Zagami delves deeply into the occult machinations and control mechanisms behind the NWO power play, exposing how Freemasonry and secret societies everywhere are being infiltrated by Satanists. He reveals that the major forces working towards a world government are Jesuits in cahoots with Zionists. But the other key hand, he says, is China with its own brand of Freemasonry operating behind the scenes. Zagami tells the ongoing story of the Dragon Family and some mysterious, confiscated bonds, among many extraordinary tales and historical details that are not for the faint-hearted.

For anyone caught up in this shady network, Zagami has tips on psychic defense. His book names names and uncovers a disturbing world that's far removed from the masses.

–Nexus

As a former 33rd degree member of the Freemasons, ranking member of the P2 lodge and born from a lineage of aristocratic Illuminati blood, Illuminati defector Leo Zagami has an acute knowledge of the powerful network consisting nefarious new world order elite and exactly what their future plans entail.

After years of grooming by the powers that be, in 2006 Leo dissolved many of his alliances and started exposing freemason beliefs, members of the elite societies and their agendas. Leo Zagami offers authentic insights into the 2016 new world order agenda and what we can expect in years to come.We know that only a privileged, nefarious few truly make the big decisions of the world. Referred to as the *Illuminati* or the *New World Order,* they are a powerful network made up of royal bloodlines, secret societies, occult orders, shady banksters, and corporate oligarchs.

–Higher Side Chats

Reviews for

Confessions of an Illuminati (Vol. I):

The Whole Truth About the Illuminati and the New World Order

Author Leo Lyon Zagami uses the Illuminati's internal documents and reveals confidential and top-secret events. His book contends that the presence of numerous Illuminati brotherhoods and secret societies - just as those inside the most prestigious U.S. universities such as Yale or Harvard – have always been guides to the occult. From the Ordo Templi Orientis (OTO)'s infiltration of Freemasonry to the real Priory of Sion, this book exposes the hidden structure of the New World Order and the occult practices of the various groups involved with it, including their connections to the intelligence community and the infamous Ur-Lodges.

Critique: A scattering of black-and-white photographs illustrates this astonishing glimpse into the power structures and occult practices of notorious secret societies, including their connections to metaphysical pioneer Aleister Crowley, hostile extraterrestrial lifeforms, the intelligence community, and more. But how can ordinary people take a stand against vested interests of money and power? Knowledge is the first step, and even the most skeptical browser will find Confessions of an Illuminati modus operandi expose enlightening!

–Midwest Book Review

Leo Lyon Zagami is an ex-member of the Comitato Esecutivo Massonico – Masonic Executive Committee (MEC) of Monte Carlo. He was, until recently, a high level member of the Italian Illuminati, a 33rd degree freemason, a true insider and a high-member of the infamous Freemasonic P2 Lodge. He was the "prince," prepared to take over after the older Illuminati "king," Licio Gelli. He is of Illuminati aristocrat bloodline and therefore involved in the Illuminati Order since childhood.

However, Leo decided he'd had enough of all the evil he was exposed to, and a part of, and the horrifying Satanic, black magic rituals, mind control and torture that was going on inside the lodges, behind closed doors. So he left everything and fled to Norway. Since he left, he's been harassed and tortured and had his life threatened. He realized that the only way to hopefully stay alive is to expose to the world what he knows and make himself known. History shows that this is one of the best ways to survive, although nothing is for certain. Leo started a website, *Illuminati Confessions,* where he reveals the secrets to the world, one by one.

–Yoga Esoteric

Leo Lyon Zagami

Confessions
of an
Illuminati
Vol. III

Espionage, Templars and Satanism in the Shadows of the Vatican

Consortium of Collective Consciousness Publishing
CCCPublishing.com

Confessions of an Illuminati, Volume III:

Espionage, Templars and Satanism in the Shadows of the Vatican

1st edition

Copyright © 2017 by Leo Lyon Zagami
Published by the Consortium of Collective Consciousness Publishing™

As is common in a historic and reference book such as this, much of the information included on these pages has been collected from diverse sources. When possible, the information has been checked and double-checked. Almost every topic has at least three data points, that is, three different sources that report the same information. Even with special effort to be accurate and thorough, the author and publisher cannot vouch for each and every reference. The author and publisher assume no responsibility or liability for any outcome, loss, arrest, or injury that occurs as a result of information or advice contained in this book. As with the purchase of goods or services, caveat emptor is the prevailing responsibility of the purchaser, and the same is true for the student of the esoteric.

Library of Congress Cataloging-in-Publication Data:

Zagami, Leo Lyon
      CONFESSIONS OF AN ILLUMINATI, VOL. 3 / Leo Lyon Zagami
      p. cm.
            print ISBN 13: 978-1888729665 (Pbk.)
            ePub ISBN 13: 978-1888729689 (epub)
            MobiPocket ISBN 13: 978-1888729696 (kindle)
            PDF ISBN 13: 978-1888729672 (pdf)

1. Religion & Spirituality. 2. Other Religions, Practices & Sacred Texts. 3. Freemasonry. I. Title
      Library of Congress Catalog Card Number: 2015930357

Printed in the United States of America.

10 9 8 7 6 5 4 3 2 1

Then the woman said to Elijah, "Now I know that you are a man of God and that the word of the Lord from your mouth is the truth."

(1 Kings 17:24)

And behold, I come quickly. Blessed is he that keepeth the words of the prophecy of this book.

(Revelation 22:7)

FIG. 1 – Masonic Tracing Board for the 3rd degree of Freemasonry (Master Mason) created by Lady Frieda Harris (1877 – 1962), artist and illustrator, known for designing The Tarot of Aleister Crowley.

About the Author

Supported by a creative environment from an early age, Leo Lyon Zagami's devotion to the study and research of esoteric, historical, and philosophical subjects has yielded his unique perspective. This ran parallel to his passion for music, which led him to collaborate with radio and television stations around the world. Since 2006, Leo began circulating, first-hand, information regarding his direct involvement with the New World Order and various secret societies connected to it; often referred to as the Illuminati. From 2009 to 2013 he authored six books published in Japan, all of which were bestsellers in their genre; and together selling over seventy thousand books. From 2012 to 2015, Leo published seven books in Italy with great results— results that have made him a household name in his native country.

Dedicated to the members of the Ordo Illuminatorum Universalis *and the Brothers of my Lodge. We are sowing the seeds for a harvest that will be enjoyed by future generations.*

Translation: Leo Zagami, Jennifer Fahey
Adaption: Christy Zagami
Editing: Christy Zagami, Brad Olsen
Cover and Book Design: Mark J. Maxam

CONTENTS:

8 . . . . About the Author
13 . . . . . . Introduction by the Author

Chapter I: In Search of the Perfect Knighthood

29 . . . . . . Awaiting a Holy Empire
35 . . . . . . From Ancient Egypt to the Strict Observance
41 . . . . . . The Rite of Strict Observance vs. the rest of Freemasonry in
         the hands of Islam
48 . . . . . . The threat of a pro-Islamist New World Order
52 . . . . . . The False Prophets of "the Noble Sanctuary" and Ataturk
59 . . . . . . The Goddess
68 . . . . . . The Templars, the Holy House and the Japanese Princess
78 . . . . . . Is Oblast the "New Israel?"
82 . . . . . . Palaprat Johannite Foundations
85 . . . . . . Loreto's Holy House
89 . . . . . . The dispute in the Neo-Templar world after the appearance of
         a mysterious parchment

Chapter II: The Holy Grail

96 . . . . . . The Seborga Files
100 . . . . . The Holy Grail revealed
103 . . . . . *In memory* of Rocco Zingaro: A Templar in possession of
         the Holy Grail
112 . . . . . Padre Pio and the Holy Grail
116 . . . . My experience with the Holy Grail
118 . . . . . The Spiritual Alchemy of the Knights Templar
122 . . . . . The Threicia
125 . . . . . Loreto and Medjugorje ... awaiting the Antichrist

Chapter III: Blood Lineages and Gnosticism
130..... The DNA of the Illuminati
141..... Initiates on the dark side of the force
149..... The Neo-Templars and the Gnostic Church with a Jesuit flavor
160..... Richard, Duc de Palatine and the Pansophic Rite
163..... The Tau, the Gnostic Church and the Patriarchate of Antioch
172..... The Jesuits, the Rosicrucians and the Catholic Origins
         of "Scottish Freemasonry"
177..... Dom Martinez De Pasqually, the mysterious Illuminati ...
181..... Papus and the Orders & Societies of the Theosophical Society

**Chapter IV: The Magical World of the Illuminati: from Abramelin
  to Wicca**
184..... The magic of Abramelin
195..... Jung and Sacred Magic
202..... Jung and Mind Control
205..... Jung and the wife of Tutankhamun
210..... Pazuzu
212..... Domizio, Monte Carlo, and the Grand Lodge
213..... Franz Bardon, the 99 lodges, and Adolf Hitler
218..... Wicca Witchcraft: another creation of the Illuminati

**Chapter V: Espionage, Freemasonry and Satanism in
  the Vatican**
227..... Father Malachi Martin, a Jesuit who served the Mossad
230..... In Defense of Father Malachi Martin by William H. Kennedy
233..... The secret mission entrusted by Padre Pio to
         the heroic Don Villa
237..... The Vatican and Masonry: a ballad of hypocrisy
239..... The "Post-Conciliar Church" and Rock Music in the Illuminati
242..... Satanism in the Vatican: not a hypothesis but a certainty!
247..... From Rome to the Boston "Spotlight"
250..... The world of spies in the shadow of the Vatican
253..... Graham the Vatican Jesuit Spymaster
255..... A strange encyclopedia of spies
258..... Aldo Conchione, Gabriella Carlizzi, and Satanism of
         the NWO in the Vatican

Chapter VI: Beneath the Vatican the Darkest Secrets are Hidden

264 . . . . . Pope Montini the Freemason
269 . . . . . *The Elixir Vitae*
271 . . . . . Cardinal Siri
274 . . . . . The Vatican Mafia 666: obey or die!
275 . . . . . A brief tale of a Masonic human sacrifice piloted by the Vatican
278 . . . . . The Knights of Colombus, the Knights of Malta, and the Jesuits
285 . . . . . Satan the alien enemy, and the New Age
292 . . . . . UFOs and SciFi: instruments of Illuminati propaganda
293 . . . . . Confessions of a Pilgrim: Paulo Coelho
300 . . . . . From Zecharia Sitchin to Satanism in the Vatican
305 . . . . . This is the End
308 . . . . . Arcanissima
314 . . . . . Explaining the Magical Door
316 . . . . . From Straw Man to the New Cornerstone
321 . . . . . Trilogy Conclusion

Introduction by the Author

I n this project called *Confessions of an Illuminati*, I have carried out a complex and in-depth study, based on my direct experiences, creating in this way a sort of hybrid project. It can serve as a curious reading, but also as a manual and an inspiration, for even deeper future studies for those willing to go further in search of the truth. Moreover, this is an innovative way of showing the true history of the hidden controllers of the NWO. I not only speak about their origins and their past, but demonstrate the direct influence of certain past events, to the present, and what they plan in the future. I call this format **"Conspiracy reality."** It offers readers a much broader knowledge without boring them to death, because it's projected in the here and now, *Hic et Nunc* as stated in Latin. We are now living in a crepuscular time in history, where the publication of the third volume of my *Confessions,* will finally unveil the hidden truth about the Templars and their modern imitators. Over time they have been divided into two factions, a truly enlightened and benevolent one, and an infernal, malevolent, and obscurantist side, that seems to be prevailing today. When we speak of the Templars, the original ones born in the lap of the Catholic Church, we must be careful not to confuse the Order with individual knights. These knights were real monks, who made the three vows of chastity, poverty and obedience. In fact, the much celebrated wealth, power and ambition must be exclusively attributed to the Order, and understood as a super individual body, their motto: *Non nobis Domine, non nobis sed Nomine tuo da Gloriam.* As far as we know, historians have searched the archives of the past, and have not been able to find a single piece of evidence that the Order acted in their own self-interest, rather than for the universal and Catholic defense of Christianity; the safety of roads and traffic to the Holy Land, and the protection of the needy.

It can be said that the Templars were advanced for their time, and as it usually happens in such cases, they became misunderstood, and envied for their work and their perceived mission. This is obviously what we know from the official and "profane" side of history, but of course there is also another side to the story, the occult path of these problematic Knights. I will explain deeper the mysterious teachings and traditions in this volume of the trilogy, and in *The Invisible Master,* that helped the Templars understand the laws that govern the historical cycles of humankind. They understood fully the beginning of the downward slide of the current phase of civilization, what the Hindu tradition defines as the Kali-Yuga, and they dared to challenge and oppose it, or at least attempt to delay the fatal conclusion of this cycle. The occult and underground struggle was titanic, and these monks failed to triumph. But something happened that we can not yet fully understand, that stopped this wonderful project that the Templars had in part begun to realize. Perhaps a most dazzling revelation informed them that certain laws, although cruel and absurd, are present for the final Well of Cosmic manifestation, of which man is part of the same symbol. Yet, at the same time, when they were invited to submit to the Church, and obey the Pope, they refused.

Many centuries later, a similar episode would take place with the Jesuits, after the *Dominus ac Redemptor,* the apostolic Letter of Pope Clement XIV, that suppressed the Society (or Company) of Jesus, until the papal bull *Sollecitudo omnium ecclesiarum* on August 7, 1814. They were admitted back into the Vatican by Pius VII, and in 2013, they were even able to place one of them on the papal throne for the first time in history with Pope Francis. This situation makes me think of the *Götterdämmerung,* which concludes the *Tetralogy of Wagner.* The subject of the opera (i.e.: the *Götterdämmerung*), is the Armageddon of the world in Norse mythology, and that is where we are today, mainly because of our parents and of the generations that preceded, since the end of World War II, who lived in the spirit of compromise with this illusory lie. Social tension is increasing more and more each day, and you can clearly notice this since the tragic events of 9/11. These are the signs of a new "strategy of tension," manipulated by the usual architects of control, which for the occasion, create a new "Cold War" with the usual enemy: Russia, the only possible ally in the conflict with so called Islamic "fundamentalism." That is another big farce, packaged by the New World Order, in which Russia is also obviously seeking their role without underselling in any way, their sovereignty or their Christian tradition, something the rest of the world seems to be submitting to, in order to embrace a One World Religion.

Let us remember what the late Count Licio Gelli, former Worshipful Master of the famous Lodge Propaganda 2 said in relation to the "Muslim lands," and their relation to the Knights Templar:

> *"The great strength of the Templars, however, was the ability to dominate the Muslim territories with very few men. Their diplomacy enabled them to rely more on this, or the other Muslim factions, taking advantage of the hatred between the various Islamic sects and the various cities. Promising their protection to a powerful city or a Muslim faction, they had allies at all times and played skillfully on the division of Islam. If Muslims were united, and it is also the history of today, the Templars and the other crusaders would not have resisted for so long in the Holy Land."*

This is what happens in fact even today, where the same technique is applied each day in the Middle East. They lean from one faction to the other, dividing Islam, and manipulating them for the interests of the New World Order. On top of all this, those in the U.S. risk a new confrontation with the Russian Federation, and a possible clash with Christian Orthodoxy, that although fragmented, is attempting to stop this vulgar globalist ideology that is promoted by **George Soros & Co**. After the end of the monstrosity called Communism, Russia seems to be the only true conservative faction that is willing to fight terrorism and Islamic extremism, and defend the values of true Christianity. Liberal atheists have helped to create and promote Communism, and are now sitting at the top of a pyramid that seems more like a "New World Disorder" than a "New World Order." This Communist ideology was secretly promoted by the Jesuits in the 60's and 70's, and they are now the true Masters. To fight such an abomination we would like a "total Revolution," if not by us, at least by those who govern us, but this is still a difficult and dangerous utopian vision to be realized. The great Italian Sardinian initiate Vincenzo Soro, in a curious commentary on the French work of the eighteenth century, entitled *The Great Book of Nature,* spoke of the hidden operators that lie behind the most important revolution, discussed brilliantly by **Gérard Encausse (1865 – 1916) (FIG. 2)**, known also as **Papus**:

> *They were faced with the need of the revolutions in the same spirit of physicians to address the need for a surgical operation. They do not think about the operation itself but of the consequences of the same, of the pain that the patient would suffer, of the weakness that occurs and that we must fight, and so on; and they previously study the consequences and the painfulness, to minimize the loss of blood, and especially to comfort the patient in the most serious hours of the disease, and in the*

FIG. 2 – Papus, aka Gérard Encausse (1865
–1916), a great popularizer of occultism and
founder of the modern Martinist Order, one of
the most important emanations of the Western
Illuminati network.

most dangerous stages of the operation. But it happens very often that
revolutions do not take place as the
initiates would have wanted: and
sometimes its precursors and train-
ers are also the first victims. [1]

In the course of my *Confessions*
series, it has been of fundamental
importance to me, to study the genesis and development of the secret
societies commonly referred to as
the "Illuminati," a term of course
not restricted to the **Order of the Illuminati** of Adam Weishaupt, but
in my view, a description of a much
wider "New Age" network ranging
from Wicca to Thelemic sects, all the
way to the knighthoods of the Vatican, and Occult Freemasonry. In my
research I have found important and
influential groups created by the elite
of the Royal Houses, other times I
have encountered irrelevant groups
playing a very dangerous geopolitical game. Even worse, I have found
sects manipulated by the big shots of
Occult Freemasonry, and the Intelligence services operating in the magical arena, often affecting the world
negatively without the knowledge of
their practitioners. These are groups
such as the *Ordo Templi Orientis* or The Golden Dawn, who often live on the edge of a
parallel magical world, which interferes (not always successfully) with our reality through
their growing contribution in the countries where they operate. For this reason a further
analysis of their structure is not only interesting, but necessary, for those who want to
fully comprehend the true ideologies of the Illuminati that form the astral body of our
society that has been called *Unicuique suum*, a definition by Gérard Encausse. (FIG. 3)

Papus was, as I mentioned earlier, his magical name, chosen to obtain contact with
the gods. He took this name from the *Nuctéméron* of Apollonius from Tiana, a figure
appreciated by various luminaries of the occult world, like Franz Bardon. It was therefore
a name of a *genius*. Genies, or *jinn* as the Romanized Arabic word, comes from a long line
of mythological creatures dating back to 2400 BC. According to the Qur'an, God created
jinn out of the "fire of a scorching wind." Papus is the *genius* of the first hour, an entity
dedicated to medicine and healing. Papus was also a worldly man, taking part in *Le Chat
Noir* (French for "The Black Cat") a nineteenth-century entertainment establishment
on the hill of Montmartre (a club in vogue between the late 1800's and early 1900's), but
spent a lot of his time in libraries to research ancient texts, just as I have done at times.

1   See. Vincenzo Soro, **The Great Book of Nature**, (Rome: Atanor, 1921), footnote 1, p. 13.

FIG. 3 – Above: a Kadosh Knight (30th degree A.A.S.R.) wields the dagger, and vows revenge against the papacy and monarchy for the death of Jacques de Molay, the last Grand Master of the Templars.

This knowledge allowed him to oppose the Eastern tradition being promoted at the time by the Theosophical Society, with an equally strong Western tradition.

In Paris, he surrounded himself with the main esotericists of the time; among those closest to him we find the French magician, the Marquis **Stanislas de Guaita (1861 – 1897)**, a noble of Lombard origin considered by Papus himself to be one of the greatest initiates and Illuminati of his time, who wrote some very interesting things which I will return to shortly. **Sedir** (who worked for the *Bibliothèque Nationale de France*) and **Joséphin Péladan (1858-1918)**, who would leave the group shortly after to create his own group (without success). In 1888, Papus met Pierre-Augustin Chaboseas, who he hoped would transmit to him an initiatic lineage dating back to L. C. de Saint-Martin. This was a "strange" coincidence, or at least a syncronicity, that will give him the power and authority to form a new order (the Martinist Order), and the structure that will be permanently established in 1891, based on that of the already existing *Kabbalistic Order of the Rosicrucians.* He wrote more than 160 books with the name Papus or Gérard Encausse. Papus affirmed the following thought on Secret Societies describing them: *"as a real social astral body"*,[2] a kind of invisible aggregate formed by various egregore that operate through them.

Egregore is an obscure term that I have used a lot in my trilogy, which seems to have originated and developed as a word describing a group thoughtform in the Hermetic Order of the Golden Dawn, and the early works of the Rosicrucians. The first author to adapt such a term in modern language was the French poet Victor Hugo, in his *La Légende des Siècles* ("The Legend of the Ages"), a collection of poems published back in 1859, where he uses the word "égrégore" first as an adjective, then as a noun, while leaving the meaning obscure to his readers. It was Eliphas Levi, pseudonym of **Abbé Constant,**

2   See. Papus (Gerard Encausse*), Martinez Pasqualis,* (Paris: Chamuel, 1895), pp. 108, 109.

a remarkable character of the esoteric and political scene of his era, who promoted this term a decade later, in his book *Le Grand Arcane,* where he identifies "egregore" with the tradition concerning the "Watchers," the fathers of the Nephilim, describing them as *"terrible beings"* that *"will crush us without pity because they are unaware of our existence."*[3] The word "Egregore" derives in fact, from the Greek word *egrégoroi,* meaning "watchers," present in the *Book of Enoch,* a biblical apocrypha where it designates the fallen angels who, for love of the daughters of man, lived on earth, teaching humanity art and science. But in contemporary esoteric phraseology, reminiscent of the work done in the highly influential Hermetic Order of the Golden Dawn, this term indicates a collective psychic entity that is produced both from a ritual or naturally, by any human congress of at least three people together. The *Egregore* characteristic therefore consists not purely of its mathematical sum, but on the sum of its geometrical energies, which is why it manifests itself more strongly through Sacred Geometry, so dear to the Templars.

There are those who are skeptical of this "weird" reality that I am proposing to you through my trilogy, and despite all the evidence and truth which I have brought to you in the first two volumes, there will always be the skeptical person who refuses to accept such truths, because it's easier for the majority of the population to live in illusion and ignorance. I quote in this case a classic episode of the New Testament that involves St. Thomas contained in *John 20, 24-29,* known as "the disbelief of Thomas." Thomas, who doubted the resurrection of Jesus, then came to meet the risen Lord. Addressing him, Jesus says: *"Put your finger here, and see my hands; and put out your hand, and place it in my side; do not be faithless, but believing."* Thomas replied: *"My Lord and my God!"* Jesus said to him: *"Have you believed because you have seen me? Blessed are those who have not seen and yet believe."* To my dear readers, you have learned uncomfortable truths thus far, about the various sects of the New World Order and their intelligence networks, and information denied to you by the powerful elite of this Earth. I present to you this trilogy of truth, through much sacrifice, after years of injustice and oppression, suffered precisely because of my opposition to these injustices, that are part of the system. It's been over 10 years since June of 2006, when I began my open confrontation with the Monte Carlo Lodge of the P2, which pushed me later that year to publish my *Confessions* online, with a small but successful blog. It has been over 15 years since the beginning of my war against the Satanists of the *Ordo Templi Orientis,* and other Crowleyan Illuminati sects. They were important choices in my life, as was joining Freemasonry in 1993, with Prince Gianfranco Alliata di Monreale, aware of what could happen if I went down the **"rabbit hole,"** the popular phrase used in *Alice's Adventures in Wonderland*, that defines a sort of *catabasis*, which literally means "descent into Hades." Freemason and author of several books Gianmichele Galassi writes the following:

> *The theme of the descent into the underworld, or more exactly the catabasis, is certainly not new, there are many examples in various cultures since ancient times. It's sufficent to recall Hercules, Pollux, Orpheus for the Greeks, the Babylonian Inanna, the hero Hittite Kessi, Xolotl in Mexico, the Aeneas of the Latins or Dante in Italian literature. Jesus himself would die and then rise again, so it is clear how the ability to go down to the underworld before returning to that of the living is an expression of an ancestral need of human beings. Of course, the various myths and stories likely to give rise to different interpretations, but at the same time they are always related to an ego-soul transformative cathartic process or the idea of eternal life with the consequent defeat of death.*

3   See. Eliphas Lévi, *Le Grand Arcane* ("The Great Mystery," 1868) pp.127-130, 133, 136.

But as the same Galassi writes in his excellent essay on the subject: "*The concept of death can take on various meanings: the end of it all, as the last act of existence without any possibility of extension, a simple transmutation, through the migration of the soul, until the rebirth to a new life, a spiritual life that lasts for eternity.*"[4]

I open the last volume of my trilogy with Plato's *Allegory of the Cave* and its two interlocutors, Socrates and Glaucon. I would like to present to you the correct interpretation of the most beautiful and famous metaphor in Western philosophy, thanks to my father Dr. Elio Zagami (1939 – 2010).

Elio wrote about it in his unpublished essay entitled *The Experience,* where he states:

> Socrates, after comparing our nature, in regards to education or lack of education, described the following picture of mankind, in Book VII of The Republic,[5] where we find the famous description of Plato's experience, perhaps among the most beautiful pages ever written, undoubtedly among the most cited, although not equally understood. It is a "catabasis" and later a mental "rise," with specific reference to various degrees of initiation.

On the myth of Plato's Cave contained in the work *The Republic,* I will attempt, with my fathers help, a cautious analysis and description in connection with the initiation rites of the time, which have always been the basis of the Western Initiatic Tradition, and in this way I hope to help you, my reader, understand its importance in the eyes of the Illuminati Masters. My father used to tell me that Plato was blamed (by the Sicilian Pythagoreans), for having created such an important allegory and putting it into writing. They were a sort of forerunner to the "mafia" of today, where they obviously wished to control such secret knowledge and monopolize it in order to facilitate their personal goals. They did not agree with Plato showing such truths outside certain initiatic circles in the hands of the elite, blaming him for revealing to the masses the secrets related to the control of the *Matrix,* a bit like Jesus did. Elio writes: "*Recall how Socrates, his teacher, was punished and accused by his opponents of having aroused the youth protest, which his disciple Plato still denied—here we go again, we want to always stay prisoners of the system. The truth scared to the mafia back then as it does today, and Socrates was condemned to die by taking hemlock, do not forget, thus becoming a 'guided suicide.'*" My father Dr. Elio Zagami also wrote:

> It is a descent into hell, which was already made by Ulysses, Aeneas, Jesus, and Dante, made to meet with a thousand possible faces of ourselves. It is the heart of the Platonic esoteric transmission, the place of ideas, the mental point of constant reference of our civilization. It is time then to reinterpret the "Myth" or "Allegory of the Cave" in a modern way for it to be made accessible to all. With an underground dwelling in the shape of the cave, thinking to see men who have been trapped in there since they were children, with chained legs and necks, so as to have them standing only able to see forward, unable, because of the chain, to turn around their neck. Unable to see other levels of existence beyond their own. The man, enslaved, only looking ahead. But in front of him there is usually nothing (only shadows). There will never be a sun shining in the depths of the cave! We have become specialists of the dark. And now we want to go to other planets, systems, galaxies like we are able to move when we cannot truly move ourselves mentally from our present position,

4   Gianmichele Galassi, *V.I.T.R.I.O.L. ed il tema della discesa negli inferi*, brief essay from the site: http://www.riflessioni.it/riflessioni-iniziatiche/VITRIOL.htm Archived 27th of September 2016.
5   Plato, *The Republic, Book VII,* translated by Franco Sartori (Bari-Rome: Laterza, 1973) pp. 237-241.

we want to travel the universe to defeat nature, confusing such things with reality. We are all wannabe Icarius. High and far behind us shines the light of a fire, and between the fire and the prisoners raises a road. Along this road you think you see a low wall built, like the screen that the puppeteers put in front of people to show above them the puppets. And who are the puppet masters of this reality?

If we look at the Platonic metaphor **"we must not overlook anything,"** Dr. Elio Zagami urges us, and he continues his analysis by writing:

Man enslaved, tied, prisoner in the bottom of the cave, is actually us, or at least most of us. So the question arises, 'Who are these puppeteers?' Glaucon replies to the Allegory of the Cave, "I see." At that time this meant hear and see. Imagine seeing men carrying along the low wall objects, all sorts protruding from the edge, statues and other figures of stone and wood, crafted in all sorts of ways; and, as is natural, that some carriers talk, others are silent in the process.

So Plato described to us in his *Allegory of the Cave,* the power, and men of power, who continually stun us with their ideology. Some of these men speak during their work, while others are silent. My father wrote that the silent ones are those who rule the system:

Those are the ones who lead or command humanity (linked at the bottom of the cave) which provide to us a glimpse or "projection" of false things built for us, proposing this as the only possible reality. Even the sun (= fire) in their eyes is constructed for them. Perhaps cousins of Prometheus, they think they are so close to God as to believe to know that God does not exist. The world, maneuvered out of their hands, gives them vertigo and therefore they believe from their glorious heights to be the gods of this world. But this is not the case: they are only a visible manifestation of the infinite loop chain of this prison planet. "Some people talk" and write and bombard us in so many ways, in their own words (political, religious, prophets, psychologists, critics.) Others prefer to manage the power in silence, never saying anything (business magnate, esoterist, Masons, courtesans, friends and friends of all these). [6]

An excellent description of the *Allegory of the Cave* made by my father Elio, in his unpublished essay written in the mid 70's, just as good, if not superior to what we find in more recent times.

In the movie *The Matrix,* a 1999 American-Australian science fiction action film written and directed by The Wachowski brothers, a film that as some of you already know, I consider of great importance in the initiatic process of the masses at this crucial time for humanity. The film in question revolves around the opposition between real and fictional worlds, between truth and falsehood, between truth and appearance, a central duality in all of Western philosophy. The truth is not as it appears to us, a nice game of empty phantasmagoria, to deceive us and keep us subjugated in chains. This is what the dark side wants. The film in question may partly be relied upon as a representation of Plato's thought. *The Matrix* seems to rewrite the myth of Plato's Cave with a new interpretation, with of course a technological upgrade, which is compelling when you refer to the sleeping masses of today, lost in the virtual world of the internet. If a slave could escape, says Plato, initially he would be blinded by the sunlight, but he would then be able to see the truth clearly, which the shadows concealed, and finally he would understand the prison planet that surrounds him. If he wanted to go back into the cave to reveal such truths to the other slaves, he would not be believed, and indeed he might even be killed. Neo, the

6   *Elio Zagami, **The Experience** (unpublished essay), various extracts from the chapter "The Prophets of Experience."*

protagonist of the film, somehow represents the ultimate man-philosopher of this age, who manages to escape the cave *(The Matrix),* and finally realizes the true nature of reality that surrounds him. At first he is dazzled by the light outside, but once he gets used to it and recognizes the truth that it hides, he returns to the cave (the Matrix), and tries to free other men. In this context, after you take **the red pill** described in the film, you reach the enlightenment experience, however some, after reading my words, will ask in the way Glaucon did in the *Allegory of the Cave*: *"But, what is this experience?"* It does not really simplify life, if anything, it makes it more difficult, and often controversial at a social level, and sometimes it can even cause you to die if you are not cautious in the way you proceed after your "illumination."

Some may not want to dissolve the chains of human existence that lead to the truth. They are the poor prisoners of Plato's ideal cave, with the realization that this is still a **"Prison Planet,"** and knowing that one could be opposed and persecuted by the controllers of the famous "Matrix" for ones choice, or even be killed by the "slave gods." This term was defined by the discarnate entity named *Aiwass*, that dictated the ***Book of the Law*** to English magician Aleister Crowley, and his wife Rose Edith Crowley, in Cairo in **1904.** If the elite could have it their way, they would try to stop any future mutiny of "cavemen," as they did with me over and over again in the past, hoping I would eventually give up. The truth is so scary that most ordinary people prefer to refuse it, and not all men have the courage to face the risk involved in fighting such a battle that involves a radical choice in one's life, and in the life of one's family. This has happened to me when I suffered the betrayal of people close to me after my dramatic choice over a decade ago. I suddenly found myself in isolation in a prison in Norway. In the end, there will always be an infamous character like **Cypher "the traitor,"** the Judas of *The Matrix* movie, the companion of Neo and Morpheus, who reveals secret plans to artificial intelligences. The gist of the speech made by Cypher is that humanity is lazy, fearful, tied to its false security, and they feel it's better to remain ignorant than to know the truth that could radically disrupt their lives. [7]

I saw this reflected particulary in contemporary Scandinavian society, which I consider the most subdued and conditioned in the world, although it is considered by many to be an example to follow. It is actually the first society to sell out to the globalists with various initiatives. Norway and Sweden, for example, are eliminating cash in favor of electronic currency, thus promoting the latest trend of the New World Order, and to global slavery, where we are treated more and more like a number or bar code. In every era of humanity that dares to go against the system, to bring men to rebel consciously against this age old slavery, as Socrates did, there are those that are unfortunately betrayed and usually murdered. This happened not only to Socrates, who Plato of course was referring to in his *Allegory of the Cave,* but we also have Jesus and many others in the same position: **Joan of Arc, Giordano Bruno,** and before them **Boethius,** imprisoned in Pavia in September 524 for allegedly practicing witchcraft. There is **Ramon Llull**, who is said to have been stoned to death by the crowd, **Cagliostro** the "Magician" of the Masonic tradition, who died in solitary confinement in the Castle of San Leo, to limit ourselves to only some of "the real Illuminati," as my father used to call them. Characters who were persecuted, ridiculed, insulted and eventually brutally murdered by the "smart" pseudo "Illuminati" elite, simply for revealing the truth about the system that governs our physical and spiritual world. And remember it is not the crowd that

---

7   Fabio Balic, ***Matrix, A philosophical interpretation*** from the site http://www.greendayfactory.it/ cult. htm **(no longer online)**.

decided the death of Jesus, but it was the notorious demagogues; who were obviously instructed by "someone" behind the scenes. They are the hidden manipulators from the dark side of the Illuminati, the slaves of the occult elite that still dominate this world, just like in Jesus' time, those who manage to brainwash and control the sheeple with their lies: *"Away with this man, and release unto us Barabbas. Crucify him! Crucify him!" (Luke 23:18).* Socrates, in turn, the inventor of logic, was condemned by a totally illogical verdict, issued by men who acted in the name of a supposed justice that keeps defending the system and its controllers regardless of the outcome: *"At this point the judges vote a second time. They had to choose between the sentence proposed by Meleto and the fine proposed by Socrates. Says Diogenes Laertius: (II, 42) Socrates was sentenced to death with 80 votes more than those who had him pleaded guilty; and so he had been found guilty by 280 votes to 220 but was sentenced (to death) with 360 votes against 140!"*[8] In all this, it is hard to see the good in man. You see, the idea of good in the physical world is in fact, extremely rare.

For this reason, the experience of enlightenment depends on several impalpable factors, and hopefully at some point in our lives we understand the true master we have been searching for resides within us. Once activated, you will quickly develop the feeling for the reality that surrounds you that is invisible to the majority of people. This is described in the movie *The Matrix,* when the protagonist chooses the "Red Pill" after Morpheus tells Neo: *"You take the blue pill, the story ends. You wake up in your bed and believe whatever you want to believe. You take the red pill, you stay in Wonderland, and I show you how deep the rabbit hole goes."* So with the closing introduction chapter of this trilogy I hope I will lead some of you to become true masters of your life in this crepuscolar moment in history. This is the ultimate purpose of this trilogy, where you are resurrected in a new life made of awareness, just as it happens in the initiation to a *Master Mason*: which some say was originally inspired by the cult of Osiris, and the third degree of the Egyptian initiation, that was called the "Gate of Death." This practice was later introduced into the Pythagorean school, founded by Pythagoras in Crotone (in today's south of Italy), around 530 BC. In this ancient form of initiation into the Egyptian mysteries, we find the coffin of Osiris, who is like Hiram Abiff, the central character of the allegory presented to all the candidates of Freemasony during the third degree. This allegorical figure is lead to a truly dramatic experience for the initiate, where he is asked if he took part in the murder of Osiris. After showing evidence to him, and despite his denials, they impose on him the feeling of being hit with a blow to the head.

The initiate is then wrapped with bandages like a mummy; he hears moaning around him; lightning is flashed in front of his eyes covered by the bandage, sounds and noises are created around him, to alienate and scare him even further. Then the candidate is wrapped in fire (and not just symbolically), and suddenly after the ordeal has terminated, they bring him symbolically back to life, obtaining in this way mastery, and with it, the full awareness of **the cave/Matrix** that surrounds us. In today's world such knowledge and understanding should be promoted well beyond the sectarian realities of the Illuminati mystery schools or speculative Freemasonry. Living free, or at least aspiring to live outside "Plato's Cave," should be an essential part of the realization of every human being on earth, not the privilege of a few brilliant minds. This evolution could and should happen if a new humanity is capable of rejecting materialism, and idolatry, so prevalent in our present society. We need to help the elite of today lose their vice and pervesion, to embrace instead **"spiritual alchemy,"** and the noble practices of a true initiate.

8   Elio Zagami, *Ibid.*

Francesco Brunelli, a leading figure of the Italian and European Illuminati in the 1970s, known in Martinism as **Nebo** (1927 – 1982), who in 1973 was named by the famous French initiate **Robert Ambelain** his representative to Italy, wrote the following:

> *Once his true nature is known, man will aspire to leave such prison, and after inquiring about the means at his disposal, will begin the job of deconditioning, decanters and purification that will lead him, after realizing the well-known fourfold motto:* **dare,** *to be silent, to know, to will, ready to operate the transmutation of spiritual alchemy whose finality is the structuring of a different kind of man from average humanity, surely he will be hunger for evolution and possibilities, "he will reconcile and reinstate his primitive" quality and power. Regardless of the "techniques" used by the initiate, he will also act "operationally." This work, which involves putting into action such operations, following the traditional patterns (purifications, diet, prayer magically understood, installation of an operating place, etc.) and rituals (in my case Martinezist rituals) that brings all operators who have a pure heart and a sincere faith to start living sensitive effects, consisting generally in a direct vision of flashes and glyphs (steps) that represent the signals on the path of reintegration and which confirm the validity of the work and its progression.*[9]

Returning to Speculative Freemasonry, it is generally divided into what is standardly agreed upon as the "Blue lodge"—linked to the Order and its first three degrees, whose symbolic color reminds us of the infamous **blue pill** offered by Morpheus to Neo in *The Matrix,* to stay in "blessed ignorance"—and the **red pill** to find out "how deep the rabbit hole goes," as in the "Red lodge" that can be defined in Masonic terminology as either the Scottish Rite or the York Rite of Freemasonry, depending on where you are in the world, seeking improvement beyond the degree of Master Mason (3rd degree). (see FIG. 1, in front matter, page 5) In reality, the only true initiation in Freemasonry is the one obtained in the **Apprentice degree,** as all the others are just stages of Masonic improvement. After Mastery, you can remain in the administration of a "Blue Lodge," and have little more than a social club experience, or if persistent, you can push forward for further knowledge, and ultimately to the "Invisible Masters"... I will discuss this mysterious topic in the follow up to the *Confessions* trilogy, in a book known as *The Invisible Master.* In the "rabbit hole" of Freemasonry, we find the Martinist Order, an expression of the teachings of Martinez de Pasqually (1727?–1774), the father of the Martinist lodges, and his student Louis Claude de Saint Martin. A hundred years after the death of Saint Martin, various prominent figures of the occult establishment of the Illuminati network, including the aforementioned Papus, with the help of Stanislas de Guaita, and other French esoterists who had their roots in the Egyptian-Atlantean tradition of the Illuminati, with wide esoteric wisdom deriving from different channels, from Gnostic-Christian to Kabbalistic, to Neo-Templar Freemsonry, of which the above were dignitaries and reformers.

The Martinist Illuminati, who were born mystic and still remain mystic, are in contrast to the majority of the Masonic orders, which are to this day rather rationalist, often succumbing for this reason to black magicians, simply because they are not able to prepare the necessary psychic protection, forgetting their esoteric roots in favor of a social approach to the Craft. The essence of all the teachings of the Martinist Illuminati are found in the works written by various Grand Masters, but their initiations and their knowledge is transmittted through a rather simple ritual initiation ceremony. There are many Illuminati sects open to both men and women, but women do not seem to have access to the highest levels in Europe. Martinism is an initiatory group that owns a phil-

---

9   Collection of Articles from 1927 to 1982 of the Grand Master Francesco Brunelli Alias "Nebo"

osophical and mystical doctrine, a method of individual work and group work, where members must operate according to their individual possibilities. The main aim of the Martinist Order are essentially two:

1. Reconciliation and personal reintegration,

2. The universal reintegration.

The Martinists will later deepen these purposes not stopping at the letter, but penetrating behind the hidden anthropomorphism used by the Masters.

The means that they provide for the attainment of these goals are individual and collective, that is, the Martinists were placed in a position to make both individually and in communion with the other members of the Order, the work of reintegration. Scholastically—and therefore not initiatically—we can describe it on this assumption, constructed on the following scheme:

1. Individual work.
  a) Discovery of the true nature and the true being of man.
  b) Liberation work to free man here "at the bottom," of the "cave" with inside and "operational" work.
  c) Contribution to the universal personal reintegration through participation in the spiritual workings of the order.

2. Collective Labor through active participation in the magical chain having as effects:
  d) Energy exchange between the members of the chain.
  e) The use of individual energies for the expansion of the initiatic chain and for healing and cleansing the earth's aura. For this reason daily, monthly, and equinoctial rites are practiced.

This scheme, regardless of being "Martinist," has a central role in the ***Ordo Illuminatorum Universalis*** (also known with the acronym **O.I.U.**) which I founded in 1999 within the Monte Carlo Lodge of the P2. Summarily, I can say that the inner depth of the teachings of the past masters and those still living "at the bottom" are essential for a true evolution of man, especially in this day and age. Louis Claude de Saint Martin wrote: "*It is in fact the sum of all the problems, being himself a problem, the enigma of enigmas. One can not understand man by means of nature, but nature through man.*" With these words, Louis Claude de Saint Martin invites you to analyze for yourself the reality that surrounds you. So that man finally discovers his true rank and position in the universe and perceives the harmony of the world according to the famous motto of Delphi: **"Know Thyself and Know the Universe and the Gods!"** [10] Remember that mankind, in spite of its "degradation," will always carry the signs of our divine origin from the stars. Chained to this planet like Prometheus, exiled from his original kingdom, the **conscious beings** of mankind hope one day to overcome this stage and possibly rejoin one day the "Creators." For the good side of the Illuminati, it's important at this point to contribute to the cleansing of the Earth's aura, to fight the work of the Satanic enemy. The Martinist chain for example, when it is genuine, and it is not infiltrated by evil elements, as is unfortunately more and more often the case nowadays, can establish a positive energy exchange between Freemasons and other Illuminati, as I try to do in my own Order. One must understand that currently the astral atmosphere is haunted by negative thoughts

10   Leo Lyon Zagami, ***Confessions of an Illuminati Vol. I REMIX***, (Montevarchi –Arezzo: Harmakis Edizioni, 2015), p. 186.

emitted by man, by the negative forces of non-corporeal beings, and these forces generate the evils of humanity, and hinder rapid evolutionary ascent with racial hatred, religious, social, caste, selfish desires, etc.

Only true theurgic operations, and real exorcisms, are able to successfully fight such negativity. Collectively performed theurgic operations have a force that increases in a geometrical sense in relation to the number of operators that perform it. Believe it or not, moving the polarity in the astral environment even slightly, contributes to the great work of universal reintegration. Following the Martinist teachings, the initiatory chain I created within the **Ordo Illuminatorum Universalis,** can naturally devote its positive energy to fight the negativity on all levels, and particular attention is also paid to the healing operations that are not only addressed to the members of the Order, but also to their families, and to the society around us that often requires our intervention on the astral plane. That's why we, as well as Martinism and certain Masonic Rites, are constantly infiltrated by the dark side of the Illuminati, and it is for this reason, that Martinism as a mystery school was incorporated in the O.I.U. activities and teachings, to ensure transmission and to adjust its Egregore outside the harmful influences of the dark side of the Illuminati. The initiate who embarks on this positive initiatic path, does it initially through the understanding of the esoteric teachings present in my books, and later through the practice of them, essential for a proper understanding of the ultimate truth and the practice of transmutation, which in a more current and understandable term is referred to as **Spiritual Alchemy.**

Francesco Brunelli wrote that:

> *The transmutation is reached through the practice (and never through pure theory) also fideistic, which through the intervention of the Egregore chain allows that the small arcane, even the inexpressible, is sensed by the adept or revealed to him. The possession of small natural arcane allows the beginner to move to a further stage of the work. Without this there is no possibility of intuition or revelation or progress because no living being, no instructor can simply explain the secret, of course.* [11]

You must live certain realities to understand them. But remember how Brunelli had to point out several times in his writings that only an initiatic Order can guarantee the application of the rule, and only constant practice can open these possibilities gradually. It is laughable that many modern orders or fraternities define certain rites of acceptance as "initiations," without the actual possession of any major or minor teaching, stating they will raise you to new heights of understanding, or even promise to reveal to you the ultimate truth of the universe with a simple initiation, when this is far from possible. In this context I recall the words of a true initiate, De Guaita, who said to his masters to meditate profoundly: *"we will 'start' them out: but the role of initiators must stop here."* The initiate receives input, but not the ultimate truth, which must be reached on his own. Only in this way will he be able to reach the intelligence of the Major Arcana, and the title of **Adept.** But know well that it is in vain that you will attain the supreme formulas of science and knowledge from the wisest of the Masters in a book or speech; each person must summon it, create it and develop it as an experience. Once you are initiatically "opened," you are one with the others, and have been put on the path to become a true adept; i.e. one who has conquered the science of self, or, in other words, the son of his works. [12]

· ·

11   *Ibid.*, pp. 187-188.
12   *Ibid.*

I am in fact transmitting to you not only the necessary information, but also the oldest of initiations with this work. It is then up to you to deepen the knowledge, unknown to most. At the end of this introduction, and returning to the teachings of a Master Mason, the historical figures or symbols over the centuries might change, but I assure you that in the end there is a common truth to all the mystery schools and traditions, and not just Western ones. The Judeo-Christian power axis, which as we know dominates this historical moment and currently dominates Freemasonry worldwide, simply wants to be identified at this juncture of Space-Time, in the biblical Hiram Habif, or in the case of Christian-Masonic Rites in Jesus. But remember that beyond appearances and names that change (as we also saw in the previous volume, where I explored the subject of Chinese Freemasonry), the initiatic valences that these above figures represent, since ancient times, is the initiatory path of rebirth "of the One" that is in all of us, and the mysteries they represent, are the same. Plato explains in *Phaedrus,* that for those who want to reach such beautiful ideals it is also acceptable to suffer to obtain them. [13] The philosophic truths of such distinguished figures such as Plato or Pythagoras, and their teachings, play a central role in understanding the Matrix around us, especially after the final meltdown of the transcendent metaphysical world in our society with the work of materialists and Satanists. The *Allegory of the Cave* has become a helpful tool in our analysis of reality. A world where nothing is as it appears, where everything is studied, watched, controlled and manipulated by the usual Jesuits in cahoots with their Zionist allies.

In this third volume of my *Confessions,* I do an in depth study of the elite bloodlines, showing you secrets known until now, only to a select few. Finally there is a topic that is close to my heart present in this book, the Holy Grail and the Knights Templar, and their famous curse and supposed revenge. Many do not know that Count Licio Gelli, former Worshipful Master of the controversial lodge Propaganda 2, dedicated a small booklet (FIG. 4) to the Knights Templar and their revenge: *"A conspiracy born in the dawn of 1314, when the last Grand Master of the Temple, Jacques de Molay, was sent to the stake launching the famous curse, a revenge that was extinguished, according to some with the beheading of Louis XVI. While for others it is still in place. On this episode there has been a lot of literary, pseudo-esoteric and even historical speculation."* To the supposed "Revenge" of the Templars, the 30th degree of the Ancient and Accepted Scottish Rite is dedicated. It is judged as being controversial by some Freemasons, who have applied for a review of it in some jurisdictions, perhaps without having understood its true essence. For this reason I would like to open this book mentioning my first "experience" with the Templar legacy, when I was still a child in the family library, (FIG. 5) and found an old book published in **1891** entitled *Le Temple du Satan,* whose author was the famous French occultist Stanislas De Guaita. I began to read this book, and I discovered many initiatic teachings and hidden historical facts under the bright veil of Pythagorean philosophy, but it was only a few years later, during a very heartfelt initiation into a lodge with a strong Templar tradition, that I understood in fullness its importance, and its secret teachings, thanks to an old member of the Priory of Sion that pointed out to me a particular passage.

Let's read together this passage and you will understand why:

> Still we stand in shock for the quick summary of the trial of the Templars, for their relentless description of their infamous persecution. They were sorcerers? Listen. Rich and powerful, for the more ambitious, the trustees of surprising and frightening powers which were conferred to some of them by a partial initiation of an arcane science often questioned, at times ridiculed, but always forbidden by priesthoods

13   See. Plato, **Collected Works, Vol. III: Phaedrus**, translated by P. Pucci, Roma-Bari, Laterza, 1974.

FIG. 4 – Cover of the booklet by Licio Gelli entitled "Revenge of the Templars" published by ENAM a Club of Art Operators and Culture Academy.

and absolute governments, the Templars could clearly determine in the political and social, sudden and unexpected upheavals, such as to change the face of Europe and even the world. ... that's what was vaguely sensed by the Pope and the King of France. Following the superficial logic of the facts understood in their apparent meaning, Clement V should have seen in the Knights of the Temple at the time those valiant defenders of Catholicism and zealous supporters of the papal throne; Philip the Fair, only the loyal subjects and fervent supporters of the monarchy. But a singular intuition in the heart of the two powerful, protested against this apparent situation. Frightened, the monarch and the Pope (the latter even before his election), decided the total destruction of the Order and pursued this objective with licit and illicit means, despite rumors of conscience and humanity. The persecuters were from time to time, evil and violent, hypocritical and merciless.

In this particular passage it seems we are dealing with a new perspective of the Templar legacy:

Idolatry and witchcraft! What did it matter? What did they bury under the ashes of the fires of 1311-1313, it was the possibility of a policy and revolution, and a plan still vague of a social and religious reform. But they had reckoned without the laws of impact and balance. The persecuters were ignorant of the fact that you do not suffocate an idea, even in germ, in the blood of those they are made apostles and legatees of such idea, that ferocious prudence was illusory and the infamous trap they prepared will condemned them both very soon, and more importantly, in the future they aroused almost five centuries later, a return shock of which the earth still trembles; a belated

FIG. 5 – The author at work during the writing of his Confessions trilogy in the family study that was his father's, Dr. Elio Zagami, using the same desk that belonged to his grandfather, Senator Leopoldo Zagami.

shock that caused suddenly the most complete and colossal collapse in recorded human history: 1793 was the shocking reply to Inquisition judgment of 1312! Clement V and Philip the Fair were undoubtedly clairvoyant when they sensed the living threat urging in front of them in the person of the Templars, and this in spite of all imaginable protests of fidelity and love, but they were blinded in their absurd barbarism if they could flatter themselves with the hope that an act of faith, for rapid and complete that it had been, would eliminate the Templars, their power and the Word of which they were carriers. Both will be invited to appear before God— the Pope within forty days and the King within the same year—history shows how ominous was such appointment with death. Two apostate knights, traitors of the Order, the first, in an obscure process, were hanged by a Court, the other was found bathed in his own blood. Fellow prisoners of the Grand Master that had betrayed the Templars after his death persisted in their confessions, no less died miserably later on. An immense secret society was formed from the ruins of the Templar Order. Now the revenge prepared in the shadows whose explosion will terrorize Four Hundred Fifty years later: waiting for this terrible and late response, it decimated one after another, all the murderers of Jacques de Molay.

Stanislas De Guaita then explains the genesis of something that is born from "the ashes of the Knights of the Temple" and is spread over four centuries following their secret "orders," to manifest themselves fully only in the second half of the seventeenth century, when:

Secret societies are multiplying in a surprising manner; they swarm everywhere like a multitude of swarms that you saw out of the land, vibrating in the sun in the effervescence of an unusual job. The time left is played. Noon of punishment; and the industrious bees revenge prepare the golden sting for the great battle. ... Already the century tasted the intoxicating honey whose aroma rise to the brain, subtle poison that blinds and makes us delirious ... stay still a moment, listening, and what is felt is a buzz of insects and the noise of the hurricane always getting closer; a confused and growing noise of millions of human voices crying vengeance and Freedom! Especially **Germany seems the nursery of the Illuminati, the meeting place of these sects.** *Powerful lords, greedy beyond the grave revelations, dripping favors in good faith from some mystics that call them "my son," but especially the many charlatans who mock them and exploit them.*

De Guaita clearly explains to his readers who the infamous Illuminati really were, and such info came from what he experienced first hand. Given their central role in the secret societies of the time, he does not limit the "Illuminati" term to the **Ordo Illuminatorum** of Adam Weishaupt, which he is highly critical. Instead, he has a much broader view of the *Illuminati* in line with what I have taught you in the first two volumes of my *Confessions.* De Guaita says that among these "many societies" that make up the network of *Illuminati,* "there are a few good ones," but let's read his words:

Adam Weishaupt, a professor at the University of Ingolstad, founds its Areopagites. Arousing the curiosity of the public and become fashionable for some time. Emanuel Swendeborg preaches in Sweden; Georg Schröpfer evokes in Leipzig, Johann Heinrich Jung known as Heinrich Stilling foretold elsewhere. Karl Von Eckartshausen teaches in München the highest speculations of Pythagoras magic numbers, Lavater, the Zurich theosopher, goes to Copenhagen to participate in the mysteries of the Northern school. It is nothing less than the **physical manifestations of the active Intelligence cause** *(The Word!) In intervals to keep fit Danes theurgists evoke St. John, Moses, Elijah, not counting the minor characters of one and the Old Testament. In short, the followers abound and it would be folly to pretend to list them all.* **Of all these Illuminati there are a few good ones (except Von Eckartshausen),** *many mediocre as Jung-Stilling, Swendeborg and Lavater and even more detestable as Schröpfer, Weishaupt and all the others.*

As you can see I am not the first Freemason to criticize the "Illuminati" sects, although I am definitely the first to come forward to publicly denounce the corruption of this millennial sectarian system, as explained in part by *De Guaita*, who showed the Templars as the main protagonists, especially after their tragic ending. In spite of my enemies who have tried to stop me several times, I present to you the third episode of my *Confessions*, where you will finally take the red pill, and thus becoming a Master.

⟋◠

Leo Lyon Zagami

Chapter   I

In Search of the Perfect Knighthood

Awaiting a Holy Empire

Maurizio Blondet writes:

*T*he Western civilization has reached its terminus momentous—or its dead end—it is common sense (hopefully for them) also for the atheists to feel the terminal crisis of capitalism that does not know how to escape this mess having consumed their whole bag of tricks and moral degradation, social dissociation, consumption of individual hedonism, nihilism and a wish of death permeates it. The new "achievements" and "rights" that are being pushed by the progressives in their latest battles do not have the force of optimism of their old "magnificent and progressive" ideologies that seem now mortuary and funeral conquests like abortion, euthanasia ... Maybe the atomized masses get it too (perhaps), and now confused about their desires, and insatiable consumers of standard-products while their "leaders" act as psycho-cops of progressivism. What they reject with fury and mad rage (seem therefore suspicious and hides their fear) is the diagnosis that Buchanan stated sometime ago with such frank simplicity: our civilization is the last stop because it refuses Faith. Christianity, specifically. The irrational hate, drooling, that radical progressivism has towards Vladimir Putin is the feeling that the salvation of civilization requires a "correction," a daily moral code demanding dogmas founded in people's history, the renunciation to that microscopic and swarming hedonism of today; the end of this vacation and those standards to which the atomized masses believe (and they are made to believe) they have been "liberated," emancipated from the "dogmas and taboos."

And symptomatic comically, by contrast, the adoration of such intellectual managers of terminal and their whole body of left wing journalists—who bestow upon Pope Francis the high clerical hierarchy—committed to frantically pull down the building that created civilization, civil morality, culture, noble costumes (Chilvary) now torn and trampled, to dismantle the Church destroying its sacrality, to turn it into an auxiliary of the generic religion that adapts to the One World Government— these lost unbelievers, adoring him, and expect "Francis" to bring them out of the dead end they ended in. The left wingers have become clerical, at every opportunity they cite the phrases of Pope Francis obviously the most anti-Christian, such as "who am I to judge?" They drink from him their new catechism, confirming their secular approach. What a funny and sad sight.

But this does not exempt us—the few true Catholics left behind—to focus on the last word of Buchanan. "Unrecoverable." We, too, who "believe" to have faith, are hurt by the present climate, by the collective Satan raging on the Western world as a roaring lion. Not enough to recognize that it takes the Christian faith to maintain and rebuild civilization; faith, you have to have and live. Do we truly have such faith we who go to Mass? Supernatural protections ruined by the treacherous hierarchy that conducts the liturgy leaves us exposed to the roaring lion. Our faith is really more than a crumb?Recently a "traditionalist," a militant Catholic character, which is not worth to mention by name, a co-founder of the Catholic Alliance, announced the organization to renounce to all charges because—he left his wife and four children—and at 61 years old he goes and lives in the USA with his mistress. In New York, the capital of the sunset, a very symbolic move.

Maurizio Blondet is referring above to **Massimo Introvigne,** the co-founder of the *Alleanza Cattolica* (**Catholic Alliance**), and infamous Jesuit agent I talk about in Volume 1. Blondet continues:

After the inevitable evil grin (he was my opponent, Israeli supporter, and known figure of the Interdisciplinary Center Herzliya, i.e. a Mossad recruiting center). I asked myself, can this happen to me? He stripped himself of his "Catholic faith" like you take off a dress ... why I say, a dress? More like a carnival mask, a fake nose made of paper applied to the face with a rubber band, of which he has been freed without any difficulty so he can chase a little sex and pleasure of which he should know—from his doctrine—deceives and does not last, and will bring him to repent soon. His true face was therefore this, cheesy and standard hedonism; and the faith in Christ was only his carnival costume, his mask.

This is a pretty strong criticism by Maurizio Blondet against Massimo Introvigne, one of the most influential contemporary figures within the sectarian world of the Illuminati, controlled by the Jesuits and Pope Francis, with the support of the CIA and the Mossad. However I always considered him, as you know from my previous writings, a Satanist and not a true Christian. People like Blondet should have realized this earlier:

I can attest to one thing. Very true. In these times, with this Church in dissolution, with a Catholicism that has given up their mission and priests who teach the "ecumenical pastoral" way—There are young people who are called. Are chosen one by one, they receive calls through meetings and messages that it is impossible to describe—because they are unmistakably supernatural. I met, last year, at least three. They were young, lost, mixed up in standard pleasures; young people to whom no one has ever even spoken of faith (unless an old grandmother) specifically Catholic. Yet, after answering the call, they rediscovered everything I meant everything Catholic. Traditional, Thomistic, liturgical and Gregorian, the ones abandoned by the hierarchical Church, are traditional Catholics. One of them called to me to visit him a few weeks ago, now married and with children, teaching (teaching!) Thomas Aquinas, the perennial philosophy in a Spanish university with holy audacity and true doctrine. The doctrine that the person who called him in, must have taught him. I have a bit of faith that will not endure the persecution. But I see that Christ is calling one by one those who will rebuild, in the very near future that I will probably not see; He is enlisting his commandos, his martyrs, his virile he-

roes—and sometimes ferocious amazons—for the last battle. So, I am serene. There will be a civilization tomorrow, after the catastrophe. **Christians will be strong then. There will be a Christian Empire, as some prophecies say—not a republic. A holy empire. Not a democracy.** [1]

And from these words written by the famous Italian journalist Maurizio Blondet, once linked to Opus Dei, we understand that we are living in what is commonly called the end times. The apostasy of the Church itself, and the will to destroy the Catholic Church, which is now apparent to everyone. With this third volume of my *Confessions* we arrive to the complete removal of the veil of Isis, that was presented to the initiate in ancient Egypt, by the revelation of the light of ultimate truths.

Imagine the Egyptian burial place of Isis, in a place close to Memphis, where there was a statue covered by a black veil. On the base of the statue is engraved: "*I am everything that was, [QUID FUIT], everything that is [QUID EST], that will be [QUID ERIT] and no mortal has yet dared to lift my veil.*" In the journey of initiation in ancient Egypt, what followed was voluntary, and concerned only the development of the individual, the Egyptian religion was never promoted with a missionary spirit. They were tolerant and benevolent towards the world, but Egypt never wanted to impose their religious practice elsewhere, the exact opposite of the subsequent Abrahamic religions, invasive and too often oppressive. Rightly so, Egypt did not wish to impose on others their religion with the force seen later on with Christianity and Islam; but the cult of Isis and Osiris, were gradually absorbed by the nascent Christian faith, only to be rediscovered and used in secret, centuries later, by the Jesuits. It is the Jesuits who became the new priests of Heliopolis in the Vatican, with the most powerful network of secret agents in the world, to help their faith expand and develop. Remember, there is a huge obelisk in St. Peters Square in the Vatican, in the center of Christianity, that is dedicated to the "sun god," from Heliopolis. The Jesuit Order is therefore the new secret Brotherhood of Heliopolis (the Sun City) within the Church, the High Priests of the God **On** (which is another name for the sun god Osiris communicated in secret to the Minervals of the O.T.O. at their initiation). The Jesuits are the sons of the sun, who for 500 years have been structured as a sect, and military operation, with unconditional support of the papacy. Obedience to their immediate supervisor is total, and closed occult deals are made among their adepts. The commander is defined as Superior General, but there is also a **"Black Pope,"** given the black robes he wears and his position in the shadow of the "White Pope," although now we have an anomaly with Pope Francis, as he is a Jesuit, and everything about him becomes much more complex and precarious. The "Society of Jesus" was originally used by the Vatican to counter the various movements of the Protestant Reformation, but of course with time they became something much more powerful, as we shall read in this book, but I want to focus now on Helipolis.

The area of the ancient Egyptian city of Heliopolis is located today in the northeastern part of the Egyptian capital **Cairo**, which constitutes the district of **Mataria**, a place I once visited, in November of 2004, for an exorcism by a holy lady of the Coptic Church. The ancient magical practices of Egypt are still alive today thanks to Christianity, the Coptic faith is the closest to its original source. Egyptian Magic in its more dark connotations, scared the Roman aristocracy when they arrived in the town of Cleopatra. At the time, Cleopatra was able to dominate many men and make them her slaves by using the magical art of seduction and also red magic, often sex magic. However after Cleopatra

––

1   http://www.maurizioblondet.it/senza-cristo-crolla-la-civilta-solo-putin-lha-capito/ ‡ Archived 27th September 2016.

arrived in Rome, Egyptian magic spread throughout the empire. Pliny the Elder, a well-known Roman author, naturalist, and natural philosopher in the first century AD, never missed an opportunity to thunder against the impiety of such magicians, but meanwhile advised people to wear a dried beetle, as an amulet for the health of their children, in imitation of Egyptian scarabs. In short, even Pliny was not exempt from these practicing forms of magic. In the beginning of the third millennium, **Knowledge and Light** seem to be covered by darkness; myths and gods disappeared, giving way to a growing obsession with movie stars, sports figures and entertainers.

Homer, best known as the author of the *Iliad* and the *Odyssey*, would no longer be able to write today, about the appearance and many adventures of the gods with mankind, and a pharaoh doesn't welcome the sun officially among large crowds, like it was in ancient times. However, the elite of today and our government officials still practice (or try to practice) certain rituals in the secrecy of their lodges, and in the narrow circles of a select few, in temples inaccessible to ordinary people. Therefore, when night falls on our consciousness, we return to ancient Egypt for answers. As stated by **Guillaume Apollinaire: "now is the time to rekindle the stars."** The Illuminati of the various sects of today and "Occult Freemasonry," hide their true knowledge, in various mystery schools and secret societies, the mysteries of ancient Egypt, as I have shown you in the previous volumes of the *Confessions* series. When I was myself initiated into the mysteries of the invisible world linked to the ancient Egyptian Illuminati and joined the A∴A∴ of Aleister Crowley, who some call *Argentium Astrum,* back in 1993, I was told by my initiator some of the secrets of Heliopolis. I was told that it was no coincidence that my now deceased father was named Elio, and I am named Leo. Basically our names put together in Latin describe the period known in English as **the Dog Days**, the hottest, most stifling days of summer. They are 40 days, beginning on July the 3rd, and ending on August 11th, that coincide with the heliacal rising of **the Dog Star, Sirius**. For the ancient Egyptians, Sirius appeared just before the Nile's flood season, so they used the star as an indicator of the flood. Since its rising also coincided with a time of extreme heat, the connection with hot, sultry weather was made. This period also coincides with the Sun in Leo among other things. Four years after this important event in my life in 1997, the same character, the initiator who had introduced me to the secrets of this brotherhood of the A∴A∴(of which I spoke of in depth in Volume I), gave me a mysterious text to read written by someone who he said would help me figure out a few things on the true situation of the world. Here is the content and the words written by, who I discovered later on, was none other than the Grand Master of the Order of the Illuminati Knights **Frank G. Rippel:**

> *I remember the particular state of political tension that had been created in Italy in December 1988, something was happening. The evening of Monday 12th of December we witnessed, the Scarlet Woman and I, the manifestation of a divine sign. We were in an area of Veneto and saw darting in the sky a green energy sphere. The heavenly Ark of the Covenant (not to be confused with the terrestrial one) had projected a force field around the earth. This was the signal announcing the fall of communist ideology. In July of 1989, we visited Licio Gelli (the former head of the disbanded Masonic lodge P2). In a previous letter he wrote:* "**The time of our meeting was brief and could not offer us the opportunity to know each other better, though, if you believe you can, in the near future, and if you have the opportunity to pass through Tuscany, it would be of my satisfaction to have a meeting with you.**" *In his villa, a manor house in the green of nature, we were welcomed with great courtesy. Gelli led us into a huge hall and made us sit on two of the twelve chairs arranged in an arc, six on each side. We began to talk, and at one point in the*

conversation he said: **"We have two enemies: the Communists and the Catholic Church. ... And especially the Jesuits,"** *Then I made a ritual question: "When will be the end of these two ideologies?" "You have to have patience," he replied. "Maybe because I'm young I have a lot of patience," I replied. And a few months after that the Synarchy overthrew communism in the world. The Cold War was over. It seems that no one had realized the rapidity with which it had crumbled, the Soviet Union and its satellite countries. Even the most pessimistic political scientists believed that communism would last even for a hundred years and yet in a few months everything was shattered, weird right? Since December 12, 1988 there have been almost ten years, and a new world disorder reigns in the world, for a new world order can be born. A New Dawn will rise soon and the world will change. The evening of Monday the 6th of January 1997, there has been another Divine sign. In the sky of Rome a green energy ball darted from east to west. The heavenly Ark of the Covenant produced another force field. This is the signal that announces the fall of this fideist religious ideology, the signal of the beginning of the Great Return. The beginning of the Great Return is marked by the Knight of Space announcing the end of the old days and the start of new ones. The Knight of Space is a comet, discovered on July 23rd, 1995 by amateur astronomers Alan Hale and Thomas Bopp. The minimum distance from Earth occurred on the 22nd of March, 1997. In late 1996, astronomers around the world have found a body, defined Companion, who was following the Hale-Bopp comet. Later, with their primitive tools, they have been no more able to detect the Companion. The Companion is a force field that came into collision with the Aura of the Earth, to the transmutation of the same Energy collision occurring on March 19, 1997, and the transmutation of the Aura was completed on 29 April, 1997. The Return of the Gods is marked in time, but few are those who know how to interpret the Divine Signs.*

After handing me this revealing text, my initiator recited these words he told me were written by the **Antichrist**.

Well my dear readers, I am not to sure the "Antichrist" he was referring to was Frank G. Ripel, but here they are:

In all these years I have not done more
than revealing the Absolute Science of Magic.

But now, My children, Sons of Vengeance,
listen to what I'm about to tell you.

For some time now there as has been constituted a New Order,
a New Line of Magicians. We are the Psionics.

We can use the power of our mind
to change the surrounding reality,
but always in deep respect of the Laws of Nature.

We operate in Justice, above the law of man.

We abhor all forms of brutal violence carried out by the wild human.

We are the antibodies of the Earth,
opposing the madness devastating
the wild men.

We can kill with just a mental effort
and there is no human law that can hit us,

since there is no law that rec-
ognizes our faculties.

And this in our favor and it is
our strength.

We are beyond good and evil.

The term **Psionics** is the study
of paranormal phenomena in relation to the application of electronics. This modern term derives from
psi ('psyche') and the -onics from
electronics (machine). It is closely
related to the field of radionics. Of
course there is no scientific evidence
that psionic abilities exist, however
from that day on I wondered what I
had to do, and although I felt to be
part of "a New Line of Magicians," as
the supposed "Antichrist" revealed
in his message to his adepts, I certainly did not want to serve him in
any way, because as you know the
devil and his acolytes are sons of
lies and deception. It took however,
many years for me to understand
fully that the only answer was in Jesus Christ, and that the promises of
"justice" and not "violence" of the
supposed Antichrist in his message,
were part of that great deception
perpetrated on mankind called the
New Age, that I described to you in
Volume I. New Age is a term coined

FIG. 6 – Cover of The New Age Magazine
that was "the official organ" of the Supreme
Council 33°, Ancient & Accepted Scottish Rite
of Freemasonry Southern Jurisdiction (**not the**
Northern jurisdiction as errouneously written
by the author in Volume I). *The magazine was*
inaugurated in 1904 and still continues today,
but in 1990, the title of the publication was
changed to the Scottish Rite Journal.

in the Masonic field, (FIG. 6) that is now a global movement that has been amplified in
recent years, with an obsession for the mysteries of the ancient Egyptian civilization. This
growing interest was originally promoted by certain Illuminati sects within Freemasonry
in much narrower circuits, but is now alive with the expansion of the New Age creed, a
kind of planetary revival, not always positive, as most New Age practitioners are in the
hands of the perverse ideology and beliefs of the aforementioned Aleister Crowley and
his cult of **Thelema.** Crowley, who was a violator of the true teachings of alchemy and its
sacred notions, in recent years was able to influence more people thanks to his disciple
Paulo Coelho, a character who despite presenting himself to the world as an innocent
intellectual figure and writer, is someone we should not trust. Coelho, as I will show you
in detail later in this book, was also for a time a devout disciple of Crowleyanity, and was
tied to **Marcelo Ramos Motta (1931 – 1987)** of the S.O.T.O., and the mysterious brotherhood of the A∴ A∴. In addition to all this, he received his education from the usual
Jesuits, which makes us understand a lot about his perverse psychology. Today, the mysti-
fying philosophy of the Jesuits reigns supreme, and man is living in a growing realization
that he actually lives on a prison planet, where freedom does not exist.

From Ancient Egypt to the Strict Observance

L et us now revisit ancient Egypt, and the ancient initiatic tradition that was partly transmitted to the mysterious Rosicrucians, at the center of Western initiatic tradition in the last four centuries. In the pseudo-autobiography of **Christian Rosenkreutz** (ie *The Chemical Wedding*, attributed to **Valentin Andreae**), we find in this initiatic tale, a description of a king and queen crossing the sea and reaching a sacred island. This story is reminiscent of the journey of the sarcophagus of Osiris, in Plutarch's version of the events. Egyptian influences became even more evident in the **Golden and Rosy Cross**, which appears in 1757, as a faction of the Illuminati sectarian network secretly piloted by Jesuits. Egyptian secret doctrines are simply Christianized, according to their legend, credited by a supposed Alexandrian priest named Ormus (in Persian Ormuzd), who I have already spoken of in detail in the first volume of my *Confessions*, a key figure of the ancient Illuminati, who is worth mentioning again because of his importance, to this day, in the mysterious Brotherhood of the Rosicrucians. Ormus was baptized a Christian by the Evangelist Mark, and his secret teachings were passed down through the centuries, so says the legend, by a secret school of sages and Illuminati, which finally manifest themselves to the world as **Rosicrucians** through the Rosicrucian Manifestos: *Fama Fraternitatis* and *Confessio Fraternitatis*. These two masterpieces of propaganda were published anonymously in 1615 and 1616. Soon after we find the Golden and Rosy Cross, a secret fraternity linked to the Jesuits, whose maximum representative of the time, according to Erik Hornung, was a Venetian magician who lived in Egypt. [2] Indeed, legend or myth, all this simply leads us back to Egypt, the land of Hermes Trismegistus. I should also mention that the brief, but intense success of Count Cagliostro, and his **Egyptian Rite of Freemasonry,** was not only tied to the Jesuits, but also to the elite of the Freemasons of the time, involved in the Strict Templar Observance, a Templar Masonic order later infiltrated and sabotaged by the Jesuits, that was eliminated and absorbed partly, by other Masonic rites in 1782 in the famous **"Convent of Wilhelmsbad,"** of great importance for the future of Freemasonry and all Masonic rites.

The rite of the Strict Observance Templar was reactivated by the author of this book in 2016, along with other truly enlightened Freemasons, to establish a new initiatic base that can facilitate the future reconstitution of a true aristocracy, based on merit and enlightened by noble souls ready to help forge the future empire of God. Madness or reality, we oppose this drift towards the humanist, liberal and communist New World Order. We propose something different than the elite, just as Cagliostro did in his day. Let's not forget to mention in this context, the great fear that the legendary Count Cagliostro instilled with his magical and esoteric practices in the Roman Catholic Church, thanks to his Masonic / magical rite, the aforementioned Egyptian Rite, clearly inspired in part by the work of the Jesuit **Athanasius Kircher**, who promoted a very thorough research of Egyptian themes. He was the only one to conduct a serious and profound study of ancient Egypt before the famous discovery of **the Rosetta Stone** hieroglyphics, deciphered by Jean-Francois Champollion in 1822. This changed the whole approach to the subject, and a few years later Champollion met Napoleon Bonaparte (his brother Jacques was a supporter), while he was passing in his ascent from Grenoble to Paris, and had the opportunity to talk to him of his own studies, captivating the enlightened emperor.

We recall that Napoleon was a disciple of Cagliostro and the Illuminati of Adam Weishaupt, and therefore everything is connected perfectly to the esoteric and occult current that expanded from the Egyptian Rite and Cagliostro the "Great Copt," a title

---

2 See. Erik Hornung, **Egitto Esoterico**, (Turin, IT: Edizioni Lindau, 2006), pp. 157-163.

used by him, instead of Grand Master, that some say was inspired by Rabbi Falk, another key figure of the "Invisible Masters" in those days. During the infamous Inquisition trial of Giuseppe Balsamo aka Count of Cagliostro, he had even proposed to the Vatican and the Pope (who assisted behind the scenes at his trial), that his Egyptian Masonic Rite could become a new Order of the Catholic Church just like the Knights of Malta. This offer was rejected because it obviously would have risked showing to the world the most occult and secret side of the Catholic Church which obviously must remain secret. The Jesuits, heirs of Kircherian thought, and in part, the role of the Templars, are the only ones that are still in charge, to this day, of such secret knowledge within the Vatican. That is why the Jesuits are also important for their influence on what is called Neo-Templarism, although of course the Jesuits, who are the secret service of the Church, are distant in their actions and in their ideology, from the true spirit of chivalry, and of the aristocracy that originally moved the real Templars, and are increasingly inclined to communism and devilish compromise instead. This is the current context in which I reawakened the rite in Italy, as other luminaries of Freemasonry are doing in other countries around the world. The **Strict Templar Observance**, is a Christian, chilvaric Masonic Rite of great importance for the history of Freemasonry. This long lost rite was described this way by two of the biggest experts in contemporary Freemasonry, namely **Arturo de Hoyos** and **Alain Bernheim,** who dedicated a thorough study in *Heredom Magazine*, or "Heredom," the annual of the Scottish Rite Research Society (Volume 14, 2006):

> *Of the many rites, systems and orders that have appeared in the arena of Freemasonry, few have attained the level of notoriety or controversy of the Rite of Strict Observance. Its history is a tapestry of mystery, knighthood, glory, intrigue, deception, and fragmentation. Its influence upon the development of High Grade Masonry is undeniable, and it has left an imprint upon many of the important Masonic orders of the present day, foremost the Rectified Scottish Rite, but also the Swedish Rite, the York Rite, and the Ancient and Accepted Scottish Rite. Its mystique continues to beckon investigation and speculation, and writers seem unable to leave it alone, whether they recycle earlier notions, or offer genuine contributions to the subject. Few would argue that the Rite of Strict Observance has a rightful place in the pantheon of Freemasonry. Yet for all this, it remains something of a phantom to the English-reading Freemason, as its rituals somehow escaped translation and publication. Thus, like a phantom, it is something often talked about, but seldom seen. One reads about the Rite, but one does not read the Rite itself. With a view of bringing our phantom into the light, this paper presents, for the first time, the first three degrees of the German Rite of Strict Observance translated into English, with a history of its origins.*

Arturo de Hoyos is the Grand Archivist and Grand Historian of Scottish Rite Freemasonry; Director, Department of Education and Heritage The Supreme Council, 33°, Ancient and Accepted Scottish Rite of Freemasonry, S.J., USA, while **Alain Bernheim** was awarded two times the Norman Spencer Award by the English premier Lodge of Research Quatuor Coronati Lodge N° 2076. He is a Freemason since 1963, and not only belongs to the Regular Grand Lodge of Belgium and to the Swiss Grand Lodge Alpina, but was awarded the 33° by the Supreme Council of the United States (Southern Jurisdiction), and is a member of the prestigious **Royal Order of Scotland**. Certainly de Hoyos and Bernheim are two heavyweights of Freemasonry, and ten years after this historic publication of their invaluable research on the Strict Templar Observance, that was published for the first time in 2006, the official reawakening of this lost Masonic Rite in Italy took place, **in the Orient of Tivoli on March 5th, 2016 at the Castle of Rocca Pia in the year 898 Anno Ordinis**. To give you a quick general idea of the beliefs of this lesser known

Christian Masonic Rite, I will show you part of the teachings reserved to the **Inner Order** of the Rite of Strict Observance, that gives you the true superior meaning of the **Entered Apprentice** tracing-board of the S.O.T.: "*The Order which is concealed within Masonry is the Order of Knights Templar, and therein lays its source and origin. Below there are seven steps which lead to the closed door of the so called hall of the Temple ... The two pillars refer to the last Grand Master of the Order, namely Jacobus de Molay, native of Burgundy, and the letter J signifies the name Jacobus.*"

And here is an illuminating passage that explains the meaning of the Master's degree tracing-board in the Strict Observance secret tradition of the inner order usually given in the secular chapter of the Order:

The Masters' tracing-board has two different, although closely connected, parts of the Order's history in its different emblems as topic, The coffin located in the middle is not that of de Molay who was burned and could not be buried, but is rather that of Carolus a Monte Carmel Commander of the Province on the Po and Tiber, who was slain by Noffodei and Squin de Florian as taught in the history of the Order. He is the real Hiram of whom Masonry speaks. This story was contrived to approximate the true history of the Order that only the names are lacking. The blackjacks located below signify the murder weapons of the ruffians, and the hill with the Cassia upon the rubbish signifies that the corpse of Carolus de Monte Carmel, who was buried in the garden. The flames which are located on the floor, and which must be 61 in number. signify the tragic death of our Brethren whom Philip caused to be burned- in particular, 59 who were burned in one day in the field of St. Anthony. and also de Molay and Guy, who languished slowly over a fire on the Isle of St. Louis. The two letters M. B. do not signify May Beinac, as in Mabeignac, the adopted name of Aumont but they are once again, as in the first two Degrees, the name of the last Grand Master, MOLAY BURGUNDUS.

Let's remember that Adam Weishaupt, as well as Baron Adolph von Knigge, respectively the founder, and the person who structured the main rituals of the Illuminati Order, were both initiated in the **Rite of Strict Observance.** In the introduction of the book *The Secret School of Wisdom – The Authentic Rituals and Doctrines of the Illuminati,* we find information that confirms the importance of this rite in the Masonic life of Baron Adolph Knigge:

Following the example of his father, he had joined the Kassel lodge 'Zum ge- krönten Löwen' (Crowned Lion) in February 1773, at the age of twenty. Having witnessed its 1778 convention in Wolfenbüttel, he became a member of the Strict Observance, where he was given the name 'Eques a Cygno.' ... After moving to Frankfurt, he frequented the two lodges operating there, 'Zu den drei Disteln' (Three Thistles) and 'Zur Einigkeit' (Unity). Knigge was disenchanted with the Strict Observance with its spurious pretensions of unknown superiors and even sceptical as to whether the basic degrees of Freemasonry were worthy of reform at all, but he nevertheless lobbied for a full transformation of the Illuminati Order into a Masonic system. With Weishaupt's consent, he added some unmistakably Masonic elements to the Minerval degree, such as the layout of the assembly room, the use of a tracing board, and the practice of knocking with the gavel to gain the members' attention. In April 1781, he asked for specific instructions concerning the development of a fully fledged Masonic system. The degrees used by the Frankfurt lodge, he said, were too garbled to be of much help, but he had other sources at his disposal. He also recommended not to worry about supposedly authentic constitutions. At the time, the Strict Observance was the dominant Masonic system in much of Germany, its sphere of influence even extending into Switzerland, France, northern Italy, and Hungary. However, there were grave doubts concerning the central tenet of its high degrees, namely the supposed historical link between Free-masonry and the Knights Templar. The much-anticipated forthcoming convention of the Strict Observance was expected to deal with this and other crucial questions, and Knigge, who was pursuing the plan of a merger of this expansive yet ailing system with the Illuminati, initially wanted to wait for the results of the congress before working on an entirely new body of Masonic degrees. The convention was due to be held in Oc-tober 1781, in Frankfurt. When the news reached him that the date was postponed, Knigge immediately set out to write his own version of the three basic Masonic degrees. He also suggested that Weishaupt should finish both the Illuminatus major and diri-gens degrees which he could then cloak in the manner of 'Scottish' degrees. Some three months later, in late August 1781, Knigge had finished work on the Masonic degrees and an accompanying book of constitutions. The result was deliberately eclectic, and since Knigge did not divulge any of his sources, a meticulous comparison of all the de-grees he may have had at his disposal, in printed or manuscript form, would be neces-sary to fully appreciate it. Suffice it to say that some elements are typically German, such as the three lamps and rapier lying on the altar, some are taken from the Strict Observance rituals, such as the Master of Ceremonies carrying a sword rather than a baton, some are of English origin, such as the office of the Stewards. [3]

So Knigge seemed fed up with the "spurious pretensions of unknown superiors." But how could the "unknown superiors" of the time, that included many powerful royals, and even certain Jesuits, reveal themselves to the world, in this whole Masonic affair? The Jesuit abbate **Giuseppe Marotti**, who was later to become the secretary of Pope Pius VI, was for example, directly involved in the layout of the Masonic teachings of the Order of the Illuminati. So the Stuart family, and many other royal figures, at one point simply opt-ed out of this Templar system of Freemasonry, using the Unknown Superiors' controversy as an excuse, as they hide the secret teachings and rituals of the Strict Observance in other Rites. Let's remember that even Weishaupt's "Illuminati" degrees devised by Knigge had their own "Secret Superiors" and they are mentioned in the *Illuminatus Dirigens*, the "Directing Illuminatus," or **Scottish Knight degree** in *ADDENDUM A. FORM FOR THE LODGE CONSTITUTION:*

We, Delegates authorized by the Illustrious Worthy Secret Superiors of ancient true Freemasonry, under the invisible protection of the Secret Grand National Lodge in the Orient of Germany and its subordinate Provincial Lodge of this District, have decided, after the urgent request of several Brethren in. ... and after consulting with the Higher Superiors, to establish a true Lodge of secret Freemasonry there.

Of course, if you read superficial books like *The Templar Code For Dummies* By Christopher Hodapp, and Alice Von Kannon, you might think Baron Karl Gotthelf Hund made the whole "Unknown Superiors" thing up, like the majority of today's Free-masons, but of course that's not the case, and in my next book *Invisible Master*, I will prove this point further. However, the Strict Observance members who were initiated into Weishaupt's Order apparently believed that they were being initiated into the high-est echelons of the real Illuminati, or Brotherhood existing from time immemorial. Once initiated under strict vows of secrecy, a great deal of political and anti-monarchial phi-losophy were revealed to members. Weishaupt's "Illuminati" was soon attacked.

3   Joseph Wages, Reinhard Markner, Jeva Singh-Anand, *The Secret School of Wisdom* (Surrey, England, GB: Lewis Masonic, 2015), p. 26.

Its headquarters in German Bavaria was raided by the Elector of Bavaria in 1786, and many radical political aims of the Illuminati were discovered in documents that were seized during the raid. The Duke of Brunswick, acting as Grand Master of German Free-masonry, finally issued a manifesto eight years later, in 1794, to counteract Weishaupt's "Illuminati," after the public scandal could no longer be contained. Joining in the suppression of Weishaupt's Bavarian "Illuminati," were many Rosicrucians. Despite the repression, Weishaupt's teachings survived, and still exist today in many off shoots of his order, that use his unique techniques of mind control and manipulation, but also his more reasonable and intelligent teachings.

Having said this, people have mistakenly believed that Weishaupt's order was the only true Illuminati, and that it took over all of Freemasonry, when in fact it was only one of its manifestations. I already explained this in Volume I, that the real Illuminati mystery schools are many, and they form a network that has existed, in one way or another, since the times of **Atlantis**. One can still find books today, which theorize that Weishaupt's order was, and still is, the source of nearly all of mankind's social ills. A careful study of the evidence, indicates that *Spartacus,* a.k.a. Adam Weishaupt, and his order of "Illuminati," did contribute with their new ideas and their secret structure, to inspire some of the most important revolutionary organizations, and the agitations manifesting later in the world. Its direct impact on history does not appear to have been as great as some people believe, as the *Illuminati Order* was not the only Illuminati sect in existence, even in Weishaupt's time. There were, for example, the Illuminati of Avignon. The dark, Satanic side of the elite has existed since the beginning of human history, and Weishaupt's Illuminati order took a clear turn to the dark side only decades later, with people like Theodor Reuss, who later co-founded the *Ordo Templi Orients,* and his one-time representative Aleister Crowley, known as "The Great beast 666." In fact, the social ills which have often been blamed on Weishaupt's Illuminati order, existed long before the birth of Adam Weishaupt, and others were still being formulated and took place long after the end of Weishaupt's original order, that lasted not very long. What did take over nearly all of Freemasonry in the eighteenth century, was the obsession with the **Templar degrees,** which were not the same as Weishaupt's "Illuminati," who were actually opposed to them and proponents of an Age of Reason, whose purpose was to expand man's knowledge by questioning the church's teachings, their surroundings, and the society. They disliked all Templar and Rosicrucian traditions, as being the fruit of bigotry and superstition, and eventually such a position lead them to atheism.

But atheists, my dear readers, have been promulgating their wish to establish an atheist One World Religion for, at the very least, three centuries, so Weishaupt's *Ordo Illuminatorum* was simply picking up on a popular trend of that period, supported by the usual Jesuits. The true significance and purpose of the Bavarian Illuminati was an anti-monarchy faction, allowed to operate right out of Strict Observance lodges, becoming a sort of virus. Meanwhile, the Strict Observance was, and still is, generally considered pro-monarchy and it supports pro-monarchy causes. All this made the Strict Observance a source of secret agitation on both sides of the monarchy, versus anti-monarchy conflicts for a number of years, until the death of their founder Karl Gotthelf von Hund in 1776, and the defeat of the Stuart/Catholic mission, plus the upcoming French Revolution and the rise of the new middle class in Europe, that made it necessary for the Strict Obedience to seek refuge in other Masonic bodies or transform their entire aristocratic Christian Chilvaric Masonic tradition into something different, at least on the surface, or risk complete extinction. This was done with the adoption of much of the Strict Observance tradition by the **Swedish Rite**, later present in the whole of Scandinavia and Germany, and the creation of the **Rectified Scottish Rite** founded by **Jean Baptiste de Willermoz**, present in France and Switzerland.

The transformation of the Strict Observance into something else, obviously omitting the open use of the word **"Templar"** in their new public denominations, was said to be a strategic and deliberate choice worked out in the various Masonic Convents of those turbulent years, to hide their Neo-Templar origins. That's why the French Templars of the Strict Observance, that gave birth to the Rectified Scottish Rite, took the name of "Chevaliers Bienfaisants de la Cité Sainte" or "Knights Beneficent of the Holy City," commonly referred to as "C.B.C.S.," instead of calling themselves Knights Templar. After this reformation, Willermoz decided that it would be right to expand this revision into the bosom of the Mother branch of the German Strict Observance. It was with this initiative in mind, that he went to the Convent of Wilhemsbad in 1782. He found supporters of his plan in the Princes Ferdinand of Brunswick and Charles of Hesse, but found stiff opposition on the part of the Illuminati of Bavaria of Adam Weishaupt, and met hostility in the character of Francois de Chefdebien de Saint-Amand, representative of the **Order of the Pilalethes**, as well as resistance from Savalette de Lange. After heated arguments, Willermoz and his supporters won the day, and succeeded in having the title of C.B.C.S. adopted by all members of the Inner Order. A committee was formed under Willermoz to prepare the high degree rituals and those of the secret degrees of the *Profession*. This work was well advanced when the French Revolution interupted Willermoz's task.

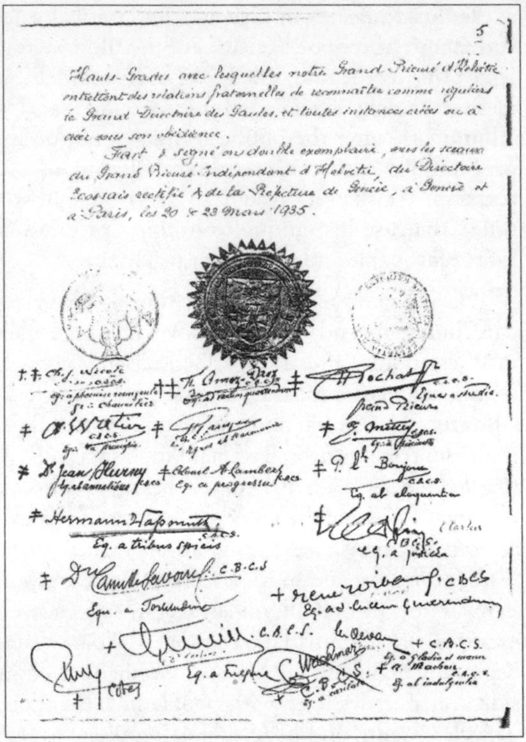
5

Hauts-Grades avec lesquelles notre Grand Prieuré d'Helvétie entretient des relations fraternelles de reconnaître comme réguliers le Grand Directoire des Gaules, et toutes instances créées ou à créer sous son obédience.

Fait & signé en double exemplaire, avec les sceaux du Grand Prieuré Indépendant d'Helvétie, du Directoire Écossais rectifié & de la Préfecture de Genève, à Genève et à Paris, les 20 & 23 Mars 1935.

FIG. 7 – Rare image of the 5th page of the charter issued by the Grand Priory of Helvetia C.B.C.S. for the French reactivation of The Knights Beneficent of the Holy City and the reawakening of the **Rectified Scottish Rite** *in March, 1935 that officially gave birth to the* **Grand Priory of the Gauls (GPDG)**, *that is said to have hosted from the beginning of their activites in France, the first manifestation of the modern Priory of Sion.*

The "Rectified" temples of the C.B.C.S. which were still active, had to suspend their works, the brethren being dispersed by the events of the period. After the Revolution, in 1806, the C.B.C.S. became active again in France, but the many problems and the death of Jean-Baptist Willermoz in May 1824, forced them to move in 1828, part of their archives and their most important founding documents from the Directoire of Burgandy in Besançon, known as the 5th province, to Geneva, the second most populous city in Switzerland; where the **Grand Priory of Switzerland** still resides and became the driving force of this new Masonic body "Rectified" with occult elements planted there by the occult elite, that later expanded in various countries including the United States of America. So the Rite of Knights Beneficent passed into Switzerland when the Directoire of Burgandy transmitted its occult powers to the Directoire of Helvetia, commonly referred to as the **Grand Priory of Helvetia**, and it is from this Swiss Jurisdiction, that has remained active ever since, that the C.B.C.S. would later be re-activated in France in March 1935, (FIG. 7) with the **Grand Priory of the Gauls** (GPDG), and became the headquarters of *The Alpha Galates,* that later became the Priory of Sion. During World War II, as a result of the anti-Masonic legislation of the so-called *Etat français* (French State) of Marshall Pétain, Masons were declared outlaws and Masonic temples and archives were confiscated. After the Liberation of France, Masonic workings began again and, in 1958, the GPDG and the *Grande Loge Nationale Française* (GLNF) signed a Treaty (Convention) of mutual recognition and cooperation: the GPDG entrusted the GLNF, by formal delegation of powers, with the management of the first three Masonic degrees—the 4th Masonic degree and the Chivalric Order remained under its own jurisdiction. An official statement by the GPDG on their website says:

> *In June 2000, the GLNF broke off suddenly, and with no regard to its legal obligations, the Treaty. For that behavior it was condemned twice by the civil Courts of Paris (the judge on first hearing had even formally forbidden it to practice the Rectified degrees!) The GPDG therefore retrieved the direct management of its Masonic lodges and in this way brought together again all the elements and both classes of the Regime, restoring it as it was originally during its first years 1778-1782. In the interim, the GPDG had received:*
>
> *– the degrees of the Order of Malta from the Great Priory of England and Wales*
>
> *– those of the Order of Knights Templar from the Great Priory of Scotland, and*
>
> *– those of the Rose-Croix from the Dutch Order of High Degrees.*
>
> *So the GPDG decided to practice those Systems in full from the Masonic degrees upwards, thus creating, besides the Scottish Rectified Regime (Rite Ecossais Rectifié), two other bodies: the Scottish Rite of Scotland (Rite Ecossais d'Ecosse) and the French Rite (Rite Français), using the purest original rituals of each. Today, the GPDG is recognised by all the Masonic Obediences and Great Priories in France (except of course that of the GLNF) as a Masonic Obedience and Chivalric Great Priory. Many other Masonic Obediences and Great Priories outside France are in amity with the GPDG—the latter entertaining the very best relations possible with all of them.*

For the famous occultist **Arthur Edward Waite** (1857 – 1942), the Rectified Scottish Rite was the one Rite he craved the most. He *"had come to see the Régime Ecossais et Rectifié as maintaining, more than any other rite, the essence in ritual form of that secret tradition that tells us that the Soul 'cometh from afar' and that the Soul returns whence it came, but it delineates the Path of Ascent."* It was, for him, the true secret tradition in practice.

The Rite of Strict Observance vs. the rest of Freemasonry in the hands of Islam

To this day, these two Christian Masonic rites (Rectified Scottish Rite and Swedish Rite), are proud of their Christian Masonic heritage, and only accept Christians amongst their brethren, but they are also more discreet and secretive about their practices, and their beliefs in the original Rite of Strict Templar Observance. This was done so they could comply with the rules of the newly expanding English Masonic network, and their all inclusive religious version of the Craft promoted by the English "Moderns." Such vision will open Freemasonry to non-Christians after the unification between "Ancients" and "Moderns" in 1813, that took place after the installation of Prince Augustus Frederick, Duke of Sussex as Grand Master. The term "Moderns" defined the non-Christian Masons, more close to the thought of Adam Weishaupt's "Illuminati," and the Age of Reason, during the period of time before this historic unification. The "Moderns" never claimed a Christian heritage, but instead had set up lodges that promoted values other than those espoused in Christianity, even in the predominantly Christian USA, creating a feud between the anti-Christian Freemasons and their Christian counter-parts, that involved some of the Founding Fathers. Obviously the new "United" Grand Lodge of England in 1813, did not recognize any Masonic links with a supposed Tem-plar tradition, and generally covered up, dismissed, or minimized, the Christian origins of the Craft altogether, to not offend their non-Christian members. In the meantime, the Rectified Scottish Rite (known also with the acronym R.E.R.), and later the Swed-ish Rite, included in their reform from the Strict Observance, a lot more occultist and gnostic elements into their teachings and high degrees (from the teaching of the Order of Elect Cohens in the R.E.R. to the teachings of Emmanuel Swedenborg in the Swedish Rite), at times jeopardizing in my view, their traditional Christian values and beliefs, or at least creating in the average Freemason, the possibility of an alternative interpretation of Christianity, facilitating the expansion of Crowleyanity, especially in the Swedish Rite.

In any case, I want to include in this book some rare images from an almost impossible to find publication by the Masonic historian Klaus C. Feddersen, entitled *Rituale des hohen Ordens vom heiligen Tempel zu Jerusalem, auch Strikte Observanz genannt, weltlicher Zweig nebst Ordensregeln und vielen Abbildungen aus dem Jahre 1764. I. bsi VII. Grad.* Published in 1999 by the German Masonic Research Group Forschungsvereinigung Frederik, it digs deep into the Strict Observance roots, showing the way it shaped the Swed-ish Rite and its symbols. (FIG. 8) Even after the collapse of the Stuart cause, the Templar degrees originally promoted by the Strict Observance remained popular and spread rapidly, inspiring the birth of the Ancient and Accepted Scottish Rite and the York Rite. The pro-Stuart slant vanished in favor of an antimonarchial philosophy in some Templar organiza-tions, and a pro-monarchial sentiment in others. Without a doubt, Freemasons practicing the Templar degrees played important political roles on both sides of the monarchy vs. anti-monarchy battles going on in the 18th century, thereby helping to keep that issue alive in such a way that people would find it something to continuously fight over.

For example, King Gustavus III of Sweden and his brother, Karl, the Duke of Soder-manland, were initiated into the Strict Observance in 1770. In the following year, one of Gustavus's first acts upon assuming the Swedish throne, was to mount a *coup d'etat* against the Swedish *Riksdag* [parliament] and reestablish greater powers for the Crown. According to Samuel Harrison Baynard, writing in his book, *History of the Supreme Council*, Gustavus was assisted largely by fellow Freemasons. The Knight degrees also found a home in Ireland when they attached themselves to **The Loyal Orange Institu-tion**, more commonly known as the **Orange Order**. The Orange Order is a Protestant fraternal organization based primarily in Northern Ireland, patterned after Freemasonry. It was founded to ensure the Protestant Ascendancy of Northern Ireland, but it has a sig-nificant presence in the Scottish Lowlands and lodges throughout the Commonwealth and the United States. Members of the Orange Order vowed to support the Hanoverians (now called the Windsor), as long as they continued their support of Protestantism. The Knight degrees were grafted onto the Order of Orange in the early 1790s, by which time the Stuart cause was nearly dead. The Orange Order's Templar degrees were, and still are today, called the **"Black Preceptory."**

Although the Orange Order and the "Black Preceptory" are supposed to be equal in status and link, entry into the Black Preceptory is accomplished only after a person has

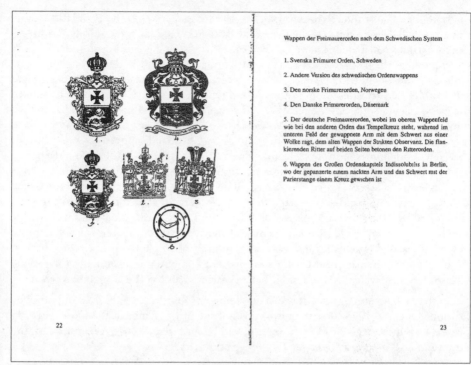

Wappen der Freimaurerorden nach dem Schwedischen System

1. Svenska Frimurer Orden, Schweden

2. Andere Version des schwedischen Ordenswappens

3. Den norske Frimurerorden, Norwegen

4. Den Danske Frimurerorden, Dänemark

5. Der deutsche Freimaurerorden, wobei im oberen Wappenfeld wie bei den anderen Orden das Tempelkreuz steht, während im unteren Feld der gewappnete Arm mit dem Schwert aus einer Wolke ragt, dem alten Wappen der Strikten Observanz. Die flankierenden Ritter auf beiden Seiten betonen den Ritterorden.

6. Wappen des Großen Ordenskapitels Indissolubilis in Berlin, wo der gepanzerte einem nackten Arm und das Schwert mit der Parierstange einem Kreuz gewichen ist

FIG. 8 – The coats of arms of the various Swedish Rite Masonic Bodies shown in relation to the Strict Templar Observance on page 22 and page 23 of the book by Klaus C. Feddersen, Ritual des hohen Ordens vom heiligen Tempel zu Jerusalem, auch genannt Strikte Observanz, weltlicher Zweig nebst Ordensregeln und vielen Abbildungen aus dem Jahre 1764. bSI I. VII. Grad Published in 1999 by the German Masonic research group Forschungsvereinigung Frederik.

first passed through the degrees of the Order. According to Tony Gray, writing in his fascinating book, *The Orange Order: the Black Preceptory* today has eleven degrees and *"a great deal of secrecy still shrouding the inner workings of this curious institution."* Approximately 50% to 60% of all Orange members become members of the Preceptory. The Orange Order itself continues to be strongly Protestant and anti-Catholic, and in this way it contributes to some of the conflicts between Catholics and Protestants in Ireland to this day. In the meantime the worldwide transformation of human society was announced by the *Fama Fraternitatis*. This anonymous Rosicrucian "Illuminati" manifesto published in 1614 gained momentum as Freemasons and other mystical network members led numerous revolutions around the world.

The uprisings were not confined to Europe, and not always with positive results; but they spilled across the Atlantic Ocean and took root in the European colonies in North America, where they gave birth in 1776 (the year of Baron von Hund's death), to the single most influential nation on Earth today, the United States of America, the guiding force of this New World Order. Unfortunately, such well "Crafted" revolutions were not always as positive as the American and the French revolutions, and they sadly destroyed the Russian Empire, that is now being reconstituted by Vladimir Putin, and they also brought us that disgrace of Communist China.

Don't worry, the last "Revolution" to end them all will bring us the most Holy and the most powerful Empire of all time, that is already on the horizon, and that's the Empire of our Lord Jesus Christ and His followers during the Second Coming. This is said to be something that will defeat ultimately the rise of the Antichrist, and the present New World Order, that is indeed of a Satanic nature, as you can notice by simply turning on your TV. Let's remember that the first recorded Freemasonry under the Grand Lodge of England (now United Grand Lodge of England), was the formation of four Lodges within one square mile within the City of London on the 24th of June, 1717. Therefore Freemasons around the world celebrate the Tercentenary i.e. 300 years of Masonry in England in 2017, a very important event indeed for the New World Order. We should use this historic moment to lay the cornerstone (or foundation stone) of our new Christian Empire, when everything in this New World Order seems to be leading instead towards a soulless One World Religion, with no hope for the Christian faith or the future of this civilization. This can be done with the help of the reawakened Rite of Strict Observance, the oldest of all Masonic Christian Rites, that we should use to shape the new aristocracy of the future Empire, the one announced by the journalist Maurizio Blondet, who I cited earlier, that will finally defeat the seemingly unstoppable Islamic take over of the West. The Strict Templar Observance never really ceased its activities and was only waiting for the right moment to come back in the open on the international Masonic stage for a new important mission, this time saving Christianity and laying the foundations of a new aristocracy for **The Kingdom of God.**

In the *Instruction Manual* of the Strict Templar Observance published in France by Editions Opéra in 1997, after the restoration of the 3rd province of the Order in 1995 headed by our illustrius Brother, Reverend, and Knight, **Jean-Marie Auzanneau**, in the *Order Eques Professus a Stella per Ensem* we find written:

> But the Templar Strict Observance will never cease to exist under its particular form but far more occult in many Germanic countries and Northern Europe; its survival explains its influence on the most used Masonic "Templar" system, using individual transmission for the qualification of "Knight of the Temple" it has allowed an original authentic affiliation always ensuring the integrity of the message with the fidelity to the Holy Christian religion.

The historic reawakening of the Rite of Strict Observance that took place in France on the 3rd of September, 1995 was an event supported by many ex-Brothers of the *Grande Loge Nationale Française* (GLNF), fed up with the invasive policies of the United Grand Lodge of England that eventually forced their French minions of the GLNF, in the year 2000, to establish their own Priories of the Rectified Scottish Rite C.B.C.S. after the GLNF, in an unprecedented move that derecognized the home of the Rectified Scottish Rite in France, the *Grand Prieuré de Gaules.* This is a Masonic body that has been recognized since 1958, and is a not-so-clever move, accomplished to form their own Rectified Scottish Rite controlled by the Brits and the British Royals. The excuse was the birth of the supposedly competing **Grand Priory of the Scottish Reformed and Rectified Rite of Occitania,** chartered in 1995 by the *Grand Prieuré de Gaules* (which was, in turn, chartered by the Great Priory of Helvetia in 1935, and is said to be the birthplace of the Priory of Sion). I know it's all very complicated, even for Masonic experts, but don't worry, just let me say one thing, Masonic politics are the biggest waste of time in the history of mankind, and often many intelligent individuals leave the *Craft,* as Masons call it, for this reason. However the main reason to join the Strict Observance for many high level Freemasons and dignitaries in that turbolent time, above all the Masonic conflict and policies, was the real possibility to finally return to the original source of their teachings beyond the "Rectified version," and being able to work the Templar degree in its true format; not corrupted by mainstream Freemasonry and its "Modern" style non-Christian

Masonic elite policies, that are influenced by the darkness and ignorance of this modern age we live in. Since 2013, the Rite of Strict Templar Observance brought back to life by **Jean-Marie Auzanneau**, whom remains the regent and co-restorer of this Order, is lead by the illustrious Brother **Didier Pestel,** known in the Order as *Eques Professus a Tempora Modernis*. Didier Pestel made an important statement on the 3rd of June 2013, during a ceremony at the Templar Church of Beaussiet in Mazerolles, a commune where Didier Pestel resides, based in southwestern France.

Pestel said to all his dignitaries present from the various provinces for this solemn occassion, that he Didier Pestel, was now the *sérénissime Grand Maître général de l'Ordre de Stricte Observance et de toutes ses provinces templières répandues sur la surface de la terre.* This means Pestel declared himself to be the General Grand Master of the Strict Observance for all the provinces of the world. Of course such claim might be regarded as pompous by some and will not be recognized by everyone for sure, especially as his unique brand of the *Stricte Observance Templière* accepts also women, a problem for many "Regular" Freemasons working in male only lodges, who would like to join this unique Masonic tradition. Having said all this, in one way or another, it proves once again that the Strict Observance never really ceased to exist, and their message of fidelity towards the Christian faith is considered today stronger than ever in Masonic circles all over the world. That's why Christian Freemasons are trying to bring back to life in recent years, the most pure and original form of the Rite of Strict Templar Observance. Like I am doing in Italy for example, and even Freemasons of so-called "Regular Freemasonry," are constituting in secret in the last decade their own Strict Observance, disenchanted with the Rectified Scottish Rite. They are doing this with the secret backing of key figures of the Supreme Council of the U.S. Southern Jurisdiction of the Ancient and Accepted Scottish Rite. This is done to oppose the expansion of the Strict Observance in "Irregular" circles, but also to offer an alternative to the expanding Rectified Scottish Rite linked in the USA, and other countries to the York Rite. Back in 1934, with the secret support of the elite of the **York Rite** in the USA, a charter had been given to the Grand Priory of America C.B.C.S., which was originally granted by the *Grand Prieuré Indépendant d'Helvetie* (Great Priory of Switzerland) C.B.C.S.

The problem is that the Grand Priory of America, established in Raleigh, North Carolina by Dr. William Moseley Brown and J. Raymond Shute II, is to this day an invitation only group, and its constitution limits the membership to just 81 Freemasons at any one time in the U.S., and since its chartering it seems there have never been any more than 45 or 50 members following this tradition in the U.S. at the same time. Limiting the structure to a very elitist group recruited in the top positions of the U.S. York Rite, however creating discontent in the long run amongst the brethren left out, that finally decided to change things. So it's no wonder U.S. Freemasons interested in the teachings and traditions of this Christian Masonic Rite went initially abroad to seek initiation in the Rectified Scottish Rite, but by doing so they created an internal schism in the U.S., and chaos within the U.S. Grand Encampment of Knights Templar supporting such a move. The known Masonic author and blogger **Christopher Hodapp** wrote in 2010 on his popular website *Freemasons For Dummies*:

> In 2009, the Great Priory of America objected officially to a group of American Ma
> sons being initiated into the English CBCS by the Great Priory of Anglia (England)
> as infringing on "their" territory. If they were nothing but a supper club for Masons
> in need of more fancy dues cards in their wallets, why would they object to the English
> priory actually conferring degrees on Americans?... After meetings, letters, and not
> a few heated emails, Grand Master William H. Koon II of the Grand Encampment
> of Knights Templar of the USA issued the following statement on May 5, 2010: "The

Great Priory of America is an unrecognized Templar Order operating within the United States of America, in direct conflict with Section 3 of the Constitution of the Grand Encampment of Knights Templar of the United States of America. Accordingly, membership in the Great Priory of America is incompatible with membership in the Grand Encampment of Knights Templar of the United States of America and any Grand, Subordinate, or Constituent Commandery under its jurisdiction or owing allegiance to the same." Now, all of this would just be so much stuff and nonsense over nothing, except that some of the most respected Masons in the U.S. are members of the CBCS. Brothers Reese Harrison and Thomas W. Jackson serve as officers in the GPA, and both men are highly regarded in the Masonic community.

The truth is that the York Rite wants to stay in control of the U.S. "Christian" Masonic scene, and does not want the Masonic advancement of Brothers initiated abroad if not fully controlled by them, that's because the York Rite only wants a watered down version of the Masonic Christian ideal, but also because the Grand Priory of America C.B.C.S. wished to establish themselves more openly as Knights Templar, becoming a sovereign and independent Templar order in the U.S. That meant the sovereignty of the Grand Encampment of the York Rite was being challenged, and this motivated the actions of the Grand Encampment of Knights Templar of the U.S. York Rite.

So the York Rite went as far as announcing on its website in 2011, that the Grand Priory of the Scottish Reformed and Rectified Rite of Occitania had issued a charter to form a new "Grand Priory of the Scottish Reformed and Rectified Rite of the United States of America," without taking into account the position of the previous existing Great Priory of America (GPA) established in the 1930's by the Swiss Priory. Now the problem is that Rectified Rite of Occitania is considered by many longstanding, recognizing Templar organizations in Europe, and the rest of the world to be spurious and irregular, since its foundation in the middle of the 1990s. This means the whole thing is a scam from the start, mostly driven by the Masonic policies and interest of the New World Order, that can now give to the interested Freemasons in the U.S. and abroad, the genuine teaching of Christian Freemasonry if they stay in the firm hands of the York Rite Grand Encampment of Knights Templar of the United States of America, a Masonic Christian body that works now more than ever before, with the secret Blessing of the Catholic Church. In April 2011, they happily announced *Grand Encampment Adopts an Ancient Order of Templary*. A few months later, Christopher Hodapp, who is a member of the Grand Priory of the Reformed and Rectified Rite of the United States of America wrote:

A tiny group of men who want to see that the only CBCS body in America remains nothing but a supper club for a handful of self-appointed elite Masons, while holding the 230 year degree system of the Rectified Rite hostage in the U.S. The Great Priory of Helvetia (Switzerland) was desirous of having the Rectified Rite practiced, with full conferral of the degrees, in the United States, and they were and remain well aware of the "supper club" dead end of the GPA. The Swiss desire to have their Order's degrees worked properly as it is all over the world except in the United States. Unfortunately, the GPA changed its mind after the agreement in place since 1932 and became desirous of becoming a sovereign and independent Templar order in the U.S. That meant the sovereignty of the Grand Encampment was being challenged by them. That is what motivated the actions of the Grand Encampment to seek a charter.

The York Rite's decision to relaunch a new Rectified Scottish Rite, obviously under their control would like to appear legitimate in the eyes of Freemasons worldwide, but the truth is that their actions are only driven by power and interest in territorial control, and the will of international Freemasonry to destroy or closely control its Christian heritage and hide certain secrets. favoring the growing interest of young Freemasons for Thelema and dangerous Illuminati sects with nothing to offer except black magic and lies. Going back to the Rite of Strict Observance, and the various attempts to restore it around the world; other people in the Masonic community linked this time to the U.S. Southern Jurisdiction of the Supreme Council of the Scottish Rite, obviously in competition with the York Rite, appear to be interested in restoring the oldest Chilvaric Christian Masonic tradition. This is happenining particularly in South America, in places, like Costa Rica, where Freemasons like **Emmanuel Mora Iglesias** of the *Lodge San Juan de la Persever-ancia # 20,* practicing the Rectified Scottish Rite under the Gran Logia de Costa Rica (GLCR), have created a parallel Strict Observance Lodge called *Amadeus der drei Sau-len,* recognized by **Thanos Christopoulos**, and his Grand Lodge, a close friend of our illustrius Brother Arturo de Hoyos, who is doing the same thing in Greece on a slight-ly larger scale, with the reawakening of what used to be the 9th province of the Order (Greece and Arcipelago). Unfortunately for Brother Arturo that I respect very much, his friend Brother Thanos Christopoulos is a truly controversial figure, and somebody who openly admitted on his Facebook that he is a member of the Ku Klux Klan. Yes my dear readers, Brother Christopoulos who used to be once upon a time a member of the Greek Supreme Council of the A.A.S.R. is a member of the infamous KKK.

On top of all this, Brother Thanos Christopoulos' supposed Masonic lineage for his Rite of Strict Observance is coming from a dubious source in Italy called **Gran Loggia d'Italia UMSOI,** an acronym that stands for *Unione Massonica di Stretta Osservanza Iniziatica* (Masonic Union of Strict Initiation Observance), a spurious Masonic body with no legitimacy, headed by the self-styled Grand Master and Sovereign Grand Com-mander **Gianfranco Pilloni,** a dangerous agent of the New World Order, who was ac-tually kicked out of the original UMSOI in 2011, to establish his own version of this Obedience, trying, with no luck, to get accepted in the inner circle of the late Count Licio Gelli, who never really liked him. There is also another important detail regarding "Grand Master" Gianfranco Piloni, and that is he never even worked the Rite of Strict Templar Observance in his small Obedience, he only pratices and knows the Ancient and Accepted Scottish Rite, so what kind of S.O.T. lineage can he have? None of course, but Piloni is also known in the Illuminati world for nominating in his Supreme Council many VIPs, that later on function as Satan's little helpers, like for example the well-known Turkish ex Anti-Masonic figure, and Islamic leader, called **Adnan Oktar,** also known as **Harun Yahya**, someone who has radically changed his tune in regards to Freemasonry since 2010. This was the year Mr. Oktar, a very popular person in Turkey, started a sort of "dialogue project" with various high level figures of the Masonic and Neo-Templar world like **Timothy Hogan,** the Grand Master of the Neo-Templar order called *Ordre Souverain du Temple Initiatique* (**OSTI**), who runs **CIRCES** (*Cercle International de Recherches Culturelles et Spirituelles*), the organization built to convey the mes-sage of its founder, the late U.S. Illuminati initiate and Knights Templar Grand Master **Raymond Bernard** (1923 – 2006), who basically created CIRCES International as an outward Templar vehicle to eventually prepare people for initiation into the inner Order of the OSTI, where they are said to have a Johannite belief system in place. CIRCES International also continues to protect and perpetuate *L'Ordre Martiniste of Papus,* now headed by Grand Master **Emilio Lorenzo**. Timothy Hogan, who is a Democrat and a member of the Grand Lodge of A.F. & A.M. of Colorado, is a Past Master of *East Denver #160 Masonic Lodge (AF&AM)* and an active member of *Enlightenment Lodge #198*, two lodges he used to actively promote his new Islamic friends from Harun Yahya's organization in the U.S. as he candidly admitted himself with no shame on page 152 of his book, *Entering the Chain of Union,* published back in 2012. Hogan is also a member of *Pythagoras Lodge #1841,* in Lebanon, founded in June 2014, and one of the newest Lodges in Lebanon, working under the Grand Lodge of Scotland, where there is to my knowledge, a predominantly Muslim Shia brethren, showing in this way the typical "Templar" manipulation on all sides of Islam indicated earlier by Count Licio Gelli. Hogan who is also listed as a speaker at the *Colorado Masonic Speakers Bureau* (CMSB) for the Grand Lodge of Colorado AF&AM, and both a Knight Templar in the York Rite, and a 32nd degree *Knight Commander of the Court of Honor* (KCCH) in the Ancient and Accepted Scottish Rite (SJ), has also been knighted into the **Royal Order of Scotland** as a *Rosicrucian Knight of Kilwinning,* and is an active officer in the *Societas Rosicruciana In Civitibus Foederatis,* and much more initiatic rubbish from the sectarian world of the Illuminati, even if he is in secret a full-on Muslim believer.

The threat of a pro-Islamist New World Order

Timothy Hogan, who likes to be presented as the worldwide Grand Master of the "original Knights Templar," met Harun Yahya in 2010, and the two seemingly got on like a "house on fire." In the following years, Hogan occasionally appeared on Harun Yahya's TV channel promoting and supporting enthusiastically Harun Yahya's vision of Islam, and how Freemasonry was deeply connected with the values and traditions of Islam. Really? I don't think so, or at least not in the overly enthusiastic way portrayed by "Grand Master" Timothy Hogan, who appears to be after close analysis, a closet Muslim more than a Christian Templar, as he should be by tradition. Of course, the topic of Islam and Freemasonry is a very sensitive topic, for both Freemasons and Muslims, because of the Shriners, who are often called the "playground of Freemasonry," employ Islamic symbolism, philosophy and the entire general theme of Islam for their Shrindom, which was perhaps the first step of the elite of Freemasonry, in promoting a more general acceptance of Islam in the U.S., before today's full on support in proximity of a possible Muslim take over. This however, did not work out as planned, and the Muslim author and researcher Mustafa El-Amin, a pioneer in the field of Islam in relation to Freemasonry, who wrote such books as *Al-Islam: Christianity and Freemasonry* (1985), *Freemasonry: Ancient Egypt and the Islamic Destiny* (1988), and *African-American Freemasons: Why They Should Accept Al-Islam* (1990), was most critical of Shrine Masonry. El-Amin accused Freemasonry of using the religion of Islam in a profane manner. He considered the Shriners to be totally heretical and described how they were eventually banned from Makkah, which in my opinion is fully understandable, as the description of the Shrine rituals and their initiations in detail by El-Amin in his books, points out on the obvious incompatibility of Shrine Masonry with true Islam. Many passages of their rituals might even be considered blasphemous by Muslims, so why continue to offend them, why not join them instead, like Hogan and his "Templars" seem to have done in recent years.

I know it's crazy, but Timothy Hogan has done that, and was once again seen with the Islamic leader Adnan Oktar/Harun Yahya, on his satellite TV station A9, as recently as July, 2015. This time Hogan was not the only Freemason on air with Mr Harun Yahya, as he brought two other senior members of the Grand Lodge of A.F. & A.M. of Colorado, **Scott Ammerman** Chemistry Teacher at West High School (WLA) and Paster Master of *Union Lodge #7,* who is also the General Secretary of the Knights Templars, OSTI (*Ordre Soverain du Temple Initiatique*) and of the CIRCES, a member of the Research Lodge of Colorado, and a speaker of the CMSB, plus Brother **Paul Dickerson,** who is a more mysterious figure, another 32nd degree Freemason from the Scottish Rite, and a Past Master of the *East Denver Lodge #160.* A Knight Templar in OSTI, Dickerson lectures on symbolism and esotericism for the CMSB, and works with Timothy Hogan for the Denver-based **Elite Sterling Security LLC.** This company, where both Hogan and Dickerson work, is the only U.S. authorized seller for the Miguel Caballero line of exclusive ready-to-wear bullet resistant clothing solutions *for Corporate and Governmental Executive Leadership, as well as military, security, rescue, and law enforcement,* obviously with many connections to the United States intelligence, and security community. Their public discussion with Harun Yahya that took place on the 20th of July 2015, touched on some very interesting points, amongst them the arrival of the "Grand Grand Master," meaning the Messiah that Freemasonry has been waiting for 5,000 years. This is a written extract of the TV show conversation published by Mr. Adnan Oktar's organization with the relative video on YouTube: [4]

Bülent Sezgin: *Yes, we are continuing with our broadcast. In our studio we have Mr. Timothy Hogan, current Grand Master of the Knights Templar and Freemason and Templar guests from Colorado, America. Welcome.*

Adnan Oktar: *Someone needs to introduce them by name, though.*

Oktar Babuna: *Mr. Timothy Hogan has visited us before. He is currently the Great Commander, the Grand Master, of the Knights Templar. He is the current leader of the original Knights Templar who go back to the 12th century under the name of the Sovereign Order of the Initiatory Temple* [Ordre Soverain du Temple Initiatique]. *He is a senior Mason from the Honorary Board of the Scottish Rite. He is the author of several books on Freemasonry and regularly holds conferences in lodges. He is also affiliated to many Masonic groupings, such as the Rosicrucians.*

Welcome, Timothy Hogan. We also have here Freemason and Templar guests from the USA, Colorado. Welcome, Mr. Paul Dickerson and Mr. Scott Ammerman.

Adnan Oktar: *You do us an honor. We are delighted. It is a great pleasure to have you here among us.*

Timothy Hogan: *We are very happy to be here.*

Adnan Oktar: *We are delighted to have our friends here with us. But let us not give such long breaks and let us meet up with shorter intervals.*

Timothy Hogan: *Yes, it has been too long.*

Adnan Oktar: *Yes. What have you been doing? Could you give us some information about the activities of our friends?*

Timothy Hogan: *Well, we have been doing a lot of travelling around the world and actually we have had the opportunity to share our great experiences in Istanbul and with you to a lot of people. We have a whole bunch of people out here in Istanbul right now. They were all here because of the things we've shared about how wonderful it is.*

Adnan Oktar: *Yes, Istanbul is a city full of mysteries. You have done exactly the right thing. What a great idea!*

Timothy Hogan: *Yes.*

Adnan Oktar: *Is there something that you would like to tell us?*

Sadun Engin: *If you like I can give some information about our other guests here, Mr. Paul Dickerson and Mr. Scott Ammerson.*

Adnan Oktar: *You go on, I am listening.*

Sadun Engin: *I would like to introduce Paul Dickerson. He is a 32nd degree Freemason from the Scottish Rite. He is a past Master of the East Denver Lodge. He is a Knight Templar in OSTI (Ordre Soverain du Temple Initiatique) and Masonic Order. He is also a member of the Masonic Rosicrucian Society. Mr. Scott Ammerman is a past Master of the Union Lodge and Research Lodge of Colorado. He is the General Secretary of the Knights Templars, OSTI (Ordre Soverain du Temple Initiatique), General Secretary of the CIRCES (Cercle International de Recherches Culturelles et Spirituelles) and District Lecturer of the Grand Lodge of Colorado.*

Adnan Oktar: *How nice, how beautiful posts these are. What a nice honor it is to assume them. Insha'Allah, we will make the world a more beautiful place together. We will lead the whole world to peace, brotherhood and love. Wars and bloodshed will end and arms will be eradicated. Only love will remain in the world.*

The problem with all this is that Adnan Oktar aka Harun Yahya, who seems a nice guy, was originally a Sunni zealot influenced by the books of the Kurdish Mullah, **Said Nursi,** the same evil Mullah who influenced Fethullah Gülen, who I wrote about in Volume I. Gülen, who presents himself to the world as a humble, self-denying cleric, in private is an entirely different kind of person, just like Adnan Oktar, vain, megalomaniacal and demanding total obedience from his followers. Gülen's sect is divided into seven levels, with Gülen of course at the top. Adnan Oktar, who is in reality a minor player compared to Gülen, but still a key figure of the New World Order in Turkey, and an active collaborator with the Turkish and U.S. Intelligence, who also has a very large Islamic organization at hand, full of wealthy individuals who totally believe in media censorship. The Adnan Oktar organization holds a lot of influence over what Turks can and can not watch on the internet today, frequently talking about the immorality of the West on his satellite TV channel **A9 TV**, while at the same time secretly controlling an Islamist sex cult positioned at the inner circle of his **mens only** Illuminati sect.

Does Brother Timothy Hogan, or his organization know about all this? Does his Order of "Knights Templar" know about all this? Or do they simply blindly support this move to corrupt the soul of true Islam? I hope not, because this is digraceful to say the least. Just watch Hogan's quasi religious farce during the last public meeting with Harun Yahya in the summer of 2015 (FIG. 9), and check out his dedication towards this typical NWO project in the YouTube video entitled *Mr. Adnan Oktar's Live Conversation with Grand Master of Knights Templar.*[5] Of course, the other two guys with Timothy Hogan on this TV debate looked quite frankly like they were two U.S. Intelligence operatives, especially one of them, but of course that's just speculation on my side, so please forgive me if I am wrong.

In his book *Entering the Chain of Union,* Timothy Hogan talks in detail about his experience with Harun Yahya, from the time they first met, and exposes his esoteric thought, that shows him not only as very close to Islam, but as a full-on closet Muslim: *"In the years of 2010 and 2011, I had the good fortune to organize initiates from Templar, Masonic, Martinist, and Rosacrucian backgrounds, to go on a series of historic trips to Istanbul, Turkey, to meet wih Islami leaders and initiates, and to help clear up misconceptions about Templarism and Freemasonry, in particular for the Islamic*

FIG. 9 – From your left Adnan Oktar (born 2 February, 1956), also known as Harun Yahya with his Neotemplar-Masonic guest **Timothy Hogan, Paul Dickerson,** *and* **Scott Ammerman** *on his own satellite TV channel A9 TV in July, 2015. —Lily Lynch: Followers of Harun Yahya wear drag make-up and practice a "sexed-up, Disney version of Islam" that helps promote conservative Prime Minister Recep Tayyip Erdogan's vision of a modern, Muslim Turkey. Step inside this surreal world where religious piety meets psychedelic softcore porn, led by the world's foremost Islamic creationist. Image from the website: https://www.sott.net/article/278696-Meet-the-bizarre-Islamic-sex-cult-propelling-Turkey-towards-a-neo-Ottoman-Turkish-Islamic-Union*

world, while at the same time gain new light on Islam. In attendance were brothers of many different religious faiths from around the world."[6]

Timothy Hogan talks about his mentor, the French philosopher Raymond Bernard, a Grand Master of the Knights Templar, who after his earlier initiatic encounters in Rome in 1955—where Bernard was initiated in the *Sovereign Order of the Initiatory Temple* (OSTI)—an experience that inspired his esoteric masterpiece: *A Secret Meeting in Rome*, originally published in the early 1960s, he then went on to meet certain "High Adepts" in Istanbul back in 1966. These "High Adepts" instructed Bernard specifically on certain secrets, and told him to wait for a **"SIGNAL"** to happen—and 40 years later in early 2006, just before his passing, Bernard wrote about it: *"Important historical connections which would unfold between initiates from around the world and certain initiates within Instanbul, (which is a sacred center in the future as it has been in the past), and as Templars we were responsible for helping to guide these associations which will bring about the start of important connections for the Aquarian Age we are going into."*[7]

Either "Aquarian Age" or the "New Age"—one thing is for sure, the OSTI–CIRCES Freemasons (FIGS. 10, 11, 12, 13) presented themselves as pious Knights Templars to their Muslim counterparts and their TV audience, not knowing the infinite hypocrisy of the person they had in front of them (FIGS. 14 and 15), their new "Brother" Adnan Oktar, known in Turkey as Adnan Hodja (Preacher Adnan), and to his followers as Adnan Agabey (Big Brother Adnan), who is the leader of an **Islamist sex cult**, whose headquarters

6   Timothy Hogan, *Entering the Chain of Union,* (Amazon Digital Services LLC, 2012) p.121.
7   *Ibid.* p. 124

FIG. 10 – At Denver Scottish Rite Consistory, Freemasons, Paul Dickerson, Scott Ammerman and Timothy Hogan showing a member sash of Pythagoras Lodge #1841 working in Lebanon under the Grand Lodge of Scotland. In many Scottish Lodges the Office-bearers wear sashes over the right shoulder and under the left arm. A chilvaric tradition also in use in various Masonic rites including the Swedish Rite and the Rite of Strict Observance.

are in Oktar's residence. A lavish building built in the image of King Solomon's Temple, fueled with young ladies eager to work for him and appear on his TV stations (FIGS. 16 and 17), and always ready to please the various influential men at the core of his organization with some "extra services," and for this reason he has been involved in many public scandals. Indeed, Adnan is a very smart individual. After being arrested in the 1980s, and to save himself from any future legal issues, since 1986 he has managed to get a report from the state mental hospital in Turkey saying that he has a severe mental disorder..

The False Prophets of "the Noble Sanctuary" and Ataturk

Edip Yuksel, a Kurdish American intellectual considered one of the prime figures in the modern Islamic reform and Quranism (Quraniyoon) movements and author of many books on the Qur'an and Islam, was someone who knew Adnan Oktar very well back when he wrote about him in a controversial article entitled *Harun Yahya or Adnan Oktar: The Promised Mahdi?*:

I met Adnan in the prison clinic. I was taken there by the doctor who happened to recognize me from my books and conferences; he wanted to save me from the crowded ward which was filled with convicted murderers and burglars. Adnan was there for a different reason, a much different one. He was acting like a paranoid schizophrenic in order to get a medical report to dodge the draft. It was ironic, since he was indeed mentally sick; he was a delusional megalomaniac, yet he was cunningly acting for another mental illness. He was successful; he dodged the draft and since then

FIG. 11 – Timothy Hogan and Paul Dickerson with a senior officer of the the Grand Lodge of the State of Israel, at the Masonic Temple of Haifa (Israel) located on Mount Carmel, 119 Hanassi Blvd. The Mount Carmel Lodge of Haifa works their ritual in the English language.

he has been found lacking mental capability to be the subject of criminal law. So, he is getting away with sexual abuses, fraud, libel, blackmailing schemes, and other criminal activities. If Adnan has demonstrated a miracle as a Mahdi, this must be his miracle: he is officially insane and criminally teflon! ... Knowing him before the 1990s, I could not believe that he would be indulging in promiscuous sexual activities, since at that time he was a devout Sunni who was very scrupulous about interacting with women. He would not even shake hands with women. However, according to the media reports and published confessions of his former followers, Adnan has evolved and transformed since. His sexual abuse of girls around him has been the frequent topic of Turkish media and acknowledged by the defectors. He reportedly claims the right to have sexual intercourse with every female member of his cult. He has even invented a name for those females: MOTOR (engine). Reportedly, his male followers are feeling lucky in letting him taste their girl friends first.

Edip Yuksel makes this strong statement in a comment to his own article: "*Adnan Oktar is a cult leader who has enslaved many children of rich and elite. His sexual and mental abuse of his subjects is a well-known fact to Turkish people. His confession in police alone, which is corroborated by his former followers to details, is sufficient to put him behind bars.*

But so far, money, connections, blackmail and all the tricks available to his well-connected and super rich followers have kept him out of trouble."

So for recruiting new members and promoting his brand name, Harun Yahya uses **sex, money, popular symbols**, and famous people. But the main tool he uses is deception, Yet

FIG. 12 – *Timothy Hogan in Jerusalem indicates Warren's Gate as one of the four western Wall entrance gates to the Temple Mount from the Second Temple period, discovered by Freemason Charles Warren.*

he thinks he is doing this deception "righteously," justifying his deceptive ways with the abused Quranic word **TAQIYYA,** a sort of holy hypocrisy permitted by the belief system of a Shiite sect, but Harun Yahya is supposedly a Sunni. He recruits young and rich boys, possibly good looking, arranges for them beautiful models (whom he calls *Motors*), and leads them into a sex trap, filming them from a secret camera, or at least this is what he used to do. Harun Yahya has been charged and was even prosecuted for these unlawful pratices and other crimes related to his sect, but of course nothing happens these days due to his "insane" status obtained in the 1980s, by his powerful friends in the present Turkish government who will always rescue him from the occasional scandal or crime or impeachment. He is now considered a sort of "untouchable" of the Turkish scene, and has been working on developing a sort of Islamic Scientology in line with the coming "One World Religion" concept promoted by the New World Order, where he presents himself as the Mahdi, the prophesied redeemer of Islam, who is preparing the second coming of Jesus. With his powerful charisma, a pool of unlimited and gullible rich people, a market of more than a billion Muslims, and the support of high level Freemasons and Illuminati, he looks like the ideal Antichrist candidate. In an interview in 2008, Oktar said, *"I want to resemble the Prophet Solomon."* He added, *"His palace was beautiful; there were beautiful people around him. [The] aim of a Muslim should be beauty."*

    "According to their interpretation 'vaginal' intercourse was 'haram' but 'anal and oral intercourse' was 'halal' when not married." For those not familiar with Islamic religious terms, the only rule for everybody in Harun Yahya's sex sect is simply no vaginal penetration, only oral and anal sex are permited by the Grand Master Adnan Oktar, who is also said to be an expert in sexual magick (maybe Crowley style?) I guess the 33rd degree Grand

FIG. 13 – From your left, Grand Master and known French illuminati **Emilio Lorenzo** *who has led since 1979 one of the leading* **branches of the Illuminati Martinist sect** *created by Papus in 1888. With him, amongst others, is Michael Pearce, Paul Dickerson Ramzi Abou-Hassan and Timothy Hogan at the Cimetière du Père-Lachaise, at the resting place of Papus Dr Gérard Encausse, Jacqueline Encausse and his son Philippe Encausse.*

Inspector General patent given to Oktar from a small irregular Scottish Rite Masonic body from Italy, assumes in this Illuminati context, a whole new meaning. I am sure Aleister Crowley, who even called his only son **Randal Giair Doherty** with the nickname **Aleister Ataturk**, (FIG. 18) and certainly would have loved being on Adnan Oktar's satelite TV A9. Poor Aleister Ataturk however, who later self-styled himself **Count Charles Edward D'Arquires (1937-2002)**, who I was able to meet once personally in London in front of the Atlantis bookshop, a year or so before his death, lived a terrible life, victim of his father's daunting legacy, who died tragically in a car accident in Chalfont St. Peter, UK, on November 20, 2002. Aleister Ataturk spent some of his teen years in California, with O.T.O. members from *Agape Lodge*. He was deported from the USA for failure to pay a medical debt (his handler Germer refused to pay it, actually). Up to that time Aleister Ataturk had made some effort to attract a following in the O.T.O. as Crowley's successor, but without success. He later attempted to help convince Germer to allow resumption of O.T.O. initiations and temple work, also without success and possibly contributing to Germer's refusal to pay his medical bills. After that, in Paris and London, he occasionally attempted to argue for a role as successor to *The Beast*, but that petered out in the 1980s, especially after he founded in the middle of the 1970s a **"Supreme Council of Great Britain"** with himself as the "Adjudicator," wishing to take over the governance of the UK by persuasion. Harold Wilson was Prime Minister at the time.

In 1976, Aleister Ataturk hired a posh limousine, complete with Supreme Council pennants and, with his Private Secretary, Peter Bishop, was chauffeur-driven to London. They arrived in all their finery; Aleister in his dress uniform jacket with gold trimmings, epaulettes and velvet cape. They tried to get into Downing Street for an audience with Wilson, in order to persuade him to join the Supreme Council. The message was delivered to Wilson who, unsupportingly, declined the offer. I wonder who gave them the money to do all this? Perhaps the Illuminati? The O.T.O.? The C.I.A.? We will never

LEFT *FIG. 14 – Adnan Oktar meets Harun Yahya in July, 2015, along with American-born Israeli rabbi Yehuda Joshua Glick (b. 1965), who campaigns for expanding Jewish access to the Temple Mount. Glick was awarded the 2015 Moskowitz Prize for Zionism.*

know but it makes an interesting story, nevertheless. Harun Yahya admired Aleister Crowley and Freemason Mustafa Kemal Atatürk, the founder of modern Turkey; who had connections with the British intelligence services whom Crowley served for a time. Well, as you can see, we always find a few skeletons in the closet of these elitists and their fake interfaith dialogue, that's why I have long held that ecumenism and dialogue are just tools of the New World Order. People like Harun Yahya should preach Aleister Crowley's Thelema, not Islam, as their version of Islam is to expert eyes, a total joke and mockery of this faith, as well as his claims of being the Mahdi, and his lies about being recognized as "his spiritual son" by the late Sultan al-Awliya Maulana Sheikh Nazim (1922 – 2014), commonly known as Shaykh Nazim, who was the spiritual leader of one of the most respected Sufi Orders: the Naqshbandi tariqa. This incorrect information was reported by Timothy Hogan in his book *(Op.cit.*, p.137), but is not supported by the Naqshbandi Order, who made a clear statement coming from an authorized Naqshbandi source on the matter called Shaykh Abdul Kerim Kibrisi, known as the Lion of Haqq, Ottoman Khaliphah and the U.S. representative of Sheikh Nazim, spoke clearly about this impostor named Adnan Oktar, saying in a YouTube video that Harun Yahya's Shaykh is Shaitan. Check out for yourself the video present on YouTube, as it is in the English language. [8]

This means Mr. Oktar, as Edip Yuksel likes to call him, could truly be the Antichrist, and Timothy Hogan has either been fooled by Adnan, or is a willing accomplice to all this, as a Neotemplar-Masonic tool of the pro Islamist New World Order used to destroy Christianity. If this is the case, we should all start getting worried, especially because, in a revealing TV show broadcasted on A9TV, Hogan's Turkish guru made some unprecedented statements about his meeting with "Knights Templar" and "Masonic Grand Masters"

on a video you can still find on YouTube entitled *Freemasonry and the Knights Templar will support Hazrat Mahdi! (Adnan Oktar)* https://www.youtube.com/watch?v=GaAuI6oUrow

We find Adnan in front of his trashy Turkish bombshells wearing things like false rainbow eyelashes, wigs, and diamond-studded Versace bondage gear, often referred to as "the girls," or "angels" or "kittens of Adnan Oktar" by the Turkish media. He explains to his viewers and followers, that Freemasonry has only been created to support the Mahdi in the end times. This means that the Freemasons or the Knights Templar exist since time immemorable only to support him, the Turkish sex guru.

RIGHT *FIG. 15 – Temple Mount activist Yehuda Glick hands Prime Minister Benjamin Netanyahu a copy of the guidebook Arise and Ascend only a month after meeting Mr. Oktar on August 19, 2015. It would be interesting to ask, "did Netanyahu know this?"*

Are you insane dear Brother Timothy Hogan and friends from the GL of Colorado? How can you believe in such a charlatan? Ok, I am ready to stand in front of your Grand Lodge and prove every point I am writing in this book. Dear Freemasons of Colorado, you are serving another "false prophet" remember what Jesus said, *"Beware of false prophets, who come to you in sheep's clothing, but inwardly they are ravenous wolves. You will know them by their fruits"* (Matt. 7:15-16b). "Beware" means to be on alert—to discern what is being said, and Adnan Oktar replies in the above mentioned TV show to a viewer's letter, who asks him: *"Dear Adnan Oktar, you said the Mahdi will be a Freemason?"* He replied: *"Freemasonry will support the Mahdi. They say that is why they are here. The Knights Templar say that is why they are here."* Masonic grandmasters came and said, *"We exist so the Mahdi can rule the Islamic world."* They explicitly said that Freemasonry had been established for that end. They said they exist to give the sacred relics to the Mahdi. They said many of the sacred relics were with them. The Knights Templar have been around since the time of the Prophet Solomon. They say that many sacred relics are preserved in special places where they concealed them. They say they have concealed them for thousands of years for the Mahdi, and that they will give them to him when he appears. They have some original copies of the Torah. I asked whom they will give them to in our time. They said they will only give them to the Mahdi. Adnan Oktar clarifies his view with the following passage:

And they said there is something special in Istanbul. They said that is why they founded the first Knights Templar in Istanbul hundreds of years ago. They said the Knights Templar were first founded here, in Istanbul. They said that Istanbul is a very important city, and that the one who will save the world will appear from here. They said that this information was in their books dating back a thousand years. It is really there. They say

Sincerity is a subject that gets overlooked.

FIG. 16 – Adnan Oktar talks about the subject of "Sincerity" with his ladies and the rest of his followers on satellite TV Channel A9.

they have relics from people you can never imagine. They say they have original and special information dating back to past civilizations and that they will give this to the Mahdi. This is part of what I am free to say. They say that the first purpose of the foundation of Freemasonry was the system of the Mahdi. They also say they exist for the global reign of Islam. And the time has come. The say the Masonic calendar has expired. They say they have come to the end of their calendar. They say they will serve the Mahdi. As clearly as that. I never said the Mahdi is a Mason. The Mahdi is a power over and above Freemasonry. Freemasonry will serve the Mahdi. The Mahdi will not serve Freemasonry. Our brothers fail to grasp that. There are other details I shall give when the time is right.

What should we do now to fight all this decadence in the Western initiatic system? The answer is simple, let's bring back to life the original Rite of Strict Observance, with its true Templar degrees, and let's get the real **Knights Templar's Revenge** going, the one that will eliminate once and for all the hypocrites of their faith like Harun Yahya, and his false Islamic ideals, promoted and supported by the New World Order. Back in 2014 I tried to get in contact with Brother Timothy Hogan, both through a common friend and member in both hour organizations (CIRCES and OIU), and through Brother Sean Stone (son of film director Oliver Stone), so I could warn Hogan of the dangerous mistakes he was making with this high level Turkish crook and irregular Freemason, (FIG. 19) but he never replied. Maybe he was too busy with Mr. Adnan Oktar? Or he thought I was not respectable enough to talk to as Grand Master like him, serving the Great Work of the New World Order.

I can only say the truth is now here in this book for you and everyone else to read, prove me wrong if you can dear Brother, if not accept the fact that my Order, the *Ordo Illuminatorum Universalis*, is now here in the USA to bring truth and clarity upon the initiatic world, as we are not only real Illuminati, but we are also true hereditary Knights Templar of the Rite of Strict Observance (FIGS. 20 and 21) **and we are Christian, not Muslim. *Get it?*** Believe me, I know what true Islam is made of Brother, and I think that as Templars, even if we have a superior understanding of things, and can, and should, dialogue with them, we have to ultimately protect Christianity now more than ever, from complete extinction, because "dialogue" does not mean "submission." In the meantime, interest for

FIG. 17 – Harun Yahya and a couple of his "apostles."

the Rite of Strict Observance is growing everywhere, (FIG. 22) even in the atheist and more liberal version of Masonry represented by the *Grand Orient de France* (with the acronym GODF). Between the 12th of April and the 23rd of October 2016, at their prestigious *Museum of Freemasonry* in Paris, at number 16 of Rue Cadet, the GODF offered a glimpse into the unseen world of the Rite of Strict Templar Observance of Baron von Hund, with a unique exhibition called *Templiers & Francs-maçons, De la légende à l'histoire* "Templars and Freemasons, from legend to history," (FIG. 23) in which they show not only the Masonic regalia or jewelry of the Order, and other esoteric writings, but also a rare illuminated manuscript on the Strict Observance from 1775, (FIG. 24) recently purchased by the GODF for a huge amount of money (some say 60 thousand euros). Let's hope all this will eventually bring something positive, that will help save what's left of the Christian civilization, because without Christianity the West is doomed to end in disgrace, conquered by false Islamists and Communist mercenaries of the NWO, that are in reality just agents of the Antichrist with no real God, but money and control in their heart.

The Goddess

The birth of the so-called "Egyptian Rites of Freemasonry" within NeoTemplar Freemasonry was based on the **myth of an underground and secret transmission of true ancient wisdom**, through channels that date back to Roman times, passed on to the Middle Ages and through the Renaissance, in an unbroken chain of Illuminati sects and mystery schools to this very day. Adherents are held to the strictest secrecy, which only occasionally would manifest outwardly, and these secret traditions were always practiced in very small groups, except in the case of the legendary Knights Templar. As the *Association for Studies and Research on Traditions* writes about the word myth, in the initiatic context we use the word "myth" in its true meaning, according to the definition of Attilio Mordini: *"The term mythos (ie myth) means, at least in the original sense, 'word,' a word that is manifested from the silence in the secret act of initiation into the Mysteries; and hides, but at the same time holds out discreetly and reveals the truth that the great primordial silence is enclosed."*[9] We lift the veil to try to understand

9 Attilio Mordini , *The Temple of Christianity*, (Vibo Valentia, IT: Edizioni Settecolori, 1979), p. 10.

the true meaning of what the myth really means, and initiation into the Illuminati, especially the ones devoted to the mysteries of the Goddess Isis. For this reason, I want to begin this third and final chapter of my *Confessions* trilogy, uncovering more sides of this invisible prison that surrounds us, this more or less divine "Matrix" that oppresses us.

I would like to speak first about the Shrine of Loreto in Italy, and a story that involves once again our old Japanese friend Princess Kaoru Nakamaru, who I have mentioned in the first two books. Loreto is a city located in central Italy on the Adriatic Sea, and one building called *Santuario della Santa Casa* is a local sanctuary, supposedly the original home of the Virgin Mary. Her house is said to have been miraculously transported there by a group of angels, at least this is the official version given by the Church of Rome, but there is also a very different and more credible story be-

FIG. 18 – *Aleister MacAlpine known also as Ataturk Crowley, Randall Gair, and Count Charles Edward D'Arquires (1937 – 2002).*

hind these "angels," involving the mysterious Knights Templar, which have been at times gatekeepers to much older belief systems. In the meantime, the supposed modern heirs of the original Templars, these days divided as you may know into various warring factions, invited my friend Kaoru Nakamaru to visit the sanctuary in question. The Neo-Templar faction that invited her is probably the only one operating officially inside the Vatican, as the basilica and the alleged "Holy House" of Mary is also within Vatican territory.

This house was the place where Catholics say the Virgin Mary heard the words of the Annunciation, and where she uttered the *fiat*, and they say **the Word became flesh**, where the purity and virginity were fused with motherhood for the Christian tradition. However Mary, the Mother of Jesus for the Illuminati, received the "divine seed" for the creation of the Messiah from a High Priest of the Illuminati, a sort of divine inseminator. This happened during a specific ritual, used to capture the divine Spirit, containing what Christians call the Holy Spirit. The **"Holy House,"** is where this sexual magical ritual took place, which then produced Jesus, the greatest initiate of all time. According to an archaeological study conducted by the architect Nanni Monelli, and Father Giuseppe Santarelli, director of the "Universal Congregation of the Holy House" of Loreto, the stones that are in the grotto of the Annunciation in Nazareth, have surely the same origin of the stones on the altar of the Holy Apostles of the Holy House of Loreto. This discovery confirms the genuinity of the Holy House of the Virgin Mary and has reopened the discussion on the historical validity of the transfer of the Holy House of Nazareth to Loreto in Italy, and the mystery of how this relocation had taken place. [10]

....

10   *The Holy House of Loreto: Mary's "real House of Nazareth"* article published by www.zenit.org on March 28th, 2006.

FIG. 19 – 33rd degree patent of the Ancient and Accepted Scottish Rite of Turkish Anti-Masonic figure and Islamic sex cult leader Adnan Oktar, also known as Harun Yahya.

This location is definitely a destination for pilgrimages, but what is behind this from an esoteric point of view? Through an enlightened perspective, we lift the veil of mystery and secrecy where the mystery of the Holy House and the Order of the Templars is hidden. The miraculous angelic-thesis of the translation of the Holy House has taken shape in the folkloric tradition only after 1625, more than three centuries after the mythical deposition of the stones in the Piceno area in Italy, and especially after the publication of the book by Father Andrea Gelsomini, *The Celestial Treasure of the Virgin Mary's devotion*. The legend of the intervention of the angels has also tapped into the existing narrative of the local town of Recanati's mysterious *Antici Brothers,* as well as the fact that the Templars in Recanati were called angels because they are allocated in the city's district of St. Archangel. So in light of these findings, the structure relocation would be simply a symbolic account of an event that happened in real life, where the Knights Templar transported from the Holy Land, the home of their beloved Virgin Mary, who the Templars are particularly devoted. If we search for a magical connection with the supposed angels in the legend of the mysterious knights, we find that the Templar leaders would evoke angels. Some of their modern heirs still evoke them today within certain Neo-Templar branches, with an esoteric inclination, which increasingly often degenerates in the use of black magic and demonic figures, instead of angels.

There are now rare cases where modern Templars have had a real angelic connection through the Holy Spirit, and through the spiritual purity of its members. In the late-medieval grimoires you can trace clear kabbalistic influences and Muslim mysticism, which obviously reached our culture thanks to the Templars, who long lived in the Middle East in direct contact with Jews and Muslims. To make concrete contact with these mysterious entities, evocation must be made respecting the parameters of sacred geometry, in sacred places related to such entities, such as Loreto has been since ancient times.

An Illuminati prayer reported by the key figure in occultism Eliphas Levi, pseudonim of Alphonse Louis Constant (1810–1875), in his small booklet *Sactum Regnum,* opens with the following words:

> O caput mortuum empire tibi for vivum Serpentem Kerub empire tibi for Adam Aquila tibi empire alas Tauri. Serpens empire tibi for Angelum et Leonem.

These opening words in Latin are followed by the invocation of certain angels and kabbalistic spirits that are made in relation to various demons. This passage gives us a clear idea of how the occultists of the Illuminati networks dominate, or at least try to dominate, the forces of evil using their angelic allies:

In the name of Michael, whom Jehovah decrees to command Satan!

In the name of Gabriel, whom Adonai decrees to command Beelzebub!

In the name of Raphael obey Elohim, thou Sachabiel.

By Samael Tzabaoth, and by the name of Elohim Gibur, lay down thy weapons, thou Adramelek.

By Zachariel and Sachiel Melek, submit to the power of Eloah, thou Samgabiel.

In the divine and human name of Shadai, and by the power of Anael, of Adam and of Chavah, thou Lilith retire, leave us in peace, thou Nahemah. By the holy Elohim, and by the power of Orifiel, in the names of the spirits Cassiel, Schaltiel, Aphiel, and Zarahiel, turn back, thou Moloch, there are no children here for thee to devour.

FIG. 20 – Coat of Arms of the Rite of Strict Observance Templar, a Masonic-Knightly Order that was "reawakened" on March 5th of 2016 e.v—corresponding to the Anno Ordinis 898 of the Strict Observance.

These practices are unknown to most, but not to the Templars, or their modern imitators. They were passed down after the dismantling of the Templars, and especially within the teachings of Occult Masonry, a term coined by the same Eliphas Levi. Unfortunately, such rituals in the wrong hands end up becoming obscure and perverse practices, linked, as revealed in the first volume of my *Confessions,* to the dark side of the force, and the evil of black magic. In one way or another, the origin of these seemingly Christian practices, are polytheistic in their essence, because the secrets are, and remain always, for the privileged few who may pose as devout Christians. Many of those who recite these dark conjurations, are often sitting at the heart of the Vatican hierarchy. Even the roots of the "Santa Casa," the supposed "Holy House" of Mary, are nothing more than pagan, not monotheistic or "Christian." The historian Hans Vogel, a writer from the eighteenth century, faithful to the miraculous theory of the translation of the place by the "angels," originating from a deep-rooted popular tradition, that the angels laid the "Holy House" right above the ruins of the temple of the **Goddess Cupra.** (FIG. 25) She was a local goddess with impressive vestiges at the time of the so-called translation, actually operated by the Templars. The epithet "Cupra" dates back to antiquity, in the paleo-Umbrian context, and serves to designate royal divinity.

The reports show us that the local population of the *Piceni,* were people of the sea, and the etymology of the name derives from the greek Kupria or Cypria used to describe the goddess **Aphrodite,** who to the Egyptians was **Isis**, and to the Phoenicians **Astarte**, a deity linked to, and associated with, the planet Venus and copper, a metal that is abundant in Cyprus, the native island of Aphrodite. The Goddess Cupra is shown with a copper-colored leather, like the Madonna of Loreto, and often with a baby in her arms, true to the Hellenistic style of Isis. This is an *ante litteram* depiction of the Christian Virgin

FIG. 21 – Mons. Ireneo (Mons. Vitaly) Bishop of the Italian Orthodox Church, the Sovereign Grand Master Leo Lyon Zagami and various O.I.U members and their dames along in the historic day of the reawakening of the Rite of the Strict Observance on March 5, 2016 e.v.

Mary, linked to the cult of the Mother Goddess, that the Templars revered as the principle of wisdom, the female **Sophia, Shekinah,** but not necessarily to the worship of a true woman, but rather an idealized Goddess, as European society has always been patriarchal in nature. However, the allegory of the Mother Goddess, so important for the Templars, was later represented in the sublime esotericism depicted in the writings of Dante Alighieri. This vision has been gradually distorted by the Society of Jesus, that wants to establish in today's world, **a twisted matriarchal vision in line with the precepts of counter-initiation promoted by the New Age, that wishes to castrate masculinity and destroy traditional family values and identity.**

This distorted concept reminds me of a certain Lady Caithness, referred to as "the Duchess" by her many followers. She was a woman that was believed to be the reincarnation of Mary Stuart, and later presented herself as a sort of "inspired" guide in the very early days of the **Theosophical Society**. She promoted the advent of the era of the **"divine feminine"** with the leaders of this important new Illuminati group, which I have written about in Volume II. Rene Guenon, one of the highest authorities in the field of esotericism of the past century, also revered by Catholic scholars, wrote about Lady Caithness and this supposed "divine revelation" in his ***Theosophy: History of a Pseudo-Religion***:

> *Charged to announce and prepare the coming; It was a new revelation, an era that was meant to succeed Christianity that succeeded the old law; she was in a word the "coming of the Holy Spirit" agnostically known as the "divine feminine." It was still, "the manifestation of the sons and daughters of God," not so much as a unique being but as a plural one: this most perfect race will humanize the earth, of which we know had already passed through the periods of mineral, plant and animal development ... the Duchess adds this point: "We can probably say that the old world is finished in 1881, and that the Lord has created a new heaven and a new earth, and that we are entering the year of our Lady, 1882."* [11]

11   Rene Guenon, Theosophy, *Il Teosofismo storia di una pseudo-religione*, (Turin, IT: Arktos, 1987) p. 188.

Guenon seems to be focused on the problems concerning the growing distortion of the "sacred feminine" concept in the modern world. Italian Freemason, author, and well-respected member of the scientifical community **Professor Mariano Bizzarri**, in his book on the mysteries of Rennes le Chateau, explores this subject, commenting on the passage above by Guenon stating that: *"Undoubtedly, one can not be but struck by the extraordinary coincidence that this 'message' shows with the one that was trumpeted by Lincoln, Baigent and, especially in fictional form by Dan Brown. It is clear that you are talking about the advent of an era characterized by a goddess figure, giver of wisdom and nurse to that mysterious 'perfect race' of which Nerval or Bulwer-Litton spoke of, intending to supplant the human race (concepts later taken up again by National Socialism, author's note)."* [12]

FIG. 22 – Jean-Marie Auzanneau, regent and co-restorer of the Rite of Strict Observance reawakened in France in 1995.

Guenon illuminates us further, when he notes the "singularity" inherent in the idea of a **"collective messiah,"** by stating: *"whose conception, however, is not completely new ... it is precisely the messianism that, under one or the other form, seems to offer the key to this 'identity purposes' mentioned by the Duchess of Pomar towards the 'Theosophical Society' which has long prepared for the appearance of a 'the future messiah' and indeed works to form 'a body,' comprising a large number of members joined together and ready to welcome the new bearer of the Torch of Truth. ... Here, however, the 'common goal of the Duchess of Pomar and Madame Blavatsky that ... had assigned to their society a secret mission, not only to prepare the way to the One who is to come' but also to provide for his appearance in the same time it would be considered more favorable."* [13] Professor Bizzari adds this conclusion: *"this allusion to 'the One who is to come' could not be more disturbing, especially if one remembers that the 'Torch Bearer' or 'Bringer of Light' is a euphemism that stands for Lucifer."* [14] **Meaning the Messiah of the Illuminati is Lucifer.**

We are living in the kingdom of evil and "Counter-initiation," but let me explain to you briefly what "Counter-initiation" is. "Counter-initiation" is a term invented by the aforementioned Rene Guenon. He spent a long time in the occult underworld of France between the two world wars, and came out understanding that a lot of dark stuff was going on in the Illuminati network. Basically our civilization is distorting the mother goddess con-

12   Mariano Bizzarri, *Rennes le Chateau. Dal Vangelo perduto dei Cainiti alle sette segrete*, (Rome: Ed. Mediterranee, 2005) p. 86.
13   *Ibid.*, pp. 188-189.
14   *Ibid.*

FIG. 23 – Poster of the exhibition Templiers et francs-maçons, De la légende à l'histoire dedicated by the Grand Orient of France to the Rite of Strict Observance taking place from April 12 to October 23rd, 2016 at the Museum of Freemasonry, based at 16 Rue Cadet 75009, Paris.

cept, to use it in the New World Order project, and this happens because of certain liberal forms of Freemasonry, the same ones that gradually, in the last hundred years, led to the atrocities of contemporary feminism. This modern abomination, that on February 21, 2012, pushed five members of the musical group **Pussy Riot** to stage a highly indecent performance in Moscow's Orthodox Cathedral of Christ the Savior. It is no coincidence that the first international congress on women's rights was organized by **Maria Deraismes,** who later became one of the founders of co-Masonry, in Paris in 1878. This event apparently took place in the hall of the Grand Orient of France, and for sure the Masonic-esoteric theories, propagated by the leadership of the Theosophical Society of Helena Petrovna Blavatsky, that I wrote about in Volume II, were already present. Both Madame Blavatsky, who founded the Theosophical Society on November 17, 1875, and Alice Bailey, her heir, were both key figures in the development of the future of feminism, a movement that in the long run proved nefarious and unnatural, especially after it progressed well beyond the simple discourse of equal rights between men and women.I know my words will not be well-received by the usual leftist-thinking idiots who appreciate and love feminism, but know for a fact my dear feminists, that Condoleezza Rice and Hillary Clinton, are actually two of the worst expressions of what feminism and being a woman is, and they are the result of this evil work crafted for over a century by the Illuminati and liberal Freemasonry, to bring the human race to its self-destruction.

And what about the appointment in August, 2012 of the first U.S. General to be openly gay, the lesbian **Tammy S. Smith.**

Rene Guenon wrote prophetically about *deviation and subversion* in his ***The Reign of Quantity and the Signs of the Times:***

We treated anti-traditional action, THE ANTI-TRADITIONAL ACTION by which the modern world has in a sense been "manufactured" and hitherto been considered as an operation designed primarily to bring about a deviation from the normal state, that is, from the state normal to all traditional civilizations whatever may be their particular forms, something easy to understand and requiring no further comment. On the other hand, there is a distinction to be made between deviation and subversion: deviation can be regarded as comprising an indefinite multiplicity of degrees, so that it can go to work gradually and imperceptibly; this is exemplified by the gradual passage of the modern mentality from "humanism" and rationalism to mechanism, and thence to materialism, and again in the process whereby profane science has elaborated successive theories, each more purely quantitative in character than the last. This makes it possible to say that all such deviation, from its earliest beginnings, has steadily and progressively tended toward the establishment of the "reign of quantity" But when deviation reaches its limit, it ends by being a real "contradiction," that is to say a state diametrically opposed to the normal order, and only then can "subversion" in the etymological sense of the word properly be spoken of; needless to say, "subversion" in this sense must in no way be confused with the "reversal" referred to in connection with the final instant of the cycle, it being indeed the exact opposite since the "reversal" actually happens after the "subversion" and at the moment when subversion seems complete, and is really a rectification whereby the normal order is re-established, and whereby the "primordial state," representing perfection in the human domain, is restored.

FIG. 24 – A rare picture from a manuscript dated 1775 recently aquired from the Museum of Freemasonry of the Grand Orient of France for their exhibition Templiers et francs-maçons, De la légende à l'histoire.

As against this, it could be said that subversion, thus understood, is but the last stage of deviation and is its goal, or, in other words, that deviation as a whole has no tendency other than to bring about subversion, and that is true enough; in the present state of affairs, though it cannot yet be said that subversion is complete, the signs of it are very evident in everything in which the special characteristic of "counterfeit" or "parody" is conspicuous. This characteristic has already been mentioned more than once, and is to be dealt with more fully later. For the moment no more need be said than that this particular characteristic affords by itself a very significant indication of the origin of anything that shows it, and consequently of the origin of the modern deviation itself, the "satanic" nature of which is thus brought out very clearly. The word "satanic" can indeed be properly applied to all negation and reversal of order, such as is so incontestably in evidence in everything we now see around us: is the modern world really anything whatever but a direct denial of all traditional truth? At the same time, and more or less of necessity, the spirit of negation is the spirit of lying; it wears every disguise, often the most unexpected, in order to avoid being recognized for what it is, and even in order to pass itself off as the very opposite of what it is; this is where counterfeit comes in; and this is the moment to recall that it is said that "Satan is the ape of God," and also that he "transfigures himself into an angel of light." In the end, this amounts to saying that he imitates in

FIG. 25 – The goddess Cupra in a painting by Adolfo De Carolis in the Government building of Ascoli Piceno.

his own way, by altering and falsifying it so as always to make it serve his own ends, the very thing he sets out to oppose: thus, he will so manage matters that disorder takes on the appearance of a false order, he will hide the negation of all principle under the affirmation of false principles, and so on. [15]

When Guenon wrote these words in the mid-forties, of course the "subversion" of our society and its civilization was not yet complete. We can now say with certainty, and in light of recent events, the "reversal" mode of the system is accelerating, as we are in the grip of a hellish society. In this context of increasing disintegration and loathing encouraged by the so-called New Age, in 2011, Princess Kaoru Nakamaru, which as some of you may know I co-wrote books with, published in Japan, officially paid a visit to the Holy House of Mary. It was the early days of September, and the gesture took on a very important meaning, beyond the mere diplomatic gesture given by the fact that Loreto, the place where the sanctuary of the House of Mary is located, is on Papal territory. Karou was officially invited by the Pontifical Delegation of what is considered the home of the mother of God by Christians. Mary means "loved by God" and Loreto is actually in a very important Sacred Alignment linked to the Marian cult in Europe, inspired originally by the Mother Goddess, especially in the context of the famous **Black Madonnas**. Many of these Madonnas are famous, such as the one in Loreto (near Ancona), the one in Tindari, a fraction of Patti near Messina, the one in Czestochowa, Poland, the Spanish one at Montserrat in Catalonia, and the Virgin of Candelaria in Tenerife, the patron saint of the Canary Islands. Many sanctuaries of Black Madonnas, however, are replicas of the most famous ancient cults. In particular, there is a clear reference that Isis is the Black Madonna, as she is not only Mary the mother of Jesus, but **Isis** (or rather, to be exact her embodiment, **Hathor**), is represented with the solar child in her arms.

The expanding Marian cult has been steadily growing in the Far East for sometime now, and has considerable importance in the distant land of the rising sun, even though the Catholic Church, as we shall see later, is widely disliked in this country. That is because Japan has been an important asset of Jesuitry for centuries, and has always embraced the fundamental role of a women's Divinity, as does the New Age. In Shintoism in particular, we find the goddess **Izanami,** that in Japanese means **"She who invites,"** as well as another important deity in the mythology of Japan, the creator goddess Amaterasu-ō-mi-

15   René Guenon, *The Reign of Quantity & the Signs of the Times*, (Hillsdale, NY. Sophia Perennis; 4th Revised ed. edition June 9, 2004), pp. 197-198.

kami, that means literally "Great Goddess shining in the heavens," whose name is usually shortened to **Amaterasu, the Sun goddess,** a deity from which all the things decend in the Shinto religion. Amaterasu is therefore considered to be the direct ancestor of the legendary Japanese imperial family, from which **the alleged granddaughter of the Emperor Meiji, (FIG. 26) who Kaoru Nakamaru derives from.** She has even declared herself to be the reincarnation of Amaterasu, as well as the legendary Cleopatra.

I know sometimes the eccentricities of some characters makes them less credible, but this kind of externalization is typical of the elite immersed in the most delusional New Age philosophy, of which the princess is part of, although she loves to say otherwise. And even if the statements of Kaoru Nakamaru must be rightly taken with skepticism, the strange experience of Nakamaru and the Vatican may be of some interest to my readers. The Vatican "templars" headed by Dr. Antonio Leonardo Montuoro, and the former **Prefect Enrico Marinelli,** former head of security for Saint John Paul II, together with Bishop Domenico Sigalini Palestrina, even named Kaoru as an ambassador for the Work of the Holy Spirit Divine Power of Love. An unusual gesture for the Church, that could have risked ridicule because of Kaoru Nakamaru's unusual statments as the mother goddess, and her apocalyptic vision on December 2012, where of course nothing happened, despite the Princess announcing three days and three nights of darkness, but as you know in the New Age landscape the demonic forces often interefere with even the best people.

However, despite the initial acceptance by Princess Kaoru of her new role as "Ambassador of the Holy Spirit" she quickly resigned shocking almost everyone, for what proved to be not only a personal choice due to the growing scandals of the Vatican, but as an act performed under the growing pressure of the Japanese security apparatus, who acted to discourage her initiative with direct suggestion by the CIA in late February of 2012, convincing her to give up her new role as "Ambassador of the Holy Spirit" for the Vatican. All this happened in an interesting sequence of events that related mainly to her connections to North Korea, and her links to the mysterious Knights Templar residing in the Vatican, who claim to be in possession of the Holy Grail and the ashes of Jacob de Molay.

The Templars, the Holy House, and the Japanese Princess

Behind the Neo-Templar mysteries that revolve within the Vatican, we find the ashes of the last Templar, Grand Master Jacques de Molay, and a lot more, including a possible new truth about the Holy Grail, and a broad discussion by the so-called Gnostic churches created by the **Brotherhood of the Illuminati,** the supposed spiritual side of the Illuminati. A journey that will lead us in the following pages, to discover the most intimate secrets and untold stories of my adventure with the Holy See, and as usual, the involvement of the Jesuits, the secret agents of the Vatican, obsessed in controlling every Neo-Templar revival in and out of Freemasonry. Who is promoting Neo-Templarism? According to Rene Guenon, the suppression of the Order of the Temple was implemented by Pope Clement V in 1313, with the killing of the last Grand Master, Jacques de Molay on 19 March, 1314, by order of King Philip the Fair of France. Europe broke their last initiatic chain, that for the Illuminati goes back to Atlantis, and with it the possibility of a real transmission of true esoteric knowledge, which encouraged the spread of black magic and Satanism. After that date, according to Guenon, in Europe you can no longer speak properly of initiation, but only of pseudo-initiation, or worse, counter-initiation, as Guenon calls it. For this reason, those who appear today as "the real Templars," even if there are of course genuine formations, there is no real transmission of the mysteries, just a fragmented version. In a comment made in relation to the initiatic reality of our day, Guenon, who later in his life became involved with Sufi Islam wrote: "*In Islamic esotericism ... it is*

FIG. 26 – Emperor Meiji (1852 – 1912) the alleged grandfather of Princess Kaoru Nakamaru, was the 122nd emperor of Japan.

said that he who shows up at a certain door, without being received through a normal and legitimate preparation, sees this door close in front of him and is forced to go back, however, no longer as a simple layman, which is now impossible, but as a saher (sorcerer or magician); we would not know to express more clearly what it is."[16]

I would say it is certainly true that nowadays there are many magicians and sorcerers who received the worst type of initiation, and are used as agents of destruction by the New World Order.

As Luca Gallesi wrote recently in the Italian newspaper *"Il Giornale"* in 2016, to clarify who Guenon was to the uninitiated, and those who do not know who he is: *"Think of a French intellectual converted to Islam and immediately these days you imagine that it may be a potential terrorist, as well as knowing that the same character is also a high rank Master Mason immediately evokes his participation in dark conspiracies or casual banking speculations. Curiously enough Rene Guenon, despite having embraced the Muslim faith, climbed the summits of Masonic esotericism, and did not become neither a terrorist nor a banker, but was instead a sleek and appreciated thinker, leader of the so-called traditional thinking, which counts among its ranks Julius Evola, Schuon, Titus Burckhardt, SH Nasr and other masters of the 1900s."[17]*

For some traditionalists this description of Guenon is a bit too simplistic, especially for people like me, who have studied him in depth, and who appreciate his traditional thought and his almost prophetic criticism towards modernity that was made decades ago, when the West was still in good shape, but it is however a good synthesis concerning this controversial figure, who I invite you to study further. Gallesi also notes:

> The thought of Guenon is the most anti-modern imaginable: for him, as for other "traditional" thinkers, the decline began about ten thousand years ago, and this entire historical period is but the last phase of something much bigger. The fall, or expulsion from the metaphysical world, has become even faster since the Renaissance, and the Enlightenment, and the twentieth century has only further accelerated the decay.[18]

Who were the Templars, and how are they tied to this place called Loreto? Pope Clement V, with a minor bull dated July 18, 1310, indirectly confirmed the authenticity

16   See. Rene Guenon, *Tradition and Traditions*, (Rome: Edizioni Mediterranee, 2003).
17   http://www.ilgiornale.it/news/spettacoli/gu-non-sul-disastro-delloccidente-aveva-capito-tutto-1217679.html
18   *Ibid.*

of the Holy House, and the popes in the centuries that followed confirmed again and again their devotion to the Virgin of Loreto. This is especially since the dramatic circumstances we are experiencing now for humanity, in proximity to the real turbulance of 2020-2025, which is the turning point according to many, for the fate of humanity, as I have exposed in part in the previous volumes of my *Confessions*. We are going through many years of "Tribulations"—even according to the loyalists of the Loreto Shrine, which are also very attached to the messages given during the famous alleged apparitions in Medjugorje, an important place for the Marian cult, which I will dwell on later in the course of this chapter. For hundreds of years, worshippers journeyed to the grand sanctuary of Loreto, which contains according to tradition, the Holy House, becoming what Pope John Paul II defined as: "The Marian heart of Christendom." Just think, since the beginning of the fourteenth century, this was an important place of pilgrimage, even for those taking the coastal road, who were actually heading toward the Holy Land, and, even in the aftermath of the crusades in the XV and XVI centuries, Pope Leo X, equated the Sanctuary of Loreto, to that of Jerusalem, because it was much safer and had virtually replaced the great penitential pilgrimages, that saw until then Rome, Santiago de Compostela, and Jerusalem, as the only crucial places for Christianity.

The so-called striking prodigy of the supposed translation of the Holy House, hides one of the most heroic gestures of the mysterious Knights Templar, and caught the attention and relative pilgrimage of kings and queens, princes, cardinals and popes, who left lavish gifts for the spiritual favors they received from the Virgin Mary of Loreto. In later times, they have been joined by political leaders, poets, writers, inventors, founders of religious orders, philosophers, artists, and saints. In this V.I.P. context, you can understand the importance the symbolic gesture represented with the official visit of the alleged Japanese Princess Kaoru Nakamaru. An absolute novelty definitely out of the norm for the rigid Vatican tradition, as Kaoru speaks openly of UFOs, and apocalyptic events, the New World Order, and other topics. At the time of her visit in 2011, the producer of a well-known Italian television show that aired on Berlusconi's TV Channel *Italia Uno*, was quite shocked by the fact that "the Japanese Princess" would actually be received officially by the Vatican in Loreto. She was genuinely surprised by the unusual gesture by the Holy See, and wanted to send a television crew, but unfortunately, budget and resources increasingly scarce for Italian television, prevented it. The producer would be even more shocked and surprised if she had known the truth about the connection between the invitation to the Princess, the Neo-Templars and the Holy House, followed by a sudden wave of strange events that lead the Japanese Princess to ultimately reject her appointment as ambassador for the Vatican, commissioned by Dr. Montuoro and Bishop Sigalini. A story was revealed, that at first glance might seem downright fantasy-politics, but I have all the evidence and related documents to prove otherwise. (FIG. 27 A & B)

It was the summer of 2011, as reported by Vatican expert Gianluigi Nuzzi, Archbishop Alberto Bottari de Castello, Apostolic Nuncio in Tokyo, wrote to his superiors a note entitled **"Reflections on my mission in Japan"** dated 15 August, 2011. It is a confidential document to the Vatican, which reflected deeply on the relationship of the Japanese with Christianity and the Catholic Church, that stated: *"Japan has a high culture, and a glorious history, a strong national identity tied to certain symbols (the Emperor) and religious expressions (Shintoism, Buddhism). Japan has become one of the most powerful countries in the world with their might, with the values they received through the centuries. They are proud of their identity, and do not feel the need for teachings coming from outside."*

FIG. 27 (A) – The official Vatican document attesting to the appointment of New Age guru and staunch alien believer Kaoru Nakamaru as Ambassador of the Holy Spirit Divine Power of Love on the 25 day of December 2011, with an official approval by the bishopric of Palestrina and the signature and stamp of his Bishop Monsignor Domenico Sigalini.

But there is one point in particular that I consider interesting in the words written in the reflections of Archbishop Alberto Bottari reported by Nuzzi: *"Certain images and ways of the Western world, constantly disseminated by the media: violence, materialism, corruption, are perceived as part of the Christian world, and are so very difficult to accept."* [19]

It seems obvious that the Japanese want to preserve their way of life, and they can't be bought by the Holy Father and his futile theater. The note criticizes with some irony, the Catholic tools to find new believers, judged incompatible with the Japanese population and their values. However in the summer of 2011, Bishop Domenico Sigalini at the time the General Chaplain of the influential Catholic organization *Azione Cattolica* ("Catholic Action"), and Dr. Montuoro, *Grand Officialis* of the Knights Templar in the Vatican, decided to invite Kaoru Nakamaru to Italy, to possibly shake things up, in hopes of gaining more interest for the Catholic Faith.

Princess Kaoru Nakamaru is a figure very close to the present Imperial family, as well as the founder of the **International Affairs Institute for World Peace** in New York in 1985. Kaoru has also been an exceptional diplomatic mediator in the past for the New World Order due to her long-standing friendship with the leaders of controversial countries such as North-Korea and Iran. Nakamaru exerts a kind of "personal diplomacy" lending herself sometimes as VIP mediator between warring countries, often financing her own missions. A gesture certainly commendable, which the princess wished to repeat for her new mission with the Vatican, arriving at her own expense from Japan at the end of August of 2011, for a series of important meetings with senior representatives of the Holy See, both in Palestrina near Rome, and in Loreto, for the above mentioned official meeting. The arrival of the Princess was described in this way by the Vatican:

Princess Kaoru Nakamaru, granddaughter of the Japanese Emperor Meiji, paid a visit to the Holy Spirit Center. She arrived on the evening of August 31, accompanied by two Japanese television operators, remaining our guest until the 2nd of September. The Diocese of Palestrina and the Pontifical Delegation of Loreto have issued two press releases to announce the important visit that has had so much echo in all the newspapers and local television stations. Princess Nakamaru, contacted us after be-

19   See. Gianluigi Nuzzi, *Sua Santità*, (Milan: Chiarelettere Editore, 2012), pp. 22, 244, 245.

OPERA DELLO SPIRITO SANTO
Potenza Divina d'Amore
Laici-Religiosi-Religiose

Discepoli e Apostoli dello Spirito Santo

Il Presidente

The Order of the Holy Spirit "Divine Power of Love"

founded on the basis of Canonic Law, with the pastoral blessing of the Bishop of the Suburbicarian Diocise of Palestrina, led today by His Excellency the Bishop Domenico Sigalini, would like to express extreeme gratitude to Dott.essa Kaoru Nakamaru for her visit to our Order where she was deeply impressed by its spiritual aims and the construction of a Temple and Citadel to the Holy Spirit, whose first stone was placed and blessed by His Holiness John Paul II.

In recognizing her zeal in presiding over the Foundation "The International Affairs Institute for World Peace", defending those ideals of peace and fraternity among nations; appreciating the spiritual sensitivity, whose deep courage leads to the realization of a route on the "Path of Life" of brotherly love, in opposition to the "Path of Power" of egoism in the individual;

confer the charge for the year 2012 of

AMBASADRESS IN THE WORLD OF THE ORDER OF THE HOLY SPIRIT "DIVINE POWER OF LOVE"

so she can help the Order to promote interreligeous dialogue between nations, to universally spread the spiritual rebirth of the whole world through intervention of the Holy Spirit according to the teachings of the Holy Roman Church, led by His Holiness Benedict XVI.

Palestrina, 25 Dicembre 2011, foundation of N.S.G.C

The President of the Order of the Holy Spirit　　　　　*Bishop of the Diocise of Palestrina*

Dott Antonio L. Montuoro　　　　　　　　　　*S.E. Mons Domenico Sigalini*

For a copy of the original issued in italian

Opera dello Spirito Santo
Potenza Divina d'Amore
Il Presidente

Opera dello Spirito Santo "Potenza Divina d'Amore" Via delle Piagge,68-00036 Palestrina-Roma Tel 0039 06 9535262-
www.spiritosanto.org
Casa di Riposo "Oasi Ave Maria" Via Leonessa, 3 – 60025 Loreto –Ancona tel 0039 071 977281 –
www.oasiavemaria.it

FIG. 27 (B) – The official English translation of the Vatican document attesting to the appointment of New Age guru and staunch alien believer Kaoru Nakamaru as Ambassador of the Holy Spirit Divine Power of Love on the 25 day of December 2011, with an official approval by the bishopric of Palestrina and the signature and stamp of his Bishop Monsignor Domenico Sigalini.

ing in possession of a booklet in English "Divine Power of Love." She was struck by the message on the Holy Spirit which mentions that with the worship due to him, you will make peace and concord among peoples, and its action of love will radiate in the world especially through the building of the Temple of the Holy Spirit. The princess came to visit Palestrina to make a television report on the Work of the Holy Spirit "Divine Power of Love." On September 1, she interviewed the bishop Mons. Domenico Sigalini and the President of the Opera, Antonio Leonardo in Montuoro in an atmosphere of cordial friendship on the issues that affect humanity in the search for a meaning in life that is not power, or pleasure, but the peace and harmony with ourselves and with others. The princess has been very satisfied by sharing some similarities with her Shinto faith and our Christian spirituality. At the end of her experience at the Opera, the princess said she found the spirituality she was looking for for at least a decade, wanting to learn even more about our reality in the world. Then the princess visited Loreto and the nursing home "Oasi Ave Maria," and then traveled to the Pontifical Delegation, where she met the Archbishop Mons. Giovanni Tonucci. At the end of the interview with him she has been welcomed by the Franciscan Friars of the Basilica of the Holy House where she could admire our artistic beauty. The Mayor of Loreto Paul Niccoletti and councilor for culture Mariateresa Schiavoni, greeted the princess donating her the "Book of Princes" an exclusive publication that next year will include also Princess Nakamaru's visit to Loreto. The princess (married to actor Tadao Nakamaru with two children) specialized in international politics at Columbia University, and from 1970 began her many activities as a journalist, interviewing kings and presidents, prime ministers and businessmen from all over the world. In addition to writing several books, she worked in television as an international commentator for Political Affairs. In 1973, she has been hailed by the U.S. magazine "Newsweek" as the best interviewer in the world, while the "Washington Post" described her as a woman with "a strong international sensitivity." She later became a producer and director of a talk show and she began to travel to war zones around the world by opening positive discussions with the heads of state of those countries. The primary objective of Princess Nakamaru is to promote world peace through human renaissance. Wealth, fame, power, Nakamaru says, do not make man happy, true happiness is sustained rather, by a heart full of love, harmony and peace. [20]

Dr. Antonio L. Montuoro, and Bishop Sigalini immediately wanted to recruit Kaoru Nakamaru for their projects. Suddenly, however, a mysterious accident took place in a mountain near Subiaco. The Bishop of Palestrina, Monsignor Sigalini, wound up in the hospital in a coma, that some say was not really an accident at all, but an attempted murder linked to the present battles of the Vatican's inner power structure with Sigalini's intentions of bringing Kaoru into the equation. A few days earlier, during the visit of Princess Kaoru to Palestrina, Bishop Sigalini revealed to a few of those present, including myself, that we would see him with a cardinal ring soon. After recovering from his coma, and returning to the scene after a long hospital stay, Sigalini communicated to his loyalists, and his parishioners of Palestrina, that he had a mystical- revelation, and that he was no longer ready to become a cardinal, and wanted to simply remain the Bishop of Palestrina, as he wanted to focus on his diocese. That was of course a lie, as many knew he had been threatened by somebody in the Vatican, who was nearly able to kill him, and for this reason Bishop Si-

20   http://www.spiritosanto.org/mensile/347/page5.htm (no longer online)   For more information see also: http://www.ilrestodelcarlino.it/ancona/provincia/2011/08/29/571026-manda_imperatore.shtml and http://www.cronacheanconetane.it/la-principessa-del-giappone-kaoru-nakamaru-in-visita-a-loreto/ ‡ Archived 28th September 2016.

galini gave up the possibility of ever becoming a cardinal. I also want to specify, that the request to visit the Vatican organization, *Work of the Holy Spirit Divine Power of Love* in Loreto and Palestrina, contrary to what was stated by the Vatican in their propaganda lies, was an idea of Dr. Montuoro, after reading the previously mentioned note of Archbishop Alberto Bottari, and not Princess Kaoru's idea. She never heard of the *Work of the Holy Spirit*, nor had she ever appreciated this little booklet in English entitled: *Divine Power of Love,* of which they are boasting in their article above. This booklet was actually donated to Kaoru during her visit to Loreto.

We even have evidence of this in the various images that were taken that day by the Japanese photographer accompanying the princess, Taro Nakamura. Kaoru was also not impressed by the "Book of Princes" that was given to her in Loreto, and

> ### ORDER OF THE HOLY SPIRIT
> "DIVINE POWER OF LOVE"
>
> IN COLLABORATION WITH
>
> **"THE INSTITUTE FOR INTERNATIONAL AFFAIRS WORL PEACE"**
>
> PRESENTING THE CONFERENCE
>
> **"THE HOLY SPIRIT IN THE HEART AND GIVER OF PEACE AMONG NATIONS"**
> -A WORLD OF LOVE AND TRUTH-
>
> BONUS PASTOR HOUSE VIA AURELIA 208 - ROME -
> extraterritorial area-
> - Vatican City-
>
> FRIDAY 'May 11, 2012 AT 15.00
>
> MODERATOR AND INTRODUCING
>
> DOTT.SSA KAORU NAKAMARU-
> PRESIDENT "THE INSTITUTE FOR INTERNATIONAL AFFAIRS WORL PEACE"
>
> GREETING THE AUTHORITIES 'VATICAN
>
> SPEAKERS
>
> -MONS. RENZO LAVATORI
>
> INTERVENTIONS
> THE TEMPLE OF THE HOLY SPIRIT:
> CENTER OF IRRADIATION AND RESIDENCE OF A NOVEL STABLE PENTECOST.
>
> DR. ANTONIO LEONARDO MONTUORO

FIG. 28 – Invitation issued by Dr. Montuoro for the event planned in the Vatican for Kaoru Nakamaru on May 11, 2012 that was meant to have as special guest Kim Jong-un, the North Korean dictator.

she actually gave it to me before leaving Italy. This is just the usual disinfo typical of these strange characters that revolve around the Vatican. For those interested in knowing more, and having ulterior confirmation about the "accident" that involved Bishop Sigalini, there are a few articles present online.[21] The following is an email from Montuoro to Kaoru that announces his intention of organizing a conference in the Vatican for Kaoru on the 11th May of 2012, (FIG. 28) where they would also host the infamous North Korean dictator **Kim Jong-un,** (FIG. 29) and other personalities invited by Kaoru:

> *Kindest Princess Kaoru Nakamaru,*
>
> *I enclose the appointment of Ambassador in the world of the Order of the Holy Spirit also signed by S.E. Bishop Domenico Sigalini. I will send the original via air courier. We rely heavily on your support for peace in the world through the knowledge of the Holy Spirit, the Divine Energy that will change the world. I remain at your disposal throughout the organization of the conference. The date given by the*

21 http://www.lastampa.it/2011/09/07/vaticaninsider/ita/news/monsignor-domenico-sigalini-in-gravi-condizio-ni-per-una-caduta-in-montagna-bX9294h3QYfdnZmjLKBlvM/pagina.html ‡ Archived 28th September, 2016.

FIG. 29 – Kim Jong-un, the third son of the late Kim Jong-il photographed in front of a million people in Pyongyang, on the second day of the solemn state funeral for his father the "Dear Leader," which also functioned as the official ceremony for the handover of power to the new dictator of North Korea.

Bishop is the day May 11 at 15.00 p.m. The submission of a draft program of the Congress that we can modify to your liking. According to the authorities invited by you, we will join personalities from the Vatican to the same level. I ask you kindly to send me as soon as possible, the list of personalities that you will invite and then the list of persons who agree to participate. So I can arrange time for the calls of the Italian and Vatican. A warm thanks from the Order of the Holy Spirit and Bishop Sigalini. With the hope that God will guide you always in your way.

Dr. Antonio Leonardo Montuoro
President

Remember, of course, that behind Montuoro and the **Opera of the Holy Spirit Divine Power of Love,** is the powerful Neo-Templar faction of the deceased Rocco Zingaro (1941 – 2011) and the Italian organization *Azione Cattolica*. Princess Kaoru, however, despite being Japanese, and an outsider to the Italian scene, understood pretty clearly that behind this supposed Marian devotion, and the many beautiful words of these zealots from the Vatican, in reality, were only partly genuine, made with great economic interest and many compromises. This of course, had very little to do with spirituality, and a lot to do with the present decline of the Catholic Church, and their sordid affairs. Kaoru Nakamaru's exclusive relation with Kim Jong-un and her intention to bring him to visit the Pope in the Vatican eventually caused her big trouble with the agents of New World Order. A situation of high international tension and intrigue suddenly erupted around the princess, who was eventually forced to give up her collaboration with the Vatican, and I have documents signed by the princess to prove it. All this happened in order to maintain a constant strategy of tension in South-East Asia, favorable to the USA. **Jennifer Lind** of Dartmouth College once wrote in *Foreign Affairs* magazine that Westerners always overestimate their ability to penetrate the mystery of North Korea. Kaoru's direct relation with North Korea's dictator could have changed all this. So in this tense geopolitical scenario, the Neo-Templars of Montuoro and former Prefect Enrico Marinelli, realized a great opportunity in the possible arrival of the young Korean dictator with which Princess Kaoru has had a long-standing relationship, due to her close friendship in the past with both his dictator father, and his dictator grandfather, the one who first invited Kaoru to visit North

FIG. 30 –Page 1 of the LETTER OF RESIGNATION sent to Dr. Montuoro by Princess Kaoru Nakamaru in February, 2012, that mentions an earlier visit by the Japanese security forces that threatened her for wanting to bring Kim Jong-un to the Vatican, and also advised her to not collaborate any longer with Dr. Montuoro, Bishop Sigalini and the Holy See.

FIG. 31 – Page 2 of the LETTER OF RESIGNATION sent to Dr. Montuoro, where Princess Kaoru Nakamaru also mentions the New World Order, and the possible influence of the U.S. in the act of intimidation exercized against her by the Japanese Security forces, who forced her to stop her collaboration with the Vatican. This important document written in the Italian language will be available to journalists and historians for any further research at www.leozagami.com or by written request sent to CCC Publishing.

Korea, after hearing her inspirational speech at the **United Nations.** Certainly Kaoru was a great opportunity to relaunch the Vatican diplomacy for Montuoro, and his Templars in the Vatican, however her sudden choice to give up her position came after a visit to her house and at her office, by the Japanese security services, and what became a clear threat to her life, and the life of her Japanese co-workers.

Antonio Leonardo Montuoro has also promoted for years, the idea of a Temple Work of the Holy Spirit, another of his projects I spoke about in detail in my book *Pope Francis: The Last Pope?* This strange place, which has been long under construction, was said to become a sort of emergency Vatican, a "Vatican 2" of the Holy See, if its territory in the center of Rome were somehow destroyed or irreparably affected by the terrible events of the period that we are experiencing, in which various catastrophic prophecies of the Catholic world, seem, according to Montuoro, to converge towards a grand Apocalyptic finale, which will see a devastating terrorist attack against the Vatican (perhaps ISIS?) There are a couple of videos based on Montauro's project that are still present on YouTube for you to

FIG. 32 – From your left, Dr. Antonio Leonardo Montuoro, Princess Kaoru Nakamaru and Giovanni Tonucci, former apostolic nuncio in Scandinavia and titular archbishop of Torcello—prelate of Loreto and pontifical delegate of the Sanctuary of the "Santa House" during the official visit of Princess, at what is supposed to be the Holy House of Mary.

check out, one by the title of the **"Monument of the Holy Ghost —The Temple"** *Opera dello Spirito Santo - Il Tempio,* [22] and the other entitled the **"Holy Spirit—The foundations of the Temple"** *Opera dello Spirito Santo - Le fondamenta del Tempio.* [23]

After my revelations on their supposed "Temple of the Holy Spirit" were made public in various books I published in Italy and abroad, in 2014, the City of Palestrina confirmed the abandonment of this project by the diocese of Palestrina and Bishop Sigalini. Even their chilvaric order of the *Knights of the Temple of the Holy Spirit* seem to have lost *momentum* and slowed down their operations, having no longer a temple on which to base their Neo-Templar project.

Princess Kaoru instead moved towards an absolute condemnation of the Vatican activities in a book we co-wrote together, as the Holy See seems increasingly distant from God. However in her resignation letter sent to Dr. Montuoro, (FIGS. 30 and 31) she even mentions the remarkable pressure she suffered in early February of 2012, by the Japanese secret police, that came close to threatening her life, if she did not immediately interrupt her dangerous relationship with North Korea and the Vatican representatives and the Holy See. (FIG. 32) So do not be manipulated by the media lies and the propaganda that is regularly brought to us by the U.S. Department of State in regards to North Korea, because it is all crap. Regarding American interests and the tension between the two Koreas, the U.S. does not want any kind of real peace deals, especially one made by an independent figure like Kaoru Nakamaru. They, along with the "Architects of the New World Order," just want to use the situation to their advantage in any way possible. This is a classic example of the U.S. Military Complex applied strategy in the geopolitical /

22   http://www.youtube.com/watch?v=FRkKPyzAJWM ‡ Archived 28th September, 2016.
23   http://www.youtube.com/watch?v=V2AP9s1357g ‡ Archived 28th September, 2016.

military field moved by unscrupulous characters who obviously want to maintain their power at all costs. They wish to maintain influence in the area, to justify their presence and military bases, using the North Korean "danger card" as a propaganda tool to spin their own rubbish. The New World Order prepared a bad joke for the young Korean dictator, who had stated he wanted to come to Rome as a guest of the Vatican and the *Opera of the Holy Spirit Divine Power of Love*, along with his then powerful uncle Jang Song-Thaek, aged sixty-five, who was later executed by his nephew, by what some say was an attempted coup in December, 2013. Sacha Noam Baron Cohen (born in London in 1971), known for having created the exhilarating character of "Borat," who is in reality a British actor of Jewish origin, and a renowned international comedian, launched one of his more demented acts to date, towards the North Korean leader during Oscar night of 2012, pouring on the famous Hollywood red carpet the fake ashes of the father of the North Korean dictator, Kim Jong-il, who had just died recently. Sacha will later be removed by the security services in place for the event, but he will continue until he was brought away to recite his unworthy and offensive show that evening against North Korea, stating with his provocative jokes, that the old dictator had always dreamed of coming to the Oscars and to appear on the red carpet. Imagine what this gesture of bad taste, to say the least, did to his troubled son, the new dictator of North Korea, Kim Jong-un. This is the unjust and criminal world promoted by the Zionist Masterminds of the New World Order propaganda, where there is no respect, even for the dead.

Is Oblast the "New Israel?"

The Israelis are planning a strategic exodus that will position them rather close to North Korea. In fact, the Zionist lobby is buying large slices of territory in the northeast of China to create an autonomous province in accordance with the Chinese authorities. This has been the case for some years, and the details about it come directly from agents within Mossad, and the lesser known ShinBet,[24] the Intelligence agency for the state of Israel Internal Affairs. It seems that secretly for years, the Israelis have been preparing internally for mass evacuations, if the situation with Iran or other Muslim countries or terrorist groups like ISIS degenerates, perhaps by being nuked, which would thus compromise the entire area for thousands of years. The Iranian Supreme Leader Khamenei made it clear in the past what the level of conflict would be if tensions escalate. Is this a piloted strategy of tension? Maybe, but in Tehran in the past, they have shown to not fear the risk of a military escalation on a large scale.[25] If this "Armageddon" scenario was to happen, such as an Israeli war with the use of nuclear weapons, who are always ready for anything from the days of Moses, would be ready for the next exodus of the Jewish people, with a pretty good back up emergency plan. Among other things, the location for such a colossal move wasn't chosen at random by the Jewish elite.

It's a Chinese territory bordering with **The Jewish Autonomous Oblast,** also referred to as "Yevrey" or "Birobidzhan,"[26] an Autonomous Province created for the Jews in Russia by Stalin in 1934, according to his political vision of giving a territory to every ethnic group in the USSR; called **Birobidzhan.** It is obvious that Israel would like to create a new state in this area, which would be, "incidentally" bordering with the fastest emerging economy in the world, that of the Far East, with whom they already do a lot of business.

24   http://it.wikipedia.org/wiki/Shin_Bet † Archived 3rd October 2016.

25   http://www.meridianionline.org/2012/06/07/israele-e-iran-si-preparano-per-la-resa- dei-conti-atomica/ ‡ Archived 3rd October 2016

26   http://it.wikipedia.org/wiki/Oblast'_autonoma_ebraica ‡ Archived 3rd October 2016.

FIG. 33 – The main square of the city of Birobidzhan, the capital of the Jewish Autonomous Oblast in Russia, located on the Trans-Siberian Railway, close to the border with China. According to inside sources close to the Israeli intelligence services, this region would be annexed as a future homeland based in the northeast of China, created by Israeli Jews, a back-up state in case of a nuclear emergency in the Middle East.

The Jewish Autonomous "Oblast," a term that is analogous to "state" or "province" in the USA, has important deposits of gold and silver, and has developed a good local craft for jewelery. Also, Birobidzhan has important mechanical industries, textiles, footwear, clothing and wood; and in spite of the Stalinist persecution of the Jews, today things have changed. Yiddish and modern Hebrew is again taught in the schools of this Oblast, and business with the international Jewish community is now possible and frequent, and bring in many people from abroad. (FIG. 33) Since 2003, the Birobidzhan synagogue has taken on an important role in the worldwide Jewish community, and **seems ready for Plan B if Iran and the Arab world in general, move towards a more aggressive position towards Israel and their "Holy Land."** Meanwhile, the **Bank of China** in 2008, entered the capital of *Compagnie Financière* of Edmond de Rothschild, with a stake of 20%, becoming the largest China-Jewish alliance in the history of high finance, where for some time things have been moving in this direction, thanks to influential figures such as Henry Kissinger.

The New World Order is preparing to leave the American "democratic" model in favor of Chinese dictatorship for their global goverment. The transaction, which has asked the Chinese group for an investment of 2.2 billion yuan, or about 236 million euros, is accompanied by a partnership which provides for the creation and promotion by the historic French bank, of French products for distribution in the Chinese market. Thus the bank of **Edmond de Rothschild,** will have access to the 130 million potential Chinese customers. **Bank of China**, one of the top four banks in this country, will become an important partner in this deal, but the *Compagnie Financière Saint-Honoré*—parent company of *Compagnie Financière*—will stay with the majority of capital. The internationalization of the historic French brand also sees an Italian figure involved. In fact in the supervisory board of the Rothschild bank we find the Italian Carlo De Benedetti, another key shadow figure of the present New World Order. Meanwhile another historical alliance has been created between the Rothschilds, and the other major funder and supporter of the New World Order, **Rockefeller**. [27] So two of the world's largest industrial dynasties, the first in America, the second in Europe, decided in 2012, to merge at least part of their economic forces, to form a "strategic partnership," as defined by the *Financial Times*. The "strategy" in question, of course, is to make even more money, although they already have quite a lot: 34 billion dollars in goods and investments in the case of the Rockefeller group, and a more modest 1 billion and 900 million pounds for the Rothschild group, operating under Edmond de Rothschild. This "marriage" between billionaires of the NWO elite that sees also the involvement of the infamous George Soros lurking behind the scenes, was mainly born out of the the personal relationship between the two elderly patriarchs, the late **David Rockefeller,** traditionally closer to the "Republicans," who used to be a member of the San Francisco-based Bohemian Club, and **Lord Jacob Rothschild IV,** traditionally closer to the "Democrats." Seemingly distant politically speaking, this historic alliance is of course part of a plan to destroy the sovereignty of most nations in favor of their demented New World Order.

An email dated January 9, 2012, from Hillary Clinton, published by Julian Assange's *Wikileaks,* discusses a meeting that would take place at Jacob Rothschild's historic estate, Waddesdon. [28] In 2016, Hillary Clinton attended a $100,000-a-head fundraiser hosted by another member of this powerful family, Lynn Forester de Rothschild, a prominent New York businesswoman, and supporter of Mrs. Clinton. She was introduced to her third husband Sir Evelyn de Rothschild (b.1931) by Henry Kissinger, at the 1998 Bilderberg Group conference in Scotland. Lady Rothschild wrote an email on April 18, 2010, in which she tells her friend Hillary she would *"love to catch up"*—and *"I remain your loyal adoring pal."* Clinton responds *"let's make that happen,"* and signs her response, *"Much love, H."* Later, on the 23rd of September 2010, Clinton emailed Lynn Forester de Rothschild saying, *"I was trying to reach you to tell you and Teddy that I asked Tony Blair to go to Israel as part of our full court press on keeping the Middle East negotiations going ..."*

The wealthy family of today descends from **Mayer Amschel Rothschild**, a court Jew to the German Landgraves of Hesse-Kassel, whose rulers played a key role in the development of Freemasonry. Prince Karl, Landgrave of Hessen-Kassel 1744-1836, was the chief organizer of the most important Masonic Congress of all time in Wilhelmsbad in 1782. Since then, the Rothschild family has, in the last two centuries, developed as one of the most important banking families in the world, and have always retained a key role in the policies of the newly born State of Israel, which they helped fund and ideologically craft. After the death of James Jacob de Rothschild in 1868, his eldest son Alphonse Rothschild, took over the management of the family bank, and was the most active in support for Eretz Israel. The Rothschild family archives show that during the 1870s, the family contributed nearly 500,000 francs per year on behalf of Eastern Jewry to the *Alliance Israélite Universelle*. In 1917, Walter Rothschild, was the addressee of the **Balfour Declaration** to the **Zionist Federation**, which committed the British government to the es-

27   http://www.repubblica.it/economia/finanza/2012/05/30/news/l_allenza_rockfeller-rothschild_europa_e_usa_alleate_negli_affari-36224333/ ‡ Archived 3rd October 2016.
28   https://wikileaks.org/clinton-emails/emailid/4475 ‡ Archived 3rd October, 2016.

tablishment in Palestine, for a national home for the Jewish people, and what would later become the state of Israel. Baron Edmond James de Rothschild, youngest son of James Jacob de Rothschild, was a patron of the first settlement in Palestine at Rishon-LeZion, and bought from Ottoman landlords, part of the land which now makes up present-day Israel. In 1924, he established the **Palestine Jewish Colonisation Association** (PICA), which acquired more than 125,000 acres of land and set up business ventures.

Today history repeats itself, and Lord Jacob Rothschild IV, who is the Honorary President of the **Institute for Research of the Jewish Policy,** is possibly one of the masterminds behind this new planned exodus of Jews towards a new land. Baron Rothschild is a key figure in Israel who controls the **Hanadiv** foundation, which was founded by Edmond de Rothschild, and has built up, for example, the Supreme Court of the State of Israel, the building of the Knesset, which is Israel's parliament, and he is building the national library. Jacob Rothschild, and the aforementioned Henry Kissinger, are perhaps two of the most influential Jews in the world today. Their friend David Rockefeller, although he did not have to my knowledge proven Jewish heritage, as a young man has worked to cultivate both public relations for the family business (oil), and U.S. Military Intelligence, working in close contact with Israel, its main ally. Henry Kissinger, Lord Rothschild and David Rockefeller, who died in March 2017 have been a legendary trio. Their influence, however, and their past work, undoubtedly constitutes the central framework of the New World Order, and have a central role in the global economy for centuries to come. In the meantime, the 80-year-old member of the Rothschild dynasty, Jacob Rothschild, must build a stronger case for his secret project in the northeast of China, that involves annexing what is at the moment an autonomous region of the Russian Federation, confident that the United States, in this new Cold War scenario with Russia, will find support in some of the Russian elites. Rothschild said on an American political TV show in 2016 later reported on October 6, 2016 by *Cenznet.com* [29] and later translated from Russian by Kristina Kharlova for *Fort-russ.com*: *"The current crisis may last much less time than the cold war. At the moment the U.S. has allies among the Russian elites, who are ready to take over the initiative. In this scenario, ordinary people will not notice anything. The course of Russia's foreign policy will change—this will be presented as some kind of achievement of Russian diplomacy."*

Meanwhile, before Trump's arrival in the White House, Rothschild was pretty sure that the so-called conflict within the Russian elite was in its final stage, forgetting however what will happen if his protégé Hillary Clinton would have lost her bid for the White House like she fortunately did. *"A part of the Russian elite insists that the Russian leadership pushes for the lifting of sanctions. Part are against concessions to the West. Next year we'll know who won,"* said Rothschild.

It is worth noting that since September 30, 2016, a video of the famous Donbass defender Igor Girkin (Strelkov) lashing out at Putin has been circulating online. Strelkov makes it clear that his followers are ready to protest, and did not shy from personal insults towards Putin. Earlier those Russian experts who favor Putin, dubbed Strelkov "the fifth column." Who Strelkov's sponsor remains a mystery, but the person is probably the usual George Soros. Kristina Kharlova adds an interesting comment to all this:

> *Every country has its patriots and traitors, and it's no doubt that Rothschild is not exaggerating. He seems very well informed for a government outsider. Strelkov is the least of Putin's worries. The tentacles of the sprout reach far and wide and there*

29   http://cenznet.com/2016/10/02/джейкоб-ротшильд-у-сша-имеются-союзни/ ‡ Archived 3rd October, 2016.

is no doubt America has its "allies" deeply planted in every strategic sector of the Russian society. But so they did in the 90's but it did not prevent an emergence of a new strong and defiant leader seemingly out of nowhere. Undoubtedly America succeeded in enslaving much of the world, but Russia is no stranger to such attempts. Whenever Russia was plunged into dark times it has found its way out.

Apparently for America a victory means complete defeat and surrender of the opponent, which is consistent with its adherence to the law of the jungle in international politics. It has worked so far as long as 95% of the global population are content with the status quo. However, everyone understands that sharing a pie is better than giving it all to one, and global leaders and their constituents are watching Putin's moves with envy and anticipation. In that regard we can safely conclude that Putin himself has many more silent allies among global elites than he is even aware of. [30]

Well, I am sure Russia is ready for its future, whatever the outcome. In the meantime, I am also pretty sure that they have been informed about Israel's intention to prepare for a back-up state in the northeast of China, that may merge with one of their autonomous regions. In October 2016, Russia and Israel celebrated 25 years since they officially restored diplomatic relations after the Soviet Union severed them in 1967, following the Six Day War. In the meantime things are changing for Israel in 2017, a great nation often misinterpreted, that deserves to exist in defence of the basic values of our Judeo-Christian civilization under threat from the daily expansion of Islam secretly promoted by the Jesuits. Israel is a nation I regard as one of the most important and influential on Earth, since **Benjamin "Bibi" Netanyahu**, the current Prime Minister of Israel, is finally fronting his internal enemies, including the Rothschild family. Of course, they will try to sabotage and investigate him for bribery, fraud and God knows what, but thanks to his new ally, U.S. President Donald J. Trump, and his team, I think Netanyahu can initially look forward to a great new alliance to oppose Iran's nuclear threat, without having to move again from the Holy Land to some distant place in Asia.

Palaprat Johannite Foundations

I'll return now to speak of Loreto, this magical place said by Antonio Leonardo Montuoro to also be an extra-dimensional portal, central to the pagan tradition, which was later transformed into a place of Catholic devotion and Marian worship, linked to the mysterious Templars, and even to the modern versions of the Templar tradition we define as Neo-Templars. These turn out to be the true leaders of the Western initiatic system in all their various emanations, from their pure Christian form, to the ones we find in the various Masonic rites originally by the Rite of Strict Templar Observance, to the blatantly Satanic and anti-Christian ones, like the *Ordo Templi Orientis* (O.T.O.) for example. Although the degenerate factions of Neo-Templarism dedicated to the black magical arts are not always regarded as genuine by the most traditional Neo-Templars. They are to be considered as influential in multiple environments prone to esotericism, but are definitely the scum of the international Neo-Templar scene, reflecting even today, if you will, the black soul and perverse practices of certain degenerate aristocrats, that often devote themselves to witchcraft and evil practices, since ancient times, as part of the dark side of the Illuminati, as I have already explained in Volume I of my *Confessions*. This situation originally facilitated even Philip the Fair, in his destructive mission against the Knights Templar, which thanks to a minority of sorcerers present in its ranks, would be banned forever after they courageously defended Christendom, receiving honors and

30 http://www.fort-russ.com/2016/10/jacob-rothschild-us-has-allies-among.html ‡ Archived 3rd October, 2016.

glory since their foundation. The Order of the Temple was thus a monastic order, whose history is intertwined with that of the Crusades, which was officially dissolved by Pope Clement V (1260 – 1314)—after the cruel persecution of the King of France, Philip the Fair (1268 – 1314)—in 1307.

CESNUR led by Massimo Introvigne writes the following explanation:

> After the suppression, the Order survived for a few decades out of France, but at the latest at the beginning of the fifteenth century the Templars have completely disappeared. The thesis of their secret continuation has been denounced by the medieval history specialists such as Régine Pernoud (1909 – 1998) as "completely insane" and linked to claims and legends "uniformly silly" (The Templars, trad. It. Effedieffe, Milan, 1993, p. 11). The idea that the Templars, officially abolished, had clandestinely continued their activity until the eighteenth century first spreads in French and German Freemasonry.

What Introvigne's Jesuit controlled CESNUR, and his friends forget to tell us, is that this Neo-Templar revival in France and Germany was inspired by the Society of Jesus, who influenced the Freemasons of the eighteenth century like no other. Of course there was also the Jesuits, as well as the Stuardist Masonic factor at the base of so-called "Scottish" Freemasonry, bound to the Templar roots of the Craft.

Thus, in 1804 the Jesuits and their brothers were formally banned by the Catholic Church, and appointed **Bernard Raymond Fabré-Palaprat (1773 – 1838)**, Grand Master of the Order of the Temple, that was established for the first time clearly outside the bounderies of Freemasonry. Fabré-Palaprat, who merged later with the Johannite Church in 1812, was born in 1773, in France, the son of a surgeon with a priest for an uncle. He was a former seminarian (as Adam Weishaupt before him), then an ordained priest, who went on to become an adventurer and a doctor. The idea of an autonomous and independent branch of the Knights Templar coming out of the rigid control of the Templar degrees of Freemasonry, was supported by the Jesuits, and at the same time Napoleon Bonaparte (1769 – 1821), an agent of the Jesuits and the Illuminati, who authorized a solemn ceremony to restart the order publicly in France in 1808. Fabré-Palaprat, had more in mind than just a knightly order, and intended to return rapidly to the Catholic Church. His idea was ambitious, and began to fully manifest in 1812, by tying the Neo-Templars into a new religion shaped to support a possible new Messiah. The importance of this sequence is clearly at odds with the Jesuits we know of today, but probably instrumental to the last period of their diaspora from the Catholic Church, because as Grand Master of the Order of the reconstituted Temple, Fabré-Palaprat even proclaimed himself to be the true successor St. John, and of Jesus Christ, which protected him with all the powers of the priesthood. The dress rehearsal for the coming of the "Messiah" of the Templars could now proceed with the foundation of a church of the Neo-Templars, which is called the **Johannite Church**, declaring itself the only real legitimate Christian Church (as would be unlawful for them to follow the "ecclesiastical" line of the Catholic Church, which comes not from Saint John but from Saint Peter). The Johannite Church, however, lasted only a few years but will have, as I will show you later, a link with what will become the Gnostic Church, or the "Secret Church" of the Illuminati, where the dangerous "Thelemic" heresy of Aleister Crowley was born, and other devilish diversions which often assume a gnostic Satanic twist. At the time of Fabré-Palaprat, all members of the Order of the Temple would take his heresy seriously, and some who did not intend to break with the Catholic Church, probably sensing the imminent return of the Jesuits in the Vatican, departed from his project.

This seemingly crazy gesture by Fabré-Palaprat to found a new religion, created a series of schisms, and the emergence of a "Catholic faction." They were dissidents since the first attempts, which also determined the separation of the Italian branch of Palaprat's order, which became independent in 1815, which I will return to later, because it is important for its subsequent connection with the Catholic Church and the Patriarchate of Antioch. The eventual end of the Johannite Church did not eliminate the growing disagreements between Neo-Templar factions. The "Catholics" wished the Order to explicitly profess the Roman Catholic religion, while the "Palapratians" (or "lay" Brothers), offered an interfaith Order open to all Christian denominations, and even gnostics. Both branches, however, declined, and more or less disappeared. In 1871, the few "Palapatrian" French survivors left the Order, taking note of the lack of success and, using a Masonic expression went into "sleeping" mode. The same applies to the "Catholic" branch in Belgian in 1890. Later, the "regent" of the Order in France is given to Joséphin Péladan, who was nevertheless, more interested in another order of its creation, the Catholic Order of the Rosy Cross. It seeks even greater convergence with the Jesuits, returning to Catholicism and renouncing the Johannite heresy, that still proliferates, despite being officially "dormant" by the figures who originally represented it.

In fact, most occult orders and churches born in the Neo-gnostic and the Theosophical milieu of the New Age, pick up from the Johannite tradition, and often we find in this initiatic context supposed lineages related to a direct succession of the Johannite Church of Bernard Raymond Fabré-Palaprat, which is said to be by some, the Mother Church of the various lineages of the Gnostic Church in existence today. One of these is the lineage transmited by the Liberal Catholic Church headed by the gay bishop of the *Ordo Templi Orientis Antiqua*, Michael Paul Bertiaux from Chicago, known also as **Tau Ogdoade-Orfeo IV,** leader of the infamous **Choronzon Club**, the first "Thelemic" secret society that openly recruites only gay men. Bertiaux writes that his supposed lineage from Palaprat was transmitted to him by his mentor and intiator **Hector François Jean Maine, Tau Orfeo Ogdoade-III (1924 – 1984).** The Liberal Catholic rite was founded in 1916 by Arnold Harris Mathew (1852 – 1919), bishop of the Old Catholic Church. Following disagreements with Mathew, the church in question was re-founded on the basis of a wider freedom of thought, and of a particular mysticism by James Ingall Wedgwood (1883 – 1951), member of the Theosophical movement. In 1918, the Old Catholic Church in Britain assumed the name **Liberal Catholic Church.**

The most important and genuine lineage of the Order of the Temple founded by Fabré-Palaprat to date, remains in Belgium, and the only one still active to this day. In 1894, they promoted the establishment in Brussels of an International Secretariat of the Templars, which was not recognized by all the foreign priories, but was a rather large coalition. In 1930, the "secular" branch in Belgium (called *"de la Trinité de la Tour"*) ends as such, but in 1932, is reconstituted as Grand Priory of Belgium, which makes the formal establishment of an association called **"Belgian Association of the Knights of Sovereign and Military order of the Temple of Jerusalem"** (OSMTJ). It is from the latter that all subsequent Neo-Templar affiliations eminate, including that of **Antonio Campello Pinto de Sousa Fontes (1887 – 1960)** father of **Regent Fernando Sousa Pinto Fontes,** and **Gabriel Inellas (1913 – 1987),** who was born in Venezuela and resided in Brazil, where he introduced himself as "Prince Gabriel Inellas Palaeologus," a disputed title of pure fantasy said his opponents. [31]

••

31   http://www.cesnur.com/gli-ordini-Neo-Templari/le-origini-del-Neo-Templarismo/ ‡ Archived 3rd October 2016.

Loreto's Holy House

The Knights Templar and their Grand Master William of Beaujeu are said to have defended with their lives the Holy House of the Virgin Mary, in the city of Acre in 1291, against the advancing Islamic enemy, the same one that Pope Francis in now welcoming in the West. The Templars acted with great skill in the subsequent removal of the stones, which they quickly transferred to Loreto, after a very difficult and risky journey from the Holy Land. It was the last great operation and act of courage of the Knights Templar in the Holy Land, and indeed it deserves some kind of recognition now that the truth is slowly being revealed.

It was these real indomitable Knights Templar, and their exploits, that inspired the former Grand Preceptor Rocco Zingaro, who is recently deceased. He had worked for years behind the scenes with the Vatican in bringing back the Templars to the Church, despite past accusations of heresy sanctioned by the infamous papal bul *Vox in excelso* issued on March 22, 1312. There is also a key document for understanding the recent developments in the previously difficult relations between the growing Neo-Templar movements and the Church of Rome, a document that was strangely "lost" in the archives of the Vatican secret archives for hundreds of years, and some say may even be a fake, conveniently presented at the appropriate times to please the present Neo-Templars at the top of the Vatican hierarchy. This document is called the **Chinon Parchment.**

True or false, this document is meant to show the acquittal by Pope Clement V, of the leading members of the Knights Templar. This supposedly long lost document was drafted in Chinon, Diocese of Tours, between the 17th and the 20th of August 1308, the original of which is formed from a single large piece of paper (70 x 58 cm2), initially provided with the hanging seals of the three papal legates who formed the special apostolic Commission ad *inquirendum* appointed by Clement V. The original was accompanied by a certified copy, still preserved in the Vatican Secret Archives, with the signature *Archivum Arcis, Armarium d 218.*

The parchment was discovered in 2002 by Dr. Barbara Frale, a historian and expert in ancient documents, who is said to have conducted this important discovery with the approval of the Vatican, that was then published in 2007 by the Vatican itself, with all documents related to the process. One thing is certain, 2007 for a number of reasons, relating also to Rocco Zingaro's work within the Vatican wall, became a very special year for Neo-Templarism. The "Chinon Parchment" if true, undoubtedly puts into question whether the past position that wrongly judged the Knights Templar, debunks the previously "official" version of the events that condemned the Templars without appeal, as heretics of the worst kind.

The Chinon Parchment shows that Pope Clement V, in secret, absolved all the leaders of the Order, and that the convictions to have them burned on the stake and arrested were actually the responsibility of King Philip IV of France, not of the Pope or the Church. A widespread misunderstanding sometimes used strategically to justify opposition to the Church of Rome by certain Neo-Templar Masonic currents, that include the Ancient and Accepted Scottish Rite, which in the 30° as I have already mentioned earlier, have members swear revenge against the "injustice done to the Templars."

The document in question discovered by Barbare Frale, contains a supposed absolution that Pope Clement V gave to the Grand Master of the Temple, Friar Jacques de Molay, and other leaders of the Order. This was after DeMolay had repented and asked for forgiveness to the church; and after formal abjuration, that was mandatory for everyone who was even suspected of heretical crimes. Members of the Templar commanderies would then be reintegrated in the Catholic Communion and re-admitted to receive the sacraments. This gesture was supposed to be the first phase of the trial of the Templars, when Clement V was still convinced he could ensure the survival of this important military-religious order. The apostolic document had to restore their image, and lift the infamy of excommunication for the warrior-monks, who had previously embroiled themselves, admitting they denied Jesus Christ by the testimonies given to the French Inquisitor, sometimes under severe torture. The Chinon Parchment was a prerequisite for a future reform of the order, but it remained a dead letter, or maybe it was conveniently set aside to prove one day the innocence of the Vatican, that even back then feared for the future "revenge" of the Templars. The French monarchy reacted by triggering a blackmail mechanism, which will force Clement V, who will not be able to oppose the will of Philip IV the Fair, King of France, who wished for the complete elimination of the Knights Templar. He heard the opinion of the Council Fathers, arriving to suppress the order "with unalterable and perpetual rule" (the papal bull *Vox in excelso*). Clement V stated that this decision does not constitute an act of condemnation for heresy, which they were not able to reach on the basis of the various inquiries carried out in the years before the Council.

To issue a final ruling, it was necessary to have a fair trial, which also foresaw the exposure of the defensive position of the Order. But the scandal spinned by the King's propaganda brought shameful accusations against the Templars, which included heresy, idolatry, homosexuality and obscene practices. Such charges would have dissuaded anyone, according to the pope, from wearing again the Templar habit. On the other hand, a delay in the decision on such issues would have produced the squandering of great riches offered by many Christians to the Order, instructed to come to the aid of the Holy Land to fight the enemies of the faith. Careful consideration of these dangers, together with pressure on the French side, convinced the Pope to eventually abolish the Order of Knights of the Temple, which since then went into hiding, searching cover throughout history in other orders, and other forms of Christianity, including the Orthodox and Protestant, and finally seeking, at least for some, a unification with the Church of Rome.

In October 2007, the Vatican managed to acquire what for some think is the real **Holy Grail,** an object that was donated to the Church by Rocco Zingaro, who was a leading figure in Neo-Templarism. The Vatican also decides to include in their collection for public display, *Exemplaria Praetiosa,* a fine reproduction of some of the major documents of the process to the Knights Templars, including the Chinon Parchment. Barbara Frale, who had discovered this precious document, conveniently wrote a historical introduction to the documents chosen for this new Vatican itinerant project, which was presented to the media with a great press conference by Monsignor Sergio Pagano, Titular Bishop of Celene and prefect of the Vatican Secret Archives. A year later, the entire corpus of extraordinary works for the Secret Archives, the Vatican Library and the Vatican Museums, was presented at the Italian Cultural Institute of New York in 2008. The *Processus contra Templarios,* was exhibited in New York, which is the unpublished and exclusive edition of the complete acts of the ancient trial of the Templars, containing the original parchments conserved in the Vatican Secret Archives, including the Chinon Parchment, inserted inside the *Exemplaria Praetiosa* project. Every Freemason and Neo-Templar of relevance was there for the event. Imagine that the project that brought the famous parchment to New York in December, 2008, was actually compiled years earlier by Saint John Paul II, who wanted to "let the world know of the wisdom and beautiful treasures" of the Vatican Apostolic Library. The historical introduction to the documents of the process against the Templars received great attention both in academic and cultural circles, and also in the more obscure chivalric and Masonic ones. This lead to several articles both in various national and foreign newspapers, as well as on websites of various Neo-Templar orders, and Freemasonry. The move was made so as to facilitate a total rehabilitation of the Templar figure, so much so that in conjunction with the discovery made by Dr. Barbara Frale, a rumor spread that the Supreme Council of the Ancient and Accepted Scottish Rite of 33 ° in Lexington, Massachusetts, which governs the rite in the jurisdiction of the northern United States, removed part of the teachings of the 30th grade, and eliminated the Sublime Areopagus of the Knights Kadosh that usually accompanies it.

The lesson of this degree teaches revenge against the Rulers and the Vatican for having eliminated the Order of the Templars. Not having direct contact with the jurisdiction in question, I can not tell you how this changed in the A.A.S.R., even though I know for a fact that this jurisdiction has reformed the 32nd degree **Sublime Prince of the Royal Secret**, omitting it in their Consistory, or at least over simplifying it. A simplification that distorts perhaps one of the lessons perhaps most revealing of this rite, a bit like the British have done a few years ago with the reformation of the Royal Arch, which I spoke about in the previous volume. The 32nd degree is:

> *The third and last of the Kadosh degrees, and consumates the Templarism of Masonry. The degree was originally a Christian degree of knighthood; its object was, for a long time, to reconquer the Holy Land and plant the Banner of the Cross once more on the ruined walls of Jerusalem. Many of the Knights of the Crusades were Masons, and thus became acquainted with the legend which Masonry had preserved.*

> *The Knights Kadosh are the legitimate successors of the Templars.*

> *None but earnest and sincere men, unselfish, and whose philanthropy is not a mere name, but a practical reality, should enter here—such as will do Masonry good service in the war which she is waging against the ancient enemies of the human race— a lover of wisdom and an apostle of Liberty, Equality, and Fraternity.*

> *No virtue is acquired in an instant, but step by step.* [32]

The Templar symbolism of the 32nd degree is linked to the military organization of the Order (FIG. 34), and the inspection of forces that could also be intepretated like those of the New World Order, and conceived of as collections to the various "camps" that will conquer "Jerusalem," and build the "Third Temple." The Temple identifies with the "Holy Empire," with the "Empire of the World" and therefore is the ultimate aim of World Unity.

From the Text book of the Ancient and Accepted Scottish Rite for Vermont:

> *This degree is the military organization of the order. The candidate is supposed to enter a camp, which is a nonagon enclosing a heptagon, which incloses a pentagon, and that an equilateral triangle, and that again a circle, the external lines of which form a figure in Geometry, and on each side of this figure is a tent with a flag and pennon, each of a different color from the others; and each tent is designated by a letter. Each represents an entire camp, and the several sides of the nonagon are assigned by our rituals to the Masons of the different degrees from the 1st to the 18th.* [33]

---

32   http://www.bradford.ac.uk/webofhiram/?section=ancient_accepted&page=32princesublimesec.html
‡ Archived 3rd October, 2016.
33   Daniel Norris Nicholson, *Text-book of the Ancient and Accepted Scottish Rite for Vermont*, published by Vermont Concistory, 1893, p. 183.

Also from what I understand they have built-in the 32° degree, a reduced version of the 30th, which thus becomes an appendant degree conferred only in a nominal form in the Consistory of the Prince of the Royal Secret, to he who receives it, without the ability to participate in any Areopagus of Kadosh Knights, and often given in a hasty manner, without a true ritual. This often happens to ensure that modern man does not lose too much time with the complexity of this degree. It is actually describing the vengeance of the Templars, something that Barbara Frale's supposed discovery seems to have put into question, shocking both the Masonic and Neo-Templar worlds. The institutional and academical credentials of Dr. Frale, who is often invited to preside at official events with various Neo-Templar groups, leaves me to question the genuinity of her intentions.

FIG. 34 – An example of one of the most intricate symbols of the Scottish Rite found on the apron of the 32nd degree "the Masonic Camp." Notice that is a nonagon, enclosing a heptagon which encloses a pentagon, an equilateral triangle, and again a circle. Within the circle is a St. Andrew's Cross.

On April 22 of 2012, the scholar Barbara Frale, headed for example, a very special visit of Neo-Templar Knights to the City Council in Rome, based in the city hall on the Capitoline Hill, where she was received by the mayor, Gianni Alemanno, a controversial figure of the Italian right wing, closely linked to Israel. The meeting in question was organized by the Unsi and the Academy of European Artists, cover names for a modern emanation of the Knights Templar knowns as the Cofraternity of Hugo de Pagani. The event saw the presence of many military relating to this Neo-Templar Brotherhood, whose Grand Prior is a guy called Francesco Russo.

As you can see in Rome, as in the USA, the Neo-Templars move at the top of the political and military establishment of the New World Order, and Barbare Frale seems to be working with them every step of the way. (FIG. 35) So let's keep that in mind when we talk about the Chinon Parchment (FIG. 36) that she supposedly discovered. Remember, there are no coincidences.

www.ilroma.net · DOMENICA 22 APRILE 2012 · ANNO CL N.111 · €1,00 · SS. SOTERO E CAIO

ROMA CRONACA

QUOTIDIANO D'INFORMAZIONE FONDATO NEL 1862 — di SALERNO e PROVINCIA

PAGANI — AL PRIMO CITTADINO DI ROMA FRANCESCO RUSSO HA DONATO UN PREGEVOLE PIATTO IN CERAMICA

I Cavalieri Templari ospiti in Campidoglio del sindaco Alemanno

Franco Russo con Gianni Alemanno

PAGANI. Si è tenuto nella Protomoteca del Campidoglio in Roma Capitale, l'interessante convegno "I Templari : verità, leggenda, tradizione " organizzato dall'Unsi e dall'Accademia Artisti Europei, organo culturale della Confraternita dei Cavalieri Templari "Ugona dei Pagani".

Illustri relatori : la dottoressa Barbara Frale, storica ed esperta di documenti antichi nonché ufficiale dell'archivio segreto Vaticano; il Generale dei Carabinieri Vincenzo Pezzolet ed il Professore Domenico Rotundo - filosofo, storico e scrittore. Dopo il saluto del Sindaco di Roma Capitale - l'On. Gianni Alemanno e del suo

Consigliere Comunale On. Giorgio Masino, hanno aperto il convegno il Mar. Magg. Arturo Malagutti - Presidente Nazionale dell'Unsi ed il Cavaliere Francesco Russo - Presidente dell'Accademia Artisti Europei, nonché Gran Priore Internazionale della Confraternita Templare "Ugona dei Pagani". Al tavolo della Presidenza l'Avvocato Pietro Barone – Presidente dell'Ass. Handicap " Noi e gli Altri " e già Presidente dell'VIII Municipio di Roma.Il Cavaliere Francesco Russo ha donato al Sindaco On. Alemanno un pregevole piatto di ceramica, recante il logo della Confraternita Templare, mentre a tutti gli altri relatori è stato donato un Crocifisso

con il cavaliere in ginocchio, realizzato artigianalmente su legno. Presente al convegno la delegazione dei Cavalieri Templari di Roma, la delegazione del Gran Priorato Internazionale di Pagani-Salerno ed una corposa delegazione del Priorato di Vicenza, capeggiata dall'attivissimo Priore Cav. Fr. Giovanni La Face. Moderatore dell'incontro storico-culturale è stato il dottor cavaliere Salvatore Scalia, vice Presidente dell'Unione Nazionale Sottufficiali Italiani. Onorava il convegno la presenza della Medaglia d'Oro al Valor Civile brigadiere carabiniere Mario Trotta, circondato da una folta presenza di associati Unsi.

FIG. 35 – Article on the special visit of a group of Neo-Templar Knights headed by Barbara Frale to the Capitoline Hill in Rome by the Italiana newspaper Roma, April 22, 2012.

The dispute in the Neo-Templar world after the appearance of a mysterious parchment

Among contemporary Neo-Templars claiming the legacy of the true Knights Templar (too many to mention here), there is always someone who uses the latest historical, or pseudo-historical findings to their advantage. There was an Order that went even further, suing the Pope himself. The *Asociación Soberana Orden del Temple de Cristo,* in the hands of the **Regent Fernando Pinto Sousa Fontes,** which is certainly a prominent figure of the Neo-Templar scene and the various emanations of the O.S.M.T.H. (*Ordo Supremus Militaris Templi Hierosolymitani*). The most influential and serious one being the **Commandery Charlemagne,** an autonomous branch of O.S.M.T.H. presided in Nice (France) by the Grand Prior Jean Pierre Giudicelli, an old friend of mine, who I have talked about extensively in Volume I.

As was explained by the Spanish newspaper *El País,* the case in question was brought against Pope Benedict XVI, because he was the holder of the papal throne and successor of Clement V. With the revision of the process, and the new revelations made in the document found by Barbara Frale, the Neo-Templars do not want the return of their immense wealth, now estimated at around 100 billion euros, but they simply demanded *"That the Court can give an idea to the size of the operation hatched against our Order."* The assets of the Knights Templar had approximately nine thousand properties, plus rights to lands, mills, harbors and boats, however the supposed heirs of the legendary order added: *"We do not want to cause the economic collapse of the Roman Church."* The *Asociación* of Sousa Fontes went on and waited for the verdict of the appeal, which produced nothing. Meanwhile, in August 2008 the Italian newspaper *La Repubblica,* devoted an entire page of their newspaper to the case, with sensational headlines like: *"The Knights Templar are rising"* and phrases like *"the Pope must rehabilitate our order."*[34] But these attention seekers are not the only ones: in 2011 the Grand Master **Walter Grandis** from Trieste, was expelled in 2002 from OSMTJ, and is now head of the Italian Grand Priory of the Knights Templar, a very influential group with extensive support in the Italian institutions, who asked the Pope for an official apology for putting Jacques de Molay, the last Grand Master of the Templars, to death at the stake. This improbable move was not given any importance by the Italian newspapers, but was instead reported by the well-known British newspaper *The Telegraph.* [35]

FIG. 36 – The Chinon Parchment, drafted in the diocese of Tours in 1308, between the 17th and the 20th of August.

Let me remind you that these Neo-Templar realities come from the same stock that was later divided due to constant schisms, and problems often linked to wars happening in the high degrees of Freemasonry, even if the vertices are all united by a common strategy: a deep devotion towards the New World Order. Surely the majority of them (but not all) are not to be taken seriously from a historical point of view, if placed in direct relation to the original Order of the Knights Templar, as was explained to me by my friend and expert Cavalier Luciano Fortunato Sciandra, one of the main living historians of this phenomenon he calls "Templarism," and others "Neo-Templarism."

The Italian edition of *Wikipedia* describes Neo-Tempalrism in this way: *"Neo-Templar groups are modern associations that go back to the tradition of the ancient Knights Templar."*

Neo-Templar groups officially recognized by the Vatican do not exist today, but there are some who have secret recognition by the Holy See. In this scenario there also plays an important role in the O.S.M.T.J.—Sovereign and Military Order of the Temple of Jerusalem, that today with the O.S.M.T.H., is testing in some countries with a possible reunification to O.S.M.T.J. In others a further division in adverse fringes, to better serve the divide and conquer geopolitical strategies of the hidden governments of the NWO. I must emphasize, however, that these orders, even if they do not have any historical continuity, with the Order of the original Templars, are linked with certain bloodlines and dynastic powers of the Illuminati. This gives them influence in certain political military and Masonic circles, and we find them often collaborating with more official knighthoods like the **Knights of Columbus,** guided by the Supreme Knight (Grand Master) **Carl A. Anderson,** deeply in-

35   http://www.telegraph.co.uk/news/religion/8579801/Knights-Templar-heirs-demand- apology-from-Vatican. html# ‡ Archived 11th October, 2016.

volved with the Vatican Bank, known as IOR, the reckless banking entity of the Holy See.

The Knights of Columbus, according to **Jean-Pierre Giudicelli de Cressac Bachelerie,** who is also the supreme guide of the more legitimate affiliation of the Priory of Sion, used a commandery of the Priory, formed years ago in New York, to keep a regular connection with the Knights of Columbus. The Priory of Sion that appeared in the 1950s in France, is the result of geopolitical games and ancient affiliations of which I have already spoken of in Volume I. Today the Priory of Sion is partially active. Periodically some who claim to be its representatives attempt to influence writers and researchers, and many people have been deceived by these lies that have been devised only to create confusion. But despite the disillusionment that many will now feel with the Priory of Sion, it is important to note, that in the world there are genuine spiritual groups and individuals who are highly developed, who operate for the benefit of humanity, and Jean-Pierre Giudicelli de Cressac Bachelerie is certainly one of them. Domizio Cipriani, Grand Prior of the *Ordre des Templiers de Jerusalem,* in the Principality of Monaco, author and leader of an important chivalrous reality based in the Principality of Monaco, also linked to the Priory of Sion, describes the mythical Priory in the following way:

> The "Priory of Sion," the Fellowship of the Rosy Cross, the Supérieurs Inconnu. Basically are schools of thought, a living energy, a primitive core from the primordial vibration, of operational alchemy. They are places where the wise men of the Ormus society find themselves in meditation to understand the arcane, identifiable as an initiatic society formed by a discreet circle, are to be considered the true Temple. They are present in different parts of the world, they do not talk to each other, the date for receptions is January 17 feast of St. Roseline, the popular places are reused existing shrines, which were previously underground temples dedicated to gnostic deities such as Isis, Mithra, Dragon, where water is present as a matriarchal principle, and often we have black Madonnas that are hidden portals to Agharta. Some examples are Mont Saint Michel, Lourdes, Chartres. ... The Holy Sacrament is one of the top American organs, the emblem is a red cross with a white rose, a symbol of the Rosicrucis, members are like the signs of the zodiac, 13, divided into nine crusaders of Saint Jean, three Noachites Principles, a **Grand Chevalier Natonnier named Jean.** In parallel there are **72 Unknown Superiors.** Other mysterious emblems are the Southern Cross of God's children on the island of Atlantis, the cosmic symbol of the octopus, that is both representing the solar movement, the matriarchal essence, the eight arms of the octagon, the cross, the wheel, the swastika; The other peculiarity is the multipersonality of some characters that have inspired films like Arsene Lupin, The Saint, 007. .... or anagrams according to the theory: if you want to hide the truth make it obvious! The Essenes mirrors on which the symbols have to be interpreted backwards. The rituals evoke primitive energies fueling inhalation and exhalation of cosmic energy, cosmic principle of positive and negative vibration, vibrational duality of red and green; the man who shares the manna with the invisible when, at certain moments of equinox and solstice, the grids of the hermetic traditions open. These rituals are performed in the three rooms where you work the seven alchemical degrees. [36]

You may wonder who Domizio Cipriani is, especially after reading his words. Well Domizio hopes to become a disciple of Jean-Pierre Giudicelli de Cressac Bachelerie, key figure of the French esoteric scene, who works today in the inner circles on the good side of the Illuminati, and holds the real secrets of international Neo-Templarism. But Domizio is also connected to Giorgio Hugo Balestrieri and Ezio Giunchiglia of the Mon-

---

tecarlo Lodge, who is his real mentor, and describes him in an introduction note to a recent booklet published by the same Cipriani, entitled **Templar Order,** in the following way: *"Domizio Cipriani is truly an enlightened sage, eclectic and vibrant, authentic and new protagonist with other Freemasons to the construction of a new path, traced for the evolution of humanity to be freed from all evil. Therefore, the Priory of Monte Carlo in the Principality of Monaco, is the spearhead for a wise evolving international group of Knights Templar that is the continuation of the new and renovated Masonry of The United Grand Lodge of England who works to help those most in need. Let us always remember that life is a moment ... and that's why when we get up every morning, we have to thank the Lord for giving us a new moment."*[37]

The Knights of the Temple are therefore present everywhere in the Western initiatic system, even in Montecarlo, and although there are plenty of scoundrels who love an easy cloak, the way of true initiation into the mysteries of the Knights Templar is still open for a privileged few.

Domizio Cipriani's view on the true Templar tradition, which he links to the Rosicrucians is the following:

From the dawn of time ancient civilizations in the vicinity of these statues would gather in a circle and were celebrated with rituals. Druids and bishops practiced these rituals around a statue, a tree, a spring, a fire. .. and the circle of Saint Jean. In Hindu Egyptian and Greek representations, the snake is placed in a circle which means the universal way, in which the magical agent, the engine and the driving force is the light; it is as the snake that is coiled around the circumference of a hermetic cross, as it represents to the alchemists the unity of matter and at the same time the universal fluid or perpetual renewal of nature. It is not the circle itself which has in it a profound sacred significance, it is the moving circle, the wheel, in fact, and for the initiated the lotus flower in the Far East. In rotation means supreme knowledge, the rose window of the cathedrals in Europe is the rose of the initiates, the "rota" the wheel.[38]

Then Cipriani adds about the "Merovingians" in a cryptic manner with a clear Apocalyptic flare:

I was on the sand of the sea, and saw a beast out of the sea, having seven heads and ten horns, and on his horns ten crowns, and on his heads the name of blasphemy. And the beast which I saw was like a leopard, and his feet were as the feet of a bear, and his mouth as the mouth of a lion: and the dragon gave him his power, his throne and great authority. The emblem of bear rampant ... depicts just that—the constellation of the Bear linked to Earth's Pole, and dance around it. The two bears, eleven bees, and the **Fleur de Lys;** *the motto reads* **et in Arcadia ego.** *Arcadia = 127, which is the number of the Egyptian Goddess Heqt. The tradition Typhonian or Draconian refers to the secret doctrine of the* **Ordo Draconis, the Order of the Dragon** *that is associated with the Rosicrucians: "In 1408 ... the Dragon Court was formally reconstituted as a sovereign body at a time of wars and general political unrest. The re-emergence of the Court has been wanted by Sigismund von Luxemburg, king of Hungary, a descendant of Lusignan Dragon King of Jerusalem. After he inherited in 1397, drew up a pact with twenty-three nobles who swore to observe 'true and pure brotherhood within the* Societas Draconis *(then called* Ordo Draconis)—In Hungary: Sarkany*

---

37   *Ibid.* p. 8.
38   *Ibid.* p. 66.

Rend in the founding document ... and stated that members of the Court could wear
the insignia of a dragon bent in a circle, with a red cross—the symbol of the original
Rosicrucis. Godfrey of Bouillon, was the first Grand Master of the Priory of Sion. The
ancient pedigree of the Dragon succession, which began with Cain." [39]

Domizio Cipriani says, as others before him, that the Priory of Sion was founded by
Godfrey of Bouillon, and actually the "Abbey of Our Lady of Mount Sion," was founded
in 1099 in Jerusalem, by Godfrey of Bouillon. They obviously had nothing to do with
the modern day "Priory" founded by Pierre Plantard, because this religious community
apparently died out in the fourteenth century. They survived until 1617, when the few
remaining monks entered the **Society of Jesus,** with the usual Jesuits. An established fact,
is that Godfrey of Bouillon founded the **Equestrian Order of the Holy Sepulchre of
Jerusalem,** which is considered by historians, together with the Order of Malta, the oldest Chilvaric Order of the Catholic Church still in existence. Godfrey of Bouillon is also
recognized by the Masonic Rite of **Strict Observance,** as the protector of the Order. The
Templars are therefore critical to understand not only Neo-Templarism, the Rosicrucians
or the High degrees of Freemasonry, and the Illuminati, but also the notion of chilvary
in the broad sense, and the aristocracy itself in the Western world, thus leading us to the
greatest mysteries of mankind and the elite bond of the royal families with the Gods, who
in Sumerian tradition were called the Annunaki. The Templars are therefore not only the
result of Christianity, but of something much older, that leads as Cipriani states, in the
handing down of *the esoteric teachings known by Jesus Himself, who was, according to
this tradition, a Great Initiate to the Ancient Mysteries.* This for the initiated, is the true
Holy Grail, which was one of the strongest myths of Christianity in the late Middle Ages.
However the Templars have always been considered the "Guardians" of an ancient holy
relic with that name, but the question is are they still in possession of this legendary relic?
From my research it seems they are indeed, even though it might have wound up in the
wrong hands after all, because many of these modern Neo-Templar emanations are corrupted by Satanism and the occult. However many esoteric traditions have understood
"the Grail" as a symbol and a vehicle for the metaphysical knowledge over the centuries,
and as Massimo Scaligero, a great Italian initiate and disciple of Rudolph Steiner, once
wrote, and is conceived by many initiates: *"an imaginative and narrative form of meditation. They take as basis a well described 'spiritual object,' they focus upon it according
to a thin line of esoteric criticism, and they believe is so well fixed into their memory,
they think they will be able to grasp it a second time, without realizing that for an effective communion with the upper level the object of meditation is secondary to the action
committed in the lower level. The object is only the pretext it can be a tree, the sun, a
tradition, a concept, a simple thing among things."* [40]

A concept for real initiates, but in addition to such a genuine form of spirituality that revolves around the Holy Grail in various schools and mystery traditions, there is also a physical reality of the object in question. A physical object, also known as the "The Holy Grail,"
that is supposedly in the hands of someone. That someone is for many, the previously cited
Dr. Antonio Leonardo Montuoro, the Neo-Templar exceptionally linked to the Vatican,
and in particular to the Jesuits, who aside from being *Grand Officialis* of Rocco Zingaro's
Neo-Templars (FIG. 37) started not so long ago that **The Order of the Knights of the
Temple of the Holy Spirit** was recognized by the Vatican (although in a rather reserved
manner), together with his friend, the previously mentioned Enrico Marinelli, former

39   *Ibid.*
40   http://www.geocities.ws/tidelar/scaligero.html ‡ Archived 11th October, 2016.

Prefect and Coordinator of Security Services for the Vatican at the time of Pope John Paul II. [41]

For others however, the Grail is in the possession of **Al (short for Alberto) Festa**, film director, around fifty, and a relative of Giorgio Festa, the doctor who operated on St. Padre Pio, and examined his famous stigmata, writing a detailed report when the unexplainable phenomena erupted. This could be the two people who today are actually holding the historical relic of the Holy

Grand Officialis
ANTONIO LEONARDO MONTUORO

FIG. 37 – Business Card from Dr. Antonio Leonardo Montuo "Grand Officialis" of the Supremus Militaris Templi Hierosolymitani Ordo – S.M.T.H.O. Casella Postale 48 60025 Loreto (Ancona)

Grail. Montuoro, that the deceased Polish Pope named "Man of the Holy Spirit," is a renowned and highly rated personality within the Church, and tied to the powerful *Propaganda Fide*, now the Congregation for the Evangelization of Peoples. The latter owns, according to the latest estimates, real estate and assets around nine billion euros, scattered in Rome and around the world among the thousands of apartments and residential luxury buildings often occupied, at least in Italy, by VIP's subservient to the Vatican. It was June 22, 1622, when Pope Gregory XV, with the bull *Inscrutabili Divinae Providentiae* founded the famous Congregation of *Propaganda Fide*, with the specific task of spreading the Catholic faith throughout the world. To this end, this Vatican institution *"coordinates and exercises jurisdiction over the Holy See's missions and promotes the formation of the clergy and the local hierarchies."* [42]

Montuoro's work with the Order of the Knights of the Temple of the Holy Spirit, whose official seat is in **Via XX Settembre 98 / G in Rome** (a few steps from the Italian Ministry of Defence) also revolves around the highly secret **Vatican Secret Services**, of which Montuoro is a liaison officer with the Italian Government, hence the convenient location of his headquarters. Montuoro also has a strong link with Rome's **Black Nobility**, heirs of ancient bloodlines related to Roman emperors and gods, that are still secretly at the apex of the globalist elite. **Nicola La Marca,** Professor of History at the Sapienza University in Rome, entitled an excellent book published a few years ago *The Roman Nobility and the Perpetuation of its Power Tools.* [43] The journalist Raffaele Gambari commented on La Marca's work in 2012, stating the following about the Black Nobility: *"It is still very obsequious to clergy, I do not know if on the basis of faith or tradition, or for duty. Pope Montini officially abolished aristocracy in the Vatican City. However in the current political situation a part of this social group sympathizes with left wing politics."*

41   https://w2.vatican.va/content/john-paul-ii/en/speeches/1999/january/documents/hf_jp-ii_spe_19990114_security.html ‡ Archived 11th October, 2016.

42   http://freeforumzone.leonardo.it/lofi/Propaganda-Fide-l-immobiliare-del-Vaticano-che-trova-casa-ai-vip-/D9296376.html ‡ Archived 11th October, 2016.

43   See. Nicola la Marca, *La nobiltà romana e I suoi strumenti di perpetuazione del potere*, Bulzoni, Roma 2000.

Surprised by the fact the aristocrats are leftists these days? Unfortunately, it is very chic for the elite to be leftist, even among the families of the black nobility traditionally linked to the extreme right in the past. A communism façade for the elite that fits in the New World Order of Obama, Hillary Clinton, Pope Francis and of course their "Masters" the Jesuits, in an attempt to make themselves more acceptable to the people-sheeple who seem to appreciate such a demented move made increasingly more obvious in the last few years. These people are the power tools of the "Invisible Masters," and represent the ultimate expression of their millennial hypocrisy, that of **George Soros,** who has now taken up the cause of a soulless technocracy—the Bilderberg Club—but uses at the same time the Church to legitimize such a terrible scenario. Jesuit Pope Francis, a communist that appeals to Democrats, and the leftists around the world, is deceived by this Satanic farce. In reality these supposed "Democrats" are nothing more than "fascists" of the New World Order. They want to impose their vision to others as the only possible way, even if made of absurd and unnatural compromises. You can see clearly watching the presidential campaign in the US., that Russia and *Wikileaks* were able to publish reserved and top secret material, and how they possibly work behind the scenes, with alien forces, to manipulate our reality, a subject I explore in my next book *Invisible Master*. Aliens want to help mankind but fear our violent tendencies, at least this is what Jean-Pierre Giudicelli de Cressac Bachelerie said in Volume I of my *Confessions*. [44] According to an email exchange revealed by Wikileaks, during the heated presidential campaign in October 2016, mails sent by astronaut Edgar Mitchell to John Podesta made public by the popular site, showed an impending space war, and confirmed once more the Vatican's knowledge of alien life. *"Remember, our nonviolent ETI from the contiguous universe are helping us bring zero point energy to Earth. They will not tolerate any forms of military violence on Earth or in space."*[45] Podesta was serving as counselor to President Barack Obama during this exchange, before he left the position to become chairman of Hillary Clinton's presidential campaign. At a 2002 news conference organized by **Coalition for Freedom of Information,** Podesta stated that *"It is time for the government to declassify records that are more than 25 years old and to provide scientists with data that will assist in determining the real nature of this phenomenon."* Why are they not doing that? Well that will show the real nature of the elite, and the great lie of democracy, which has never really existed on this planet. However, also keep in mind the gradual alien invasion from their "contiguous universe" as I mentioned in Volume II of my *Confessions*.

E-mail: segreteriatemplari@libero.it

URL: http://web.cheapnet.it/smtho/

44 See. Leo Lyon Zagami, *Confessions of an Illuminati, Volume I*, (San Francisco: CCC Publishing), p. 190.
45 See. https://wikileaks.org/podesta-emails/emailid/1802 ‡ Archived 11th October 2016.

Chapter II

The Holy Grail

The Seborga Files

Worshipful Brother **Donald Falconer**, a member of the Craft for many years, and a known Masonic author, wrote in 1999: *"Freemasonry's association with the Holy Grail began with the building of the temple at Jerusalem. The fundamental tenets of Freemasonry reflect the Grail Code, which is a desire to serve and in serving to achieve."* So how did this connection start, and why are the Knights Templar involved? Falconer describes the Holy Grail in his masterpiece entitled, *The Square and Compasses: In Search of Freemasonry,* a collection of papers on the many aspects of Freemasonry presented to various Masonic bodies over a 40-year period.

The **Holy Grail** is traditionally the cup or chalice Christ used at the last supper. **Grail** is an Anglicised form of the Old French **graal** or **greal**, meaning a **dish**, which derived from the Latin **gradalis** from the Greek **krater** meaning a **cup** or **bowl**. In a spiritual sense, the **Holy Grail** is the **Sangréal**, which in common usage is said to mean the real blood of Christ. However **Sang Réal** is French for **Blood Royal**, which in its accepted usage designates the royal bloodline of David descending through Jesus to the present day. At first sight, there may seem to be little, if any, connection between the **Holy Grail** and Freemasonry, because the popular conceptions of the **Holy Grail** have largely been fashioned by the search for the **Holy Grail,** that is a key element in the romances of King Arthur and the Knights of the Round Table. In fact, the first inkling we have of an association between Freemasonry and the **Holy Grail** is a statement in I Chronicles 17:1, when King David said: *"I dwell in a house of cedar, but the Ark of God dwelleth within curtains."* Later, when King David had subdued the Philistines, the Moabites and the Syrians, he purchased the threshing floor of Araunah the Jebusite as the site for the temple on Mount Moriah, collected building materials and gathered treasure to finance the work. In I Chronicles 22:6-8 however, we are told of King David: *"Then he called for Solomon his son and charged him to build a house for the Lord God of Israel. And David said to Solomon, my son, as for me it was in my mind to build a house unto the name of the Lord my God: But the word of the Lord came to me, saying, 'Thou hast shed blood abundantly and hast made great wars: thou shalt not build a house unto my name, because thou hast shed much blood upon the earth in my sight.'"*

The link between Freemasonry and the *Holy Grail* became a reality in the fourth year of King Solomon's reign, when he commenced construction of the temple at Jerusalem, about 480 years after the Exodus when Moses led the Israelites out of Egypt. The temple was in the area that is now called Haram esh-Sherif, which is on the east side of the *Old City* of Jerusalem, where the mosque known as the *Dome of the Rock* now stands.

In I Kings 5:17-18 we read of King Solomon: *"And the king commanded and they brought great stones, costly stones and hewed stones, to lay the foundation of the house. And Solomon's builders and Hiram's builders did hew them, and the stonesquarers: so they prepared timber and stones to build the house."*

This Authurian tale is actually not all fiction, and has direct relevance to the establishment of the Celtic Church and early Freemasonry in Britain, as well as to the formation of the crusaders, *Soldiers of Christ* who became the Knights Templar, and the guardians of the *Holy Grail*. [1] At the time of the daring research into the mysteries of the Holy Grail that was conducted in the book, *The Holy Blood and The Holy Grail,* written by the late researchers **Michael Baigent, Richard Leigh and Henry Lincoln**, as well as their controversial statements on a supposed bloodline of Jesus. A connection with ancient traditions allegedly transmitted to the mysterious Priory of Sion, a story with no real evidence, that inspired Dan Brown. The authors demonstrated to the world that the Holy Grail was linked to the Cathars and the Knights Templar. This discovery is still considered credible by most historians. A few years later, an interesting **"Open Letter to John Paul II"** surfaced, written in Toulouse, on January 26, 1998, in which the original signatories were none other than the French politician Dominique Baudis (1947 – 2014), at the time mayor of Toulouse, (repeatedly elected also to the EU parliament), and Farge Bertran, engineer, author and Cathar historian, president of the organization *Flame Cathar*, also mayor of Toulouse between 2001 and 2008. In this letter, both these politicians emphasized how the latest discoveries in science had helped to demonstrate that the Cathar religion was actually truly and deeply Christian in nature, in an attempt to change the view that contemporary historians have on the matter.

Strangely enough, Dominique Baudis was implicated in a case that seems artfully assembled relative to the serial killer Patrice Alegre, from which he was exonerated completely only three years later, perhaps to punish him for his "Open letter to John Paul II," and his inconvenient revelations about the Cathars. There is also, a direct link between the Cathars, the Priory of Sion, and a mysterious place called **Seborga**, in Italy, near the border with France, that I need to tell you more about.

Since the 1950s some members of the community of Seborga related to international Freemasonry, and the world of Neo-Templarism, claimed independence from the Italian Republic, by virtue of an alleged ancient principality status of this location, deeming the earlier annexation to the kingdom of Sardinia invalid. The citizens of Seborga elected a prince with purely symbolic function, with no way of being recognized for their independent status. From the 14th of May 1963, until the 25th of November 2009, the date of his death, the role was played by **Giorgio Carbone (George I)**, and from 25 April, 2010 to the present, by **Menegatto Marcello**. But why is a prince with no real power, assisted by a council of nine ministers, and a principality whose coins are just ridiculous currency, called the *Luigino*? The name was inspired by the coins principality, where they were originally minted in the seventeenth century, but I repeat such currency has no legal value (supposed value of the so-called *Luigino* is set to a fixed rate of 6 U.S. dollars). Why is this

1   http://www.themasonictrowel.com/books/the_square_and_compasses_falconer/files/chapter_43.htm
‡ Archived 11th October, 2016.

a place of importance to an influential organization such as the Knights Templar? Well, there are many legends and stories that bind this particular place to the Templar world, and lead us to understand that since ancient times, it has not only been a location of strategic importance for the Knights Templar, but it is linked to its origins and perhaps at one point, to the Holy Grail, that was hidden here, amongst other holy relics. The Principality of Seborga is located in the Ligurian hinterland, on the famous and beautiful *Riviera dei Fiori*. In the surrounding mountains, a Celtic tribe used it to bury their dead, and it seems that the Cathar heretics deem the area so sacred to choose it, in turn, as a burial place for their priests. That would explain the origin of the ancient name of Seborga, coming from *Castrum sepulchres*, the sepulcher. Land of the Counts of Ventimiglia up until the year 954, the castle was later traded to the Benedictine monks of the abbey of Lérins, and in the year one thousand became principality of the Holy Roman Empire led by a **Prince-Abbot,** invested by the pope of temporal and spiritual authority.

In 1117, the **Bernard of Clairvaux,** a known French theologian and founder of the Abbey of Clairvaux, who wrote down the rule of the Knights Templar, reached Seborga with two of his brothers, the monks and future abbots Gondemar and Rossal. It is said that this was done with the task of safeguarding a "Big Secret," the same one that in 1127, during a solemn ceremony that saw the participation of the Cathar priest, Giovanni de Usson. Bernard himself was sworn to protect the secret with a vow of silence. It seems that Gondemar and Rossal transmitted to posterity, the necessary information regarding this secret, and an allusion to Jerusalem by the means of an engraved stone still present in Séborga. (FIG. 38)

From Seborga, Bernard of Clairvaux expanded the Order of Cistercian monks, turning the small principality to the only Cistercian Sovereign State in the world. And, in September 1118, the prince-abbot Edward, who was the reigning prince of the time, consecrated the first nine Knights Templars who formed the famous Poor Army of Christ, that later constituted **the original nucleus of the Knights Templar.** It included the Abbots Gondemar and Rossal, André de Montbar, the Count Hugues 1st of Champagne, Hugues de Payens, Payen de MontDidier, Geoffroy de Saint-Omer, Archambaud de Saint Amand and Geoffroy Bisol.

In November 1118, eight knights left for Jerusalem, and were placed by Baudouin of Boulogne, brother of Godefroy de Bouillon, in the stables of King Solomon. Hugues de Champagne joined them six years later. The nine Knights Templar returned to Seborga in 1127. The Archives of King Solomon was repatriated, as well as certain relics linked to the temple of King Solomon, but also relics linked to the crucifixion of Jesus-Christ, and some say to the Holy Grail. At that point, Hugues de Payens was designated by Saint Bernard de Clairvaux, to be the first Grand Master of the Knights of Saint-Bernard, and was consecrated by the sword by the Prince-Abbot Edward. It is said that an oath of silence was then pronounced between the Knights of Saint-Bernard, and the High Priest of Cathar, to maintain and defend the Great Secret. [2]The legend says that Seborga's "Great Secret" miraculously defended the town from destruction, looting and even natural disasters, for centuries, and it may be linked to the sensational discoveries that have been attributed precisely to the first nine Poor Knights of Christ, who went to the Holy Land to protect pilgrims visiting the holy sites of Christianity. They were allowed by Baldwin II, King of Jerusalem, to set up camp on the ruins of the Temple of King Solomon, (hence the name of the Templars), and once there, based their headquarters. According to unofficial sources,

2   See. http://www.histoiresecretedestempliers.com/pages/eng-histoire-secrete-des-templiers/fran-b/b1-seborga. html#WboDhdUXpjr8XUDa.99 ‡ Archived 11th October, 2016.

FIG. 38 – The Engraved Stone of Séborga.

they would make many excavations in the labyrinthine foundations, in search of the sacred relics that were said to have been hidden by the priests, before the looting and destruction of the Temple of King Solomon by the Romans. Among other hypotheses that have been formulated to explain the nature of Seborga's secret, there is the possibility they even hold the bandages that wrapped the body of Jesus Christ, the authentic Shroud, the nails of the Cross, and the legendary Holy Grail. Among other things, it seems that in 1611, the last secret General Chapter of a legitimate affiliation of the Templar Order under the auspices of the Prince-Abbot of Seborga, **Father Cesario from Sao Paulo,** was held in Seborga. To sanction this occasion, they placed on every roof of the Principality, 13 tiles engraved with the date 1611, the number 13, the acronym c.s. and the Templar cross. In 1729, the Principality was sold to Vittorio Amedeo II, Prince of Savoy, Piedmont and King of Sardinia, although the transaction proves that it was never recorded or paid for. In fact in 1815, during the Congress of Vienna, it was not mentioned as being part of the Kingdom of Sardinia. Its independence was in fact not recognized until 1946, by the Italian Kingdom, but with the establishment of the Republic, the ancient Principality was automatically considered an integral part of the Italian state in 1962. But the Seborgans rebelled against Rome, proclaiming their independence—never officially recognized—electing a year later, for their prince, George I. But to understand more about Seborga and the Holy Grail, there's an interesting report on the subject by the aforementioned Domizio Cipriani:

> *In the middle of the twelfth century the Knights Templar (consecrated by St. Bernard and invested by the Prince Abbot of Seborga, Prince Edward) which then assumed the title of Sanctus Sepulchrum, erected in Seborga the "Mansion of the Temple;" the building, which I can not say more, houses the Holy Relic, the Great Secret of Seborga, which they found in Jerusalem and brought here secretly. A story, picked up two centuries ago, reports the presence in Seborga of the Cathar (Bishop?) Johann de Usson,*

which would ensure that St. Bernard and His Knights with the later contribution of the Cathars acted in defense and custody of the Holy Relic. Registries from the Abbey of St. Honore Lerino say that at the end of the fifteenth century, by order of an Abbot Prince, the Cathar community had to move to another location, which still has the peculiar name of "The Peverei," not to be confused with another building, not far away from that one, perfectly preserved, called "The Cristiai," also built and inhabited by the Seborgan Cathars.

More than a word deserves the influence they have had in Seborga's religion, the Judeo-Christianity and Celtic Christianity of the origins. Here, however, the situation is different, for the existence, well-known by Saint Bernard, of the Holy Relic hidden in Seborga and that, according to him, could be jeopardized by the Cathars; this must have been the motivation of his meeting with the Cathar Johann de Usson. [3]

FIG. 39 – The Grand Preceptor for Italy of S.M.T.H.O. Rocco Zingaro (1941 – 2011).

After realizing the importance of the town Seborga, in the long saga of the Knights Templar and its possible connection to a variety of holy relics that may have been kept there, including the Holy Grail, let's move forward now in search of the present owner and location of this legendary object that is of great importance for all the Illuminati sects operating today.

The Holy Grail revealed

To understand better where the Holy Grail is hidden, I must first trace back in history how the Templar Order has survived to this day, in the many, perhaps too many, emanations more or less fictional or legendary, which derive from both Masonry and Jesuit inspired Neo-Templarism. From the latter, the affiliation was led for many years by the Italian Count Rocco Zingaro (1941 – 2011), a very mysterious character, and in some ways controversial, not affiliated to the aforementioned succession of Sousa Fontes, who as I have already shown above, is perhaps one of the most influential in modern Neo-Templarism linked to the New World Order and the Masonic / Zionist matrix, and its American Catholic lobby led ultimately by the **Knights of Columbus**, which within their initiations, relate to the Templar history and its symbols. The affiliation of Rocco Zingaro came from the "Brazilian" Neo-Templar branch of the Inellas succession, considered close to the Catholic Church. In 1981, Gabriel Inellas, of the famous Palaiologos dynasty, who in some documents signed as "Jnellas" (1913 – 1987), will appoint Rocco Zingaro, who he ordered to become a Knight, and soon after, Grand Preceptor of S.M.T.H.O., as head of the Italian Knights Templar, for a program of rapprochement with the Catholic

3   Domizio Cipriani, *Ibid.*, pp. 39-40-41.

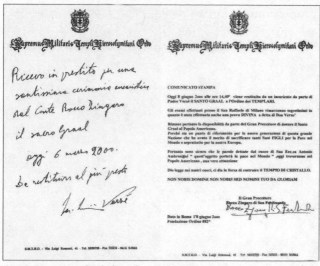

FIG. 40 – On the left, a handwritten message by Don Luigi Maria Verzè from March 6, 2000, on the letterhead of the SMTHO, given to the Grand Preceptor Rocco Zingaro, as proof of delivery of the Holy Grail used for a "holy ceremony." On the right a press release made in June 2000, which speaks of the direct involvement of Don Verzé with tests carried out at the San Raffaele hospital in Milan on the Holy Grail of Zingaro, and his intention to donate it to the American people.

Church after their historic break of 1307.

The S.M.T.H.O.—Internationally led by Gabriel César Inellas Zaccaria, born in 1947, who succeeded his father the aforementioned Gabriel Inellas, began a variety of cultural activities associated to the Neo-Templars, including the establishment, in 1990, of a University of the Knights Templar, making repeated requests to the Holy See to "rehabilitate" the Templars. But perhaps the greatest awareness at a public level of the Grand Preceptor Rocco Zingaro (FIG. 39), and his Order, will come after his controversial statement made on the 17th of August 1995, echoed later by the international press. Zingaro shocked the world by saying he was in possession of the Holy Grail, which would be presented on the occasion of his wedding, by Professor Antonio Ambrosini, a professor at the University of Rome who claimed to have retrieved it in an Egyptian Coptic monastery. Five years later, there was an attempt to legitimize this important discovery by **Don Luigi Maria Verzé (1920-2011),** a key figure of the Vatican, responsible for leading the Hospital San Raffaele in Milan, which in June 2000, did a thorough series of scientific examinations on the object in question, and used it for a ritual, as Don Verzé himself states, in a formal letter of request written to Rocco Zingaro. However, according to Zingaro, the positive results of these tests had to remain secret (both documents can be viewed in FIG. 40). The late Don Verzè spoke in the same letter of a "divine test," and Zingaro said that after these examinations **they wished to give the Holy Grail to the American people for their great sacrifice during WWII.** So I wonder why things have changed? Why did such an important discovery disappear in the maze of the Vatican, instead of being brought to the USA? This relic was held in secret for years, by Rocco and his Neo-Templars, headed by Montuoro and Marinelli, and even the scientists par excellence of the Church, the infamous Jesuits. The former General of the Order, Father Peter Hans Kolvenbach, member of "Entity," the Papal intelligence service, was also impressed. It was the former black pope, who at the time said to Montuoro, that it may be authentic, but in the absence of further testing they had to accept this item, at least for now, in the form of a testimony of faith, and for this reason, it must be kept safeguarded, which Montuoro surely has done. After the examinations made in Milan by Don Verzé, Father Kolvenbach advised them to not show this relic in public, as its nature frightened the leaders of the Church.

FIG. 41 – Claims of being in possession of the Holy Grail made in Italian Newspapers by Rocco Zingaro in the early 1990s show the image of the relic before it was again obscured by Vatican leaders and Dr. Montuoro.

FIG. 42 – The discovery of the mythical Holy Grail and the ashes of Jacques de Molay, the last Grand Master of the Templars, by the Grand Preceptor Rocco Zingaro, reported in the early 1990s in Italian newspapers.

Dr. Montuoro confided that in 2011, after the death of Count Rocco Zingaro, they were ready to relocate the object to their future Temple of the Holy Spirit in Palestrina, once the construction of the ambitious project was ultimated. However, the construction of this Temple was abandoned in 2014 for lack of funds, **so now who has Rocco Zingaro's Holy Grail?** The sudden bad state of health of the Grand Preceptor Rocco Zingaro, who died in mid-August of 2011, certainly helped the characters around him in their mission to finally obtain the supposed Holy Grail, and other relics of importance, including the ashes of Jacob De Molay (FIGS. 41, 42, 43), that wound up in the possession of Antonio Leonardo Montuoro. According to Montuoro this happened in a legitimate manner, according to ancient Templar tradition, as Montuoro was for years the *Grand Officialis* of Zingaro's Order. Montuoro then stashed everything in a safe in Loreto and later brought them to his villa in Calabria, claiming they were now property of his Order, which was founded in 2009, with former Prefect Enrico Marinelli. (FIG. 44) Montuoro started this chilvaric project at the *Casa Bonus Pastor* of Via Aurelia, 208 in Rome, on Vatican soil, to lay the foundations of his new Neo-Templar Order in Vatican territory, where he would benefit from such status. Montuoro went on to formally merge the two orders in 2011, when the late Rocco Zingaro was now out of the picture, Montuoro and Marinelli could proceed with the creation of their order from the ashes of Zingaro's Neo-Templar lineage.[4] Marinelli, who is a key figure in the Vatican, wrote a book about his experience as top security adviser for Pope John Paul II, called *Pope Wojtyla and the General.*[5]

4   http://www.spiritosanto.org/info/italiano/statuto.htm ‡ Archived 16th October, 2016.
5   See. Enrico Marinelli, **Papa Wojtyla e il Generale,** (Rome, IT: Nova Itinera, 2007).

FIG. 43 – In the magazine Gente Rocco Zingaro speaks of the Holy Grail discovery and shows it to the public. Note the strange background of the photo that seems to reflect a dark side to this character, not quite in tune with his being a Catholic.

Zingaro's Order at the time of its foundation, has the tacit approval and support of Pope John Paul II, and his successor Joseph Ratzinger, who by no accident called himself Benedict XVI, due to the fact that he would be reunited in spirit, body and soul to the Benedictine Order, and therefore to the Cistercians that emanated from it, and of course the Templars whose rule was written by a Cistercian. The Rule of the Templars, was in fact prepared in Troyes, in 1129, by St. Bernard of Clairvaux. The Templars were said to be the continuation of a secret order created by Saint Benedict, to defend true Christian values, but also to defend the origins of their knowledge that pre-dates the advent of Christianity, as reported by the Vatican scholar and historian of the Knights Templar, Luciano Fortunato Sciandra, legitimate successor of Rocco Zingaro, as I have already written in *Pope Francis: The Last Pope?*:

Cav. Rocco Zingaro died in 2011 under circumstances that some of his friends and closest collaborators, including a character who I have spoken of previously, Luciano Sciandra of the Equestrian Order of the Holy Sepulcher, consider unclear, if not downright suspicious. Sciandra, who was also involved in running Zingaro's Templar order before the Marinelli-Montuoro takeover, speaks in particular of a phone call that he received from Zingaro a week before his death in which the Grand Preceptor of the Order of the Temple told him that he was in a life threatening situation and terrorized. A conversation in which he said: "they want to kill me just like they did Jacob De Molay." [6]

In memory of Rocco Zingaro: A Templar in possession of the Holy Grail

On Sunday, January 29, 2012, in the Basilica of Santa Maria, a strange mysterious Mass was celebrated, in honor of the deceased Knight and Grand Preceptor of the Templars, Rocco Zingaro. Celebrating the Mass was a friend and collaborator of Dr. Montuoro, known Military Chaplain Monsignor Gino of Ciocco, who besides being one of the Most Rev. Honorary Canons of that Basilica, is also known for being the Military Chaplain of the Italian Contingent "Italfor Kabul 10" that operated in Afghanistan. It was definitely a Mass full of famous people from the Opus Dei, various Chilvaric Orders and the Masonic world including the author of this book, (FIG. 45) and even my mother Jessica Lyon Young, plus the presence of numerous dignitaries of the Ancient and Accepted Scottish Rite including Danilo Tiberi, in the past involved with the Ordo Illuminatorum Universalis.

Among the many representatives of military and religious institutions, stood the figure of Enrico Marinelli. In 2005, when the health of Wjojtyla became worse, the prefect went to the Vatican and shortly before losing consciousness, the Holy Father called a few friends, and among them was his "General," as John Paul II always called Marinelli, who is now the head of the Neo-Templar movement within the Vatican. This shows without a doubt that the Neo-Templar Jesuit matrix is definitely at the top of Vatican power, and that they inherited the tradition of Rocco Zingaro. He lived the last years of his life in a protected resi-

FIG. 44 – The Prefect Marinelli (at center of the photo) on Sunday, January 29, 2012 in the Basilica of St. Maria Maggiore in Rome, while they exchange a peace sign with his Knights of the Temple of the Holy Spirit during the Holy Mass in honor of Rocco Zingaro.

dence, "Oasi Ave Maria" in Loreto, and that "Protected Residence" basically was Zingaro's prison, where Montuoro could control him in the last years of his earthly life.

Dr. Antonio Leonardo Montuoro, born in Calabria in 1955, with a degree in Political Science, is the director of the rest home and Protected Residence *"Oasi Ave Maria"* based in Loreto (AN) in Via Leonessa 3, but Montuoro is also a Provincial President of the European Association of Police operators. Montuoro is therefore also a policeman, so is the rest just a cover? He also holds Institutional and Honorary professional positions such as Minister and President of the SFO—Delegation Pontifical Secular Franciscan Order of Loreto (AN). But in the official curriculum of Antonio Leonardo Montuoro available on the web, there is no reference to his past activities with the Order of Neo-Templar of Rocco Zingaro—of which I have photographic documentation. Zingaro died in his "Oasis" in Loreto in August, 2011 leaving Montauro the supposed Holy Grail and the supposed ashes of the last Grand Master of the Templars, Jacob de Molay, now hidden from the public by Montuoro.

Rocco Zingaro, born in Puglia in 1941, to an ancient family of Templar tradition, grew up in an austere and religious climate, according to the dictates inherent in his family through the social culture and education of the Salesians, where he attended, and where he graduated from in 1959. He later was immersed in the world of the knighthood, and came into contact with Prof. Don Gabriel Jnellas Palaeologus, who as I wrote earlier, made him a Knights Templar. From 1970, he devoted himself to the reconstruction of the Order of the Temple, and in 1972, dedicated his life to the Italian branch of the Brazilian S.M.T.H.O, and the prestigious *Res Gestae* Magazine, which analyzes all fiction attributed to the noble Knights of Christ. In 1981, he was appointed Grand Preceptor, and was commited to the Knights Templar, and their new mission, in the most beautiful basilicas. In 1987, he was appointed a full member of the Supreme World Council for Inter-religious Relations, a group built to obtain and achieve the wishes of the Second Vatican Council.

In the month of July, 1994, Rocco Zingaro made the first rehabilitation request of his Templars to the Vatican, and from that point onwards he began the gradual rapproche-

FIG. 45 – The Marquis Roberto Caldirola, Bishop Sigalini and Leo Zagami, on Sunday, January 29th, 2012, in the Basilica of Santa Maria Maggiore in Rome, for the Mass in honor of the Grand Preceptor of the Templars, Rocco Zingaro.

ment of Neo-Templarism towards the Church of Rome. A rapprochement, however, often thwarted by other Neo-Templars affiliations, which will lead Rocco Zingaro to be attacked publicly in the following years by other Neo-Templar branches that refused to rejoin officially with the Catholic Church, but preferred a more loose ecumenical approach, open to other Christian denominations and even Muslims. With the help of Antonio Leonardo Montuoro, Zingaro enjoyed in those years excellent relations with both the York Rite of Freemasonry, in Italy and in the U.S. with the Ancient and Accepted Scottish Rite. However, after a period of great success for Zingaro's Order, which lasted in a steady crescendo until 2005, he was suddenly isolated from that year onwards, especially after the public complaints of the powerful Cardinal Ruini towards Neo-Templarism, which he deemed too invasive and out of control. Ruini, who was at the time president of the Italian Episcopal Conference (CEI), and the Cardinal Vicar of the Pope for the diocese of Rome, communicated officially for the first time in history, to all the churches of his diocese, to not accept the so-called Neo-Templar groups and ceremonies in their basilicas and churches.[7] Behind this sudden gesture of Cardinal Ruini against Zingaro, there is actually the involvement of a group of Neo-Templars, who had suddenly split from Count Rocco Zingaro, and were led by **Francesco Dario Labate and Gilberto Di Benedetto**, respectively Grand Master and spokesman of this new Neo-Templar affiliation, that already counted over 200 Templars. They began their operation in early May 2005, in the beautiful and important church of Santa Prisca, on the Aventine Hill in Rome, which was used in a more reserved manner by Rocco Zingaro in the previous years. Among these new Templars, the Italian newspaper *Il Tempo* mentioned the presence of academics, like Bruno Brandimarte, professor of biophysics applied to the Fatebenefratelli Foundation, the Sapienza University, and the University of Tor Vergata. Prof. Benito Passangrilli, professor of dentistry at the Sapienza University and **psychiatrist Antonio Vento**, president of the National Observatory of Mobbing alongside many entrepreneurs and tycoons of American finance. Also present were aristocrats such as Jephine Borthwick, Princess Borghese, mother of Michele Borghese, and many actors,[8] as well as Al Festa, who I will talk more about soon, in connection to the Holy Grail.

At the time, seeing the unexpected success of this new order, the website of one of the leading Neo-Templar groups, O.S.M.T.J. commented with concern, emphasiz-

7 See. http://www1.adnkronos.com/Archivio/AdnAgenzia/2005/05/19/Cronaca/ABORTO-ORDINE-TEMPLARI-ANCHE-GLI-UOMINI-DEVONO-POTER-DECIDERE_140910.php ‡ Archived 16th October, 2016.
8 See. http://www.iltempo.it/2005/05/10/dame-spade-e-cavalieri-i-big-diventano-templari-1.992997 † Archived 16th October, 2016.

ing their ties with American Freemasonry and their membership in the Ancient and Accepted Scottish Rite (A.A.S.R.), which according to the O.S.M.T.J. they later renamed Ancient Scottish Rite Reunified (A.S.R.R.) referring to a Masonic meeting that was held in Cape Verde, 12 years before as the starting point of this new project: *"The U.S. Masonic Lobby, with much emphasis on the National Press, looking for a Templar legitimacy, is investing their followers in Santa Prisca on the Aventine Hill in Rome. Dario Labbate and others, are renages of Rocco Zingaro's group who are using the same cloaks and emblems. The reaction of the Vatican, in the person of Cardinal Ruini, is immediate. Prohibition of the use of the Churches of the Roman Diocese by organizations called Templars."* [9]

Cavalieri del Tempio dello Spirito Santo

Program of the annual meeting
Rome 2012

Saturday, january 28:

6.30 to 8.00 p.m   informal arrival-meeting between in Casa Bonus Pastor,
                    zona extraterritoriale Città del Vaticano, Via Aurelia, 208

                    If you want to stay at Casa Bonus Pastor over night, please
                    make your own reservation in advance, tel +06 69871282
                    or internet;

8.30 p.m.   informal dinner in a restaurant nearby

Sunday, january 29:

9.00 a.m.   breakfast (individual)

9.30 a.m.   official meeting in Casa Bonus for all cavalieri (knights) and
                    friends, Admittance ceremony for new cavalieri

12.00 a.m.   Celebration of Holy Mass in the Basilica S. Maria Maggiore at
                    the Pop's altar It will be celebrated by
                    il Canonico della Basilica, **Mons. Gino Di Ciocco**.

The Holy Mass will be dedicated to **Cav. Rocco Zingaro** who died last year
Seats will be reserved for all in front.
For a nicer ceremony, please bring your coats with you, thank you

FIG. 46 – The program of the annual meeting of the "Cavalieri dello Spirito Santo" the Neo-Templar Order of Enrico Marinelli where Antonio Leonardo Montuoro cites the Holy Mass dedicated to Rocco Zingaro.

Strangely the O.S.M.T.J. that distances itself officially from Freemasonry, is actually full of Freemasons among its ranks, with a particular inclination to recruit from the York Rite. These are the mysteries of the Neo-Templar groups, where sometimes lack of coherence and clarity seems to only push water to their mill; although in this case to tell the you truth, the condemnation of these new Neo-Templar groups by the Church is in my opinion fully justified, since the O.S.M.T.J. is certainly from the perspective of traditional initiatic groups, a more serious and legitimate body on Italian soil than the misguided attempt of Labate that went nowhere, while O.S.M.T.J. is still one of the most influential orders, although increasingly split into various factions. Subsequently, the most important of the Italian newspapers, Corriere della Sera, explained in this way the project of Francesco Dario Labate:

The Order of the Poor Knights of Christ (re) created a few years ago by Francesco Dario Labate, self-appointed Sovereign Grand Master seems, to want to unite the vast (only in Italy the groups are over 40), world of modern Templars thanks to a rich American foundation, suspended between the charm and mystery of the "sol-

9   http://www.cavalieri-templari.eu/sedicenze.htm ‡ Archived 16th October, 2016.

FIG. 47 – Pope Benedict XVI and Bishop Domenico Sigalini.

dier monks" and the easy conquest of some cheap honor. "I do not understand the
action by the diocese of Rome preventing us to meet in Churches—confirmed Luigi
Zanella, spokesman for the Order. But we can also gather in the street, that's okay." [10]

At this point, the Knights that remained with Rocco Zingaro, who were involved for
years in this difficult task of rapprochement with the Catholic Church, tired of the confusing situation created by the split with Francesco Dario Labate. They entrusted their fate in
the hands of Antonio Leonardo Montuoro, thanks to the intermediation of lawyer and
Freemason Riccardo Scarpa, who was also close to the late Rocco Zingaro, and according
to some, a sinister character tied to dark plots that would convince Zingaro to accept the
offer of retirement made by Montuoro on behalf of the Jesuits. Here the slow but inexo-
rable decline of the facade of the the the S.M.E.T.H. begins, that will result in absolute secrecy
in the Vatican creation in 2009 of the new Neo-Templar order. It is called the Knights of
the Temple of the Holy Spirit, which is not officially connected to Rocco Zingaro, and
is presided over by Dr. Antonio Leonardo Montuoro, (FIG. 46) and the aforementioned
Prefect Enrico Marinelli, who became the Honorary President, with the further support
of Bishop Domenico Sigalini, (FIGS. 47 and 48) General Ecclesiastical Assistant of the
Italian Catholic organization *Azione Cattolica*. It is in the national headquarters of this
organization in the Vatican, where the blessing ceremony of the cloaks of the new Order
of the Knights of the Temple of the Holy Spirit was held in the early months of 2011. The
Order officially kicked off its operations, while an inceasingly weak Rocco Zingaro was near
death. The official announcement was made in the monthly publication, *Divine Power of
Love* published in March, 2011 (XXI – No. 3). Zingaro, meanwhile, lived in almost total
isolation since 2007. After the Cardinal Ruini intervened in 2005, the Grand Preceptor
Rocco Zingato was in fact asked to leave the Neo-Templar scene, to retire in silence among

10 See. *La diocesi sfratta i "templari" dalle chiese romane* by Palma Ester in *Il Corriere della Sera*,
06/16//2005.

FIG. 48 – The Princess Kaoru Nakamaru interviewing Bishop Domenico Sigalini for a documentary.

the old men of the old folks home controlled by Dr. Montuoro. According to Montuoro, Zingaro was no longer reliable as Grand Preceptor, and Montuoro became the new Grand Preceptor of S.M.T.H.O. A title he still holds in great secrecy in parallel with that of the head of the Knights of the Holy Spirit. According to Montuoro, who told me the story several times, Count Rocco Zingaro of San Fernando (this was his title), was saved thanks to an act of compassion and charity towards him made by his fellow Catholics, that's why he was in Loreto in Montuoro's "Oasis," where he spent the last years of life.

This was because, after the death of his wife, Zingaro was having serious financial problems, and placed himself entirely in the hands of Montuoro, (FIG. 49) obviously after officially giving him and the Church the Grail in exchange for his new residence. As evidence of this, there a press release made by Count Rocco Zingaro back in May, 2007:

> *Epochal event—An exceptionally important event is taking place in the Holy House of Nazareth in Loreto. The Holy Grail kept by the Templars is finally back in its house. In a wonderful night of the Holy Week, before Easter, the Holy Virgin appeared in a dream to our Grand Preceptor, Rocco Zingaro St. Ferdinand, addressing him with the words: "Deliver to the house of Nazareth the Holy Grail with the same generosity with which you have treasured it for over thirty years. My house is empty and with this gesture the light of truth will return to shine. The world will be surprised: a divine sign for a new path. For the greater glory of God." Obedient to the request made in the dream by the Holy Virgin Mother of God, our Grand Preceptor, Sunday, May 13, 2007 at 12.00, 889 th year since the founding of the Templars, gave such official comunication in Loreto in the Nursing Home of St. Joseph in Via san Francesco, 44 tel. 071.7501132 stating that the Holy Grail will be delivered to the house of Nazareth when legal paperwork is completed relating to the change of ownership. It is worthwhile to point out the great generosity of our Grand Preceptor, Rocco Zingaro of St. Ferdinand, who could have obtained a*

FIG. 49 – Dr. Antonio Leonardo Montuoro, President of the "Knights of the Temple of the Holy Spirit," with the cloak of the Order, during the official visit of Princess Kaoru Nakamaru in 2011.

fortune from the sale to third parties of the Holy Grail, firmly wanting to follow his motto, setting an example for all of us. Vaucent! [11]

Note in the words above the use of the Jesuit motto: *Ad Maiorem Dei gloriam!* That's why there are many who have doubts on the last period of Zingaro's life.

Before Zingaro died, in the last few months of his life, I asked Montuoro several times if I could meet him, but my requests were always turned down, something I thought from the start was very strange. I also asked Montuoro to meet with the late exorcist, Father Gabriele Amorth (who died in 2016), but this request was also denied. This made me immediately understand I was dealing with mercenaries of the Church, not real Templars or true followers of Jesus Christ. So the abrupt appearance of the "Parchment of Chinon" with a new version of the events surrounding the last days of the Knights Templar favorable to the Church, seems also very suspicious at a time in which the Neo-Templarism phenomena is on the rise after the great success of *The Da Vinci Code* book, and movie, and the Church wants to obviously capitalize on it..

In the middle of the 1990s, the Italian magazine called *Il Giornale dei Misteri* (The Journal of Mysteries), published an interesting interview with Rocco Zingaro, Count of San Ferdinando, about his "Holy Grail."

Here is the interview translated in full for the first time in English for this book.

QUESTION: We asked Rocco Zingaro, one of the heirs of the Templar tradition, some details about the Holy Relic in his possession. How he came in possession of the Holy Grail? What is the evidence in favor of its authenticity? Will it be subjected to laboratory examination?

ANSWER: *I was given the Holy relic by Professor Antonio Ambrosini, emeritus* *professor of the University of Rome, twenty years ago on my wedding day. He unearthed this object in Egypt, in a Coptic monastery, and was sure it was the real Grail. Ambrosini was a great scholar, and produced evidence and documents to support this, but I'm sure that this is the chalice used by Jesus at the Last Supper. However, it was already appraised by a Jesuit historian who confirmed the authenticity of the finding going back to a period between the first and the second century B.C. It's completely available for any test, analysis or research.*

Q: Why have you decided to disclose the existence of it only now? You could have keep the secret without news of a similar discovery coming from England?

A: *Without the pretentious information given by Phillips lately we will have kept it secret a little longer, instead we had to rely on the credibility of the Templars from the historical point of view to give out such news. We have also broken the reserve for three reasons: 1) I could not bear the disproportionate resonance given by the media to other similar false discoveries in various parts of the world; 2) the Pope's open attitude in most fields, especially towards the female element, and his indulgence toward sinners; 3) Finally, a few years before the millennium, it seems only right to go public with this sacred object in the hope that it will reaffirm the universal values of peace and fraternity.*

Q: What exactly is the Holy Grail and what does it represent for the Templars?

A: *According to tradition, this was the chalice used by Jesus at the Last Supper. Later, the disciple Joseph of Arimathea laid it at the foot of the cross to collect the divine drops of the blood of Christ. This belief is interwoven with historical and legendary elements, Celtic and Christian traditions. At the time of the Crusades, His custody was given precisely to the Knights of the Temple. The Grail is an opportunity for people to reflect on its journey towards the third millennium, which brings the opportunity to get closer to God. It is the force of Good, and is a goal to meditate that it will bring peace to the world.*

Q: Who were the Knights of the Order of the Templars? What are their ideals and projects?

A: *The Templars were the Church's sword, the defense of the pilgrims, those that under one flag brought European unity, because they fought for the same ideals. The project of the Templars if they managed to implement it, was European unity that would have been implemented since 1200. The disappearance of the Templars, which resulted in the end of this unifying design, was due precisely to the envy and jealousy of these powerful forces that fought against each other, and they feared the extinction of their kingdoms. Today the Templars are those who intend to pursue, especially in the life of every day, the ideals of chivalry, behaving as accurately as possible with a bit of extra ethics and morals. There are fundamental values in life that can not be erased; this is what in fact is required of a perfect knight. It is important on the threshold of the year 2000 to renew the pact of alliance with God and man, because the law is only one and it was written in fire, then the human being must respect the Universal Law of God which must be equal for all without distinction of creed or race.*

Q: Because it is very important to be recognized by the Church in spite of the unjust persecution perpetrated against you?

A: *Pope Clement V brought about a suspension of the Order pro-tempore and not definitive, but temporary. Not being able to condemn the Templars because of the process*

FIG. 50 – Rocco Zingaro in the Cistercian Abbey of Casamari, in the province of Frosinone, on the throne of St. Bernard as Grand Preceptor for the Italy in the early nineties.

itself that was revealed was a farce at this point (the Pope knew this very well), then he proceeded with this temporary measure. Since the cardinals of that time refused to sign the papal bull, Clement V had to make its own motion; that's why we are interested in reconnecting with the Church: another pope can remove the Papal bull of Clement V.

As the Church is reconsidering its past history, by removing their mistakes, the facts regarding the Templars becomes a matter of justice. It would therefore be very important and appropriate that the Church ruled something about it, especially to make a clean sweep of those who have speculated for a long time on the good name of the Templars, whose real order must be re-evaluated by the Church itself. However, since 1991, we have obtained the protection and blessing of the Latin Patriarch of Jerusalem. The Patriarchs power is equal to the Pope, it is the imprimatur who is different, so if the future imprimatur comes from the Church of Rome, it would be better, for us. At the same time I personally would like to confirm, regardless of who will assume the position, the will to eventually donate the Chalice of the Grail to the Holy Father, as a tribute of filial devotion, because I come from a Catholic, apostolic Roman family with a strong Faith. Strangely, in proximity of the Year 2000, this sacred object has come into my hands, and as I have been given it, so I want to give it to the Pope, because I think he must have it.

Well it seems that Rocco Zingaro (FIGS. 50, 51, 52, 53) had the initial idea of giving the Holy Grail to the Vatican, however ten years later he changed his mind. Zingaro felt that he would like to donate the Grail to the American people instead, but in the end the Vatican managed, with Montuoro and Marinelli, to get their hands on it, and make it disappear from public scrutiny.

Padre Pio and the Holy Grail

In the preceding pages I mentioned the name **Al Festa** in my research on the Holy Grail, or rather **Alberto Festa** (b. 1958), director and Italian composer, Freemason and Neo-Templar. He is connected with Saint Padre Pio, because of his blood tie to the doctor of Padre Pio, **Giorgio Festa**, who was his great-uncle. Festa became involved with the mysterious Holy Grail, which was given to the Saint of Pietrelcina. I will now explain why this mysterious object is still in the hands of Alberto Festa. Among the various "Holy Grails" I studied during the years, it is probably the most credible, because the Vatican, and the Pope Emeritus **Joseph Ratzinger**, when he was still pope, tried in every way possible to obtain it. Indeed, their deeds are sometimes extreme, and it suggests that we could be dealing with an authentic Holy Grail, and not just the usual myth.

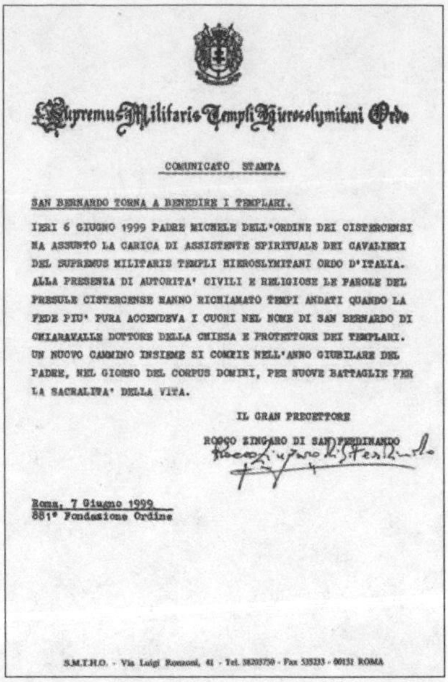

Let's begin with an article which appeared in 2008, in the popular Italian weekly **"Panorama,"** that commented on an exhibition on Padre Pio relics arranged by Alberto Festa, who owns hundreds of relics, left to him by his great-uncle:

FIG. 51 – An official document of Zingaro's Order from the 7th of June 1999, shows the appointment of Father Michael of the Cistercians Order, as Spiritual Assistant of Rocco Zingaro Templars.

It showcases nineteenth century style glass alternating with bronze busts of the saint, portrayed in all ages. Inside, relics, that include his gauzes, a lens that magnifies four hairs of his beard. On the red damask walls large photographs in gilt frames of the Saint. Above, famous phrases of San Giovanni Rotondo's celebrated monk, like: "The smile does not come on itself you have to want it." Magically propelled towards the bottom of the exhibit room by a music theme, you arrive ultimetely in front of the precious reliquary. Inside, leaning over a blood red pillow, there is a black glove of the Saint, what we have all seen on the hand of actors Michele Placido and Sergio Castellitto, depending on the TV network, in the role of St. Padre Pio of Pietrelcina. But this is the real one, which was used to cover his scars. An exhibition which presents more than 100 objects never seen, a real paradise of the devotee, for the first time on display in Rome. [12]

Alberto Festa the great-grandson of the brother of Dr Giorgio Festa, the doctor sent in 1919 by the Holy Office to verify the true nature of the friar's wounds, decided to reprint the only copy that was found in 1999, of the rare book by his great uncle called ***Mysteries of science and lights of faith, the stigmata of Padre Pio of Pietrelcina.*** Rich in annotations and curiosities on the figure of the mysterious Saint from Pietrelcina, like the episodes that saw him reach in moments of pure ecstasy and rapture the incredible body temperature of 48.5 degrees celsius, while the wound on his side, which was maintained "fresh and vermilion" over the years, could be seen "short but noticeable light radiation." After the examination conducted on the body of Padre Pio, Giorgio Festa was convinced of the genuineness of the stigmata: the wounds on his hands "are certainly not the result

12   http://archivio.panorama.it/archivio/Alla-fiera-di-Padre-Pio ‡ Archived 16th October, 2016.

FIG. 52 – Image of the Grand Preceptor Rocco Zingaro of St. Ferdinand in his post-donation Grail period at the "Protected Residence" directed by Antonio Leonardo Montuoro, visibly aged, participating in a Neo-Templar ritual with the help of Father Max Anselmi in Loreto, on September 23rd, 2008.

of a local disease"—wrote Festa—nor can they be regarded as the "expression of constitutional infirmity." The stigmata maintained "always the same size over the years," after several successive examinations. Alberto Festa said he was from the beginning: *"ready to make available to the scientific community the relics for any exam that will be considered appropriate, including the collection of DNA from traces of blood remaining on the cloth inside the black glove. … I decided to make public the existence of the glove"*—he said after he recovered it with the rest of the relics, *"only to rehabilitate the image of my great-uncle, a doctor that was always forgotten and overshadowed by the Church."* [13]

The objects in question were analyzed and considered genuine by the Vatican, and still belong to Alberto Festa, which in recent years the existence of another object deemed much more controversial belonging to Saint Padre Pio has been made known, however this one never received the approval of the Holy See like the other relics of the Saint. I am talking precisely of the supposed Holy Grail that belonged to Padre Pio. A well-kept secret that surfaced only for a brief time several years ago in the Italian media, starting with the Southern Italian newspaper, the *Gazzetta del Mezzogiorno*, dated Wednesday November 26, 2003, that coincides with the announcement made by Alberto Festa, that day, in a press conference in Rome.

Here is the full story as reported by the newpaper:

ROMA—Padre Pio was in possession of the Holy Grail, the cup of the Last Supper of Jesus with his disciples, where after the crucifixion would have collected the blood of Jesus. In an unpublished letter by Padre Pio, made public today by the grandson of the physician Giorgio Festa, in 1919, who was sent by the Holy See to investigate the stigmata of the Saint of Pietrelcina, the friar with the stigmata writes that the Greek vase, recovered from Festa, belonged to Padre Pio, it went from the hands of Peter, to those of Saint Francis. A decisive step, which introduces Festa, not to exclude that it may be the real Holy Grail. But Father Tessari

13 See. http://www1.adnkronos.com/Archivio/AdnAgenzia/2002/06/07/Cronaca/PADRE-PIO-IL-GUAN-TO-DELLE-STIMMATE-ESPOSTO-A-ROMA_163800.php ‡ Archived 16th October, 2016.

FIG. 53 – Saint John Paul II blesses Rocco Zingaro and his Templars.

urges caution and denies the object "real meaning." The "secret" of Padre Pio, presented this morning at Palazzo Cherubini, is contained in a letter, written by the Saint shortly before his death, to a Brother Christopher from Vico Gargano. In it, the authenticity of which was confirmed by the expert graphologist Antonio Bravo, it reads: *"A Father Christopher from Vico del Gargano entrust the remains of humble secrets given to me by faithful Christians. ... I leave the little Greek vase to Apostle Peter because it is a Secret Gift of God, the father, and witnessed the immense light. Guard it for the poor of faith."* In the letter, which is a kind of testament, there is also references to two other objects, a bowl and a lamp, that Padre Pio entrusted to other loved ones and now there should be one in America and the other in Japan. According to Father Tessari *"there is no doubt about the authenticity of the objects, which have been appraised, but do not have a real and material significance. They are a symbol of spirituality."* In particular, he explains, *"the vase dates from the time that Jesus and Peter could have touched it. It was probably taken from some excavations in the Holy Land and brought as a gift to Father Pio from the Christian faithful. But it is always a small jar that should not become a fetish."*

The postulator warns of an *"inopportune return to the Middle Ages,"* stating that: "there may be a special relationship with the Last Supper," he added that *"the objects are, however, to be interpreted as a reference to the Gospel scenes experienced in the heart of Padre Pio."* In summary, it would be better to consider them "spiritual symbols" without any "material value," or rather *"fragments of humanity and spirituality"* of Padre Pio. Less uncertain is Alberto Festa, who for years engaged in the reconstruction of work done by his great-uncle, who became a friend and confidant of the saint. *"I know only one object that can be called a witness of the immense light, as written in the letter, and it is the Holy Grail,"* he concludes. [14]

Five years after this announcement on May 23, 2008, in the national newspaper *Il Giornale* where the story again appears, giving us new details related to the acquisition of the Holy Grail by Al Festa:

A mysterious cup, that belonged to St. Peter and represented a "gift from God" to St. Francis, was then transmitted to Padre Pio. A handwritten letter with cryptic passages, laid in a clear and youthful calligraphy, by the stigmata saint when he actually was at the end of his life, attesting to the authenticity of the pot, calling it "Secret in me" and "a witness to immense light." Al Festa, a film director with interests in the world of spiritualism, great-grandson of the brother of the doctor who took care of Padre Pio, declares he is persecuted and fears being silenced after trying in every way to tell the story of the Grail. No, you are not reading the plot of a new fantareligious thriller, but a story on "Striscia la Notizia" the satirical News of Channel 5. The protagonist is called Al (short for Alberto) Festa, filmmaker, 50, a relative of Giorgio Festa, the doctor who operated on Padre Pio and examined his stigmata, then writing a detailed report. On Tuesday, based on some photos of the friar's burial, Festa raised questions about a possible tampering of the body, noting how the original seals did not feature on the glass at the time of the exhumation, and even giving info on an alleged transfer of the real remains in the Vatican. On this subject, the friars of San Giovanni Rotondo had no problems to clarify, deny and point out: in the days of exposure of the body before the funeral, various inspections were carried out, and a coffin change. So, immediately before the burial, the seals were not affixed on the glass lid, but the metal casing, where they stayed until 2 March. No mystery, no theft, no secret hidden in basements of the Vatican. Speaking to the Italian Satirical News Alberto Festa, however, has also re-launched the story of the letter, and of the possible "Holy Grail" of Padre Pio, which he announced with a press conference November 26, 2003, when he called it a "pot of incredible importance." All these years he has believed that his great uncle Festa had found the Grail, and the letter written by Padre Pio,were among the objects belonging to his great-uncle, doctor of the friar. In reality, things did not go exactly like that. It was a purchase, for a value of approximately 75 thousand euros. A writ of summons filed at the court in Rome on January 12, 2006, that show that Festa bought the grail, at a certain point, from Emanuele Cervone, who acted as an intermediary between the relatives of the friar, Father Cristoforo of Vico of the Gargano, guardian of the object, who in turn received it in March, 1968, from the Saint of Pietrelcina. Alberto Festa, in 2005, in the face of the many and authoritative objections received on the document of the findings, stopped paying Cervone and received by these payment injunctions. The writ wrote Festa's lawyer, Antonella Rustico, states that the "authenticity and provenance" of the two objects was "never proven" by the seller. Today the case has been abandoned due to a transaction that Cervone and the Festa later agreed upon. The letter and the Grail now fully belong to the great-grandson of the holy doctor. But are they authentic? There is a handwriting experts opinion on the letter, written by Professor Alberto Bravo, dated 2003 (thus at an earlier date to the dispute between Festa and Cervone), which concludes: "The comparison analyzes confirm that the writing comes from the hand of the Saint Father Pio."

Just as there is an expert report according to which the age of the jar, dates back to the first century. The same General Postulator of the Capuchin Order, Father Florio Tessari, pleaded in favor of the authenticity of the letter. Those who never believed its authenticity are: the late vice-postulator of the cause of beatification, Father Gerardo Di Flumeri, which branded all as a fake, noting that in March 1968 Padre Pio almost didn't write, if not just his signature, and the handwriting looks too youthful. On the Holy Grail there are libraries full of books. All legends—notes of Antonio Belpiede, spokesman of the Order of Friars Minor Capuchin s of the province of San Giovanni Rotondo say—if what Festa is presenting to the world was so important and decisive, he would find every door wide open." [15] Really? Not so sure about this last statement.

However here is the text of the letter/testament that Padre Pio supposedly wrote in March, 1968, to Father Cristofoto from Vico of the Gargano, on giving him these mysterious relics, that seem to include also a bowl used to "wet the lips of our Lord on the Calvary":

To Father Christopher of Vico of the Gargano.

Brother, God calls me, and I entrust to you the remains of humble secrets given to me by faithful Christians, to deliver to Father Fortunato Serracapriola the bowl that with this water wet the lips of our Lord on the Calvary; to Mr. Emmanuelino, who approached the Holy Table, the Lucerne that illuminated the way of the Christians at the Colosseum; for you I'll leave the little Greek vase of the Apostle Peter a Secret Gift of God to my father and witness of the immense light. Guard it for the poor ... of faith. [16]

My experience with the Holy Grail

My personal experience with the Holy Grail of St. Padre Pio, and the meeting with Alberto Festa, dates a few years after the events I just described, when in September of 2013, by chance, Mr. Festa is introduced to me during the funeral of Marco Trani, an old DJ friend also closely tied to Al, who took care of his music videos. Al Festa had just curated an exhibition in the Basilica of San Lorenzo, in Lucina, Rome, dedicated to Padre Pio, entitled: *The great light: Padre Pio between science and faith,* designed and built by Al. (FIG. 54) The Pope was invited, *"in the spirit of Christian brotherhood and renewed humility,"* for the inauguration, but he did not attend. The exhibition represented a cultural and spiritual path, as seen by a layman doctor (Giorgio Festa, Al's great uncle), who was sent to give a diagnosis on Padre Pio's stigmata, and was close to this special person, treating all his complex physical ordeals. At that point I decided to stay in touch with him, so that I could also better study the history of this supposed Holy Grail, and the privileged relationship of his family with the controversial figure of Saint Padre Pio. This was during a particularly difficult period, when I was very active on the political front in Italy with the movement of the "Pitchforks" (*I Forconi*). One evening in January, 2014 I was invited, with a dozen members of my **Ordo Illuminatorum Universalis,** to visit Albert Festa in his mansion, an hour from Rome. He wanted to bring us there in secret so we could check out his mysterious relic.

The night began at the Vatican, where we met with the various Brothers of my Order, that came from all over Italy, to the courtyard of the headquarters of the Knights of the Holy Sepulchre around 11 at night. We went almost immediately to the province of Viterbo, Sutri, to Alberto Festa's residence, where for the occasion, he took the Holy Grail from its safe, but he said it is usually kept in a nearby police station. It was indeed a very powerful experience for me, and the other brothers of the Order, that could fill up a separate book, and I definitely will focus on it again in the future. In a nutshell, the evening ended with a prayer by the members of the *Ordo illuminatorum Universalis,* as I kissed this sacred object around 2 a.m., which unleashed something at a subtle and magical level that would eventually emerge a little later in a series of important events in my life. First of all, I

15   http://www.ilgiornale.it/news/giallo-graal-padre-pio.html ‡ Archived 16th October, 2016.
16   http://www.ilgiornale.it/news/custoditelo-i-poveri-fede.html ‡ Archived 16th October, 2016.

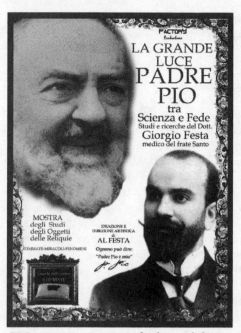

FIG. 54 – Poster of the exhibition organized by **Alberto (Al) Festa** in the Basilica of San Lorenzo in Lucina in Rome dedicated to St. Padre Pio entitled The Great Light: Padre Pio between Science and Faith.

was arrested in the early hours of the following morning by the Italian authorities, who suddenly broke into my house forcing me into a mental institution at the hands of the notorious **Tavistock Institute**, as later confirmed in front of my lawyer, **Dr. Giuseppe Nicolò**, director of the facility based in the town of Subiaco, near Rome. This wasn't a good experience, but in the months that followed, these unexpected events led myself and my soon-to-be wife Christy, to California, meeting with those fantastic people who finally believed in me and my literary projects, and gave me the opportunity to publish my books in English. The same books that are increasingly censored and sabotaged in Italy, because of my anti-government and anti-Vatican position. During the two weeks of my forced hospitalization, I experienced from the future Italian Prime Minister **Matteo Renzi** and his occult manipulators of the Tavistock Institute, one of the most interesting moments with the arrival of Alberto Festa on January 28, 2014, to the place were I was forced to stay. He brought the black glove used to cover the first stigmata of Padre Pio. Imagine such a scenario, in a hospital/mental institution based in the Italian province located in the small ultra-Catholic town of Subiaco, called "the cradle of Western Monasticism," because of its important monasteries where both St. Benedict and St. Francis lived.

At the entrance of the hospital where I was locked up for two weeks, there is even a statue of Padre Pio, and here arrives suddenly out of nowhere such a holy object related to the famous Italian saint, and it is brought to a "patient" restricted in a mental healthcare facility. Well, this was a truly unusual situation indeed, don't you think? I know this story is incredible and I cannot deny that I have a smile on my face while I write this, but you should have seen the faces of the doctors at the arrival of Alberto Festa with Padre Pio's Holy relict. It was then that Al Festa left me a card with a tiny relic of Padre Pio, with the fragment of a bandage used on his stigma, attached to it, an object that would, among other things, be used within a few days on the demand of the doctors to perform an exorcism on a patient. A so-called "refugee," a black boy from Africa, was in a state of demonic possession one night during my stay. I was asked to intervene with a short exorcism, since the monks of the nearby St. Scholastica Monastery were not able to come. I began the prayer of exorcism without success. Indeed, it seemed to have worsened the situation, but the moment I exposed the relic of St. Padre Pio, a minuscole fragment of his gauze he used to cover the stigmata wounds, attached to a card with his photo, that I was given by Alberto Festa, right then and there, the poor guy suddenly stopped having issues. The incredible power that the relics of St. Padre Pio have against demons is truly incredible, I was positively perplexed. Power of suggestion or miracle, God's ways are endless. When I left for California a couple of months later I brought with me another relic of the saint that definitely brought me luck, it was another fragment of Padre Pio bandages Alberto Festa gave to me on March 5, 2014, as a birthday gift, with a certificate of authenticity signed by the Postulator General of the Order of Friars Minor of St. Francis. (FIG. 55)

This was my brief experience with the Holy Grail of St. Padre Pio, which is still in the hands of Neo-Templar and Freemason Alberto Festa, who apparently refused a 300,000 Euro offer by Pope Joseph Ratzinger because he thought Ratzinger would eventually make it disappear. True? We don't know, however, there is also another interesting fact Alberto Festa spoke about when we participated in that mysterious night gathering with the supposed Holy Grail, which was located by the way, in a beautiful medieval golden casket with the symbol of a Lion on its base, which as you know is one of the symbols of Jesus Christ and possibly his descendants. Festa said that the mysterious cup, typical of the period in which Jesus lived, and similar to that unveiled to the world by Rocco Zingaro—but slightly smaller— had some blood, on the bottom of it, which according to Alberto Festa, belongs to Jesus Christ. Behind this blood Festa says is concealed the mystery of the stigmata received by St. Padre Pio, and before him of those of St. Francis who also received the stigmata. On these claims made by Alberto Festa, we have no certainty, although I saw with my own eyes in the bottom part of the small cup what appeared to be traces of human blood, that's for sure, but was it the blood of Jesus? Surely the saint of Pietrelcina, Padre Pio, could not lie about the origin of this object, whose public ostentation would change the face of the history of religion and humanity itself.

The Spiritual Alchemy of the Knights Templar

An important statement in relation to the famous story of the supposed descendants of the "Holy Grail" and the Priory of Sion, was made years ago by Pierre Plantard and his associates, who learned it from the previously mentioned Robert Ambelain (1907 – 1997), who **Massimo Introvigne** (also Martinist and agent of the Jesuits), said was the real inspiration behind the legend of the supposed Merovingian descendants of Jesus and Mary. He points out Introvigne was not present in the first publications of the Priory and the various falsified documents of this mysterious Order that appeared in **the years 1965-1967:**

> *The part of the story about Jesus Christ and Mary Magdalene was born between 1969 and 1970, when the story of the Priory of Sion attracts Henry Lincoln an English actor, who became later a director of documentaries on esoteric topics. This actor and documentary filmmaker comes into contact with the trio de Chérisey—Plantard—de Sede and decides to rewrite the history of L'Or de Rennes in a way more suitable to the English language form, presenting it in the first three documentaries broadcast by the BBC between 1972 and 1979 and then in a book published in 1982 with the help of Michael Baigent and Richard Leigh called the Holy Blood and Holy Grail. ... Lincoln, realizes that who is responsible for the title of pretender to the throne of France, is of little interest to the British public. At the same time he met Robert Ambelain (1907 – 1997), who in 1970 published Jésus ou Le secret des templiers mortel (Robert Laffont, Paris), where he argues that Jesus Christ had a girlfriend, and identifies this "concubine" in the dancer Salome. Lincoln puts together the story of the marriage of Jesus, which derives from Ambelain, with that of the Merovingian Plantard and "reveals" that the Merovingian protected by the Priory of Sion are important, far beyond the claim of the throne of France, because they are descended from Jesus Christ and Mary Magdalene.* [17]

Nowhere in the New Testament or surviving literature from the time of Christ does

17   http://www.cesnur.org/2005/mi_02_03.htm ‡ Archived 16th October, 2016.

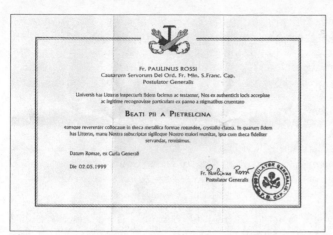

FIG. 55 – *Certificate of authenticity signed by the Postulator General of the Order of Friars Minor of St. Francis for a fragment of Padre Pio bandages that Alberto Festa gave to the author on March 5, 2014, as a birthday gift.*

it mention Jesus having wed. *So are the Royal Houses descended from Jesus?* This odd notion can be traced to the political machinations of Pope Paul I (757 – 767). During his pontificate the Vatican was besieged from all sides by roving Lombard hoards, a hostile Eastern Emperor and the emerging threat of the Islamic Empire. His only allies were the Franks (Merovingian and Carolingian cousins) whose military prowess could save the Holy See from these encroaching enemies. The Byzantine Emperors claimed succession from Julius Caesar. In 476 AD, the Western Empire fell to the Germans and the royal symbols (standards) were sent to Byzantium where the Eastern Emperor assumed all titles of the Western Holy Roman Emperor. The Muslim princes claimed noble descent from Muhammad. As a means to upstage these hostile elements, Paul I declared that the Frankish Kingdom was now the "New Israel" and addressed Frankish rulers as "David" and "Solomon." This was not a matter of blood—no surviving documents state that the Franks were of Jewish blood. The Pope used a right called *translatio imperii*—the right of the pontiff to transfer the titles of a royal house to anyone he chooses. (Pope Sylvester transferred the titles of Julius Caesar to Constantine even though he was not a blood descendant of any of the Roman Emperors). This was long established when Paul I bestowed the titles of the House of David unto the Franks. Dan Brown attempts to claim that the Franks were descended from the Despoysni, but the odds of this would be astronomical, and there are no surviving documents which mention this as a fact. It is merely a misunderstanding of the right evoked by Paul I, who never claimed that the Merovingians were Jewish or from the family of David and Jesus. If Paul I suspected that the Franks were descended in any way from Jesus, he would have bestowed upon them the title of "House of Christ" as opposed to the "House of David." It would have given him an even stronger form of propaganda to use against the Eastern Empire and potential Muslim invaders. Nor would it hinder belief in Catholic theology, if it were made clear that they were descended from Jesus' cousins. However, this was not the case. It was the real political and Vatican propaganda (Romanita) of Paul I's reign, which generated this weird notion of Europe's nobility being of Davidic origin. Furthermore, in a 2006 episode of the History Channel program *Digging for the Truth*, host Josh Bernstein performed a DNA test on the remains of a Merovingian princess, and discovered that this bloodline possessed no Semitic genes—her racial profile was purely European. [18] As the late writer and researcher William H.Kennedy wrote: *"It is clear then that **The Da Vinci Code** is based on a flawed under-*

18   See. William H.Kennedy, **Satanic Crime**, (Mystic Valley Media, 2006), p. 127-128.

standing of Petrine history and, consequently, is debunked, and can be heaped onto the junk pile of bogus ideas." However there is another claimant to the Jesus/ David bloodline, and that is Queen Elizabeth II, as the Royal College of Heralds in Britain officially accepts this direct line of descendant, at least from King David to Queen Elizabeth II as factual. The Queen is the 122nd lineal descendant of King David, who is of the tribe of Judah, and for some, the royal line of the Messiah comes through the tribe of Judah, and will continue until His second coming. Now this might only be a well-crafted myth, but Robert Ambelain was not your average researcher.

Ambelain was one of the leaders of the Illuminati of his time in the Martinist field, as well as supreme leader of the so-called Egyptian Rites of Freemasonry in the world, and was considered one of the greats of Spiritual Alchemy. The majority of contemporary Egyptian Rites derive their initiatic transmission from Ambelain.

This is what Ambelain wrote about his "alchemical doctrine," the true inner teachings of his work in the introduction to the book **"SPIRITUAL ALCHEMY"**—which does not lack a strong critical sense with respect to the inventories of the Rosicrucian—Masonic tradition that represent a unique testimony of the spiritual alchemical doctrine as one of the leaders of Neo-Templarism in the past century. No coincidence Ambelain was also the author of the book, *Martinez Pasqualis* and he truly knew the turning points of the Illuminati tradition:

Between the year 1625 and the year 1675, the energy of the Devotional Aspect and that of the Ritual and Ceremonial Aspect met in certain quarters. This meeting had the effect of bringing into manifestation, through a ritual and a visible ceremony, what in Mystics Orders was a State Within inaccessible to non-initiates. The objective of this Work of popularization was to reach and emotionally engage the mind first, consciousness then, and more wide swath of the profane outside world, always regarded by the Initiates as "brothers in sleep." The goal was to increasingly lead man through the recognition of a visible ritual, being able to play inside the Ceremonial conditions that would imply the establishment of the inner state and bring inner awakening to the consciousness of Being Aware of one for All, latent in us. The statement in the external world of certain principles, produced the same effect as that of the stone thrown into a river: the first will be the clearly visible effects of the stronger mass penetration in a weaker state, in the event of concentric circles, they soon lose their concentricity and geometric similarity, while continuing to expand, with the result then of a domino effect on the space that contains it. But in the end, despite having marked a moment of perfection in a world that does not belong to him, the geometric circles, which effect the meeting of two worlds impenetrable to each other, will first be made unrecognizable by the current and then cease to exist. I hope you understand that every work of externalization includes the sacrifice of the raw material used. Do not fret the loss, through time, the Spiritual Principles that each order possesses in origin, nor the consequent loss of the power of initiation. The first loss occurs with the effect that I have tried to explain in the above example, while the second loss must be to safeguard the principles initiatory from access of the profane hands of those who, later, will sit at the top of the now too vulgarized Initiatic teaching, of which nothing remains but a memory in the memory of his rituals. This, and much more, is part of the price paid to the profane world (the river), as always, from the Initiatic Orders to periodically awaken Brothers in sleep that are wallowing in it: exchanging a part of himself with a portion of humanity awakened. This is the real work of sowing the wheel of alchemy for humanity, of which I want *you to become aware, before you start reading these words. The decision to present the alchemical doctrine of the Elect Cohen, has been determined by a number of reasons, and with one goal. I would define the first and state the second. The first reason is that it is the Western Order of never voiced direct offshoot of the **Brotherhood of the Rosy Cross**, which, however, in the Initiation actually not existed for almost a century. Not that we will discover the secrets of those who "elected" is no longer, and this also applies to the imaginative circles the Rosicrucian Masonic Rites.* [19]

Strong words, by Robert Ambelain, that help us understand the degeneration of the **Western Initiatic System**, and here we must go back to **Rene Guenon,** to explain the distinction between the supposed existing **elite of today** and the truly illuminated ones of the past:

*There is a word, we quite frequently use on occasions, of which it is necessary to clarify at least explicitly the meaning, especially by placing a proper initiatory point of view: **this word is elite,** we use to designate something that no longer exists at the present state in the Western world, and whose constitution, or rather reconstitution, appeared the first and essential condition for the intellectual reconstruction of a traditional restoration.*

This word is one of those that is strangely abused in our time, to the point of using it currently in meanings that have nothing in common with what it would normally mean; these deformations, such as other purpose we did detect often as a true aspect of caricature and parody, that take place in such a way that deforms words that, prior to all profane deviation, were in some way consecrated by a traditional use, and it is really the case, as we shall see, in regard to the word elite. Similar words hang in a certain way, like "technical," terms in the same symbolism of initiation, and it was not for the simple fact that laymen sometimes seized a symbol, that they are incapable of understanding, they miss the meaning and make of it an unlawful application, the symbol shall cease to be what it really is; there is therefore no valid reason why the abuse of a word should oblige us to avoid using it, and, on the other hand, if we were to do so we would not see, with all the existing disorder in the current language, which terms may be available to us. When we used the word elite, as we said earlier, the false conceptions to which it is applied were not yet as widespread as we later found, and maybe they were not true because everything is visibly getting worse faster and faster; In fact, the elite is never been spoken of, at any time and from all sides, as when it no longer exists, and, of course, what you want to designate with this word. Is never the elite in its true meaning. But there's more: they talk about the elite nowadays using the term for all individuals who have even slightly exceeded the "average" level in any order of business, even if much less and far from any intellectuality.

We note first that the plural concept is not a true sense: not even out of the simple profane point of view, you could already tell that this word is for those who are fettered plural, because their meaning is somewhat that of a "superb" person, and also because they imply the idea of what, by its very nature, is not susceptible to fragment or divide; but it is appropriate to make this appeal to other considerations of a deeper order. Sometimes, for greater accuracy and to avoid any misunderstanding, we used the expression "intellectual elite," but in truth this expression is almost a pleonasm, as it is inconceivable that the elite is not intellectual, or, if you prefer, spiritual, these two words being short equivalent for us, since we absolutely refuse to confuse true intel-

19   See. Robert Ambelain, *Alchimia Spirituale*, (Genova, IT: Amenothes, 1982), *[emphasis added].*

lectuality with "rationality." the reason is that the distinction determining the elite can not, by definition itself, take place if not "from above," that is to say in the ratio of the highest possibility of being; it is easy to realize by reflecting on the meaning of the word, as deduced from its etymology. In fact, from the strictly traditional point of view, what gives this word elite all its worth, is that it comes from "elected;" and is such a reason that has led us to use it as we have done in preference to any other; but it is also necessary to specify the manner in which this has to be understood. Do not believe that we stop here to the religious and exoteric meaning is undoubtedly the sense in which you habitually speak of "elected," although it is certainly already something that could result in a fairly easy to appropriate analog transposition about in what is in effect; but there is nothing to add, that you may indeed find an indication even in evangelical judgment, well-known and often quoted, but perhaps insufficiently understood: After all, we could say that the elite, as we understand, representing all of those who possess the qualifications required for the initiation and who are naturally still a minority among men; in a sense, they are all "called," because of the situation "central" which occupies the human being in this state of existence, among all the other beings who are still there, but there are a few "chosen ones" and, in the current conditions of the time, there are certainly less than ever. [20]

The words of Guenon capture exactly the conditions of the present situation where humanity has lost the very notion of sacredness, and reminds us of a time when the elite that ruled mankind was more aware of its divine role as an intermediary between the entities of the invisible world and humanity.

The Threicia

In 1799, a violent social, political and cultural upheaval occurred in France, what I characterize as the First French Revolution (to distinguish it from the July Revolution and the French Revolution of 1848). There was a lawyer from the Illuminati called **Gabriel André Aucler,** nicknamed **Quintus Nautius,** who wrote a book called *Threicia*, which is the Latin adjective that refers to the Thrace, Hellas, region with a large diffusion of magical and shamanic values toward the underlying world of classical Greece. The Italian historian of esotericism, Vittorio Fincati, writes that Aucler however played on a game of words with *threskeia,* that in Greek means *"worship of the gods,"* as he explained himself in the book in question. As Gerard de Nerval wrote in a now rare work of that time entitled not surprisingly *The Illuminati,* Quintus Nautius was in charge of a mysterious task reserved only to a few genuine and chosen "Illuminati." Such special education is necessary for this kind of Illuminati and is transmitted to them only **"from mouth to ear."** It states: *"He places between man and God a chain of immortal spirits called Optimates and with which every Illuminati can arise in communication. It's always the doctrine of the gods, the Aeons and the Elohim of antiquity. Man, animals and plants possess an immortal monad, that animate from time to time the soul of more or less perfect bodies, according to an ascending and descending scale that materializes or deifies beings according to their merits."*

That said, Aucler is not a real pagan, but he seems to be nothing more than a follower of the teachings of the aforementioned **"Philosophe Inconnu, Unknown Philosopher"** and inspirer of Martinism, **Louis-Claude de Saint-Martin.** This conclusion is based on what Aucler himself states in his Book: *"Saint-Martin published his first book, **Des Erreurs et de la Vérité, par un Philosophe Inconnu** which I found with pleasure a large* *part of the doctrine that I present."* This is one of the main texts for reference of the followers of Saint-Martin. Aucler also speaks of his reconnection with an ancient pagan tradition tied to Orphism. *"I believe that the work of Aucler was only an attempt to revive the old religion of Rome and of the elite of the Illuminati in the author's personal perspective, a view with strong post-pagan veins."* This is how the Italian historian Vittorio Fincati describes his work, emphatically adding: *"but what an effort! After about 1,500 years since Christianity was supplanted in the heart of the state of the ancestral cults, that of Quintus Aucler was the first official position of a private citizen in favor of the re-establishment of those same cults."*

Unimaginable audacity against the Catholic Church that only the French Revolution could have allowed, since the revolutionary government wanted to erase its own motion of Constantine's edict proposing instead of Christianity, a secular religion, the foundation of which was influenced by the strong personalities of the time involved in the world of Masonry, and of course of the Illuminati. This revolutionary proposal was the only attempt to this day, since only the National Socialism of Adolf Hitler, that wanted to suppress the Christian denominations in favor of new pagan cults. An attempt that never came into fruition, however implemented with an official act, as it happened back in the time of Aucler. And we know that Italian Fascism and Benito Mussolini could not impose paganism in Italy, as their initiates of the **Group of Ur** would have liked, something I also mentioned in Volume II, because of the Vatican. Gerard de Nerval synthesizes in his book *The Illuminati,* the ideas of lawyer Gabriel André Aucler, who wanted to promote in that historical twilight period of great importance for the history of the West, the typical ideaology we find in most Illuminati sects: *"We must not believe that the rest of Quintus Aucler doctrine was the isolated event of an exalted spirit who was trying his faith through the darkness. Those who at the time were called Theosophists were not far from a similar line of thought. The Martinists, the Philaletheans, the Illuminati, and many members of the Masonic society professed a similar philosophy, whose definitions and practices varied only for the name you gave. You can therefore consider Aucler's neo-paganism as an expression of the ideal pantheist who was spreading thanks to the progress of the natural sciences. The old chemistry lovers, astrology and other occult sciences of the Middle Ages had left in that time many adepts, with the stunning news that what Mesmer, Lavater, Saint-Germain and Cagliostro, were announcing to the world, was with more or less sincerity. Paracelsus, Cardano, Bacon and Agrippa, old masters of cabalistic and spagyrical sciences, were still studied fervently."*

Gabriel André Aucler, recognized himself in the philosophy of Adam Weishaupt's Illuminati operating in that period, and views them as a kind of new salvation through a return to pantheism, but also as a way to reconnect with those original Christians of the origins known in fact as "Illuminati." As I mentioned earlier, the paganism of Aucler is not so convincing as De Nerval also seems to think, but hides a Jesuit vision of things. The ideological position of Aucler represents a well-defined type of paganism, that of a classic Roman religion, which often stands in stark contrast to other forms of pagan religion. The "religion of Rome," not surprisingly, has continued, somehow, in Catholicism, that has borrowed from the previous worship of many deities absorbed by the Roman Empire.

Is not a coincidence that a little over a century after the arrival of Aucler, Aleister Crowley, proclaimed himself "The Great Beast 666" and founded his Gnostic Ecclesia Catholica (E.G.C.), or Gnostic Catholic Church, the religious branch of his *Ordo Templi Orientis.* Always note the presence of "Catholic" in the religious aspect of its anti-Christian projects. I know it may seem a contradiction but it is not a mistake. **Arturo**

Reghini, whose name was transcribed in **the "Golden Book" of the O.T.O. in 1913**, [21] the year when Aleister Crowley formulated the *Liber XV,* which is the central ritual of his religion, was himself a staunch opponent of Christianity. Reghini was a central figure of the Illuminati in Italy, and particularly close to Crowley, who made this anti-Christian statement that shows us the vision is clearly more disrespectful and Satanic towards Jesus, than earlier paganism, stirred up by figures such as Aleister Crowley. Definitely not the vision of Aucler, but the first Illuminati or Martinists were basically always reverent and respectful of Jesus, who is considered the Master of Masters. Aucler was in fact more moderate in his pagan vision of Crowley, and his associates for sure, as you will read in his underlying words, still lays claim to a generational bond of his family to paganism, and the ancient cults, which is often the case with the elite of the Illuminati, even today:

> *We are the successors, the Keepers, of the ancient Mysteries of Samothrace, the very ones that were continued by the Romans through a special college of priests and only ones to have perpetuated, unlike all the others because they lost their values in high society and mundanity. In a passage of the book by the author of* The Thréicie, *Aucler, claims within his own family, to follow the Roman religion through the anniversaries of his schedule, stating that the origin of this family goes back "to lineages of hierophants," and he calls himself "hierophant of Ceres" adding that his descendants have crossed the centuries without mingling with secular families thanks to the gods, who preserved them in order to perpetuate a cult overwhelmed by so much time.*

Eventually Aucler's message is made even more clear by the words with which he concludes *THE THREICIA,* bringing us back to the theme of the link of the Illuminati with the Gods, and then with the Invisible Masters and Secret Chiefs which I will discuss in more depth in my next book called *The Invisible Master*:

> *Then you will see well that these rites were given by the gods to men, who are the expression of the universe, you can not neglect them without committing a crime, which the same mistake it bears the mark, and you can understand them only in the context of a universal doctrine. Then gathered in the expression of all that is, in the world analogies, not that we will form an admirable concert in the assembly itself of gods and men, the bond that unites the earth to the sky, waiting for a world of happiness, in which evil will no longer exist, in which nothing can separate us and when we can say: "O evil, where's your poison? O crime and sin, where is your ugliness? O death six deprives your scythe." Earn the name of philosophers, do not miss the most in your useless disciplines; they are nothing more than stuttering, bodies without consistency and solidity that do not cast even their own shadow, indeed they generate monsters against nature. Only one thing is useful, the regeneration of man. Anything that does not go in this direction is vain and useless. All the sciences that do not do this are not true sciences. But rest assured, you will not be idle, the real sciences that revive your genius. They contain the universe analogies and reasons of all worlds. Time flies, it flies away. You do not have more time to take care of frivolity. Those who will want to have this knowledge by an even deeper source, must know that there is strength only in unity. Men, rejuvenated! You have the chance through the Mysteries that the gods have bestowed upon you. Only through their rites and sacraments you can achieve. You have been placed on this Earth to bear fruit. If you do not give such result you will be uprooted from the land you render sterile, and you will wait in the places intended for that purpose the destruction of this world, so to go and form the world of the prince of evil.* [22]

21   Robert Gilbert, Baphomet & *Son, in Nuit Isis,* Oxford, n. 1, 1993, p. 21.
22   See . Quintus Nautius Aucler, **THREICIA THE UNIVERSAL RELIGION NATURAL** original title

This last step is particularly in line with those who think that the human being has been put on Earth to serve the "gods," or rather the alien races. According to Professor Corrado Malanga: *"For these beings, the human soul as an energy resource is exceptional. A resource that can provide them the elixir of immortality. Beyond Good and Evil, the aliens—angels and demons of ancient times—do not have any integrated consciousness, i.e. osmosis between soul, mind and spirit. Because of this lack they carry out alien abductions."* This is only the summary of a chilling interview with Corrado Malanga esteemed researcher and professor of organic chemistry at the University of Pisa in Italy. [23]

Loreto and Medjugorje … awaiting the Antichrist

I would like to close this chapter speaking again about the choice of Loreto by the Knights Templar, where it can be deduced that the deposition of the stones of the house in which the Virgin Mary lived was not coincidental, but rather made to precise indications, related to both the pagan past of those places and the peculiar esoteric connotations related to Sacred Geometry and what we call ley lines, a phenomenon connected to the power that emanates from these places. The current definition of a ley line according to **http//:Wikipedia.en.org/** is as follows: *"Ley lines are hypothetical alignments of a number of places of geographical interest, such as ancient monuments and megaliths. Their existence was suggested in 1921 by the amateur archaeologist Alfred Watkins, whose book 'The Old Straight Track' brought the alignments to the attention of the wider public."* The following natural and manmade features were suggested by Alfred Watkins, who coined the term ley line: *"Mounds, Long-barrows, Cairns, Cursus, Dolmens, Standing stones, markstones, Stone circles, Henges, Water-markers (moats, ponds, springs, fords, wells), Castle, Beacon-hills, Churches, Cross-roads, Notches in hills, Camps (Hill-forts)."*

Loreto, therefore is a truly magical place, chosen not by chance: as pointed out by the well-trained Jesuit agent Antonio Leonardo Montuoro. Loreto is a city that fits perfectly into a kind of Ley-line map of the Roman Catholic Marian devotion, with its miracles, appearances and its most important Churches, that include such places as Lourdes, Fatima, Medjugorje, and other strategically important locations for the Catholic faith. Locations such as San Giovanni Rotondo, Palestrina or Pompeii, another sacred place since ancient times because of the temple of the Goddess Isis, with very ancient ties to the lunar and feminine cults. Places that seem to form a veritable pyramid of Marian faith (FIG. 56), like Montuoro pointed out which show a link between Heaven and Earth, and therefore a sort of preferential route used to tap into very precise cosmic forces. Would these mysterious forces propelled by "Faith" manage to save the world?

Right now in the pre- and post-2020 turning point for humanity, things are gradually getting worse in the technocratic and soulless implementation of the New World Order. Of course, the faithful of the various religions are getting closer than ever before to a One World Religion headed by the Vatican, but are living in the false illusion of a positive change. Let's also remember that in 2016 a Jesuit Pope like Pope Francis ends up celebrating the 500th **anniversary** of the Protestant Reformation in Sweden praising **Martin Luther**, so the countdown for unity amongst different Faiths seems to be accelerating. In the meantime, the growing interest for the Marian cult, as well as the material interests of its alleged representatives on Earth, are simply offering spiritual pilgrimages tailored to our pockets,

Quintus Aucler THE THRÉICIE ou la seule voie des sciences humaines et divines , culte du vrai et de la morale in Paris , Chez Moutardier, Imprimeur - Libraire , quai des Augustins, An VII 28th year of the French Republic , the French translation and notes by Vittorio Fincati 2003, privately printed in Italy.

23 http://www.dionidream.com/gli-alieni-sono-tra-noi-e-vogliono-la-nostra-energia-intervista-al-prof-corrado-malanga/ ‡ Archived 30th October, 2016.

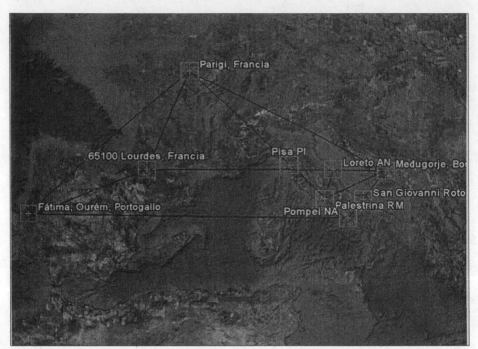

FIG. 56 – The incredible pyramid of faith created with the help of Google Maps by Dr. Antonio Leonardo Montuoro shows us the strategic position of Loreto in a serious of ley lines that include Fatima and other landmarks of Catholic belief, in what is an apparent alignment of places of significance used to activate energies that belong to the Mother Goddess.

blessing and miracles included; something that unfortunately happens even for the followers of St. Padre Pio, who come to San Giovanni Rotondo in Italy every day from around the world to find themselves in a tourist trap with no santity or sacredness **whatsoever**. In the midst of all this there are some scholars of ufology who did complex studies in relation to the **Blessed Virgin Mary,** and have even created an acronym for it, **B.V.M.** affirming that behind the Marian apparitions, there is an alien trap laid by manipulative and highly dangerous entities to manipulate mankind and vampirize him of his own soul. The subject has been dealt in the past by two famous Italian ufologists, Roberto Pinotti, and the aforementioned Corrado Malanga, two characters of whom I also spoke in Volume I, that have well described the phenomenology of the B.V.M. appartition in their book from 1990 entitled: *The B.V.M. phenomena: Marian manifestations in a new light,* [24] and before them there was a complex study on the phenomena conducted by Freixedo Salvador in Spain, who wrote the book *Defendàmonos de los dioses*, published in Spain in 1984 where we read:

> *The B.V.M. phenomena, or the apparitions of the Blessed Virgin Mary, as stated in the acronym, are closely linked to what we consider extraterrestrial phenomena for various reasons. The first aspect of the matter is related to the fact that if an entity religiously motivated actually appeared to human beings, this is something coming from outside the planet and then, according to some it should be classified as a terrestrial phenomenon. Some atheist authors consider instead the Marian apparitions that are not caused by schizophrenia or mental illnes,s something far more complex than just the appearance of a god, a demigod, a saint or other. For these authors the Marian apparitions hide a purely extraterrestrial phenomena. In other words, the*

24   See. Corrado Malanga, Roberto Pinotti, *I fenomeni BVM*, (Milan,IT: Mondadori, II edizione 1995).

Blessed Virgin Mary does not appear at all, but is instead a series of illusions driven by a race of aliens, with the use of highly sophisticated technologies, who mask themselves as Madonna to fool some humans particularly susceptible and gullible. [25]

Roberto Pinotti, who was until recently a Freemason of the Grand Lodge of Italy of the A.F.& A.M. (Antient Free and Accepted Masons) based at Palazzo Vitelleschi, via San Nicola de' Cesarini, 3 in Rome and also the co-founder of the CUN (National UFO Center of Italy) is a former NATO officer, currently very close to the Italian military Intelligence, and is very well-regarded by the Vatican despite his unorthodox theories on the Marian apparitions.

Roberto Pinotti has in fact confirmed in my presence, his view on the Marian phenomenon, in late September of 2010, during one of the conferences I organized at the Brancaccio Castle in Roviano in the Province of Rome in Italy. He explains in his book with Corrado Malanga, that some photos taken by occasional witnesses on the sites of supposed Marian appartitions show the presence, during the apparition, of strange flying objects moving in the sky, similar to genuine unidentified flying objects. This happened in Fatima in Portugal, and more recently in Crosia in the province of Cosenza in Italy. In these events, several unidentified objects can be seen moving with erratic motion, and some ufologists obviously conclude that these objects are actually real UFOs. We must question, "are they?"

Jacques Vallee describes what happened at Fatima in this way:

The crowd that stood in a field in Fatima, a small village in the district of Leiria, some sixty-two miles north of Lisbon, on October 13, 1917, were awaiting a miracle, because three children had been assured such an event would take place after a number of meetings with an "entity" that came from the sky in a globe of light.

According to the very words of the Reverend General Vicar of Leiria, who was one of the witnesses, the lady came in an "airplane of light," an "immense globe, flying westwards, at moderate speed. It irradiated a very bright light." Some other witnesses saw a white being coming out of the globe, which several minutes later took off, "disappearing in the direction of the sun." The last episode was the miracle itself. It was seen by seventy thousand persons, among who were pious individuals and atheists, clergymen and reporters from a socialist newspaper. As promised, it happened on October 13, at noon. Among the crowd was Professor Almeida Garrett, of Coimbra University, a scientist, who described the phenomena in the following terms: "It was raining hard, and the rain trickled down everyone's clothes. Suddenly, the sun shone through the dense cloud that covered it: everybody looked in its direction. IT LOOKED LIKE A DISC, OF A VERY DEFINITE CONTOUR. It was not dazzling. I don't think that it could be compared to a dull silver disk, as someone said later in Fatima. No. It rather possessed a clear, changing brightness, which one could compare to a pearl. It looked like a polished wheel. This is not poetry. My eyes have seen it. This clear-shaped disk suddenly began turning. It rotated with increasing speed. Suddenly, the crowd began crying with anguish. The sun, (disk?) revolving all the time, began falling toward the Earth, reddish and bloody, threatening to crush everyone under its fiery weight." Fatima was a modern event, yet it is already clouded with the distortions of "belief." The photographs of the object had "disappeared." The key prophecy has been suppressed. Lucia shut herself away from the world. As the years passed, the object was turned into a "dancing sun," the angel hair became "rose petals," and the entire phenomena was removed from the field of science and entrusted to the religionists. This should make us take a second look at all religious apparitions, visions and miracles. I do believe in the occurrence of true spiritual visions and miracles. Perhaps a real Mary or the spirit of Isis does appear to people, but paranormal entities (i.e. jinn) are also adept at performing such "miracles."

••

25   See. Salvador Freixedo, *Defendámonos De Los Dioses!*, (Madrid, España: Editorial Algar, 1984).

Islamic teachings about jinn say that some of them have always endeavored to make people worship them instead of God. This is called committing "shirk," and history provides ample evidence of such practices. Humans have always made various sacrifices to the "gods" and spirits. In many parts of the world they still do. On the other hand, perhaps some good jinn are trying to advance human awareness or motivate people to be more religious. Islamic history records accounts of jinn relationships with saints. And what about that Hindu pantheon? They certainly look like jinn! Four arms, blue skin, and elephant heads to boot! Messages from Mary often contain warnings about coming calamities which usually never occur. Doomsday threats are a common and well-documented type of jinn communication. Many BVM (Blessed Virgin Mary) events contain psychokinetic elements which resemble poltergeist activity. Usually it is only little children who can see the Lady. The BVM event at Garabandal involved little girls. The little seers went into trances which sometimes lasted hours. They sometimes ran BACKWARDS in a trance at incredible speeds with heads back and eyes directed upwards towards the heavens. They didn't ever trip or bump into trees or anything. How creepy, seems like something out of *The Exorcist*! Doing things backwards is characteristic of demonic possession for sure, just remember the protagonist Linda Blair in some of the key scenes from that Jesuit-inspired film from 1973. Currently, the group of beings referred to as "aliens" are portraying themselves as disparate elements of the paranormal and religious spectrum. Aliens, walk-ins, ascended masters, the hidden hierarchy, spirit guides, channelled beings and natural forces like Gaia, are all imparting a similar message of impending disaster and a need for all of humanity to unite just like the messages delivered in the B.V.M. apparitions. The "aliens" claim to be preparing the Earth for a massive evolutionary shift of consciousness, a paradigm shift, while also continuing the education that they maintain is crucial if the human race is to be spared destruction. The non-human intelligences are feigning good intentions by warning humans of their potential fate, and the offer to assist humans is all but altruistic in that it is designed to unite mankind under a global authority, with their candidate on the Throne of the World,[26] and on that throne will be of course the Antichrist, the ultimate one-man show of this increasingly Satanic New World Order that is becoming more and more evident each passing day.

As an example in this disturbing context, Detroit's Satanic Temple chapter gathered at the Michigan capitol in Lansing, on December 19, 2015, to perform what they called the "nation's first state-sanctioned Satanic Ceremony in history." The event came one week after Republican presidential candidate Ted Cruz supporters held a "Live Nativity" display on the capital grounds. As with the group's previous public demonstrations, the Satanic Temple says their ceremony was not an anti-Christian protest, but rather as a demonstration of religious plurality, as well as a stance against the breach of the separation of church and state in the government.[27] In his speech **Blackmore Jex,** director of this organization known as *The Satanic Temple,* of which I have already examined the origins and purposes in Volume II, said it has commenced a new American era. His speech began with the words: *"Hail Comrades. Hail sisters and brothers. Hail Satan. We are gathered here to celebrate the spirit of humanity and the dawn of a New American Era. In a season when many commemorate the birth of Christ, we commemorate our own genesis—the enlightenment of all humanity, a revelation of our nature as written in the annals of history, a gift from Lucifer, the light bringer, the morning star, and the rebel."*

Blackmore has also called for the total moral freedom, spiritual and sexual, personal independence and freedom of choice in all things Satanic, and lashed out at those who want to prevent the marriage between homosexuals, abortion, euthanasia, women's libera-

26 http://www.thejinn.net/marian_apparitions.htm ‡ Archived 1st November 2016.
27 https://www.youtube.com/watch?v=0r7mb4kj88w ‡ Archived 1st November, 2016

tion and liberalization of drugs by informing us to have the patriotic duty to disseminate such theories in the State, in the courts, in schools, in homes and businesses of America. They call it "Satanic Emancipation." That's why Satan has certainly found a comfortable home within the Democratic Party. If we look into the agenda of the Democratic Party today as formulated by it's current leadership, we must admit that evil is certainly running the show in that side of the political fence, and many of these battles for the so-called "Satanic Emancipation" are carried out regularly by the UN, that as I have shown you in Volume II, is a Satanic organization dedicated to a Neo-Theosophical agenda manipulated by the Jesuits.

"For too many,"—say Blackmore— *"religion has become an excuse to rule, to divide, to hate and destroy each other. The time has come for us to put aside our differences and realize that we have a common problem."*

Have you heard this recently? The same phrase is also found in a book that Pope Francis appoints and recommends often with great care, *The Master of the World*, by **Robert Hugh Benson** (1867 – 1914). The novel narrates the rise of a dark character, Felsenburgh (the antichrist), who comes to the world with political power through democratic elections, preaching humanitarianism, pacifism, tolerance, overcoming of nation states in order to impose a total control of the project through a new humanitarianism which completely dilutes the differences between religions—so to destroy them—and preaches of course universal tolerance, in the name of love. Faith, in short, should be abolished because it threatens to divide people, and calls instead for a mandatory brotherly love that can do without God. Sigh! A Catholic Church reduced to a pile of rubble, just as I have shown in my book *Pope Francis: The Last Pope?*

Robert Hugh Benson writes: *"'Oh! Once again we have a Savior!' Exclaimed Francis, a former priest who converted to the religion of the Antichrist—a Savior that you can see, praying face to face! It 's like a dream, too good to be believed."* [28] I ask myself, why does Bergoglio support this novel, and perhaps approve its contents? This is outrageous! *"Gender differences: whether religious, social, cultural rights are perceived as negative and the attempt is to achieve the unification, standardization, one might say, of the entire planet,"* admitted the Italian Bishop Luigi Negri in the Italian preface to *The Master of the World*, adding that this is: *"a massive system that brings people, social groups, nations, peoples, based on a fundamentally atheistic form of humanism, with references to common values that are deeply secularized Christian values."*

Returning to the Satanic ceremony, this is the announcement of a "New Era," the official announcement that the darkest period for humanity has already begun and it is just waiting to reveal its director. The fact that the exhibition took place in front of a public building, the temple of politics (and so with the consent of the authorities or at least a partial one), says a lot. But I am comforted by one certainty, they will not prevail!

Footage made on the 20th of January, 2017 during the national Women's March in Washington D.C, which spawned several demonstrations across the country financed by the infamous George Soros, showing a group of women wearing all black and holding the Satanic Temple sign. As they walked down the street, one member introduced herself to a reporter and briefly explained why she, along with the rest of the Satanic Temple members, are opposed to Trump. [29] "He's going to take most of our rights away. Not happy about that. We want to protect you," she said. [30] Well, we don't need their protection for sure, and now it seems clear as the light of the day that President Trump's enemies are also our enemies.

28 *Ibid.*
29 http://www.vibe.com/2017/01/satanists-atheists-protest-donald-trump/ ‡ Archived 23rd January, 2017.
30 https://www.youtube.com/watch?v=2Aa4LzpWbc8 ‡ Archived 23rd January, 2017.

Chapter III

Blood Lineages and Gnosticism

The DNA of the Illuminati

"*E*sotericism,"—wrote René Schwaller de Lubicz—"*is not a particular sense concealed in a text, but a state of fusion between the vital status of the player and the vital status of the author, in the sense of spiritual vision, spatial, synthetic, that disappears properly with the concretization of thought.*" The esoteric teaching is therefore a sort of "evocation" and can be only this. Initiation does not reside in the text we are studying, whatever it may be, but the "intelligence of the heart" by interpreting it. Nothing remains more "hidden" or "secret," even compared to the seemingly complex world of the Illuminati network. I am progressively introducing this information in this trilogy, which includes a fundamental role in the DNA of aristocracy, and is also the DNA that guides the leaders of the most influential Illuminati sects in history, and the chivalrous and Masonic institutions controlled by them. My old friend and film director, the researcher Varo Venturi, himself an aristocrat from the Piccolomini family, includes in the preface of the book of Ricccardo Tristano Tuis dedicated to the **Black Aristocracy**, and writes: "*By using the filter of scientific biochemistry and genetic engineering, if we put ourselves in the shoes of those who want to, or must colonize an entire planet and its humanity, one of the main steps would interconnect with the ruling aristocracy, implying primarily in the DNA. So in the history of the complex genealogy of the nobility, which highlights the well-known inbreeding of royal families, you can see how from a certain point, the infiltration of another DNA takes place. The modern conspiracy theorists would remind us immediately that this was done under the aquisite financial capacity by the Ashkenazi Jews, giving the opportunity to the most wealthy tribes from this strain, to lend substance to the aristocracy for some reason in ruins, (often orchestrated in a certain way, as demonstrated by the French revolution and the Russian one), and through the negotiation of huge debts with the union of one of its own members, and a scion of the various families of the nobility. Sure not a noble way to conduct things, but most likely there is another intention that goes beyond the mere interests of political economic power. This process would have led to the current genetic condition of House of Windsor, which brought together all ruling aristocracies from the Eurasian region (from Egyptian Pharaohs to Genghis Khan so to speak starting from deities and mythologi-*

Alexandre de Dánann

Mémoire du sang

"contre-initiation", culte des ancêtres
sang, os, cendres
palingénésie

ARCHÈ
MILANO
1990

FIG. 57 – Cover of the book of Alexandre de Danann, Mémoire du sang. "Contre-initiation," culte des ancêtres, sang, os, cendres, palingénésie.

cal characters), where both William and Kate's families have in their recent family lineage, the Red Shield of the Rothschilds, the most powerful family of the Ashkenazi Jews, in this case represented by the Roche family." (Author's Note: An authoritative source noted how Diana's mother Frances Ruth Burke Roche, was possibly part of the Rothschild family.) "*Jewish presence is strong both in the maternal line of Lady Diana—she was perhaps 100% Jewish, if the rumors of her father being the banker Goldsmith are real—and the mother of Kate.* (A/N: Also a Goldsmith related ro the Rothschild.) *While playing stupid* about *the Jewish law the woman transmits and imposes 100% the 'Jewish' gene, this leads to the evidence that George Philip Alexander, the result of two parents from 50% by the same family, carries a overwhelming increase of that DNA. Now it will be enough for the future King of England to marry another representative of the Jewish family and 'bingo!' ... One wonders if the reflection of this genetic strategy could better explain why recently the U.S. has imposed that the white race is termed 'Caucasian.' Anyway, back to the real spouses, when the family trees in question will be of public domain, the world could officially welcome the 'Rothschild Royal Family.'*"[1]

The eliterian Varo Venturi says that the aristocracy DNA is "a more informed DNA" and describes it this way: "*DNA is more informed when transported by individuals who have had access to different and 'high-level' information, political, cultural, military, scientific, etc.; a 'database' that is handed down and enriched after falling downwards. And for representatives of the nobility, it was possible to write in the genes the largest and specific amounts of information. Because if we see the integral family tree of certain aristocratic families, they even claim to descend from the gods, those are the 'first' destined to rule the world, to influence humanity. Developing within an environment of power, which will always be overwhelming on any other human circle, because it is nourished generation after generation, because it has always more 'glory' than anyone else can claim, because it descends from the Kings, from the princes, because from the very begin-*

1   1 Malachi Martin, *Windswepthouse,* (New York: Broadway Books, 2001), p. 493.

ning they had territories, that can only be taken by individuals, or families of the same power, so they can be handed to their offspring. Basically they had sense of what Aristotle theorized, a government of aristocrats, is a government of beings with more information, so more suitable, ready to face any high-level situation, because in the genes they may have even data from medieval leaders, who not only commanded armies because of rank, but they fought bravely on the battlefield, ready to die, drawn into the glory of immortalizing their name for posterity. In the DNA of the nobles there is also this: the blood, the dust, swords, terror, violent death, oppression, hardness and the fragility of the matter."[2]

Alexandre de Danann, who is the "pen name" of a duo of Italian researchers working in the field of esoteric societies called **Alessandro Boella and Antonella Galli,** are authors and editors of numerous works in both the French and Italian languages, who have dedicated their lives to the study of esotericism as a "spiritual aspect of the world" and the authors of the excellent book ***Mémoire du Sang "Contre-initiation," culte des ancêtres, He sang, os, cendres, palingénésie,***[3] (FIG. 57) where they show the biblical origins of **counter-initiation,** and the dark side of what I call the Illuminati sectarian network, originally born from the union of humanity, with the fallen angels. So on the one hand the emergence of lineages whose "special" bloodline preserves the memory of the elite via the ancient cults like the one of the ancestors; on the other, the dispatch made by the rebel angels, of certain knowledge regarding blood, in the broadest sense of the term. These lineages who refused and still refuse the traditional interpretation of the redemption and the doctrine of Christ, use the operational tools of evil, and counter-initiation on the dark side, to promote their agenda during the course of human history. However, the fading away of "blood memory" with the passage of the centuries, these lineages emerged from their traditional field, to offer to other individuals judged worthy, knowledge that aims to "deify" luciferically, mankind. It was important then, to integrate them with methods such as the blood pact, certain *"palingenesis"* made of bones and ashes, the use of human seed, the "marriage" with the elementary spirits, etc. I want to point out that the text of "Alexandre de Danann" is based on documentation from sources most rare or unpublished, and is a text studied in the context of the studies carried out by members of the *Ordo Illuminatorum Universalis,* so it is an important book, although little known, followed by various schools of contemporary Illuminati. In the book, *Memoire du Sang,* whose underlying theology is Christian, and Christian esoteric (or even pseudo-gnostic) there is a revealed truth, that the reader can trace, and in the same Bible, in particular chapter VI of *Genesis.* This truth, in essence, says that in ancient times, the angels who sided with Lucifer, after being defeated by the Angels of the Lord, came down to Earth and joined sexually, in the form of incubus, with women. From this **psychic union,** but no less effective, were born races of Heroes and Giants—the martyr Giustino did not hesitate to identify them as demons—of which we have a memory in pagan mythologies.

Although it is not explicitly told, the authors seem to understand that the chosen people are the only ones that were created by God, while other breeds descend directly from these semi-human beings, children of the fallen angels, here is the point I don't totally agree on, but I will focus on it in my next book *The Invisible Master.*

To put an end, later, to the disproportion between the two lineages, de Danann writes that the Savior, through Baptism, was allowed to heal the imbalance that had arisen. This is the last and final goal, Christian evangelization, according to a vision in vogue in cer-

2 *Ibid.,* pp. 15-16.
3 See. Alexandre de Dánann, *Mémoire du Sang "Contre-initiation," culte des ancêtres, sang, os, cendres, palingénésie,* (Milan, IT: Arché, 1990).

tain Christian circles. However, it seems that by mating with Earth women, these angels transmitted all their magical knowledge, but also "every kind of turpitude." What's more, apparently because of women, mankind is haunted by demons and the spread and exercise of magical arts. Because, according to the mentioned literary sources, these fallen angels were sentenced to remain on Earth (including its astral sphere) until the end of time. They also have visible dwelling in seven key points, partially identified, with the specific purpose to damn humanity. Do not forget that the reason for the rebellion of Lucifer was because he refused to bow down in front of Adam, made in the image and likeness of God. From these **seven key points**, Rene Guenon imagines a semicircle around Europe, and it is no accident that from here, all the religions and magical currents would spread, according to some traditionalist speculations, that aim to stop the correct understanding of spiritual realities, including the correct part of the teaching taught by the Catholic Church. However, the tip of the Luciferian offensive diamond is embodied by those human beings more or less indirect descendants of those ancient semi-divine and semi-human beings, who were the Giants and Heroes, and the children of women.

This offensive by the dark side of the Illuminati is produced through knowledge of the magical arts, and in particular, **Blood Magic—bone and semen [4] which as you know from "Spirit Cooking" is in vogue with the dark Illuminati sects. [5]** By the above biblical passages, we can draw palpable certainty to consider the fall of the angels on Earth as the explanation for the origin of evil in the world. After making broad dissertations of the most diverse Jewish and Christian sources, to the comfort of this "historic" event, the authors of *Memoire du Sang* come to clarify that these angels incarnate, these demons aim, from those remote times up to today, to combat and disrupt everything that represents the correct way of life, and the true conception of spiritual realities, with the sad epilogue to destroy man in his own psycho-physical harmony. Until not long ago, this infernal program would be carried out by the so-called **"bloodlines," that is, the elite families who have over the centuries maintained close communion of intents and purposes, through the celebration of certain rites, originally transmitted down to them, by the founder of the demon dynasty.**

The author identifies these families with the ruling elite of the ancient world, those who I have spoken about since the first volume of my *Confessions,* and to which I am also personally connected. The ones that have preserved their crypto-demonic origin through royal and aristocratic bloodlines, connected among themselves, and later mixing with the modern lineages of the industrial and financial elite, the ones that people often generalize without distinction and call them "the Illuminati," basically the proponents of this New World Order, that is in fact an "Old World Order." However, because of the difficulty in celebrating exactly, the rituals that connect the first male offspring with the parent, difficulties led over time, to the depletion of the same lineage, as the rite poorly executed would have the affect of severing the "link," these fallen angels, who rush for cover to find a solution, making sure that among the surviving lineages a few individual personalities were able to incarnate and/or evoke them (types as **Cagliostro, Saint Germain** or **Aleister Crowley**), who spread throughout the world, all sorts of magical practices (especially the ideas of "free thinking"), in order to annihilate, as their purpose, the human lineage. Indeed Alessandro Boella, and Antonella Galli, remind us in their book, that according to ancient Jewish tradition the angels in question rebelled against God when he wanted them to serve and revere Adam, who he made in his exclusive image. All the action of harmful sub-standard angels condense into **envy, which is the root of many evils.**

These lineages, holders of a particular bloodline inherited from an ancient pact with such angels, recreated or awakened secret societies, mystery schools, and sects, through the intermediary of certain individuals specially equipped. We could consider these individuals as a particular kind of "possessed" persons, who are loaded with the necessary powers, as were figures like **Martines Pasqualis (1727 – 1774)** advocate of **Martinism (the Elus Cohens),** or Giuseppe Balsamo, aka Count Cagliostro who founded the **Egyptian Rite** of Freemasonry, who with their powers, resulted in phenomena ranging to form the catalyst element around which such groups were formed. But today, we don't have the well-defined groups or charismatic occult individuals of the past, instead we have a whole myriad of schools of thought and action (indeed, almost all of them with impersonal impulses), that are numerous in number and dangerous in their path, forming what is the current network of the Illuminati, that now after my trilogy I hope will be more identifiable because of my publications devoted to this unusual subject. Throughout the book *Memoire du Sang,* they describe for the first time with historical proof and references, the DNA of the Illuminati from an esoteric point of view. The authors are relying on a Judeo-Christian point of view, but show the most controversial side of "counter-initiation" and / or "pseudo-initiation." These realities related to the dark side, are said to exist in parallel with the destructive forces of the truly divine and spiritual forces, that are opposing these lineages of evil since ancient times, and it is from these subjects that I continue recruiting new members every day for the *Ordo Illuminatorum Universalis.* They are working with genuine initiatic forces, that all over the world, under different names and secret organizations, are opposed to the evil takeover of this Satanic age, and driving human beings towards a true spiritual ascension. We are still far from the mystic asceticism of certain characters of the Middle Ages, or a certain **"Brethren of the Free Spirit,"** always misinterpreted and persecuted by the official Apostolic Succession of the Catholic Church. However, in chilvary by the most "Sacred" sense of the term: *"We find on the contrary"*—writes Boella Alessandro and Antonella Galli, a.k.a. Alexandre de Dánann—*"an example of traditional lineage, especially in certain medieval chivalry in particular that of the Grail tradition. For the intermediation of the chivalric initiation rite, then, of a divine covenant, the quality of a lineage is transformed, transfigured: the rider was given the means to sublimate and make ethereal his own blood, thus highlighting the highest quality and spiritual ancestry."* They then add: *"The knight who embarks on a heroic way of purification and is ready to shed his blood, for a liter of blood from a knight equals a thousand liters of blood from poor people, so to eliminate the original sin, with the content of his blood which is common to all men."* [6]

In practice, there is still linked to the Bible, a description of the serpent of Genesis that could not be other than a downgraded angel, if not Lucifer himself, which for "Alexandre de Dánann" passed on to humans through the turmoil of original sin, his legacy, because he would be psychically present in the blood of all of us. This ferment or gluten, is what the "counter-initiates"—that is, all those who deal with black magic without believing in countless warnings from my books—try in every way to revive, as the blood would be one of the ways through which they can implement contact with demons or entities, or better yet "alien beings," to use a more current term. Eric Gajewski a well-known traditional Catholic blogger writes:

6   Alexandre de Dánann, *Ibid.*

Pope John 23rd was supposedly aware of the "aliens" (they are demons) during his time and was the first to lay down the hammer on Catholics resisting any potential new changes in the Church. Catholics forever would be seen as "prophets of doom" or fundamentalists or Pharisees (take your choice). Even the verbiage had to change from Rome in relation to that, which was once believed because they themselves have been changing. [7]

In order for the masses to ultimately embrace this new tower of babel, that is everything in the Catholic Church that runs the New World Order under a Jesuit Pope, had to be gutted and changed, by the Vatican 2 Council, including the philosophy, the theology, the Orwellian new verbiage and of course the liturgy. Fr. Malachi Martin warned we are entering a New Age. They have existed since biblical times, and would have been also related to Jesus' bloodline that for some, wound up in France, and spread throughout Europe, in various aristocratic dynasties antagonizing, those of pagan derivation. It goes without saying that this thesis, as great as it sounds, is absolutely not accepted by the Church, but in the end has a strange variation of the official verison of the event, considered almost Sacred by nobility, which is why this is an issue of primary importance to the real Illuminati, which I will introduce in this book, as I'd like now to stress its importance. The operating mode with which the members of the "deviant lineages," and all evocative magic lovers in the various sects of the Illuminati, is the maintained contact with their arch-demonic entities since prehistoric times, with the use of the ritual human blood sacrifices, the bones of the ancestors or their ashes, and finally, the magic techniques of the palingenetic and avataric sphere, that use sperm and menstrual blood in their practices, even using urine and feces, as you can read in the secret documents of Aleister Crowley, and his disciples from the O.T.O.; or in the Illuminati group headed by the Italian **Giuliano Kremmerz, pseudonym of Ciro Formisano (1861 – 1930),** as well as **Georges Le Clément de Saint-Marcq** in his *Eucharist,* and in some tantric texts of witchcraft. Polytheistic religions, the magical doctrines, and esoteric cults, have done nothing but "nurture" the human psyche and the planet; more for ill than for good, as the psychic art of magic was revealed by downgraded angels, or rather substandard aliens. The incarnation of Christ and his earthly life have allowed man, only from that moment, to escape the evil aura of the Earth, and look towards more transcendental dimensions. All those who do not recognize the cosmic and salvific role played by Christ—and the truth contained in the traditional Judeo-Christian texts—automatically side with evil and often flounder in low level psychic activities, believing they are rising in authentic spiritual dimensions, but instead, often end up supporting the downgraded angels and their "New Age." However, there is also angelic possession, not only demonic, which occurs when an initiate is attracted into the sphere of influence of an archangel, or a holy person, or a saint, that brings select people to serve at great sacrifice, sometimes with their martyrdom to the forces of good, in this eternal struggle with evil. On the one hand, man and the true initiates of light are working for other planes of existence (naturally pure and spiritual), and on the other hand there are those who follow the dark side, that binds man to his earthly existence.

For the Illuminati and the different initiatic schools, at the moment of death, the human component breaks down and dissolves into the vortex of the elements, unless man is able to maintain their conscience and memory (perhaps most importantly the latter), above the body, and able to maintain, a *ligament dei vincula, as* **Giordano Bruno** would have called it, with the world of tangible forms. According to Dr. Henri Favre, the Roman tradition guaranteed this with the cult of the **Manes, Lares, and Penates, that**

7   http://tradcatknight.blogspot.it/2016/11/fr-malachi-martin-we-are-entering-new.html#more ‡ Archived 5th November, 2016.

are obviously all demonic deities. When a being dies, this "dries" and does not disintegrate if his relics are well-preserved, and he can be revitalized with appropriate libations (blood, semen etc.). Ancient Romans were accused of wallowing in this kind of practice, that, in reality, reconnected them to their demons and entities, which have always been linked to the elite. After the Christianization of the Roman Empire, these "pagan" practices survived in the patrician families and, secretly, in secret traditions of many European noble lineages, up to this current day.

That's why this is one of the secrets never revealed, and the object so jealously guarded by the elite. So, to this day, the worship of demons, indeed, their livelihood, still happily survive among us, thanks to the Millennial network consisting of the multiple sects of the Illuminati network. These practices have actually occurred and have continued to exist in their purest form, only in several noble strains because, at the social and popular level, the Christian religion prevented the masses that performed them almost every day. If not, even the common man would have continued practicing them. The passing practice, down the family tree, was once a common tradition, and not a dark and forbidden one. In fact, in ancient times, the whole thing took place in broad daylight, and these age-old practices were common, even among the elite, much more conscious of how the world really worked. Of course, times have changed, and now the common man believes that all this is a fairytale, and such traditions are simply superstition, now that he is immersed more than ever, in ignorance and materialism. This is increasingly present amongst the slaves of the system, the sheeple, while the elite of the Illuminati secretly continue to maintain such traditions, granting them the superiority of their psychic energy, and control over the ignorant masses. Well wake up and smell the coffee my dear readers, as time is running out. The manipulation of psychic energies, of whatever nature they may be, is in fact considered essential by the elite in power, for they conduct them not only for their daily lives, but also for the creation of conditions of survival, and for a possible immortality card, that some of them try to play even as they are still alive in this life.

Transmigrating their soul in another body in the last period of their existence, is a complex concept known and practiced in India for thousands of years. It was later embraced and expanded by the western Illuminati, in particular, the already mentioned Kremmerz. Technically, the condensation and manipulation of psychic energies by the Illuminati is done through the scent of blood and other materials, which attracts these energies mixing them with thicker psychic emanations from the operator or the bystanders. The result is a regenerating aerial energy called **pneuma** dear to the Gnostics, which we could compare, with the necessary distinctions, to what they called in the east **avatars.**

A key characteristic of theological thought is in the Gnostic tradition, the dualism between the God of Light and the God of Darkness, between God, that in itself is inaccessible and unknowable, and man. Creation is an event created by the God of Darkness, or lower powers somehow emanated from God, called Archons or Aeons, whose seat is in the heavens. For the Gnostics, man is composed of three elements, **a divine spark that is mostly pneuma or spirit,** subtracted in some way to God by the Archons, and locked in earthly prison, while the other two components are the psyche and the body. We were created by the Archons to prevent the pneuma to recognize themselves as belonging to this world; the psyche in particular is an aggregate of passions arising from each one of the archonics skies. The pneuma, in the world is obscured by the veil of the psyche and the body, so men are ignorant of their true origin, and to free themselves from the chains of matter require the knowledge of its true origin, and this knowledge is *gnosis*. Based on this division of the human being, the Gnostics distinguished man into three categories: **the hylic, the psychic and the pneumatic,** i.e. the Gnostics themselves as keepers of the fullness of the pneuma. The first ones are the individual materials, in which the divine spark is perhaps part of. They make up the vast majority of humanity: they are narrow-minded, indolent, incompetent, lazy, indifferent, treacherous, envious, greedy, slaves, always devoted to materialistic pleasures.

The psychic man are those who are torn between the lure of the world, and need to attain knowledge to raise their spirit—often these people need to be stimulated so that the spark which glimmers in them becomes a flame that illuminates the darkness of ignorance. The psychic man, while not forgetting pleasures, relish in it. They fail to discern the invisible side in corporeality, and vice versa. Finally, the pneumatics are the masters and the initiates. In traditional Christianity, pneuma translates to the Hebrew word חור **spirit** ("ruah"), the name of the female gender that means wind and breath. Christian theology then will use the term pneuma to indicate the "Holy Spirit" which in Hebrew is named **חור שדוקה**, "**the Ruach HaKodesh.**" When we wonder why the world, despite the flamboyant proclamations of "scientists" and "politicians," is now close to self-destruction, we need to reflect on who has almost always decided on the fate of the people, the vulgar foolish and ignorant slaves unconsciously subservient to the elites, who never really wanted, or could rebel. We return to the theme of "the Platonic cave" that I mentioned in the Introduction. From my point of view, the elite of today, and the so-called "Iluminati," even if this term is only partially correct, are more than ever, slave to counter initiation, black magicians, and real inductors to what is literaly a collective mass suicide—as they instill in the minds of the people living on this planet the idea, that their false "spirituality" is the true way, which is nothing more than a bunch of ruminations, without support to reality. The origin of all this is unfortunately to be found in organized religion, that has always been misguided for geopolitical and military purposes, and has nothing to do with real spirituality, or the genuine teachings of the mystery schools of the truly enlightened, infiltrated and corrupted from within by the Satanic forces.

How does the dark side of the "Illuminati" keep in touch with the fallen angels and their demonic powers?

Mainly through an altered state of consciousness, which allows them to establish contact between their astral body and that of the world. It is clear that in this way, the conscience, freed from the bonds of their opaque embodiment, acquires those psychic powers which are the only means to establish the *ligamen*. Mind you, that great Master and teacher called Rene Guenon, distinguished the psychic powers and the world of the spirits. Such psychic powers often derived by the possession of demons, on the human personality, that with such practices, have opened their inner doors, so not an angelic force, but a demonic one, is helping them. It's the same explanation that the Church has always made, about miracles made by the Saints, and the already discussed Blessed Virgin Mary, where the miracles of God are performed through an intercession. This explains exoterically an esoteric truth. To achieve these powers, in addition, we must undergo a placement that is analogous to the schemes of traditional purifiers and religious initiations—with the important difference, that this purification, capable of separating the fine from the coarse consciousness, is purely instrumental. That is, there is a true Ascended Evil working for Evil. When you read, here and there, of practices that allow the development of supposed "astral travel," that is precisely the separation of the subtle consciousness from the body, we must keep in mind that this is the best way to end up possessed by these damn demons, that will never leave us in peace. These are practices used by some Orders of the Illuminati network, and mystery schools linked to the teachings of Aleister Crowley, or the aforementioned Kremmerz.

Marco Massai, a black magician and leading figure of the dark side of the Illuminati operating in Florence, in recent decades, in a mysterious booklet distributed amongst his followers, describes what is actually the exact repetition of the ancient pagan sexual practices writing: *"But if the individual could largely find in this world the way for perpetual happiness, wouldn't he try to endure the abandonment to the delights of the flesh for a continuation of this status for as long as possible? You would prefer to have at that point an evolution of MATTER instead of the one of the SPIRIT, giving to each his new and desired incarnation, choosing the circumstances in which to be born? This is possible and has been done by many people, who like to REIGN on the delights of this land rather than face a new spiritual dimension or the unknown."*

These godless ideals are already typical of the Babylonians (hence the famous saying *Babylon the great harlot*) and the Assyrians, whose religions centered on the interest for life and its continuation. At the moment of death, with all the memories and all the baggage of experiences made in the world, he focuses on the pneuma, the breath that survives bodily death. Various sects of pseudo Illuminati, improperly defined Gnostic as the *Ordo Templi Orientis,* teach their members at the higher levels, the practice of eating the menstrual blood and semen during dark magic practices, when, at the height of some of these rituals they blasphemously recite the phrase: **"We know the Truth and his God."** They are fools who do not realize they are owned by the fallen angels, the **Nephilim!** This possession is evident even today in what is undoubtedly the most bizarre Wikileaks revelation that surfaced during the 2016 U.S. elections, where the Hillary Clinton campaign chairman John Podesta was invited to a "spirit cooking dinner" featuring menstrual blood, semen, urine and breast milk, by Satanic performance artist **Marina Abramovic**. Podesta was invited to basically take part in an occult ritual the media said was inspired by Aleister Crowley. During their sex cult practice, "Spirit Cooking" includes chanting the following: *"With a sharp knife cut deeply into the middle finger of your left hand, eat the pain."*

So Clinton's inner circle includes child traffickers, pedophiles, and of course members of the usual elitist "sex cult," and the Podesta emails revealed from Wikileaks are pretty clear on the matter. Marina Abramovic says to Podesta's brother Tony: *"I am so looking forward to the Spirit Cooking dinner at my place. Do you think you will be able to let me know if your brother is joining? All my love, Marina -- ABRAMOVIC LLC."*[8]

It is no wonder Marina Abramovic was mentioned as a top contemporary artist in HBO's anti-Christian TV series *The Young Pope*. In hard core Crowleyan, and other types of deviant Illuminati organizations where such practices are encouraged, you can see practitioners change their human name with that of a demonic entity. I wonder what Hillary's demonic name is? However, the Italian Illuminati Ciro Formisano, became Giuliano Kremmerz, on the basis of a complex astrological calculation of Chaldean origin, that sees the origin of the incarnation of the soul, not in the time of delivery, but in that of conception. Of course the entity in question sucks all the life force, advising him to devote himself to unnerving sexual practices, including masturbation sacred to the *Ordo Templi Orientis,* an obligatory practice for members of the eighth degree. Once the person has been used and worn out, the entity changes lodging and finds another of these unfortunates, perpetuating its own existence over the centuries. And to think that it is man himself who welcomes voluntarily this scourge, is truly unbelieveble. For God has not given Lucifer the power to enter freely in people—but these occult practitioners like the ones from the Clinton entourage, often offer their cum to these demons, jerking off and viewing their demonic seals as I also mentioned in Volume I. But what I have not told you earlier is that depending on the

FIG. 58 – **Tantra Magick** book published in India in 1992 where you will find the first three sets of instructions for the Tantric group AMOOKOS (the Arcane and Magickal Order of the Knights of Shambhala).

"purity" reached by these Illuminati seekers in refining their sperm, with a complex alchemical process, they are later able to attract more and more powerful entities. In fact, in their own ungodly doctrines, sperm maintains the imprint produced by the brain; so if while masturbating they meditate on the seal of **Lilith** or **Astaroth,** this sperm will be the catalyst and then draw these entities—where somehow there will be a kind of astral conception—which must then be fed until it is developing with his own blood or with the menstrual one of a partner. So man—for these particular Illuminati beliefs—is a kind of astral androgyn, able even without a woman, to create the shapes that then will return to act in the bodily sphere. They argue that there is a close connection, as we just said, between consciousness and semen.

Where are the historical and geographical origins of these strange doctrines and practices of witchcraft used by the Illuminati?

One part of such tradition comes from **Kurdistan,** where there are influences of Egyptian-Atlantean origin. From Kurdistan these doctrines descended into the Chaldean world, influencing Iran, and spreading into Syria and later returning to Egypt, and then Alexandria, where the various mystery schools related to the Illuminati had their most important base in ancient times. Orphism, which created the hermetic ferment that went on to influence the whole of Europe in the following centuries, and it is here that the demonic intercourse with Platonism took place. I'm not going to delve deeper into this, but even in Asia such doctrines were already widely attested, just think of Tantra and Taoism. A prevalent idea amongst contemporary Illuminati including the O.T.O. is that the development of the origins of shamanism and Tantra come precisely from the area of the Gobi Desert. In some documents of the dangerous **AMOOKOS sect** (FIG. 58) of which I wrote of in detail in Volume II[9], speak of satellite photos which prove the existence of a civilization in the Gobi desert whose epicenter was in the **Ananda Valley,** but since it would be too expensive to make the excavations in the desert to receive confirmation of this, the mystery remains. Instead, what I would like to point out is the prevailing opinion in the various schools of the Illuminati, the divine light is in the sperm (actually just a spark is contained), and man can manipulate this light as he likes, to create one form or another. This is obviously a heresy, as unclean man should never touch the work of God. Man has no right to manipulate life, nor the means to employ the knowledge of demons, like some of the latest scientific discoveries, including the progress of the deviant side of the Illuminati elite in the dangerous realm of nuclear power and nuclear weapons that could unfortunately end our civilization. Now we even have an advanced Russian nuclear missile called **"Satan 2"** and an English tabloid, *The Sun* reported in the Fall of 2016, that: *"RUSSIA'S 'Satan 2' warhead is the world's most advanced nuclear missile and is reportedly capable of destroying the UK in one swoop. The 40-megaton nuke will replace Vladimir Putin's Soviet-era Satan missiles which can already carry payloads 1,000 times more powerful than those used on Japan at the end of WWII. It has been reported the weapon could even wipe out the vast state of Texas in the U.S. – an area twice the size of Britain. But what would actually happen if tensions with Moscow spilled over into atomic armageddon?"*

There is a strong relationship between semen and the astral world, underlined in numerous references ranging from Aristotle to Gurdjieff, but we must reiterate that the astral is a perishable part of the human being, and therefore is too controversial to make any theurgical work and attempt to achieve immortality with a human body. Yet this is the firm conviction of initiatory and traditional schools working on the dark side of the Illuminati. In the higher degrees the disciple must assume the sperm of the teacher, since this substance also conveys the power that will act in the neophyte fermenting the corruption of his moral and spiritual ways. Just think of the so-called **"Cake of Light,"** the eucharistic host found within Thelema, the religion founded by author and occultist Aleister Crowley in 1904. [10] This is also attested in the Tantric Lamaist and initiations, however sperm manipulated alchemically, as I mentioned earlier, and as is done in some sects of these Illuminati sects, like the one headed by Hillary Clinton's supporter Marina Abramović (even if she likes to disguise her work into the convenient realm of "performance art"), plays a central role into these dark practices. The mysterious author **Senciner** writes the following critical to such practice:

*The occult practitioners purify the sperm through a series of ingestions in order to eliminate from it the so-called "spirit of the forms" and make it "essential," that is, devoid of specifications and ready to undergo the astral coverings operated by the **tinctura solis**, the power creator of the mind. Then this sperm, or mercury in alchemical terms, is made dynamic uniting the red egg of a pigeon and nourished with menstrual blood. These are the same theories of some pseudo-Gnostics and their aberrant practices with menstrual blood and semen that they say contain the soul of man, so that if they are harvested and eaten at the source, such substances can grow and regenerate man. This was done in the usual ways I have already mentioned in conjunction with special breathing techniques. Of course, for all of them, their evil seeds must be first expelled from their bodies, since it is only following the altered state (called **Mag**) produced by an orgasm where the mind can engrave its will in this substance and what they call **Logos spermatikos**. Also they claim to have within themselves a potential androgenic state, that would be in place during their unseemly practices, when, copulating with themselves and with their own hands, separate their perception of the erotic act, in a sentient part and an embossing and debossing part . This is false because by the time of the creation of Eve, this possibility was no longer granted to man—even if there are those who argue that she was literally created with such practice as was the very substance of Adam. These deviant masturbation and sperm eating practices have been symbolized by the ancient*

10   https://en.wikipedia.org/wiki/Cake_of_Light ‡ Archived 5th November, 2016.

idolaters with myths of Cronus swallowing their children (i.e. their ejaculation) and of the Egyptian god Set.

The abomination of these doctrines is evident, and above all, this Luciferian willingness to go against the will of God is clear. What kind of impulses drive them to want to postpone the terms granted by God to human life? They want to recall from their sleep, the astral bodies of the dead, or artificially bring back the astral body of their masters with unclean sexual practices, using a specific kind of priestess devoted to demons and orgies, burning their semen and blood in the process. I dare to point out to the readers, these are not the mere practices of some pseudo-initiates, but I am indicating to you the very essence of the counter tradition and perversion that in Europe is embodied by the **Osiridean Egyptian Orient** of Giuliano Kremmerz, that I described in Volume I, and in the U.S. by the *Ordo Templi Orientis,* founded in the same period by Theodor Reuss and Carl Kerner, later highjacked by **Aleister Crowley**, representing the diabolic gathering of those who are controlled and work for the fallen angels.

Initiates on the dark side of the force

The black magicians of the various sects of the Illuminati are the true and only descendants of the servants of the fallen angels, those who have entered into a diabolic pact since the dawn of time. The purpose of the Illuminati sects that I have introduced in this trilogy since Volume I, is to return to this dimension simply to serve the fallen angels. For the purpose of re-establishing the kingdom of darkness, of which all sacred texts speak of extensively, to coincide with the full institutional arrangements of the New World Order. As I told you in the first pages of Volume I, the *Agape-Prometheus Group* [11] finally unmasked the existence of the mysterious Illuminati inner circle called **Osiridean Egyptian Orient,** making known to the world the real covert purposes of the Kremmerzian tradition, based on the secret teachings of the Illuminati **Ciro Formisano aka Kremmerz.** This gesture is certainly important, given the worsening of the international situation that has occurred in recent years, that saw thanks to the spread of the internet, further accelerating in the occult field among Crowleyan orders, obviously much more popular, and the more elitarian Kremmerzian schools. Paolo Fogagnolo, ex Red Brigade terrorist turned occultist, began in his introduction to the first three books of the *Corpus* of Giuliano Kremmerz, stating that *"some of these realities, have brought their wealth of occult knowledge to the various O.T.O. groups, scattered around the world, particularly in France and America."*

This is important to clarify and help the many who naively, superficially and erroneously practice esotericism and magic, often believing to reach illumination, when in reality they only enslave themselves to dark uncontrollable forces. I advise my readers to never practice such rituals involving magical seals and obscure teachings that sometimes, if not fully understood, could be dangerous in the wrong hands. For this type of occult teaching there is already an extensive occult publishing reality, that is usually controlled by the most influential secret societies and the so-called "Occult side" of Freemasonry. But what is worse, is that these secret practices, so far only known by a restricted circle of persons, are now being spread by the internet, to the four corners of the globe, and anyone can abuse such practices. The truth is, that with the dissolution of the Order of the Templars, the Western world actually broke ties with the last remains of a genuine initiatic system. This point was also reiterated by Rene Guenon, as I mentioned to you at the beginning of this book. Since that time they have made their appearance on the

---

11   *Confessions of an Illuminati Vol. I,* pp. 15-16.

scene to be a myriad of counter-initiatic organizations, **pseudo-Rosicrucians, wannabe Knights Templar, pseudo-Freemasons, deflected orders, etc.,** With them, we receive a corollary of new arguments into the equation, that have nothing to do with pure metaphysics or true illumination, but only with the manipulation of power and dishonesty, a world with no ethics and culture that we see in their present representatives, that lead astray their followers. These villains manipulated by the occult elite, have had in reality the task of overthrowing the social field, destroying real initiation in favor of groups of pseudo Illuminati that have nothing to do with the true tradition, rather the reverse, like for example, the *Ordo Templi Orientis*. To do so they were forced to conceal these eminently political projects that have become more evident in recent years, behind the veil of the preservation of a fictional and incommunicable secret. The political project of the dark side, continues to this day, as we all saw during the Wikileaks revelations on Hillary Clinton, made before the U.S. elections of 2016, with ninety percent of the work for the establishment of the New World Order is in place. What is next, if not a global market collapse, of this surreal and dramatic farse we call the New World Order?

Looking back we can see how many so-called martyrs of free thought roasted at the stake or persecuted by the Church, were actually exponents of certain initiatic societies such as Giordano Bruno, who was tied to the Rosicrucians, a group that was infiltrated, and deflected later from its original purpose, in which politicians and black magicians and various Jesuit intriguers, work to control the revelations made in those famous **Rosicrucian Manifestos**: *Fama Fraternitatis* and *Confessio Fraternitatis*, a product of the anti-Catholic Protestant world, that ended up succumbing and serving the usual Company of Jesus and the infamous Jesuits. They became secret authors of pseudo-initiatic literature, where it is claimed that man should be able to initiate himself with his own strength, a Promethean way of seeing things initially promoted by figures like Baron Munchausen. The most striking example we have perhaps, is with Abbot **Montfaucon de Villars,** who wrote the famous *Count of Gabali*. In this book (which I will return to in *The Invisible Master*), there is the theoretical justification for the demonic and anti-traditional practices which deal with the famous "marriage" between the entities of the psychic sphere, or if we want to use a more current term, the alien and extradimensional sphere with man.

Now, the requirement (covenant) of this crypto-demonic marriage to the alien entity consists of the waiver, by man, of sexual intercourse with women, because these secret practices require to nourish the entity in question with your own orgasmic vitality and the erotic activity of your brain—taking often the form (also tangibly) of a beautiful woman. Those who betray this secret pact with the entity are put to death, and amongst both Kremmerzians or Crowleyian practitioners in their secret teachings, there are warnings concerning the threat of dying from "exhaustion" if they are in violation of this secret union. A similar relationship with the entities is also created within the animist culture, especially in Africa, where if one marries to such entities they should dedicate at least one day a week, or suffer the immediate penalty of death, if you miss your appointment.

Abbot de Villars was later assassinated it is believed, for precisely disclosing this secret, even in its most intimate meanings. Returning to the mode of union with the elemental entities, it also cites the possibility that he might, however, have a regular sexual relationship with another human being as long as the practitioner pictures or displays in his brain the symbolic form (such as a seal) of the entity with which they are uniting. The latter can also intervene directly in their mental sphere when it has already established a close relationship. It remains to specify that for the sorcerers of the Illuminati, what in hermetism is defined as the **Androgynous** state, is obtained by absorbing in oneself the qualities of the opposite sex. This is a typical Luciferian deviation, not the real tradition.

In fact, androgynous archetype comes from the need to combine the ability to generate (feminine principle) and to fertilize (male principle); and despite the Bible, affirms that God's creation was made exclusively using his word, and after the eighth pronunciation made with the creative word (and "God said," in the first chapter of Genesis), can not but reveal its double nature—of which man was created "in the image and likeness"—masculine and feminine at the same time. Numerous other mythological traditions take on an identical conception of the dualism in the divinity, as the Egyptian tradition, and most of Eastern tradition, that are all born from a gesture of the primordial god. Hapi, the god of the Nile, in whose waters lie the fertilizing of fire, is portrayed as a fat man with breasts; Mut, the great mother, has a set of male and female sexual organs, in representation of nature and is connected to what, in Greek mythology, is known as Cybele. The two deities, however, were generated by a primordial sun god who, *motu proprio,* creates the Ennead, which owns, among others, Geb and Nut (heaven and earth) and Osiris and Isis (sun and moon). The issue of coexistence of opposites in the divine dimension is not insignificant.

Luciferian power of the fallen angels is in fact engraved in women, such as in the character of **Lilith,** which is one of its most important aspects, suggesting woman is equal to man. Not by chance, that great initiate and illuminati called **Gustav Meyrink**, would speak of a type of chthonic-Pelasgian initiation of which there's still a trace in the Anatolian peninsula. These twisted polytheistic initiations see in the relationship between a man and woman a sort of fight, which is won only by the one that can absorb the other's sexual astrality. Furthermore, the existence of female magical-priestly colleges has the principal task of cultivating entities (fallen angels) for purposes that we can all imagine also included the induction of will in subjects rendered passive by highly refined sexual techniques. These forces are destined to incarnate in a material woman, however, so that together with the male element, they can finally accomplish the Great Work. The latter, on the one hand, entails the total insensitivity of the woman, and on the other, her ability to bring to the height of orgasmic climax, her male partner several times, so as to induce him into a hypno-erotic state suitable to receive external will. It also explains the sacred prostitution of ancient times that was intended to direct the people's collective orgasmic energies, embracing the male population with sacred prostitutes. More technically, this secret was exposed by Kremmerz in private manuscripts, when he says that in the moment of female exaltation, the lunar body of the male is shaped in the form of the person coveted. In occult practice, it is the same thing that happens with wax statues, when they are magically imprinted with the will of the operator, so that the priestess can impress her will in the human psyche, without them being aware of it.

In the *Bruce Codex* which is a papyrus manuscript codex present in the British Museum, and containing Gnostic texts in Coptic, which are named "Bruce," from the name of its discoverer James Bruce, who aquired it in 1796 in Thebes, in upper Egypt, and is written not to reveal the mysteries to those who serve the eighth power of the great archon namely: **"Those who eat the impure menstrual blood and the male sperm."** So John Podesta and possibly his boss Hillary Clinton are serving the eight power.

I have established that the confidential Crowleyan teachings of the high degree of the *Ordo Templi Orientis* or the internal ones of the Brotherhood of Miriam written by Giuliano Kremmerz, are mainly to make contact with extradimensional entities, or produce an artificial hyperphysical body, relating to these practices rightly considered impure in the *Bruce Codex*. Practices that concern the sexual manipulation of energy in order to reach that state of active trance called by Aleister Crowley **Eroto-comatose lucidity,** and Kremmerz defined as the **state of Mag**, which is the particular state of consciousness that allows you to make this extra-dimensional contact. A state which is maintained by a variety of practices and regulations seemingly pious and ascetic, with sexual continence for a certain period, before copulation. One of these entities dear to the dark side—however subject to even more powerful ones—in the case of the followers of Ciro Formisano alias Kremmerz is called **Myriam,** hence the name of this secret society. So here below are some details about the secret ritual that is made to establish contact with this entity in **The Magical and Therapeutic Brotherhood of Myriam,** or, more bluntly, **Myriam Brotherhood** or **Miriam Brotherhood** often referenced with the acronym **SPHCI FR+ TM + of Miriam:**

> *By the power of the sacred word, which changes the Earth to fire and water in the air: for the virtue of the power in place that allows the Supreme brother and teacher to reveal the secret in our work: to the strength of a love ineffable that binds us in a current of good for the health of the people of Myriam, I [name of the celebrant] summon the invisible world of living ideas, of living spirits, creatures of love, of unknown peoples to the human senses, that all obey the power of good, adraan coropazin zealous, love generators, saliel adriar Hormuz, archangels of light, kons-sindar, unique spirit of regeneration of the flesh and spirit health, will evoke in me, on me, around me; I will evoke the earth, the water, the spirit of fire, air, aspiration, breathing in the visible and invisible world; will summon because the shadow of the Supreme myriam, eternal queen and eternal rose, descend upon me, you confuse my shadow, they protect the force, it centuplichi the power of good, it intensifies the miracle of a single thing, it determines the combative character of all evil, it numbs uncleanness of every pain. esefi uri gnomes in the east, besufi caturbi roberis and let the waters of the West, micris, salamanders and buri dell'orsa, abenibusi sylphs jellyfish scorching Empire of the South, come! Come! Come!, which the prodigy's great that Myriam appear, that the fate of the triumph is quick as lightning a thousand times, like a hundred and thousand more times the light.*

According to the authors of *Mémoire du Sang,* the visions and the same powers that come from the mastery of these occult practices, which I might add are typical of many sects of the Illuminati, are not of the initiate, but they are induced by the entity with which they are connected or re-connected to, in some cases. Proof of this is in the fact that these occult initiates assume an occult name, which would correspond to the sphere of influence of an entity, if not to an entity itself, becoming in this way a conscious medium for extradimensional entities. All this takes place for the Illuminati members not without a complex calculation of the astrological doctrines which originally belong to the *Trutina Hermetis, which is* of Assyrian-Babylonian inspiration. Since ancient times the dark side of the Illuminati attempted to crystallize and revitalize the astral remains of the dead and their pneuma in order to allow the mundane consciousness to remain tied into the material world in which they lived, and eventually they will return, through the practice of **avataric-vampiric magic.** This is the medium of choice that allows the entity to remain tied to the earthly sphere—while the initiate would almost never be aware of what actually happens to him, the entities nourishment comes from his life force, the sperm of the initiated is transformed through its etherification (burning) on the coals. Among other things, the combustion of the blood or semen allows you to create a real entity. And curiously enough there is also another possibility, burning the sperm of a deceased initiate, collected and stored when they were still alive, in order to be able to keep them "connected" with the material world. In the highest levels of these perverse organizations, the dark initiation is transmitted—just as is the case of certain Hindu sects, with an alchemical process. Through the absorption of the Master's sperm generally with anal or oral sex, the transmition to man of magical knowledge occurs. When man gives his "substance" to such entities, it permits them to materialize and thus makes them able to dialogue with *the state of Mag* mentioned by Kremmerz. I repeat, this is a particular state of consciousness achieved by the initiate during the sexual act. Here we are not dealing with pseudo-initiatic sects recently established, but with the very essence of counter-initiation, and the evil side of the New World Order. These obscure practices may also be glimpsed in the myths of the Egyptian earth god Seb who masturbates or in the more obscure—but no less evident— Greek god Kronos devouring his children. Incidentally, in the latter context, we can point out that there is an explicit assimilation to the philosopher stone, and seed. Going into operational details, the extraction of this alchemical "mercury" would take place according to certain parameters which, in ancient times, were connected to Sacred prostitution and certain priestesses.

These priestesses had a duty, during the copulation with those initiated into the mysteries, to impose on them, by means of very sophisticated techniques of sexual magic, and with an energetic act of will, the orders that came from the power of the priesthood. ... these women were taken to a very intense degree of hypersensitivity and blunting at the same time, by means of drugs or other means, reaching this, through contacts with initiates, not for desire nor love, but rather a state of separation that allowed to condition the other deeply. [12]

These procedures and others, which allow you to reach what has been called by magicians the "marriage with the faeries," was "advertised" since the early years of the Rosicrucian era, with the already cited book of Montfaucon de Villars entitled, *The Count of Gabali*. It seems that from time immemorial man has had some kind of relationship with these faeries. We can find stories going back to the dawn of time, where the relationship of man and faery have excited the phantasy of many men. The faeries expect a particular behavior from humans, they expect humans to honor the faery ways and beliefs, they set standards of orderliness for human homes, which they visit often, however they forbid us to see them or watch them work. They like cheerful, generous humans. They enjoy all kinds of human food and wine but I will talk more in detail about this in my next book *The Invisible Master*. We must recognize, however, that these ancient teachings, apart from helping us understand the true occult beliefs of the most twisted and perverse side of the Illuminati, also provide a further explanation to this erotic trade with alien entities, often happening for reasons connected to the sentimental realm, and not the intellectual one. While wanting to accept the idea of being able to have an exchange of fluids with such beings, we remain perplexed about the total lack of doctrinal justifications given by de Villars, who attempts to hide the true nature of the game, so as to give rise in the actual reader a shrewd suspicion that the book was actually written by the Jesuits to expose and / or denigrate the initiatic operation of Rosicrucian groups, showing their most secret practices that bound them to entities of which the Jesuits have always wanted exclusivity. Senciner writes in *The Count of Gabali*: *"The ideals of the book seem always just blatantly sentimental (i.e.: it is this way not because it is right and proper, but because is nice to be so.) Now, it's possible that there's never been anyone who has noted this? Even nowadays, in which reigns the sentimental superficiality of the New Age, there are many who refuse to be blurred by this vision. So why is it so? Is it not a proof of our suspicion? So it's easier to think that the infamous Abbot of Villars was assassinated in the street not by the initiates of his time because he had betrayed them, but by the initiates who wanted to punish him for having done a service (perhaps historically, completely useless or even counter productive) to the Jesuits!"* [13]

12   Alexandre de Dánann, *Mémoire du Sang, Ibid.*, p. 150.
13   Senciner, *CORPUS LIBRORUM MAGIAE SEXUALIS DISCIPLINAE, Ibid.*

But was it really "counter-productive" for the Jesuits in the work of Montfaucon de Villars? As I will show in my next book, the notorious Jesuits have actively helped the propagation of this book long after the death of the supposed author, because it was considered valid and important for their occult work. Whatever the case, the book—that I propose to examine even more closely in *The Invisible Master*—tells us of events that have a true doctrinal foundation. It clearly states that it is the virile member that attracts and coerces the hyperphysical beings; that through intercourse with them you can generate other hyperphysical beings, but generated in human form, as the Italian initiate **Count Umberto Amedeo Alberti Catenaia (1879 – 1938)**, the last Grand Master of the Brotherhood of Erim (a Christian esoteric brotherhood) known as **Erim of Catenaia**: "*occult schools to be avoided include those formed by intellectuals bandits, the most dangerous ones that have magic pacts with more demons.*"

Erim Catenaia once wrote under the name of Lorenzo De Guberti to Papus and other occultists, exposing the wrongdoing and low magical operations made by Giuliano Kremmerz, inviting them to be wary of him. The letter of which I speak is at the Papus archive in the Library of Lyon, cataloged with the number 5486. Also Erim Catenaia explained why they do it, and what the dark side wants to accomplish: "*Extraphysical accomplishments profit on keeping alive the ghost at the expense of the credulous and naive mass of affiliates attracting them with the purest and attractive names such as the Osiridean Egyptian Orient, the goddess Isis, Shiva, the goddess Diana and similar. Nor turn from bestial promiscuity, artificially fertilizing an egg from hatching the desired demon with an evil and vile pratice known as 'in interiora mulieris' or the 'homunculus.'*"[14]

That is why Crowley entitled *De Homunculus Epistola* the secret instruction to the 9th degree of his version of the *Ordo Templi Orientis* dedicated to this shameful practice. In *Mémoire du Sang* the authors hinted at what the correct doctrine is, the traditional sense of the "marriage with the fairy" or the marriage to a benevolent entity in opposition to the evil associations I just mentioned, making it clear that this is the way followed by a certain nobility which militate the true initiates who fight the forces of evil and counter-initiation:

> It should be specified that the fairy protector of a lineage is not only this, but also a complement not made of flesh of another being incarnated on earth belonging to the same lineage. ... When the first is ready to incarnate, and this generally occurs within lineages which can be considered as the counterpart to those of Luciferic origin, then, it is the true marriage of two complementary beings, transformed by divine grace that allows these beings alone to reconstitute their primordial androgynous status. Within these lineages, the fairy of the house is the same force, that protects the family and his descendants, until it reaches a certain degree of maturity that will allow her to be embodied in the form of an earthly woman.[15]

Here is the text of the letter of Erim (Umberto Amedeo Alberti Catenaia) sent to Papus (Gérard Encausse), a testimony of a struggle between good and evil in the occult side of the Illuminati.

Read and form your own opinion on the matter:

Naples September 13, 1910

To Mr. Dr. Gérard Encousse (sic)—Paris

14   This quote, in the book *Mémoire du Sang* (p.25) has been just shot, as it comes from the "reserved" Attainment of The Celestial Erim, that still is not available in its entirety outside a very limited circle of people.
15   *Mémoire, Ibid.*, p. 145.

Master Papus,

It's with the commotion of all my spirit that I address these lines. You are the beloved teacher who gave to my spirit light and the right distrust towards those writings, when I fell into the abyss of a terrible bad association. I understood then the terrible way in which I was pushing, after three years of a terrible battle with the elements of evil, my manuscript will come under your eyes as a thank you gesture, and feedback of your good work.

Read, teacher and benefactor, the summary of three years of continuous struggle, standing alone against the evil, evil sect of "Miriam." Your spirit will be moved and will answer me giving peace to my poor tormented spirit.

I ask you: I do not have to publish this manuscript because I could not quite conceal the terrible mysteries to the uninitiated? If I do it in good faith, will you give me the backing or your protection word or at least a prefatory letter? I expect an answer that puts on the right path the poor disciples in good faith, that a perverse will can detract from the right path. I expect from lovely France and by you, the light and the freedom that your ancestors have given us through the sacrifices of the "Terror." I hope in the help of those good men that propose to combat evil in all forms in which it presents itself.

I greet you with all my soul

Dr. Lorenzo De Guberti (sic)

At the Sign. Puzziello via Flavio Gioia, 23 NAPLES

Dr. Lorenzo De Guberti, the false name chosen by the Count Catenaia, obviously living in Naples where also Ciro Formisano known as Kremmerz was from, and of course Catenaia was probably reluctant to reveal his real name to the famous Papus for fear of retaliation. Turning to the subject of sexual continence, it is clear that most of the time this state is extremely conducive to the manifestation of the astral entities, which, appearing under the guise of the opposite sex, who involve the psyche of the subject they want to link to them. However in the magic of the Illuminati there also exists the "opportunity to take the place of the entity"—so to speak—and even to nourish the vitality of another human being. Of course same entity opening such a possibility to the magical operator "plays" with people who undergo the rituals in question, so there is always a downside for certain choices. It is what is called, in a word of Eastern import, *Avataric magic*. It consists precisely in the detachment of the soul from a living person and the introduction of the intelligent body in place of the conscious principle of the magician. An assumption, whose simple statement seems to go beyond the capabilities of all the magic in the world, but that can be documented from different sources, being able to trace it, in its imperfect forms, in the same clinical cases of psychiatry and of exorcisms.

It's clear that *Avataric magic* can also be made to encourage the incorporation of an entity—also for a magician who survives in the lower astral realms—with the aim of perpetuating his survival. A kind of immortality conditioned by the possibility of renewing the ritual. It seems that this magic is a derived from Chaldeism and especially Egyptian esoteric knowledge, where they had become experts in setting the vampire vitality of the ancient priests to their own mummies. The latter was used as "astral anchor" for the pneuma of the priest, so he was able to continue to "live." One means of avataric transmigration could also consist in acting upon a pregnant woman, ousting the soul of a child, which is precisely documented in Kremmerz writings in

the *Corpus Philosophorum totius magiae*, as one of the features of this magical practice, and is precisely to define "he's not born of woman," but in the sense of what was
said just above. In a passage of the *Dialogues on Hermetism* by Giuliano Kremmerz,
citing the words of a "friend," with any approximation appears to have been the Grand
Master **Prince Don Leone Caetani**, the driving force of the Osiridean Egyptian Orient, the following, significant words that finally reveal the truth about immortality
and certain Illuminati practices:

> *My original sin, because I saw the light many centuries ago, when times were not
> these but the truth was the same. From that time, I did not die definitively, and I can
> say, like Hermes, that I am as I was, and I am now, not by being born of a woman's
> uterus, but changing the body, reborn by mutating the body, hiding jealously my
> old person, my identity, and, even in saving the same, changing approximately the
> external shape and never saying to the layman what was, what I thought, what I
> think, what I did, if they are between the names of the history of humanity. You
> see that my experience is longer than yours, not because you are a new soul, you are
> all old souls to my knowledge, but at each rebirth you first descended into the hell
> of a very dark womb and then formally drawn to light through the oblivious water
> of Lethe, you were left no memory of your past, without the awareness of what you
> were, being instinctively tending to an ancient facticity that is perpetuated in you
> alone for sympathy or an already experienced attitude to life. And I listen to it sus-
> pended between belief and unbelief. And I thought anxiously: poor and dear friend,
> an almanac wheel does not turn smoothly, perhaps? Is he suffering schizophrenia
> from dreaming while talking? Is he deceiving me? Then am I left questioning myself:
> what if Thomas Aquinas, and if Pico della Mirandola, and if the Borri, the Phila-
> lethes, the Rupescissa, the Trevisano, the author of the Turba philosophorum, were
> alchemists, did they not find a secret unthought, a Great Arcanum that enables man
> to eternally live as an Avatar, as the Indians say, changing only the physical body,
> with the youngest, entering the body of a teenager?*

On the techniques of this operation mode, which is, as we have seen, the real big
arcane of magic, the authors of *Mémoire du Sang* relate to the manner in which this is accomplished, and you will be surprised to learn that the best opportunity was supplied by:
*"therapeutic way, understood as claiming to effectively treat disease by magical means;
something that is always well accepted, the patient not being able to evaluate the nature
and mode of administration of the drug since it has the result to the heart, that is, its
possible cure. But it is just so that the pseudo-initiation has the opportunity to act on a
large number of people who are ... particularly subject to the action of the forces to which
these organizations constitute the vehicle."*

In fact, for the fulfillment of this magic it is necessary that the person act upon
both the presence of the magician and in a state of clouding of consciousness: *"In such
a state of passivity, it happens that the vital spirit withdraws from the head in the
region of the heart: when it is completely withdrawn, then the other's soul can project
and penetrate the body."* [16]

So what better way to implement *Avataric Magic* if not by founding yet another sect
of Illuminati engaged in such occult practices, this is basically what Kremmerz and Aleister Crowley did at the beginning of the last century with a certain degree of success.

---

16 *Mémoire, Ibid.*, p. 128.

The Neo-Templars and the Gnostic Church with a Jesuit flavor

When speaking of the legendary Knights Templar, and the links between Neo-Templarism, the so-called Gnostic Church and the Vatican, a prominent figure in the Italian Illuminati comes to mind. Grand Master **Gastone Ventura (1906 – 1981)**, a high level Italian Illuminati born into a noble family, in the city of Parma, in the Veneto region, who lived in Venice, and was a high dignitary of Freemasonry and Martinism, as well as a key figure in Neo-Templarism. Count Gastone Ventura, who was in life a vice admiral of the Italian Navy, died on July 28, 1981, but his studies are fortunately still with us to help us understand more. His books unfortunately never were translated in the English language, include amongst the most important ones, *The Masonic Rites of Memphis and Misraim,* published by Atanòr of Rome in 1975, and *Templars and Templarism,* originally published by Gasparoni Venice in 1963 (now reissued by Atanòr with an introduction by my friend Fortunato Luciano Sciandra). Ventura decided in 1964 to "reawaken" as they say in Masonic language, the **Italian Grand Priory of the Sovereign Order of the Knights of the Temple,** called in short **"Italian Temple"** in which to train its future Neo-Templars, mainly enrolled in the European Masonic Martinist milieu of that time. Being a member of the Black Nobility in Venice, and respectful of the Catholic belief prevalent in Italy, despite his Masonic ties, may have you believe otherwise. Gastone Ventura found himself heir to an important branch of the pro-Catholic Neo-Templars, thanks to a foundation charter he received by the **Marquis Alessandro Vettori,** nephew of the former Marquis Vettori, who was Grand Master of this Catholic Neo-Templar Order from 1860 to 1880. Vettori was an old fascist killed in 1945 by the communist partisans in the last hours of the Second World War. He was in charge of the Italian Grand Priory, that more than a century before, dissociated from the Johannite of the previously cited French Grand Master, Bernard Raymond Fabré-Palaprat. On the 14th of September 1940, when the war took over Europe, the regent Vettori, unable to summon a regular Great Convent of the Knights and Squires of his Order, as would have been his original intention, met in Venice those who were closest to him, a total of six knights including himself, who I quote below:

Eques Justitiae ex Val Illiria Count Vincenzo Cavalli della Torre;

Eques Justitiae ex Val Pezzola Count Gastone Ventura;

Eques Justitiae ex Val Sile Liutenent commander Giuseppe Manfroi;

Eques Gratiae Luigi Valfredi;

Armiger Gino Vianello Moro.

On that occasion, the Regent reminded the five Knights to enlist more volunteers for the war declared one year earlier, as the oaths provided by the Order when joining stated such mission for the country in case of war. Each one of those present in the meeting was handed a copy of the statute with an attached statement from the Regent, where it was stated that after the war the survivors of the meeting would elect the new regent, and if lacking the possibility for a new election due to the death of all five Knights, the only survivor would inherit the succession, with the obligation to attend to the duties relating to his position. Here is an excerpt of the declaration of the Marquis Vettori made on September 14, 1940 (the day dedicated to the Holy Cross): *"We Alessandro Vettori of St. Mark and Val Dorica, have entrusted copies of this letter to the members of the Order indicated below, we convened in Venice before doing our duty as volunteers in the war for the defense of the Fatherland. So we do this in order to ensure the continuity of*

the Order itself in the event of our demise. ... if none of us survives abide by the Divine
Providence, we have done this in the hope that we have done everything in our power
to ensure the continuation of the Order, as well as it was our obligation and right as a
result of the solemn promise which we have done about assuming the Regency."

Alessandro Vettori, like the ancient Grand Masters of the Temple, was killed in
Bologna in May 1945, by the Italian partisans (communists!) After the war, of the five
Knights, two died, another one disappeared, and a fourth was reported missing in Russia.
The only survivor was in the end the aforementioned **Conte Gastone Ventura**, who now
had the right to the Regency. On the 1st of December 1964, he convened the General
Chapter, which marked the "re-awakening" of the Order (after the Second World War),
from which Ventura received the confirmation of his dignity, and inherited the broadest
powers to carry on this Neo-Templar tradition. A few decades later two figures connected
to the Vatican, took on Ventura's Templar legacy, creating two separate entities.

The first affiliation is the current **Magister Mauro Giorgio Ferretti,** born in Reg-
gio Emilia in 1954, who graduated in law at the University of Parma, and who is now
the leader of a Neo-Templar branch completely controlled by the Jesuits. Of course, the
Jesuits have been trying to accomplish this since the year 2000, a form of Catholic Neo-
Templarism, less esoteric and more acceptable to the Vatican with its **Order of the Catholic Knights Templar of Italy.** Until 2006, this Order was known as the Grand priory
of Italy of the *Supernus Ordo equester Temples* (SOET) abbreviations used by Gastone
Ventura in 1981.

Ferretti, of course, hides the Masonic origins of his Order, and any past association with Freemasonry and the previous Grand Master, Count Gastone Ventura. It is
why they have also changed their name in 2006, preferring nowadays a more popular
approach in line with Pope Benedict XVI, who initially blessed Grand Master Mauro
Giorgio Ferretti during a Mass at the Vatican, where Pope Francis blessed the Order
publicly during a parade. (FIG. 59) Something truly unusual for a Neo-Templar Order
that was born originally in a Masonic lodge, called *Chevaliers de la Croix (in English*
Knights of the Cross) belonging to the Grand Lodge of France, a lodge that openly
disagreed with the prevalent Masonic thought of the time. Thus was born in France
the Old and the Sovereign Military Order of the Temple of Jerusalem, on November
4, 1804, from an idea of Bernard Raymond Fabré-Palaprat, appointed Grand Master of
the Order, by several influential figures of the **Lodge Chevaliers de la Croix,** including:
Dr. Philippe Ledru (personal doctor of the Duke of Cossé-Brissac), the notary de Cour-
champ, Prosper de Charpentier Saintot, and a mysterious character named **Claude-Mathieu Radix de Chevillon,** Grand Master of a pre-existing Templar Order and regent
of it during the French Revolution. He inherited this position from the previous **Grand
Master Louis Hercule Timoléon de Cossé-Brissac, Duke of Brissac** (1734 – 1792),
who was Commander in Chief of the constitutional guard of the French King from
1791, and was brutally killed in Versailes during the French Revolution. It was actually
Claude-Mathieu Radix de Chevillon that gathered key members of the Lodge Chevaliers de la Croix, with the intention of transmitting this genuine Templar lineage transmitted to him by the Duke of Cossé-Brissac shortly before his death, in order to make
it possible in the post-revolutionary era to have a "regular" Templar succession. True or
false, this version of the events given by Palaprat, kickstarted the very first non-Masonic
Neo-Templar Order, independent of both the Church and Freemasonry, and it is from
here that the future branches of Neo-Templarism are born, even those who openly embrace the Church, like the one of Magister Mauro Giorgio Ferretti.

FIG. 59 – Order of the Catholic Knights Templar and Pope Francis during a parade, an event that has not happened in the field of Neo-Templarism since Pope John Paul II, and his loyal knight Rocco Zingaro.

In 1804, Palaprat came into possession of a Gnostic manuscript, written in Greek, called *Levitikon* and another text, called *Evangelicon,* with a version of the Gospel of St. John—probably false, from the fifteenth, or, according to others, the eleventh century—heavily modified (without miracles and resurrection: in fact missing, chapters 20 and 21), showing that Jesus was initiated in Egypt to the great mysteries of Osiris, who had given to his favorite disciple (John) divine knowledge, or *gnosis.* In addition to this, Jesus was painted certainly not as the son of God, but as a simple man, moreover the illegitimate son of Mary! For Palaprat, the Christian Church founded by Peter and Paul and the other apostles did not understand the secret teachings of Jesus, and was of course twisting the real story about the Great Master of all Masters.

However, the truth for Palaprat was retained by the Patriarchs of Jerusalem, at least until the arrival of the Templars in the Holy Land, which, later, would have assumed the role of gate keepers of these secrets. It was the Templars in fact, after learning the true doctrines attributed to St. John the Apostle in the Holy Land, who gave up the religion of St. Peter and St. Paul, to become Johannites. On this basis, is this legend and the doctrines set forth in *Levitikon* and *Evangelicon*: a few decades later Fabré Palaprat formally founded in 1828, the ***Église des Johannites Crétiens Primitif*** (*in English* Johannite Church of Primitive Christians). In this context, to give a valid apostolic succession to the first consecrations of his Church he cleverly involved a Catholic bishop who had sworn allegiance to the French Republic, **Mgr Guillaume Mauviel (1757 – 1814)**, Bishop of Cayes (in Haiti), who was consecrated bishop on July 29, 1810. In turn, Fabré-Palaprat consecrated Primate of the Church Monsignor Jean Machaut (1770 – 1845) on the same day of his investiture. Machault was to finally consecrate on February 20, 1831, the most famous member (at the time) adhering to the Fabré-Palaprat church, namely the former dissident radical Catholic priest (suspended *a divinis*) **Ferdinand-François Châtel**, founder of the so-called French Catholic Church. [17]

Châtel did not last long in the Fabré-Palaprat Johannite Church, from which he was expelled, after a trial for "heresy." The church itself did not survive, in fact, the death of its founder took place on the 18th in February 1838, although former members of the Johannite clergy emigrated to other formations to form what will be later called the **Gnostic Church**. Already in 1815, the "Catholics" escapees of Palaprat's Order, who at the time started fomenting the Johannite heresy with a removal of the Church of Rome by the post-revolutionary France, declared the only faith for a true Templar was the Apostolic Roman Catholic Church. However, since 1815 when the Company of Jesus returned to the Vatican Palaprat's Templar Order, they broke into a series of irregular Regencies with the decision of the Grand Priory of Italy to constitute an independent association. Proponent of this decision was Count Giovanbattista Ventura, who was the last Grand Master appointed to organize the Italian Grand Priory of the Order, and felt a duty to stand firm on the an-

FIG. 60 – Document of the Orden del Antiguo y Masónica Egipcio Primitive Rite of Memphis Mizraim y (O.M.A.P.R.E.M.M.) Declares the worldwide leadership of self proclaimed Antichrist and 100 ° degree of Freemasonry Frank G.Rippel.

cient traditional principles increasingly misrepresented in the French Templars. So the Italian branch of the Neo-Templar Order that representative Count Gastone Ventura was officially born on March 1st 1815.

The second Neo-Templar affiliation currently linked to Gastone Ventura, is instead much more covert and secret than the one presided by Magister Mauro Giorgio Ferretti, and is linked to the mysterious Italian Count, **Salvatore de la Moneda Olivari,** born in Camogli (Genoa), on January 21, 1940. He was the Chancellor of the Order of Patriarch Ignatius of Antioch, and advisor to the Public Prosecutor of the Patriarchal Church of Antioch of the Syrians to the Holy See. Graduating from the School of Genealogy, Heraldry and Documentary Sciences, de la Moneda was a member of the Italian Institute of Heraldry, and a member of the College of Arms. The count was a leading figure of the *Real Academia de Estudios Mallorquina Genealogicos,* of the Academia Melitense Hispanica and the *Academia de Letras de Lisboa and Arts,* and a member of the *Societe d'histoire et de genealogies* of Moscow; and an expert on the history of the Orders of Chivalry, and also associate member of the ***Académie Internationale de Généalogie***. And if all of this was not enough academic pomposity, Olivari Salvatore de la Moneda is also a prominent figure of the hidden network of the Martinist Illuminati, with the initiatory name of **"Ignis."** This is certainly a controversial and influential character linked to Italian naval Intelligence, and is considered up to now a prominent figure of the Italian Illuminati in

17   See. http://www.eresie.it/it/Gioanniti.htm ✝ Archived 15th November, 2016.

FIG. 61 – Mass Celebrated by Freemasons lead by "the Grand Hierophant" **Vladimir Frederic Lillo Mardones** *of the irregular Masónica Orden del Antiguo y Egipcio Primitive Rite of Memphis Mizraim y (O.M.A.P.R.E.M.M.). An irregular Masonic body headed by the Illuminati and self proclaimed 100 ° degree of Freemasonry* **Frank G.Rippel,** *with the help of a dangerous Mossad agent and Israeli representative of the Illuminati called* **Alexander Rybalka,** *known in the initiatic world as Frater Sephariel.*

the last 50 years. Salvatore La Olivari is still very active, and is currently an adviser of the Holy See to the Catholic Patriarchate of Antioch of the Syrians, and the **Patriarch Grand Master SBR Ignatius Youssif III Younan,** Patriarch of Antioch of the Syrians, a role that would show a real and concrete link between the Vatican and high degree Freemasons which are after the 66 degree of the Masonic Rites of Memphis and Misraïm, admitted in *Grand Consistory of Great Consacrator Patriarchs,* with a **Episcopal Consecration.** The teaching in this Section finds its study and research in classical gnosis and its Christian derivation **that are linked with the Church of Antioch,** intimately connected with the early history of the gospel. It was the great central point from where missionaries to the Gentiles were sent (presumably following the Great Commission). It was the birthplace of the famous Christian father Chrysostom, who died A.D. 407. This link was confirmed to me by **Professor Giancarlo Seri,** Sovereign Grand General Hierophant of the Italian Sovereign Sanctuary of the Egyptian Rite, that regularly works under the auspices of the Grand Orient of Italy, and the only one in the world working such Rites within the strict bounderies of a "Regular" Masonic Obedience. However, there are a bunch of "Irregular" Egyptian rites working under the auspices of various Illuminati sects, full of black magicians and theurgy, and homosexuality, in a reality that is as far as possible from "Masonic sanity" let alone "Regularity." For example, Fabio Sebastián Cruz who signs himself with 33 degrees 66 ° -90 ° 95 ° 97 °, Grand Master of the Sovereign Sanctuary of the *Rite for Uruguay Antiguo y Primitivo Memphis-Misraïm* consecrated in Santiago de Chile, in November, 2011 by the Frenchman Michel Gaudart de Soulages, and tied to the Federation project by Frank G.Rippel. (FIGS. 60 and 61) Cruz is the founder of the first Masonic gay lodge in the world.

Fabio Sebastián Cruz founded the first gay Masonic lodge in the world in 2008,[18] and at the same time he devoted himself actively to black magic and Satanism, which he often uses against his enemies. I have a photo that was sent to me by a friend, in which we see objects from a black magic ritual (FIG. 62) allegedly operated by Cruz against Freemason **Hector Lascurain 33 ° 97 ° 99 °** tied to a unrecognized branch of the *Fraternitas Rosicruciana Antiqua.*

Let's return to the hidden link between the Patriarchate of Antioch and the Egyptian Masonic Rites, a very interesting connection unknown to most, that leads the members of such rites not only to the highest mysteries of Gnosticism, but in some cases to a secret recognition by the Vatican, linked to a supposed apostolic succession deemed valid by the Holy See, which then allows these Freemasons not only to celebrate Mass in their lodges (as I did even myself once), but recognizes them secretly as bishops by the Church of Rome. Certain Masonic Rites and the Martinists have in fact an Episcopate Gnostic transmission that often interfaces with other small religious groups, like the *Old Catholic Church,* or those of the various branches of the Patriarchate of Antioch. All this is a reality that sprang originally from the Gnostic Church, the *Ecclesia Gnostica Catholica,* launched at the time by a former Jesuit and Freemason named **Jules Doinel-Benoît,** a dubious character born in Moulins (France) on December 8, 1842 to a deeply Catholic family who entered the Jesuit order in 1859 (a bit like Weishaupt a century earlier), and after a growing obsession for women and frequent mystical visions of the "Eternal Feminine," eventually Doinel was dismissed by the Jesuits in 1861. In 1874 Jules-Benoît Doinel, a widower since 1873, remarried, and through the family of his second wife, joined Freemasonry. He was initiated in 1884 by the Grand Orient of France, and subsequently oversaw the archive and library of the Masonic Museum, a prestigious position. Meanwhile, his skills as a valiant archivist brought him a promotion in 1875 to the Archives of Orléans, and as a researcher he discovered in the library of the city in 1888, a medieval manuscript written by Stephen, a canon of the Church of the Holy Cross of Orléans, burned at the stake in 1022 for his pre-Cathar Gnostic doctrines.

The discovery kindled the interest of Doinel for various Gnostic movements of the Middle Ages, like the Manichean, the Paulicians, the Bogomils and of course the Cathars (he believed, in fact, that the Gnostic religion was at the base of Freemasonry), and such interest made him resume his mystical visions. One night, he recalled later, he had been visited by **the Aeon of Christ**. Aeon, in the Gnostic tradition, bear a number of similarities to Judaeo-Christian angels, including roles as servants and emanations of God, and exist as beings of light—basically benevolent aliens. In fact, certain Gnostic Angels, such as Armozel, are also Aeons. The Gnostic Gospel of Judas, recently found, purchased, held, promoted and translated by the **National Geographic Society**, also mentions the concept of Aeons, and speaks of Jesus' teachings about them. So the Aeon of Christ consecrated him spiritually as Bishop of Montségur (the place where we find the famous fortress, and the last bastion of the Cathar resistance in 1244), and Primate of the Albigenses, ordering him to establish a new church. Following this vision, Doinel came into contact with high level **esoteric circles, theosophists and spiritualists in Paris.** In particular, he was introduced in the living room of the Countess Maria de Mariategui (1832 – 1895), later Duchess of Medina Pomar and Lady Caithness, a follower of **Anna Bonus Kingsford (1846 – 1888), founder of the Hermetic Society,** as well as a theosophist and passionate spiritist involved in séances: she considered herself the reincarnation of Mary Stuart Queen of Scots (1542 – 1587).

18   http://fabiosebastiancruz.blogspot.it/2008/01/primera-logia-gay-del-mundo.html ‡ Archived 15th November, 2016.

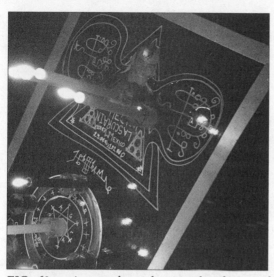

FIG. 62 – A rare photo showing the objects of a black magic operation carried out against Freemason **Hector Lascurain** *by* **Fabio Sebastián Cruz** *Grand Hierophant for South America, of an irregular Memphis–Misraïm branch.*

The communication sessions (séances) were attended by key figures in the esoteric circles of that time, like Stanislas de Guaita, Gérard Encausse (which ushered in the Martinist Order with Doinel in 1890), and Joséphin Péladan founder of the Kabbalistic Order of the Rose-Cross in 1887. In these spiritualist séances, they evoked various characters of the past, such as the previously mentioned Canon Stephen and the Cathar bishop of Toulouse, Guilhabert de Castres. The sitting that was most memorable was on September,1889 (another source cites June, 1890), when 40 Cathar bishops manifested and consecrated Bishop Doinel, as part of the Assembly of the Paraclete, later called the Gnostic Church. Doinel is then consecrated through a medium, which is unusual, but crucial to understand the nature of this reality, transmitted by what Illuminati call their "Invisible Masters" or "Secret Chiefs."

For the management of this new religious movement, Doinel was supported by a female figure, a "Sophia" (the Aeon, whose name means wisdom) on Earth, but, after the rejection of some candidates (including the same Countess), they had to settle for a spiritual Sophia. Perhaps Doinel hoped for a sexual encounter with the Countess, the Gnostic Church was already linked to an idea of sexual magic since its origins. A 33rd degree Freemason, **Dr. Stephan A. Hoeller,** who I knew when I lived in Oslo, is one of the most important contemporary representatives of the gnostic tradition in the world, and will deny such thing, wishing to distance himself publicly to any controversial "gnostic" figures of the past, like Aleister Crowley, who definitely tarnished the image of the Gnostic Church with his sexual magick and his libertine manners. Although in truth, Crowley was not the only one in this environment to deflect towards the dark side. But let me explain who Stephan A. Hoeller is—the leading figure of contemporary Gnosticism.

Born in 1931 in Budapest, Hungary to a family of Austrian-Hungarian nobility, Hoeller ran away in 1945 from Hungary, which, unfortunately, became a communist country, until the collapse of the Berlin Wall. In 1952 he ended up in beautiful and sunny California, which as we all know was the favorite laboratory for mind control experiments in the growing New Age movement, run by Intelligence operatives secretly controlled by the Jesuits, and the various Illuminati factions of New World Order. Hoeller and his church, known as *Ecclesia Gnostica,* have certainly left a mark in the New Age movement. Secretly promoted by *Lucis Fratres,* it is a mysterious sect allegedly founded in Florence in 1498, also known as the *Brotherhood of the Illuminati,* that some say are the milder and good side of the Illuminati. I managed to obtain top secret documents, originally hidden on microfilm, later digitally converted, that seem to validate this hypothesis. Such documents prove the direct involvement of the Order of the Illuminati, the one created by Weishaupt, and not just the Brotherhood of the Illuminati. It is present in the United States and in the affairs of the Gnostic Church that Stephan A. Hoeller has inherited from **Richard Duc de Palatine (1916 – 1977)**, in internal documents called **"the Hidden Church of the Illuminati."**

But let's see how the *Ecclesia Gnostica* and Hoeller's connection are described on **Wikipedia**:

> *The organization now called the Ecclesia Gnostica was originally organized in England under the name the Pre-Nicene Gnostic Catholic Church in 1953, by the Most Rev. Richard Jean Chretien Duc de Palatine with the object of "restoring the Gnosis—Divine Wisdom to the Christian Church, and to teach the Path of Holiness which leads to God and the Inner Illumination and Interior Communion with the Soul through the mortal body of man." Born Ronald Powell, Richard Duc de Palatine had served in the Liberal Catholic Church in Australia, before moving to England. Bishop Duc de Palatine was consecrated by the Most Rev. Msg. Hugh George de Willmott Newman (Mar Georgius I), patriarch of the Catholic Apostolic Church (Catholicate of the West) who consolidated many lines of apostolic succession. Bishop Duc de Palatine also received a charter in 1953 to head an organization first called "the Brotherhood of the Illuminati," renamed "the Order of the Pleroma" in 1960. He received other esoteric lines and charters such as: the Templar Order, Brotherhood of the Rosy Cross, Memphis and Mizarim Rites of Freemasonry, and the Martiniste Order, and termed the combination with the Ecumenical Apostolic Succession "the Wisdom Religion-Gnostic Mystic Tradition." In 1959 the organization became active in the United States through the work of Stephan A. Hoeller, who served as a priest of the church in Los Angeles, and was subsequently consecrated as regionary bishop for the Americas in 1967. He became presiding bishop on the death of Bishop Duc de Palatine in 1977, although there was a falling out prior to that.*

Stephan A. Hoeller has also been for years a representative of the **Theosophical Society of America,** which the Theosophists traditionalists say is colluding with the Jesuits, and not respectful of true Theosophy, as I explained in the previous Volume II of my *Confessions.* So Hoeller is basically an agent of the Jesuits in disguise.

This is how Hoeller is personally described by Wikipedia:

> *An author and scholar of Gnosticism and Jungian psychology, Hoeller is Regionary Bishop of Ecclesia Gnostica, and the senior holder of the English Gnostic transmission in America. Hoeller was ordained to the priesthood of the American Catholic Church by Bishop Lowell P. Wadle in 1958. He was consecrated to the Gnostic episcopate by Richard Duc de Palatine on April 9, 1967. Ronald Powell (who took the ecclesiastical name Richard Jean Chretien Duc de Palatine) had established a modern-day Gnostic church, the Pre-Nicene Gnostic Catholic Church, in England during the 1950s—de Palatine received his successions from British independent prelate Hugh de Wilmott-Newman in 1953. After the death of Duc de Palatine in the 1970s, Hoeller abbreviated the church's name, in Latin form, to Ecclesia Gnostica. He has continued to serve as bishop of the Ecclesia Gnostica for over four decades.*

Something strange happened in 2004 on the centenary of the famous "gnostic revelation" received by Aleister Crowley in Cairo, when Stephan A. Hoeller, called by many "the bishop of Hollywood Boulevard" because of the location of his Church, at 4516 Hollywood Boulevard, saw suddenly its prestigious center used for 27 years, on fire.

Strange? Of course some say that the perpetrators of this act have been precisely the

Crowleyans, who apparently did not appreciate at all, the harsh criticism moved over the years by Hoeller against the Thelemic orders and their Ecclesia Gnostic Catholica, especially those made in a Official document of his Church that was to remain secret, entitled, *Ecclesia Gnostica Position Paper Concerning the Thelemite or Crowleyan Gnostic Churches By Rt. Rev, Stephen A. Hoeller Regionary Bishop of the Ecclesia Gnostica,* released years earlier among members of his Church with the following Premise: *"This position paper is issued privately for the information of the clergy and selected laity of the Ecclesia Gnostica. It is not for general distribution or publication. Recipients of this paper are requested to exercise the utmost discretion and caution in making the same available to others, which should be done only in cases when the position of the Ecclesia Gnostica versus the Thelemite or Crowleyan groups must be clarified as a matter of practical necessity."*

Obviously the disclosure document came into the hands of the perverse and dangerous followers of Aleister Crowley, who most certainly did not appreciate it. And here are some excerpts taken from the document in question, written by Stephen A. Hoeller, and later published by the site of the controversial Illuminati Swiss researcher **P.R. Koenig** that will help you better understand the situation:

A quotation from the pen of Francis King, a contemporary authority on Crowley may be useful here: *"When Crowley visited Reuss in Berlin and had conferred upon himself the chieftainship of the British section of the O.T.O., he was also consecrated as a Gnostic Catholic bishop—or so Reuss claimed."* Crowley, however, does not appear to have been aware of his new status; certainly he never made any attempt to exercise his ecclesiastical functions [wrong: see W.B. Crow], *"although, it is true, he did write a special Mass for the Gnostic Church."* (Italics by Stephan Hoeller. Francis King: *Man, Myth & Magick,* ed. Cavendish). *"Indeed, as far as one can discern, Crowley's only act that related to anything even remotely ecclesiastical is his writing of the Liber XV O.T.O. Ecclesiae Gnosticae Canon Missae, of which more shall be said later. When perusing Crowley's voluminous Opus of many volumes, nowhere does one find any indication of his interest in or knowledge of the sacraments, the mythos and ethos of the historic Christian church. He frequently uses (some would say misuses and abuses) the technical terms of the sacraments, associating them with sexual matters, but that is about all. In the following we shall undertake a systematic, point by point examination of the features of the claims of the Crowleyan succession which seem doubtful to us:"*

(1) Crowley seems never to have used the Papus successions at all if he ever received them in the first place. Crowley only operated two orders: the O.T.O. which he received from Germany, and the A∴ A∴ which he took from the Golden Dawn. At the time Crowley received his authorities from Reuss, the Gnostic Catholic Church had merged or was about to merge with the Martinist Order, in such a manner that they no longer functioned separately. There is no reason to suppose that Reuss or Crowley would have gone contrary to the rules established by Papus and separated this church from the Martinist context.

(2) Neither Papus nor Crowley had a valid apostolic succession to pass on because they had none in the first place. Reuss is said to have received the succession from Papus in 1909. ... Papus only received the unquestionably valid succession from Bricaud after July 1913, this being the date of Bricaud's own consecration. Thus in 1909 Papus may or may not have been a valid bishop depending on whether he did or did not receive the Doinel succession by this time and (b) whether one is justified in accepting the Doinel succession is valid. ... The only succession possessed by Papus which one must accept as valid, however, he simply did not have to confer on Reuss in 1909.

(3) Assuming that Papus had a valid succession to hand on in 1909, which is assuming too much—the succession may not have passed on to Reuss owing lack of proper intention. Proper intention in the ecclesiasitcal sense implies that in consecrating an other bishop the consecrator intends to do as the church has always done under such circumstances. The passing on of the Martinist and associated grades and initiations was a pro-forma honorary gesture on the part of Papus, given in exchange for a similar honorary confering of O.T.O. degrees on himself by Reuss. This sort of thing is customary among heads of initiatory orders who recognize each other in a fraternal manner, but it is a little more than a friendly formality. (A famous and controversial analogous event being the exchange of honorary grades in a like manner by Aleister Crowley and H. Spencer Lewis of the A.M.O.R.C.) While there may be honorary degrees of Masonic orders conferred at a distance or "on sight," this cannot be done in an ecclesiastical succession. Thus even if Papus may have wished to pass on some kind of an ecclesiastical succession to Reuss, the manner of conferring it would have been enough to render it very suspect indeed.

(4) There is nor proof that either Reuss or Crowley were technically capable of receiving a valid catholic episcopate. In order to be consecrated a bishop, a person must be validly baptized, confirmed, and ordained a priest and deacon. Were these prerequisites fullfilled in the case of Reuss? Were they in the case of Crowley? If not, they were not capable of receiving a valid episcopate even if the consecrator possessed a valid succession and held the proper intention.

(5) Reuss probably, and Crowley almost certainly, could not pass on any valid succession they received because they lacked proper intention. Reuss was a Mason with little or no knowledge of catholic practice, and Crowley was a passionate neo-pagan without any shred of sympathy for the catholic sacramental mythos even in its most esoteric aspect.

(6) Provided that claims should be raised to a succession descending from Papus through Reuss and through Crowley to various O.T.O. bishops, such bishops themselves could probably not pass on an apostolic succession in a valid manner for lack of proper intention. The leading members of O.T.O. organizations as a rule are so out of touch with even the rudiments of the catholic tradition that it is highly unlikely that their actions could be accepted as conforming to the doctrine of intention even in its most liberal and esoteric sense. Present-day representatives of the O.T.O. tradition at least in the United States are woefully uneducated in all matters including those ecclesiastical, and emotionally unstable to boot—at least in the majority of instances. It would be too much to expect from most of these ragtag subculture-magicians to know anything of proper intention, not to speak of holding such an intention.

(7) Whatever valid stream and current of magic, ecclesiastical or otherwise may have existed in the O.T.O. in Crowley's time is now probably absent in the present O.T.O. offshoots, owing to their lack of proper succession authority. ... Here a little insight into more recent O.T.O. history may prove helpful. According to the late Louis T. Culling (Frater Aquila), a high-ranking member of the O.T.O. as well as of its short-lived offshoot, the G.B.G., and a long-time personal friend of this writer, the only person lawfully entiteld to head the O.T.O. was Karl Johannes Germer (1885 – 1962). This man—of whom even the most rabid critics cannot say much ill—became the Outer Head of the O.T.O. upon Crowley's death as he was already somewhat the acting head during Crowley's last years. According to reliable informants Karl Germer named a man named Metzger (Frater Paragranus) as his successor.

Metzger resided in Switzerland and re-stablished the O.T.O. in the German speaking countries in a most sensible and respectable way. It would appear on the basis of this information that all other existing O.T.O. groups (exclusive of that of Mr. Metzger, Frater Paragranus) are without proper succession authority. The English writer on Crowleyana, Kenneth Grant, who claims to be Outer Head was expelled by Karl Germer from the order on July 20, 1955. An other alleged chief, Grady McMurtry of California was indeed appointed by Crowley as his personal representative in the United States and as the reformer of the order, but only subject to the approval of Germer. Germer never approved, thus McMurtry's position also evaporated in spite of his claims. Neither the expelled member Grant, nor the unapproved representative McMurtry were mentioned in Karl Germer's will. A Brazilian claimemt named Motta has similarly failed to establish any valid authority for his high-sounding titles in yet an other revival movement of the O.T.O. Unlike in churches, where schisms do not invalidate successorship, in the O.T.O. the magical current is said to go with the lawful successorship—at least so this writer was informed by the late Luis T. Culling and other informed O.T.O. members. Perhaps this factor may be held accountable for the stability and common sense of Metzger's O.T.O. and for the lamentable ways of the other, less legitimate bodies?

Then Stephan A. Hoeller makes further accusations:

The only document available that pertains to the sacramental practice of the Ecclesia Gnostica Catholica of the O.T.O. is the aforementioned Mass written by Crowley himself. It is a curious text, poetic and magical in nature, but having virtually nothing in common with a Mass as understood by Catholic tradition both orthodox and heretical. While it cannot be thus said to be either a Mass or catholic, one may also say that it has hearty little in it that could be called Gnostic either, unless the frequent use of the mystic word IAO unaccompanied by any other Gnostic feature should be accepted as atoning for the ommission of everything else. The Ecclesiae Gnosticae Catholicae Canon Missae is not what its title declares. It is a complicated magical ceremony of considerable dramatic effect written in the typical bombastic style of Crowley, and dilated with his poetry, and containing quasi-Egyptian, Kabbalistic and other elements, with the Christian sacramental mythos notably absent. It does not contain many of the essential features which make up a Mass in any and all branches of the church catholic whether in East or West. Although it does contain the necessary formula of consecration in Greek ("this is my body 'and' this is the chalice of my blood") the formula of consecration is taken out of the traditional context wherein it is identified as spoken by Jesus the Christ. Also in other portions of the Mass the consecrated host is referred to as sperm, and indeed there exists a probably well-founded rumour to the effect that the bread-like substance used in the Mass contains sperm. It is also telling that although many personages of various spiritual stature from Lao-Tze and Krishna to Rabelais, Swinburne and (naturally) Sir Aleister Crowley are mentioned by name in the Mass, the name of Jesus or Christ is never mentioned once. This ritual is clearly not a Mass in any sense of the Christian and Catholic mythos. We are not informed whether Crowley recognized or had any use for the other six sacraments, or whether he felt that one, i.e. his Mass was enough. [19]

So what better time to punish Stephan A. Hoeller for his frontal attack on the O.T.O. Church, with the centenary of the *Book of Law*, channeled and transmitted in April, 1904 to the Wizard of the Illuminati, Crowley himself. A. W. Hill wrote by no coincidence,

19   http://www.pararreligion.ch/hoeller.htm ‡ Archived 15th November, 2016.

that after the event , as reported by *L.A. Weekly*: *"On May 7, 2004, as dusk was falling, a plume of black smoke as big and ornery as a Texas twister rose above Los Angeles. And though no one later raved on local talk radio that he'd seen the face of the devil in the ominous cloud, a knowing onlooker in a sufficiently altered state might well have glimpsed the Whore of Babylon, the face of the eternal Rome to which Philip K. Dick referred when he famously wrote: 'The Empire never ended.' The rundown, two-story building at 1516 Hollywood Boulevard, which for 27 years had been the peculiar home of Bishop Stephan A. Hoeller's Ecclesia Gnostica, was in flames. No one was injured, and the vessels of communion were salvaged, but unbeknownst to most, a landmark of hidden Hollywood had been lost. In this tiny hole-in-the-wall of a chapel, to the streetside accompaniment of bleating horns, sirens and the occasional gunshot, the gnomish and erudite Dr. Hoeller had held forth most every Friday night on subjects ranging from Kabbalah and Sufism to the psychedelic sacraments of Eleusis. And on each Sunday, he'd lighted the incense, donned his vestments and conducted a mass that was Catholic in all but its subtly subversive liturgy, for Hoeller is a Gnostic, and the sole American bishop consecrated by the Duc de Palatine, mysterious bearer of the English Gnostic Transmission.* [20]

Now let's talk a bit more about the mysterious Duc de Palatine.

Richard, Duc de Palatine and the Pansophic Rite

The *"Ancient Universal Pansophic Masonic Rite"* was a rite established at the end of the 19th century by **John Yarker**, to "synthesize" all esoteric European lineages of the various Illuminati sects. It is generally known that Yarker was a "collector" of Charters, and like Theodor Reuss, founder of the O.T.O., and Papus after him, it was his dream to unite all the orders, rites etc. of the Western Mystery Tradition of the Illuminati with each other. The Ill. Bro. *Yarker*, Jn.: 33°, 90°, 96° Grand Hierophant of A.P.R.M.M., initiated and installed James Heard as the first *Vicarius Salomonis*, Conservator of the *Rite of the Ancient Universal Pan-Sophic Rite of Masonry*, (which synthesized all esoteric European lineages in the late 19th century), who transmitted to Ill. Bro. Hugh G. de Willmott, who transmitted to H.S.H. Duc de Palatine. *Pansophic Freemasonry* can operate any and all of Yarker's rites, but only by individual warrant and charter of the *Vicarius Salomonis*.

Richard, Duc de Palatine, was a seminal figure in the development, transformation, and perpetuation of the Gnostic tradition. Palatine was born Ronald Powell of French and British noble parents in 1916. His mother descended from Captain John Hancock, first signer of the Declaration of Independence. He was ennobled by H.I.H. Prince Alexander Licastro de la Chastre Grimaldi Lascaris of Deols, France, under the Seal of the Prefect of Rome, Italy in 1954, and took the name *Richard Jean Chretien Duc de Palatine*. This was to confirm his attainment of *Spiritual Nobility* as a *Prince of Light*. Richard came to England and was eventually consecrated as a Gnostic Bishop, and claimed an unbroken line of succession from the *College of Antioch*, that linked twelve lines of succession. In 1953, he received a Charter from *The Ancient Mystic Order of the Fratris Lucis*, commonly called The Brotherhood of the Illuminati (FIG. 63), to institute an *"Outer Section to be called The Brotherhood of the Illuminati*, to be dedicated to the object of restoring the mystic teaching of our, Lord Jesus Christ."

In 1960, the name of the *Brotherhood of the Illuminati* was changed to the *Brotherhood of the Pleroma* and *The Order of the Pleroma*, and a council of three was appointed. Richard held high office in many orders and was Sovereign Grand Master of the United

20   http://www.laweekly.com/news/exile-in-godville-2139968 ‡ Archived 15th November, 2016.

C·O·P·Y

"NOR THE CATHOLICATE OF THE WEST
Incorporated in India under Act XXI of 1860 in 1950

C H A R T E R
of
THE ANCIENT MYSTIC ORDER OF THE FRATRES LUCIS
commonly called
THE BROTHERHOOD OF THE ILLUMINATI

WHEREAS in the year 1493 at Florence, Italy, there was founded a non-sectarian fraternal Order called THE ANCIENT MYSTIC ORDER OF FRATRES LUCIS, which was carried on its work secretly until now.

AND WHEREAS on the day of the date hereof there came and appeared before Us in Our Chancellery in London, His Excellency Count Pietro da Costa-Malatesta, the ARCHON of the said Order, who did then and there in Our presence duly transmit his office of Archon to our well-beloved HIS SERENE HIGHNESS PRINCE RICHARD JOHN CHRETIEN de' PALATINE, with plenary powers to extend the operations of the said Order by instituting an Outer Section in addition to the existing Inner Sectio, such Outer Section to be called THE BROTHERHOOD OF THE ILLUMINATI, and to be dedicated to the object of restoring to the outer world the mystic teachings of our Lord Jesu Christi.

BE IT KNOWN THEREFORE that We, in order to facilitate and assist the said object DOE HEREBY CHARTER the said ANCIENT MYSTIC ORDER OF FRATRES LUCIS, commonly called THE BROTHERHOOD OF THE ILLUMINATI, and confirm in the Office of ARCHON him the said RICHARD JOHN CHRETIEN DE PALATINE, With full power and authority to rule and govern the said Order, to enact a Constitution for the same, to appoint all Officers therein, and to nominate and appoint his Successor.

Corporate
Seal
Affixed Here.

G I V E N under the Corporate Seal of THE CATHOLICATE OF THE WEST, this 14th day of November, A.D., 1953 by the undersigned.

(Signed) + Georgius
PATRIARCH OF GLASTONBURY
Catholicos

John, Baron Kennedy
Secretarius ad hoc.   Enrolled in Archives: 1953/28.

NOTE: His Serene Highness has been confirmed in his noble dignity by H Highness Prince Souverain Titulaire de Deols, Pretendent au Trone du Saint Empire Romain d'Orient in 1954 and was confirmed by the Prefeture of Rome, Sez. Il Pen, del 3/8/1954. R.G. 3188, vist. P.M. 15/10/1954. All documents can be seen in the Archives of the Brotherhood of Illumin.

FIG. 63 – Document 50 present in the archives of the Brotherhood of the Illuminati, also known as Ancient Mystic Order of Fratres Lucis, on their supposed origins, showing the date of their foundation in Florence in 1493. On the bottom of the document there is also a note that shows how Ronald Powell was ennobled by assuming the name and the title of Richard, Duc de Palatine by Prince Alessandro French Licastro de la Chastre Grimaldi Lascaris, Duke and Marquis de la Chastre under the seal of the Prefect of Rome in Italy in 1954.

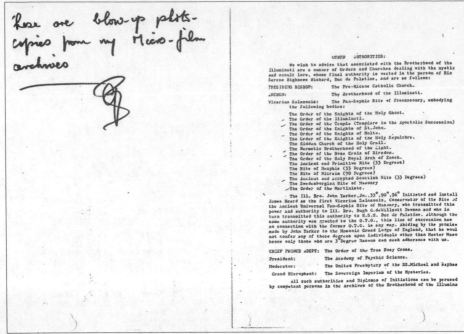

FIG. 64 – Top secret documents originally hidden on microfilm—as explained in the note written by hand on this page to your right—that would seem to show evidence, at least on paper, of the fact that Richard, Duc de Palatine, Archon of the Brotherhood of the Illuminati, was initiatic heir of a supposed lineage of the Order of the Illuminati Masonic Rite called **Ancient Universal Pan-Sophic Rite**, originally bestowed upon his Master **Hugh G. de Willmott**, by noted English Freemason **John Yarker (1883 – 1913)**, a prominent figure of "fringe" Freemasonry, and an important member also in so-called "Regular" Freemasonry, who started several Neo-Templar rites and was tied, in turn, to Aleister Crowley.

Rites of Memphis and Mizraim, *Grand Hierophant* of the *Sovereign Imperium of the Mysteries*, Sovereign Grand Master of the **Ancient and Universal Pansophic Rites of Freemasonry**, Senior Prelate and Great Prior of the *Order of the True Rosy Cross*, and Grand Master of the *United Templar Rite*.

In July, 1964, he incorporated these bodies into the *Disciplina Arcani* (Arcanum Arcanorum), an integral part of the **Order of the Pleroma**, in order to withdraw the Masonic influence, and to cleanse the Order from all taint of being a political tool. Palatine had plumbed the depths of Freemasonry through the Scottish Rite, and attained the 33° degree, then went into the esoteric *Ultra-Masonic* and **Egyptian Rites,** searching for spiritual enlightenment. Palatine preserved and perpetuated the *Pansophic* or **Ancient Rites of Freemasonry,** where John Yarker had spent his career painstakingly collecting valid charters and warrants to preserve. (FIG. 64) Palatine deleted the Masonic requirement, synthesized authorities, warrants, and charters, used spiritual discernment as a basic canon for ordination and consecration rather than seminary training, and was willing to quickly advance people to higher degrees when appropriate. These and other such Rites are mere *external* group exercises or liturgies through which *invisible* Cabalistic and Hermetic forces are contacted to potentiate the interior unfoldment of lodge members. These rites are not the essential Gnosis of any school or tradition. They are merely *ritual instruments* that were appropriate in a medieval setting, and are secondary to the essential transmission. The intent was not to revive those complex medieval European rites, but to make them available for study by Pansophic Freemasons. (FIGS. 65 and 66)

Also, one must ask, how many of those who work the *Rites of Memphis and Mizraim* still have the entire 99° degrees, and of those, how many actually do the "*Internal Alchemy*" work related to the material in the Quarantines of Cagliostro? Duc de Palatine transmitted to Bishop and Count **George Boyer**, *Grand Archon*, Brotherhood and Order of the Pleroma, Hermetic Brotherhood of Light, *Sanctuary of the Gnosis* (which have authority to transmit the following extant lineages), warranted the *Grailmaster*, on behalf of the *Temple of the Holy Grail*, to carry forth the authorities embodied in the *Pansophic Rite*, including:

- ILLUMINIST (ULTRA-MASONIC):
    1. *Fratres Lucis* (Brotherhood of the Illuminati)
    2. Order of the Illuminati (*Ordo Illuminatorum*)
    3. Order of the Martiniste
    4. Brotherhood of Luxor

- TEMPLAR:
    1. Knights of the Holy Ghost
    2. Knights of St. John
    3. Knights of Malta
    4. Knights of the Holy Sepulchre
    5. Knights of the Temple

- ROSICRUCIAN:
    1. Order of the True Rosy Cross
    2. Golden and Rosy Cross
    3. Order of the Rose Croix of Hiredom

- GNOSTIC ECCLESIAE:
    1. Order of the Ecclesiae Rosicrucianae Catholicae (Catholic)
    2. Hidden Church of the Holy Grail (Protestant, Edgar Waite)
    3. Ecclesia Gnostica Ortodoxa

- ULTRA-MASONIC and MASONIC:
    1. *Ancient and Primitive Rite*
    2. *Rite of Memphis*
    3. *Rite of Mizraim*
    4. Ancient and Accepted Scottish Rite
    5. Swedenborgian Rite
    6. Order of the Rose-Croix of Hiredom
    7. Order of the Holy Royal Arch of Enoch

The Tau, the Gnostic Church and the Patriarchate of Antioch

Jules-Benoît Stanislas Doinel du Val-Michel, known as Jules Doinel, (FIG. 67) placed in the foundation of his Gnostic Church, the mystical title of **Tau**. That's why all the bishops of the contemporary Gnostic Churches use this appellative in their own mystic name. This Greek letter reminded him of the Egyptian ankh, and he called

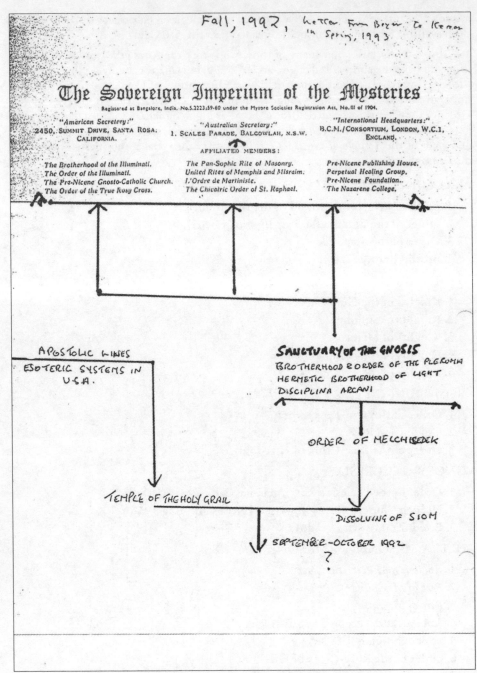

FIG. 65 – *Document from 1992, on apostolic lineages of Richard, Duc de Palatine linked to the esoteric systems of the Illuminati in various countries.*

The Sovereign Imperium of the Mysteries

Registered at Bangalore, India, No.5.2223/59-60 under the Mysore Societies Registration Act, No. III of 1904.

"American Secretary:"
2450, SUMMIT DRIVE, SANTA ROSA, CALIFORNIA.

"Australian Secretary:"
1, SCALES PARADE, BALGOWLAH, N.S.W.

"International Headquarters:"
B.C.M./CONSORTIUM, LONDON, W.C.1. ENGLAND.

AFFILIATED MEMBERS:

The Brotherhood of the Illuminati.
The Order of the Illuminati.
The Pre-Nicene Gnosto-Catholic Church.
The Order of the True Rosy Cross.

The Pan-Sophic Rite of Masonry.
United Rites of Memphis and Misraim.
L'Ordre de Martiniste.
The Chivalric Order of St. Raphael.

Pre-Nicene Publishing House.
Perpetual Healing Group.
Pre-Nicene Foundation.
The Nazarene College.

YOUR REF.:
OUR REF.:

DATE: 1st January 1960.

DECRETUM
CONCERNING THE BROTHERHOOD OF THE ILL-
-UMINATI, THE ORDER OF THE ILLUMINATI,
and THE HERMETIC BROTHERHOOD OF LIGHT

WE, RICHARD, DUC de PALATINE, PRESIDENT AND GRAND HIEROPHANT OF THE SOVEREIGN IMPERIUM OF THE MYSTERIES, pursuant to the plenary powers vested in Us by Rule XIII of the said Imperium, DO HEREBY DECREE that the organisations referred to in the said Rule XIII (4), to wit : THE BROTHERHOOD OF THE ILLUMINATI, THE ORDER OF THE ILLUMINATI, and THE HERMETIC BROTHERHOOD OF LIGHT, shall from henceforth be governed and administered by a Governing Body to be called THE COUNCIL OF THREE, to which end WE HEREBY APPOINT Ourself, The Reverend John Martyn-Baxter, and The Right Reverend George William Boyer as the first Members of the said Council of Three, with full powers, including that of appointing other Officers and of registering and/or incorporating the pre-named bodies or each and any of them in any part of the world ; Provided always that nothing herein contained shall be deemed to in any way diminish Our full powers in relation thereto as set forth in the above-mentioned Rules.

GIVEN under Our hand, this 1st day of January 1960 at London, England.

WITNESS :-

Richard Duc de Palatine.

DUC de PALATINE
President and Grand Hierophant, S.I.O.M.
Leader, Brotherhood of the Illuminati
Grand Archon, Order of the Illuminati and
Hermetic Brotherhood of Light.

John, Baron Kennedy

FIG. 66 – *Document in which Richard, Duc de Palatine was appointed as head of the Brotherhood of the Illuminati, Order of the Illuminati and of Hermetic Brothehood of Light, by a council administred by a initiatic entity called* **THE COUNCIL OF THREE.**

himself Valentin, in honor of the famous Gnostic founder of the second century named Valentin, something that was done also by my old friend the Norwegian Jan Valentin Sæther (b. 1944), a very talented painter who paints all the Grand Masters of the Order Freemasons of Norway (Swedish Rite), and is primarily responsible for the **Bruchion Center** that used to operate in Oslo on behalf of the *Ecclesia Gnostica* of Dr. Stephan A. Hoeller. (FIGS. 68 and 69) I followed this Gnostic reality for a few years when I lived in Norway, but at one point it was completely infiltrated by members of the various O.T.O factions, bringing in their perverse Gnostic liberal beliefs that were far more dangerous than those of the *Ecclesia Gnostica.* Present were Illuminati Satanists like Nicholaj Frisvold de Mattos,

FIG. 67 – *Jules-Benoît Stanislaus Doinel du Val-Michel (1842 – 1903).*

who calls himself **Tau Orphee Luchifero**, or his disciple Runar Karlsen (Bishop Tau To Logos), an XI° of the *Ordo Templi Orientis* (degree dedicated to homosexual magic), who celebrated an unlikely Gnostic Mass in the *Bruchion Center* of Jan Valentin Sæther, where under the valuable sacral vestment, he was actually naked. Definitely an unusual celebration that would have pleased the Vatican gay lobby, but later Sæther became upset by the practices, and forbid the use of his Gnostic Church to Thelemites.

Returning to Doinel, when he was appointed Patriarch of the Gnostic Church, he declared his direct descent from the Apostle John (the beloved), whose gospel was considered their main holy book. And it is precisely this reference to John, that suggests a certain continuity of the Gnostic Church with the Johannite Church of Raymond Bernard Fabré-Palaprat, that far from disappearing, was partially absorbed by the French esoteric milieu, since the Order of Palaprat and his church were transmitted down to Joséphin Péladan, which in turn transmitted them inside what was the first Martinist Order organized under the aegis of Papus or Gérard Encausse. Just see the names of the first people involved in the Gnostis Church, and you will understand right away the protagonists of the Martinist Order founded by Papus. However, Doinel was convinced that the Church should be run by couples, formed by a male and a female bishop, as was done fifty years earlier by the controversial Illuminati mystic and prophet of Lyon the French, **Eugene Vintras,** with his infamous Church of Carmel. In 1842, under pressure from the Catholic Church, Vintras was arrested by the French authorities and imprisoned for five years

FIG. 68 – Stephan A. Hoeller (b. 1931) Regionary Bishop of the Americas of the Ecclesia Gnostic.

on the trumped-up charge of soliciting donations from people that he claimed to reveal the name of their guardian angel. While he was in prison, the Abbe Marechal, known as Ruthmael, took over the community. He apparently began publicly teaching certain rituals that had a sexual content. According to some reports, he confided to his congregation, *"Those who feel love for one another should share it often. Every time they do, they are sure to create a spirit in heaven."* Well, this was yet again another connection to sexual magic, however the ancient Gnostics included both men and women in the priesthood, a tradition revived by Vintras in the Church of Carmel, and later by Doinel who chose its members, among the adepts of Papus, were the first form of organized Martinism open to both men and women (although men are still to this day the only ones that can achieve the degree of S :: I :: I :: / *Supèrieur Inconnu Initiateur*), this made possible to recruit the future male and female bishops of his church.

As the historian Richard Griffiths explains:

> *These rites were sacrificial in nature, and they enabled those who performed them to receive the merits of "redemption," and to participate in the preparation for the coming of the Paraclete. The belief in the efficacy of a specific rite in freeing man from the fetters of matter and bringing him nearer to the spiritual redemption which would announce the Third Reign is very near to that of most gnostic sects, for whom the method of redemption consisted not so much in the profession of certain opinions or virtues as in the practice of certain rites. The ancient Gnostics included both men and women in the priesthood, a tradition revived by Vintras in the Church of Carmel. Women were permitted into the priesthood of the rite, in fact they held a very important place, for it was through Woman that salvation was to come. And in the attitude towards the Virgin Mary we find a conception of her as "created Wisdom,"*

FIG. 69 – Circes / OSTI and Stephan Holler in his reconstructed Church in Hollywood.

the invariable reflection of "uncreated Wisdom." This can be seen to be very close to one form of Valentinianism, a gnostic belief in which Sophia, or Wisdom (a divine principle which had fallen from the realm of light into the realm of matter) was conceived as being a double figure. The higher Sophia remained in the sphere of light, the lower Sophia had sunk into darkness. Through this duality Sophia became the fallen divinity through whom the mingling of light and dark, of spirit and matter, in the world, had been achieved; she was also seen as the intermediary between the lower and higher worlds and an instrument of redemption.

I know it can become complex at times to follow all these names that shaped the history of the priesthood of the Illuminati in the last couple of centuries, however it's important to underline their importance. Among the various characters recruited from Doinel for his project, there was Papus himself who became Tau Vincent, Bishop of Toulouse, and Paul Sedir [pseudonym of Yvon Le Loup (1871 – 1926)], who became Tau Paulas, coadjutor bishop of Toulouse and Concorrezzo or Lucien Chamuel [pseudonym of Lucien Mauchel (deceased in 1936)], Tau Bardesanes, bishop of La Rochelle and Saintes. These three formed the Holy Synod of Ecclesia Gnostica, that as you can see was firmly in the hands of the Martinist branch of the Illuminati. The theology of the Church included elements of the Gnostic doctrines of Simon Magus, Valentin and Marcus, the Cathars (of which were recovered two sacraments: *consolamentum,* a form of complex ritual with laying on of hands, and *Aparelhament,* a public confession of their sins), of the Catholic Church (a form of Mass with the splitting of the bread) and of Masonic initiation. [21] And then through a séance, Doinel obtained the main line of consecration of contemporary Gnosticism, that became the *Ecclesia Gnostic Catholica* (EGC), whose branches, as I told you in the first volume of my *Confessions*, are particularly interested in sexual magic along the lines dictated by occult-ists like Theodor Reuss, Aleister Crowley, ending in the O.T.O. and its derivatives.

The "Gnostic Mass" unfortunately, in this environment, gradually becomes an orgi-astic ritual, of which the expert Massimo Introvigne, in his book *The Return of Gnosti-cism,* reconstructs sources, largely unknown, highlighting in particular the figure—al-most ignored today—of the Belgian knight **Georges Le Clément de Saint-Marcq**. A high level dignitary of Freemasonry in his country that was fanatically anti-Catholic, whose influence has been decisive, and a figure that I have already described to you in detail in Volume I of my *Confessions,* because of the importance in the teachings of the *Ordo Templi Orientis*, with his controversial *Eucharist* brochure. Crowley enclosed in the highest degrees of his paramasonic system, the secrets of the E.G.C, and transmitted them to a worthy successor, creating the mysterious 12th degree that was to remain a total secret even for the majority of O.T.O. members. Before his death in August, 1944, Crowley left the legacy of his Church in the hands of **William Bernard Crow,** who in 1948 declares himself Patriarch Great General Director and Grand Master of the Order, (FIGS. 70 and 71) which, however, will take place outside the traditional transmission of the O.T.O. degrees, and it seems to be rather linked to the Rite of Memphis and Mizraim, and the various denominations of the colorful Gnostic-Catholic "Fringe" Masonic milieu that involves high level Illuminati. Understanding the sectarian world of the Illuminati and their philosophy will lead to the weird world of the head of slaves of the elite, and Satanic parasites like Marina Abramović or Marilyn Manson, just to name two servants of evil. Our world seems to be heading towards a final clash with such forces, so we need to prepare, understand and comprend the level of manipulation at all levels, especially when this ends in the classical worship of the Sabbatic Goat.

Elphias Levi re-imagined Baphomet into a figure he named the Sabbatic Goat. Repre-senting the universe in the form of binary opposites, the Sabbatic Goat incorporates ele-ments of the hermaphroditic stone Baphomets and the symbolic ideals of the Templar Ba-phomet myth. He mingled these elements with Occult, Kabbalistic and Catholic imagery. [22]

The Gnostic legacy and the various Churches is confusing to the untrained and disinter-ested believer, which is orchestrated and manipulated by different factions of the Illuminati, sometimes fighting each other, that is made up of Bishops who become Masons (a quite well-known fact), but also by high dignitaries of Freemasonry recognized as bishops by the Vatican because of their apostolic succession from Antioch deemed legitimate. This was con-firmed to me by Professor Giancarlo Seri, who is one of the highest authorities worldwide of the so-called "Egyptian" rites of Freemasonry. Currently there are at least five bishops and several churches that bear the title of Patriarch of Antioch, without counting the various derivatives and sub-products of the Church of Antioch, which was derived by a splinter group present in irregular and spurious forms of Freemasonry. One of these is represented by **Archbishop Roberto C. Toca,** is tied since the second half of the seventies to the **Frater-nitas Rosicruciana Antiqua (F.R.A.),** and the *Ordo Templi Orientis* and its EGC. That is where he obtained, thanks to the Illuminati **Johannes Rider,** X°degree and OHO (*Outer Head of the Orde,)* of a branch of the O.T.O. In 1976, Toca then came into contact with a particular branch of the Patriarchate of Antioch close to Freemasonry, headed by Archbish-op **Herman Adrian Spruit.** This happened when Toca, a rather colorful character of the international occult scene, was still a resident in Cuba, where, contrary to what you might initially think, Freemasonry and the Jesuits are the masters, not the so-called communists, and this has been proven to the world once again with the arrival of Pope Francis, a South

22   http://ultraculture.org/blog/2016/02/08/baphomet-sabbatic-goat/ ‡ Archived 15th November, 2016.

American Jesuit. He has often used Cuba in recent years as an outpost for his geopolitical business for the New World Order. All those idiotic Hollywood stars that criticized President Donald J.Trump before his election in 2016, should go there, since they seem to love communism, a creation of the evil side of the Illuminati, and for this reason an ideological abomination.

Roberto C. Toca, was not that attracted to communism, and thanks to his Illuminati connections moved to the U.S., where he would form his own independent jurisdiction of the Patriarchate of Antioch in 1980. A couple of years later he joined the Archbishop Herman Adrian Spruit, founder of the Catholic Apostolic Church of Antioch-Malabar Rite, which claims valid lines of apostolic succession in the historical episcopate, which is not however, in union with the Catholic Pope in Rome or any Orthodox Patriarch,[23] and consecrated Toca archbishop in 1982. In the United States as resident since 1987, he becomes first Archbishop and later Archbishop Primate, but also a stable landmark of the Cuban community in the city of Tampa, Florida, where Toca still resides and launched a successful television career. This led him to be one of the most viewed Latin American men in Florida,

SOVEREIGN SANCTUARY
of the
Ancient and Primitive Rite
of
MEMPHIS AND MIZRAIM

In the name of the great Architect of the Universe.

Salutation upon all points of the Triangle.

WHEREAS it is universally accepted by responsible students of Masonic History that the whole authority of the Scottish, Memphis and Mizraim Rites was concentrated in the late John Yarker, and from him finally passed to Aleister Crowley, in whom it is now vested.

NOW, THEREFORE, we the said **ALEISTER CROWLEY,** by virtue of such authority, **do HEREBY APPOINT Our Brother WILLIAM BERNARD CROW** as Patriarch Grand Administrator General of the Rite, with full authority to administer all such funds as come within his control.

In witness whereof we have hereunto

set our Hand and Seal,

August 1944 e.v.

FIG. 70 – Document certifying the transfer of the Patriarchate of the Ecclesia Gnostica Catholica by Aleister Crowley to the Freemason William Bernard Crow in August 1944, present on page 484 of the book O.T.O. Rituals and Sex Magick by Theodor Reuss and Aleister Crowley, published by the Pentacle Enterprises (September, 1999) and subsequently withdrawn from circulation because of a court case and pressures received by the O.T.O. U.S. caliphate.

PATRIARCH
GRAND ADMINISTRATOR GENERAL
of the Ancient and Primitive Rite of
MEMPHIS
AND
MIZRAIM

REX SUMMUS
SANCTISSIMUS
ORDO
TEMPLI
ORIENTIS

SOVEREIGN
PATRIARCH
GNOSTIC
CATHOLIC
CHURCH

FIG. 71 – Coat of arms of the Masonic-Gnostic- Neo-Templar Sanctuary created in August, 1948 by William Bernard Crow, named by Aleister Crowley in 1944, Patriarch Grand Ancient General Director and Universal Cosmic Ritual Architecture, which included the XII ° of the O.T.O., the 33 ° 90 ° 97 ° of the Rite of Memphis and Mizraim and the title of Sovereign Patriarch of the Gnostic Catholic Church. This document is taken from p. 485 of the rare out-of-print book O.T.O. Rituals and Sex Magick by Theodor Reuss and Aleister Crowley, published September, 1999 by Pentacle Enterprises in London.

and the most delirious and improbable televangelist that you have ever seen, even in the United States. Archbishop Roberto C. Toca is one of a kind. However he seems to be globally recognized by the Ecumenical College of Metropolitans of the Gnostic Church. The Catholic Church of the Antiochean Rite of Roberto C. Toca has even an official addresss, **P.O. Box 8473 Tampa, FL 33674-8473.**

The seat of the patriarchate was formerly Antioch, in what is now Turkey. However, in the 15th century, it was moved to Syria in response to the Ottoman invasion.

Going back to what is modern Gnosticism, Massimo Introvigne writes that it is an attempt: *"of synthesis between the setting of Jules-Benoît Doinel and that of the Gnostic Ecclesia Catholica: almost all of which include secret teachings of sexual magic, though compared to Aleister Crowley—the liturgical and ritual aspects retain greater importance and the magical use of sexuality is proposed, trying to stay away from the orgiastic tone of the extreme English occultist."*[24]

So for Introvigne, there are no branches of the Gnostic Church without sexual element, they are all involved in some way in sexual magic (or magick as Crowley used to write), and there are only less obvious manifestations of the "orgiastic tone." And now before closing with the subject of Gnostic tradition within the Illuminati, I could not do so without mentioning **Joel Duez Vichery,** a contemporary author of 25 books on various elements of the esoteric tradition, and a controversial figure of the Illuminati. Duez goes from membership in the infamous gay **Choronzon Club** of **Michael Paul Bertiaux,** (FIG. 72) to a key position in almost every Illuminati sect in the world (including the mysterious and highly secretive **Order of the Dragon**), to his leading position in the ***Église gnostique apostolique,*** founded in 1953 by Robert Ambelain. (FIG. 73) Duez incredibly received an official blessing as Monsignor, from the now Saint, **Pope John Paul II,** after joining the infamous Choronzon Club, (FIG. 74) and even celebrated Gnostic Mass in a Masonic lodge in Haiti, home of Voodoo. Monsignor is an honorific form of address for those members of the clergy of the Catholic Church including bishops, honorary prelates and canons. I have included documents that will cast an even darker shadow on the nefarious John Paul II activities, and his familiarity with key figures of the occult world.

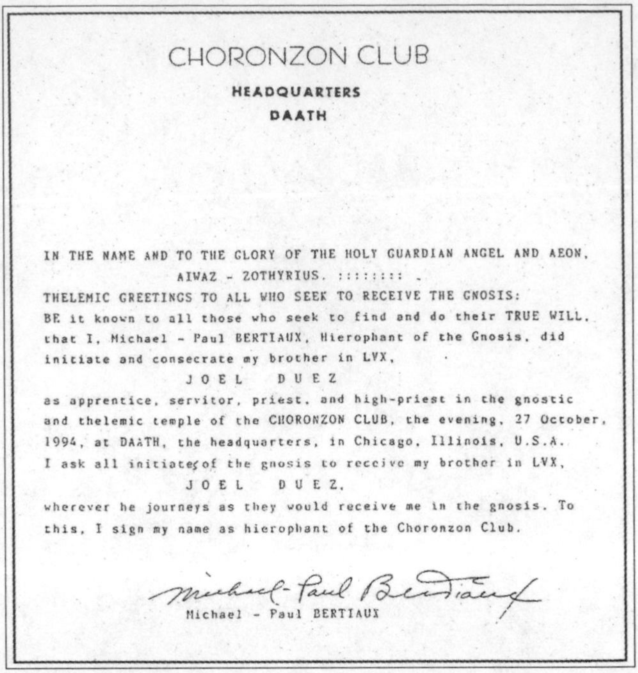
CHORONZON CLUB

HEADQUARTERS

DAATH

IN THE NAME AND TO THE GLORY OF THE HOLY GUARDIAN ANGEL AND AEON, AIWAZ - ZOTHYRIUS. :::::::: .

THELEMIC GREETINGS TO ALL WHO SEEK TO RECEIVE THE GNOSIS:

BE it known to all those who seek to find and do their TRUE WILL, that I, Michael - Paul BERTIAUX, Hierophant of the Gnosis, did initiate and consecrate my brother in LVX,

J O E L D U E Z

as apprentice, servitor, priest, and high-priest in the gnostic and thelemic temple of the CHORONZON CLUB, the evening, 27 October, 1994, at DAATH, the headquarters, in Chicago, Illinois, U.S.A.

I ask all initiates of the gnosis to receive my brother in LVX,

J O E L D U E Z,

wherever he journeys as they would receive me in the gnosis. To this, I sign my name as hierophant of the Choronzon Club.

Michael - Paul BERTIAUX

FIG. 72 – Joel Duez membership in the homosexual CHORONZON CLUB with a document signed by Michael Paul Bertiaux.

The Jesuits, the Rosicrucians and the Catholic Origins of "Scottish Freemasonry"

Athanasius Kircher plays a dual role of paramount importance, both in the growth of Marian devotion, and in the development of the Jesuit "Golden" infiltration of the Rosy Cross, that inspired later the birth of the Order of the Golden and Rosy Cross, a German Rosicrucian organization founded in the 1750s by Freemason and alchemist Hermann Fichtuld. Some say this emanated part of the Bavarian Illuminati, which then became their sworn enemies according to the law of ***divide and rule,*** dear to the Jesuits, agents of the Catholic Church to this day, as well as heads of Vatican Intelligence services, that had a major role in the development of the Brotherhood of the Rosicrucians after their infiltratation gradually moved to control the "Invisible College." Kircher in his works, attempted to establish an affinity between Pythagoras, the Greek mysteries, the kabbalah esotericism both Hebrew and Arabic, and will remain even after his death, a constant source of inspiration for many researchers of the occult sciences, and of course a key figure for his fellow Jesuits. [25]

About the strange link between the Jesuits and the Rosicrucians, Freemason and historian Furio Bacchini writes:

25 See. Frances A. Yates, The Rosicrucian Enlightenment, (London and Boston: Rutledge & Kegan Paul, 1972), p. 230.

FIG. 73 – Document of Église Gnostique Apostolique that indicates in Joel Duez the successor of Robert Ambelain (1907-1997).

This juxtaposition of the Rosicrucians and the Societas Jesu (author's note: the Jesuits), characterized by a sort of "love and hate relationship" that had roots dating back to the seventeenth century, during the Thirty Years War, may appear strange because at that time the Rosenkreutz followers were figured in, especially among Protestants, but it was since then that the Jesuits began a real strategy to bring them back "to the true faith." This aspect will certainly help Kircher in his mission, which is described in this way in the last century by the Jesuit **Pierre Theillard de Chardin (1881 – 1955),** *who had tried to reconcile Darwin's theory of evolution with religion, and is a rising hero of the New Age: a potentially predisposed world (author's note: that of Protestants) to transpose the influence of the Jesuits, who are holding a real affinity with the Rosicrucians, the values from them expressed in the same period, the seventeenth century, with the search for the Cosmic Christ, the aggregation point between the universe and all humanity, an evolution not deterministic but theological."*

Freemason Bacchini shows us the affinities that bind them:

Yet of all the religious orders of the Catholic Church, the Jesuits were the ones that looked more to the Rosicrucians. Renaissance esoteric influences acted on the formation of the Society of Jesus have never yet been examined completely. The order made use of the hermetic tradition to appeal to Protestants and to the many religious denominations with whom he came in contact during his missionary work. The hermetic and occult philosophy of the Jesuits had an extraordinary formulation in the work of Athanasius Kircher ... who always mentions with deep respect the alleged ancient Egyptian priest Hermes Trismegistus. The work of Kircher was much used in their missionary work.

Here's another gem extrapolated from Brother Bacchini's work, showing instead, the secret structure of the Golden Rosicrucians, linking them to the Jesuits: *"The structure of the Golden Rosicrucians was a pyramid, similar to that of the Jesuits, however, they were dependent on a single general and not twelve members (like the Areopagus of the Illuminati, and the twelve Apostles). The purpose of the Rosicrucians was clear and coincided with Freemasonry, and the research and the training of men to revive a fallen Christianity."*[26]

The first mention of the mysterious **Golden Rosicrucians** was made by **Samuel Richter** in 1710, who wrote an important work on alchemy under the name *Sincerus Renatus*, where the perfect description of the philosopher's stone of the Aurea Rosicrucian

26 See. Furio Bacchini, La vita rocambolesca del conte Alessandro Savioli Corbelli (1742-1811), (Bologna, IT: Edizioni Pendragon, 2011), pp. 141-143.

Brotherhood is found. The Order of the Rose Cross of Gold appears to be present in Germany between 1750 and 1790, but according to some scholars did not have much in common with the original Rosicrucians of the *Fama Fraternitatis*. Only their symbolism and mysticism remain present, the rest was Jesuit made. Jesuits were the experts of the occult, arising precisely from their Kircherian tradition, to influence the Christian symbolism of the Rosicrucians in the first years of the famous Rosicrucian Manifestos, and this

FIG. 74 – Incredibile official document of the Vatican signed by Pope John Paul II, addressing the Freemason, occultist and member of several Illuminati groups, Joel Duez as a member of the clergy.

is another of the interesting points of which Bacchini speaks in his essay. A conflict between the Illuminati Order of Weishaupt and the mysterious Golden Rosycross linked to the Jesuit leaders of the time, initially helped the creation of the Order of Weishaupt, for their occult purposes of control and manipulation. Let's not forget that the same Franz Adolph Freiherr von Knigge (1752 – 1796), who I spoke about in Volume II (because he is key figure of the original Illuminati Order), before being hired by a certain Di Costanzo for the Bavarian Illuminati, is suspected to have already been initiated into the mysteries of Rosicrucian in 1772. Certainly in 1773 he was initiated into the Masonic Rite of Strict Templar Observance, the Freemason Neo-Templar hideout of the aristocracy, infiltrated over time by the Jesuits through the mysterious Unknown Superiors, whose initials were indeed, the same initials of the Societas Jesu, or *Society of Jesus.*

This rite of the Strict Observance that I currently preside as one of the leading representatives, as I mentioned in the preface, was purified of Jesuit infiltration, and it has now been reawakened in March of 2016, under my direction. Vincenzo Soro in his commentary of the French pamphlet, *The Great Book of Nature*, shows that the Strict Observance was at one time *"the instrument more or less aware by Loyola."* Baron Heinrich von Gleichen (1733 or '35 – 1807), Minister of Denmark, in a letter dated 3 June 1781, fully supports the hypothesis that the **initials S.I.** were those of the notorious Society of Jesus, and that the Rosicrucians and Neo-Templar were *"like puppets of which the Jesuits pulled the strings."* The Jesuits have always been prone to double and triple play to accomplish supreme manipulation, that even back then saw their expulsion from the Vatican. They were intent on orchestrating dramatic revolutions, like the French one, that brought epochal social changes, in order to regain possession of their position in the Vatican. I would like to recall that a few decades before the French Revolution, there was Jesuit and Vatican support to the dynasty of the Stuarts, in their misguided attempt to re-install a Catholic monarch in England, another fundamental step to understand the origins of a certain kind of Freemasonry found in the "Scottish Degrees."

Certainly it is a difficult task to outline the distinctive terms of such a form of Freemasonry, because it is difficult to understand its essence, not only because of the complexity of the varied, and sometimes contradictory aspects that distinguish it, but by its very nature that makes it comparable, rather than a "historical" phenomenon, to a category of human thought. "Scottish Degree" implies, however, a distinction between this and the other, thereby leading to a dramatic rift that is antithetical to the unity of the phenomenon that is canonically defined a "Universal Freemasonry." It is however, an inevitable simplification and schematization of the problem in order to make possible the approach. With this background it can be said that the connotations that characterize "Scottish Degrees" and "Scottish Freemasonry" and distinguish it from the "English," may, in a very simplistic way, be summarized as follows to give you a clearer idea of the matter:

– **With a Catholic character;**

– **Linked to the dynasty of the Stuarts (hence the title "Scottish," the place of origin of the Stuarts, and the title "Jacobite" of the Lodges with reference to James II Stuart, dethroned in 1688);**

– **Aristocratic (in fact found fertile ground among the aristocracy and the high clergy);**

– **Articulated in the High Degrees, next to those of Apprentice, Fellow and Master (High degrees called "Scottish" because they would be derived from the ancient Herodom Kilwinning Lodge of Edinburgh);**

– **Of knightly origin, linked to the Crusades and the Knights Templar;**

– **Romantic or pre-Romantic;**

– **Spiritualist, devoted to philosophical research, to spiritual perfection, to a "Christian form of Esotericism."**

Conversely, you can write a parallel list with the characteristics of "English" Freemasonry: Protestant Hanoverian, bourgeois, are limited to three degrees called "blue," of Corporate origin, Enlightenment, and rationalism. In fact, in the earliest Statutes, prior to the establishment of the Grand Lodge of London in 1717, **"fidelity to God and the Holy Church" [the Roman Catholic]**, is imposed, and it should be remembered that the Grand Master of the Lodge of "St. Paul" in London, from 1685 to 1702, was the famous architect **Sir Christopher Wren,** Catholic and follower of James Stuart. The Lodges became the place of a lacerating struggle between Hanoverians and the suporters of the The House of Stuart, (originally Stewart), that took place in the seventeenth century, the place where the defeated continued to organize themselves in their political struggle. Hence the opposition of Hanoverian Masonry, inside which would be built, in June 24, 1717, the Grand Lodge of London.

The fifth Grand Master of the Grand Lodge of London was **Philipp, Duke of Wharton (1698 – 1731)**, a colorful character, of vivid intelligence, elected in 1722 in order to lend prestige to the institution. But when, in the solemn Masonic banquet of the feast of St. John the Baptist, the hymn of Stuart was played, he was expelled and his name symbolically "burned between the columns." In 1724, Wharton went to Rome with James Stuart, pretender to the throne of England, and took refuge there from 1718, under the name of James III. (FIG. 75) He converted to Catholicism, and founded a lodge in Rome, probably belonging to **The Antient Noble Order of the Gormogons** that was set up in opposition to Grand Lodge of London. The Gormogons are first heard of in a notice published in the *London Daily Post* on September 3, 1724:

Whereas the truly ANTIENT NOBLE ORDER of the Gormogons, instituted by Chin-Qua Ky-Po, the first Emperor of China (according to their account), many thousand years before Adam, and of which the great philosopher Confucious was Oecumenicae Volgee, has lately been brought into England by a Mandarin, and he having admitted several Gentlemen of Honour into the mystery of that most illustrious order, they have determined to hold a Chapter at the Castle Tavern in Fleet Street, at the particular request of several persons of quality. This is to inform the public, that there will be no drawn sword at the Door, nor Ladder in a dark Room, nor will any Mason be reciev'd as a member till he has renounced his Novel Order and been properly degraded. N.B.— The Grand Mogul, the Czar of Muscovy, and Prince Tochmas are entr'd into this Hon. Society; but it has been refused to the Rebel Meriweys, to his great Mortification. The Mandarin will shortly set out for Rome, having a particular Commission to make a Present of the Antient Order to his Holiness, and it is believ'd the whole Sacred College of Cardinals will commence Gormogons. Notice will be given in the Gazette the Day the Chapter will be held.

FIG. 75 – *The author in front of a little-known fresco of James Francis Edward Stuart nicknamed the* **Old Pretender** *painted in the Monastery of St. Scolastica in Subiaco near Rome where he stayed for a while, had lodge meetings, and even met the Pope of the time. This was only recently rediscovered by chance during a restoration of the Monastery.*

Letters appeared in the *Plain Dealer* for Monday, September 14, 1724 (No. 51) attacking Freemasonry and referring to the Gormogons; and then in the British Journal for December 12, 1724: *"We hear that a Peer of the first Rank, a noted Member of the Society of Free-Masons, hath suffered himself to be degraded as a member of that Society, and his Leather Apron and Gloves to be burnt, and thereupon enter'd himself as a Member of the Society of Gormogons, at the Castle-Tavern in Fleet Street."* This is presumed to be a reference to Philip, Duke of Wharton.

Little is heard again of the Gormogons until the edition of the *Daily Journal* for October 26 and 28, 1728:

By command of the Vol-Gi. A General Chapter of the Most August and Ancient Order, GOR-MO-GON, will be held at the Castle Tavern in Fleet Street, on Saturday, the 31st Inst., to commence at 12 o'clock ; of which the several Graduates and Licentiates are to take Notice, and give their Attendance.

The same year a letter by Wharton appeared in Mr. Mist's Journal, lampooning the British royal court in a similar Persian style as the Gormogon literature of 1724. Nichols and Stevens, editors of *Hogarth's Works* (1810) claim that the order was frequently advertised between October 1728 and 1730, but no records exist. The *Weekly Journal* or *British Gazetteer* for April 18, 1730, stated that John Dennis, poet, political writer and critic, had renounced the Gormogons and joined the Freemasons. Wharton died on May 31, 1731, and the Gormogons were not heard from again. [27] However the first known Grandmaster (or *Oecumenical Volgi*) was **Andrew Michael Ramsay of Ayr**, Scotland, a Jacobite of strong convictions that as I already outlined in Volume II was responsible for the birth of the Masonic Templar Degrees that influenced not only the birth of the Strict Templar Observance but also the much younger Ancient and Accepted Scottish Rite the most practiced Rite of Freemasonry today in the USA.

Note that the presence of "Jacobites" is also found several times in the symbolism of the first three degrees, for example in the expression "widow's sons," which are used by Freemasons, which would seem to refer to the fact that they were children of a widow both the "Old" and the "Young" Pretender. Other references can be found in the Hiram legend of the 3rd Degree of Freemasonry, where the architect's death of Solomon's Temple depicts symbolically the execution of Charles I, while attempting to lift the body of the Master Hiram, and alludes instead to the attempt to raise the young Prince Charles Edward from the tomb of exile to the throne of England. Other references about the meaning of the word in Gaelic, are even in the branch of acacia. But the Jacobite and the monarchical period leading to the Jacobin and revolutionary one, are a development of a much older initiatic reality known inside of Freemasonry and Martinezism, linked to the mysterious figure Martinez de Pasqually (1727?–1774) a theurgist and theosophist of uncertain origin, that would create the *Élus Cohen de L'Univers* **"Order of Knight Masons, Elect Priests of the Universe."** He had knowledge that went far beyond just the physical and spiritual world, that **placed him in direct contact with those we now call "aliens."** Martinez held a **Masonic Patent,** inherited by his father, that received directly from Charles Edward Stuart, in 1738, which allowed him to immediately kick start Masonic operations "on demand," and found Freemason Lodges and Chapters with no limitations of Masonic jurisdiction. I have already written of him and his possible link with the 18th of R.S.A.A. in the last chapter of Volume I. We will now delve deeper into this mysterious Illuminati figure in contact with "Aliens" and the "Invisible Masters" that guide us from behind the curtains of history.

Dom Martinez de Pasqually, the mysterious Illuminati ...

Despite the painstaking research of many historians on the mysterious figure of Martinez or Martinès de Pasqually, as he was called in France, there are still gaps in knowledge about his origins and his personality. Though his surname is in itself significant, and despite the French predicament *de la Tour,* it is reasonable to think that the family of origin name Martinez is stated to be by many historians of **Jewish and Portuguese origin.** His family was definitely converted to Christianity, as they received a "Certification of Catholicity," and was linked to the Stuart family in some mysterious way. Only Robert Amadou, specialist on the history of Martinezism and Martinism, supports the non-Jewish origin of Martinez, who is indicated as a direct descendant of the family of Bartolomé de las Casas, the famous historian of Spanish-Portuguese colonialism. Martinez Pasqualis was born in Grenoble in 1727, and died in Santo Domingo in 1774, but his lack of knowledge of the French language makes it doubtful that he was born on French soil. Lacking iconography (the picture reported by some is pure fantasy), while some report he was a black man, or at least of mixed race. However, his life and his personality are poured out in his work, and it is from this that you can deduce, above the legend and myth, his characteristics and features. Martinez alludes vaguely to his teachers, however, they remained always unknown, this trait is common to many founders of other Illuminati Orders, and esoteric sects, who do not speak as symbolic abstractions, but as real people, although with considerable power, that position them in the elite of the Illuminati close to the invisible masters. Martinez was in possession of a legitimate Masonic Patent inherited by his father, who had received it from Charles Edward Stuart, in 1738, and this Masonic Patent was recognized as valid by the Grand Orient of France, when it was presented for the ratification of the Order he founded, *L'Ordre des Chevaliers Maçons Élus Coëns de l'Univers.*

Even if the vehicle was Masonic, in fact the tradition that Martinez wanted to convey was derived from the Ancient Illuminati Priesthoods. Cohen (from the Hebrew word *Cohanim,* the priests) were a priestly class founded by Aaron, who kept the oral and esoteric tradition of the Torah, that later merged into the Kabbalah. As often happens in the esoteric orders, the terms and nomenclature of various degrees had already been used a century earlier, as recalled also by the late Grand Master Gastone Ventura:

> *(Swedenborg) would be able to coordinate the degrees of reborn Freemasonry operating with pre-existing levels of some so-called lodges of perfection ... (reserved degrees to be accepted) and those derived from alchemical and hermetic companies belonging to the Venerable Order of Golden Rosicrucians, thereby constituting a Masonic-Illuminati system consists of ten degrees divided in three sections, the last of which would have constituted an inner temple.*

The system was made up as follows:

1st section (Masonic) with grades:

> *1st Apprentice*
> *2nd Mate*
> *3rd Master*
> *4th Master Elected*

Section 2a (Enlightenment or Cohens) with grades:

> *5th Apprentice Cohen*
> *6th Comrade Cohen*
> *7th Master Cohen*

Section 3a (active) also known as the Rose + Cross section, with three degrees:

> *Cohen first Master or Grand Architect Apprentice*
> *Rose Cross*
> *Knight of the Rose+Croix*
> *Kaddosh (saint) or Rosicrucians Illuminati*

The Cohen system was as follows:

(The tables below show some differences in degree, as reported by different authors)

Freemasonry of St. John

1a table	2° table
1° Apprentice	1° Apprentice
2° Companion	2° Companion
3° Master	3° Master
∞	4° Grand Elect

Portico of the Class

4° Apprentice Cohen	5° Apprentice Cohen
5° Companion Cohen	6° Companion Cohen
6° Master Cohen	7° Master Cohen
7° Particular Master	∞

Degrees of the Temple

8° Grand Master Elect Cohen	8° Grand Architect
9° Knight of the East	9° Grand Elect of Zorobabel
10° Commander of the Orient	∞

Secret Class

11° Reaux Croix	10° Reaux Croix

The Order Cohen was shaped in the form of a high-degree Masonic system. Masonry in the St. John's degrees are the classic Blue Lodge degrees without which, of course, it was impossible to access to higher ones. He agreed to receive sisters, but only in exceptional circumstances. In the "Blue" degrees (the first three) he explained in the Masonic legend, its symbolism, followed its esotericism. The degree of Grand Elect—2nd series—was a degree of synthesis of the "Scottish degrees," and his philosophy of fidelity to the Order. Portico of the class is beginning to explain the first elements of the Cohen doctrine, translated in Masonic terms and revealed in Martinezist terms in its entirety. In the Temple class there were more initiations, linked to transmission of priestly powers. Only in this class was the operational aspect of this Illuminati sect explained and implemented. Alien connections in various aspects, the time and place of the evocations, and the final mission of the Order: **Contact.** The practice is evocative, individual or collective, sometimes carried out with the aid of a "pupil" or a medium. With considerable complexity, it brings adepts to a daily commitment with all sorts of depravations including food, and even prolonged sexual abstentions to fit into the "Cosmic scheme." The "events" and the "Contacts" are rare and obtained with difficulty, but directly testifies the existence of an "otherness" that could not be forgotten. This is truly a sophisticated form of alien "Contact," which I will talk about extensively in my next book *The Invisible Master.* The Reaux Croix is constituted in the Order's elite, and it held all of the theoretical and operational doctrines of the Order. According to oral tradition, however difficult to verify, they routinely identify themselves with one or the other of the entities from the *Shemhamphorasch* of the Kabbalistic tradition, which involves a blood oath. In the first Kabbalah, the term was sometimes used to describe the name of God consisting of 72 letters. Kabbalists proposed certain correspondences between the 72 names of *Shemhamphorasch,* and a variety of other things, including Psalms, tarot cards, and so on. It is because of the flexibility (and the numerical coefficient) of the *Shemhamphorasch,* that many ceremonial magicians consider **the key to the creation of all things and of all the Arts.**

The Seventy-Two Names of God, with a Christian diagram and the IHS, (a monogram for "Jesus"), are featured in the *Oedipus Aegyptiacus* of the Jesuits. Athanasius

Kircher, who as you know, was a key figure in the Jesuit infiltration of the Rosicrucian movement. The names used in the *Shemhamphorasch* have long been associated with 72 angels, as well as to 72 demons, (as set forth in *Lemegeton* or *Lesser Key of Solomon*). According to tradition they can make or break the organization or disorganization of the elements in the creation of material reality. The Order had great power in regards to the personality and the initiatory powers of its Master. From 1754, (according to some authors from 1758), they traveled across France, founding lodges of this system. In 1758, the Order gathered admirers and followers in southern France, in Marseille, Avignon, Montpellier, Narbonne, Toulouse and Foix, where the first chapter of **"The Cohen Temple,"** founded in the "Josue" Lodge. In Bordeaux, the first Mother Lodge of the Cohen tradition was founded, with the distinctive title *"La Française Elue Ecosséuse"* (1764), which in 1765 was recognized by the Grand Orient of France, as regular. On March 21, of 1765, **the Sovereign Court** (supreme governing body of the Order) is created in Paris, granting to Bacon de la Chevalerie the power of its universal substitute. The Court was formed by the *Reaux Croix* (Bacon de La Chevalerie, J. B. Willermoz, Duroy d'Hauterive, De Serre), called Sovereign Judges, with the last degree of the Order. Sovereign Judges are also referred to as S.I. (Unknown Superiors) and are a crucial link with the Society of Jesus.

Rene Allau, in his preface to *Les Aventures du philosophe inconnu,* cites the alchemist Petrus de Arlensis Scudalupis (1580 – 1637) called *"Hierosolymitanus presbyter,"* who in his work *Sympathia metallorum ac septem septem planetas lapidum,* rejects the previous Chaldean and Persian magic, recognizing only the Judeo-Christian traditions. Petrus states that real magic is based only on the power of the Hebrew letters that make up the heavenly figures, and the sign of the cross for which "the holy magic is demonstrated and accomplished." The volume cited the work of Dom Belin, a sixteenth-century alchemist who uses Christian terminology to describe the hermetic process, and in this title is mentioned, for the first time, the "Philosophes Inconnus," setting them in an airtight-Christian context manipulated by the Jesuits. It also seems that Martinez Pasqualis knew as I will show shortly, the famous ***Book of the Sacred Magic of Abramelin the Mage.***

In 1772, there was a complex inheritance issue so Martinez left everything to St. Domingo, a place rich in Voodoo tradition, where for the next two years he would try to complete the instructions for the Order, and where he died in 1774. Caignet de Lestere succeeded him as the new **Universal Sovereign of the Order**, dying in turn on the 19th of December, 1779. He was succeeded, by Sebastian de Las Casas, who in 1780, noticing the easing of the "Contact events" following the death of the physical plan of their Master, advises the Cohen Lodges to close their works and Temples, handing the archives to the Philalethes Order, not to be confused with the Philalethes Society, a Masonic research society, based in North America, founded on October 1, 1928. At the height of their past fortune, this powerful Illuminati Order flourished with 12 Temples, one in Port au Prince, an island in St. Domingo, now known as Haiti and the Dominican Republic. Since the death of the Master, the order began its dissolution, and since 1776 the Temple of La Rochelle, soon followed by those of Libourne and Marseille, left the system and so joined, or rejoined, the Grand Lodge of France. This Masonic tradition merged into the **Rectified Scottish Rite,** that also was heir to the Strict Templar Observance. The so-called "theurgic" part of Martinezes work is at the heart of the **Martinist Order,** that never really ceased to exist, and is still secretly present in contemporary Martinism.

The seal of Dom Martinez (FIG. 76) described by author and Freemasons Vittorio Vanni from Florence:

FIG. 76 – The seal of Martinez de Pasqually that brings us back to his animistic roots.

This seal is a light representation of the reintegration of beings. A large circle is largely opened on the infinite, as a sort of stopping point. A similar rise is explained by widening of the circumference in the form of arrow and from indicating a lower circle of the very nature of the largest, but also anticipation, after a previous action or before a next. Likely an alternate function of doors. The large circle involves another series of openings, but of different natures. Other functions, perhaps different other beings that pass through it. The circle represents the created world, the universal world. An arrow out of the universal world, and shows a particular world. This world is not indicated as the send from inside the large circle, but it is a manifestation, an emanation branch, feminine, lunar, then represented as a rising moon, yes crossed by two arrows, but not split. It is animated by a twelve-rayed star, which in the center shows a triangle formed by three points, the top of which is directed downwards. Sign of involution towards matter and also the symbol of earthly spirits in the domain of the forms. One of the two arrows coming out of this particular world and heads towards the infinite, towards the divine absolute immensity, the fourfold essence in action. The other arrow heads towards the opening of the large circle, and pointing to a star with five rays. It is the Blazing Star, the regenerated man coming out of the particular world towards Reintegration divine immensity. The interior of the large circle is the uncreated. There are, in this, multiple emanated beings, very different, that are confused together but not fused. Then they retain their individuality. They are what they are and represent the will of their creator. You would not give it a name, if not secret. This secret is their destination towards emancipation or their persistence in the bosom divine immensity founding lodges of his system.

Papus and the Orders & Societies of the Theosophical Society

At the age of 23, Papus became a member of the "THEOSOPHICAL SOCIETY." On October 25, 1887, Colonel Olcott personally announced the election of Papus to the newly formed General Council of the Theosophical Society at Adyar, India and as a propagator of Kiato Buddhism for the "T.S." Papus became a member of the Lodge-Isis, founded in July, 1887 by Dramard and Gaboriau. In 1888, Papus would leave the T.S. when he helped co-found the Lodge-Hermes in October, 1888. Papus "officially" resigned on May 19, 1890. According to many sources, his reason for leaving the T.S. was his dislike of the Society's emphasis on Eastern Occultism. Some sources even state that Blavatsky and Papus disrespected each other! (Christopher McIntosh). According to Papus' son Dr. Philippe Encausse, his father had always held Blavatsky in high esteem. Papus considered Blavatsky's Mahatma to not be the sole depository of "Sacred Science." Papus believed in a tradition conserved in the ancient temples of ancient Egypt.

Events began to turn in Papus' favor in 1887, when he was elected President of the *GROUPE INDEPENDANTE DES d'ETUDES ESOTERIQUES* ("Independent Group of Esoteric Studies"), known by the acronym G.I.D.E.E. This association attracted many popular mystics living in France at the time. Its aim was to create "Initiates;" men and women who chose to undertake the study of esoteric wisdom and occult science. "The role of the Initiatic society," as Papus conceived it, was to "encourage the student to create a personal doctrine of his own." Many of the French occultists who were collectively known as "*LES COMPAGNONS DE LA HEIROPHONIE*" were part of the G.I.D.E.E. Included were men like Victor Michelet, Josephin Péladan, Paul Sedir, Lucien Chamuel, Stanislas De Guaita, Albert Poisson, Ch.F.Bartlet (Alfred Foucheaux), Gary de Lacroze, Augustin Chaboseau, Phaneg (Descormiers, + 1946), Silva, Marc Haven, Dr.Rozier, Jollivet-Castelot, and many others. Many of them were Theosophists, as well as initiated Martinists of one or another chain. Papus was editor-in-chief at the time of a journal called "*The Veil of Isis*." The *Veil of Isis* was published under the banner of the G.I.D.E.E., published once a month, between 1890 and 1898. In 1905, the review reappeared. The review then continued its publications until 1936 (Chief-editor Charnorac; Charnorac became chief-editor in 1912, the review disappeared during 1914-1918, and reappeared again in 1920. In 1936, the "*Veil of Isis*" changed its name to "*études traditionnelles.*" Papus would describe the G.I.D.E.E. as "*the Outer court for a greater and higher Initiatic Order, comprising their recruits from this outer and predominantly theosophically oriented association (The Balzac of the Occult).*" This statement of Papus shows the obvious reason why his days in the Thesophical Society would be short-lived. He left to give way to his full-time concentration on the order that would unite all Martinists. In an article by Papus, published in the "*Veil of Isis*" of February, 1891, he stated that the G.I.D.E.E. was already "active" for a year, with more than 350 members, a headquarters, library, and conference-room included. Other contemporary members were men such as Polti, Colonel Rochas, Lemerle, Abel Haatan, Serge Basset, etc. The G.I.D.E.E. had various branches in France and Belgium: For instance, in Lyon, at 17 Rue de Sully, there was established the "*Fraternité Lyonnaise et Catalane*" (contact: Ely Steel). At Brussels, Belgium, lodge KVMRIS represented i.a. the G.I.D.E.E. in Belgium.

There are sources who state that the G.I.D.E.E. was established by Papus with the help of key Illuminati player **Saint-Yves d'Alveydre**, who according to some sources, also claimed to be the Grand Master of the original Martinist Order. Whatever the truth is, the collaboration of a man like Saint-Yves d'Alveydre would certainly have attracted many "mystics" to the ranks of a new organization like the "*Groupe Independent des Etudes Esoterique.*" But the fact is that Saint-Yves has never held any membership to any occult organization, despite claims to the contrary. He was never a member of the Martinist Order. It is claimed that Saint-Yves d'Alveydre even rejected an honorary membership into the Martinist Order, which Papus had sent to him. According to various sources (e.g. Koenig) the G.I.D.E.E. also carried a succession of Fabre-Palaprat's "Order of the Temple" that was supported by the Illuminati Napoleon Bonaparte. The G.I.D.E.E. was founded to develop research-centers of occult sciences. One of such branches was, for instance, the G∴M∴E∴I∴, *Groupe Maconnique d'Etudes Initiatiques*, which was headed by **Oswald Wirth**. According to some, the G.I.D.E.E. was later renamed "*Ecole Hermetique,*" the *Hermetic School*, others state that the "*Ecole Hermetique*" was established next (and afterwards) to the G.I.D.E.E. The "Ecole Hermetique" later allegedly developed into the "*Université libre des hautes Etudes*" (*Faculté des Sciences Hermétiques*). The university was meant for the "aces" of the Martinist Order. Some of the professors and lecturers who were appointed at the "faculty of Hermetic Sciences," that being Paul

Sédir, Serge Basset, Siséra Rosabis, Dr.Rozier, and Jollivet Castelot. The Hermetic School was led by a "council of improvement" which consisted of: Charles Barlet, Papus, Marc Haven, Victor Emile Michelet, Serge Basset, and Paul Sédir.

The Hermetic students would continue their studies in several Martinist Lodges in Paris.

1) **LE SPHINX.** The Grand Lodge for general studies.

2) **HERMANUBIS,** led by Paul Sédir, studies of the Mystic and Eastern tradition.

3) **VELLÉDA,** led by V-E Michelet, studies of French Masonry and its Symbolism

4) **SPHYNGE,** reserved mainly for Artistic adaptations.

The following text is a translation of the article *"L'Ordre Martiniste a la belle époque"* taken from the French website of the Traitional Martinist Order. The article confirms the assumptions made earlier that the *"Ecole Hermetique,"* and the *"Faculté des Sciences Hermétiques"* were indeed continuations of the G.I.D.E.E. Papus wished to renew occidental esoterism: *"As there are existing faculties where the materialistic sciences can be studied, why would it not be possible to create such a faculty where the esoteric sciences can be studied?"* Thus he creates *'l'École Supérieure Libre des Sciences Hermétiques,* a group which gives courses and organizes lectures to promote the values of occidental esoterism to the seeker. This "exterior" circle of the Martinist Order will be first known under the name *le Groupe Indépendant d'Etudes Esotériques* (G.I.D.E.E.), then as *'l'Ecole Hermétique* and *la Faculté des Sciences Hermétiques.* Many courses were presented (12 per month), with subjects ranging from the kabbala, alchemy and the tarot, to the history of hermetic philosophy. The teachers were Papus, Sédir, Victor-Emile Michelet, Barlet, Augustijnse Chaboseau, Sisera and others. A special section was devoted to the oriental sciences under the direction of Augustin Chaboseau. Another section, presided by François Jollivet-Castelot, was devoted to alchemy—this is *la Société Alchimique de France* (source: *Ordre Martiniste Traditionnel—Grande Heptade de la Juridiction Française*).

It is common knowledge that Augustin Chaboseau was very interested in Buddhism, an interest he shared with i.a. Harvey Spencer Lewis of A.M.O.R.C / O.M.T. and which he maintained all his life. In 1888, Papus and his friend Lucien Chamuel founded the *"Librarie du Merveilleux"* and its monthly journal *"L'Initiation."* Many Occultists contributed articles to the review, some of the lesser-known occultists were men such as Villier de l'Isle-Adam, Catulle Mendés, Julien Lejay, Emile Goudeau, Jules Lermina, Eugéne Nus Rodolphe Darzens, George Montiere, Aleph, with F.·.Bertrand, Bouvery, René Caillié George Delanne, Ely Star, Fabre des Essarts, G.Poirel, A. Robert, Rouxel, H. Sausse, G. Vitoux, Vurgey, and many others. The review was "banned" by the Vatican in Rome in 1891, and was put on Index. Another review of the G.I.D.E.E. was called *"l'Union Occulte de France,"* and was published in Lyon.

The journal remained in publication until 1914, when World War I broke out. Papus' son, Dr.Philippe Encausse, reconstituted the *"ORDRE MARTINISTE DE PAPUS"* in 1952, and revived the original journal again. There exists today even an English version of *"L'Initiation,"* obtainable at the following address: *GERME (USA)—4287-A Beltline Road, # 330; Addison, TX 75001—USA*; their first edition, published in 2000, was for the most part a translation of the first edition of the revived *"L'Initiation"* of Phillipe Encausse published in January, 1953. [28]

••

28   The Martinist Order (by Milko Bogaard) http://www.hermetics.org/Martinism.html ‡ Archived 15th November, 2016.

Chapter IV

~◦~

The Magical World of the Illuminati:
from Abramelin to Wicca

~◦~

The magic of Abramelin

The influence of the famous ancient grimoire *The Sacred Magic of Abramelin the Mage* over the Illuminati world became increasingly evident in the last 100 years, and is one of the key texts to understand better the very evolution of certain branches of the Illuminati network in their "Contact" with alien extradimensional beings. The first important translation into the French language in the eighteenth century was known to **Martinez Pasqualis, Louis-Claude de Saint Martin and Jean-Baptiste Willermoz,** three of the key figures in the whole philosophy of Martinism. The second translation in the English language, of the French manuscript, was extensively annotated and commented on by none other than MacGregor Mathers (1854 – 1918), co-founder of the **Hermetic Order of the Golden Dawn,** and the occult mentor of Aleister Crowley. There is a vast significance of this book for the occult elite, and we will now examine why. The book in question explains that there are evil spirits all around, although invisible, and examines whether the one who evokes them using the grimoire is brave or timid, and if he has prudence or faith in God. I attempted this ritual in 1993, and fortunately I am alive to speak about it.

The Sacred Magic of Abramelin the Mage tells the story of an Egyptian magus named Abramelin (or Abra-melin), who transmitted the knowledge of his magic system to a certain **Abraham of Worms,** a German Jew who presumably lived between 1362 and 1458. It is structured as an autobiography, in which Abraham of Worms describes his journey from Germany to Egypt, and reveals his magical and kabbalistic secrets to his son Lamech. The text inside is dated **1458.** Abraham recounts how he found Abramelin the magician, who lived in the desert, outside an Egyptian city, Arachi or Araki, which borders the Nile. He was an Egyptian magician who taught a powerful form of Kabbalistic magic to Abraham. He was a "venerable old man" who was courteous and polite. He did not discuss anything except his "fear of God," leading a regular life, and was careful about material acquisitions of goods, and not inclined to wealth. Abramelin extrapolated a promise to Abraham that they would give up the "false dogmas" and would live "in the path and in the

Law of the Lord." Then he gave Abraham two manuscripts that he was supposed to copy himself, demanding 10 gold florins with the intention of distributing them to 72 poor people of Arachi. Upon his return 15 days later, after arranging for the payment of money, Abramelin made an oath to Abraham, to serve the Lord, and to "live and die in His most Sacred Law." After this, Abramelin gave Abraham the "Divine Science," and transmitted to him his "True Magic," embedded in the two manuscripts, that he would have to follow and give only to those he knew well. The book exists in the form of six manuscripts, and an early printed edition. The origin of the text has not yet been identified with certainty. The earliest manuscripts are two versions dated around 1689, written in German, and now are in Wolfenbüttel. Two other manuscripts are in Dresden, and are dated respectively in 1700 and 1750. The first printed version, also in German, is dated 1725, and was printed in Cologne by Peter Hammer. A part copied in Hebrew is in the Bodleian Library in Oxford, and is dated around the year 1740. A manuscript copy was still in France in the *Bibliothèque de l'Arsenal* in Paris known as Library of the Arsenal today, an institution founded in 1797, but it seems that their copy is sadly missing, [1]and some say it ended up in the hands of a powerful sect of the Illuminati, but fortunately it is still available on microfilm.

Analysis of the language used in the French manuscript indicate that it dates back to the eighteenth century, and was also likely to be copied from a German original. Although the author quoted is a Jew, the version is not Hebrew, but rather from a translation of the Bible, used by the Roman Catholics of the time. All German copies of the text consist of four books: an autobiographical account of a trip by Abraham of Worms to Egypt, a book of assorted materials from the corpus of practical Kabbalah, and two books of magic that Abramelin gave Abraham. The well-known English translation of S. L. MacGregor Mathers from the French Manuscript in Paris, contains only three of the four books. The Hebrew version in Oxford is limited to Book One, without reference to the missing books. Of all existing sources, the German manuscripts in Wolfenbüttel, and Desden, are accepted by scholars as the official texts. According to the student of Kabbalah, Gershom Scholem, the Hebrew version in Oxford was translated into Hebrew from German.

The German esoteric scholar Georg Dehn assumed that the author of the *Book of Magic of Abramelin* was Rabbi Yaakov Moelin, a German Jew Talmudist, and an authority in Jewish law. The text describes a ritual whose purpose is to attain the knowledge and conversation of your Holy Guardian Angel. The preparations are elaborate, difficult to read, and long for this "alien contact" of an extradimensional nature. All German texts describe a duration for the operation of eighteen months before receiving divine, or alien contact, if we want to be more contemporary. The version translated by Mathers is a little different, and the initial period before the coveted "contact" only lasts six months, perhaps one of the reasons for the problems experienced by those who used Mathers version like myself, or even Crowley "The Great Beast 666."

During the period of work, the magician must pray every day before dawn and again at dusk. During the preliminary stage, there are some restrictions: Chastity duty is to be observed, no alcohol, and the magicians had to lead their own work with scrupulous obedience. After the preliminary phase was completed successfully, the Holy Guardian Angel of the magician appeared and revealed himself to the magician, and revealed his magical secrets. Once this point is reached, the magician must evoke the twelve Kings and Dukes of Hell (Lucifer, Satan, Leviathan, etc.) and order them to serve him. With this operation the magician is seemingly in command of these entities in his mental universe, and removes their negative influences from his life.

••

1   https://en.wikipedia.org/wiki/The_Book_of_Abramelin ‡ Archived 15th November, 2016.

Since such magical work includes the evocation of demons, the Abramelin operations are juxtaposed to Goetic magic, and are to be regarded as dangerous. However the Illuminati of the various sects, and in particular the O.T.O, tend to focus on the benevolent aspects acceptable to their New Age public. Of course, one can try to take possession of these forces, and attempt to master these dangerous demons to achieve a higher form of communication with the angelic realm. But how many words badly pronounced by a bad-intentioned person will return against that same person, who uttered them with ignorance? He who has such a character should never undertake this magical operation, because you will end up hurt, make no mistake. Many occultists of the Illuminati sectarian network even put their lives at risk to raise their psychic powers, thanks to this ritual. Of course there is the occasional person who has obtained a positive experience from the *Sacred Magic of Abramelin,* but they are few and far between.

Ramsey Dukes (Lionel Snell) has described his experiences with the *Sacred Magic of Abramelin the Mage* in the 1970s as a journey of self-discovery, that led him to a deep and subtle inner transformative process, where the effects continued well beyond the end of the magical operation. Lionell Snell, who is still a member of the highest level of the *Ordo Templi Orientis* (Caliphate) in Britain, and one of the guides of the **Thanateros Illuminati,** performed the ritual of Abramelin in Hertfordshire cottage during the summer of 1977. I can say that I agree with his description, and impression of the "Sacred Magic of Abramelin the Mage," which I wanted to experience for myself over twenty years ago. I believe it led to all the positive adventures around the world in the years that followed my experience with the Magic of Abramelin. By chance I obtained the first Italian edition of the *Sacred Magic of Abramelin* published by **Atanor,** only 13 years earlier, in December, 1980. What attracted me initially was actually the cover of the book, which was a portrait of an old man in some ways similar to **Saint Padre Pio,** a figure who I feel I have always been linked.

This book had a profound affect on me, just as it did nearly a century earlier, on Crowley, who derived from it part of the system for developing his mystical system of Thelema, and the so-called "Knowledge and Conversation of his Holy Guardian Angel," which becomes essential magic for any follower of Crowleyanity, even if there are few who have actually implemented it in its entirety, especially in the O.T.O., where the concept of *True Desire* (or True Will), is of course the basis of Thelemic religion. When you are seriously studying Magic, the first thing you want to obtain is a guide; a basic text for your own personal development. I found myself looking through the *Sacred Magic of the Wizard Abramelin,* during my stay in a small room in a puppet theatre in the area of Campo dei Fiori in Rome, owned by the Mazzetti sisters, **Paola and Lorenza Mazzetti,** [2] friends of my father, known for being adopted by the family of Albert Einstein during the war. This unusal set up was used as a Puppet Theatre for the Sunday *Punch and Judy Show* in the English language, a truly magical place, where when you turn the corner, and you are facing the statue of that great initiate of all time, Giordano Bruno.

In the Catholic tradition there has always been much talk of guardian angels. They even teach about them in catechism, but in the gospel there is no mention of a guardian angel. The Guardian Angel is a spiritual entity, a deity who protects us and guides us. In the magical tradition they speak of the Holy Guardian Angel (or even **Augeoides or Daemon**) and search for Knowledge and Conversation with the Holy Guardian Angel, as a key step for the magical journey towards contact with extradimensional beings, and mastery of your own reality. What is the guardian angel for these New Age Illluminati? The angel for them is the "Higher Self," that lives beyond the space time continuum re-

---

2   https://it.wikipedia.org/wiki/Lorenza_Mazzetti ‡ Archived 15th November, 2016.

ality. What is a space-time continuum? In 1906, soon after Albert Einstein announced his theory of relativity, his former college teacher in mathematics, Hermann Minkowski, developed a new scheme for thinking about space and time that emphasized its geometric qualities. In his famous quotation delivered at a public lecture on relativity, he announced that: *"The views of space and time which I wish to lay before you have sprung from the soil of experimental physics, and therein lies their strength. They are radical. henceforth, space by itself, and time by itself, are doomed to fade away into mere shadows, and only a kind of union of the two will preserve an independent reality."* This new reality was that space and time, as physical constructs, could be combined into a new mathematical/physical entity called "space-time," because the equations of relativity show that both space and time coordinates of any event must be combined together by mathematics, in order to accurately describe what we see. Because space consists of 3 dimensions, and time is 1-dimensional, space-time must, therefore, be a 4-dimensional object. It is believed to be a "continuum" because so far as we know, there are no missing points in space or instants in time, and both can be subdivided without any apparent limit in size or duration. So, physicists now routinely consider **our world to be embedded in this 4-dimensional Space-Time continuum,** and all events, places, moments in history, actions, are described in terms of their location in Space-Time. [3]

The Holy Guardian Angel operates beyond the limits of Space and Time, and the most famous methods published on the subject are Crowley's **Liber Samekh,** and the Abramelin system. Both involve spending long periods of time in isolation. This sort of approach probably doesn't suit a great many people, but the use of a magical retreat or sabbatical can be extremely valuable and aid in working above the restrictions and physical constructs of the Space-Time continuum. Our Higher Self knows no death, it has always lived and always will live. Knowledge of the Higher Self is the shortcut to actually developing the magic side of the Self, which is one of the great secrets of the Illuminati. The traditional magical approach, which follows the pattern of the **Tree of Life** (Kabbalah), combines the knowledge of the Angel to the Fifth Sphere (Tiphereth), after mastering skills in the Astral plane, and communications with other entities, psychic abilities and various other things. So even in the words of one of the greatest initiates of the Illuminati named **Franz Bardon (1909 – 1958)**, whose recommended approach to the Higher Self is only reached at the Fifth Sphere. But the "New Age" ideal that the Guardian Angel is "Myself Completely Developed," encourages the connection to acquire the necessary knowledge, and magical abilities, without worrying about the consequences.

Drunvalo Melchizedek, a new age spiritual authority, and author of several books on the "Flower of Life," recommends starting early with the connection to your inner guidance, your Higher Self. The magical tradition of the Illuminati of the dark side says that once the Angel is contacted, it will accompany you throughout your training, that is, until the Abyss. Here the magician must abandon himself, standing alone for the biggest test. There are many different methods to contact and communicate with the Higher Self. Bardon recommends, for example, the use of the pendulum, the planchette (**Ouija board**) or automatic writing, while others advise the use of seals, deep meditation, prayer and dreams. Clearly some practices can lead to obvious possession. What counts, in any case, is intention, and obviously, will. Although Crowley used *The Sacred Magic of Abramelin,* he stated that an adept could more or less achieve this mystical state in various ways, also with other fundamental concepts that coincide with the Abramelin system. In 1906, Crowley was not able to complete the education of the "Sacred Magic," and

3   https://einstein.stanford.edu/content/relativity/q411.html ‡ Archived 15th November, 2016.

decided to change the Abramelin operation so he could perform the ritual during a trip with his wife Rose Kelly, to China.

The manifestation described by Aleister Crowley of a bright spirit, the Order of the Silver Star (A∴A∴), was something he considered as the Knowledge and Conversation with his Holy Guardian Angel. However Crowley showed ambivalence about his use of hashish during this experience, so in October 1908, he repeated the operation again in Paris, without its use, to rework the whole process in a new light. In subsequent years, it became established in Crowley's mind that he actually completed the Abramelin operation successully with the revelation of his *Book of the Law* (the sacred text at the basis of his religion of Thelema), and the proclamation of the incoming "Age of Horus" (Aeon of Horus), that he received while he and his wife Rose Edith Kelly were visiting Egypt in 1904.

Who knows what would have happened if Crowley, or myself, would have used a different version, than the one translated by Samuel Liddell MacGregor Mather. The more recent version by **Georg Dehn with Steven Guth** published in Germany in 2001, and then in English in 2006,[4] is based on earlier, and much more erudite sources. Maybe that's why Georg Dehn, one of the two curators of this new version, felt that the translation was a mystical experience. His friend, **Lon Milo Duquette,** contributed to the introduction to this new version. He stated that the translation of S. L. MacGregor Mathers, given the missing parts of the French edition, "was practically useless, but still dangerous from an operational point of view, if not carried out with the utmost caution."[5] **Grady McMurthy (1918 – 1985)**, founder of the modern offshoot of the *Ordo Templi Orientis*, commonly referred to as Caliphate, and a close friend of Aleister Crowley wrote: "one day while Crowley was preparing his usual cup of English tea in London, I picked up Crowley's copy of the *Sacred Magic of Abramelin* opening it to those pages where they describe the famous magical squares to use in the occult operations, but when Crowley returned to the room where McMurthy was, his teacher became furious and terrorized him as only Crowley could do, and told him: *'Do not touch that book because you do not know what forces might be unleashed.'"*

In fact, in the first Italian edition we find the following **warning**:

> *The Abramelin instructions as they are exhibited by Abraham to his son Lamech involve a profound vocation to the sacred and to the good, dictate the need for technical preparation-purification that lasts six months, explain the rules to prepare the furnishings and holy places and provide all the details for the apparition of the Guardian, or Custodian Angel, who alone can help in the long work necessary to summon the Good Angels and dominate Familiar Spirits without any "tricks" by the various devils always ready to enslave the unwary operator. Concept also given by the author of the Magic of Abramelin who says in this passage: Please, therefore each be on guard, not to despise the Way and the Wisdom of the Lord, not to be seduced by devils since the devil is a liar and always will be. We must hold on to the Truth by following and obeying faithfully what I write in these three books. Not only will you obtain the Science, but you will considerably know the grace of the Lord and you will enjoy the assistance of the Angels, who feel an incredible pleasure at being obeyed and observed to see God's Commandments.*[6]

••

4   http://en.wikipedia.org/wiki/The_Book_of_Abramelin ‡ Archived 15th November, 2016.
5   See. Abraham von Worms, *The Book of Abramelin*—A New Translation compiled and edited by Georg Dehn and Steven Guth, (Lake Forth, FL: Ibis Press, 2006).
6   *La Magia Sacra di Abramelin il mago,* introduzione e note di Luciano Pirrotta, (Rome, IT: Atanor, 1980), p. 5.

Who is the author of this dangerous grimoire? According to Georg Dehn who, besides being editor of this new version in 2001, is the founder of the German publishing house Araki of Leipzig, and a member of various Illuminati sects, says it is a rabbi. They seem to have no doubt that the author of *The Book of the Sacred Magic of Abramelin the Mage*, is **Rabbi Yaakov Moelin**—a German Jew, and a noted Talmudist known as MaHaRIL, or Abraham von Worms (city in Germany in Rhineland-Palatinate where he resided). But the Jewish authorities don't accept the discovery by Georg Dehn, which according to them would undermine a charismatic figure not only of their faith, but also of their communities. Because the great rabbi helped the Jewish survivors of the terrible genocide of 1420 in Austria, and the subsequent Hussite Wars, especially in 1421, a situation which brought considerable suffering to the Jews in Bavaria, and the Rhine, in the southern part of the border between Germany and France.

That's why we find a disclaimer in *Wikipedia* on (Yaakov ben Moshe LeviMoelin): *"Recently, the German esoteric scholar Georg Dehn has argued that the MaHaRIL was also the author of* The Book of Abramelin *which he wrote under the pseudonym of Abraham von Worms. However, this is disputed."* [7]

Perhaps there will always be some dispute about who the author of this work is, but certainly there is no doubt to the Jewish origin of the work, and its profound Kabbalistic matrix. It is even written: *"This takes from the Most High Wisdom foundation and the Holy Kabbalah, which is only given to the first-born."* [8] Luciano Pirrotta writes a footnote on the same page about the relationship between Kabbalah and Sacred Magic: *"The subordination of theurgic magic is here reaffirmed than the body of doctrine of the Kabbalah that integrates and surpasses it. The same opinion, argues that the entire Western esotericism and particularly the ceremonial magic, find their theoretical foundation and practice base in that immense sum which is the Kabbalistic system."* [9]

Another significant testimony on the use and abuse by certain occultists of this grimoire is present in the letters of H. Campell, published in December 1929, in the monthly magazine *"The Occult Review"* by Ralph Shirley (1905 – 1951). (FIG. 77) Among other things, Francis X. King was the known British occult student who courageously published the secret rituals of the *Ordo Templi Orientis* in 1973, included this precious testimony in his *Ritual Magic in England: 1887 to the Present Day* (1970), with some minor variations:

> *Desiring some information which I could not get in any ordinary way, I resorted to the System of Abramelin, and to this end prepared a copy of the necessary Talisman, perfecting it to the best of my ability with my little stock of knowledge. The ritual performed, I proceeded to clear my "place of working." A little knowledge is a dangerous thing; my ritual was imperfect and I only rendered the Talisman useless without in any way impairing the activities of the entity invoked. This looks like nothing else than gross carelessness on my part; and to a certain extent this is true—but the point I wish to make is this, that my knowledge of this particular system, and therefore my ritual, were imperfect; and in any case, I had been shown no method of combating this particular entity when once aroused. Now note the results. ... Unfortunately I have no account of the date when these occurrences began, but the first hint of trouble must have come on or about March 3, 1927. I can guess the date with fair accuracy because, as I was to learn, the manifestations were*

7   https://en.wikipedia.org/wiki/Yaakov_ben_Moshe_Levi_Moelin ‡ Archived 15th November, 2016.

8   *La Magia Sacra di Abramelin il mago,* Atanor, *Ibid.* p. 40.

9   See. Dion Fortune, *The Mystical Qabalah, Fraternity of the Inner Light*, London 1957; trad. it. La Cabala Mistica, (Rome,IT: Astrolabio, 1973).

always strongest about the new moon, and after I had gone to sleep. Upon this occasion I can remember waking up suddenly with a vague feeling of terror oppressing me; yet it was no ordinary nightmare terror, but an imposed emotion that could be thrown off by an effort of the will. This passed almost as soon as I stood up, and I thought no more about it. ... Again on April 2, or thereabouts, I was troubled by the same feeling, but regarded it as nothing more than a severe nightmare, though the fact that my sleep was distorted towards the time of the new moon had occurred to me; while as full moon drew on, the nights were peaceful again. The new moon of May brought a recurrence of the trouble. This time very much more powerful, and necessitating an almost intolerable effort of will to cast if off. Also it was about this time that I first saw the entity which was rapidly obsessing me. It was not altogether unlovely to look at. Its eyes were closed and it was bearded, with long flowing hair. It seemed a blind force slowly waking to activity.

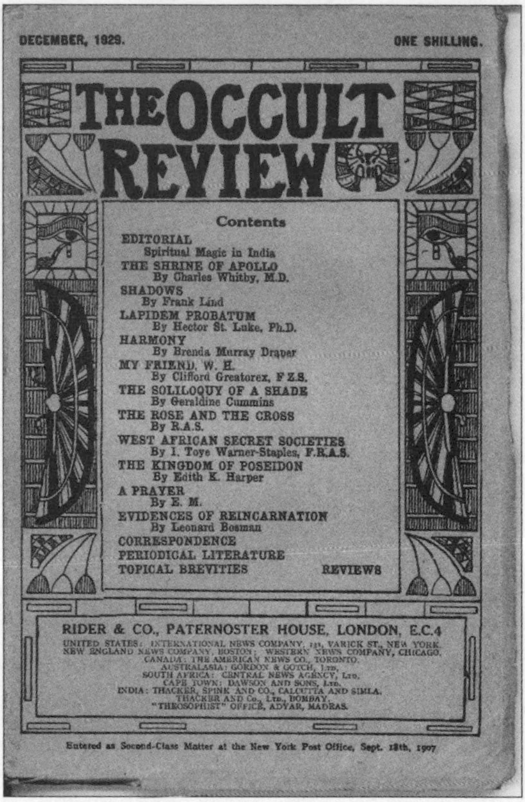
DECEMBER, 1929. ONE SHILLING.

THE OCCULT REVIEW

Contents

EDITORIAL
Spiritual Magic in India
THE SHRINE OF APOLLO
By Charles Whitby, M.D.
SHADOWS
By Frank Lind
LAPIDEM PROBATUM
By Hector St. Luke, Ph.D.
HARMONY
By Brenda Murray Draper
MY FRIEND, W. H.
By Clifford Greatorex, F.Z.S.
THE SOLILOQUY OF A SHADE
By Geraldine Cummins
THE ROSE AND THE CROSS
By R.A.S.
WEST AFRICAN SECRET SOCIETIES
By I. Toye Warner-Staples, F.R.A.S.
THE KINGDOM OF POSEIDON
By Edith K. Harper
A PRAYER
By E. M.
EVIDENCES OF REINCARNATION
By Leonard Bosman
CORRESPONDENCE
PERIODICAL LITERATURE
TOPICAL BREVITIES REVIEWS

RIDER & CO., PATERNOSTER HOUSE, LONDON, E.C.4
UNITED STATES: INTERNATIONAL NEWS COMPANY, 131, VARICK ST., NEW YORK.
NEW ENGLAND NEWS COMPANY, BOSTON; WESTERN NEWS COMPANY, CHICAGO.
CANADA: THE AMERICAN NEWS CO., TORONTO.
AUSTRALASIA: GORDON & GOTCH, LTD.
SOUTH AFRICA: CENTRAL NEWS AGENCY, LTD.
CAPE TOWN: DAWSON AND SONS, LTD.
INDIA: THACKER, SPINK AND CO., CALCUTTA AND SIMLA.
THACKER AND Co., LTD., BOMBAY.
"THEOSOPHIST" OFFICE, ADYAR, MADRAS.

Entered as Second-Class Matter at the New York Post Office, Sept. 18th, 1907

FIG. 77 – Cover of the monthly magazine ***The Occult Review*** *of December, 1929.*

Now there are three points which I must make quite clear before I proceed. In the first place, I was never attacked twice in the same night. Secondly, when I speak of physical happenings, the smashing of glass and voices, they were never, with one absolutely inexplicable exception, actual, but pure obsessions; and this leads to the third point. Not one of these incidents happened while I was asleep. Always I found myself awake with the terror upon me and struggling violently to cast off the spell. I have had nightmares before, but no nightmare that I have ever had could hold my mind in its grip for minutes at a time as this thing did, or send me plunging through a ten-foot-high window to the ground below. ... The first indication I had that these visitations were absolutely out of the ordinary course of events came on May 30. About midnight I was suddenly awakened by a voice calling loudly, "Look out," and at once I became aware of a red serpent coiling and uncoiling itself under my bed, and reaching out onto the floor with its head. Just as it was about to attack me I jumped through my window, and came to earth among the rose bushes below, fortunately with no more damage done than a badly bruised arm. After this there was absolute peace until June 30, when the real climax came. I had seen the thing again on the night of the new moon, and had noticed considerable changes in its appearance. Especially it seemed far more active, while its long hair had changed into serpent heads. *The night after I was awakened by a violent noise and jumped out of bed. I then saw the noise was caused by a great red obelisk which crashed through the west wall of my room and leaned against the wall at the east end, smashing both that and the window to pieces but missing my bed, which was in an alcove to the left of its path. In its transit it had smashed all the mirrors, and the floor and top of my bed were strewn with broken glass and fragments of wood. This time the obsession must have lasted some minutes, I dared not move for fear of cutting myself, and to reach the matches—wherein, I knew, lay safety—I had to lean across the bed and again risk the glass. Yet in my heart I knew that all this was false, but had no power to move. I could only stand there, incapable, looking at the shattered room in a state of hopeless terror. ... And now comes the most extraordinary part of the whole business. When I had finally mastered the obsession, I went to bed again dead tired, and I know that the only sound I made that night was jumping to the floor, also my room is at least a hundred yards from the rest of my family, yet next morning at breakfast I was asked what was the terrible noise in my room during the night.*

After that I realised that the game was up. I had not taken these occurrences lying down, but I knew that it was impossible for me to try and control the force which I had set in motion. In desperation I turned to a good friend, who, I was aware, knew much of these things. She did not hesitate, but came at once to my assistance, and from that day to the present the trouble has absolutely gone from me. Such is the case; and I only hope it may warn those who are contemplating my folly to treat with the greatest of care any printed systems of magic, and not to use them at all unless they have the fullest control over the entities invoked. This testimony, published by The Occult Review in December 1929, was considered very important by various authors of esotericism and began the last century linked to the world of the seven of the Illuminati, so much so that he was picked up by **Dion Fortune**, who takes her back fully in his excellent guide Psychic Self-Defense *commenting in this way: Among the general public, who do not dabble in occultism, the results of a magical mishap are never seen, and the only doctors who ever see them are fellow-initiates who happen to be medical men, and they, naturally, keep silent. The catastrophes are of varying degrees of severity, ranging from a bad fright to a fatality. I cannot say much upon these subjects, for they are among the most secret paths of occult lore. Enough must be hinted, however, to reveal what, under certain circumstances, may be experienced. I do not think it in the least likely, however, that the Qlippotic demons will be encountered save through the use of ceremonial magic. They are as rare as anthrax in England, but it is as well to know the manner of their manifestation so that, when encountered, they may be recognised. The great majority of dabblers in occultism are protected by their own ineptitude. They fail to get results, and consequently come to no harm; but if they should succeed in getting results they would find that they had their hands full. The serious student, unless he is working under skilled guidance, may also find himself in difficulties, and for various reasons. He may be insufficiently experienced in the operation he has undertaken, for in magic theory is one thing and practice is another. A student of occult science will often take a formula out of a book and try to use it. He might just as well study the instructions in a book on surgery and try to operate. Most formula are incomplete, there is always unwritten work. Some of the "barbarous names of evocation" which the uninitiated use as Words of Power, are really the initial letters of a mantric sentence or formula. I came across an invocation once in which the Word of Power was Tegatoo. On investigation this turned out to be the battered remains of The Great Architect Of The Universe. Even an experienced occultist may get into difficulties if he attempts*

*magical work when he is in bad health, over-tired, or has had even a moderate amount
of alcohol, for very little is too much when the Invisible Forces are being handled.
Equally does this apply to each of his assistants. A chain is no stronger than its weakest
link, and if one of the team cannot handle the forces, everybody is going to suffer. A
ritual lodge is no place for the well-meaning ineffectual. There is an immense amount
of dabbling in occultism going on today. Most of it is innocuous because it is totally
ineffective; but there is never any knowing when one is going to strike a live wire. Take,
for instance, the advertisers in various occult papers who offer to supply "charms that
work." One of two things is certain. Either they do not work at all, in which case one is
wasting one's money on them; or they work by means of some power with which they
have been charged. What is the nature of that power, and did the persons who made
the charm or talisman really know what they were about? Did they take the precau-
tion to bind the baser aspect before magnetising with the higher aspect? These are the
elementary precautions of the practical occultist who has been properly trained. Did
the maker of the talisman know them? Again, one buys second-hand books on magic.
Who was the previous owner and for what purposes were these books used? Or one
buys a new book which has been brought out by some occult school for propaganda
purposes. These books are often magnetised before they are sent out, and so form a
magnetic link between the purchaser and the Order which caused them to be issued.
Or someone may join a group who has previously been associated with another occult
group whose contacts were debased. Unless the proper precautions are taken, that person will bring the psychic contagion in with him, and his fellow-members may have
unpleasant experiences. I well remember it being said to me by an occultist of great
experience that two things are necessary for safety in occultism, right motives and
right associates. We lull ourselves into a false security if we believe that good intentions
are sufficient protection. My advice to the would-be student is to invoke the Master to
send him an initiator, and to refuse to attempt any practical work until he is fully
satisfied that the initiator has been found. I cannot here enter into either the precautions to be taken against untoward happenings in practical occult work, nor the rem-
edies to apply if they take place; I will merely indicate the signs by which such an
eventuality may be recognised. This is all that can be done, and all that is necessary in
a book of this type; the initiate knows what to do without need of guidance from me;
the non-initiate cannot do anything, and must seek assistance. It is enough for him if
he knows when such assistance is needed. ... If things go wrong in the course of a magical ceremonial, the power "shorts," and someone, it may be the operator, or it may be
the weakest person in the team, gets "knocked out" as if he had received a punch from
an invisible pugilist. When picked up, he will be very dazed and badly shaken, and
will certainly be some days, possibly weeks, before he gets over it. He will be in a state
of complete prostration and considerable mental confusion, which will gradually wear
off. Unless there is some organic defect, such as hereditary mental instability, a bad
heart, or hardened arteries, there will be a complete recovery, given time; but naturally it is a bad outlook should one of these conditions be present, and those who have
them should not take part in occult experiments. Personally, I do not believe that the
invisible forces alone will ever actually cause the loss of life or permanent disability in
the absence of any physical lesion. The person who goes out of his mind as the result of
a psychic shock would have gone out of his mind if he had been in a railway disaster or
any other drastic emotional experience. Unless the psychic atmosphere indicates otherwise, it is not necessary to do any banishings, or take precautions against obsession,
because the power has dispersed itself in the very act of inflicting the shock. During my
early days of occultism I developed my powers very rapidly because I recovered the*

memories of previous incarnations en bloc, and with them the capacities acquired in previous lives, and I shook myself up severely on numerous occasions before I learnt the technique of handling the invisible forces. I never experienced any permanent ill-effects from my mishaps, though I admit that upon occasion I have been extricated by my friends from a considerable amount of debris. During the early days of my occult career a girl was brought to me by a mutual friend, who told me that the mother of this girl, an ardent student of occultism, seemed to have a terrible effect upon her daughter. The mother was a widow, and mother and daughter lived together under very comfortable material circumstances; but whenever the girl made a friend, or showed any desire to leave home, the mother performed extraordinary antics, coming to the daughter's room at night and drawing signs in the air about her bed. The effect of all this upon the girl was most peculiar. She felt unable to free herself from the mental domination the mother had obtained over her, and she was wasting away in a most curious fashion. When I saw her, although able to get about, she looked like nothing I have ever seen, save a famine victim. I made a psychic investigation, and formed the opinion that the mother was working by means of an entity of which she had obtained possession. How this had been accomplished in the present instance, I do not know, but such things are common in occultism. I determined to take on the case, and to chase and, if possible, break up this artificial elemental. I was away from the group I was accustomed to work with, but among people keenly interested in occultism of every sort, size and description, and I had no difficulty in picking up a team to help me with the undertaking. I had no qualms about the undertaking. A second-hand elemental, directed by a woman with only a rule-of-thumb knowledge of magic, did not appear to me to be a formidable opponent. I had seen a good deal of practical occultism, had lent a hand at similar operations, and possessed the necessary formulae. So I went round the town, asked certain friends to lend a hand, and others to come and see the fun. To be frank, our attitude was that of a party of small boys going ratting. We met at the appointed time and place. Formed our circle, and went to work. The method I meant to use made it necessary for me to leave my body, and the group were really there to look after it while I was out of it, and see it came to no harm. I got out on to the astral readily enough, did my job, and returned, feeling very pleased with myself, for it was the first time I had operated entirely on my own, without the supervision by my teacher. ... As I began to recover physical consciousness, which is just like coming round from an anaesthetic, I had a sensation as of machinery running, and felt as if I were lying on something very lumpy. I opened my eyes, and saw something brown towering above me to an enormous height. As I gathered my senses together, I discovered that I was lying on the floor, close to the skirting, across the feet of an unfortunate man, who was thus securely pinned against the wall, and it was he, shaking in his shoes, that had felt to me like the vibration of machinery. Various other members of the circle slowly and reluctantly reappeared from behind the piano and sofa and other heavy articles of furniture. They had seen some practical occultism for once in their lives, but they did not appear to like it. It appears that, after I had gone out and left them with my unconscious body, they got a good deal of phenomena in the way of bells and voices outside the circle. If they had kept quiet, it would have been quite all right, but they lost their heads and scattered. Then, the circle being broken, I began to perform antics, arching up on my head and my heels and, in some way that has never been explained, arriving at the far side of the room at the feet of one of the circle, which, of course, did not improve matters. Then an extraordinary thing happened. We were just gathering ourselves together, thinking that everything was over, when a force of what nature I have never known suddenly rushed round the circle, and one member seemed to take the *brunt of it. He went flying across the room and landed, fortunately for him, face down-wards in an arm-chair, and was ill in bed for three weeks. While all this was going on, the father of one of the people taking part became uneasy about her, and walked across from where he lived at the far side of the little town, to see what was happening. Like most little country towns, this one usually went to bed early, but he told us that as he came along he saw that innumerable windows were lit up, and he heard the sounds of children crying all down the street. When I think of the risks I took and the conditions under which I worked in those early days, I wonder that I or any of my friends are alive to tell the tale. It is said that there is a special Providence to look after fools, drunkards and little children. I think there must be another that looks after inexperienced occult-ists and their friends. It may be interesting to note that as a result of this operation which I so rashly undertook, the girl was entirely freed from the domination of her mother, and began forth with to put on flesh and rapidly became normal. That end of it, at least, was entirely successful.* [10]

Psychic Self-Defense is a very interesting manual that I explained in depth in Volume II. Returning to the new edition in English of *The Sacred Magic of Abramelin* promoted by the *Ordo Templi Orientis*, that dates back to 2006, there is a very clear and explicit warning on the dangers in a **note to readers** at the beginning of the book:

Readers should contact a medical professional whenever they have health con-cerns and before attempting any procedure that may affect his or her health. The publisher and the author assume no responsibility for the results that can be ob-tained by improper use of the described methods.

These warnings issued in this new edition may seem a bit ridiculous, but they have good reason to be there, as it is much worse to pretend this is simply a harmless "New Age" book, like some of the more recent editions out there. At this point I prefer the first edition I obtained in Italy, introduced by Luciano Pirrotta. (FIG. 78) At least it explains the importance of this text in certain circles, where he warned the reader at the end of his introduction clearly and effectively about the dangers of what he was about to study.

Here it is the warning of Pirrotta at the time:

Against this background, we can not by ourselves strongly advise the reader to prac-tice the Magic of Abramelin, before having complied with skill and conscientiousness all the preparations. The road leading to the Holy Guardian Angel or Higher Self, has ramifications that reach up to the dark regions of the Demons, or as modern scholars say of deep psychology, the atavistic unconscious tanks. We hope that any-one who wants to embark on a journey of inner knowledge, of which the Magic of Abramelin is one of many methods of approach, they consider fully the potential and implications, so as it was for others who walked this path, the exhilarating thrill of a misleading and fictitious contact with the "divine," not concealing a tragic and ir-reversible ego descent into chaos domains and darkness. [11]

It is said that **Carl Gustav Jung** was involved, even if only partially, in the occult prac-tice of the *Magic of Abramelin.* He was interested in the experience of those who had preceded him in it, in this case Aleister Crowley, who practiced it to receive "Contact" with his **Secret Chiefs** in Cairo, in 1904. In various occult movements, Secret Chiefs are said to be transcendent cosmic authorities, a Spiritual Hierarchy responsible for the operation and moral calibre of the cosmos. They oversee the operations of an esoteric

10   See. Dionne Fortune, *Psichic Self Defense*, (Milan, IT: SIAD, 1978).
11   *La Magia Sacra di Abramelin il mago,* Atanor, *Ibid.,* p. 14.

LA MAGIA SACRA
DI ABRAMELIN
IL
MAGO

Introduzione e note
di L. PIRROTTA

ATANÒR

FIG. 78 – Cover of the first Italian edition of the Sacred Magic of Abramelin published by Atanòr in December 1980, (with a foreword by Luciano Pirrotta) used by the author in 1993, at the age of 23, to run this long and exhausting ritual with uncertain implications. Note the strange resemblance of the figure on the cover to Padre Pio.

organization, which manifests outwardly in the form of a magical order or lodge system. Their names and descriptions have varied throughout time, dependent upon those who experience contact with them. They exist on higher planes of being, or to be incarnate; if incarnate, they may be described as being gathered at some special location, such as Shambhala, or scattered through the world working anonymously. One early and influential source on these entities is **Karl von Eckartshausen**, whose *The Cloud Upon The Sanctuary*, published in 1795, explained in some detail their character and motivations. Several 19th and 20th century occultists claimed to belong to, or to have contacted these Secret Chiefs, and made these communications known to others, including H.P. Blavatsky (who called them the "Tibetan Masters" or Mahatmas), C.W. Leadbeater and Alice A. Bailey (who called them Masters of the Ancient Wisdom), Guy Ballard and Elizabeth Clare Prophet (who called them Ascended Masters), Aleister Crowley (who used the term to refer to members of the upper three grades of his order, **A∴A∴**), Dion Fortune (who called them the "esoteric order"), and Max Heindel (who called them the "Elder Brothers"). [12]

Jung and Sacred Magic

Unpublished and little-known truths about Carl Gustav Jung, the occult, and Abramelin, are definitely hard to find, but they are present in the excellent essay from 1995 written by the Swiss researcher **Peter-Robert König**, entitled *Abramelin & Co.* (FIG. 79) in which we find interesting data on the contact points Jung had with this hidden reality, if not directly, then indirectly through one of his dearest friend, **Traugott Egloff**. This research is of great importance for those who want to study and further deepen the many realities and occult experiences that lurk behind *the Sacred Magic of Abramelin the Mage,* the primary text of importance to the Illuminati.

· ·

12   https://en.wikipedia.org/wiki/Secret_Chiefs ‡ Archived 15th November, 2016.

We find the unpublished extracts from the diary of Aleister Crowley, with references to the Choronzon Club, and the worship of the image of LAM, his famous alien looking painting that Crowley created in 1917, 10 years after he completed the Abramelin ritual. König speaks of the work of occultists, Franz Bardon Koenig, Emil Stejnar, Dr. Michael Aquino (which we know is tied to the CIA and the MK-Ultra project), Walter Jantschik, Claas Hoffmann, describing in the process the O.T.O.A., demonstrating its degrees and rituals of this lesser known branch of the Franco-Haitian Illuminati, dedicated to conversation with these entities, following the precepts dictated precisely by the *Sacred Magic of Abramelin*. There is also a description by Krumm-Heller, founder of the *Fraternitas Rosicruciana Antiqua* (FRA), which I mentioned in my past books. König's work also contains the faithful reproduction of a rare copy from 1725 of the *Sacred Magic of Abramelin,* (FIG. 80) and two unpublished manuscripts of the Golden Dawn, adding the

FIG. 79 –Cover of **Abramelin & Co.** by Peter-R. Koenig (Hiram-Edition, 1995).

strange practices related to the sexual magical circle of "vampires" from the **Fraternitas Saturni**. It reproduces even the gods of ancient Egypt in connection with the Enochian Tablets, in an interesting piece of research conducted by Frater A.P.S. of the Illuminati, and another unpublished document of the Golden Dawn by Dr. Pullen-Burry dating back to 1895. Finally he mimics Israel Regardie related Addendum of the *Book of the Concourse of the Forces*. In short, an excellent text, it's a shame that it states on the official website of König that it is now "Sold Out Sold Out Sold Out Sold Out." [13]

Jung was connected to the mysterious work of the Rosicrucians, which was tied to his passion for alchemy and the occult, and the origins of his family. In fact it would seem that he had an ancestor who was part of the mysterious Rosicrucian Brotherhood, with the same name, and he too was a doctor, **Dr. Carl Jung from Mainz** who died in 1645. We learn in the biography dedicated to him by Frank McLynn, that suggests his descent from this character that he portrays as a follower of none other than the **Count Michael Maier**, one of the greatest authors and Masters of Rosicrucian thought. But it was probably Carl Gustav Jung, born in 1784, and his grandfather, who was an important representative of Switzerland Freemasonry, that influenced him to become himself a Freemason and Illuminati one day. This happened within a lodge linked to *Monte Verità* (literally "Hill of Truth"), a mount (350 meters or 1,150 feet high) in Ascona (Swiss canton of Ticino), a place that seems to be an important portal for extradimensional forces from the invisible plane. It is no coincidence that in June of 2016, at the opening of the Gotthard base tunnel that connects the cantons of Uri and Ticino, the prime ministers Matteo Renzi, François Hollande, and Angela Merkel, the puppets of George Soros, were strangely all present at

13   http://www.parareligion.ch/dplanet/html/abrameli.htm ‡ Archived 15th November, 2016.

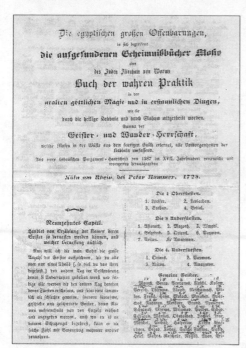

FIG. 80 – Page extracted from a rare copy of 1725 of the Sacred Magic of Abramelin reproduced on the book *Abramelin & Co* by Peter-R. Koenig.

the event. They attended the representation of a dance-drama that seemed to be a **sabbatical** ritual of hellish nature, where among the witches, a goat **devil** appears. There is also an image that resembles the main figure in the *Lucifer Rising, a* movie by Kenneth Anger, which was projected on a giant screen for full effect. Switzerland, is the seat of the most important Grand Priory of the Rectified Scottish Rite, which has a central role in the world of occult Freemasonry. Let's not forget there is also CERN, where occult rituals take place, but let's return to Monte Verità, whose original name was Mount Monascia, which is just over the hill above Ascona in Ticino, who assumed the Monte Verita name in the early decades of the twentieth century. It is here where the foundation of a diverse community of Illuminati / utopian / vegetarian / theosophers was formed, where Anarchists, aristocrats, intellectuals and artists, began arriving in large numbers to the place, attending the Mount assiduously. There was Prince Peter Kropotkin, the "Cosmic" Countess Grafin Franziska zu Reventlow, the famous choreographer and dance theorist Rudolf von Laban aka Rudolf von Laban and Laban Váralja (1879 – 1858), and his "art school" built in an individualistic cooperative which provided for the initiation to all modes of expression and human genius, to the important member of the Illuminati Theodor Reuss, the theosophist co-founder of the O.T.O. who summoned a major event for his Illuminati known as **"The Anational Congress for Organising the Reconstruction of Society on Practical Cooperative Lines"** that took place from the 15 to 25th of August, 1917 at Mount Verita. [14] The event outlined by the communistic and liberal-minded Reuss were the following: *"Forms off non national companies and cooperatives, conforming to the modern age education, emancipation of women in the future society, mystical Freemasonry, new forms of sociability, art, dance and cultural ritual."*

It would appear this important event for the Illuminati of the nascent New Age, culminated in a celebration known as the **Festival of the Sun,** a kind of dance drama from dusk to dawn staged by one of the founders of European Modern Dance, Rudolf von Laban and his school. In short, Monte Verità was probably the most important laboratory that the New Age movement had, before officially landing in California, there is no doubt about this. The colony was regularly visited by numerous internationally renowned personalities, and some also resided for a time in this magical place including, Karoly Kerényi, Erich Maria Remarque, Hermann Hesse, Filippo Franzoni, Marianne Werefkin, Alexej Jawlensky and obviously Carl Gustav Jung, who seems to have joined the irregular lodge opened by Theodor Reuss and von Laban in Zurich in 1917, called *Lodge Libertas et Fraternitas* (which later became a regular Masonic lodge). It seems that Jung initially obtained the

Rosicrucian degree that was apparently the *Cernau* schismatic version of the Ancient and Accepted Scottish rite. There are those who say that Jung obtained the Rosicrucian degree in the *Ordo Templi Orientis* system, where this degree is present as the 5th degree, and others who are very critical of this possibility, or the fact that Jung was ever a Freemason at all. Jung's Masonic membership was never officially confirmed by the **Grand Lodge Alpina of Switzerland (SGLA)**, but the information probably spread by a key figure of the Italian Illuminati, Francesco Brunelli, who apparently learned it from Robert Ambelain, his teacher, who indicated Carl Gustav Jung as a member of the *Freimaurerloge Modestia cum Libertate* of the Rectified Scottish Rite. Jung is present on the list of famous Freemasons published on the website of various lodges operating today in Italy. [15] Jung is also identified as a Freemason by the **Italian Symbolic Rite (RSI)**, [16] confirming his Rosicrucian rank and his willingness to go "beyond" the physical realm of appearance. Freemasonry aside, in 1916, the paranormal entered into Jung's life with automatic writing, which produces a very strange work: *The Seven Sermons to the Dead,* written officially by Basilides in Alexandria, the City where the East toucheth the West. We are in the postwar period, and Jung is 41 years old. The book is written rapidly in three nights, in a trance state, a bit like Crowley a few years earlier in **1904**, in Cairo, with his *Book of the Law,* which was received mediumistically through the entity Aiwass. From an early age, Jung had entered into communication with invisible presences. After the age of 40, however, the entities literally seem to have invaded his life. In his house Jung experienced paranormal phenomena, where there was a worrying presence that involved not only Jung, but also his daughter. His child had unusual nightmares, the doorbell rang by itself, and Jung felt surrounded by many spirits in attendance, where he asked them what they wanted.

The answer was: *"We return to Jerusalem, where we did not find what we were looking for."* The book *The Seven Sermons to the Dead* begins with these words explaining that *"Jerusalem is the center of Christianity, the spirit you are looking searches for something that he does not find, because Christianity has changed, it has become something else. Jerusalem is the spiritual city that must be liberated, is the soul, but there is a heavenly Jerusalem made by God and an earthly Jerusalem made by men; the first is the sacred, the second the historical religion. Through time the symbols of earthly Jerusalem have moved away from their original purpose, which is why one of the first Christians philosophers writes bringing back the basics."*

When Jung began writing in a trance, the energies cease to manifest themselves in his house, because they have found their channel. Jung privately publishes this automated dictation in a booklet form and gives it only to friends. It illustrates phrases and concepts typical of **Basilides,** a gnostic philosopher who lived in the second century, where the script has the same hermetic style. Gnosticism through the sacred knowledge and the object of the dictation is the Supreme Being and its manifestations. *The Seven Sermons of the Dead* is a mediumistic writing that conveys the invisible energies of the alien world around us, giving them a voice. Jung called this phenomenon, which is external and internal together, *"an unconscious constellation, whose atmosphere is the numen, of an archetype that runs around here, in the air."* The archetype is not just a psychic matrix, it can be an energy living in another time and another space, or a historical memory reactivated and channeled through another subject that brings it back to light, even two thousand years later. The Christian era seemed for Jung and the Illuminati that gathered in Monte Verità, was born out of a mistake, that mistake became evil, slowly spreading and leading

15   http://loggiadedeo.altervista.org/joomla_dedeo/index.php/massoni-celebri ‡ Archived15th November, 2016.
16   http://www.ritosimbolico.net/studi1/studi1_34.html ‡ Archived 15th November, 2016.

to dissolution. Everything was contained in its origins; the sin of the origins of Christianity was not the original sin of Eden. He wanted to separate the totality of universal energy, male-female, that privileged the male. Gnostics in the first centuries of Christianity respected the whole being, the two sides of the cosmic energy, but the established Church that followed broke the covenant of balance, denying Christ and his saving wholeness, and breaking the world in an unresolvable antinomy between male and female. The glyph of Pisces with his two contrary motions indicated in reality an opposition never really resolved, which would lead eventually to the final collapse, the Apocalypse, the end of the world, or of an era. The forgotten values of the Mother, the exile of the Goddess, the denial of nature, the love oblivion had unbalanced the world in denial and in the war; rationality, malfeasance, and greed were risking an end to the planet.

Whenever Jung was restless, he questioned his soul, the soul sent an image, and that sense of oppression vanished. The soul is the unconscious messenger, and communicates with an even larger reality, extra-temporal and universal. For years Jung converses with his soul when he was upset or worried, and this is something that was also practiced by my father Elio, also a disciple of Jung's thought, using this strange modality. It was something I tried to understand since childhood, when for hours and hours I could hear my father talking to himself in his study, in an unusual dialogue with his soul, to ask what was happening, what was new, what disturbed him. The soul produces an image in this process, and, as soon as it appears, the sense of oppression vanishes. Jung analyzes the image and the soul and acted at times like a kind of shaman who questions his spirits. It is no wonder my father's friend, the late Lorenzo Ostuni (died in 2013), also well-versed in analytical psychology, and a leading figure in the Italian esoteric scene, who called my father a sort of "Witchdoctor."

The emotion for Jung acts as an intermediary for conscious communication with the unconscious. As this happens the emotions subside, the order returns and energy finds its rhythm. Jung writes down his path of consciousness in the *Black Book*, six small volumes bound in black leather, which then assume a more artistic tone in the *Red Book*. Jung will work on the *Red Book* for 6 years, taking care and great attention to the designs, colors, mandalas, and the Gothic features, penned thoroughly with Indian ink so to render it a masterpiece. Towards the end of his life, Jung wrote to his friend and Masonic Brother, Traugott Egloff, "If the meeting with the shadow" (the inner aspects of life by a person not recognized) is the "apprentice work" in the development of the individual, then the encounter with the soul is the "masterpiece" (9 Feb., 1959). Jung was definitely part of the Illuminati establishment and the correspondence with Traugott Egloff, a cultured and erudite Mason, and a Swiss member of the Order of the Illuminati, proves it. No wonder Egloff was especially fond of the *Sacred Magic of Abramelin*.

Jung's secret work with the *Sacred Magic* allowed him to meet his muse Anna Antonia "Toni" Wolff (September 18, 1888 – March 21, 1953). Traugott Egloff later disappeared in the jungles of Brazil, where he had gone ostensibly to seek the ideal place for contacting his Holy Guardian Angel in the final stage of the *Sacred Magic of Abramelin*. Unfortunately, it seems that Egloff died on this occasion, as with other unwary O.T.O. members before, and after him, who dedicated themselves to the dangerous practices of the *Sacred Magic of Abramelin*. This includes Dr. C. H. Petersen, known to the initiates of the O.T.O. as *Frater Fines Transcendam,* high dignitary of the Order in Germany. After the war he wanted to embrace the ritual, but violated the strict rules of the grimoire by bringing in his cousin Frau Pingwill called "Kama-rupa" who practiced sexual magic with him. The Sacred Magic is clear on this point: *"we must not admit a woman in this operation."* Kama-rupa committed suicide in 1956 and Dr. C. H. Petersen died in the hospital in Hamburg on April 4, 1957. Although, to be fair in the case of Traugott Egloff,

Jung's friend, the certainty of his death was never proven, despite extensive research, the body was in fact never found. It's almost like he vanished or was abducted to another dimension. And although he was in the end given up for dead, there is always the possibility (however remote) that he may still be alive, or absorbed by an interdimensional door. A door that perhaps Egloff the Illuminati, was trying to open to get in touch with certain extradimensional entities, and maybe having witnessed his insistence, totally absorbed him in their own reality with a permanent abduction. In the *Sacred Magic of Abramelin* it is written: *"I dare say, in truth, dear son Lamech, that I have done for you what no one has done in our time, especially by telling you the two signs without which (I swear on the True God) out of a hundred who embark upon this operation, there would not be that two or three that we would succeed."*

Another important source of information on Jung's connection to the occult was definitely **Oskar Rudolf Schlag**, an important figure of the Swiss Illuminati, who I wrote a lot about in the first volume of my *Confessions*. He was used as a medium by Jung for a series of experiments, and was tied to the Hermetic Society of Zurich. Jung was secretly fond of occultism and saw in ceremonial magic the means to open contact with certain unknown forces, those same entities that dictated the mysterious Gnostic text *Septem Sermones ad Mortuos,* or *The Seven Sermons to the Dead* I mentioned earlier. This brief booklet, which as we know was never published officially by Jung, will become part of those mysterious writings never published during his lifetime, like the mysterious *Red Book. The Sermons* are 14 pages of philosophy dictated by the spirit and life of the Gnostic philosopher Basilides; summarizing themes that Jung will analyze over the following years. Gnosticism came to Carl Gustav Jung in 1916 through mediumship, and if knowledge of the Gnostics had arrived to him with the beginning of this study of automatic writing, his knowledge of alchemy was dictated by an act synchronism, in 1929. When he was ready, Jung received by mail a Chinese book, a Taoist alchemy text called *The Golden Flower.* From that moment on he stopped writing the *Red Book* and began to deal with alchemy in a vast study that was to last 30 years. However, the *Red Book is* not a monument to psychology, although Jung began writing it almost immediately after the break with Freud in 1914. But it's not even a simple document as academics claimed it to be. Jung called it a "confrontation with the unconscious" in the period between 1912 and 1918. In the following years he worked on the principles of his psychological theories, the archetypes, the collective unconscious and the identification process, transforming psychotherapy from a simple treatment of a possible mental disease, to a medium for the development of the higher personality. Analytical psychology became a theoretical discipline and a form of psychotherapy. At the center of this was the *Liber Novus,* or the *Red Book.* Here Jung tried to derive the psychological principles with fantasies. He also tried to understand the symbolic form of events and how they would present themselves in future developments in the world. The material was revised several times, only to be copied in an ornate Gothic script in a large volume bound in red leather, to which he added not only all sorts of ornaments but also many interesting figures and designs made by him. Even if the work in question was inspired by the Illuminated manuscripts of the Midde Ages, the texts and images used by Jung is strongly reminiscent of the work of the Illuminati master **William Blake (1757 – 1827).** William Breeze, born on August 12th, 1955, and current **Patriarch of the E.G.C** *(Gnostic Ecclesia Catholica),* the Gnostic Church linked to Aleister Crowley and the Illuminati of the *Ordo Templi Orientis*, also known by the initiatic name of *Hymenaeus Beta*, was basing his judgement on an essay in 1997, that Crowley himself had dedicated to Blake as a sort of saint, and officialized William Blake's position as a "Saint" of his so-called "Gnostic Church." He achieved the dual objective of including Blake in the list of saints and at the same time being able to celebrate his own onomastic in memory of this extravagant and ingenious character beloved by Freemasonry and the Illuminati. Furthermore, the O.T.O followers (a bunch of communists and satanists of the worst kind) on February 17 of 2000, also inserted Giordano Bruno in the list of the Saints of their infamous Church. I say poor Giordano Bruno, whose memory should not be in any way linked to this dangerous Illuminati sect. **William Blake** according to some well-informed British researchers is present in an alleged official list of Grandmasters of the **Druid Order** (from 1799 to 1827).

Blake was certainly prone to certain esoteric disciplines, and was inspired by magic and the occult, from which he drew profusely his visionary works and his deep research on the soul of man, which inevitably will bring him into contact with the subtle reality, which also influenced and inspired Carl Gustav Jung. The dangerous Satanist of Jewish origin Marilyn Manson, who made a disgraceful music video in 2016 where a figure resembling the Republican president-elect Donald Trump was decapitated, together with other left wingers of the occults, including the Grand Master of the *Ordo Templi Orientis* William Breeze, enthusiastically participated a few years ago (in June, 2010) in an exhibition titled *The Alchemy of Things Unknown (and Visual Meditation on Transformation)* that took place at the prestigious Khastoo Gallery of Sunset Boulevard in Los Angeles, contributing in various ways to this event created by the political and cultural milieu of the *Ordo Templi Orientis* and the dark and perverse side of the Illuminati, to promote the release of the *Red Book* by C.G. Jung. Maybe someone should tell these communist freaks that Carl Gustav Jung was not one of them, and for this reason at one point he was even accused of being a "Nazi sympathizer"—accusations which, in some respects, seems justified for some researchers. [17]

However the Hollywood exhibition I just mentioned promoting C. G. Jung's *Red Book,* was described as a sort of art exhibition, a modality many satanists often use to promote their occult events (i.e. Marina Abramović, Zeena Schreck, just to name a couple). This "exhibition" was said to explore and expose individual works of art in relation to theosophy, the sacred tradition, and devotional practice. I guess one thing is to be illuminated by the works of divine imagination created by the genius of William Blake, or the designs of Carl Gustav Jung's collective unconscious, as visual art is undoubtedly a great creative tool to achieve illumination; but this context was built instead to submit to dark forces and promote their occult liberal agenda amongst the elite. Analyzing deeper the relationship between Jung and Blake, in 1948 Carl G. Jung began to study the works of William Blake, where his studies of some Gnostic texts and his vision of reality turned out to be very similar in some respects to those of Jung. Even the imaginative art of Blake seems to come close to Jung. In fact, there are so many similarities, that Jung according to various experts, included Blake among his favorite figures of all time, along with **Dante, Goethe, Wagner** and **Nietzsche.** There is a particular episode in C. G. Jung's life, found in a acclaimed documentary from a few years ago produced by Werner Weick for the Italian Swiss public television channel, where we find mentioned a certain Atmavictu: *"In the great images that filled his soul. He had erected a monument to the creative demon that had driven him all his life to pursue their own visions and to give the world some brilliant psychological insights perhaps not yet fully understood and accepted; he called him 'Atmavictu' that is, 'breath of life.' On the pediment of his home in Küsnacht, Carl Gustav Jung, had engraved an inscription in Latin:—'The first man is of the earth and is earthly, the second man is from heaven and it is spiritual. Whether you call him or not, God will be present.' His daughter Gret told us: 'He remained motionless for 24*

----

17   See. http://pandc.ca/?cat=carl_jung&page=jung_nazis ‡ Archived 15th November, 2016.

*hours before he died and did not respond to any stress. ... It was very far away now. His
last breaths were so wonderful and free that there was no room in my heart for sorrow.
Fifteen minutes after his death with a frightening roar a bolt of lightning tore along its
length of the garden poplars.'"*

It seems that a similar event took place after the death of Aleister Crowley. **Patricia
"Deirdre" MacAlpine** mother of Aleister Ataturk, present the moment the "Great Beast"
passed away, told an interviewer from British television that a sudden gust of wind, and
crash of thunder came at the exact moment of Crowley's death. Adding that it seemed
to her that the gods wanted to pay homage to him in the moment of his passing away, to
what Crowley used to call *the greater feast.*

In Jung's *The Red Book: Liber Novus (Philemon)*, the Master and founder of Analytical psychology (sometimes called analytic psychology), also known as Jungian psychology, allows us to all participant in a fundamental aspect of his spiritual and intellectual growth linked to the occult: *"When, in October 1913, I had the vision of the flood,
I was in a period of importance for me personally. Then, at the age of forty years, I got
everything I had hoped. I had achieved fame, power, wealth, knowledge and all human
happiness. Thus ceased in me the desire to further gains by those assets, I was lacking
the desire, and I was filled with horror. The vision of the flood overtook me and I felt the
spirit of the deep, without understanding it. But it forced me making me feel unbearably
intimate longing, and I said, 'My soul, where are you? Can you hear me? I speak, I'll
call you. ... Are you there? I'm back, I'm back again.'"* And of one thing we are sure, Jung
is still here, and today his thinking is more relevant than ever despite the compromises
that he might have been forced to make within the academic world and with those "Architects of control" and manipulation involved in "mind control."

Jung and Mind Control

My father, Elio Zagami, was for a time, one of the leaders of the Jungian school
worldwide. In fact, he studied and worked in Switzerland with **Carl Alfred
Meier (April 19, 1905 – 1995),** the successor of Carl Gustav Jung, who had great esteem
for my father, and offered him the post as his successor at the Zürichberg Clinic (Clinic
and Research Centre for Jungian Psychology)—an offer that my father refused. He returned to Italy, where he founded, as some of you may know, the Independent **Group of
Analytical Psychology (GAPA).** Years later he also refused to take over the patients of
another great teacher of Jungian thought, the Italian **Aldo Carotenuto,** who contacted
him by telephone shortly before he passed away. Difficult and unusual choices, that only
years later I fully understood, given the rebellious and independent nature of my father,
and his work. His research went well beyond the boundaries of psychoanalysis, where in
a single year in Zurich, only five years after Jung's death in the period 1966-67, he shocked
the local academic world. Meier remained in contact with my father in the following
years, and up until the mid-seventies, regularly visited him in Rome during his time in the
Italian capital; a bond made of true friendship between researchers of deep thought. My
father declined the offer of becoming the successor of Jung and Meier because he found
the Jungian world corrupt and manipulative.

I would like to explore a few lesser known aspects of Jung's work in relation to mind
control, and its hidden manipulators, including those of Freemasonry. In 1948, the *National Association for Mental Health* of Montagu Norman announced the great **International
Congress on Mental Health,** in London. Under the patronage of the Duchess of Kent,
widow of the Grand Master of the **United Grand Lodge of England,** (a position he held

from 1939 to 1942) and mother of the future Grand Master (since 1967), the Congress saw the participation of C. G. Jung and key figures of the growing New World Order. **Julian Huxley**, the American anthropologist Margaret Mead, **Winfred Overholser**, head of the American delegation, that some sources indicate as senior member of the U.S. Scottish Rite, and the director of the **St. Elizabeths Hospital in Washington, D.C.**, that usually provides **mental health** care **services** to members of the U.S. armed forces and presided over the Office for Strategic Services (OSS, that after the war became the CIA) began a project in search of the ultimate "truth serum," i.e. psychotropic substances to use in the interrogation of prisoners. The clinic was used in the 1950s to experiment various drugs on U.S. Army recruits, to identify subversive subjects. Among the famous doctors were Thomas J. Lord Horder, personal doctor of Edward VIII, and president of the *Eugenics Society* and the *Anglo-Soviet Public Relations Association;* Dr. Alfred E.Tredgold, member of the *Committee for Sterilization* at the Ministry of Health; and psychiatrists Cyril Burt and Hugh Crichton-Miller, an expert in paranormal research and first vice president of the C. G. Jung Institute, Zürich, both founders of the infamous **Tavistock Institute** in London.[18]

Let's not forget who engineered this, the aforementioned Montagu Norman, an English banker, best-known for his role as the Governor of the Bank of England from 1920 to 1944, as there is always a connection between the banking system and Psychological operations (PSYOP).

In 1921, The Tavistock Institute, formally a psychiatric research clinic, became the perfect place to study mental disorders derived from continuous exposure to terror generated in battle by British soldiers, especially those who survived World War I. It became a laboratory of psychological warfare for the British army during World War II, and later settled as a world center of mass brain washing and social engineering for the New World Order. Working closely with experiments to create methods to control the masses, widely-used on American citizens, a sneaky and outrageous attack on freedom by means of applied psychology, imposed with no authorization on circumscribed areas of the brain. The object of the fiercest studies of the Tavistock in recent years is, for example, the creation of "paradigm shifts," or the means to induce "new" values in society through collective traumatic events (*turbulent environments*). For example, a cycle of lectures at the Tavistock Institute in 1989 had as its central theme the following: *"The role of NGOs in weakening national states."*

In 1948, a key role was played by **John Rawlings Rees** (1890 –1969) in the International Congress for Mental Health, when he was nominated President of the World Federation for Mental Health. He was a British civilian and military psychiatrist, and one of the key figures at the original Tavistock Clinic, where he became the medical director from 1933: *"After leaving Tavistock, Rees' first role was as the chief organizer of the 1948 International Congress for Mental Health, held in London. At this congress, the World Federation for Mental Health was founded, and Rees was elected as the first president."*[19]

Rees' part in the colossal CIA program called MK-Ultra is unclear. In 1943, the Rockefeller Foundation created in Canada (i.e. in British territory) a clinic, called the "Allen Memorial Institute," linked to the McGill University in Montreal. Donald E. Cameron, a Scottish psychiatrist who was head of psychiatric services, became known when chilling details about the experiments of MK-Ultra began to leak out, causing a revolt by the American public in the 1970s. Cameron was a specialist in inducing sleep in his patients

18   http://www.disinformazione.it/psichiatrimassoni.htm ‡ Archived 20th November, 2016.
19   https://en.wikipedia.org/wiki/John_Rawlings_Rees ‡ Archived 20th November, 2016.

(or victims) using drugs, and then woke them with electric shocks. Cameron's research pinpointed topics that interested the CIA, and The Army Chemical Center financed, always under MK-Ultra, including research with LSD. Paul Hoch, a psychiatrist and Freemason who collaborated with German pro-Nazi eugenicist Franz Kallmann, in studies on schizophrenia sponsored by some members of the Masonic elite. Kallmann wrote *The Genetics of Schizophrenia: A Study of Heredity and Reproduction in the Families of 1, 087 Schizophrenics,* (New York, 1938). Kallmann began his research in Germany under the eugenicist of the Third Reich Ernst Ruedin, but in 1935, he was identified as a "half Jew" and had to emigrate to the USA to avoid persecution. Here he found employment at the New York Psychiatric Institute, whose director Nolan D. C. Lewis, was a Freemason. Robert Hanna Felix, a 33 ° Scottish Rite, and the founder of the *National Institute of Mental Health,* was involved in some of the scandalous experiments into "brainwashing" conducted by MK-Ultra, along with his student Harris Isbell. The CIA made extensive experiments with a variety of illegal drugs given to drug addicts in its Addiction Research Center in Lexington (Kentucky). Finally, after the press revelations on MK-Ultra, the program was officially halted in 1973. An investigation, which went nowhere, was conducted for the media. It's no coincidence that the head of the relevant Senatorial Committee appointed to the case was none other than Nelson Rockefeller. The Rockefeller Commission closed its work on the subject in 1975. However, since 1961, Robert H. Felix assembled the leading researchers of MK-Ultra under the umbrella of a new institution with the more respectable name: *The American College of NeuroPsycopharmacology.*

In 1967, the College held a conference called **"Effects of psychotropic drugs on a normal human,"** whose introduction fell on two former actors of the MK-Ultra: **Wayne O. Evans,** military psychiatrist from the U.S. Army Stress Laboratory in Natik (Massachusetts); and **Nathan S. Kline (1916 – 1983),** a eugenicist of Columbia University, and a scholar of Haitian Voodoo,[20] whose best-known work was with psychopharmacologic drugs,[21] to which a well-known clinic in the industry, the Nathan S. Kline Institute for Psychiatric Research found in Orangeburg in the State of New York is dedicated to him.[22] The beginning of their relationship reveals, with dazzling clarity, the very reason why the financial oligarchies have for so long funded psychiatric research:

> *The current range of psychotropic drugs seems almost trivial when we compare it to the possible number of chemicals that will be available for the control of selective aspects of human life in the millennium. American culture moves towards a "sane society." The emphasis regains more and more on the experience sensory and less and less on rationalist philosophies. This philosophical vision, together with the means to separate sexual behavior from reproduction, will step up without question, sexual freedom. It seems obvious that the youth of today are no longer afraid of drugs or sex. Still, philosophers and avant-garde commentators advocate the personal sensory experience as the* raison d'etre *of the next generation. We are going towards an era in which a significant work will be possible only for a minority: in that era, chemical aphrodisiacs will be accepted as a common means to occupy your time. If we accept the position that man's mood, his motivations and emotions, are reflections of the state of the neurochemical brain, then medications may provide the simplest, quickest and most practical way to produce any state neurochemical you wish. As soon we cease to confuse the scientific and the moral claims on the use*

20   See. Rebecca Stefoff, *Vampires, Zombies, and Shape-Shifters,* (Salt Lake City, UT: Benchmark Books 2007), p. 44.
21   https://en.wikipedia.org/wiki/Nathan_S._Kline#cite_note-1 ‡ Archived 20th November, 2016.
22   http://www.rfmh.org/nki/ ‡ Archived 20th November, 2016.

of drugs, the sooner we can rationally consider the types of neurochemical states that we want to be able to provide to the people. [23]

These characters are skillful and cunning at the apex of the New World Order, with the intention to maintain control over the system of so-called mental health. This was one of the main reasons why my father, in the end rejected psychiatry and Jung's legacy. He could not tolerate the fact that this science that should have helped man in the next evolutionary step, was subject to control and manipulation from a central power as that of Tavistock. This was often repeated to me in our long talks.

Jung and the wife of Tutankhamun

For further study, we find the book by **Frank McLynn** called *Carl Gustav Jung,* [24] where many interesting facts about Jung surface, that also include his privileged relationship with the **Rockefeller family**, which also had a direct involvement with his studies in psychiatry. Jung even met the famous Standard Oil founder **John D. Rockefeller,** after treating his elder sister **Edith Rockefeller McCormick (1872 – 1932)**, who visited Jung in 1913, after suffering terrible depression, and from that point onward became a fan of C. G. Jung, donating a substantial sum of money for the psychological Society of Zurich. Edith Rockefeller McCormick, who was the daughter of John D. Rockefeller and his wife, Laura Spelman, found herself making headlines in February, 1923, when she claimed to be the reincarnation of the wife of Tutankhamun. She was quoted as saying: *"I married King Tutankhamun when I was only sixteen years old. I was his first wife. Only the other day, while glancing through an illustrated paper, I saw a picture of a chair removed from the King's Chamber. Like a flash I recognized that chair. I had sat in it many times."* [25] The Rockefeller family must have reacted to stories like this with a collective cringe. She followed up by stating *"My interest in reincarnation is of many years standing."*

It can be seen the Rockefeller's have a pretty obvious occult side, and the **Rockefeller Archaeological Museum** is even hiding alien artifacts. A coincidence or something more sinister, in the aftermath of the opening of the tomb of Tutankhamun, the discovery ended with a bizarre set of murders with mysterious circumstances. But while in the intellectual salons of the twenties and thirties in London, there was talk of supernatural powers of the ancient Egyptians at work behind the sudden deaths. The historian Mark Beynon argues that contemporary researchers should actually focus on Aleister Crowley, the infamous black magician and driving force behind the dark side of the Illuminati.

Incredible parallels between Crowley, and Jack the Ripper, have been discovered during research by historian **Mark Beynon.** Throughout the 1920s and 1930s, London was gripped by the mythical curse of Tutankhamun, the Egyptian boy-king, whose tomb was uncovered by British archaeologist Howard Carter. More than 20 people linked to the opening of the pharaoh's burial chamber near Luxor in 1923, all died bizzare deaths over the following years—six of them in the capital. Victims include Carter's personal secretary, Captain Richard Bethell, who was found dead in his bed from a suspected smothering at an exclusive Mayfair club. Bethell's father, Lord Westbury, plunged seven floors to his death from his St James's apartment, where he reportedly kept tomb artifacts, as gifts from his son. And Aubrey Herbert, half-brother of Carter's financial backer Lord Carnarvon, also died suspiciously in a Park Lane hospital, shortly after visiting Luxor. At the time, a frenzied press blamed the "Curse of Tutankhamun" for the deaths, and specu-

....
23   disinformazione.it *Ibid.*
24   See. Frank McLynn , *Carl Gustav Jung,* (New York: St Martin's Press 2008), p. 347.
25   https://en.wikipedia.org/wiki/Edith_Rockefeller_McCormick ‡ Archived 20th November, 2016.

FIG. 81 – Aleister Crowley and Sir Ernest Alfred Thompson Wallis Budge as they were portrayed in The Telegraph.

lated on the supernatural powers of the ancient Egyptians. But Mr Beynon examined unpublished evidence to conclude the deaths were all ritualistic killings masterminded by Crowley, an occultist dubbed "the wickedest man in the world." After a unique analysis of Crowley's diaries, essays, books and inquest reports, the armchair detective argues that he was a Jack the Ripper-obsessed copycat killer. Crowley, who called himself **"The Great Beast 666,"** apparently had his own motives in tarnishing the legacy of Carter's legendary discovery. The gods and goddesses of Crowley's own religious philosophy, Thelema, were derived from ancient Egyptian religion, and he believed himself to be a prophet of a new age of personal liberty, controlled by the ancient Egyptian god, Horus. It is likely that he would have found Carter's escavation sacrilegious, and wanted revenge, according to Mr Beynon, in his book *London's Curse: Murder, Black Magic and Tutankhamun in the 1920s West End.*[26] For many occultists and pseudo-Illuminati, the secret bond between the supposed "Curse of Tutankhamun" and Aleister Crowley could be judged false and without foundation, especially as your average follower of "The Great Beast 666" never likes to accept unpleasant truths about Crowley. He is considered a prophet and the guru of sexual freedom, and of course "The Magician of all Magicians." But in November 2011, with his new thesis, Beynon disrupts the magickal-esoteric scene of the Illuminati linked to the "Beast 666," especially after he received an excellent review by the English newspaper *The Telegraph.* (FIG. 81) However, **Alessandro De Angelis** writer, researcher of the history of religion and early Christianity states that these deaths, served to cover up the discovery of secret documents that would change the course of history.

In 1924, there is testimony by Lee Keedick, who witnessed a harsh argument between Carter and another British official, in the British Embassy in Cairo, during which Carter threatened to publicly reveal the burning of documents found in the tomb. (FIG. 82) He later justified the disappearance of the documents by saying that he had misclassified

26   http://www.telegraph.co.uk/news/worldnews/africaandindianocean/egypt/8878314/Curse-of-Tutankhamun-may-have-been-work-of-Satanist-killer.html ‡ Archived 20th November, 2016.

FIG. 82 – *The famous British archaeologist and Egyptologist Howard Carter (Swaffham, May 9, 1874 – London, 2 March 1939) pictured with his Egyptian worker in the period following the opening of the Tutankhamun sarcophagus, dating from the 16th of February, 1924. Inside contained the mummy of the pharaoh child in a solid gold sarcophagus weighing 110 kg, with the face covered by a solid gold mask reproducing the likeness of the deceased.*

some bandages of the pharaoh as papyrus because there was "little light in the grave." An implausible explanation as his team would have become immediately aware of such an error given the interest that these documents had aroused. But this concealment is also evident from a letter sent by Lord Carnarvon in 1922, to his friend Egyptologist Alan H. Gardiner. The Count spoke of the presence of "a box with some papyrus," an assertion later confirmed by a further letter by Carnarvon to Sir Edgar A. Wallis Budge, who worked for the British Museum Department of Egyptian and Assyrian Antiquities, and was responsible for displaying the artifacts from Luxor. Mr Beynon states there is evidence that Budge and Crowley were associates on the London occult scene. Further confirmation was found in a telegram sent by Arthur Merton November 30, 1922 which read: *"one of the boxes found in the tomb contained the papyrus rolls from which it is expected to find a large amount of historical information."*

Howard Carter did not deny the statements of Lord Carnarvon about its existence. Only after the death of Lord Carnavon was the first modified version of the facts presented, which led the Egyptologist, Alan Gardiner, to claim that those documents could shed light on the change of religion of Pharaoh Akhenatun and *"The real hidden story of Israel."* The conspiracy involving suppressed papyri (relating to the Jewish Exodus) from the tomb. Aleister Crowley's involvement in this supposed series of assasinations could be quite plausible, seeing his important position and role in occult hierarchy, and his links to various Jewish

Freemasons. Carter was threatening truly explosive disclosures on ancient documents that would do nothing less than re-write the history of Judaism and Christianity. This was at the same time as tensions were rising over plans to establish a Jewish homeland in the Middle East. What Carter was suggesting would throw the Middle East into turmoil. The secrets he may have stumbled upon would have completely overturned key elements in the Bible.

The implications are enormous—forcing us to ask whether the person we call Moses was in fact a renegade Egyptian priest. I will explore this topic in *The Invisible Master*, and whether Christianity has its roots in a religious revolution initiated by a heretical pharaoh. The contents of these papyrus documents are so contentious that if they had been made public, they may well have changed the course of the 20th Century completely. The missing papyri have been the subject of speculation from the time the tomb was opened. Lord Caernarfon mentioned the discovery in two letters to friends. A report in *The Times* also mentioned their existence. It is odd that later the official story changed, and everyone began insisting that these documents never existed! Carter alleged that the find was in fact "loin cloths" —the boy king's "underwear!" And that poor light made for the misunderstanding. Too many people saw these documents before they "disappeared," perhaps in a secret Masonic vault, an astounding "blunder" for someone of Carter's standing. Lord Caernarfon himself states that, on their first entry into the room, it was fully illuminated by electric light. Looking a little closer at this discovery, the official version has Carter uncovering a secret sunken staircase in the Valley of the Kings. Then penetrating a doorway sealed with the jackal emblem of Egyptian royalty, and clearing a rubble strewn corridor leading to another doorway. Making a small hole, he peers through this doorway to reveal strange animals, statues of gold, everywhere the glint of gold. [27]

The public revelation made by Edith Rockefeller McCormick the following year, in 1923, about being the wife of Tutankhamun, seems a bit strange in regards to Howard Carter, and his discovery. The number 23 is also a very important number for the Illuminati. There is an obsession for many occultists with Egypt, that will lead us to discuss the links between ancient Egypt and Satanism. Obscure practices and perverse rituals are part of this, and because of their infatuation with ancient ritual, that include human sacrifice, the more perverse sects of Illuminati are often fixated with Egypt, as with other ancient cultures. Rituals dedicated to Isis described by Dion Fortune, including those of the Sumerian culture and the Mesopotamian culture, as well as those practiced by a large part of the European and Asian societies (at least up to the Bronze Age), all practiced human sacrifice with the objective to appease the gods. The Royal Cemetery of Ur, discovered in the 1920s, with its 16 majestic filled tombs rich in gold and jewels, is not only a tangible document of the apex of the civilization of Ur, it's also evidence that human sacrifice was practiced on a large scale to please their alien gods. And if you think about it, even today, in areas of Iraq, death and brutality dominates with human sacrifice being practiced on a daily basis with ISIS, the evil Islamic thugs and mercenaries of the New World Order.

Crowley was an eccentric, bisexual, heroin addict, who gained notoriety as a supporter of sexual promiscuity and prostitution. Beynon describes him in his book as a dangerous schizophrenic, known for murdering his servants in India. In his diaries, Crowley never speaks of deaths relating to him, but as I have mentioned earlier he describes how he felt "relieved" in the days after they occurred. Beynon describes a Crowley haunted by the figure of **Jack the Ripper,** who not only wrote many poems and essays about him, but even came into contact with Walter Sickert, who was suspected of being Jack the Ripper. Beynon states that he based Jack the Ripper's crimes as a source of inspiration, for his own crimes years

*FIG. 83 – Pontus Lindqvist, VII ° of the Ordo Templi Orientis, sitting next to the **stele of Ankh-ef-en-Khonsu** (also known as **a pillar of Revelation**). He is the alleged contact of the Order with Carters' family and certain hidden relicts supposedly found in Tutankhamun's tomb.*

later. In Crowley's diaries we find that he was convinced that the places of the five murders committed by Jack the Ripper in Whitechapel in 1888 (the year of the founding of the Golden Dawn), formed a pentagram, a symbol of great importance in the mystery schools since antiquity, but also connected to the practice of Satanism, as well as Freemasonry. Crowley also believed that the murders of Jack the Ripper would provide him the special powers he needed, including invisibility, and in that period he practiced experiments in public.

For Crowleyan followers, these truths are considered uncomfortable and therefore are strongly denied, even today, they often promote the erroneous interpretations of Crowleyan thinking and his "eccentric" ways, but remember that these sacrifices are performed to meet an evil Egregore, which aids the *Ordo Templi Orientis*, and other Crowleyan sects in a demonic mission to promote the Kingdom of the Antichrist. Aleister in fact died in the grips of his addiction to heroin on December 1st, 1947, while the O.T.O. will be gradually absorbed in all its emanations by American military intelligence for a much larger project, piloted by the elite, and certain branches of Freemasonry, and the Illuminati, connected to mind control and mass manipulation. (FIGS. 83, 84, 85)

For this reason, at the end of the 1960s and the first half of the 70s, several particularly diabolical films came out that shocked a whole generation and were introduced by the dark side into the collective consciousness. Three of them have been described in America as "Satanic blockbusters:" *Rosemary's Baby*, 1968; *The Exorcist*, 1973; and *The Omen*, 1976; as well as dozens of smaller films of the same style. Surely the three I just mentioned were the more successful, and terrorized the masses starting with *The Exorcist*, which is clearly inspired by the infamous Jesuits. The influence of the Society of Jesus in the art of propaganda is massive and not understood by the average person. However, many New Age and satanic sects that originated from the Theosophical milieu are under Jesuit influence. A key element in the movie *The Exorcist* is definitely the figure of the exorcist/archeologist **Father Lankester Merrin SJ**, a distinguished Jesuit played by Max von Sydow, who in the first scene of the film finds himself in the desert in the North of Iraq, where he discovers a strange amulet. Let us dwell on this very scene because beyond the fictional film, these ancient relics can have a supernatural power and a specific demonic quality highly regarded by the Illuminati. [28]

28   See. Leo Lyon Zagami, Enrica Perucchietti, I *Maestri Invisibili del Nuovo Ordine Mondiale*, (Rome,

FIG. 84 – Satanist of the Ordo Templi Orientis and high level dignitary of the Swedish Rite of Freemasonry Henrik Bogdan while visiting Egypt with Pontus Lindqvist.

FIG. 85 – Carl Abrahamsson, a leading representative of modern Satanism and European heir by initiation of Church of Satan founder Anton LaVey is Pontus Lindqvist O.T.O. lodge Master.

Pazuzu

In the movie *The Exorcist*, power is derived from a relic linked to the ancient Assyrian Babylonian demon called **Pazuzu,** the king of air, and in some religious sects is interpreted as Satan. Pazuzu is represented as a man with a monstrous face in the shape of a jackal with wings. Pazuzu was invoked to protect pregnant women from evil spirits—as, for example Lamashtu, his eternal rival who is the origin for the biblical **Lilith,** kidnapper of children. But it is also the wind demon, which brings death by hypothermia and wind destruction. In the follow-up film *Exorcist II: The Heretic* 1977, Pazuzu is represented as the lord of the locusts, which brings destruction on crops. Eric Marple, in his book *The Dominion of Demons,* believes that Pazuzu spreads diseases with his breath. And William Woods in *The History of the Demon* says: ***"In Mesopotamia the horned demon, Pazuzu, rode the winds carrying malaria. ... By emphasizing its destructive role of Lord of fever and the plague."***

In 2008, Her Majesty the Queen of England gave permission for one of her Crown Estate buildings in The Mall, the main road to Buckingham Palace, to be home for a statue of Pazuzu, which portrays what is the premiere effigy of evil from ancient Iraq.

FIG. 86 – The statue of Pazuzu by Italian artist Roberto Cuoghi during and after installation on the "Nash House" in the road leading to Buckingham Palace, within the legendary area called The Mall.

Italian artist **Roberto Cuoghi**'s scupiture of the god Pazuzu was hoisted on to the roof of London's **Institute of Contemporary Arts (ICA)**. (FIG. 86) The statue was craned into place on the roof of the "Nash House," a building that is part of Carlton House Terrace, built by John Nash, who was also responsible for Buckingham Palace, Trafalgar Square and Marble Arch to name a few, and is home to the aforementioned Institute of Contemporary Arts. The entire building is of course personal property of the Monarchy, so this monstruosity obviously had to have Royal backing. The face of Pazuzu is scary, the Chinese dragons also have the same snarling face, but that does not necessarily mean that they are cruel. The role of Pazuzu however is negative. It was thought the air, with the wind, often brought diseases, which were once believed to be the work of evil spirits, and consequently even death.

Many deities associated with storms are also associated with fertility and change, and not only with destruction. An interesting figure associated to air is the Genius, in Arab-Persian mythology called the ğinnī (*Jinn*). The best-known of these *Jinn* is the genie in Aladdin's fairy tale, and the magic lamp. [29] The presence of air creatures is not lacking even in classical Greek culture. In this context, this element does not intervene actively in the creation of man, but, like all the other elemental forces is represented by a god, that personifies and dominates. In this case it is Aeolus, the legenday son of Poseidon and Arne (or Melanippa) that was commissioned by Zeus to keep control of the winds, which were released in the past causing the detachment of Sicily from the mainland. Aeolus kept safe in a bottle hidden in a cave in Lipari, an island that is part of a volcanic archipelago, made up of seven islands placed in front of the upper part of Sicily. The same **Lipari, Vulcano, Stromboli, Panarea, Salina, Alicudi and Filicudi. A cluster of islands denominated Aeolian, from which the god Aeolus took his name, and is where part of my family comes from.**

The Zagami's from Lipari, like other inhabitants of these magical islands, are said to have descended from the same god Aeolus, who gave to his descendants the gift of manipulating the winds by using prayers secretly transmitted from father to son. Aeolus, like Pazuzu, is a god from a divine race, a breed that originates in the extraterrestrial and extradimensional realm, with special powers over the elements. Last but not least, Pazuzu is a member of the Annunaki, a revered race not only by the Sumerians, but by the elite of the Illuminati, who are related by blood affinity with these gods, which over the centuries and millennia have become a kind of karmic and spiritual affinity. It is possible they helped me rise in ranks within the world of the Illuminati and Freemasonry.

Domizio, Monte Carlo, and the Grand Lodge

I n 2006, I exposed the existence of the Monte Carlo Lodge of the P2, which closed down a couple of years later due to my revelations. This lead to the consecration of a new Grand Lodge. It's fair to say that Freemasonry in Monaco had been lowkey for a number of years following its conditional acceptance by the Monégasque authorities in the first half of the twentieth century. However the *Port of Hercules Lodge* was formed in 1924 under the English Constitution. Many Monégasques wished to become Freemasons and sought membership outside the principality. In more recent years, three lodges were formed under the German Constitution, but it became apparent that the Monégasques, who had joined lodges in France, would like one of their own. At that point the first steps were taken to establish a Grand Lodge in Monaco, and this meticulous planning came to fruition in 2011, on the 19th of February in Monte Carlo, when the **Grande Loge Nationale Regulière de la Principauté de Monaco** was formed by seven lodges, one formerly meeting under the English Constitution and three each under the German and French.

The consecrating officer was Pro Grand Master, Peter Lowndes, assisted by the Grand Master of the United Grand Lodge of Germany, Rüdiger Templin, as Senior Warden; and the Past Grand Master of the National Grand Lodge of France, Jean-Charles Foellner, as Junior Warden. The ceremony was directed by Oliver Lodge (Grand Director of Ceremonies) with the help of Nick Bosanquet and Sebastian Madden (Deputy Grand Directors of Ceremonies) and Malcolm Brooks (Grand Tyler). The team from UGLE also included Nigel Brown (Grand Secretary), Alan Englefield (Grand Chancellor), Reverend Dr John Railton (Grand Chaplain) and Ron Cayless (Grand Organist). The consecration ceremony proceeded without a hitch, and included the unveiling of the lodge boards, the familiar scriptural readings from the Bible, the symbolic use of corn, wine and oil, and the censing of the lodge and its officers. It was conducted almost entirely in English, but the Rulers-designate took their obligations in their own languages. Jean-Pierre Pastor was installed as the first Grand Master, and he then appointed and installed Claude Boisson as Deputy Grand Master, and Rex Thorne, Knut Schwieger, Renato Boeri and John Lonczynski as Assistant Grand Masters. Other Grand Lodges were represented by more than a hundred delegates and many presented gifts to the newly installed Grand Master, including a magnificent ceremonial sword from the United Grand Lodge of England. The new Grand Master appointed and installed his officers, before the UGLE team withdrew, leaving the Grand Master and his new team to complete essential business. Monaco's Grand Lodge had been launched in splendid style but soon after it was infiltrated by the now ex-Brothers of the P2 lead by Ezio Giunchiglia and his protégée **Domizio Cipriani,** the prior of MONACO of the *Ordo Supremus Militari Templi Hierosolimitani* O. S. M. T. H. (FIG. 87) Cipriani is a strange character, and he makes some interesting revelations in the book *Templar Order* in line with what we all know about the Illuminati and their "alien" connections. Cipriani mentions Tutankhamun in his research: *"The Dog Star, Sirius, was the location of intelligent beings who visited the Earth in ages past and taught humanity the sacred alchemical traditions preserved in the Egyptian mysteries. It is said that Tut-*

FIG. 87 – On the left is Domizio Cipriani, the current Grand Prior of Monaco's Ordo Supremo Militari Templi Hierosolimitani, who welcomed in June, 2015 various Neo-Templar delegations to Saint Paul's Anglican Church in Monte Carlo, defined as a "Christian home for English speaking families in the Principality of Monaco."

ankhamun's sister named 'Scotland,' in order to escape the conspiracy against them, bringing to Scotland their knowledge hidden in her DNA."[30]

An interesting revelation for the author of this book, a descendant of the Lyon family (now Bowes-Lyon) Earls of Strathmore and descendants of the King of Scotland which traditionally hid a terrible secret that was revealed only to the male descendants on their twenty-first birthday. Nobody knows what the secret is or how old it is, because the tradition eventually died out, but when a former gardener of the 14th Earl of Strathmore and Kinghorne was questioned about it by the granddaughter of the Earl, he simply replied: *"you are lucky not to know it, and you'll never know it, because otherwise you'd be the unhappiest of women."* For the first time in 1904, the XIII Count Claude Bowes-Lyon, at twenty-one, publicly admitted the existence of a terrible secret to his friend stating: *"If you only knew the nature of our secret it would throw you on your knees and you would thank God to be immune."* So what was this secret? Perhaps the fact that they descended from the Annunaki, and Tutankhamun's sister named Meritaten whose nickname was "Scotland" could be the answer. Lorraine Evans from *CarlaNaylan Website* writes: *"A medieval manuscript called the **Scotichronicon**, or **Chronicles of the Scots**, written in AD 1435 by a monk named Walter Bower, gives the following legend about the origin of the Scots: In ancient times Scota, the daughter of a pharaoh, left Egypt with her husband Gaythelos and a large following. For they had heard of the disasters that were going to come upon Egypt, and so through the instructions of the gods they fled from certain plagues that were to come. They took to the sea, entrusting themselves to the guidance of the gods. After sailing in this way for many days over the sea with troubled minds, they were finally glad to put their boats at a certain shore because of bad weather. The manuscript goes on to say that the Egyptians settled in what is now Scotland, and were later chased out by the local population and moved to Ireland, where they merged with an Irish tribe and became known as the Scotti. They became High Kings of Ireland, and eventually re-invaded and re-conquered Scotland, which gains its name from their founding princess, **Scota**.'"*

Franz Bardon, the 99 lodges, and Adolf Hitler

In this chapter devoted to the "magical world of the Illuminati" I would like to introduce to you **Franz Bardon**, (FIG. 88) a lesser-known figure of the vastly discussed esoteric side of Nazism. Some time ago I had a discussion about Franz Bardon with my friend Sean Stone from RT (also a Freemason). I later decided to dedicate a few lines in my book about his work, to clear up a few points on this mysterious member of the occult world. He was born in Sudetenland, now Czech Republic, near Troppau in 1909, and died in 1958, while he was in police custody in the then Soviet Czechoslovakia. His mother said that Bardon had always been a strange figure from the time of inception. He was born dead and after numerous attempts to resuscitate him the midwife was eventually able to return him to life. He was the son of a mystic named Viktor, a disciple of theosophist Karl Weinfurter, founder in 1891 with **Gustav Meyrink** of the

FIG. 88 – Franz Bardon (1 December, 1909 – 10 July, 1958) was a Czech occultist, student and teacher of Hermetics.

Lodge of the Blue Star in Prague. The Theosophist influence never abandoned Bardon, and this is present as a constant reminder, in his writings. Between the 1920s and '30s he became known in Germany as a magician and illusionist in popular shows, perhaps in the wake of the success achieved by the renowned illusionist Erik Jan Hanussen. He traveled frequently between Prague, Austria and Germany, where he gained most of his knowledge in the esoteric field, mainly in the Illuminati groups of **Friedrich W. Quintscher** and **Franz Sattler,** the first was influenced by the teachings of **Pascal Beverly Randolph** and by the *Ordo Templi Orientis.*

Ms. Otti Votavova, former disciple of Weinfurter, and faithful secretary to Bardon, had the task of transcribing his books that were dictated to her by tape recorder, which seems to be partly responsible for the spread of improbable, legendary news on Bardon. This info is still promoted by the Theosophical group that holds the commercial rights of his books, and is firmly in the hands of the elite. For reasons that escape me, Votavova created a legend using supposed links between Adolf Hitler, and the esoteric group of Friedrich W. Quintscher and Franz Bardon. Mr. Bardon was promoted as the most important of the two by Votavova, who reported that the Führer himself gave important positions in the Third Reich in exchange for Bardon's magical collaboration during the war. Bardon apparently refused, despite being horribly tortured. True or false, Bardon wound up in a concentration camp, and was able to escape, thanks to an allied bombing. Votavova wrote a galloping fantasy about Quintscher that is not totally correct. Her biggest counterfeit was to identify the Quintscher group (which for some reaserchers was actually a branch of the O.T.O.), with the supposed *Der Freimaurer Orden des Goldenen Centuriums* (F.O.G.C.), a mysterious and secret illuminati sect linked to Bardon, that she reported was a brotherhood of 99 Lodges with 99 members each, devoted to black magical practices. Its existence would be historically proven between 1840 and 1933, and had Adolf Hitler himself as a member. I have not been able to ascertain the validity of such allegations. Some people, even students who have tested and verified the efficiency of Bardon's system, hold the view that this detail of Bardon's life was likely a fabrication created by the over-zealous Oti Votavova. In some ways, it does not really matter whether the story is true or not. But, if we deny this story as fanciful, then we are also closing ourselves off to one of the few pieces of information that we have about Bardon's magical career. Likewise, if we deny this story, then we no longer have a viable explanation for how the hell Franz Bardon became such an accomplished magus. The task had been given to provide an alternative means to Bardon's meteoric and youthful rise to a mastery of magic. Bardon, for some, appears to have been a normal initiate, but for others he certainly was not. The most sure and direct approach is to try and identify who Bardon's "superiors" could have been, therefore who he learned from. I have heard some of the most fantastic stories, many of them less believable than even those legends of Bardon's magical powers. According to these people, without verification, Bardon was a member of virtually every occult Order which was operating in Germany at that time. Some of them care little for the factual dates of Bardon's development, attributing his membership to Orders which are part of the Illuminati network, and are difficult to research in a serious way.

So conspiracy theories suggest he was even a member of the F.O.G.C. Lodge, that was of course villanized in his attempted biography, *Frabatto the Magician*. He was a Mason, he was an Anti-Mason, he was a Rosicrucian, he was a Satanist, a Pagan, a Sex-Magic addict. Without direct references to Quintscher, Votavova wrote, pretending to be Bardon, that this brotherhood possessed an extraordinary electronic machine called **The Tepaphon,** that was able to kill at a distance, using electro-magical currents. The son of Quintscher declared to Tegtmeier that this machine, whose real name was simply **Tepa,** in fact existed and had been invented precisely by his father, and was simply "an electrical device for remote magical manipulations having as target the photograph of a person." This exaggeration by Votavova has some basis in reality. The son of Quintscher always declared to Tegtmeier to have a reliable witness that told him that when Franz Bardon, viewed the manuscript of *Frabato the Magician* he became so unwell that he definitely forbade the future publication. Did he get upset because of too many revelations? Or too much rubbish?

The alleged link between Hitler and Bardon, however, cannot be denied after a photographic comparison, recently proposed by a French scholar known as *Evisul,* which showed that **Bardon could have even belonged to the Nazi Party,** considering the similarity of the symbols on the lapels of the jackets of both Bardon and Hitler. When Bardon returned to his country of origin after the war, he became known as a healer and practitioner of alternative medicine, while officially he played the role of handwriting expert. He also had relationships with people behind the Iron Curtain, like Mrs. Maria Pravica of Graz, who had also been a disciple of Weinfurter, and it was she who first spread in the West, the writings of Franz Bardon. She often traveled to Prague, where Bardon met members of the mystical group who followed Weinfurter known as **Master Arion.** Here Bardon, in the kitchen of his apartment, evoked the entities mentioned later in one of his books. He used to draw in the air with his hand the seals of the entities, which gave rise to a series of more spiritualistic phenomena for this transcendent character. During an evocation, Bardon rolled up his eyes and entered into a semiconscious state. The exercises were practiced alone, which seems less esoteric and ascetic, and closer to the practices of a faker. These magical practices eventually brought the secret police of the Communist regime to imprison him in 1958. During his months in prison, his health condition worsened (he suffered from pancreatitis), and died in the hospital. His death gave rise to another legend, where he commited suicide in prison to avoid being sent to Russia, where the KGB was very interested in the paranormal phenomena he was able to manifest, and where he would have undergone innumerable and exhausting experiments. The seals of the Entities and description were derived in part by the teaching of his friend, the previously mentioned Quintscher Friedrich Wilhelm (1893 – 1945), who was an enthusiast and Crowley supporter, and a member of the O.T.O. who obtained them in 1931 with the help of Joseph Schuster, a medium known as Silias. The well-known German occultist Adolf Hemberger, known as Klingsor, had indeed found among the papers Quintscher left, a manuscript with the "František Bardon" header, proof that Bardon received loan notes from Quintscher, who was obviously in contact with Bardon. Quintscher was among the most influential personalities of an Illuminati group called the "Order of Mental Builders," the core of which was magic-psychic-evocation and sexual practices that demonstrate the infatuation of Quintscher with this O.T.O. style.

According to a report by the usual Swiss scholar Peter König (*Das O.T.O. Phänomen, 100 Jahre und ihre Maghische Geheimbünde Protagonisten vom 1895-1994*), in the 1930s Bardon wrote to Aleister Crowley to ask his permission to translate into the Czech language, the book *Magick Theory and Practice*. Bardon's unpublished correspondence attempting to connect with one of the most legendary and controversial figures of the Illuminati, is currently held by an Austrian scholar, writes König. All the important objects and documents seized at the time of his final arrest by the Communists, including the 960 books that he had—was never returned to the family, said his wife. His unpublished works could be in the secret archives of the KGB. Finally, his body was exhumed for a second autopsy, and the police forced the family to give notice of his death. His tomb can be seen in the cemetery of Opava, a city in the northern Czech Republic on the river Opava. Here is the original list of his works, including the last, controversial one partly produced by his secretary Otti Votavova:

Der Weg zum Wahren Adepten. 1ª ed. 1956, Herman Bauer.

Die Praxis der Magischen Evokation 1ª ed. 1956, Herman Bauer.

Der Schluessel zur Wahren Qabalah 1ª ed. 1957, Herman Bauer.

Frabato: Ein Okkulter Roman 1ª ed. 1979, Herman Bauer.

The works of Franz Bardon have not been published in their entirety, and there are many obscure points, such as his likely memberhip in a sect called **H'abrat zerech or boh'er** (**Descendants of the Primordial Light**), present in Prague. They did not practice Judaism, but used Jewish as their sacred language, for the invocations and ceremonies, to remedy the alleged initiatic deficiencies present in the Western languages. A fact that would explain much of Bardon statements about the Kabbala. Examining the comparative characteristics of the entities he used, their names, and their seals, makes you seriously think that these entities don't come from a different planetary sphere but only from the astral plane of Earth. We find them in a kind of jigsaw puzzle of entities present both in the Upper and in the Lower realm, ready to be dominated and evoked, by the magician, as an intermediary for certain elemental spirits, gnomes, Ondine, Salamanders and other seemingly alien beings, close to us, and proof of his trust in black magic. Important demonic entities: **Aschmunadai (Asmodeus), Lilitha (Lilith)**, and **Asamarc (Asamarac)** are present in his work.

It's obvious that Bardon is card shuffling and playing with dark forces. Bardon's inconsistencies aside, he is yet another figure of the dark side of the Illuminati, who operated in the shadow of Crowley. The influence of Aleister Crowley in contemporary magic movements clearly began a long time ago, even before the start of what we now call "neo-paganism," that in recent times is experiencing a colossal acceleration. Even in my personal experience over the past eleven years, I have noticed a growth of interest in the esoteric, new religious cults, Freemasonry, and everything that revolves around the Illuminati and the neo-paganism, in general. I not only noticed an increase in the programs on TV, magazines, specialty stores, but also the variety of types of people who approach me in relation to these topics. Until a few years ago, if you entered an esoteric shop, the average customer that you met would have strictly respected the cliché Tarot reading girls with a Wiccan look, or the long-haired guy dressed in black from the O.T.O. Today we find either your next door neighbor who is interested in naturopathy, or the student who practices martial arts and loves yoga and meditation, plus all kinds of people that have a normal life, but are getting sucked in, little by little, in one way or another, into the New Age trap that opens up the world of occultism and magick with a K, the one Crowley promoted. In this context, **Edward Alexander Crowley** better known as **Aleister Crowley** was one of the figures, if not the key figure, conducting this change, that the Illuminati crafted in the last decades, to better control humanity. All this of course, before the dramatic turning point in 2020, and what might be the ultimate war and for many the possible rise of His Imperial Majesty Jesus Christ the Messiah.

Crowley lived and practiced his magic in a period when the Illuminati had already begun the process of transformation of society and spirituality towards the New Age, that coincided with a rebirth of the occult on a massive scale, that also saw the involvement of Franz Bardon. Long before him, there was **Éliphas Lévi, born Alphonse Louis Constant** (1810 –1875), a French occult author and ceremonial magician who Crowley is said to be the reincarnation. Levi was a character that had to some extent, reshaped magic and the occult, although it was on a very limited scope based only on medieval traditions. It was **Levi who coined the term "occult,"** because he already felt the need to start talking about the occult sciences in a more modern and specific way. Another important figure was a contemporary of Crowley named **James Frazer,** the author of the well-known book *The Golden Bough: A Study in Magic and Religion* (1915). He was not an occultist, but in his monumental work, he is now recognized as the first true anthropologist. With this book, all religions and cults of the present and the past are no longer of interest, except to the individual who practices them. You can study and compare, draw your own conclusions, and so on. This method will be a fundamental part of Crowley's work, proving himself to be superior to all those who had preceded him. In this climate of a more analytical approach to the spiritual life of man, we find the *Hermetic Order of the Golden Dawn,* the first Illuminati group Crowley joined. This order, which we know was founded at the end of the year 800, was based on occult aspects which included the Kabbalah, alchemy, tarot, and all the major currents of the Hermetic thought. It was a comprehensive doctrine that pleased Crowley, and was the pillar of his studies. In turn he created an even broader and more analytical approach for his own work, and the future work of the O.T.O. branches he took over from Theodor Reuss. The approach to magic, Science and Psychology in **Crowley's** *Scientific Illuminism,* was both simple and brilliant for those who appreciate the dark side of the Illuminati and Freemasonry, so it was ideal for Crowley's O.T.O. system. He took the goal of all religions and mystery schools of the world, which were to spiritually elevate man, and combined the widest variety of possible schools of thought, alchemy, medieval magic, Christian mysticism, yoga, and more. He brought everything together in twentieth century Europe, doing the only thing that made sense to do in a society that lived in the middle of the Industrial Revolution, applying the scientific method of Weishaupt's pragmatic Illuminati, in a simple and thus effective way for his own evil goals. He realized, studying virtually all the cults on the face of the earth, that beyond the differences in form, they had much in common, all deriving from a common source, that of the Secret Chiefs or *Invisible Masters.* The use of symbols to direct the thinking towards an idea, meditation (or prayer, depending on the cult), are used to connect with the divine.

In short, all the spiritual exercises of all religions, including those of the **Jesuit Ignatius of Loyola**, so important for the Illuminati for his meditative practices, have a lot of common points. He put together the best of each practice, and created a new system.

Crowley practiced on himself various spiritual exercises, experiencing firsthand, and constantly throughout his life. He put into writing all the magical or spiritual proceedings, without the use of symbolism, but with a language that was clear to everyone, allowing others to implement those same practices. He made all this public with his books, inviting everyone not to simply repeat its practices, but to follow his methods, and apply them to their own practices. Crowley was one of the first in Europe to import Yoga, and to use discipline applied to simple experimental methodology within the occult realm. The scheme was simple—train your mind to focus on a single thought for a long period of time, and focus your will until you obtain it. In the process, taking note of the physical and environmental conditions that surround you, trying different positions, recording the difficulties encountered, and the results achieved. You must re-read everything, to deduce what are the best conditions for the best results. The next time you change the position, time of day or any other factor, until the technique used is perfected. The basis of his work was how he mixed medieval magic and hidden grimoires with tantra, and the most diverse techniques from a variety of places and traditions brought to Europe in the twentieth century. Crowley practiced "Magick" for a lifetime, acquiring every year new techniques, writing new books, but the real turning point in his life was in 1904, when he became the "Prophet" of his new religion based on Will. It was that same Will that helped Adolf Hitler in his nefarious mission born in the occult world. So Otti Votavova may perhaps have exaggerated with her speculations on F.O.G.C. and the Franz Bardon connection, especially in regards to the alleged membership of Hitler, but no doubt both Bardon and Hitler were influenced by Aleister Crowley, and Thelema. And now let's talk about Wicca, founded in the milieu of Aleister Crowley and the O.T.O., whose rituals are in fact often indicated by occultists as a creation by the same Crowley, and not his disciple **Gerald Gardner,** who would have paid Crowley to obtain certain rituals from him, in a time of deep crisis for "The Great Beast 666." The rituals put together by Crowley suited this new neopagan movement, rituals that will end up in Gardner's *Book of Shadows,* the main book of Wicca rituals.

Wicca Witchcraft: another creation of the Illuminati

Wicca witchcraft was not originally connected to medieval witchcraft, nor to profane acts and the typical sacrifices of Satanic sects, as it is not linked to the worship of the devil, but to neo-paganism. It has been promoted with increasing insistence from the first decades of the last century, by **the various sects of the Illuminati in the nascent New Age.** The term "New Age" has been used since the 1920s, first coined by the theosophist Alice Bailey, when she stayed in Ascona (Switzerland) at the Monte Verità. A place of fundamental importance for the Illuminati, as I wrote previously in relation to Carl Gustav Jung and Theodor Reuss, and defined by Massimo Introvigne of CESNUR and Pierluigi Zoccatelli as a **"Sanctuary of a new religiosity that represents the prehistory of the New Age."** The New Age scene was born on Monte Verità nearly in parallel with the birth of Wicca witchcraft, both exponents of a syncronistic cocktail of diabolical proportions. Remember, those who practice low level spiritual practices such as magic and witchcraft, will always be easy prey of sorcerers and the pseudo-Illuminati. I think of the orgiastic gatherings of Wicca witches and wizards of the *Ordo Templi Orientis,* as I have often witnessed in Norway myself. This is because both the New Age movement and Wicca were born in the theosophical milieu that gave birth to the *Ordo Templi Orientis* to destroy Christianity—their ultimate goal. Authors Massimo Introvigne and

Pierluigi Zoccatelli give this brief but significant summary about the world of New Age, that I want to show you before unveling the truth about Wicca:

> *Bailey began in the 1920s to use the "New Age" expression in the present sense. A few years after the death of Alice Bailey, some of her most brilliant English students— Sheena Govan (1912 – 1967), daughter of John George Govan (1861 – 1927), founder of the fundamentalist group* Faith Mission, *and under the guidance of an independent group of "Christian esoteric" students; Dorothy Maclean, who belonged to the Order founded by Western Sufi Pir Hazrat Inayat Khan; Peter Caddy (1917 – 1994), husband of Govan; and Eileen Combe (1917 – 2006), who became the second wife of Caddy—began an adventure that leads the most representative figures of this original group into a pilgrimage that takes them from Glastonbury, linked to the legends of the Arthurian and Celtic past of Great Britain, to Forres, in Scotland—where they manage to get hired as promoters of the tourist center at Cluny Hill Hotel, which they will transform into a theosophical center—and eventually went to* **North Scotland, in Findhorn,** *where in 1962 they founded a garden community. A "Global Village" and an ecological community according to the typical models of the New Age, Findhorn is also the place of meetings and messages that spouses Caddy and Maclean, along with numerous followers that flow in numerous and force to build permanent structures— thanks to the generous support of two British patrons of alternative forms of spirituality: Sir George Trevelyan (1906 – 1996) and Sir Anthony Brooke (1912 – 2011), heir to the dynasty of the "White rajah" of Sarawak and great-grandson of James Brooke (1803 – 1868)—a real-life historical figure and well-known to Italians as implacable opponent of the Salgarian fictional pirate figure Sandokan— they receive various types of "entities:" God, devas—nature spirits associated with the plants—angels, fairies and create even a "center of light" that consists of a group of Soviet political prisoners, dying or already dead, able however to communicate from the bottom of a Siberian salt mine. The fame of Findhorn grows up to spread quickly overseas and in 1962—the foundation of the same Findhor inspired the more convincing date of birth of the New Age phenomenon as we know it today—when they founded Esalen, in California, a center of meetings and seminars inspired by similar principles; and always from the United States arrives in Findhorn David Spangler, who contributes greatly to making this new reality in the Americas through the publication of the most influential manifestos of the New Age during the 1970s, thus promoting the spread and success on a global scale of a reality originally born in Europe.*

This is the official history of the New Age, which was the creation of a certain branch of Occult Freemasonry and Theosophy, as I outlined in Volume I and II, which flows later into something even more open and public, that goes from neo-pagan druids to the so-called "kitchen witch." This movement is now so widespread and was originally inspired by the dark side of the Illuminati and guys like Gerald Gardner, and the works of Aleister Crowley and Theosophy. Remember that Aleister Crowley boasted of being born in the year when Theosophy was founded, and he used the vast network of theosophy to impose its unhealthy ideas on the *Ordo Templi Orientis*. One can therefore safely say that Wicca generated by Gardner is certainly a byproduct of Theosophy and Crowleyanity, although its practitioners admit it only in part. Other authors who have contributed significantly to the advancement of Wicca were; Patricia Monaghan, Silver Ravenwolf and Doreen Valiente. Wicca calling themselves Wiccan, believe in deities and natural entities—primarily, a "Mother Goddess" in its various emanations just like most New Agers. Devoted to the "Mother Goddess" its neo-pagan author, a witch known as **Starhawk** in San Francisco, alias **Miriam Simos (b. 1951)** is a typical exponent of

"Spiritualism Feminist" linked to that evil witch Hillary Clinton that fortunately failed in her confrontation with Donald Trump, even after a massive use of black magical rituals against him during her presidential campaign.

So fortunately black magic is not always winning lately, however Starhawk was actually listed **in 2012** by the magazine *Watkins' Mind Body Spirit* as one of the 100 most influential people living in the spiritual field. She writes that "the Goddess has infinite aspects and thousands of names ... she is the world and all things in it." But in some cases Wiccans are also devoted to a "Horned God," her husband who some say is **Osiris**. This thesis focused on the syncretic worship of a horned god considered central to a cult of witches whose forerunner was initially **Margaret Alice Murray (1863 – 1963),** an Egyptologist and British anthropologist. The Goddess and God are generally seen as personifications of the divine source of all things, that in itself can not be known or understood, but it is imminent in all creation: rocks, trees, living beings, etc. Some Wiccans have abandoned the personification in recent decades, preferring to understand the gods as mere metaphysical concepts driven by the increasing atheism also promoted by the New Age movement. Most Wiccans still accept them as personifications or emanations—the Mother Goddess is associated with the moon and called by different names (e.g. Astarte, Diana, Artemis, etc.), and at times linking her to the Holy Mary. God is instead associated with the sun, and unlike the Goddess, dies and is reborn every year. Christian author (Larson) writes:

> *In many ways, the Wiccans are a protest movement against those religions which accept only comprise and male leadership. The movement attracts especially those women who are looking for a form of spirituality that honors the female desire to breed, celebrate and be in a community. These groups attract the romantic that is in all people, the reverential awe that one feels in the presence of nature. They also attract those who consider the ritual an important part of worship. Wicca is a religion whose adherents usually embark on a journey with a strong desire to assert the individual and the natural world. They wish to embrace the community and creativity. The pagan system, however, strangely ends in a world apart from any understanding that links together these needs and give it value.*

Having an imminent vision of the deity (i.e. the lies coincide with nature and with man), Wiccans mistakenly conclude that the Christian God is not accessible to man. The scriptures teach instead that he is not part of His creation, and it is not an impersonal force, but He is a living God who can and wants to be known personally by each. McCann, a former warlock turned Christian today, explains: *"The pagans of each extraction revere nature. In fact, many individuals are attracted to Paganism as a direct result of the connection that they have with the world around them and the beauty of the world they see. This feeling of reverence towards nature leads many pagans to the conclusion that the world itself is divine. It saddens me to see how the pagans and Wiccans look at the world around them, they see in it the power of God, but rather go further and seek the Creator, look to creation itself. It's like admiring a sculpture instead of praising he who carved it."*

Most Wiccans, given their anti-Christian origins, have an obvious and distorted idea of Christianity, which they are often at odds with, and of course tend to be the leftists of the Antichrist. They believe, for example, that the Roman Catholic Church is the Christian Church. In fact, superstitions and persecutions of the church hierarchy have nothing to do with Christianity, which for centuries have indeed persecuted themselves with ferocity. Jesus Christ is Christianity—He is the center and the whole, nothing else. This is when a true Christian belief is not the result of an obsession with the dogmas and rites of different institutions and religious denominations, but is the tangible reality of a personal encounter with the living God; a new life accessible to any person, big or small, ignorant or educated, who wants to once again look to the One who gave Himself for our sake. The fires and inquisitions are the highlight of many books and pagan websites and neo-pagan groups. Starhawk the author speaks of nine million persecuted witches in an arc of four centuries. This idea was widespread in the 18th century by a German historian, feminist Matilda Gage. Today, historians are in agreement that the number is much lower (about 40 thousand). Robin Briggs, historian at the University of Oxford, recently highlighted that **most of the persecution of witches took place between 1550 and 1630, for the most part restricted to France, Switzerland and Germany**. Perhaps it would be appropriate here to recall again the hidden role of Switzerland in occult history, as they always have been dedicated to witchcraft, well before Mount Verità and the arrival of the Illuminati and the O.T.O. An examination of the documents of Briggs illustrates that typically the accusers were common citizens (often women), and that none of the people accused of witchcraft were ever associated with the practice of a pagan religion. McCann writes:

> Many Wiccans do not know that they were not persecuted witches. Even another group was persecuted. Who were these people? True Christians. Over the centuries, many wicked men burst into the professing church and have been led to apostasy. True Christians have been separated from it, and are seen savagely persecuting. Those who have persecuted pagans and Christians were not Christians, but corrupt men who took advantage of every opportunity for their selfish gain. The true Christianity does not seek the evil of his neighbor, but rather to obey Christ who said: 'Love your neighbor as yourself.' ... True Christians, whose lives have been transformed from a personal experience with Jesus Christ, leave any form of violence, hatred or persecution of others. The fact that someone you define as 'Christian' or frequents a church does not automatically mean that he is a disciple of Jesus Christ, no matter how famous or in view of both. Indeed, even the Bible repeatedly warns us that many false Christians will do so to shift the shame on the Gospel of Jesus (See. 2 Pet. 2: 1-3, 2 Cor. 11:13, Gal. 2: 4, 1 John. 3:15, Phil. 3: 18,19, etc.). Meanwhile, many pagans and Wiccans tend to look to the "professing Church" for mistakes and use them as an excuse to reject what they believe to be Christianity. On this basis, unfortunately, they lack to know Jesus himself.

A little knowledge of Christianity is often the instrument practitioners as Silver Ravenwolf use to define their reality. L.P. Harvey professor emeritus of Spanish at the University of London and a fellow of King's College, London, adds that for them: "*Christ was just a wise teacher, God is a human invention, and of course Satan is only a myth (remember well the many years that I myself have spent with these beliefs). it remains nothing of Christianity when it comes down to your personal beliefs that rejects the biblical message, it becomes hypocrisy even to talk about 'Christ,' since at that point is only a name as any other.*"

And let's talk now about what the Wiccans call **"the myth of the devil"** used by the occult elite to cover up their satanic roots and their evil intentions. McCann writes: "*The majority of Wiccans do not believe in an entity called Satan, or the devil. Many of them argue that it is just a myth that the Christian Church has invented to frighten people. In fact, many hundreds of centuries before the Christian church, the Jews already believed in its existence. He speaks right from Genesis (the year 4004 BC), and also in the book of Job it is clearly described as an entity intelligent and malignant. Some pagans admit that there is such an entity in the world, but believe that this is just an impersonal force. Yet we know that he speaks (Job. 1: 6-2: 1-5; Matt. 4: 1-11); has a will (1 Chron. 21:*

1; Luke 22:31; 1 Thess. 2:18; 2 Tim. 2:26); He knows groped (Matt. 4: 1-11; 1 Cor. 7: 5); and oppresses human beings (e.g. Acts 10:38); all of which they are certainly not attributable to a symbol or an abstract force. Throughout history, millions of people to this day have witnessed or have met the spiritual powers of evil; many of these people did not come from a Christian background, and therefore they had not been previously inculcated the concept of the devil and the spirits at his command. The truth is that the devil was not invented by the church, but it is a reality in the world today. One of his most successful deceptions is just convince people that he does not exist. This should not surprise us, since Jesus called Satan 'the father of lies.'"

The testimony of the former black witch De Souza offers considerable food for thought on the subject. Several Wiccans are brainwashed by the idea implanted by the Illuminati sects that Wicca is itself an ancient form of pre-Christian spirituality; i.e., the direct continuation of ancient pagan fertility cults—especially in northern Europe and the British Isles—preserved over the centuries by the same witches (for this is called Wiccan "traditions"). Numerous other Wiccans recognize that Wicca refers to paganism and has modern origins. The theories on witchcraft as a continuation of the ancient pagan religions, were spread between 1921 and 1933 precisely by the said Margaret Murray, who introduced them as a historically established fact. Numerous scholars have shown, however, that the theories of Murray have no real historical basis, and that there are no connections between the Bronze Age cults and witchcraft described by Murray. **Greer, Cooper, Ginzburg, and other scholars have denied that Wicca is the continuation of those cults.** In 1998, professor Davis, from the department of religious studies at the University of Prince Edward Island, published a detailed critical assessment of the theological statements, anthropological and historical of the neo-pagan movement, proving that the idea of an ancient pre-Christian worship of a Mother Goddess is a myth. The same conclusion is reached in 1999, by the historian R. Hutton, renowned scholar of British pagan religions. So the whole thing is the result of a plot tailor made by occultists like Crowley and Gardner, to promote the nascent New Age that needed a witch department for their New World Order Magic. Speaking at a conference on the history of Wicca in England, the Wiccan J. Phillips commented: *"In 1954, Murray's work was still taken seriously, and she remained for several years the reference point on the subject of witchcraft for the* Encyclopedia Britannica. *Today of course her statements (of Murray) have been widely discredited, and she remains for us, if not a source of historical accuracy, at least a source of inspiration. ... Murray may have a faked historical veracity so that her work was published in her day."*

Nevertheless, the theories of Murray influenced many of his contemporaries, including **Gerald Brosseau Gardner (1884 – 1964)**, who later created modern Wicca, which he called "Wica," and was disseminating it as a form of ancient paganism as suggested by Murray. For this purpose Gardner claimed to have made contact with a coven of witches, and in particular, with the old Dorothy Clutterbuck, who he said initiated him to Wiccan rituals in 1939. Several scholars, even pagans, believe that the "old Dorothy" (which, according to the birth certificate, was just little older than Gardner) was not a witch, and probably was only used to support this fake myth of the ancient witchcraft lineage crafted by the Illuminati. **The late Stewart Farrar, and another well-known Wiccan author called Gavin Bone stated that:** *"We believe that Aidan [Kelly] conclusions were correct; Gardnerian Wicca was created by Gardner and his high priestess; and even more, a creation of Doreen Valiente, who converted much literary material in poetry for Rites. A good example of this is, of course, 'Charge of the Goddess,' which in its original form is in Aradia, of Charles Godfrey Leland. Most of the Gardnerian material derived*

*from literature—also 'the Triple Goddess' was a synthesis made by Robert Graves of the
traditional nine Greek and Roman goddesses."*

The Wiccan T. Paajanen, curator of an internet portal on Wicca, said: *"Many Wiccans—usually novices—often talk about the ancient origins of Wicca, or as Wicca has
been practiced for thousands of years. In 1954, Gerald Gardner published the first book
on Wicca,* Witchcraft Today. *Many today are not convinced of Gardner's claims, and believe that his writings were more his invention than the true and ancient practices handed down for generations. Gardner's interests in occultism and ceremonial magic gave him
a lot of basic material to work with. Although Wicca may contain ideas and concepts
based on the ancient cults, modern wicca was born not before the 1950s."* the Wiccans
Farrar and Bone point out that: *"It is important to remember that the traces of a 'fake
story' abound. For example, for many years Alex Sanders claimed it to have been started
by his grandmother. A bit as in the case of the New Forest coven of Gardner."* Lady Sheba
published in her own *Book of Shadows: "(a typically Gardnerian term) in the 1980s, it
was almost entirely a Gardnerian Book, but—as often happens—she said that she had
been handed it down from her grandmother."* New Age permits such scams unfortunately.

Gardner drew from the most diverse forms of occultism, from the mysteries of Freemasonry and the Rosicrucians (he was a member of both groups), from Theosophy, ritual
and sexual magic, from various esoteric texts (like *the Key of Solomon*), and doctrines of
both Eastern and Asian religious occult practices. Relying on them, Gardner introduced
in Wicca concepts such as reincarnation and ceremonial nudism (Gardner had become
a convinced nudist after a trip to Ceylon). It was based particularly on the doctrines of
his occultist friend Aleister Crowley, who called himself "The Great Beast," or "The Antichrist," and of course "The most evil man in the world." In a book he wrote in 1910
entitled *The World's Tragedy,* he made a statement that reflected his life's goal: *"That
religion they call Christianity; the devil they honour they call God. I accept these definitions, as a poet must do, if he is to be at all intelligible to his age, and it is their God and
their religion that I hate and will destroy."*[31]

Aleister Crowley went on to write dozens of books that would help him achieve his
stated goal—the destruction of the Christian faith. Already at the time of his first book
on witchcraft, Gerald Gardner was affiliated to Crowley's *Ordo Templi Orientis.* In his
book *High Magic's Aid* (1949), published by London's *Atlantis Bookshop* based at **49
Museum Street in London,** founded in 1922 by Michael Houghton, a Jewish immigrant
and occultist with a passion for the mysteries and poetry, Gardner placed in the opening
page next to the pseudonym **"Scire"** the degree held by himself in Crowley's Order. (FIG.
89) No wonder this address on Museum Street is still the secret base of the O.T.O. in London. As Geraldine Beskin, an old aquaintance of mine and longtime owner of *Atlantis
Bookshop* once said, *"it was founded by magicians for magicians."* Geraldine's daughter
was, at least during my time in London, engaged to one of the driving forces of the O.T.O.
in the UK, **Stephen Schofield**, at one time a member of my lodge of the *Fraternitas Rosicruciana Antiqua* in London, and a Freemason present at my initiation in the United
Grand Lodge of England. Some of the most well-known occultists and witches from the
Illuminati have passed through the doors of *Atlantis Bookshop*; including Aleister Crowley, Gerald Gardner, Dion Fortune, W.B. Yeats and so many more.

The researcher and journalist Federica Serra writes: *"Different personalities from
the Wiccan scene such as Farrar and Valiente recognize the close link between Crow-*

31   Aleister Crowley, *The World's Tragedy*, pp. xxviii-xxxi (preface).

ley and Gardnerian rituals, but I want to emphasize that 'Crowley was not a Satanist.' It would be more correct to say that Crowley was not definable 'technically' as a Satanist; in fact, he was deeply attached to the satanic symbolism. Crowley did not just practice ceremonial magic. The ceremonial magic of the Golden Dawn included not only the kabbalah and the medieval grimoires, but also Egyptian gods, Greek gods, and yoga. Crowley emphasized the Egyptians elements, belittled as 'Christian,' and there he added a number of others—for example, the invocations to Satan in L. Samekh, in addition to the constant references to himself as the 'Beast 666' and other similar statements." [32]

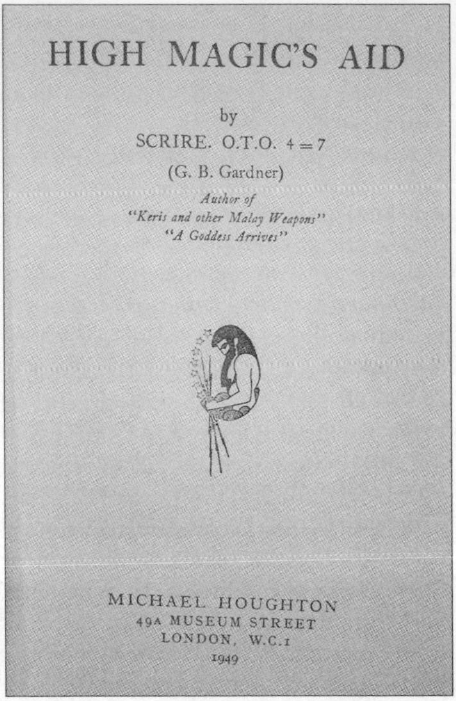

"Not a Satanist" is a remark Serra made as part of the occult establishment and she will never admit her Master was a full-on Satanist as others did. Crowley's literary executor and biographer, **John Symonds**, wrote: "Crowley's philosophy takes a bit from here and a bit from there ... but ... he was more a Satanist than anything else. 'I serve my great Master Satan,' he wrote in one of his franker confessions, 'and that august Council composed of Beelzebub, Lucifuge Asmodeus, Belphegor, Baal, Adrammelech, Lilith and Nahema.'"

HIGH MAGIC'S AID

by
SCRIRE. O.T.O. 4 = 7
(G. B. Gardner)

Author of
"Keris and other Malay Weapons"
"A Goddess Arrives"

MICHAEL HOUGHTON
49A MUSEUM STREET
LONDON, W.C.I
1949

FIG. 89 – Opening page from High Magic's Aid (1949), published by Michael Houghton of London's Atlantis Bookshop.

No matter if Crowley asserted that Satan was an invention of the **Blacks Brothers** and represented essentially the "independent man" and "God himself," Crowley was a denier of God and voted himself to a sophisticated use of lies, worthy of Satan, to whom Crowley had devoted his life, like all those who follow the dark side of the Illuminati. Crowley's attitude was in line with the literary tradition of the Satanic 19th century, where we find the most sophisticated form of Satanism. The name Satan is understood also as "ironic," and Crowley was always very ironic. Still others argue that Crowley's Satanic symbolism can be reinterpreted and read in pagan terms, but this is all too true for many forms of Satanism found in the elite of the New World Order. Gardner met Crowley in 1946 through Arnold Crowther. Becoming a member of both the O.T.O. and the A∴A∴, Gardner commissioned rituals for his Book of Shadows (the book of Wicca rituals) to Crowley who was in desperate need of money after his well-known legal troubles. Before the beginning of the last century there is no historical evidence of this book. **Alex Sanders,** founder of the **Alexandrian tradition of Wicca,** and a tool of the Illuminati said: "The Book of Shadows is one of the most controversial books in modern witchcraft. Many modern witches believe that parts of it have been adapted from the rituals of the Golden Dawn, which was formed in 1888 by MacGregor Mathers, Westcott, and Woodman. Others believe that there are parts added by Aleister Crowley and Dion Furtune and Francis King, author

32   Aa.Vv., La stregoneria Wicca origini della wicca e del neopaganesimo.

of **Ritual Magic in England**, *who claims to have read the letters of Gerald Gardner, in which he commissioned Aleister Crowley to produce parts of the* Book of Shadows."

So Bingo! And the case solved once and for all—Wiccan is a creation of Aleister Crowley—full stop! In order to confirm this, it is also interesting to note that in the Wiccan *Rede,* there is a statement that provides the key moral system in the Neopagan religion of Wicca, and in their only rule of life. They believe that there is no absolute moral rule binding, it is basically "do what you want, without doing harm to anyone." And the phrase **"Do what thou wilt"** was Crowley's only law (note the sharp contrast with the words of Jesus, which teaches that the whole of the law is "Love the Lord your God with all your heart, with all your soul, with all your strength, with all your mind, and your neighbor as yourself"). Priestess Doreen Valiente recognized that *"The Crowley influence was very evident in rituals"* (the words of the Wiccan third degree for example are practically equal to the relevant passage from the Gnostic Mass of Mr. Crowley. Gardner explained that this was due to the fact that the rituals "handed down" were so fragmented as to be unusable, and so he was forced to supplement them with other materials. Later, Valiente claimed to have persuaded Gardner to replace part of Crowley's texts with other mainly drawn from Aradia, or the Gospel of the Witches a book composed by the American folklorist Charles Godfrey Leland (1824 – 1903) that was published in 1899. Sadly, from the first paragraph a glimpse of this book shows its affiliations of its doctrine to Lucifer: *"Diana greatly loved her brother, the god. ... Lucifer who was very proud of her beauty, and who for his pride was driven from Paradise"* (the biblical references, albeit distorted, are undeniable here). The remaining elements of the Thelemic doctrine are in any case sufficient to give Crowley a decisive role in the creation of Wiccan rituals. [33] We must also say that influential authors such as Murray, Leland and Frazer, were based on the work **La Sorciere,** by **Jules Michelet.** Among the neo-pagans and the Illuminati of today, Michelet's influence is almost always unspoken, probably due to the fact that *La Sorciere is* a **work of literary Satanism,** in which Satan and medieval witches are enhanced passionately, and provided the basis for the current Satanic ideology promoted by the Illuminati sects of the occult elite; basically a parody of the Catholic mass secretly practiced to this day in the heart of the Vatican.

In many Wiccan traditions there is the concept of "Guardians," taken from the **Golden Dawn.** Although the concept varies from tradition to tradition, **Raven Grimassi (born in 1951),** stage name of a famous Italian-American Wiccan author, who has published a number of books on witchcraft and neo-paganism has described them as a "an ancient race beyond the physical form," that assist and watch over Wiccans during their magical practices. Grimassi linked them directly to the "power of the air" mentioned in the Bible. The New English Bible calls him *"commander of the spiritual powers of the air now at work among God's rebel subjects."* The "prince of the air" is Satan working on what he wants in those who do not submit to God and do not stand up to the devil, causing them to commit all sorts of sins. That's why he is called *"the prince of the power of the air, of the spirit that is now working in the sons of disobedience"* (Ephesians 2: 2). The reason why men are slaves of all sorts of vices and sins is that there is a spirit or rather as I see it an evil alien called Satan, which stops their evolution. Grimassi also cites *The Book of Enoch*, where they are referred to as *"the rebellious angels that followed the adversary in its war."*

Well Gardnerian tradition is just another form of devotion to Fallen Angels and their forces. These extra-biblical writings explained evil in terms of revolt, and Wiccans are in their own minds rebelling to the restrains of Christianity . Gardner's work influenced

33 *Ibid.*

Alex Sanders, Sybil Leek, Raymond and Rosemary Buckland, in addition to Farrar, Cunningham, etc.—Who made themselves spokesmen and further modified the teachings to satisfy the growing Wicca frenzy. Sybil Leek, for example, modified Gardnerian rituals and teachings, and popularized her own version of neo-pagan witchcraft, making converts in the United States in the 1960s (the Bucklands however remain the main architects of the spread of Gardnerian Witchcraft in the U.S.) In the same period, Alex Sanders gave birth to the Alexandrian tradition, combining the ideas Gardnerian, and many occult pagan elements from the Kabbalah, from the Golden Dawn, and other occult Illuminati doctrines cleverly filtered for the average New Age foolish player. Between the 1960s and 1980s, behind the input of the nascent New Age, dozens of new Wicca traditions were created. Generally they were built from folkloric elements, or the Celtic paganism (such as the Celtic tradition or *faerie*), kabbalah, Druidism, and naturalism, all added to medieval witchcraft. Today, there are many congregations inspired by different traditions, but their origins can ultimately be traced to the writings of the Gardnerians. Politically Wiccans have encountered opposition from some politicians and Christian organizations in the USA, including former president of the United States George W. Bush, who stated once that he did not believe Wicca to be a religion. If you thought only Hillary supporters were witches, you were wrong, as Bernie Sanders has even more supporters amongst Wicca witches. A Wiccan ceremony was even advertised on a *"Sanders volunteer website, calling on Wiccans, pagans, goddess worshipers, atheists or anyone who is spiritually open-minded to engage with a community of like-minded individuals."* [34]

However it's important to revisit information relayed by Clinton insider Larry Nichols in 2015, where he claimed Hillary regularly attended witch gatherings during Bill's presidency. In a mini-documentary shot exclusively by my friends at **InfoWars** dubbed "The New Clinton Chronicles," Nichols commented on Hillary's fascination and participation with the Satanic occult. Nichols recounted to InfoWars a conversation he had with Bill Clinton, who told him Hillary was part of a witch's coven that met in California. *"I know nothing about the Bohemian Grove with Bill,"* Nichols told InfoWars. *"I know about once a month Hillary would go out to Los Angeles. And she did it so regular that it became a bit of an issue ... 'Why's she always going?' Bill told me that she was going out there, she and a group of women, and she would be a part of a witch's church. Man, when Bill told me that, you could have hit me with a baseball bat. I tried to point out to him, 'Do you realize what would happen if that got out?' Of course my job was to make sure it didn't get out."* [35]

Hillary could have been the first Wiccan in the White House but fortunately Donald J. Trump stopped her, that why our new president needs all our prayers to protect him constantly from these evil doers and their witchcraft.

34   http://www.dailywire.com/news/5754/if-you-thought-only-hillary-supporters-were-amanda-prestigiacomo ‡ Archived 28th November, 2016.
35   http://www.infowars.com/hillary-regularly-attended-witchs-church-clinton-insider-claims/ ‡ Archived 28th November, 2016.

Chapter V

Espionage, Freemasonry and Satanism in the Vatican

Father Malachi Martin, a Jesuit who served the Mossad

I would like to open this chapter with a rather well-known person in the United States, the late **Malachi Brendan Martin (1921 – 1999)**. Father Martin, who I mentioned, albeit too briefly, in my book *Pope Francis: The Last Pope?*, became a Jesuit in 1939, and a close collaborator of Cardinal Bea under the papacy of John XXIII, and for the first phase of the papacy of Pope Paul VI. What is even more interesting and known only in intelligence circles, is that Malachi Martin was working as a liaison officer with the Israeli Mossad for the Jesuits, since his days of attending the University of Jerusalem. Gradually between 1961 and 1962, he entered into the good graces of **Rabbi Abraham Heschel**, particularly in light of his work as a translator for the Jesuit **Cardinal Bea**. He became from 1958 to 1964, the private secretary of Cardinal Augustin Bea, SJ, a key figure of the Second Vatican Council, and Jesuit agent of Zionist Freemasonry in the Vatican. In 1964, Father Malachi Martin accompanied the pope Mason Paul VI to the Holy Land, and soon afterward he left the Jesuits, (at least officially, asking to be released from the votes he had contracted with the Society of Jesus), before he launched his career as a writer and Vatican expert, full of disputes.

As for Freemason Pope Paul VI, he was a friend of Freemason Roberto Caldirola 33° ASSR, which years ago introduced me to the secrets of Montini's Masonic papacy, revealing certain truths about his old friend Pope Montini, a.k.a. Paul VI, who was to be the second homosexual pope in history (after Pope Roncalli), something that later became almost of public domain, and that apparently has made him a vulnerable subject to blackmail by liberal Freemasonry. However, guided and defended (I always hope) by the Holy Spirit, which should protect those searching for the truth, I became devoted to this mystery, after I saw with my own eyes an important document attesting the membership of Masonic Pope Montini in Caldirola's home in Zagarolo near Rome. (FIG. 90) In this brief research of mine, I stumbled several times on the works of Father Malachi Martin, and also a certain **Don Luigi Villa (1918 – 2012)**. Perhaps he is not known in the U.S., but I can assure you he is a leading figure in the fight against evil, before, during, and after the infamous Second Vatican Ecumenical Council. Villa managed to stop the beatification of Pope Paul VI, aka Giambattista Montini. Father Malachi Martin and Don Luigi Villa are for me, two heroic and unusual priests who described, each in their own way, an uncomfortable reality, when most of the media ignored it. The truth was concealed by the fiction of his novels, in the case of Father Malachi Martin, but both of these priests, even if on different positions, were ready to question the decadence of the Church of today. Villa and his book trilogy dedicated to Pope Montini, unfortunately hard to find these days, is a truly unique work. The three volumes *Paul VI: Blessed?*; *Paul VI: Trial of a Pope;* and *The "New Church" of Paul VI*; all published by the Italian independent publishing house *Casa Editrice Civiltà* made him a dangerous priest for the postconciliar Vatican. Despite the many difficulties and risks to his life, over the years he conducted his research

FIG. 90 – Pope Paul VI, born Giovanni Battista Enrico Antonio Maria Montana, makes a special dedication to 33rd degree Mason Roberto Caldirola addressing him in a typical Masonic style using the three dots ∴ that are often found in Masonic language.

with serious arguments, and exemplary documents, made public to combat the Masonic infiltration in the Vatican on behalf of Padre Pio, who commissioned his mission against **Ecclesiastical Freemasonry.** As Villa, and Father Malachi Martin his contemporary, made us realize quite often with their books, and specifically in this passage, one of his last works published in 1996 entitled *Windswept House—A Vatican Novel,* Father Malachi Martin offers a truly unprecedented insight into the Vatican for that period, and words which back them seemed like bombs for the Vatican of future Saint John Paul II:

> *In and of themselves, the grim fact Glaclstone and Slattery had documented in their reports did not surprise the Slavic Pope. Homosexuality and Satanism were among the oldest viruses lurking in the body politic of the Church. The difference now was that homosexual and Satanist activity had attained a new status within that body politic. In certain sectors of the Church, its members had come up from the underground and claimed the right to be represented in the public forum of Church life. Their apparent acceptability to their colleagues and associates was a signal that all inolved had ceased to believe in Catholic teachings. Some had beliefs so alien that effectively they could no longer be rekoned as Catholics. And yet, none wanted to quit the Church as Martin Luther had done. Nor did they intend to live somehow within the Church according to its laws and doctrine, as Erasmus had done. Suddenly it became unarguable that now, during this papacy, the Roman Catholic organization carried a permanent presence of clerics who worshipped Satan and liked it; of bishops and priests who sodom-*

ized boys and each other; of nuns who performed the "Black Rites" of Wicca and who lived in lesbian relationship within as well as outside of convent life. ... Suddenly it became clear that during this papacy the Roman Catholic Church organization had become a place where every day, including Sundays and Holy Days, acts of heresy and blasphemy and outrage and indifference were committed and permitted at holy Altars by men who had been called to be priests. Sacrilegious actions and rites were not only performed at Christ's Altars, but had the connivance or at least the tacit permission of certain Cardinals, archbishops and bishops. Suddenly shock set in at the actual lists of prelates and priests who were involved. In total number, they were a minority— anything from one to ten percent of Church personnel. But of that minority, many occupied astoundingly high positions of rank and authority in chanceries, seminaries and universities. Appalling though it was, however, even this picture wasn't the whole cause of His Holiness' crisis. The facts that brought the Pope to a new condition of suffering were mainly two: The systematic organizational links—the network, in other words—that had been established between certain clerical homosexual groups and Satanist covens. And the inordinate power and influence of that network. [1]

And despite these controversial publications followed by many other controversial admissions discussed live on radio programs such as *Coast to Coast* with Art Bell, Father Malachi Martin was still received in the last years of life in a private audience by Pope John Paul II. A fact which testifies to the credibility of his allegations made by a character so close to the most hidden secrets of the Vatican.

When John F. McManus, for *The New American*, June 9, 1997, asked Father Martin if the Black Mass in South Carolina had actually happened, it led to an enlightening Q and A:

McManus: Your book begins with a vivid description of a sacrilegious "Black Mass" held in 1963 in Charleston, South Carolina. Did this really happen?

Martin: Yes it did. And the participation by telephone of some high officials of the church in the Vatican is also a fact. The young female who was forced to be a part of this satanic ritual is very much alive and, happily, has been able to marry and lead a normal life. She supplied details about the event.

McManus: In addition ... you depict numerous other cardinals and bishops in a very bad light. Are these characterizations based on fact?

Martin: Yes, among the cardinals and the hierarchy there are satanists, homosexuals, anti-papists, and cooperators in the drive for world rule. [2]

Surely, it is no coincidence that in Charleston, South Carolina on the 31st of May, 1801, the first Supreme Council of the Ancient and Accepted Scottish Rite (A.A.S.R.) was founded, but I insist that not all Freemasons are in league with evil and darkness. However many, especially in the A.A.S.R., are linked with the Jesuits. Apart from the speculations of Father Malachi Martin that could help him pass for a new "Leo Taxil," he added in the same interview, another important statement that in recent years has proved to be more and more real:

"Among the cardinals and the hierarchy there are satanists, homosexuals, anti-papists, and cooperators in the drive for world rule." With these words he cleared the link between the New World Order and Satanism. Yes, the shadow of Satanism lingers for years on the Vatican, and in an interview by Stefano Maria Paci to the

1   Malachi Martin, *Windswepthouse,* (New York: Broadway Books, 2001), p. 493.
2   https://www.newswithviews.com/Horn/thomas130.htm / ‡ Archived 28th November, 2016.

late **Father Gabriele Amorth (1925-2016)**, who was the Vatican's leading exorcist who stated: *"Gradually, as requested by the Second Vatican Council, the various parts of the Roman Ritual were edited, we exorcists were waiting for it to be treated on Title XII, that is, the old Ritual. But evidently it was not considered a relevant topic, as the years passed and nothing happened. Then, suddenly, on June 4, 1990, the Ritual arrived and it was a real surprise for all of us, as we had not been consulted before. Yet by that time we had prepared many questions in view of a revision of the Ritual. We asked, among other things, to touch up the prayers and add invocations to the Holy Mary that were completely missing, and to increase the specific exorcism prayers. But we were completely cut off from the possibility of giving any contribution."*

The interviewer then adds another interesting question that helps us understand how the Catholic Church is truly in the hands of the devil these days: ***"Does it mean that the new Ritual is useless in the fight against the devil?"***

Amorth replied: *"Yes. They wanted to deliver a blunt weapon. effective prayers have been deleted, prayers that had twelve centuries of history were substituted by new, ineffective ones."*

The complaints of Father Amorth are not a trivial matter, especially when calculating what is happening now in the new church of Pope Francis, increasingly secular, and a continuation of what Don Villa called the *"new Masonic Church of Paul VI."* For the action exerted by the Vatican II against the Church of Christ, one can say that the real goal of the occult elite, who directed Vatican II and oversaw the post-conciliar period, is to complete the work of destruction of the Church of Christ, and everything can be expressed by the formula: **replacement of "the Catholic priesthood" with a "Liberal Masonic priesthood."** Yes, the worst form of Freemasonry, for the worst kind of Church. In the early days of Speculative Freemasonry, it is said that the only form of Freemasonry accepted by the Church was Christian Freemasonry, but now things are quite different. We find ourselves in front of a Post-Vatican II Church ready for the "End Times," and Don Luigi Villa and Father Malachi Martin understood all this a long time ago.

In Defense of Father Malachi Martin by William H. Kennedy

The primary objective of this examination is to respond to recent attacks made against the late Father Malachi Martin. Fordham University social scientist Michael Cuneo and veteran Vatican journalist Robert Blair Kaiser, among others, have recently published information which makes some harsh and unfounded claims concerning Father Martin and, for the sake of historical accuracy, it is necessary to offer rejoinders to these allegations.

In *American Exorcism: Expelling Demons in the Land of Plenty* (2001) Cuneo reviews Martin's career and offers some astounding accusations concerning the validity of Malachi's scholarship. Cuneo was correct in his initial review of Martin's life and work, but missed some important details. In his formation as a Jesuit, Martin received three earned doctorates in Semitic languages, archaeology and Oriental history and was subsequently made Professor of Semitic Languages at the Pontifical Biblical Institute in Rome. Ordained in 1954, Martin was a top-level advisor to Popes John XXIII, and Paul VI, as well as working closely with the Jesuit Cardinal Bea. Martin worked in the Vatican's intelligence division and conducted secret missions into Eastern Europe to fund the oppressed Church which suffered under Communism. During the Second Vatican Council, Martin drafted the document which exonerated the Jews from culpability in the execution of Jesus Christ for which he received universal approval from the council and international accolades. Martin left the organizational Church in 1964, and resigned from the Society of Jesus, but he in no way shape or form ever stopped being a priest of the Roman Catholic Church. Pope Paul VI released Martin from all his vows, except for chastity, and agreed to allow him to act as a Roman Catholic priest in other ways. The Pope gave Martin permission to say Mass privately, and he continued to conduct the Tridentine Mass, which was formalized at the Council of Trent, for the rest of his life.

The same permission was granted to Saint Padre Pio who distrusted the New Mass. Under canon law the Pope has the right to limit or alter the faculties of any priest. Martin falls into the category of a fully functioning (i.e., allowed to administer all the sacraments) Roman Catholic Priest whose faculties (rights) excluded him from working full time in a parish or in a religious order. ... Martin was required to wear normal clothing as opposed to a Roman Collar so that he would not be mistaken for a local parish priest. Apart from this minor restriction in dress, Martin was in every respect a Roman Catholic priest. As those who knew him can tell you, Martin never slowed from his priestly duties—saying Masses at his apartment chapel, hearing confessions, conducting marriage ceremonies, administering last rites etc. on a daily basis. ... Father Charles Fiore, who knew Martin for years, states that when Martin came to New York his written faculties—which Fiore saw—were accepted by then Cardinal Cooke. Consequently, Martin's status as a bone fide Roman Catholic Priest with legitimate faculties is beyond reproach.

Martin's stated reason for leaving the Jesuits and the institutional Church was that he felt that Roman Catholicism was changing too fast and the institution he had grown up with was becoming an alien form of religion for him. People today do not realize how many drastic changes erupted in the Church in the wake of the Second Vatican Council. This seemingly solid monolithic institution crumbled into an unrecognizable heap by 1970. Even the Mass was radically altered into vernacular hybrids which were unrecognizable to even the most devout of Catholics. Despite what critics may contend, these radical changes were the only reason Martin left the Jesuits as will be evinced below. In this regard, Martin never really left the legitimate Church of Rome or the Jesuits, but rather the institutions over from orthodoxy that, inasense, they left Martin. Martin remained true to the original intent of Saint Loyola and his earliest followers while other Jesuits—like J.C. Murray, SJ—sought to alter the very foundations of the Christian Faith. With some Jesuits of Martin's era even claiming to be atheists, Martin was loyal to the True Faith. Having been left without an income after leaving the Jesuits, Father Martin worked a variety of odd jobs while conducting academic research. He published his reflections on Paul VI called *The Pilgrim* (1964) (under the pseudonym Michael Serafian). Martin first moved to Paris and worked as a translator for various Jewish groups—a job he got because he was such a master of languages and as a reward for his pioneering work on Catholic/Jewish relations. Martin then moved to New York and won a Guggenheim Fellowship to support himself while he wrote *The Encounter* (1969) which explores the relationship between Judaism, Christianity and Islam and which predicted the crisis into which the world's three great religions have fallen. During this period, Martin became the priest for a Greek family in the shipping field at the suggestion of Cardinal Cooke. Americans are for the most part unfamiliar with the European practice of wealthy and aristocratic families adopting a priest as a personal spiritual advisor. Such priests become part of the family. A case in point is that of the Von Trapp Family Singers who adopted Msgr. Franz Wasner as their family priest in Austria. Msgr. Wasner became so much a part of their family that he fled with the Von Trapps to the USA after the Nazis sought to conscript Baron Von Trapp as a U-Boat commander. Msgr. Wasner was written out of the Hollywood version of the Von Trapp family's life entitled *The Sound of Music*, but was buried in their family plot in Vermont.

Rumors continue to fly that Father Martin was having a romantic affair with Kakia Liva-nos, the lady of this Greek family and Cuneo repeats this falsehood. From all reliable ac-counts this is clearly a blatant lie. Father Martin's relationship with this woman was purely Platonic in nature. Again, Americans cannot relate to this practice of having an adopted family priest as very few well-to-do Catholic families in the USA ever have such a spiritual advisor. In this instance the lady in question emphatically and categorically denied having any romantic involvement with Father Martin. It is horrible that anyone should promote such lies. Perhaps there is far more to this untruth than is commonly realized. After settling in the USA, Martin began to produce bestsellers that included both factual scholarship and fact-based fiction—a concept Martin borrowed from Norman Mailer et al. who called this genre "faction." Martin's books were extremely well-received and influential. Although the institutional church either ignored or dismissed Martin's work, his books found a huge audience. William Buckley hired Martin to write for the *National Review*. Even the re-nowned author Saul Bellow quoted Martin in his 1976 Nobel Prize acceptance speech. In his many tomes, Martin pointed out that the Vatican was allying itself with Global Elites in various schemes to control international politics and the World economy. Cuneo denies that Father Martin had the proper sources within the Vatican to back up his then seemingly absurd assertion. However, Martin's own brother was a priest who remained in the Holy See many years after his departure and Martin himself remained in contact with a variety of other high level Vatican sources. As will be demonstrated, Martin had accurate infor-mation from some top Vatican officials concerning a banking cabal and the current priest pedophilia crisis rocking the Catholic Church. There is absolutely no way Martin could have known of the details of these conspiracies within the Church without high level infor-mants. Cuneo never realizes this hard fact and, consequently, his attacks against Martin's "insider" status are moot. It must be recalled that Martin was making these assertions about the Holy See both in print and in public talks years before the famous Vatican Bank scan-dal which erupted in the 1980s. Martin definitively described the major players in various corrupt Vatican banking plots in his 1978 best-seller *The Final Conclave* (pages 24-31). In 1982, the Italian government uncovered a money laundering scheme wherein the Vatican Bank, the P-2 Freemasonic Lodge, and factions of the Mafia united in a criminal cabal to launder ill-gotten money derived from illicit drug running, gambling and extortion.

This resulted in the removal of gangster/Archbishop Paul "The Gorilla" Marcinkus as President of the Vatican Bank and prompted his deportation back to Chicago where he reunited with the equally vile Cardinal Cody who operated as an international bagman for the Accardo Crime Family. **All of this culminated in the dramatic Masonic ritual murder of gangster/banker Roberto Calvi from a London bridge in 1982.**

Martin mentioned Marcinkus and Cody in relation to corrupt banking practices in *The Final Conclave* on page 27—some four years before the fall of these two Vatican wheeler-dealers. Factions of this cabal may even have a hand in the untimely death of Pope John Paul I in 1978.

This Masonic/Mafia/Vatican conspiracy has been conclusively documented. Martin believed that the Freemasonic Lodge was Satanic in nature and that those various factions all took blood oaths to support each other in their various banking scams. For a complete record of this cabal, see David Yallop's *In God's Name: An Investigation into the Murder of Pope John Paul I* (1997). Martin also contended that this cabal was involved in even more heinous acts against children. In 1996, Father Malachi Martin reported that the Vatican was involved in an elaborate cover-up to protect child molesting priests and that predatory homosexuals had covertly gained control of the major seminaries in Europe and the USA. Martin further claimed that "secret gay sex cults" were being formed within these seminaries, which involved both child sex acts and homosexual relations between gay adult priests and seminarians. One of the worst culprits, in Martin's estimation, was Cardinal Bernard Law of Boston. This fact was reported to the author of this piece in January of 1996, at a meeting with Father Martin. Martin also claimed that these secret sex cults employed mind control techniques and various forms of brainwashing to keep victims in line. ... Martin's reason for not publishing this revelation was that he feared for his life having received repeated death threats from a variety of anonymous channels. Martin's anxiety was not unfounded as his associate Fr. Alfred Kunz who was investigating reports of Satanic child abuse by priests was murdered in a occult ritual fashion in 1998, after repeatedly being warned to halt his research. Fr. Kunz's murder has never been solved. Now that the child sex cult ring in the Archdiocese of Boston and the rest of the U.S. Church has come to light, much of Malachi's claims in this area are confirmed. Most alarming is the case of Paul Shanley—a Boston-based diocesan priest who for 30 years molested pre-teens, as well as adolescent boys, and was even a founding member of the perverted North American Man/Boy Love Association (NAMBLA). Even though a variety of individuals reported Shanley to Bernard Cardinal Law, Shanley was allowed to continue his sick lifestyle. When reports surfaced in one parish of Shanley's activities, the Chancery merely transferred him to another, and paid off the victim's families and once more transferred Shanley to another parish where he resumed his pedophile lifestyle. The Archdiocese of Boston never sent Shanley for cogent psychiatric help in the course of what Shanley called his 30-year "youth ministry." Martin alluded to this child-molesting cult several times in his writing and they are worth reviewing at length considering that much of what he claimed has recently come to light in the popular press.

Most frighteningly for John Paul, he had come up against the irremovable presence of a malign strength in his own Vatican and in certain bishops' chanceries. It was what knowledgeable Churchmen called the "superforce," the incidence of Satanic pedophilia—rites and practices—was already documented among certain bishops and priests as widely dispersed as Turin, in Italy, and South Carolina, in the United States. The cultic acts of Satanic pedophilia are considered by professionals to be the culmination of the Fallen Archangel's rites. (Keys of this Blood: 632) ... every day, including Sundays and Holy Days, acts of heresy and blasphemy and outrage and indifference were committed and permitted at holy Altars by men who had been called to be priests. Sacrilegious actions and rites were not only performed on Christ's Altars, but had the connivance or at least the tacit permission of certain Cardinals, archbishops, and bishops. In total number they were a minority—anything from one to ten percent of Church personnel. But of that minority, many occupied astoundingly high positions or rank. The facts that brought the Pope to a new level of suffering were mainly two: The systematic organizational links—the network, in other words—that had been established between certain clerical homosexual groups and Satanist covens, and the inordinate power and influence of that network, (Martin quoted from the site www.theharrowing.com/martin.html **no longer available**). In at least three major cities, members of the clergy have at their disposal at least one pedophiliac coven peopled and maintained exclusively by and for the clergy. Religious women can find a lesbian coven maintained in a similar way. *(Hostage to the Devil: XII)* [3]

The secret mission entrusted by Padre Pio to the heroic Don Villa

I n 1952, close to the Second Vatican Council, the aforementioned Don Luigi Villa, (FIG. 91) received from the future saint, Padre Pio of Pietrelcina, the commission to dedicate his life to fighting ecclesiastical Freemasonry. He received the order to visit the Archbishop of Chieti Mons. Before accepting this position, however, Msgr. Bosio warned Don Villa to have nothing to do with Giovanni Battista Montini, the future Pope. Shortly afterward Pope Pius XII approved the assignment of Don Luigi Villa to this important mission, appointing the powerful Cardinal Alfredo Ottaviani as his supervisor. Remember to be a Freemason is not a crime, as many Freemasons help the community and are decent people, but for a priest, being a Freemason is a big problem of incompatibility, and behind this dual membership often lies a corrupt reality; to some extent anti-Masonic, if seen through the eyes of a true Mason. How can you officially condemn Freemasonry like the Church does, and then practice it behind closed doors? **Well in the kingdom of hypocrisy, and the Vatican, everything is possible, but this is clearly another manifestation of irregular Freemasonry.** That is why I fully support, although I'm also a Freemason, the difficult mission of the late Don Villa. A unique figure,

FIG. 91 – Don Luigi Villa (1918 – 2012), priest, doctor of theology, author, and above all secret agent on a mission for Saint Padre Pio, who said: "Courage, courage, courage! because the Church is already overrun by Freemasonry," adding: "Freemasonry has already arrived at the Pope's slippers."

as a man and as a priest, who for decades was like a secret agent for St. Padre Pio, fighting against the growing infiltration of Freemasonry within the Vatican. However it was a Freemason and journalist named Carmine Pecorelli (1928 –1979), known as Mino, that made the most incredible inquiry into what is referred today as *Lodge Ekklesia*. The Masonic membership of hundreds of senior officials of the Catholic Church and high-level Vatican officials practicing Freemasonry in the Vatican was all documented and published. When, in September 1978, the so-called "Pecorelli List" appeared in the periodical *Osservatore Politico* (OP), a newsletter that specialized in political scandals, that would publish many first-hand stories that Pecorelli was able to obtain through his numerous contacts. Pecorelli was brutally mudered by the mercenaries of the New World Order.

Carmine Pecorelli died a year after former prime minister Aldo Moro's 1978 kidnapping and subsequent killing. He was described as a "maverick journalist with excellent secret service contacts." According to Pecorelli, Aldo Moro's kidnapping was organized by a "lucid superpower" (ie. Henry Kissinger), and was inspired by the "logic of Yalta." **Pecorelli's name was on Licio Gelli's partial list of Propaganda Due Masonic members,** discovered in 1980 by the Italian police. In 2002, former prime minister Giulio Andreotti was sentenced, along with Mafia boss Gaetano Badalamenti, to 24 years imprisonment for Pecorelli's murder. The sentence was thrown out by the Italian Supreme Court in 2003, and no one was imprisoned for it. So shortly after publishing a comprehensive list of Freemasons in the Vatican, Pecorelli was murdered. It was certainly not a surprise to Don Luigi Villa, since many names of those senior officials had already been investigated by him. Villa gave his list of suspected Masons to the Holy Office, together with his allegations, documents, and therefore the evidence of their membership in Freemasonry, attempting to prove their membership against any reasonable doubt. Don Villa worked in his mission with factual data on hand, not mere conjecture or speculation, and this is clear to most. Don Villa cited the following people in his books: Monsignor Pasquale Macchi (the pope's personal secretary at the time), Cardinal Jean Villot, Secretary of State under Paul VI, John Paul I and John Paul II; and even Cardinal Agostino Casaroli, whose membership of Freemasonry was apparently known by Pope John Paul II, who did nothing to stop him. Don Villa was also convinced like many others, that Pope Luciani, the Pope that lasted only 33 days (33 as we know is the central symbolic number of the AA.S.R.). He wanted to clean up the Vatican from its strong Masonic presence, and this would have been in part the cause of his sudden death. The list published by the late Mino Pecorelli was in fact issued by its periodic OP, coinciding with the election of Pope Luciani, and included a list of 131 clergy with membership in Freemasonry. Among these names we find Jesuit Roberto Tucci, who was the director of Vatican Radio in the best Jesuit tradition, as even today the Company of Jesus still controls Vatican media. Returning to Don Villa, for his mission, he needed a magazine, and so in 1971 *Chiesa Viva* was born.

In memory of Don Luigi Villa, I would like to include a brief biography written by his close friend **Franco Adessa,** his esteemed collaborator for many years:

For many years, Don Villa, worked as a secret agent for cardinal Ottaviani, with the specialty of documenting possible Masonic memberships of senior officials of the Catholic Church, and to deal with certain sensitive issues of the Church. This role made Father Villa a very well-known figure by police and other security agencies. When, in September 1978, during the brief pontificate of Pope John Paul I, the "Pecorelli list" appeared on OP, Mino Pecorelli's Magazine, it was not a great surprise for Father Villa to read many names of those senior officials that he had in some cases already exposed and in some cases even sent back home, after supplying to the Holy Office the documents of their membership in Freemasonry. One of the most famous cases was that of Cardinal Joseph Suenens, driven from its headquarters in Brusselsnot, a Mason, married and with a son named Paul. ... Another "painful," case was that of the cardinal Lienart Achilles. In Paris, as Villa waited, near a Masonic Lodge, the man who was to confirm the existence of documents attesting to the cardinal membership in Freemasonry, Don Villa, suddenly, saw a young man running towards him, who attacked him and punched him in the face, shouting: "A devil exists on earth!" Badly injured Don Villa was brought unconscious to a nearby pharmacy, with a mouth full of blood, his jaw broken, and without a tooth left in his mouth. Even in Haiti, one day, he risked his life. He went to that country for a mission, he was taken away by the military who were preparing to shoot him. But Don Villa had an inspiration and asked the officer in charge to speak with one of his dearest friends, the local Seminary Superior. The officer, disturbed by that request, went to his superiors and soon returned, saying: "We were wrong," and released him. Among the sensitive issues delegated to him by Cardinal Ottaviani, there was the meeting with Lucia of Fatima. One day Cardinal Ottaviani told Don Villa: "I thought I would send you to speak directly to Sister Lucia of Fatima." He gladly accepted. He was accompanied by a businessmen, Mr. Pagnossin, a convert to Padre Pio, who offered him the journey and stay in Portugal. Cardinal Ottaviani had equipped Villa with a personal letter signed by him, at the time Prefect of the Holy Office, to be delivered to the Bishop of Coimbra, so they should grant him a meeting with Sister Lucia. But the Bishop of Coimbra, before granting a meeting with the Sister Lucia, picked up the phone and called the Vatican. Replied Msgr. Giovanni Benelli, who, before giving a definite approval, wanted to hear Pope Paul VI, because Rome had given strict orders about the possibility of interviewing Sister Lucia that was allowed only to Royals and Cardinals. Msgr. Benelli transmitted to the Bishop of Coimbra the prohibition of Paul VI to the interview request with Sister Lucia. It was useless, then the insistence of Father Villa, in highlighting its role as envoy of the Prefect of the Holy Office. He remained in Portugal, trying to overcome the resistance of the Bishop. After about ten days, however, he had to give up. He only obtained by the Bishop to celebrate Mass in the Chapel of the cloistered convent where Sister Lucia was residing. Back in Italy, Don Luigi went immediately to report the incident to Cardinal Ottaviani. The Cardinal was offended by the behavior of Paul VI, and immediately wrote a letter of protest. He returned later in Rome. Cardinal Ottaviani said that Paul VI had made excuses, saying, however, that the decision had been taken by Msgr. Benelli. But the Cardinal pointed out that this was the usual excuse method used by Paul VI. However when Pius XII was alive, the Vatican, for Don Villa, was more than a welcoming environment. In addition to meetings related to his activities as a secret agent, Don Villa lunched and dined at least fifty times with Cardinals and Bishops. But when Paul VI rose to power, Villa lost every hospitality and precluded any possibility of launching initiatives for the defense of the Catholic Faith. [4]

The documents proposed by Don Villa were often censored by the media but he never received any complaint for the accuracy of his accusations. But as we have seen from the testimony of his colleague Franco Adessa, it seems that Villa was the subject of several attacks and even bombings during his mission. But he went on his way, continuing to fight Freemasonry in the Vatican as indicated by Padre Pio, and made no discounts even to the dangerous **Opus Dei sect,** which he called "White Freemasonry," as did the late Count Licio Gelli. To the Opus Dei, Father Villa devoted an entire section of one of his publications, where the priest declared that: *"Professor Vittadini of the Lateran University and president of the beatification office had made a terrible relationship against Escriva as saint. And when the Cardinal of the Congregation of Saints said it would be necessary to talk to the Pope. And he did. When Wojtyla received him, he looked at him and said: 'The pope is me, I want him to become Sanctified!'"*

An unsual attitude for John Paul II, who seems more in line with a "mafiosi" than a supposed "Holy Man," but the Opus Dei is a force that is difficult to challenge in any way. I remember reading an article that Frank Morales wrote a few years ago, during the presidency of George W. Bush, where he highlighted the ties of the Opus Dei, with the U.S. Government. And let me tell you that even today, there are still many links to the Vatican, links of a personal nature as well as institutional ones, that might push Trump to eventually rediscuss, unfortunately, some of his brilliant proposals made during the electoral campaign, probably viewing them in a new light now. Keep in mind that his own son, Eric Trump, is a Jesuit-trained from Georgetown University, who serves as board member of Georgetown's Business, Society, and Public Policy Initiative, and even Ivanka Trump, attended Jesuit Georgetown for two years. And without putting into question the clever Mike Pence, he is however a self-described "evangelical Catholic." Remember that all this is not necessarily evil, as even in the Catholic Church today, there are two different schools of thought fighting for supremacy, and Trump belongs to the more traditional one, secretly driven by **Raymond Leo Burke (born June 30, 1948),** an American Cardinal prelate of the Catholic Church, who is an archbishop and also serves as the patron of the **Sovereign Military Order of Malta.**

Burke is often perceived among prelates of the Catholic Church, as a voice of traditionalism, with an "unwavering passion for the integrity of Catholic doctrine." It is useful to highlight these links, which in part also shape the policies of the U.S. Government, trying to understand what is the origin of this fervor to war and conquer, that has nothing to do with the people of the United States, but rather with their hidden controllers, some of whom are located in the Vatican, as well as in Israel, along with those in the U.S. Military Industrial Complex, to go along with their decisions. I hope that President Trump will be able to overcome this challenge, probably the most difficult.

Let's try to understand more about the Church and Freemasonry. Few outside of Freemasonry know of a historic speech delivered over ten years ago by Grand Master Fabio Venzi, of the Regular Grand Lodge of Italy, held in Rome on the 25th of June 2005, at the Grand Hotel St. Regis. A speech, carried out by Anglo-Saxon Masonry in Italy, a group traditionally very close to the Opus Dei, that of the Regular Grand Lodge of Italy, marking a memorable day for Freemasonry, once again servant of the Vatican lead New World Order.

In short, a Catholic priest officially becomes the first Grand Chaplain in the history of the Free World of Freemasonry with the approval of Pope Ratzinger (now *Pope Emeritus,*) officially hostile to any form of Freemasonry. Hypocrisy? It is the usual two weights and two measures, which is two ways to judge and treat Freemasonry. There is the outward image, crafted for Catholic believers tending to slander Freemasonry, to condemn it without appeal, and to treat it bad publicly. This is while on the inside, the Church tends to justify it and to minimize it. Freemasonry that is not anti-Catholic or hostile to the Church, and maybe with hands and feet tied to Opus Dei or its rivals, the Knights of Columbus; related to Neo-Templar groups like the OSMTH and OSMTJ, and powerful Illuminati lodges like *Skull & Bones.* Complicated? Well yes, but in all this mess of orders and names, that often fuels the New World Order and its scenario, it seems that gradually in the last few years, since I started my *Confessions,* people are starting to wake up. These troubled times are inspiring a growing movement of traditionalists, especially in matters of religion and faith—a whole new population of people are rising from the ashes finally bringing Neo-liberalism to its epic fail. We are here to claim back a society that is unfortunately in the hands of a great evil, but with divine revelation and traditional instruction, we hope to preserve our values and tradition. In these unprecedented times, we are building the base for a future Christian Empire that will possibily include U.S. and Europe, and reshape what is left after George Soros and Pope Francis finish ruining the planet. In the meantime, let's hope Cardinal Raymond Leo Burke and President Donald Trump manage to bring back a bit of Christianity to the Church of Rome, and possibly with the guidance of his Military Intelligence, finally bring to justice Jesuit/Islamic agent Fethullah Gulen, who deserves the maximum penalty as a key Islamist of the rising "Caliphate."

The Vatican and Masonry: a ballad of hypocrisy

In 2016, the present Grand Master of the Grand Orient of Italy, Stefano Bisi, who was involved in a massive scandal involving one of the main banks in Italy Monte dei Paschi di Siena, and has publicly given his support to the Democratic Party and their mondialist agent Matteo Renzi (ex Prime minister) , wrote an open letter to the newspaper *Il Sole 24 Ore* in relation to the article "Dear brothers Masons" written by **Cardinal Gianfranco Ravasi, a senior Vatican representative,** that appeared as a cultural insert on the 14th of February, 2016. There is something sick and twisted in this new love relation between the Grand Orient of Italy, in the hands of Club Bildeberg mafia, and Cardinal Ravasi, mentioned in the past as a papal candidate. On the site of the Grand Orient of Italy the Grand Master states that: *"The letter expressing interest and appreciation for what is written by the President of the Pontifical Council for Culture on some common values, beyond the positions and official documents of the Church on Freemasonry, do not prevent a peaceful future dialogue between the two institutions."*

Stefano Bisi never mentions in his long letter that in the Vatican there are various Masonic lodges present from the end of World War II. Cardinal Ravasi writes: *"These various declarations of incompatibility between the two memberships to the Church and the Masons do not prevent, however, the dialogue, as is explicitly stated in the German bishops' document that already had listed specific areas of confrontation as the Community dimension, the charity, the struggle materialism, human dignity, and mutual understanding."*

Both are blatantly lying as there were at least two popes whose Masonic memberships were proven against any reasonable doubt. **Angelo Giuseppe Roncalli,** who became **Pope John XXIII** in 1958, and **Pope Paul VI** in 1963, born Giovanni Battista Enrico Antonio Maria Montini, two Popes who left a clear Masonic imprint during the important Vatican II. *Lodge Ekklesia* works with at least four lodges, appears to have received a regular Masonic patent to work the "Emulation" rite released by an American Masonic Authority, a little-known Masonic reality, still operating today in the Vatican, under the patronage of the Grand Master of the United Grand Lodge of England. Obviously Cardinal Ravasi can not admit such a truth, and even the current Grand Master of the Grand Orient, Stefano Bisi, knows very well this is all a charade. The reality is that clergy and Freemasons all meet together in places like the local building of the Grand Orient of Italy in Perugia, or in some Churches in Assisi, and even conduct occult rituals together on top of Mount Subasio. This is fact, not fiction-as a Catholic priest in 2005 became the first Grand Chaplain of the Regular Grand Lodge of Italy, this is something Catholics and Freemasons should investigate further. However the tone of the message sent to Ravasi, by Grand Master Bisi, suggests that the Grand Master knows things, but wants to keep the hidden deals between Freemasonry and the Church secret, and probably also speaks on behalf of some prelates of the Roman Curia, the ones that obviously pushed Cardinal Ravasi to open up with the rest of Italian Freemasonry, and the Grand Orient of Italy, at the dawn of what could be a pivotal year in 2017, when the United Grand Lodge of England celebrates 300 years after the founding of the first Grand Lodge. It will probably recognize the Grand Orient of Italy (Palazzo Giustiniani), after the P2 scandal took away their UGLE recognition, that now is in the hands of the Regular Grand Lodge of Italy, that in 2005, stated, after installing the first Catholic priest to the office of Grand Chaplain:

> *Today, in confirmation of this, I would like to end this my discourse, with the appointment of a Grand Officer who will likely remain in the history of Italian and possibly worldwide Freemasonry. The Officer I install in the office of Grand Chaplain is a priest of the Catholic Church. With this act, the Grand Lodge of Italy and its Grand Master, perform the most significant gesture ever, opening a Masonic Obedience to the Roman Catholic Church, distancing itself from other irregular Masonic Lodges, that with their anticlericalism did so much damage and harm caused to the image of the entire World of Freemasonry. This, in my opinion will be good for the Catholic Church, which probably ignores the vastness of the Masonic phenomenon in the world (million members, the largest form of secular association), and especially their imposing presence in the Grand Lodges of Central America and Latin America (Grand Lodge of Cuba, the Grand Orient of Brazil, etc.) We have done our part*

and expect in the future that the Catholic Church can find the motivation and the patience to know the peculiarities and differences within the diverse world of Free-masonry, which, in its traditional and regular expression is not hostile.

I think the Jesuits should stop intruding in Masonic matters, focusing instead on their Church. However in Italy, they have continued to mess up things for Freemasonry with their support of the CIA, even during the first years of the Obama administration, thanks to the well-known Masonic leader of the P4, **Luigi Bisignani**, who is now supporting President Trump.

The "Post-Conciliar Church" and Rock Music in the Illuminati

I would now like to open a short discussion on why after Vatican II, the Church seems increasingly indifferent to Satanistic tendencies, especially in the world of music and entertainment. This delicate and unusual theme of the relationship between rock music and the Catholic clergy, is written by the head of the Cultural Center of San Giorgio, **Pietro Bruno** in an article entitled *Men and the Church of Satanic Rock,* posted in 2012. Here is one particularly enlightening excerpt:

The lackadaisical attitude of so many consecrated people—bishops, priests and religious people in general—in the face of such a violent and macroscopic attack on the figure of Jesus Christ and the Catholic religion launched by a big slice of modern music is without a doubt one of the most difficult to deal with, especially for people like me who are believers and practitioners. Before moving to the treatment of the subject in its various aspects, I say that as a child of the Holy Roman Church, although a poor sinner, I feel a certain uneasiness in dealing with a phenomenon in some ways incomprehensible. I would also point out that while not wishing to judge anyone (task that belongs to God alone), I can not in good conscience turn a blind eye to certain behaviors and pretend that deep down it does not concern me, or is not of much relevance. When in 1986 I met in Rome Father Jean-Paul Regimbal o.ss.t. (1931 – 1988), the first author in Catholic circles to address the issue of satanic rock I exposed to him my intention to dig deeper into it, following his example, to bring this topic to the next level, he blessed me and spurred me to continue resolutely in this direction. Only a few years later, when I began to propose conferences or meetings in the parishes or ecclesial circles, I understood the reasons of his encouragement. The reality that I began to experience with my own eyes was not very rosy. Except in some commendable cases, most of the priests or leaders of religious communities were not interested at all in exploring the issues, and in many cases they slammed the door in my face without much to say. Some priests have hidden behind their refusal with futile excuses: "If we talk to the young people of these arguments we will end up advertising evil!" *Others have told me that if they had spoken negatively of modern music they were in danger of demonizing it and pushing away from their oratory, many young people who listened to it (or that even played this music in the sacristy, turned at times into a rehearsal room), and so on. Although sometimes it can be painful or unpleasant, as Saint Paul teaches, when there is at stake the salvation of souls and the honor of God's truth, the time is always right.*

So the question that arises is *"How did the clergy react to this terrible tragedy?"* **Pietro Bruno** explains:

Indeed, the magnitude of this disaster and its dire consequences have been felt by many pastors of souls. Unfortunately, many of them for fear of being viewed as disobedient, retrograde, and possibly being isolated or ridiculed by the brothers of their own own parish pastoral council, who don't share these views with the profane world, and most of the time they end up closing themselves in an impenetrable silence. My personal experience has shown me that only a small part of consecrated persons had the courage to openly go against this.

In over twenty years of activity a few zealous pastors or religious community leaders have generously opened the doors of their churches and allowed their flock to discuss such issues, and eventually entrusted them to know more on the danger of occultism conveyed by some music. In any case, it was always the individual initiatives, and— except for a few cases—never encouraged by their superiors in the Catholic Church. But there is another factor that has contributed greatly to facilitate the acceptability of Rock to many priests. With a gesture that has no precedent in the history of the church, Paul VI, in order to promote a more active participation of the faithful in the Eucharistic celebration abolished at one point the sacred language (Latin) and the traditional Gregorian chant, with serious damage to the sacredness of the religious rite itself. The void left by the great artistic heritage of centuries-old songs and hymns (some of which are even in the vernacular language) has been filled by a increasingly silly musical production and the daily consumption of songs of little theological content, with banal melodies and always predictably monotonous and boring lyrics, which are imposed in today's liturgy as a musical seasoning with no real sacredness. Predictably, following the horizontal spirit inherent in the liturgical reform, the majestic sound of the organ and polyphonic choral was replaced by the guitar of some boys of the parish. Within a short time, thanks to the introduction of the "liturgical experimentation," inspired in many cases by the "creativity" of the celebrant, we have basically seen everything in Churches, from jazz Masses, to Masses with drum beat, to Masses with clowns, or even DJ's in churches turned into nightclubs, etc. in some cases, the offertory was accompanied by the music of the film Jesus Christ Superstar or other horrors of the same kind. [5]

In too many cases, the Holy Sacrifice of the Mass has been transformed into a festive meeting with music and dance, in a climate of total anarchy favorable to the destruction of certain values. Many faithful offended by these disgraceful performances have denounced this abuse to the competent authorities, which have intervened (belatedly) to curb this phenomena with poor results. One can say that *the stable doors were shut after the horse had bolted long ago.* Perhaps the only one who tried to fight this now rampant degeneration, even within the Catholic Church, or at least monitor it, was the now deceased **Monsignor Corrado Balducci (1923 – 2008),** who was a very ambiguous figure with perhaps one too many friends in Satanism. A well-known demonologist, (later turned ufologist), Balducci thought differently than the rest of the clergy, when in 1994 he declared bluntly to the Italian newspaper, *Il Corriere della Sera* that: "Rock is the son of Satan" and after heavy criticism moved against the famous Beatles, and made some very interesting and shocking revelations on various artists of the time: *"Many Rockstars are members of Satanic sects; guys like Alice Cooper, Mick Jagger of the Rolling Stones, and Ozzy Osbourne of Black Sabbath, who also wrote Satanic songs."*

Balducci noticed many of the musical groups that dominated the scene, including the Eagles, Led Zeppelin and Queen, had launched subliminal messages in their songs. I think he would be even more shocked by today's attitude in the music business. The majority of artists from Jay Z to Rihanna, to the infamous Madonna, practice occultism in the open, without trying to mask this trend. As for the Rolling Stones, they even

5   http://www.centrosangiorgio.com/rock_satanico/articoli/pagine_articoli/uomini_di_chiesa_e_rock_satanico.htm ‡ Archived 28th November, 2016.

performed a concert in Cuba, a few days after a visit from former president Obama, who some referred to as the Antichrist, and for sure he is a Jesuit stooge. Monsignor Corrado Balducci in the early 1990s declared: *"I think that cults and Satanic rock fall in a plan of enormous proportion existing but unknown to people to destabilize the Western world."* Indeed, some deep thinking and ahead of his time by this high-level Vatican official. Balducci had until then dedicated his life to fight evil with exorcisms. Balducci was known in the last years of his life, as a sympathizer of ufology and friend of **Zecharia Sitchin (1920-2010)**. Before embracing the UFO phenomenon, Balducci was the author of a book entitled *Adoratori del diavolo e rock satanico*, that forced the Catholic newspaper (and official organ of the Italian Episcopal Conference), "Avvenire," and its spokesman, **Father Claudio Sorgi (1933 – 1999)**, to react, by expressing in no uncertain terms his disapproval of this editorial initiative by stating: *"It is false and silly the equation that rock equals the devil. ... Modern music is part of that first famous 'Areopagus' of evangelization to which the Pope has drawn the attention of the Church. There's a whole world that receives messages from Rock. I do not understand the importance and desirability of this offering, it means closing the Church again in an ivory tower."*

So the Catholic hierarchy moved the most improbable attacks against Balducci's work, demonstrating unequivocally that they were, and are to this day, on the side of evil. This does not mean ordinary Catholics or the clergy are necessarily evil, as there are still good priests who want to fight Satanism, but the situation has become truly decadent and corrupt in the Vatican. On the 29th of August 1986, Vatican Radio publicly manifested its appreciation for the positive influence of The Beatles, and the behavior of young people, stating that: *"With their long hair and unconventional language which highlight themes such as love, peace and even religion."* I still remember in the 1980s, when things were changing in the Church, when I met with the well-known Catholic media personality, Don Mario Pieracci (now Monsignore), at the end of Vatican censorship on certain books and songs, including The Beatles, who as many of you know, featured the image of Aleister Crowley on one of their covers. This private celebration took place at a local restaurant with the rest of the staff of Radio Valle Aniene, directed by Don Mario, who launched my career in the media and music world. [6]

The Vatican has too many weaknesses, to avoid the siege of evil fomented by Satan and his infamous "Legion" today, which is why the Jesuits were able to place one of them on the Papal throne for the first time in history, with Pope Francis. However this move has not helped the steady decline of the Catholic Church, and the constant support of the Vatican to anti-Christian music remains too antithetical to faith to ignore, as Pope Francis is trying to do. And let's not forget the **XXIII National Eucharistic Congress held in Bologna** in 1997, (FIGS. 92 and 93) when Bob Dylan, who was announced as the recipient of a Nobel Prize for Literature in 2016, created some controversy for his snobbish attitude. He performed for the now Saint John Paul II, smoking a great big joint on stage next to the Pope. Dylan received the prompt reaction of a Swiss guard, who advised him to move a safe distance from the old Pope.

Dylan shocked the world in an interview to the television program *Sixty Minutes*, where he stated that he basically sold his soul to the devil.

When Bob Dylan was asked in the interview why he keeps touring at his old age, he replied: "It goes back to the destiny thing, I made a bargain with it a long time ago, and I'm holding up my end."

6   Leo Lyon Zagami, *Illuminati and Music in Hollywood*, Harmakis Editions, Montevarchi Arezzo-2014, p. 257.

Question: "What was your bargain?"

Answer: "To get where I am now."

Question: "Should I ask who you made the bargain with?"

Answer: "With the chief commander."

Question: "On this earth?"

Answer: "On this earth and in the world we can't see."

Many fans have argued that Dylan was talking about God. But who makes a pact with God to get ahead in this world?[7] For sure playing in front of a controversial pope like John Paul II, who endorsed and helped the implementation of the New World Order and turned a blind eye to its pedophilia rings, does not play in his favor regarding the accusations against him, and in the end receiving a Nobel prize is just a final confirmation of this.

FIG. 92 –Bob Dylan performing for Pope John Paul II.

Satanism in the Vatican: not a hypothesis but a certainty!

The Last Exorcist is a book by the late Father Gabriele Amorth, (regarded by many as the number one exorcist in the Vatican), that was co-written with Paolo Rodari, and published in Italy in 2012. Amorth raised a considerable fuss in the media in the following months, with his note on the inside of the book, on the **case of Emanuela Orlandi,** the Vatican, and a thesis that according to him, related her disappearance to an alleged Satanic cult operating in the Vatican. For those who have never heard of Emanuela Orlandi's disappearance, she was the young daughter of a Vatican citizen working for the Prefecture of the Papal Household, who disappeared at the age of 15 in 1983, under mysterious circumstances. This is a case that shocked the entire world at the time, has never been resolved, steeped in a thousand mysteries, and they say is linked to turbulent events in the geopolitical arena.

The disappearance of Emanuela Orlandi, born in Rome on January 14, 1968, is an unresolved cold case. The incident dates back to June 22, 1983. The young victim was a Vatican citizen, not an Italian one, who definitely disappeared under mysterious circumstances. At first it seemed like the "usual" death of a teenager, but soon became one of the darkest cases in Italian history. It involved the Italian State spanning to the Vatican, even the **Institute for the Works of Religion (IOR)**, the Banda della Magliana, Banco Ambrosiano, and of course the secret services of several different countries. The disappearance of Emanuela Orlandi was linked to the disappearance of another teenager, named Mirella Gregori, who disappeared on May 7, 1983, never to be seen again. Emanuela

7   http://www.henrymakow.com/does_bob_dylan_worship_satan_1.html ✝ Archived 28th November, 2016.

FIG. 93 – Musician Bob Dylan personally greeting Pope John Paul II with extreme reverence.

attended a Roman school of music in Sant'Apollinare square, and on the day of her disappearance, on the street that connected the Vatican institute, she came upon a stranger, driving a green car. He attracted her with an offer of employment in the cosmetic marketing industry, to be carried out during a fashion parade, with an outrageous paycheck (375,000 liras, about the equivalent to a salary of the time). The 15 year old, before accepting, said she would have to get permission from her parents. Later, at 7 PM that evening, she exited the flute lesson she was taking, and phoned home to report the proposal to her dad. Her sister told her to be wary of an unprovoked and tempting project, and to return home as soon as possible to discuss it in detail with her mother. This was the last contact Emanuela had with her family. The late Father Gabriele Amorth, although having no direct knowledge of the facts, connected the disappearance of Emanuela to a Satanic cult operating in Vatican. Amorth then recalls in the aforementioned book, another priest who launched a similar crusade against evil infiltrating the Vatican, the deceased and mistreated Monsignor **Luigi Marinelli,** (FIG. 94) who published a book in 1999, that had a great international resonance entitled *Gone with the Wind in the Vatican,* in which he revealed the perverse life of the clergy within the Vatican. His charges included the integration of Freemasonry, sex, money, careerism, cowardice (small and large), and even Satanism, in what seemed like a true scoop at the time.

Marinelli was discovered by the Vatican's Holy See, who initially decided to convene Marinelli to the **Sacred Rota** to clarify the reason for writing his book. Monsignor Marinelli, however, decided not to appear at the trial, because he rightly believed that the Holy See had no rights under canon law to sentence, or pursue him in any way. So the Vatican changed their strategy and brought general attention to the case to push Fa-

ther Marinelli into oblivion. His book, however, went on to be a huge success—but there
were those who said that the Holy See bought
all the copies, and then burned them to avoid
circulation—Marinelli's name was included
on a black list of "unwanted" people in the
Vatican. Monsignor Marinelli never returned
to the Vatican, and died not long after that,
alone in his house under mysterious circumstances. As with the controversial figure of
Monsignor Marinelli, Father Amorth, seems
to agree on a Satanic haunting presence within the Holy See itself. Here are some shocking
revelations about Satan in the Vatican, delivered by the late Father Gabriele Amorth:

FIG. 94 – Monsignor Luigi Marinelli.

*It is the number one enemy, the tempter
par excellence. We know this being to be
dark and disturbing, and actually still
acts with treacherous cunning: he is the hidden enemy who sows errors and misfortunes in human history. Finally, February 3, 1977, again at a general audience,
It's no wonder if the Pope was bitterly writing warning us that "the whole world lies
under the power of the Evil One." Paul VI often spoke of the devil, and often linked its
figure to the Church. Why? Perhaps because he simply wanted to warn the Church,
ask her to be prudent, to escape the temptations of Satan. But, in my opinion, there's
more. Paul VI somehow realizes that Satan is in the Church, perhaps even within the
Vatican. It sounds the alarm. The second thing I want to say concerns a book. In 1999,
a book was published called* Gone with the Wind in the Vatican. *The, anonymous,
author was a monsignor in the Roman curia. Soon everyone knew his name, Luigi
Marinelli. Before the publication of the book Marinelli came several times to confide
in me. He was undecided whether to publish the book or not. Why this indecision?
Because the book is a collection of spicy anecdotes. Stories of careers, social climb-
ing, amorous adventures. It also shows unclear rites and practices that were close to
Satanism. Of course, not everything that is written in that book is true, but mostly
it is. ... This is my opinion. Now, this book, soon after being published, disappeared
from the shelves of the book stores. The Vatican bought all the copies. And then, even
more curious, the output of all this made very little appearance in the papers. Why?
How was it possible that such revelations would not trigger the explosive media?
Difficult to answer. Certainly there is a fact: this book confirms that when Paul VI
spoke in some way of the presence of the devil in the Church he had a point. It was
to be a warning for the Church, but it was not. I would like, in this regard, to show
you an example. Talk about a relatively recent affair in which, in my opinion, we see
that within the sacred walls there is an evil, not for good, and a minority that may
have taken over. It is the story that takes the name of Emanuela Orlandi. Emanuela
Orlandi is a fifteen year old girl, daughter of an employee of the Vatican and of an
employee working in the prefecture of the pontifical household, that for short, in his
work often had occasion to see closely the Pope. Emanuela is a lively sunny girl. Suddenly on June 22 of 1983, she disappears. She has still not been found. Disappears
after going to a music lesson. Emanuela, in fact, playing the flute at the church of
Sant'Apollinare in Classe, where there is a sort of conservatory. According to the lat-*

FIG. 95 – Padre Amorth.

est information gathered before her disappearance, Emanuela jumped in a black car. But it is not certain. It is sure that at 19.15 she was seen for the last time by two school friends, going to Corso Rinasci. After that Emanuela disappears.

"Through some crack" Pope Paul VI (Giovanni Battista Enrico Antonio Maria Montini, 1897-1978) announced "the smoke of Satan has entered the Church." These words and this historical statement, were also mentioned by Father Amorth, (FIG. 95) who before his death in September 2016, entered the history of the Church with his unusual, but important mission as the Vatican's chief exorcist. However no one seems to understand, including the late Amorth, that the Pope of Jewish origin, Pope Paul VI, who spoke these heavy words of condemnation against the Devil, could have facilitated this decline. Some say Paul VI was also the victim of blackmail of unspeakable proportions by the agents of the New World Order, that gathered evidence on his homosexual encounters. In any case, the book by Father Amorth *Memoirs of an Exorcist. My life fighting against Satan,* claims to have evidence on the presence of Satanism in the Vatican by people close to him, saying: **"Yes, also in the Vatican there are members of Satanic cults."**

This is a brief part of an interview with Father Amorth about this shocking topic present in his book:

Q: **Who is involved? It is simple priests or laity?**

A: There are priests, monsignors and also cardinals!

Q:**Forgive me, Father Gabriel, how do you know all this?**

A: I know from people that have been able to report it to me because they knew directly. And it is something "confessed" several times by the devil himself during exorcisms.

Q: **The Pope is informed?**

A: Of course he has been informed! But he does what he can. It's a chilling thing. [8]

And this presence of Satanic clergy in the Vatican—which should be really frightening for us, after the statement of Amorth is part of this growing Satanic Mafia worldwide—"There are priests, monsignors and also cardinals!"—something that was also confirmed by **Pietro Orlandi**, Emanuela's brother, who I know well, and I interviewed

8   See. Gabriele Amorth, Marco Tosatti *Memorie di un esorcista. La mia vita in lotta contro Satana,* (Milan,IT: Piemme Edizioni, 2010).

FIG. 96 – *The author and Pietro Orlandi, the brother of Emanuela Orlandi, and on your right the author with a poster of a public march dedicated by her brother to his sister.*

many times. [9] Pietro told me that Father Amorth reported to him in private conversation that the infamous Black Masses in the Vatican are usually held in the **Church of San Lorenzo in Piscibus** in the Borgo rione of Rome, just a few meters from St. Peter's Square, and also from the headquarters of the General of the Jesuits in Borgo Santo Spirito. One must ask, how does Pope Francis tolerate something so sick happening so close to him, unless he is in some way a participant?

Pope Francis was not even in his office for twenty-four hours when he warned about the devil to his brother cardinals at Mass celebrated in the Sistine Chapel in the aftermath of his election to the Papal Throne. *"When you do not confess Jesus Christ you confess the worldliness of the devil."* Francis quoted Leon Bloy, a writer who, ironically, a Jesuit magazine years earlier excommunicated as "impatient, sometimes exalted and increasingly extremist," and who said, *"Those who do not pray to God, pray to the Devil"* These words were more or less repeated and reinforced ten days later, on Palm Sunday, in St. Peter's square, in front of the Vatican basilica, when Pope Francis said *"With Jesus we are never alone, even when the way of life collides with problems and obstacles that seem insurmountable. And at this time arrives the enemy, who is the Devil."* This mysterious entity is "**the root cause of every persecution**," something he reiterated once again in one of the usual homilies held shortly after dawn in a small chapel of Santa Marta were he lives. (9) The late Father Amorth's assumptions on the possible murder of Emanuela Orlandi, whose body was never found, was partly confirmed by Pope Francis, when he told Pietro that his sister *"was in the sky."* An emblematic answer from the Pope himself, that must know she is dead to make this assertion. For this reason a film was made recently in Italy entitled *La verità sta in cielo*. [10]

However Monsignor Simeone Duca in an essay by Mary A. Turi, made some pretty

9   http://www.ilfoglio.it/articoli/2013/09/02/diavolo-esiste___1-v-94816-rubriche_c352.htm

10   http://www.mymovies.it/film/2016/laveritastaincielo/

FIG. 97 – The veil of Isis covering the mysteries and secrets of the Vatican, continues to unfold.

interesting revelations on the Orlandi case and the people behind her disappearance: *"As a rule they organized the feasts, which happened also in the headquarters of foreign embassy to the Holy See. In the matter was involved a Vatican gendarme. The idea of the girls was to have fun and earn some money. As for Orlandi, after being exploited, she was made to disappear, and then killed."* [11]

Going back to Amorth, he kept saying privately to Pietro Orlandi (FIG. 96) that he knew nothing directly on the Orlandi case, and that these were his own intuitions, but were they? Amorth was an idealist, but he remained loyal to the Church, so he couldn't tell everything I'm afraid, as they were constantly monitoring him.

Pope Francis did not clarify the case further, after his words to the brother, Pietro. "Emanuela is in the sky." The remains of Emanuela were never found, so how does Pope Francis know with certainty that "Emanuela is in the sky" and not in some cloistered convent? Who told Pope Francis that Emanuela is dead, because only in that way she will "go to the sky" that means basically "to heaven." Bergoglio obviously does not want to talk about it because of the involvement of the Illuminati's Satanic sect within the Vatican. It says a lot about the Satanic spirit that lingers today more than ever in the Vatican, where everywhere you look, you can see disturbing scenarios.

On June 4th of 2012, the Italian newspaper *Corriere della Sera,* published an article by famous Italian journalist Fabrizio Peronaci, author of one of the most recent books on the case of Emanuela Orlandi, written with her brother Pietro, who reported on a new link with the infamous pedophile priests in Boston. A link which binds the case in some way to Amorth's speech and Satanism, although Peronaci initially does not investigate the Satanic link through Boston, not knowing, as he told me himself, the occult background of the Boston pedophile priests and their passion for Crowleyanity, that I reported in my book *Pope Francis: the Last Pope.* Dangerous anti-Christian beliefs, which I write about on several occasions in my trilogy, have infiltrated the Church at the highest level, and are linked to the infamous Freemason, occultist and Satanist Aleister Crowley, accused of obscene practices and sexual perversion when he lived in Sicily, in his so-called Abbey of Thelema, before being kicked out by Benito Mussolini. Fabrizio Peronacci, in his investigation, links the Orlandi case to to the scandal of pedophile priests in Boston, now a well-known reality around the world, thanks to the movie *Spotlight.* [12] (FIG. 97)

From Rome to the Boston "Spotlight"

A clue that emerged in the case of Emanuela Orlandi leads us to Boston, in the city of Archbishop Bernard Francis Law, who was brought to court (almost 20

11   See. Maria A. Turi, *Emanuela nella braccia dell'Islam?,* (Tavagnacco, Udine, IT: Edizioni Segno, 2011).
12   http://roma.corriere.it/notizie/ cronaca/16_febbraio_28/spotlight-sequestro-orlandi-prova-legami-boston-gregori-garramon-1f49f024-de2b-11e5-8660-2dd950039afc.shtml ‡ Archived 28th November, 2016.

years later), for allegedly having covered up, in the early eighties, sexual abuse by dozens of prelates. A rumor in ecclesiastical circles that many knew. The first point of contact, discovered by Peronacci, was the fact that one of the **four letters that the kidnappers of Emanuela sent to Rome was from Boston**, where they announced the hostage's killing, and had the stamp of Kenmore Station, the same post office where this coven of pedophiles in cassocks had opened their own mailbox to contact victims. Perhaps they were sending encrypted messages to their opponents in the Vatican, letting them know that they were aware of the ongoing scandals, and therefore they should have accepted their demands. One was put on the official police report, the other was not. The first letter dates back to the first days of Emanuela's disappearance, Pietro Orlandi claims, while the second one was used by the pedophile NAMBLA (*North American Man Boy Lover Association*) and emerged 19 years later.

Peronacci and Orlandi exposed this with the help of a Napolitan scholar who specialized in the sixteenth century secret brotherhood, a guy named Anthony Goglia, who at the time was 43 years old, a graduate of Political Science and public servant to the City of Naples. He noted that the date of the 20th of July 1983, (the *ultimatum* given to Orlandi from Boston) adding the number 158 (direct dial telephone to the Holy See) gave some extra clues to solve this case connected to the mysteries of a "strange ancient brotherhood." Satanism in the Vatican have ancient origins and maybe this was the infamous **"Black Lodge"** mentioned several times by Aleister Crowley in his studies. However in the late afternoon of September 4th, 1983, a person nicknamed *the Amerikano,* an anonymous character, called the Italian news agency claiming to hold Emanuela Orlandi hostage. He had a strong Anglo-Saxon accent in his not-so-perfect Italian. The date of the 20th of July was not a coincidence, but a sort of Memorial Day. Goglia explains why: *"In the second half of the sixteenth century at the church of San Giovanni in Porta Latina, with the complicity of some friars, was constituted a secret circle of men who experienced bonds of affection with each other and consecrated themselves to homosexual marriage. The brotherhood was dissolved on July 20th, 1578, after the arrest of 11 males of the sect. The process of the criminal court formed by the governor ended with eight convictions for offenses of sodomy, and for the desecration of the institution of marriage and the sentence imposed was hanging, executed on August 13th at Sant'Angelo bridge, with subsequent burning of the bodies. Is this possible? The kidnappers of Emanuela Orlandi possibly alluded to that 20th of July?"* [13]

Pietro, who dedicated years of his life to this case, emphasized during our first of many meetings that the different thesis carried out over the years by various investigative journalists and experts, even if valid, are increasingly focused on a one-sided version of the event, without ever finding links between the various versions. In this way you never have an image of the whole case which can unite the different elements of the truth of this complicated puzzle, to finally find a possible concrete answer about the disappearance of Emanuela Orlandi. Jealous accusations by the different super experts, where everyone wanted to be right, caused everything to be discarded as disinformation. This created disappointment and anger in Pietro Orlandi. We hope that soon things will change and clarity can be brought to this mystery. There needs to be synergy between experts and those who are interested in the case of Emanuela Orlandi, who could lead us straight to the heart of the problem, i.e. Satanism in the Vatican.

And here's the final indication I received on the Illuminati/Satanic link to this case. Pietro Orlandi in our first face-to-face meeting told me that in the early days after the

13   *Ibid.*

FIG. 98 – Cover of the pamphlet entitled Viaje al mundo de lo oculto Pius Freddo.

disappearance of Emanuela, the family received an anonymous message from a person linked to the still operating spiritualist group called **"Navona 2000,"** created in the 1970s by the famous Italian medium and occultist **Fulvio Rendhell** (Marilyn Manson's teacher), who pointed out the involvement of a Satanic cult in the disappearance of Emanuela, mentioning the name of the famous Italian **Satanist Efrem del Gatto (pseudonym of Sergio Gatti, 1945 – 1996).** This is what Pietro Orlandi told me, confirming another Satanic element in the case. Among the members of "Navona 2000," were the well-known Satanists Efrem del Gatto, and Evaldo Cavallaro, hypnosis expert and master of subliminal communication, who indicates on his website to this day, Sergio Gatti a.k.a. Efrem del Gatto among his "Life Masters."

It seems that some members of the group "Navona 2000" had very strong ties with the nascent Italian offshoot of the *Ordo Templi Orientis* Caliphate, that will develop officially in Rome in 1987, but has its origins in 1982, when the Freemason and Illuminati agent **Alberto Moscato** receives initiation into the Minerval (0 °) degree in Germany. Then there is a very rare Spanish pamphlet from a few years ago, linked to a traveling exhibition called *Viaje al mundo de lo oculto* of Pius Freddo. (FIG. 98) In it are many interesting illustrations involving Efrem del Gatto with Satanic ceremonies, witchcraft, evil spells, Satanic artifacts, old prints, and there is a picture where you see clearly the self-proclaimed Satanic leader Efrem del Gatto, and Monsignor Corrado Balducci, while practicing an exorcism together. (FIG. 99) Why this odd partnership for an exorcism? And who is the hooded girl being exorcized in the picture? Perhaps we'll never know, but Balducci, in 1996, declared that there was a growing number of sects who worshipped the devil and even do human sacrifices. Balducci knew personally, prominent personalities of the Satanic milieu, like Alberto Moscato of the O.T.O., and Efrem Del Gatto, who even supervises an exorcism conducted by Monsignor Balducci. Another interesting element in this case is that Efrem Del Gatto, mentioned in the mysterious message sent to the Orlandi family only a couple of days after Emanuela's disappearance, had been appointed Commander of the spurious Sovereign Military Order of Saint George in Carinthia through its Grand Master, Luciano Pelliccioni, a Freemason linked to the New World Order, along with subversive plots of NATO's secret services in Italy. This pseudo-chivalric order linked to the Vatican was investigated by magistrate Giovanni Tamburino, who was investigating the subversive organization "Rosa dei Venti," an organization similar to Gladio, a sort of local branch of a NATO intelligence service operating in parallel—and on a higher plane—than the officially recognized Italian Intelligence services. The matter will fall into silence after the now deceased prosecutor invoked the "State secret" option to walk out of it untouched. Recently, continuing to investigate the matter, I came to know a mysterious place where Efrem Del Gatto apparently conducted his perverse Black Masses, in the lost city of Antuni in the ruins of **Castel di Tora,** based at the artificially created Lake Turano, **in the province of Rieti.** This isolated place, was used for a long time as a Satanic temple by Del Gatto. Another interesting link in this case was also between Efrem and the Magliana Gang, who regularly supplied him with drugs—mainly cocaine, according to people who attended these events and knew him very well. Efrem was working as a drug dealer, to guarantee the constant supply of drugs for his perverse Satanic ceremonies, that may have killed Emanuela Orlandi. However, we concluded that the disappearance of Emanuela might be one of the biggest contemporary mysteries involving the Vatican. (FIG. 100) One, that unfortunately, has no answer to this day, mostly because of the high level people involved. All these years later the Italian authorities seem to have lost interest in the Orlandi case, pushed in this direction as Pietro told me, by the Vatican. I hope my dear readers will keep Emanuela's memory alive, without giving up on wanting to know the truth about this victim of the Satanic side of the Church of Rome.

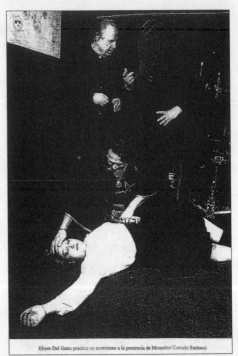

Efrem Del Gatto practica un exorcismo a la presencia de Monseñor Corrado Balducci

FIG. 99 – Efrem Del Gatto, famous Roman Satanist, and Monsignor Corrado Balducci, known Vatican demonologist while practicing an exorcism together, in a rare photo by Laura Lucatelli and John D'Aco, taken from a pamphlet entitled Viaje al mundo de lo oculto. P. Cold, published by Edizioni del **Centro Cultural Divulgaciòn Investigaciones históricas,** *Madrid, for a traveling exhibition on the occult presented in different cities of the world between 1988 and 2000.*

The world of spies in the shadow of the Vatican

Padre Robert A. Graham, S.J., died in California in a nursing home at 84 years of age, on the 11th of February, 1997. I will speak now of this unknown person, because he was not only one of the most influential figures in modern Vatican diplomacy, but also a key figure in the Intelligence and counterintelligence world. *L'Osservatore Romano,* in an article in 2011, act to diminish the world of espionage in relation to the Vatican, however they acknowledge the books related to Father Robert Graham and David Alvarez, who are considered one of the world's leading experts and historians on Intelligence matters. The late Father Robert Graham, after his collaboration with Alvarez, retired to California, and it is here, however, that something strange happened after his death, an event that Alvarez meticulously recounts in the book *Spies in the Vatican.* After the death of Father Robert Graham in California, his personal library was first transferred to the local archives of the Society of Jesus in Los Gatos, where the various documents and files were indexed in classic Jesuit style, and later boxed and sent to Rome. The Vatican had in fact ordered the California Jesuits to send the immense amount of documents gathered by Graham during his years of work, instantly to the Sacred Palaces of the Holy See in the Vatican. And that's where they are now, according

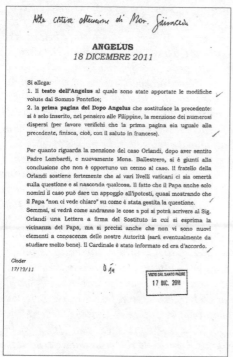

FIG. 100 – A note on the case of Emanuela Orlandi is attached to the official text of the Angelus read by the Pope on the 18th of December 2011, that shows how the Jesuits advised the Pope of the time, Ratzinger, to not make any mention of the Orlandi case during his public speech.

to Alvarez, still under the careful custody of the Vatican Secretariat, without any possibility of access granted to potential external researchers.

Alvarez even says in his book: *"Now that the Vatican has decided to confiscate the whole documentation produced by Robert Graham, all that remains are small pieces of information that I managed to salvage."* [14] In short, the Vatican, as usual, does not like external eyes on their own internal affairs, and in what it considers its "State Secrets," especially those concerning a possible aid to former Nazi's given at the end of World War II. Alleged **Top Secret** documents are even said to prove that the Sovereign Military Order of Malta participated actively in the Holocaust. Returning to the Jesuit Father Robert Graham, who obviously worked for the infamous Company of Jesus, an Order which has as its main purpose, the defense of the Holy Father and his interests, which do not always include the truth, even when there are serious shortcomings, or even criminal acts involved. Graham for me is certainly not a new name. In May of 1993, I noticed by chance, in the Italian newspaper *Corriere della Sera,* an article explaining the true role of the Jesuits in the field of espionage and Intelligence. In their actions, the Jesuits are at times completely opposite with the content of the Gospels, and are often attracted by Satanism, demonstrating a kind of bipolarity, which for me goes far beyond the Machiavellian quote **"the end justifies the means."** This inconsistent aspect, is at the heart of the Intelligence world, made even more perverse by their priestly status. Now it's time to learn more about the network of spies in the ecclesiastical cassock.

Graham was called to duty in the 1990s as a 007 from the Vatican, to go on the hunt for Communist spies in the aftermath of the collapse of the Soviet Union, and was also working with various literary projects with David Alvarez. In an article by Bruno Bartoloni in *Corriere della Sera,* dating from the summer of 1993, Father Graham speaks, giving us important specifics on the Intelligence services in the Vatican:

> *Hitler controlled Pius XII, but there were also 007's in recent conclaves. The Jesuit Robert Graham tells in a still unpublished volume,* Vatican Secrets. *The masterpiece by Robert Graham, the hunter of the Vatican spies, will probably never be read because it will never be published. "It's boring, no doubt, is just boring. Blame my style,"* explains the now octogenarian American Jesuit. But perhaps it is not necessary to read his spy story. There are six hundred pages that tell the adventures of the Nazi agents

••
14   See. David Alvarez, *Spies in the Vatican*, (Rome: Newton & Compton Publishers, 2003).

who were spying on Pope Pacelli. What he was supposed to reveal has been already revealed on the pages of Catholic Civilization, America and other magazines of the Society of St. Ignatius. For half a century it goes on hunting down spies behind the Bronze Door. Rome has always been and continues to be a city full of spies. The Vatican is certainly guarded and the last conclaves have been, in a particular way. We know that the technicians were called in 1978 to sniff around every corner of the Apostolic Palace with sophisticated equipment. "Nothing can stop a laser or modern technologies listening at a distance," Father Graham assures with great serenity. It is very likely that not many people know what really happened in the Sistine Chapel, when the electors chose a pope from the East. A 007 Jesuit, who does not love the novels of espionage Le Carre or Ken Follett, is one of four researchers privileged to which Paul VI opened the Vatican secret archives. They were all Jesuits: Angelo Martini, Pierre Blet and the now disappeared Burkhart Schneider. Pope Montini called them to rewrite the eleven white papers designed to respond to attacks launched by the German playwright Rolf Hochhuth against Pius XII for his silence on the Jewish genocide. Would Pope Pacelli have to speak up rather than act on welfare and on a local level? A historical question that will never find definitive answers. For Father Graham there are no doubts whatsoever. A small moral power as the Vatican would immediately pay the expenses of a more energetic action, losing its independence. "The Holy See was not the pontifical of Bonifacio VIII was. They could not launch crusades and large-scale convictions without being immediately put to rest. It would not be difficult or impossible for Hitler to militarily occupy Vatican Hill. The danger for a few months was real." It had to be, it seems, there was SS general Karl Wolff to deal with. At the Nuremberg trial some witnesses have referred to a physical elimination project of Pius XII. But many Jews think that a word more might have forced the managers of the final solution to reflect, as the world "knew." Historians such as Arno Mayer, however, are convinced to unleash "Judeocide," was not only the Semitic ideology, but also an almost casual reason: the turning point of the war and the dimming of the Hitler star deep in the steppes of Russia. Father Graham is from San Francisco. He is considered an heir of Piedmont Jesuits expelled by Cavour in 1848, who ended up on the coasts of California, to be an apostolic space for Alaska among the Indians. He entered the Society and finished his studies, the 007 of the future is to write for an America magazine. Between '48 and '63, he is commuting between Geneva and New York. With a scholarship he goes around the world to find all former diplomats who during the war had played roles.

... For almost ten years, the three Jesuits spend their lives locked in the Borgia Tower in the Vatican listening to sound files. In addition to the documents for the official volumes, there remains sufficient material to identify tracks and traces of the agents of the five Nazi services: the Ministry of Foreign Affairs, the Gestapo, the SS, the military intelligence, the Registry of the party employed Martin Bormann and the personal office of Goering interception They are almost exclusively cross-checks. "Some journalists are liars" The temptation to lie for them is very strong. But they were poorly paid. The most reliable were the agents of the SS, who were badly paid. Now father Graham knows almost all about what he calls the "hard job." He discovers fake students in Roman ecclesiastical colleges, employee infidels, men like Scattolini, fake journalists, as Domenico Russo, a journalist and classmate of Cardinal Secretary of State Maglione, who found himself, against his will, to be an unexpected and unsuspected agent of the Gestapo. "The best network of agents had been put up to Himmler's service, Colonel Herbert Kappler, the executor of the Fosse Ardeatine, Von Ribbentrop, jealous of its effectiveness, says father Graham, asked the systematic duplicate reports for the Foreign

Ministry." The control around Pope Pacelli was so tight that she had to use the white telephone to speak with confidence with a partner in the consulting room, as revealed to him by the daughter of general Simon, murdered at the Ardeatine. ... The stories of the California Jesuit have become legends. Every now and then back on the pages of newspapers like the Soviet agent in the Vatican "don" Alexander Kurtna, the prototype of the KGB agents as Catholic seminarians and priests, denounced by Graham in 1981 and came back in the news a few weeks ago. "The department is my hobby," he says before leaving for Lourdes. "It is time that you think a little more for my soul."[15]

Graham the Vatican Jesuit Spymaster

We now turn to the content of some excerpts from an article by the same Father Robert Graham SJ, on the subject of espionage originally published in 1991 for the journal *La Civilta Cattolica,* which is among the oldest existing in the Italian cultural scene belonging to the Society of Jesus. This article was republished in the now defunct intelligence and professional culture SISDE magazine called *Per Aspera ad Veritatem* in January-April, 1996. It demonstrates the more serious side of the now defunct and professional spymaster of counterintelligence for the Vatican: Robert Graham SJ. Remember, while reading the article, that he is not only a priest, but writes as a Jesuit. Confirming the Jesuit professionalism in the field of intelligence, Graham in the premise of this article shows complete familiarity with the world of international espionage and intelligence, and the fact that he describes in this premise an International Symposium on *"The Power and the Secret Service,"* which took place in Spain, where the Jesuits have always had the world's largest archive in the intelligence field, located at the Basilica of St. Ignatius of Loyola in Azpeitia. The news originates from the *Encyclopedia of Espionage* by G. Muratori, and should help us to contemplate the central role of the Jesuits in the scenario of an international 007. "Introduction on Espionage" by Father Robert Graham SJ:

For some time now the experts prefer to use the term intelligence instead of "espionage." Not only that, the main agents of this clandestine industry are ready to come out, to the point of appearing in public without hiding their true identity. In fact, last summer, in Spain, an international symposium on "power and the secret services," was held, which was attended by a large group of former heads of intelligence of different countries, in order to expose, according to their point of view, the meaning and the correct function of what is called "the second oldest profession in the world," even referring to biblical roots. It was a three-day round table organized at the end of August at the Escorial in Madrid by the Universidad Complutense de Madrid Cursos de Verano. The rank and level of the guests from various secret services was a guarantee of seriousness and reliability. Among those who took the floor were the former head of the French DST (Direction de la Surveillance du Territoire); *the former vice president of the Bundesamt für Verfassungsschutz (BfV), the domestic intelligence service of the Federal Republic of Germany; the former head of the Belgian State Security Services and the former head of the Mossad of Israel. ... They had accepted the invitation from a Soviet KGB general and a former head of the U.S. CIA (Central Intelligence Agency), but both eventually gave up (it was the time of the coup in Moscow). The former head of the Defense Intelligence Agency (U.S. military) took the floor. Last but not least the former head of the Italian intelligence services (SISMI), Admiral Fulvio Martini, also intervened in the debate. At the end of the Symposium, the current general director of Span-*

ish military intelligence (CESID), Emilio Alonso gave his analysis on the mission of Intelligence. The presence of a surprisingly large part of the Intelligence community means certainly that, in the intelligence environment, they agreed on the need to offer the public an authoritative presentation on the work of intelligence agencies.

Of course this was in the early 1990s, and the internet was around the corner, as well as a total reformation of the Intelligence system, but let's continue with the article:

This does not mean that participants have made indiscreet revelations. Typically, they seemed to agree in saying that the Mata Hari style, the legacy of the First World War, was outdated, unproductive, counterproductive and even dangerous. This, despite at the Escorial there had been set up a special session dedicated to the role of women in espionage and though the chairman was a woman, a former agent of the OSS (Office of Strategic Services) in Spain during the U.S. war. No one mentioned James Bond or Smiley, perhaps because at the symposium British intelligence experts did not attend, unless you want to consider Christine Keeler (involved in the Bouquet case), who in statements to the press, however, was said to be a prostitute and not a spy. All present were unanimous in saying that the challenge posed by international terrorism required close cooperation between the secret services, including the Soviet one. For once, organisms normally in competition with each other have identified a common goal under which to unite their efforts.

Father Graham then speaks of espionage within the Vatican by declaring:

The attempt on the life of John Paul II, made by international terrorism, has attracted the greatest interest on the Vatican secret services around the world. ... But it is an interest that precedes the rise of terrorism. In recent months, the long supervision exercised by the secret service of the Vatican has become a matter of public knowledge. Last summer we read that Robin Robinson, until recently one of the British intelligence chiefs, said in front of a large British television that "many times" British intelligence intercepted communications of the Holy See. A similar statement has probably surprised no one at the Vatican. The phone, in fact, is notoriously the Achilles heel of privacy. Thanks to technological progress, the wiretaps have become increasingly easy and the telephone communications are more prone to interference, especially through laser beam. Two recent publications are worth quoting to try to understand the interest rationale that nourished intelligence against the Vatican. In the last months of World War II, the American OSS, the head of which was General William J. Donovan, sent an agent to the Vatican with orders to investigate the possibility of a contribution from the Holy See to the process of peace they were trying to accomplish in the Pacific. The agent was almost about to successfully complete the mission, with the help of an official of the Secretariat of the Papal State. The events of this dramatic period are narrated in a book by the agent himself, entitled Peace without Hiroshima. *The author is Martin S. Quigley.* [16]

Father Graham wonders what there is to know in the Vatican:

The organizers of the Symposium on "Power and the secret services" have also invited observers, historians, journalists and others. One of the contributions (delivered by the writer) was entitled: "The foreign intelligence and the Vatican. As nations have spied on the Vatican and why. For that purpose we propose to draw in broad outline some of their points in the script. What is really to spying in the Vatican?" It is pos-

---

16   See. Quigley M. S., *Peace without Hiroshima. Secret Action at the Vatican in the Spring of 1945,* (London: Madison Books, 1991).

sible that this question can be asked by the profane observer. One way to answer and explain this apparent anomaly is to remember that most of the governments have a diplomatic mission accredited to the Holy See. Their ordinary task consists essentially in intelligence work in a "normal," i.e. to provide to their respective Governments, on an informed basis, reliable and secure relations, related to issues affecting their countries. That is sometimes, especially in time of war, the critical situation and the need for information beyond the legitimate ambassador possibilities. Then enter the scene secret services with their illegal methods. The famous dictum of Clausewitz on war could be read as follows: "Intelligence is the continuation of diplomacy by other means." An ambassador, at the dawn of diplomacy, was considered nothing more than a "spy." This profession has since become a respected and recognized instrument of international society. It is possible that Intelligence is heading towards the same process of legitimation? Global intelligence within the Vatican, and then the Holy See, occupies today a much more reliable place. This however is not a consolation for the Pope, who sees his confidential business exposed to the eyes of strangers. [17]

Finally here is the conclusion by Graham, where we return once again to reflect on the role of espionage and its link with the world of diplomacy:

We suggested earlier that there is an analogy between intelligence and traditional diplomacy. The history of espionage at the Vatican tends to confirm this view. There is only a difference of means and methods. But intelligence is not limited to passively collect more or less reliable information, it also has the role of facilitating the difficult negotiations. In 1939 and the following years, the German intelligence service, the Abwehr, headed by Admiral Canaris, tried to negotiate peace through contact with Pius XII, without informing Hitler. In 1945, the Second World War came to an end thanks to the work of Allen Dulles of the OSS in Switzerland. It is not surprising that would automatically extend their "tentacles," even the Holy See, especially in wartime. The neutral countries were at the crossroads of this traffic. We should therefore remain puzzled or surprised by the fact that the headquarters of a world religion, with deep roots and traditions in every corner of the known world, also attracts the attention of the intelligence organizations? [18]

A strange encyclopedia of spies

I introduce below, another valuable article that appeared in the early 1990s in the Italian newspaper, *Il Corriere della Sera,* (FIG. 101) that reviewed the extraordinary essay of the late Spymaster Giuseppe Muratori, which is entitled *Encyclopedia of Espionage, Intelligence, spies, terrorists and surroundings,* released in 1993 by **Edizioni Attualità del Parlamento Ore 12 Il Globo.** (FIG. 102) At the time, this book was very useful to me, and thanks to it I could deepen my studies on the reality that surrounded me after my initiation into the Craft in **April 1993,** when I was catapulted by Prince Alliata, as I wrote in Volume II, into the heart of the international world of spies and intelligence, as well as "irregular" Freemasonry, and the Illuminati, that is to be found at the heart of the New World Order. And even in this article, Giuseppe Muratori speaks of the Society of Jesus. However Muratori, who became one of my mentors, was always very close to the Vatican secret service, which occasionally used him as an external consultant.

This is the article, full of incredible information, translated for the first time in English:

....

17   See. *"La Civiltà Cattolica,"* 1991, IV, pp. 350-361.
18   *Ibid.*

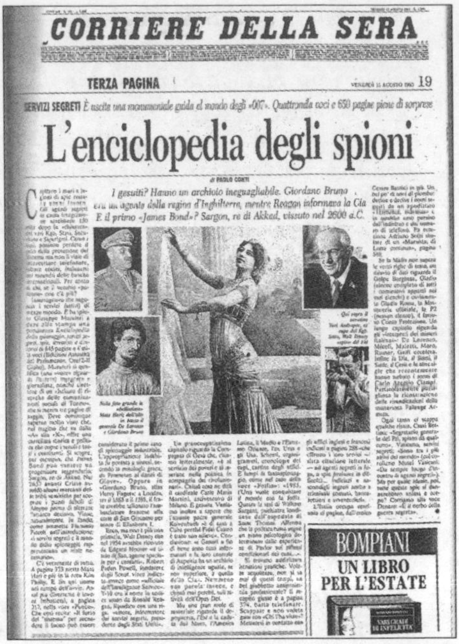

CORRIERE DELLA SERA

TERZA PAGINA 19

SERVIZI SEGRETI È uscita una monumentale guida al mondo degli «007». Quattromila voci e 650 pagine piene di sorprese

L'enciclopedia degli spioni

di PAOLO CONTI

I gesuiti? Hanno un archivio ineguagliabile. Giordano Bruno era un agente della regina d'Inghilterra, mentre Reagan informava la Cia. E il primo «James Bond»? Sargon, re di Akkad, vissuto nel 2600 a.C.

BOMPIANI
UN LIBRO PER L'ESTATE

FIG. 101 – Image taken from page 19, from the 13th of August 1993. Article by Paolo Conti, The Encyclopedia of the Spies, dedicated to the book by Giuseppe Muratori.

SECRET SERVICES: A MONUMENTAL GUIDE TO THE "007'S IN THE WORLD" 4 THOUSAND VOICES AND 650 PAGES FULL OF SURPRISES

The Jesuits? They have a unique archive. Giordano Bruno was an agent of the Queen of England, while Reagan informed the CIA. And the first "James Bond?" That is Sargon, king of Akkad, who lived in 2600 BC. The Cold War collapses and legions of spies remain jobless. Secret agents in layoffs are said to be 150 thousand after the "closure" of the various KGB, STASI, Securitate and Sigurigmi Intelligenc agencies. Like wolves, they may lose their hair but not the habit of intercepting phone calls, stealing codes, creeping into the intricacies of international banks. On behalf of who will they work for now, if the old "Owners" are gone? A question that arises these days amongst (active) services all over the world. This drove Giuseppe Muratori to print a ponderous Encyclopedia of espionage, intelligence, spies, terrorists and the likes, with around 645 pages and 4000 items (Edizioni Attualità del Parlamento, Ore12 Il Globo, 1993-Out of print).

*Giuseppe Muratori qualifies himself as an engineer and a journalist, as well as director of a "Research Institute of Social Communications in Turin," an organization that deserves three pages in his essay. Still Muratori must have learned a lot because, in the route that goes from "A" to "Z," he offers a historical overview and policy that covers all ages and all continents. It turns out, for example, that James Bond can boast a legendary ancestor: Sargon, king of Akkad. In 2637 BC, some merchants were hired from the Semitic tribes to discover the weak points of Aleppo before delivering the decisive attack on this city. He won, of course. After all, as Flaminio Piccoli admits in the introduction **"the secret services and the world of espionage are a necessary evil."** There really is everything in this book. On page 373 stands Mata Hari and after her there is Kim Philby. So far we are in the field of the obvious. Much more fun is "Fire" on page 217, that states: the theft of the "system" to start a fire, can be considered the first case of industrial espionage. This operation was carried out, according to Greek mythology, by Prometheus against Jupiter. The friar Giordano Bruno, aka "Henry Fagot" who lived in London, between 1583 and 1585, was closely following the French ambassador at the court of St. James on behalf of Elizabeth I. And it is no longer a novelty, that Walt Disney in 1954 would receive from Edgard Hoover "the title of Sac, special agent for the contacts." **Robert Baden-Powell, founder of the Boy Scouts, is referred to as "Official intelligence Service." T 10 was the code name used by Ronald Reagan, dismissed with one line in the archives of the Intelligece: "actor, informer of the secret service, president of the***

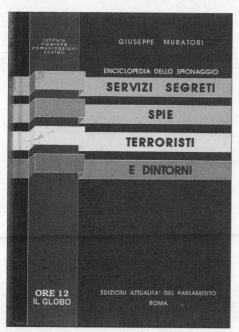

FIG. 102 – Cover of Encyclopedia of Espionage published in Italy in 1993, by Edizioni Attualità del Parlamento Ore 12 Il Globo.

United States." A disturbing chapter covers the Company of Jesus, whose purpose, "is to serve the poor and work in politics in the company of revolutionaries." I wonder what Cardinal Carlo Maria Martini, Archbishop of Milan and Jesuit would say about this? We also know that the current General Father Kolvenbach "is at home in Cuba because Fidel Castro has been his pupil."[19] Conclusion: "The Jesuits for the good of humanity, are all informers and their Headquarters in Azpeitia have equal Intelligence archives, if not superior, to that of the CIA." Not a word, and who knows why, on the activities of Opus Dei. But a great deal of material regards the war with the Communists and the fall of the Eastern Bloc, Latin America, the Middle and Far East, the former USSR and the USA. Diagrams, organizational charts, histories of the leaders, maps of the offices. And flashes of spy-fi, as in the case of "Madness:" in 1985, when the USSR wanted to conquer the world with madness. This is the thesis of William Sargant, a London psychiatrist in Saint Thomas.

He says that Russian policy follows a psychologically determined direction inspired by the experiences of Pavlov on the conditioned reflexes made by dogs. ... there are even practical instructions. Do you want to buy a good professional bulletproof vest? The right address is on page 374, just call them. You want to run away and do not want trouble with the "Missing Persons Unit"? Get in touch with the British and French offices listed on page 288 "offering their services—other literal quotation—to secret agents on the run, freelance spies in trouble. ... addresses and hiding secrets even for common criminals, bankrupt individuals and adventurers." Italy occupies hundreds of pages of the book, by the heroic Cesare Battisti down. Quite a few years of leads are present in this unusual publication: dozens and dozens of names followed by the description "Terrorist; Marxist" and in some cases even their address and phone numbers. With the exception of Adriano Sofri, a "Marxist from Lotta Continua," present at page 568.

If the Mafia does not exceed twenty lines of text in Muratori's book, a deluge of data is given, however, about the Golpe Borghese, Gladio (complete list of all the names that appeared in the various lists) and of course the Red Gladio, the official Freemasonry, P2 (no list given), the famous "Protection account." A long chapter deals with the "interpreters of Italian mysteries": De Lorenzo, Miceli, Maletti, Moro, Rumor, Gelli, et cetera. Finally, Dia, SISMI, the Sisde, the Cesis and other acronyms that have recently troubled the sleep of Carlo Azeglio Ciampi. Particularly meticulous recon-

---

19   Fidel Castro (1926-2016) was also a 33rd degree Freemason 33° Mason in the A.A.S.R. working under the auspices of the Gran Logia de Cuba.

struction of the claims of the mysterious Falange Armata. Bettino Craxi: "General Secretary of the Socialist Party, spied on by someone." Vatican Secret Service: "They are among the most active in the world" (with the corollary of the Vatican Museums: "Always been a good place for meetings of secret agents"). But for what ideals, all these spies will damn their body and soul? "Money: it is the backbone of the secret war." [20]

I believe that analyzing this side will reveal a lot more about who the Jesuits really are, the "Secret Chiefs" of international espionage: ***The Jesuits are all informers and their Azpeitia Central has an equal intelligence archive, if not superior, to that of the CIA."*** (FIG. 103) Maybe this will come as a total surprise to most people, but the Jesuits are in the end not only the New World Order's Backbone, but the inspiration for Nazism. Adolf Hitler's word on his close ties to the Jesuits were recorded in 1939 by Hermann Raus-chning, former national-socialist chief of the Danzig government: ***"I learned much from the Order of the Jesuits,"*** said Hitler, *"Until now, there has never been anything more grandiose, on the earth, than the hierarchical organization of the Catholic Church. I transferred much of this organization into my own party. ... I am going to let you in on a secret. ... I am founding an Order. ... In my 'Burgs' of the Order, we will raise up a youth which will make the world tremble."* According to Rauschning, Hitler then stopped his speech, abruptly saying: "I can't say anymore."

However, after the war, Walter Schellenberg, former chief of German counter-espionage, finished Hitler's speech, confirming Hitler's strong behind-the-scenes ties to the Vatican and the Jesuit Order: *"The S.S. organization has been constituted by Himmler according to the principles of the Jesuit Order. Their regulations and the spiritual exercises prescribed by Ignatius of Loyola were the model Himmler tried to copy exactly. Himmler's title as supreme chief of the S.S. was to be the equivalent to the Jesuit General and the whole structure and direction was a close imitation of the Catholic Church's hierarchical order."* [21]

In 1948, French writer **Frederic Hoffet** wrote: *"Hitler, Goebbels, Himmler and most of the members of the party's old guard were Catholics. It was not by accident that because of its chief's religion, the Nationalist-Socialist government was the most Catholic Germany ever had. This kinship between socialism and Catholicism is most striking if we study closely the propaganda methods and the interior organization of the party."* [22]

Quote by Hitler about Himmler: *"I can see Himmler as our Ignatius of Loyola."* [23]

Aldo Conchione, Gabriella Carlizzi, and Satanism of the NWO in the Vatican

I turned one day to my old friend, the Marquis Roberto Caldirola, a 33rd degree Freemason, and ex-**Gladio operative,** to ask him more about Satanism in the Vatican. He replied by talking about the late Aldo Conchione (who died under mysterious circumstances), and who was the central figure of a special tribute/exhibition that took place in Rome entitled *One week with James Bond.* It was dedicated to the aforementioned Spymaster, Giuseppe Muratori, after his death. Caldirola revealed to me that Conchione was also a former priest, defrocked in order to arrive at the top of the Italian intelligence services, a very unusual story that attracted my attention because of his apparent ties with

20   Conti Paolo, *L'enciclopedia degli spioni* August 13th 1993, *Corriere della Sera*, p. 19.
21   Hermann Rauschning, *Hitler m'a dit*, (Paris: Ed. Co-operation, 1939), pp.266, 267, 273.
22   http://vaticannewworldorder.blogspot.it/
23   ~Adolf Hitler: "Libres propos" (Paris: Flammarion, 1952), p.164.

FIG. 103 – Basilica of St. Ignatius of Loyola in Azpeitia. According to The Encyclopedia of Espionage by the late Giuseppe Muratori, who was one of the world's leading experts in the field, this place would be the Jesuit equivalent of the C.I.A. headquarters which is located in Langley, Virginia, and with an equal archive, if not bigger.

the Vatican, and some Masonic groups linked to Satanism. So to finally understand a bit more about Satanism in the Vatican beyond mere speculation, I started investigating **Aldo Conchione**, who as I mentioned, died under unclear circumstances in 2006. Caldirola told me the reason was an alleged blackmail operation involving the Vatican. Such a stunning affirmation by the Marquis was recorded by me on a small camera to guarantee the genuity of my research in the future. Conchione knew too much, and stupidly tried to blackmail the Vatican, asking them for 500 million euros to stay silent about a certain secret affair of unprecedented gravity related to the secret Satanic practices that some priests held both within the Vatican leonine walls, and near Castel Gandolfo. Shocking but true, this actually happened and still happens to this day, unfortunately.

I wondered what could have required his physical elimination, and Caldirola told me clearly that he "was bumped off" without receiving the 500 million euros he requested, and was found dead with foam coming out of his mouth (typical sign of poisoning), and his pants rolled up only above the right knee. This practice looked typically Masonic, and is usually implemented on an apprentice candidate during the more traditional and classic Masonic rituals, that symbolically signify the sense of compassion that will always be there to oversee his pursuit of knowledge. In this case it seems to me that there was no compassion for Conchione from his alleged Vatican killers, employed by Vatican Freemasonry. This detail and other characteristics far more gruesome, prove some sort of outside signal sent by the people who had eliminated him, to ensure that there would be no subsequent investigation by the judicial authorities and Italian police, who ignored Conchione's murder.

Gabriella Pasquali Carlizzi published an article that talked about Aldo Conchione on Sunday, March 14th, 2010. She died two months later. Carlizzi was a good investigative journalist and researcher of the many unsolved mysteries of Italy, including the brutal murder of a certain **Simonetta Cesaroni,** a young girl from Rome found in Via Poma on Tuesday, August 7, 1999. An unsolved case to this day which the 007, Aldo Conchione, proved in some way linked. A case which eventually will lead us directly into the maze of Vatican Satanism, and its Illuminati sects devoted to perverse practices and Devil worship. The late Gabriella Carlizzi died of an incurable disease, like a fast-moving cancer.

She wrote this article about Conchione knowing she had nothing to lose, and without fear of reprisals looming in the future. I must admit that Carlizzi, however eccentric in her ways, and at times too fundamentalist in her chaotic views of Freemasonry, was always ready to denounce the enemies of humanity, which she did until the last minute of her life with great courage, beyond the disease that unfortunately led to her premature death. I only spoke to her once, so I knew her only superficially, but some of her close collaborators have speculated about her death. The hospital where she died showed a friend of mine 12 different medical findings soon after her death, a very unusual thing indeed.

Carlizzi revealed that: *"In 2004 I was contacted by Aldo Conchione, publisher of the book written by Salvatore Volponi, Simonetta Cesaroni's boss. He told me many things, and we saw each other for a couple of years. One day he came to my house and when he was about to leave, expressed the following: 'If they have followed me, this is the last time we meet. They will kill even me.' It was the month of July, 2006. Conchione was found dead in August of that year. Many people ask me what idea I may have of this crime, and many will judge my idea as fanciful, or far-fetched. However, because I'm dying of cancer, I answer equally without fear of judgments from other people. I think Simonetta Cesaroni of Via Poma was working for the Intelligence services of the time on a 'private affair,' and that the documentation involved interested the dark sides of the Intel community, for deviant purposes."*

Simonetta's murder seems to have a strong link to the Emanuela Orlandi disappearance. Simonetta Cesaroni had discovered, almost by accident, in the archives of the same **A.I.A.G. (The Italian Association of Youth Hotels**), some confidential documents that bore witness to the alleged favors done by the association to the infamous Magliana Gang (*Banda della Magliana*) linked to the Vatican, the P2 Lodge, and of course Emanuela Orlandi's case.

In an interview with Conchione's old colleague, Alessandro De Vanni, (FIG. 104) a former Italian secret agent of the Italian Military Intelligence and a collaborator of the Central Intelligence Agency, that took place on **August 23, 1996**, where in addition to the interviewer, journalist Paolo Cantarelli, Ornella Mariani, and the same Gabriella Pasquali Carlizzi were present. Alessandro De Vanni described the true nature of Aldo Conchione and his job in this way:

Aldo Conchione is a senior officer of the Services.They are all characters that approach the person they need to involve, doing often the same game, to the subjects they care to involve in their operations, they promise them media contacts, implementing a fake press conference for them, organizing lunches, dinners. I can guarantee that instead they are all Freemasons connected to international Freemasonry. They have offices abroad, they are part of a homicidal group, that ultimately provide physical elimination of their victims. Aldo Conchione told me one night, that Fabrizio De Iorio was so ruthless as to rape his victims, after which he slowly tortured and killed them, dismembering the bodies, cutting them to pieces and throwing them into the Tiber. He told me that they were brought to the north of Rome, over the barrier, the dam, and there made to disappear forever. [24]

In short, the 007 Aldo Conchione operating for Italian Intelligence, was certainly somebody who knew a lot about the macabre ritual of his colleagues, relating to a mysterious international group of killers and their untold secrets operating in the shadow of the Vatican. In the end Conchione dared the impossible, blackmailing **the Vatican** and its

24   http://www.cieliparalleli.com/Politica/ustica-il-caso-taciuto-Paolo-cantarelli.html (site no longer available).

FIG. 104 – Alessandro De Vanni, the former Italian secret agent of SISMI, and collaborator of the Central Intelligence Agency.

intelligence services known as **The Entity.** As a result, Conchione the ex-priest and secret agent/assassin was poisoned. One can not blackmail the Vatican. You end up dead, that's for sure. Anyway, thanks to Conchione we also realized that unspeakable blood pacts and secret deals possibly connect the Vatican with professional groups of assassins, that of course belong to deviant Masonic lodges operating even inside the Vatican. Ties that go far beyond legality, and demonstrate, how sadism and perversion is present in the occult groups operating for the New World Order, dedicated to the physical elimination of their victims, implemented in the most terrible ways.

And here is an Open Letter to President Donald J. Trump (20 January, 2017) written by his Catholic supporters that I regard of great importance to understand the many doubts of traditional Catholics towards the Jesuits Pope and the Intelligence game being played now in the Vatican.

Dear President Trump:

The campaign slogan "Make America Great Again" resonated with millions of common Americans, and your tenacity in pushing back against many of the most harmful recent trends has been most inspiring. We all look forward to seeing a continued reversal of the collectivist trends of recent decades.

Reversing recent collectivist trends will, by necessity, require a reversal of many of the actions taken by the previous administration. Among those actions we believe that there is one that remains cloaked in secrecy. Specifically, we have reason to believe that a Vatican "regime change" was engineered by the Obama administration.

We were alarmed to discover that, during the third year of the first term of the Obama administration your previous opponent, Secretary of State Hillary Clinton, and other government officials with whom she associated proposed a Catholic "revolution" in which the final demise of what was left of the Catholic Church in America would be realized. [25] Approximately a year after this e-mail discussion, which was never intended to be made public, we find that Pope Benedict XVI abdicated under highly unusual circumstances and was replaced by a pope whose apparent mission is to provide a spiritual component to the radical ideological agenda of the international left. [26] The Pontificate of Pope Francis has subsequently called into question its own legitimacy on a multitude of occasions. [27]

During the 2016 presidential campaign we were astonished to witness Pope Francis actively campaigning against your proposed policies concerning the securing of our borders, and even going so far as to suggest that you are not a Christian. [28] We appreciated your prompt and pointed response to this disgraceful accusation. [29]

We remain puzzled by the behavior of this ideologically charged Pope, whose mission seems to be one of advancing secular agendas of the left rather than guiding the Catholic Church in Her sacred mission. It is simply not the proper role of a Pope to be involved in politics to the point that he is considered to be the leader of the international left.

While we share your stated goal for America, we believe that the path to "greatness" is for America to be "good" again, to paraphrase de Tocqueville. We understand that good character cannot be forced on people, but the opportunity to live our lives as good Catholics has been made increasingly difficult by what appears to be a collusion between a hostile United States government and a pope who seems to hold as much ill will towards followers of perennial Catholic teachings as he seems to hold toward yourself.

With all of this in mind, and wishing the best for our country as well as for Catholics worldwide, we believe it to be the responsibility of loyal and informed United States Catholics to petition you to authorize an investigation into the following questions:

– To what end was the National Security Agency monitoring the conclave that elected Pope Francis? [30]

– What other covert operations were carried out by U.S. government operatives concerning the resignation of Pope Benedict or the conclave that elected Pope Francis?

– Did U.S. government operatives have contact with the "Cardinal Danneels Mafia"? [31]

– International monetary transactions with the Vatican were suspended during the last few days prior to the resignation of Pope Benedict. Were any U.S. Government agencies involved in this? [32]

– Why were international monetary transactions resumed on February 12, 2013, the day after Benedict XVI announced his resignation? Was this pure coincidence? [33]

26   http://www.wsj.com/articles/how-pope-francis-became-the-leader-of-the-global-left-1482431940 ‡ Archived 11th December, 2016.

27   http://remnantnewspaper.com/web/index.php/articles/item/2198-the-year-of-mercy-begins ‡ Archived 11th December, 2016.

28   http://www.cnn.com/2016/02/18/politics/pope-francis-trump-christian-wall/ ‡ Archived 11th December, 2016.

29   https://www.donaldjtrump.com/press-releases/donald-j.-trump-response-to-the-pope ‡ Archived 11th December, 2016.

30   http://theeye-witness.blogspot.com/2013/10/a-compromised-conclave.html ‡ Archived 11th December, 2016.

31   http://www.ncregister.com/blog/edward-pentin/cardinal-danneels-part-of-mafia-club-opposed-to-benedict-xvi ‡ Archived 11th December, 2016.

32   http://www.maurizioblondet.it/ratzinger-non-pote-ne-vendere-ne-comprare/ ‡ Archived 11th December, 2016.

33   https://akacatholic.com/money-sex-and-modernism/ ‡ Archived 11th December, 2016.

– What actions, if any, were actually taken by John Podesta, Hillary Clinton, and others tied to the Obama administration who were involved in the discussion proposing the fomenting of a "Catholic Spring"?

– What was the purpose and nature of the secret meeting between Vice President Joseph Biden and Pope Benedict XVI at the Vatican on or about June 3, 2011?

– What roles were played by George Soros and other international financiers who may be currently residing in United States territory? [34]

We believe that the very existence of these unanswered questions provides sufficient evidence to warrant this request for an investigation.

Should such an investigation reveal that the U.S. government interfered inappropriately into the affairs of the Catholic Church, we further request the release of the results so that Catholics may request appropriate action from those elements of our hierarchy who remain loyal to the teachings of the Catholic Church.

Please understand that we are not requesting an investigation into the Catholic Church; we are simply asking for an investigation into recent activities of the U.S. Government, of which you are now the chief executive.

Thank you again, and be assured of our most sincere prayers.

Respectfully,

David L. Sonnier, LTC US ARMY (Retired)
Michael J. Matt, Editor of *The Remnant*
Christopher A. Ferrara (President of The American Catholic Lawyers Association, Inc.)
Chris Jackson, Catholics4Trump.com
Elizabeth Yore, Esq., Founder of YoreChildren

---

34   http://sorosfiles.com/soros/2013/03/soros-funded-catholic-groups-behind-african-socialist-as-next-pope.html ‡ Archived 11th December, 2016.

Chapter   VI

❦

Beneath the Vatican the Darkest Secrets are Hidden

Pope Montini the Freemason

Pope Montini, the Pope of the infamous Second Vatican Ecumenical Council, played a key role in the Masonic transformation of the Church even if he was a Freemason. There are still voices of dissent in Italian Freemasonry on Montini's actual Masonic membership. However Bishop Annibale Bugnini, who Paul VI entrusted with the "Liturgical revolution" of the council, (despite the earlier removal of the Bugnini by Roncalli, John XXIII), was a proven Freemason, as well as his bodyguard, Bishop Paul Marcinkus, later linked to the Lodge P2 and the Monte Carlo Lodge of Ezio Giunchiglia. Montini has left many traces of his Masonic links, as I will show you shortly, especially in art works dedicated to him. It is unfortunate that few have noticed such things except a few Catholic traditionalists. I would like to begin with the direct experience of Don Luigi Villa, who denounced them to the competent authorities in the Vatican. An episode of particular interest in his discovery is the five-pointed star on the hand of Paul VI, that was originally inserted in the "bronze door," made for the Second Vatican Council, present in the 12th section of the door, with its Council Fathers. However, while John XXIII and the other 5 Council Fathers were carved with the face looking forward, Paul VI's (on the far right) was carved in profile, so as to present, clearly visible, his left hand up, incidentally having on it a clear symbol of his belonging to Freemasonry: the **"Five-pointed Star,"** or **"Masonic Pentalfa."** (FIGS. 105, 106, 107)

Don Luigi Villa describes in his Trilogy the images in question in the following way:

> Shortly after the inauguration of the "new bronze door" of St. Peter's Basilica, the undersigned (Don Luigi Villa) went to see it. Watching it closely, I immediately noticed that Masonic sign on the back of the left hand of Paul VI. Then, immediately, I went to a Cardinal to report the matter. He assured me that he would proceed in inspecting it. In fact, when I went back, a short time later, returning to Rome, just to see the "bronze door," I noticed that the Masonic insignia on the back of the left hand of Paul VI had been scraped off. You could see only the red copper now instead. It was clear to me they realized they had been discovered, and those responsible for the fact scraped off the Masonic symbol of the hand, then,—as I saw later myself in another of my trips to Rome—they had replaced the N° 12 panel altogether with another

FIG. 105 – Original image of the 12th section of the bronze door dedicated to the Second Vatican Council taken by Don Luigi Villa from http://www.chiesaviva.org/don-luigi-il-vittorioso.html

FIG. 106 – The current representation in the new censored version, which has done away with all Masonic references. From the site http://www.vatican.va/archive/hist_councils/ii_vatican_council/index_it.htm

completely new one—the current—on which, however, they will not appear to have the same six figures of before, but only five, as everyone now can see.

At this point, Don Luigi decided to expose this in his literary work against Montini, and managed to highlight some very interesting data indeed. And I would like to say that he does this with a great sense of duty, despite the cover-up implemented by the Vatican in relation to Montini's close relation and fascination with Freemasonry. A secret they still want to cover up, even today. I do not always agree with Don Villa's totally Satanic vision of Freemasonry, I found it a bit too generalistic and confused, when this institution has a large presence of true Christians operating for the good of the world. The majority of members are victims of a system that at the top, is at times, ambiguous and false, just like the Vatican hierarchy itself. There is a good and bad side to Freemasonry, also the Jesuit influence on certain types of Freemasonry and their link with the Rosicrucians, or at least certain Rosicrucians is undeniable, and the link between Freemasonry and Western Monasticism is historically proven. Remember my dear readers, Freemasonry was born Christian, but unfortunately the elite transformed it into something of a hybrid, ready to create with its huge and influential network, a support to their growing **One World Religion project.** Don Villa was basically a good disciple of Padre Pio, a sort of secret agent of the future Saint, who as we know was a simple person, but for many of the faithful, someone on the frontline of the battle against evil and Satan. No wonder Saint Padre Pio was identified as the most dangerous enemy in the den of hypocrites that is Freemasonry in the Vatican, which has nothing to do with true Freemasonry.

Don Villa illustrates the heart of the problem when he writes: *"Now, the Church never had any uncertainty or doubt in its fight against Freemasonry; it was only with the advent of Vatican II, and especially with Paul VI, that this 'new attitude' reversed the previous position of the Magisterium of the Church, by adopting a more 'ecumenical' and 'liberal' position with Masonry arriving to the point of saying 'hope for peace between the two' A Masonic magazine reads: 'the Grand Master Gamberini, on the day of Montini's election to Pope, said: 'This is the man who does it for us!'"*

FIG. 107 – Closely framed image of Montini's Masonic symbol of the Five Pointed Star on his hand, inserted in the first version of the 12th section of the "bronze door" made to commemorate the Council Fathers of the Second Vatican Council.

And after the death of Pope Montini the "obituary," or better stated the eulogy, of the former Grand Master of Palazzo Giustiniani, Giordano Gamberini, on the *Masonic Magazine* was unequivocal: **"For us it is the death of the one who dropped the condemnation of Clement XII and his successors on us. It is the first time—in the history of modern Freemasonry—that the dying Head of the greatest Western religion was not in a state of hostility with the Freemasons."**

He concluded by making a shocking statement: **"For the first time, in history, the Freemasons can pay homage to the tomb of a pope, without ambiguity or contradiction."** Villa added:

There was a private letter, written by a Freemason, a friend of the famous French writer, Count Léon de Poncins, who was an expert on Masonic matters, and co-author of the famous book **The Occult War,** *where we read this sentence: "With Pius X and Pius XII, we Freemasons were able to do very little, but with Paul VI, we have won."... And what about the unusual gesture of November 13, 1964, when Paul VI*

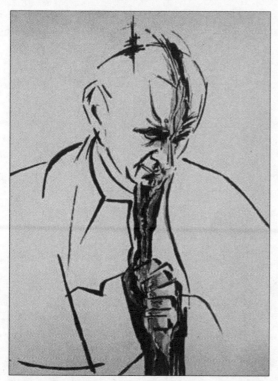

FIG. 108 – Ernst Gunter Hansing—"Paul VI in prayer" (1969). Tempera on paper, Brescia, Collection Art and Spirituality.

laid the triregnum, the high triple crown that symbolically laid claim to papal supremacy over all the kings of the earth, on the altar, definitively renouncing to it? ... A gesture, that was a supposed goal of the "French Revolution" and that binds in part with the findings of the Freemason Albert Pike, known reformer and Supreme Commander of the Ancient and Accepted Scottish Rite when he wrote: "The inspirers, the philosophers and historical leaders of the French Revolution had sworn to overthrow the 'CROWN' and 'TIARA' on the tomb of Jacques de Molay." Then Montini during his trip to the Holy Land in 1954, the Mount of Olives, in Jerusalem, embraced the Patriarch Orthodox Athenagoras I, who is said to be a Mason of the 33rd degree. In fact, on the eve of the close of Vatican II, they both took off their respective "Excommunications," launched in 1054, so as to make a "gesture of Brotherly Love."

The views that Montini had with the "Liberal Masonic plan" was not a coincidence for the late Don Villa, but can this be proven? Well the latest developments in Church policies implemented by Pope Francis seem to indicate Villa's worst fears might have actually materialized. However, let's go back to Montini and his connection with Freemasonry through art, exploring a "masterpiece" of occult mold based on him entitled "The Papacy," painted by Ernst Günter Hansing (1929 – 2011). (FIGS. 108 and 109) A great documentary still available online, was produced by **Ulrich Schmitz.** [1] Ernst Günter Hansing was a well-known painter of VIPs, and was also a member of the **Pontifical Equestrian Order of St. Gregory the Great,** an important order of chivalry of the Papal States and still one of the five pontifical orders of the Catholic Church, that precedes the Order of St. Sylvester. I know that this painting will leave you more perplexed with the presence of its occult symbolism. It is an unconventional portrait of Pope Paul VI, to which Ernst Günter Hansing, in the late 1960s and early '70s, dedicated several portraits, but on the contrary of other portraits dedicated to the pontiff, it was in fact the least known to the public, just because it was deemed inconvenient.

The *Smithsonian Magazine,* in their April, 1977 issue (pp. 60-61), wrote the following about this controversial work of art:

> Great patrons of the arts, the Renaissance popes, usually commissioned the artist in their employ—Raphael, Titian, Velazquez—to paint their portraits. The result

1 Schmitz U., Hansing E. G., "Papacy 1970" available at **http://www.youtube.com/ watch?v=9AEFbr2fm3I** ‡ Archived 11th December, 2016.

was some of the greatest paintings ever produced. Since then
the practice has fallen off (along
with the art of portraiture). So
it was with some surprise that
the world learned last fall that
a portrait had been painted of
Pope Paul VI, even though he
did not commission it, for that
matter, sit for it. Moreover, it
was in a semiabstract style unlike that of any previous papal portrait. The artist was a
42-year-old German named
Ernst Gunter Hansing. Pope
Paul did not at first respond to
having his picture painted with
any enthusiasm, but he later
relented. Hansing was given
a small studio in the building
that houses the Vatican gas station, and for the next two and
a half years, during 13 separate
visits to Rome, he observed his
subject from the front row at
papal audiences. The finished
portrait has been accepted by

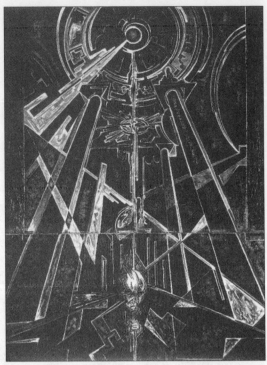

FIG. 109 – Ernst Gunter Hansing—"The
Papacy," painting on canvas from the early 1970s.

the Pope. His Holiness described the painting as "a mirror of the situation in the
Church today." Earlier, on seeing a working sketch, he made what was probably his
closest approach to art criticism. It was gracefully oblique: "One almost needs a new
philosophy to grasp the meaning of this in its context."

From the Nov. 8, 1971 issue of *TIME* magazine:

> Behind a locked door in Vatican City waits a present for Pope Paul VI that may
> conceivably please its recipient but has already shocked many who have seen pho-
> tographs of it. The gift is a large (about 71 ft. by 12 ft.) portrait of His Holiness,
> painted in a semi-abstract mode, in which the Pope's emaciated, suffering face
> and folded hands are the focus of splintering shafts of light. German Painter Ernst
> Guenter Hansing, 42, sketched his subject during twelve protracted stays at the
> Vatican over a period of 21 years. Though he never had a private sitting, he was
> given a front-row seat at papal ceremonies in which to work. "I wanted more than
> just a picture of a person," says Hansing, a Lutheran. "I wanted to show the ten-
> sion-fraught situation of the church, caught in a multiplicity of issues, as reflected
> in the countenance of the Pope."

The following is an interesting analysis of the Masonic and Demonic Symbolism in
the 1977 "Portrait" of Giovanni Montini/Paul VI made by occult researcher and author
Craig Heimbichner. I don't agree with all of it of course, as I don't like generalizations
in the case of Freemasonry, indicated as only evil, however I find that some points made
below by Craig seem to confirm the occult nature of the painting.

1. *Three pillars*

2. *Two columns*

3. *Cresent moon*

4. *Various Pentagrams*

5. *Sphynx at the top of the pillar*

6. *The columns and angles combine to form a square and compass*

7. *The point within the circle at the top is an old Illuminati symbol*

8. *Above Paul VI's head appears an abstract "eye in the triangle" I.E. the Eye of Horus or Set*

9. *A dagger is thrust in the papal tiara in the 30th Knight Kadosh Degree; here the pope clutches a dagger with a malevolent look.*

10. *Inverted crosses are Satanic, but so is Freemasonry*

In the cemetery of **Verolavecchia** in northern Italy, some members of the maternal line of Pope Montini's family (who are by the way of Jewish descent), are buried. On the grave of the mother of Paul VI, **Judith Alghisi,** there is **clear evidence of Masonic symbols.** (FIG. 110) It seems that the Second Vatican Council, between Pope Paul and the influential Jesuit **Cardinal Bea,** who was also of Jewish origin, was firmly in the hands of the influential Jewish Masonic world, and their new secret deal with the Jesuits. A deal made to implement the New World Order since the end of the Second World War. Going back to the fatal attraction of Paul VI to Freemasonry, which was confirmed to me more than once by different sources within Italian Freemasonry, that also mentioned a Masonic monument dedicated to Paul VI in northern Italy.

The Elixir Vitae

In 1962, **Maurice Pinay** wrote a mysterious book about the Vatican II. Here's an excerpt: *"What was accomplished was the most perverse conspiracy against the Holy Church. ... It will seem incredible to those who are ignorant of this conspiracy, which the anti-Christian forces continue to have. Within the Church hierarchy, we find a real 'fifth column' of agents controlled by Freemasonry, by Communism and the hidden power that governs them. These agents are found among those cardinals and bishops who form a kind of progressive wing within the Council."* [2] Under a pseudonym, Maurice Pinay wrote to a large group of clergy of various nationalities (mainly Italian but also South American), led by the well-known conservative Jesuit **Father Joaquin Saenz y Arriaga SJ,** who strangely enough opposed the council in contrast with the liberal agenda of fellow Jesuit Cardinal Bea. In 14 months, the group of Father Joaquin, compiled a detailed and huge dossier called *Conspiracy against the Church,* and then sent it to all the Council Fathers of the Second Vatican Council. This was done with the intention to initiate a discussion in the Church about what was happening. Unfortunately, they did not succeed in their mission to stop Cardinal Bea, his Masonic allies were intent on shaping the Second Vatican Council in the shadow of the **New World Order.** The text begins with these chapters:

– *Communism*

– *Freemasonry*

– *The synagogue of Satan*

– *The fifth column in the Church*

2   Maurice Pinay, *Complotto contro la Chiesa,* (Rome, IT: Linotypia - Tipografia Dario Detti - Via Girolamo Savonarola 1, 1962), p. 1.

In 1962, the first edition was given to the press in Rome, in the Italian language. It was followed by editions in Austria (January 1963), Venezuela (late 1963) and Mexico. **Archbishop Marcel François Lefebvre (1905-1991)**, who had even participated in the Second Vatican Council, was not however part of this trend of degeneration. His refusal to obey the Holy See arrived soon after the reformed Roman Missal published by Paul VI in 1969, with the apostolic constitution *Missale Romanum* of April 3, 1969, when Lefe-

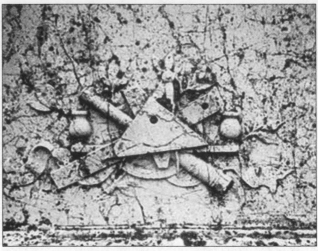

FIG. 110 – Detail showing Masonic symbols on the grave of the mother of Paul VI, Judith Alghisi. Taken from the site http://www.chiesaviva.org/don-luigi-il-vittorioso.html

bvre became dissatisfied with the end result, and announced to his seminarians in 1971, the decision to refuse to accept the post-conciliar liturgical reform for reasons of conscience. From that point on his loyalists gathered around the *Society of St. Pius X.*

Archbishop Lefebvre was somehow linked to the **Priory of Sion,** as suggested by Michael Baigent, Richard Leigh and Henry Lincoln in their book *Holy Blood, Holy Grail,* that raised various hypotheses, like the one that Pope John XXIII would have been a Grand Master of the Priory before he was elected Pope, and Archbishop Lefebvre would have been one of its members. On the Internet one finds also another author—anonymous as far as I could verify—who defends that Archbishop Lefebvre would have been the Great Master of the Priory of Sion, instead of Fr. Ducaud-Bourget. The whole history of the Priory of Sion is open to discussion, but various sources suggest it was either Ducaud-Bourget, Catholic rightist Archbishop Marcel Lefebvre, or some sort of triumvirate involving Plantard, an Italian (Merzagora), and an American banker (Gaylord Freeman, from Chicago First National). The "prieure documents" suggest there was a "schism" within the PoS in 1956, between some sort of "Anglo-American contingent" (apparently rightists connected to the **Shickshinny Knights of Malta**) and the main group. Whatever this "schism" was, it led the schismatics to register the group and its statutes with the French bureau of organizations, giving people their first traceable existence of the group in this year. Plantard claims he healed the "schism" and reunited the group. However to this day two separate lineages exist of the Priory worth mentioning, that seem to represent the two minds of the Order.

Philippe Chérisey's lineage, whose legitimate affiliation is now in the hands of Jean-Pierre Giudicelli de Cressac Bachelerie.

Gino Sandri 's wellknown lineage spread in different orders, and heir to the most controversial Pierre Plantard.

Lefebvre was connected to Chérisey's lineage, and although the Priory is a fairly recent creation, in some cases it is the repository of much older traditions, especially in the branch directed by my old friend **Jean Pierre Giudicelli,** (FIG. 111) who works with alchemy,

FIG. 111 – The author and his old friend Jean Pierre Giudicelli de Bressac de la Bachellerie in the headquarters of the Grande Loge Nationale Française in Nice (France) in May, 2016.

and is adamant that the true Priory resides in Andorra. As the **Brotherhood of Light** teaches *"The Truth Shall Set You Free,"* and this is for the true Master, is the touchstone of alchemy. But as an intellectual process it has no freeing power. True knowledge reveals its spiritual significance in the life of man. Such truth is freeing, and becomes a transmuting power, when the spirit is completely realized, and there is more than an intellectual perception or opportunity that needs to advance. When correct knowledge is passed on, it inevitably conditions reality for a higher and better method of living. This truth is the Philosopher's Stone—**the Elixir Vitae**. It is the fountain of eternal youth that has been sought in many lands. The alchemists, instead of exploring the earth in the hope of finding it already prepared by nature, undertook its manufacture. They diligently worked to prepare a fluid which they styled the elixir of life, in which to bathe would indefinitely prolong both youth and existence. With the philosopher's stone they would change other metals into gold. But to be able to enjoy this gold they must have life. To reap its advantages in fullness, old age must be defeated and death defied. Therefore, to perpetually rejuvenate themselves, they must prepare this most precious elixir. It was the policy of these alchemists, whatever they sought, to follow closely, though striving to accelerate the processes of nature. One of the biggest contemporary experts on the *Elixir Vitae* is my old friend, the aforementioned Grand Master and Grand Prior, Jean Pierre Giudicelli, a true Master of life, who I have the honor and the privilege to have known for many years.

Cardinal Siri

It is worth mentioning the strange events surrounding the alleged papal election of a dear friend to Marcel Lefebvre, Cardinal Giuseppe Siri, who renounced his papacy in 1958 in favor of another Cardinal, the Freemason, Giuseppe Angelo Roncalli. This unusual event was kept secret, but confirmed in 2003 by the investigative journalist and FBI consultant **Paul L. Williams,** in his now extremely rare book *The Vatican Exposed: Money, Murder, and the Mafia.* Williams wrote that he has reviewed a secret FBI report dated April 10th, 1961 that clearly states that the U.S. intelligence services were aware of the fact that Cardinal Siri had been duly elected Pope on the 26 of October, 1958. The secret dossier called **"Cardinal Siri"** was compiled by the **Federal Bureau of Investigation** in 1961 for the U.S. State Department, and seems to have been briefly declassified on 28 February, 1994, right at the deadline of the classification, thanks to the law *Freedom of Information Act.* Paul L. Williams was able to access the document that later seems to have disappeared permanently.[3] Williams, considered

FIG. 112 – Cav. Fortunato Luciano Sciandra, Leo Lyon Zagami, and Father Walter Trovato, Honorary Canon of the SMOM and the last seminarian of Cardinal Siri.

by some an unreliable source, is the only journalist to capture three first-place Keystone Press Awards in three different categories in the same year. He has penned articles for major news outlets, including *USA Today, The Wall Street Journal,* and *National Review.* A regular guest on such news outlets as *Fox News, NPR,* and *MSNBC,* Williams wrote celebrated articles concerning Islamic paramilitary compounds, such as Islamberg, that have been established throughout the country and remains an overall a popular speaker on the Christian circuit. In 2010, he was quoted as saying he had become "a pariah in the publishing world."[4] Prior to this, he served for seven years as a consultant to the FBI about terrorist and mafia criminal organizations.[5] Williams has even been known internationally in the field of security for avoiding an attack on the Canadian parliament and the Canadian Prime Minister, however it seems that the alleged FBI report that documented the papal election of Cardinal Siri is completely untraceable, and, therefore, is not verifiable, and Paul Williams when urged to show this document always refused to do so. On another occasion, the same Williams was sued by McMaster University in Hamilton, Canada, for defamation and for spreading false news. The publishing house that had published his books had to apologize in the end to the university, admitting that Williams' claims had, indeed, no verifiable sources. In any case, this report on the supposed papal election of Siri, which still remains a mystery, being perhaps reclassified as top secret, is something that can unfortunately happen sometimes. In this alleged FBI version of the events, Siri would have been legitimately elected Pope and would have even accepted the election initially, and even chose the name Gregory XVII, but was utimately forced to renounce to the papacy because of his traditional position often in line with Lefebvre. True or not true, the Second Vatican Council which arose from Pope Roncalli election in 1958, and Pope Montini in 1963, was truly disastrous for the Church. The enemy was literally able to change the Church to favor its nascent ecumenism, like with Pope Francis, who is clearly a globalist and pro-Islamic Pope, which he promotes seemingly every day.

3   https://it.wikipedia.org/wiki/Ipotesi_sull'elezione_papale_di_Giuseppe_Siri ‡ Archived 11th December, 2016.
4   http://ibloga.blogspot.it/2010/01/american-paul-williams-being-tried-in.html ‡ Archived 11th December, 2016.
5   http://www.coasttocoastam.com/guest/williams-paul/6543 ‡ Archived 11th December, 2016.

FIG. 113 – Cardinal Siri, as the well-informed **Pope Gregory XVII** *at the conclave of 1958.*

There is also a **diabolical synchronicity** linked to the name chosen by Siri, **Gregory XVII**, perhaps a co-incidence, but surely a very strange one, and liable to create confusion about the identity of the true Pope elected in 1958. The fact that twice in the period immediately following the Second Vatican Council, due to some revelatory visions of a "Divine nature," two eccentric characters abused, without any real authority, the name of Gregory XVII, appointing themselves as anti-popes through a medium. It is pretty weird, and as many of you know from my writings, such practices are often the gateway to demonic possession. The first claimant was the Canadian **Jean-Gaston Tremblay (1928 – 2011)**, from the schismatic Catholic community, leader of the Apostles of Infinite Love, developed in collaboration with a former French priest, Michel Collin, ex-communicated by Pope Pius XII in 1951, for having once appointed himself as Pope with the name of Clement XV, after receiving a message from the Virgin Mary. It was his deputy **Jean-Gaston Tremblay,** to self-appoint with the name in question. This happened after having a mystical revelation in 1967, claiming to be the legitimate successor despite Pope Paul VI, when Pope Montini was still alive and well at the time. A few years later, the strange phenomenon was repeated by **Clemente Dominguez y Gómez (1946 – 2005).** In May 1976, Domínguez lost his vision in a car accident. He claimed further visions, including visions from Jesus, who he claimed told him: *"You shall be the Peter to come, the Pope who will consolidate the Faith and the Church in her integrity, who shall battle against heresy with great power, for legions of Angels shall assist you ... Great Pope Gregory, Glory of the Olives ..."* He also claimed that Christ had named him His sub-Vicar, with the automatic right of succession to the papacy after Pope Paul VI. On 6 August 1978, Pope Paul VI died and Domínguez claimed the papacy, proclaiming himself *Pope Gregory XVII.*

All this sounds crazy, but it is part of a devilish syncronicity. As the duly elected Pope, Cardinal Giuseppe Siri could never carry out his mission, and his name was instead put into disrepute. In fact, even **Wikipedia** has the courage to include in the list of anti-popes naming Cardinal Siri as Pope Gregory XVII, you can check for yourself at: *Other claimants to the name 'Pope Gregory XVII.*[6]

The ultimate confirmation that Cardinal Giuseppe Siri was actually made Pope were given to me by his last seminarian Monsignor **Walter Trovato,** (FIG. 112) a chaplain of the State Police and Honorary Canon of the Sovereign Order of Malta. A singular figure who in 2010, created a movement for the defense of the crucifix inspired by the late Licio Gelli, who described the project in this way: *"This is my new battle and the color chosen for the symbol refers to the sea, the sky and the apron of the Madonna, the rest is inspired by Saint Francis and the arrows represent the cardinal points."*

I have met several times with Walter Trovato, ending inevitably with a mention of Cardinal Siri, (FIG. 113) who Father Walter Trovato got to know very well as his last seminarian. And I guarantee you that the first thing I asked him about when we got to talking

6   https://en.wikipedia.org/wiki/Clemente_Dom%C3%ADnguez_y_G%C3%B3mez ‡ Archived 11th December, 2016.

was the election history of Cardinal Siri becoming Pope on October 26, 1958, (FIG. 114) and if it was true or false what Dr. Paul L. Williams (FIG. 115) asserted. To my astonishment, father Walter without hesitation and with his classic smile, not only confirmed the story was true, but also added that almost the same thing happened in the following election in1963, the one that brought to the papal throne Cardinal Montini as Paul VI. Siri had in fact achieved once again

FIG. 114 – The white smoke from the Vatican for Cardinal Siri on 26 October, 1958.

the majority of votes said Father Walter, confirming the fact that Cardinal Siri did take the name of Gregory XVII. So it would appear that Siri was actually elected Pope twice, and twice he was forced to give up his post by Vatican Freemasonry. The French Masonic magazine *Humanism*, No. 186 of 1989, reports a meeting between the future Pope, Msgr. Roncalli, and Alexandre Chevalier (who became Grand Master of the atheist Grand Orient of France in 1965), in which they reveal the hypothesis that the liberal *Lodge L'Etoile Polaire* (called the *Atelier*), was possibly at the origin of the Second Vatican Council. Let me remind you that the Grand Orient of France, is the enemy of "Regular" Freemasonry, especially because of its dangerous diversion from the principles of True Masonry.

The Vatican Mafia 666: obey or die!

In 1958, before the conclave, Cardinal Siri was the designated successor of Pope Pius XII, but shortly before the conclave, in September 1958, the journalist and author of the book *Nichitaroncalli*, Franco Bellegrandi, received confidential information showing the sudden change of course in the Vatican: *"I was in a car with a person who I knew was a high-ranking Mason who had contacts with the Holy See."* He told me: *"The next pope will not be Cardinal Siri, contrary to what you whisper in some Roman circles, because he is considered too authoritarian. A Pontiff prone to a conciliatory attitude will be elected; and has already been chosen, it is the Patriarch of Venice, Cardinal Angelo Roncalli."* Bellegrandi replied by asking: *"Are there elements of Freemasonry in the conclave?"* The Mason interlocutor promptly told him *"Certainly, the Church is in our hands."* After a short silence he said again, *"No one can say with certainty where the head of Freemasonry is. He lives hidden."*[7]

The mysterious events at the conclave of 1958, had as its aim the achievement of the objective that the para- Masonic organization B'nai–B'rith was established for members of the Jewish faith alone. It seems that before the King of the Jews could establish His kingdom in the world, it would be necessary that the Pope is deposed from his seat. See in this regard

---

7   Franco Bellegrandi , *NICHITA RONCALLI CONTROVITA DI UN PAPA,* (Rome, IT: Edizioni Internazionali di Letteratura e Scienze, 1994) p. 62.

FIG. 115 – Investigative journalist Dr. Paul L. Williams.

the book entitled *The Talmud Unmasked,*[8] by Reverend I. B. Pranaitis, who was a great scholar of all Talmudic texts. Do not forget that if we are to believe the many testimonials on the election of Siri to Pope, this would lead to a sad observation, namely that the popes from John XXIII, are in fact anti-popes decided by the New World Order, including the current Pope Bergoglio. Although on the list, I don't consider the poor Pope John Paul I, born **Albino Luciani (1912 – 1978)**, who I think is legitimate and a victim of his position, was killed by Masonic mercenaries. Pope Luciani was killed on the 33rd day of his pontificate, a thesis shown in part by the author **David Yallop Anthony**, in his bestseller *In the name of God,* concerning the possible death of Pope John Paul I. The interesting thing is that the same Cardinal Siri, while believing the natural cause of the death of Pope Luciani as he explained in a private seminar in Genoa during a dialogue with a group of seminarians in 1987, saw him as a person too weak to deal with that environment. In 1987, during the television show called *Yellow*, there was an interview with one of the private secretaries of John Paul I, Don Diego Lorenzi, who asserted that the night before his death, around 6:30 PM, the Pope had received in a private audience the Vatican State Secretary, Cardinal **Jean-Marie Villot** also a Freemason, dismissing him an hour later, at 7:30 PM. At the end of the hearing, however, a strange thing happened, and Luciani would complain to Lorenzi of symptoms of a sickness in terms of aches and pains in the middle of the chest, with a strong sense of weight and oppression. Secretary of State **Cardinal Villot, Masonic name Jeanni,** Lodge number 041/3, initiated in a Zürich Lodge on August 6th, 1966, seems to be in tune with the 666 current, that of the Antichrist, which led him inexorably to act as the evil hitman in the murder of the poor Pope, and not anti-pope, John Paul I. Maybe if Pope Luciani had been alive today today we would not be in this situation both inside the Vatican, with the recent scandals linked to *Vatileaks* 1 and 2, and outside the Vatican, with the so-called economic crisis created by the unethical and truly satanic system implemented by the international banks. In Europe, each coin of one and two Euro has in fact 6 stars, 6 lines and 6 stars, which is precisely 666, the mark of the Beast. Another victory of the devil and evil in this ignorant civilization full of diabolic hypocrisy and materialism, although gradually the powerful of the ground floor will show their Satanic nature in the coming years more and more, and eventually you will meet the first of the fallen angels.

A brief tale of a Masonic human sacrifice piloted by the Vatican

To further understand the role and the power of Freemasonry in the Vatican, I will speak now of Carmine Pecorelli, better known as **Mino Pecorelli (1928 – 1979)**, (FIG. 116) a member of the mysterious lodge Propaganda 2, who courageously released the only detailed list of Vatican Freemasons ever published. (FIG. 117) Mino was

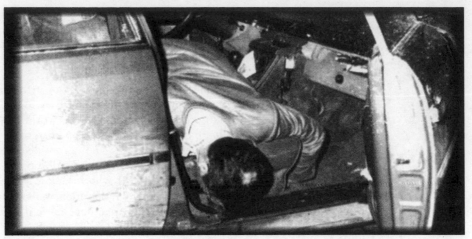

FIG. 116 – P2 Freemason Mino Pecorelli killed in his car on March 20, 1979 by a group of Vatican assassins, headed by gangster Massimo Carminati of the infamous Magliana Gang.

a journalist in charge of political and social inquiry, with his own very unique way. For this purpose Mino Pecorelli created the *Osservatore Politico,* better known by his initials *OP,* a controversial monthly newsletter in which he published, up to a few hours until his terrible murder, which occurred on March 20, 1979. Certainly his last article was a strong denunciation towards a certain type of Freemasonry, and is still precious testimony of the true causes which undoubtedly brought him to his tragic death. In his last article he wrote referencing Freemasonry:

> *Gentlemen and clergymen increase their membership, bloodline princes did not disdain to become its Grand Masters. ... In the premise of* **The Constitution of the Freemasons (London, 1723)** *Reverend James Anderson wanted to prove the ideal descent of Masonry from Pythagoreans, the Essenes, the followers of Zoroaster, by the Chaldeans or even by the ancient Egyptians and Chinese. But these connections with theories and institutions go so far back in time, beyond a common trend in the mystery and symbolism, do not help to explain the Masonic origins. As well as it does not help the filiation established by the Templars, the connections with the medieval heretics, with the Renaissance academies, with the so-called Charter of Cologne, with the Rosicrucians of the seventeenth century. More reliable research on the descent from previous guilds, especially builders, from which names and rites would then be passed to a speculative association.*

So you can notice from his writing that Mino Pecorelli's position towards Masonry was a very pragmatic and traditional one, indeed. He also wrote in the same article that *"Freemasonry was called The Society of Jesus of the Enlightenment."* However, Pecorelli was dealing with irregular Freemasonry and untold rules and compromises at the heart of the Vatican, not your average lodge problems. I wonder if he knew this when he wrote: *"English Freemasonry wanted to establish itself outside and above political and religious fanaticism struggles, and with such commitment, wanted to enlight tolerance."* But Pecorelli found out there was little tolerance for him in Freemasonry, especially after he exposed the infamous Freemasons operating in the Vatican. Strangely enough at the end of this otherwise Masonic article, that at times seems more of an essay, (FIG. 118 and 119) Pecorelli mentioned the name of somebody who probably wanted to stay secret. I am talking about **Antonio Viezzer,** colonel from the Italian Military Intelligence, and

FIG. 117 – The historic cover of OP dedicated to Vatican Freemasonry entitled **THE VATICAN GRAND LODGE.**

a big player of the Intelligence game of those days. Some sources have indicated it was Viezzer himself, who actually arranged with the infamous Magliana Gang (*Banda della Magliana*), Pecorelli's murder. As *Wikipedia* writes in regards to the Magliana Gang:

> *The Banda della Magliana was involved in criminal activities during the Italian years of lead (anni di piombo). The Italian justice tied it to other criminal organizations such as the Cosa Nostra, Camorra or 'Ndrangheta, but most importantly also to neofascist activists such as the Nuclei Armati Rivoluzionari (NAR), responsible for the 1980 Bologna massacre, the secret services (SISMI) and political figures such as Licio Gelli, grand-master of the freemasonic lodge Propaganda Due (P2). Along with Gladio, the NATO clandestine anti-communist organization, P2 was involved in a strategy of tension during the years of lead which included false flag terrorist attacks. These ties, underground compared to their standard (i.e. "run-of-the-mill") activities (drug dealing, horserace betting, money laundering, etc.), have led the Banda to be related to the political events of the conflict which divided Italy into two during the Cold War, and in particular to events such as the 1979 assassination of journalist Carmine Pecorelli.* [9]

This was an assassination commissioned by Italian politician and Opus Dei agent, **Giulio Andreotti**, Grand Master of a secret Illuminati sect called "**The Ring.**" The only person who tried to stop Pecorelli from being assassinated by "The Ring," was Pecorelli's Worshipful Master, **Licio Gelli**, (FIG. 120) who tried several times to convince Andreotti to not proceed with his murderous plan against Mino Pecorelli, warning him about the danger of killing one of his own Freemasons. This is something that went against the unwritten rules and codes of the New World Order. However, even in the years following his brutal murder, Pecorelli's memory was persecuted with terrible accusations and infamies, whose family never received any true justice for his death. In fact Giulio Andreotti, and Mafiosi Gaetano Badalamenti, initially charged with his murder in 2003, were completely acquitted. In 1999, gangster **Massimo Carminati** of the infamous Magliana Gang (the assassin who actually shot him), was proclaimed innocent, becoming later on one of the key figures of the so-called **Mafia Capitale** scandal in Rome, that involved in recent years, a network of corrupt relationships between politicians and criminals in the Italian capital, that misappropriated money destined for city services. I know this all sounds very Italian, but unfortunately this is why the administration of the city of Rome is so impossibly inept today, and tourists from all over the world can see rubbish and crime at every corner. The Vatican gangsters are to blame for this situation, that's for sure.

The Knights of Colombus, the Knights of Malta, and the Jesuits

Thomas D. Williams, PH.D. wrote in an article for *Breitbart.com* in November, 2016:

Cardinal Raymond Burke insisted that Pope Francis must clarify serious doctrinal doubts arising from his teaching letter, Amoris Laetitia, or the Cardinal will be forced to initiate "a formal act of correction of a serious error." ... In September, four top Catholic cardinals including Burke wrote a private letter to Pope Francis asking him to clarify five serious doctrinal doubts proceeding from his 2016 apostolic exhortation Amoris Laetitia (The Joy of Love) concerning Holy Communion for the divorced and remar-

FIG. 118 – The cover of the last number OP, YEAR II—11, released March 20, 1979, the day of Pecorelli's murder dedicated to the military–industrial complex (MIC).

ried, the indissolubility of marriage, and the proper role of conscience. When the Pope failed to reply to the Cardinals' letter, they proceeded to publish it online on Nov. 14, hoping to solicit a response. In an interview with Edward Pentin of the National Catholic Register, Burke said that although it is "quite rare," Catholic tradition allows for the practice of correction of the Roman Pontiff, something that may become necessary.

In recent years in the Vatican, there has been a titanic clash between **Opus Dei**, the **Knights of Columbus** (commonly referred to as **K of C**), and their boys in the **Sovereign Military Order of Malta** (commonly referred to as **SMOM**), competing for influence over the Vatican's spiritual and financial assets. Carl Anderson, 13th supreme knight of the Knights of Columbus, was appointed in 2009 by Pope Ratzinger to a five-year term on the board of supervisors for the Institute for Works of Religion (IOR), also known as the Vatican Bank. This was a period that saw various scandals and ultimately the resignation of Pope Benedict XVI, after the Vatican bank's board had Gotti Tedeschi, from the Opus Dei, removed from his role as president of the IOR in 2012, with a communiqué signed by the same Carl Anderson which was generally seen as an unprecedentedly harsh document in the history of the Holy See. The Knights of Columbus, though only founded in 1882, with their headquarters in Connecticut in some remote abbey or church, boasts a wealth of $17 billion, and 1.8 million members. In an article by the Italian Journalist Marco Lillo, posted in the Italian newspaper, *Il Fatto Quotidiano* (07/06/2012), entitled *The Cold War between Opus Dei and U.S. Lobby*, we find this description for the Knights

FIG. 119 – Opening page of Pecorelli's last article / report on Freemasonry, published in the last issue of OP, released the day of his assassination.

of Columbus referred to as: "A sort of brotherhood similar to the institution of Freemasonry, which nevertheless has its own task to cope with the increased weight of Masons in the Church." This statement is only partly true, but let's focus on the origins of the Knights of Columbus, to understand who they are and who is behind them, and behind their Supreme Leader Carl Anderson.

The Knights of Columbus was founded by **Father Michael J. Mc-Givney (1852 – 1890)**, (FIG. 121) the American son of Irish emigrants, and trained by the Jesuits at Saint Mary College in Montreal, Canada. In an excellent biography by Douglas Brinkley and Julie M. Fenster entitled *Father Michael McGivney and American Catholicism* (HarperCollins, 2006), it stressed the fact that he wanted to become a Jesuit at all costs. So Father Michael wanted to become a Jesuit, but then for some "strange reason" he became instead the classic priest of a small church in some remote town that somehow creates one of the most powerful organizations in the Catholic Church. There must be a specific project that made this man and his creation, the Knights of Columbus, so influential in less than a hundred years, giving them in recent years the possibility to control the much older order of the Knights of Malta. The Jesuit connection is, of course, crucial to our history, as Michael J. McGivney had been trained to become a future Jesuit priest, and it can't be found, in any publication, that he actually didn't become one.

Perhaps his mission for the Company of Jesus was different, how it often happens for the Jesuits. Discretion and camouflage presented him to the world as a "simple" secular priest, but he certainly was more of a Jesuit in his mindset and spirituality. The Knights of Columbus is one of the Orders in charge of the New World Order, and it is good to immerse ourselves in a deeper study, even if Jeb Bush, one of its better known members, fortunately didn't make it to the White House. The symbolism used by the Knights of Columbus seems to me to be pretty obvious, and overtly fascist. They are known by the initials **K** which stands for **Knights**—and **C**, that is **Columbus**, (FIG. 122) who inspired them, and was led, as we know from recent studies, in his voyage to the Americas, by secret maps put together centuries earliers by the Knights Templar. They are considered the long arm of the Catholic Church, and the true head of the Knighthood is not Anderson, still an influential figure, but behind him, according to some American researchers, the General of the Jesuits is concealed. Therefore, the Knights of Columbus would only be mere executors of the Jesuit agenda for America and the rest of the world, where they act using as their henchmen the Sovereign Military Order of Malta. Of this I have had confirmations both in my research and in my personal experience with them, and the Jesuits. The skull and crossbones that appears in ritual clothing of the Knights of Columbus in their Chapters (their lodges) is very eloquent indeed, (FIG. 123) and the Bush family, which as you know is involved with the management of the Order of Skull and Bones, one of the most infamous and discussed U.S. secret societies (which has its headquarters at Yale University), is directly involved, although they are

FIG. 120 – Giulio Andreotti and Count Licio Gelli.

Protestants, with the Knights of Columbus. Jeb "the low energy guy" who has unsuccessfully tried to achieve the presidential nomination, was named Knight of the third degree Knights of Columbus in 2004, and his brother George W. Bush, maintains close ties with the former Supreme Knight of the Knights **Virgil Dechant the twelfth Supreme Knight of the Knights of Columbus from January 21, 1977 to September 30, 2000** (George W. Bush admitted this at the 132nd annual Convention of the order.) So are the Knights of Columbus and Freemasonry compatible? Paul F. Boller, Jr. and John George write in *They Never Said It: A Book of Fake Quotes and Misquotes, & Misleading Attributions*:

> *Sometimes, those seeking to encourage hatred and dissent try to ferment trouble between groups whom they think are, or should be, "natural enemies." This tactic can garner interest but in the end, it is always revealed as a hate tactic. Such have been the attempts at pitting the honorable Catholic religious fraternity, the Knights of Columbus, against Freemasonry. A bogus Knights of Columbus oath was circulated in the early 1900s as an anti-Catholic tactic designed to inflame Protestants and others. Although branded by a U.S. Congressional Committee in 1913 as a fake used by American bigots, the bogus oath was used against Democratic candidate Alfred E. Smith in the 1928 presidential campaign and again against John F. Kennedy, in 1960, in the West Virginia Democratic primary. This oath resurfaces from time to time to be used by—strangely enough—individuals whose hatred for the Catholic Church seems exceeded only by their hatred for Freemasonry. The fake oath reads:* "I do promise and declare that I will, when opportunity presents, make and wage relentless war, secretly and openly, against all heretics, Protestants and Masons, as I am directed to do, to exterminate them from the face of the whole earth; and that I will spare neither age, sex, nor condition, and that I will hang, burn, waste, boil, flay, strangle, and bury alive those infamous heretics; rip up the stomachs and wombs of their women, and crush their infants' heads against the walls in order to annihilate their execrable race." *The Knights of Columbus organization has a proud history. There are a number of Masons who are also involved members of the K of C and it is not unusual for K of C Councils and Masonic Lodges to share an annual 'Fellowship Breakfast' or other activities in the interests of fraternalism.* [10]

10   See. Paul F. Boller, Jr. and John George, *They Never Said It: A Book of Fake Quotes and Misquotes, &*

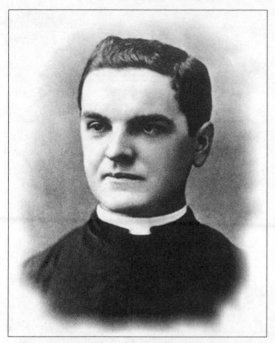

FIG. 121 – Father Michael J. McGivney, the founder of the Knights of Columbus (1852 – 1890).

Both the SMOM and the K of C were crucial in their support to Republican politics in recent decades. George W. Bush would never have become President without rigging the elections, thanks to his brother Jeb, who as I mentioned earlier, is a member of the Knights of Colombus. Donald J. Trump has the full support of part of the K of C, and the SMOM, for his presidential project, but with Donald J. Trump, the New World Order will have their biggest challenge to date. The Vatican seems to be reacting, waging a war against the SMOM, suddenly trying to limit their power and sovereignty. This means that when the Masonic Brothers are not in line with the Jesuit agenda, like in the case of their support of Trump, they are immediately restricted with some excuse. So let's see what has happened in recent months to the Order of Malta, always keeping in mind that the Knights of Columbus are the real controllers of the Order, and that many of them are Freemasons, as leading experts Paul F. Boller, Jr. and John George have stated in their work also cited by *Masonic Info*. [11]

Has a war against President Trump reached the Knighthoods and Freemasonry? In January, 2017 the *Catholic Herald* writes shocking news that involves the Knights of Malta:

> *The Knights of Malta, the ancient Catholic lay order, is refusing to cooperate with a Vatican investigation into the sacking of a top official over a condom scandal—and is warning its members to toe the line if they choose to speak with investigators. In a statement released on Tuesday, the Knights called the investigation legally "irrelevant" and aimed at limiting its sovereignty. It insisted that the ousting of its grand chancellor, Albrecht von Boeselager, was an act of internal governance that in no way involves religious superiors. The order told its members that if they speak with Vatican-appointed investigators, they cannot contradict the decision of the order's leadership to replace Boeselager. Boeselager was suspended on December 8 after he refused a demand by the top Knight, Fra' Matthew Festing, to resign over revelations that the order's charity branch distributed tens of thousands of condoms in Burma under his watch. Church teaching forbids the use of artificial contraception; Boeselager has said he didn't know about the condom distribution program and eventually stopped it when he learned of it.* [12]

Misleading Attributions, (Oxford, UK: Oxford University Press, 1989).
11   http://www.masonicinfo.com/kofc.htm ‡ Archived 11th January, 2017.
12   http://www.catholicherald.co.uk/news/2017/01/11/knights-of-malta-refuse-to-assist-irrelevant-papal-probe/ ‡ Archived 11th January, 2017.

So what is happening in the Knights of Malta as a result of this new confrontation between the different factions of the elite? It has emerged that during a meeting between Pope Francis and Cardinal Burke in November 2016, about the scandal of the Knights of Malta distributing condoms and oral contraceptives in Africa, **the Holy Father instructed Cardinal Burke to "clean out" Freemasonry from the order**. The Holy Father gave this order to Cardinal Burke in his role as patron of the Knights of Malta, by papal appointment. The Vatican journalist Edward Pentin revealed details of Pope Francis' concerns about the influence of Freemasons on the Knights of Malta:

FIG. 122 – The symbol of the Knights of Columbus also known as the K of C.

> Hope that the contraceptive scandal would be addressed came on Nov. 10, when Cardinal Burke was received in private audience by Pope Francis. During that meeting, the Register has learned, the Pope was "deeply disturbed" by what the cardinal told him about the contraceptive distribution. The Pope also made it clear to Cardinal Burke that he wanted Freemasonry "cleaned out" from the order, and he demanded appropriate action. The concern was followed up by a Dec. 1 letter to Cardinal Burke, in which the Register has learned that the Holy Father underlined the cardinal's constitutional duty to promote the spiritual interests of the order and remove any affiliation with groups or practices that run contrary to the moral law.

Edward Pentin also reported that:

> The ongoing wrangle, which Vatican Secretary of State Cardinal Pietro Parolin has described as an **"unprecedented crisis,"** first became public after the grand master of the Knights of Malta, Fra' Matthew Festing, dismissed Albrecht Freiherr von Boeselager as grand chancellor (the order's third-ranking official) on Dec. 6, accusing him of being ultimately responsible for the distribution of contraceptives through the order's humanitarian agency, Malteser International. [13]

So Boeselager was dismissed as grand chancellor following an internal investigation by the Knights of Malta, but the situation is still chaotic in the Order of Malta and it is the reason why the head of the Knights of Malta, Fra' Matthew Festing agreed with Pope Francis' request to resign from his post at the end of January, 2017. For some experts it is not clear why Pope Francis specifically identified Freemasonry as a problem in his response to the evidence presented by Cardinal Burke during the November, 2016 meeting, but the truth is that the Jesuits and Pope Francis know very well who is pulling the strings behind the Knights of Malta. That is, of course, their own creation, the Knights of Columbus, who are full of influential people in the Church, and the Jesuits in particular, recluted amongst Freemasonry, and now want to prevent them from staying within both worlds. With the

13　　http://www.ncregister.com/daily-news/disorder-in-the-order-of-malta ‡ Archived 11th January, 2017.

FIG. 123 —Members of a Chapter of the Knights of Columbus in New York. Note the skull and cross bones present in the ritual clothing of one of the members.

election of Donald J. Trump, Pope Francis and his Jesuits are basically in front of a growing Masonic rebellion within the New World Order. Already during his in-flight press interview back in July, 2013 Pope Francis expressed his first concerns about the influence of Freemasons on the Church: *"The problem is not having this [homosexual] orientation. No, we must be brothers and sisters. The problem is lobbying for this orientation, or lobbies of greed, political lobbies, Masonic lobbies, so many lobbies. This is the most serious problem for me."* [14]

In all this mess made up of secret societies and knighthoods there is also **The International Order of Alhambra.** (FIG. 124) This pseudo-Muslim Order is what the **Shriners** are to Freemasonry. They even wear fez hats like the Shriners, but they are white instead of red. We are now in full swing with the era of the *Antichrist,* that will soon be fully revealed to the world in the shape of a man. [15] An era where nothing is as it appears, because Satan for the Illuminati is actually what you define today as an alien entity. Remember the words of UFO expert Dr. Jacques Vallee: *"What the public learns about the [UFO] phenomena comes from that small portion of the facts that has been preselected by believers to promote enthusiastic support for the extraterrestrial theory."* However despite efforts to control what you know about UFOs, the occasional warning does leak out. A few years ago, a former head of the Armed Forces helped to form a pressure group, warning of the Satanic nature of many unidentified flying objects. Admiral of the Fleet **Lord Hill-Norton**, Chief of Defence Staff, 1971-73, was involved with UFO Concern, worried that some UFO encounters are **"definitely antithetical to orthodox Christian belief."** The Rev. Paul Inglesby, a sub-deacon of the Orthodox church, who was the secretary of UFO Concern, said the truth about UFOs had been suppressed for many years. He had never seen a UFO himself but knew many who had. **"It is what they do and the messages that come from them are anti-Christian, or demonic."**

Gordon Creighton, a Buddhist who edits *Flying Saucer Review*, said the group's founders were right to be concerned: **"I do believe that the great bulk of these phenomena are what is called Satanic."** [16] Satan has devised the delusion that mankind is entering into an important evolutionary phase—a New Age. The push for "global enlightenment" has now extended to the vast reaches of the universe, into what could be deemed as a "space" religion. However, once this nebulous veil is lifted, a definite correlation emerges between the UFO/

14   See. https://www.ewtn.co.uk/news/europe/pope-ordered-card-burke-to-clean-out-freemasons-from-the-knights-of-malta ‡ Archived 11th January, 2017.

15   http://www.infowars.com/the-coming-antichrist/ ‡ Archived 11th January, 2017.

16   http://www.arpnet.it/ufo/aufora.301 ‡ Archived 11th January, 2017.

*FIG. 124 – Notice the white Fez **Order of Alhambra**, the elite of the Knights of Columbus, during their official ceremony officiated by the Catholic clergy (including a bishop!), Who actively support this shameful pseudo-Muslim theater, at least in appearance.*

Alien phenomenon and occultic/satanic activity. The ancient civilizations of the Egyptians, Babylonians, Aztecs, Mayans, and Incas share several intriguing characteristics:

1   They were extremely advanced scientifically and technologically.

2   Animal and human sacrifices were performed at an alarming rate, preceding their demise.

3   They believed they had acquired metaphysical knowledge from the "gods," whom they perceived as coming from the stars and also the subterranean level of the earth.

4   These cultures disintegrated or became abruptly extinct while at the pinnacle of their existence. Many of these revered and feared entities were described as winged-reptilians or dragons. Similarly, Satan and his minions were depicted in an identical manner, as seen in artwork throughout the centuries.

A monograph entitled, **Reality of the Serpent Race**, by Commander X and Branton, reveals, *"In Genesis 3 we read about the 'Nachash;' Hebrew word for 'Serpent.' The original Nachash was not actually a snake as most people believe, but an extremely intelligent, cunning creature, possessed with the ability to speak and reason."*

Another significant parallel from the Holy Bible is shown in Jeremiah 8:17, *"Behold, I will send serpents, cockatrices among you, which will bite you, saith the Lord."* The definition of a cockatrice is a reptilian bird-like creature or winged-serpent. This could very well represent the Phoenix, described in Egyptian mythology. A theory proposed by Bible scholar I.D.E. Thomas, who asserts that the race of the "Nephilim" (meaning Giants and/or fallen ones), mentioned in Genesis 6:4 and Numbers 13:33, closely resemble the alien race of the blond Pleiadian Nordics, reported to be eight to nine feet tall. The Nazis attempted to revive this mystical Aryan race in the 1930's and 1940's. Mr. Thomas believes that a hybrid offspring culminated from relations between the Nephilim and the "daughters of man" resulted in increased wickedness upon the earth; and thus evoked God's wrath in the form of the "Great Flood." Interviews taken of ex-Wiccans and Satanists (now Christians), indicate a high level of personal contact with various alien types, especially during coven meetings and holiday rituals. **Those coming from the highest echelon of Satanism known as the Illuminati,** believe the original people who inhabited the earth descended from Mars via the Moon. They believe the first established civilization was Atlantis. [17]

17   http://www.conspiracyarchive.com/UFOs/demons_aliens_clothes.htm ‡ Archived 11th January, 2017.

Satan the alien enemy, and the New Age

Author Davy Russell wrote:

> For over 200 years in England, thousands of men and women were found with strange marks on their bodies, mysterious illnesses, or what appeared to be supernatural abilities. They were sentenced to death by the church for being witches and making covenants with the devil. In December of 1997, a 17-year-old boy was brought before a Romanian priest after coming down with a mysterious illness. The priest performed an exorcism on the youth believing that his unexplainable condition was caused by a demon. In January 1998, a New York mother and her older daughter were indicted after suffocating a younger member of the family during an attempt to exorcise a demon from the teenage girl. There are thousands of stories throughout history similar to the affore mentioned ones, all of which are negative or unexplainable phenomena blamed on evil figures of every religion in the world. Christians attribute addictions, bad habits, temptations, and illness to Satan. Pagan cultures have their own evil spirits or angry gods who take the blame. **However, others who deem the belief in God or Satan as unscientific will readily ignore the fundamental laws of physics, biology, psychology, logic, etc. and blame negative paranormal phenomena on extraterrestrial beings from other worlds.** Many UFO believers blame cattle mutilations, crop circles, abduction experiences, some nightmares, electronic disturbances, strange creatures such as Mothman and the Chupacabra, even some human disappearances and deaths on sinister gray aliens. If they don't blame the otherworldly, governments often take the blame. **Is this the roll of the extraterrestrial in today's society—the evil devil tormenting mankind?** There is often a direct link from the UFO phenomena to the occult. They appear to coincide and are similar in many aspects. Some believe that alien beings are actually demons, while the Skeptic's Dictionary *makes a great observation suggesting that aliens have taken over the Devil's role. **What do you think? Please read the following statements from Ufologists and paranormal researchers:***

JOHN A. KEEL—Author of *Mothman Prophesies* and other books on UFO phenomena said, *"The UFO manifestations seem to be, by and large, merely minor variations of the age-old demonological phenomena."*

RAYMOND FOWLER—Author of five books on UFOs wrote: *"I (have) watched in dismay as a number of respected UFO researchers moved from a physical to a parapsychological interpretation of the bizarre UFO phenomena. ... Now, I am being forced to reexamine the UFO phenomena in light of its apparent paraphysical nature."*

DR. JACQUES VALLEE—Prominent UFO researcher who made several statements on the subject: *"We are dealing with a yet unrecognized level of consciousness, independent of man but closely linked to the earth. ... I do not believe anymore that UFOs are simply the spacecraft of some race of extraterrestrial visitors. This notion is too simplistic to explain their appearance, the frequency of their manifestations throughout recorded history, and the structure of the information exchanged with them during contact. ... an impressive parallel can be made between UFO occupants and the popular conception of demons. ... The 'medical examination' to which abductees are said to be subject, often accompanied by sadistic sexual manipulation, is reminiscent of the medieval tales of encounters with demons. It makes no sense in a sophisticated or technical or biological framework: any intelligent being equipped with the scientific marvels that UFOs possess would be in a position to achieve any of these alleged scientific objectives in a shorter time and with fewer risks."*

LYNN E. CATOE—Senior bibliographer for a publicaton listing over 400 pages of UFO literature in 1969 claimed that, *"A large part of the available UFO literature is closely linked with mysticism and the metaphysical. It deals with subjects like mental telepathy, automatic writing and invisible entities, as well as phenomena like poltergeist manifestations and 'possession.' Many of the UFO reports now being published in the popular press recount alleged incidents that are strikingly similar to demonic possession and psychic phenomena."*

DR. PIERRE GUERIN—Scientist with the French National Council for Scientific Research stated that *"(UFO) behavior is more akin to magic than to physics as we know it.* Adding also that, *"the modern UFOnauts and demons of past days are probably identical."*

TREVOR JAMES—UFO researcher said *"A working knowledge of occult science ... is indispensable to UFO investigations."* [18]

The New Age, according to the objective of neo-theosophist Alice Bailey, would have to "transform" and influence the mass consciousness as I demonstrated in Volume II. For the Illuminati network behind the New World Order, this is the advent of the New Age, in which the old world dominated by Christianity would give way gradually to a polymorphic spirituality without dogma, thanks to a "leap in consciousness" where everyone will be illuminated and will have no further need for mediations or hierarchies; but it is also, perhaps, the advent of the Aeon of Horus envisioned by occultist Aleister Crowley, (whose libertarian views, deeply inspired the "counterculture" of the 1960s), preparing for the arrival of' the Antichrist, who would merely be the "liberator," the bearer of the new law, as quoted by Crowley himself in the *Book of the Law.*

The so-called "counterculture" of the 1960s was in fact dominated by this "Messianic" thought, and the advent of a new spirituality destined to omit old religious traditions. The same guru of the psychedelic movement, **Timothy Francis Leary (1920 – 1996)**, founded a kind of brotherhood where **LSD** became the acronym for *League of Spiritual Research,* and in which this controversial drug was proposed as "the new sacrament" which would open the doors of consciousness for the men and women of the Age of Aquarius. To celebrate the entrance in the Age of Aquarius, on the 14th of January 1967, the various hippie "tribes" and their leaders gathered in San Francisco to celebrate the famous Hindu Kumbh Mela, a mass Hindu pilgrimage of faith in which Hindus gather to bathe in a sacred or holy river. This event that would go down in history as the *Human Be-In,* that saw thousands of people hypnotized by LSD and dressed to resemble the Indian sadhu celebrating the birth of a "new religion without churches or cults." Proposing and organizing all this was one of the most prominent leaders of the counterculture of the time, including John Starr Cooke, tied to high finance circles and of course the CIA, as well as an early proponent of Crowleyanity. In *Acid Dreams,* Martin Lee and Bruce Schlain, wrote that Cooke had a deck of tarot cards that belonged to Aleister Crowley, with notes written on them by Crowley himself. Cooke was born in 1920 to a wealthy Hawaiian family, and traveled the world in search of mystics and magicians. Today we can finally understand that back then, globalist powers, intelligence agencies and occult orders, were intertwined in the psychedelic movement, and at the same time creating a new paradigm of man, functional to the development of the New World Order. The New Age produced a "State of mind" —a way of understanding the relationship with the "Sacred" dominated by absolute individualism, and in which ele-

18   http://www.xprojectmagazine.com/archives/ufo/alnstn.html ‡ Archived 11th January, 2017.

ments taken from ancient traditions are reassembled in ever new forms, possibly compatible with the "tastes" of post-modern man.

The heart of New Age thinking is neither recent nor original. It is, essentially, a very "vulgarized" form of Theosophy in which elements borrowed from Eastern traditions are immersed in a melting pot where we find many different elements. We have the Mayan tradition, the Sufi one, the Celtic, the Egyptian, and even a touch of Gnostic and Chinese. We may find in this New Age mess traces of supposed "revelations" received by extraterrestrial beings, often through "self-initiations" of various kinds. However the term New Age long preceded the era of so-called "flower children" in the Summer of Love, in fact it is even found in the "spiritualistic revelations" received by the Fox sisters in 1848, (the creators of the modern Spiritualism), and as I mentioned earlier, it was also the name of an official journal of the Ancient and Accepted Scottish Rite published in the USA.

Kate Fox (1837 – 1892), Leah Fox (1814 – 1890), and **Margaret (Maggie) Fox (1833 – 1893)** were three American sisters who played a key role in the birth and the spread in Anglo-Saxon countries of the Spiritualist movement. And one of the first "revelations" received from them explicitly announced the coming of a New Age. In the 1930s, the term New Age was adopted by Alice Bailey, who more directly inspired the gurus of the 1960s counterculture. Whatever its essence, the spirit of the New Age has become, in recent years, a widely present reality in public opinion, that points to absorbing those poor souls disillusioned by certain forms of Christianity like Catholicism, reduced to mere moralizing systems full of hypocricy and double standards in the hands of the usual "Jesuit Mafia." According to Michel Lacroix, philosophy professor and researcher at the University of Evry, and the author of a controversial essay entitled *The ideology of the New Age,* the New Age phenomenon, apparently libertarian and individualist, hides in fact a "totalitarian" trend that pushes to "annihilate" and destroy people's spiritual identity, drowning its followers in a relativistic amalgam that, according to the scholar, is the ideal spiritual form **"for those who want to impose a single world power."** Another interesting element in the New Age saga is that towards the end of his career as "psychedelic guru," Timothy Leary suddenly became interested in **contact with "alien intelligences."** [19] Leary and other psychedelic gurus manipulated by the Illuminati Network will be neither the first nor the last to move from "alternative spirituality" to "alien" belief, a fate indeed shared by much of the New Age galaxy of today, that seems to have found, in the extraterrestrial "Faith," a real substitute for God.

Terence McKenna and his brother Dennis, both New Age gurus of DMT, and proponents of paraphysics, **John Keel (1930 – 2009)** and **Jacques Vallee (b. 1939)** , have brought the issue of extraterrestrial contact to its primitive scope, that being **the altered state of consciousness.** Jacques Vallee, who worked for NASA in the early 1960s, and had taken part in the NSF computer networking project which was to give birth to the first conferencing system, ARPANET, long before the advent of the internet, published *Passport to Magoni : From Folklore to Flying Saucers* (Henry Regnery & Co., Chicago, 1969). Bringing together elements of medieval European folklore and contemporary "extra-terrestrial" phenomena, he attempts to prove a structural continuity between them. Vallee was chosen by Steven Spielberg as his model for the character of the French scientist Lacombe in *Close Encounters of the Third Kind*, a propaganda movie showing the "good side" of the "aliens." However, Vallee disapproved of the Jewish filmmaker's presentation of extraterrestrials as harmless "brothers." "What is the purpose of the ap-

19   See. Leo Lyon Zagami, Enrica Perucchietti, *I Maestri Invisibili del Nuovo Ordine Mondiale,* (Rome, IT: Terre Sommerse, 2013), pp. 119, 120, 121.

pearance of the UFO's?," asked Italian Illuminati Julius Evola. For Jean Robin, there is absolutely no doubt this phenomena is meant to prepare public opinion worldwide for the coming of the Antichrist, which, according to Christian tradition, will pretend to be the "Second Coming' of Christ." McKenna was especially keen to rail against the limited and "materialist" vision of the ufologists, sarcastically inviting them to experience a trip with DMT, to understand the true "nature" of the aliens: *"The feeling of doing DMT is as though one had been struck by noetic lightning. The ordinary world is almost instantaneously replaced, not only with a hallucination, but a hallucination whose alien character is its utter alienness. Nothing in this world can prepare one for the impressions that fill your mind when you enter the DMT sensorium."*

Terence McKenna proposed that the transpersonal dimension of the Wholly Other that one can experience on psilocybin or DMT/ayahuasca, is in fact, the true Alien, and that Humanity was approaching an event-horizon where we were increasingly making contact with this "alien intelligence" in the psychedelic realm of pure information. [20] For Terence McKenna, the UFO—the shiny disc in the sky—is actually an object from the Human Unconscious, from "this murky region, beyond the end of history, beyond the end of life" that is a premonition of the arrival of this singularity, the Eschaton, and the realization that the Alien was Us all along. When McKenna questioned shamans about the creatures who he met each time he was under DMT influence, they said to him: "You have just met the spirit allies. They can help you heal and to find missing objects," confirming the "reality" of these entities. Shamans even came to speculate that they might be their "ancestors," moving away from the extraterrestrial hypothesis that has crept into our collective imagination, as we have seen, only since the last century, born from the influence of the Theosophical Society and the nascent New Age. It was from these occult circles that the extent of the intermediate floors deliberately acquired an alien "mask" for the outside world. McKenna concluded: *"We will never get away from a spider hole in stories like those of UFO abductions and similar episodes, unless we acknowledge the obvious psychedelic evidence. If we recognize that, the evidence would look very differently."*

Professor Gianluca Marletta, former student of the Jesuits states that the "UFO cult," is a real "post-modern religion," explaining:

That the alien is a "faith" that in recent years seems to have rubbed a bit all, even some of those "hard-core materialists" who, although skeptical of other aspects of the New Age culture, seem possibilists on the more "practical" perspective that beings from other planets are visiting us. If we used the expression "post-modern religion," however, because it really is the "myth of the aliens," it seems to take on the characteristics of an all-embracing faith that purports to explain everything. According to its practitioners, in fact, the alien's existence would make reason of all or most of the aporias of modern science and would explain our origins as a species (through genetic modification, as claimed by authors such as Zecharia Sitchin and the Italian Mauro Biglino); the origin of ancient civilizations and their knowledge; the angelic and divine phenomena described in all religions (which would be merely misinterpretation on the part of our ancestors of those we now call "UFO phenomena"), etc. But do not think that such suggestions can be confined only to the level of a certain popular culture, as there are more and more scientists and even religions who tend to marry those assumptions. A myth for all seasons, therefore, that of the extra-terrestrial. Perhaps the only modern myth able to get people of different ideological and cultural backgrounds to "reach an agreement."

20   http://www.dmtsite.com/dmt/speculations/ ✝ Archived 11th January, 2017.

The "alien myth" was born and developed in the occult circles of the Illuminati at the turn of the nineteenth and twentieth century, and these environments end up winning the imagination of masses. See the late Terence McKenna conference in Esalen, in February 1992, or the conference he made in New York, in June 1993. Francis Crick, co-discoverer of the structure and function of DNA, in an article published in 1973 (F. Crick, L. Orgel, *Directed Panspermia,* in *Icarus* No. 19, London 1973), assumed a radical version of the Panspermia hypothesis, which he characterized as Directed Panspermia.

Crick, in essence, argued the possibility that life was "seeded" from planet to planet from extraterrestrial intelligence in a sort of "Program setting"—a hypothesis that would allow him to do without (or at least to postpone indefinitely) the unpleasant questions regarding the existence of a creator God. However there is another aspect of extraterrestrial cults that Professor Gianluca Marletta highlights, which belongs to the globalist doctrine advocated by the dark side of the Illuminati. The second aspect of "extraterrestrial myth" that interests us seems in fact to have been "cleverly spread" through the mass media, in order to instill voluntarily fear in the collective imagination. Some particularly sensitive ufologists seem to have married this intuition; **Jacques Vallée,** for example, after years of study of the UFO phenomenon, even said: **"I believe that behind the UFO phenomenon exists a plan to manipulate the masses, to achieve political and social goals, and create a new form of faith."** The plan referred by Vallée, was confirmed at a distance by **J.Allen Hynek** (U.S. astronomer and ufologist used often as a consultant for large cinematic creations on the theme of aliens), who, in an interview shortly before his death, to the researcher Italian Roberto Pinotti, as recalled by Marletta, revealed his belief that certain techniques of persuasion could have been used over the years to "familiarize" the general public with the theme of the aliens. [21] To do that, Hollywood could be used to promote certain ideas promoted by the Illuminati: *"Hollywood, expertly piloted, is beautifully serving and serves the purpose of the aliens. So here is the production-oriented or O.P. (Oriented Productions) in the field of cinema and television. With them the establishment informs and 'shapes' public opinion as in the times of those films made with blatant propaganda purposes during the war. Films like 'Close Encounters of the Third Kind' in which Spielberg has used me as a consultant and 'ET the Extraterrestrial' were not made by chance."* [22] It was a "road to Damascus" experience for the Mad Men era:

> *In 1966, the respected astronomer J. Allen Hynek had gone—seemingly overnight— from a determined debunker to an ardent apostle of the UFO gospel. A longtime consultant to Project Blue Book noted for his skeptical stance toward UFOs, Hynek suddenly began telling anyone who would listen that the UFO phenomenon merited serious scientific scrutiny. The great film director Stanley Kubrick was among the many who listened. In a 1968 Playboy interview promoting his science-fiction epic 2001: A Space Odyssey, Kubrick spoke approvingly of what he termed Hynek's "belated but exemplary conversion" (Phillips 2001, 58). In fact, the professor's apparent transformation from skeptic to UFO proponent was not quite the conversion event that it appeared on the surface. Since his teens Hynek had been an enthusiast, though closeted student of the occult. The French-born Jacques Vallee, a computer scientist and UFO author, was one of the few persons who knew Hynek's secret. Hynek once told Vallee that he had become an astronomer in order to discover "the very limitations of science, the places where it broke down, the phenomena it didn't explain" (Vallee 1996, 232). Nonetheless, the scientist's public U-turn gave*

---

21   *I Maestri Invisibili del Nuovo Ordine Mondiale, Ibid.,* p. 122.
22   Roberto Pinotti, *UFO: il fattore contatto,* (Milan, IT: Mondadori, 2007), p. 100.

*a big boost to the UFO movement, lending it a measure of credibility, and made
Hynek into a celebrity as the nation's "foremost expert on flying saucers" (O'Toole,
1966). For two decades people could point to Hynek and say, "He's a trained scientist, an astronomer no less: if even he believes in this UFO stuff then there must be
something to it."*

*Who was Josef Allen Hynek? He was born on Chicago's West Side on May 1, 1910,
only a little over a week after Halley's Comet had swung around the sun. Hynek's
Czech-born father made cigars for a living while his mother, Bertha, taught at a
local grammar school. Josef credited his mother for his early interest in astronomy.
"When I was seven, I had scarlet fever and was quarantined with my mother in our
apartment at 15th and Ayers," Hynek explained. "There was nothing to do except
read, and since I was so young, my mother read to me. Pretty soon we ran out of
children's books and she started reading textbooks. Among them was a high school
astronomy book. I guess it interested me the most" (Berland 1962). Maybe astronomy textbooks didn't give him the answers he wanted, and so, as a bookish teenager,
Hynek began to study what he called "esoteric subjects." After reading widely in the
occult, he developed a particular fondness for the writings of the Rosicrucian secret
societies, with their tantalizing promises of hidden ancient knowledge, and those
of the so-called hermetic philosophers, especially Rudolf Steiner. The high schooler
spent over $100—roughly $1,300 in today's dollars—to purchase the Canadian
mystic Manly Hall's massive, richly illustrated tome,* An Encyclopedic Outline of
Masonic, Hermetic, Qabbalistic and Rosicrucian Symbolical Philosophy: Being
an Interpretation of the Secret Teachings Concealed within the Rituals, Allego-
ries and Mysteries of All Ages, *better known simply as* The Secret Teachings of
All Ages. *"All my student friends thought I was crazy: why didn't I buy a motorcycle
instead, as they all did," Hynek later told Jacques Vallee (Vallee 2010, 64–65).* [23]

In my previous works, I have explained my ideas on the dangers of practices such as
channeling, spiritism, automatic writing, hypnosis, etc. Without going into these issues
already largely developed elsewhere, and anticipating the research of John Keel and Vallée on the "psychic" and psychotronic component of the UFO phenomenon, it is good
to remember the conclusions drawn by Keel after repeated Moth Man sightings in Point
Pleasant between 1966 and 1967. Keel had the intuition to investigate the psychic component of the UFO phenomenon (including ORBS and creatures from the unknown).
Keel studied closely many "contactees," coming to the conclusion that the set of symptoms experienced during a sighting or a real abduction (known as the **Oz Effect**) can
actually be the effect of a form of hypnosis. In particular, the paralysis and the missing
time reported by all observers and abductees would be a form of trance due to the flashing
light that emanates from the UFO (and glowing balls). For this Keel speaks of "contactee
syndrome," defining it as a form of reprogramming that undergoes the subject through
the blinking light, sound or buzz that cause a form of trance accompanied by "elaborated
hallucinations." [24] This form of hypnosis would explain, according to John Keel, all the
symptoms of the so-called "Oz effect":

*When a contactee comes out of the trance, he is often found to suffer from headaches
and muscle aches, which are spread over several days. Another common symptom is
a strong lethargy: the subject, exhausted, over-indulges in sleep. These symptoms are
comparable with those of epileptics who suffer from muscle spasms. The excessive thirst*

23   http://www.csicop.org/si/show/the_secret_life_of_j_allen_hynek ✝ Archived 11th January, 2017.
24   John Keel, *The Mothman Prophecies*, (Milan, IT: Sonzogno Editori, 2002), p. 174.

is another symptom, probably caused by exposure to intense electromagnetic radiation at low frequency (VLF), which penetrate into the tissues and dehydrates them. [25]

The flashing light can be subjective or objective and be spotted by most observers, thus giving rise to multiple sightings. Keel says:

Investigating multiple UFO sightings, I am not interested in the random witnesses of an objective light. Rather I look for people who have been directly effected by the light. Rarely they report their sightings, or because the hallucinations that have accompanied them have been too weird or too scary, or because they simply have no memory of the entire event. They are suffering from partial amnesia. When I can find people like that, I'll tell the whole story of their lives and remain in contact with them for a long time, in order to observe any changes in personality or in perception. In some cases there is a rapid deterioration, just as it does to those who have taken LSD and have unexpectedly another trip, weeks after. The individual may suffer mental imbalances, abandoning the family and work, become fanatical and, in some unfortunate events, have a nervous breakdown and commit suicide. The other side of the coin is that some people have a profound expansion of consciousness, a large increase in IQ and a complete change in lifestyle ... for the better. [26]

John Keel examines the similar "mystical light" phenomenon, comparing it to the experience of "alien contact." Both, in fact, can lead, in the best cases, to an expansion of consciousness, to a change for a better way of life, a greater awareness of nature and society, or, conversely, to degenerate, into fanaticism, violence, isolation or suicide. Keel indirectly separates the planes of the psychic / astral and spiritual, returning to the first context, the phenomenon of enlightenment. John Keel explains: *"In its purest form, the enlightenment is not a religious experience. For a few moments the subject fully understands the operation of the entire universe. He perceives all history, past, present and future. He feels part of, and is one with the cosmos. Unfortunately, in the short-term experience, he does not remember everything: most of the information has been deposited in the subconscious. And what he remembers is too fragmented to be articulated. But in the meantime the individual has been reprogrammed, or even prepared for a new role in life."* [27] The dynamic of the "real" enlightenment, Keel bridges with the UFO phenomenon, assuming there is mental reprogramming (or possession) of the observer by infernal forces, In this case would be a "false" illumination, that is, driven by the lower degree of forces. He writes:

Every cosmic force has its imitators. The UFO contacts victims often suffer from false illuminations, because their mind has misinterpreted the experience, or because they are in a reprogrammed state, by forces who have used this mechanism. In a sense, they are "possessed." Suffering from hallucinosis, i.e. repeated hallucinations, and their life is manipulated in a disastrous way. When a person has been subjected to a false light, he becomes vulnerable to repeat the experience. Just like a person who has been hypnotized once can be easily hypnotized again. [28]

This happens in many occult movements and Illuminati sects in their use of mental manipulation, but also in the induction of shamanic trance or spiritualist evocation. In addition to the deliberate pursuit of the possession of the victim whose mind must be deconstructed, fragmented and then reprogrammed, the trance induced by psychotro-

---

25   *Ibid.* p. 177.
26   *Ibid.*
27   *Ibid.*, p. 178.
28   *Ibid.*

pic substances or meditation, as well as hypnosis, allows the operator to induce hallucinations in the victim thus easing the reprogramming. But Keel does not stop there, clarifying what might be the causes and especially the effect of the spread of the UFO phenomenon. The phenomenon has a strong ability **"to manipulate humans and to generate propaganda,"** i.e. to spread their beliefs in public opinion. In this sense the UFO phenomena should be understood as a form of counter-initiation that, led by forces of the underworld, seems determined to spread their faith in the world's population in this specific moment in history dominated by the Satanic elite and the forces of darkness. Jean Robin wrote this: *"The phenomenon is related to beliefs. As many people believe in flying saucers from other planets, especially the lower force is subject to be manipulated through false illuminations. I have observed with great consternation the worldwide spread of the faith in UFOs and the consequences thereof. If this phenomenon continues unchecked, we might one day have to deal with the universal acceptance of these 'aliens' as a modern religion that will allow them to interfere openly with our business. Just like the ancient gods, from the heights of mountains, ruled large segments of the population in the East, in Greece, in Rome, Africa and South America."* [29]

UFOs and SciFi: instruments of Illuminati propaganda

René Guénon explains how the counter-initiatory forces use the traditional vestiges and other components (like inferior psychical elements) to their advantage. In many cases, the activity of the counter-initiatory forces are well hidden, and normal people don't notice it in plain view. This activity develops in the subtle domain, being an activity of suggestion aiming at modifying the mentality of human society. There are circumstances when the effects of the counter-initiatory activity are very visible, and a notorious example is the "SciFi phenomenon." This phenomenon, which is in fashion even today, has many faces, all of them having as an objective to influence people's mentality and manipulate the crowd. Reading SciFi "literature" or watching SciFi movies, the modern individuals receive anti-traditional suggestions regarding what to eat, how to behave, etc. Yet this was just a trivial facet, even though not negligible. The main attack is directed towards the religious domain. The counter-initiatory forces have no access to the spiritual domain, but they can corrupt "beliefs" and "views" in many ways. The SciFi phenomenon contained an aggressive component—a theory that explained all religious "myths" of gods would be considered as extraterrestrial visitors. There was a double purpose for that. First, the religious tradition became a collection of legends; second, the legends were an illustration of some very materialistic facts. The reason why such a theory could be accepted by some was that the intellectual level of the majority of modern individuals is low, and for decades the public at large accepted all the scientific hypotheses and theories as realities and proven facts. Another SciFi component, the so-called "literature," tried to replace the traditional vestiges represented by myths and fairy tales (those that remained uncorrupted by the Christian religion), supplying a mockery of pseudo-tales and pseudo-initiatory voyages; all the SciFi tales are profoundly materialistic—the initiatory and postmortem voyages being substituted with corporeal interplanetary trips. Also, especially present in SciFi movies, with a large young audience that promoted a type of hostile alien having as objective of the domination of the terrestrial world, to manipulate people so they are under constant fear.

In the past, there was "the yellow danger," then the "Communist danger," and, with the SciFi phenomenon, "the extraterrestrial danger" was born. There is no difficulty in

29 *Ibid.*, p. 179.

seeing that the same scenario was used against Masonry and the Templars, in connection to conspiracy theory. And to enhance the credibility of this SciFi phenomenon, a materialistic component was strongly advertised—the UFOs. This last element was in concert with the mechanistic and corporeal views of the modern world, and helped in influencing the acceptance of the new technologies as beneficial, and indispensable for a decent life. Finally, the SciFi phenomenon has another hidden reason to exist. Being open to the public at large and having a materialistic character, it was used to help the "solidification" of the modern mentality, yet, as Guénon said, after this phase there is another one, more dangerous. Due to its superficial and materialistic characteristics, the SciFi phenomenon was expendable and it was used to create the illusion of credibility for its critics. [30]

The best example is Carl Jung, who wrote the book *A Modern Myth*, in which he reinterpreted the UFO problem from a psychoanalytical perspective. We can see here two anti-traditional currents opposing each other, yet the subtle idea was to make one of the theories more trustworthy (and its author, in this case, Jung). In 1979, Jean Robin published a book about UFOs. [31] Robin wrote a year earlier, in 1978, *René Guénon, Témoin de la Tradition*, a work that consecrated him as a "guénonian." In fact, for some, Jean Robin is a suspicious author who cannot be trusted, and some people considered him even as anti-traditional and an instrument of the counter-initiatory forces of the New World Order. However, Robin tries to prove that UFOs represent a pseudo-religion and are part of the last phase, the pseudo-spiritual, a point of view I support, but Robin thinks the majority of the world's population are UFO "believers," which, of course, is not the case. The UFO phenomenon in the eyes of the majority of the world population is however a materialistic one, and is part of this age of superficiality and confusion. For this reason we need to analyze more deeply the phenomena, using the esoteric point of view typical of the Illuminati network in order to have a real understanding of it.

Confessions of a Pilgrim: Paulo Coelho

Wikipedia describes Paulo Coelho (FIG. 125) in this way: *"Paulo Coelho de Souza (born August 24, 1947) is a Brazilian lyricist and novelist. He is the recipient of numerous international awards, amongst them the Crystal Award by the World Economic Forum. His novel* The Alchemist *has been translated into 81 languages. According to* The Washington Post, *Paulo Coelho has sold an estimated 350 million books and is the all-time bestselling Portuguese-language author."* [32]

In a 1999 interview with the journalist Juan Arias, the famous writer Paulo Coelho stated: *"For me, the greatest danger in the spiritual quest are the gurus, the masters, fundamentalism ... the globalization of the spiritual quest."* [33] Except that Coelho himself has created in recent years a sort of virtual pseudo-religion based on his books. Just check out his booklet *Manual of the Warrior of Light*, and the many inconsistencies of the Brazilian writer become evident to the initiated eye. Yet, as the same Arias points out in the introduction to his long interview, Coelho is not only a novelist, but he is an eclectic and emblematic character, who lived with passion the opposite extremes that life offers us. So almost all of his novels have an autobiographical core: **the psychiatric hospital, prison, kidnapping, initiation, conversion to Catholicism.** The transition from his

30   Volume 2 Number 5-6 *ORIENS* June, 2005.

31   See. Jean Robin, *Les Objets volants non identifiés ou la Grande parodie*, (Paris, FR: Éditions de la Maisnie, 1979).

32   https://en.wikipedia.org/wiki/Paulo_Coelho ‡ Archived 11th January, 2017.

33   Arias Juan, *Paulo Coelho: le confessioni di un pellegrino.*, (Milan, IT: Bompiani, 2000) p. 29.

FIG. 125 – The best-selling Brazilian writer Paulo Coelho.

early Jesuit education to atheism, then to magic, and the return to Catholicism rests on his unusual spiritual quest. However, the occult seems to pull the strings of his journey. From his experience in a "Satanic" cult (the O.T.O.) to his "rebirth" within Christianity, Coelho admits that he has never sought balance, a real harmony in his life, but he has been living in an "extreme" modality.

This is the exact opposite of the traditional path of an initiate: *"In my life I have never tried harmony. I believe that life ends when you stop struggling and you say, 'Now I got it.' So that would be happiness, which I do not like nor do I try."* The extreme negative led him on the path of magic, first by joining the O.T.O. Here he hit bottom, he sunk into the abyss of evil, but as Dostoevsky's hero, he rose up again. However something remains of his Jesuit formation of those teachings and practices. Coelho talks about his experience as follows, starting from his education in a Jesuit boarding school: *"My training was Jesuit, a formation that gives me a certain concept of God. For me—I do not know for others—has been a rather negative experience: it was at a Jesuit college that I lost the faith of my childhood. Trying to import a faith is the best way to bring rebellion and make you move to the other side."* Coelho for this is far from the "innocent figure"— a manipulator of consciences and his education by the Jesuits makes us understand a lot about his perverse psychology and contradictions of his being. Religion imposed by the Jesuits led him as a young man to seek shelter in Marxist literature, but Coelho ends in a clear Theosophical matrix hippie movement that for many unfortunately became the antechamber of occultism and Satanism: *"I was attracted to the world of spirituality and was looking for the distant experiences, because I had not found any belief in religious training sets. I turned to Indian cosmology, in which I forcefully entered. I began to recite the mantra, doing yoga and meditation, to take care of everything related to Eastern spirituality."* The thirst for spirituality led him to attend, *"many masters, many sects, many philosophies, until it came a time which my extreme value has led me to seek something stronger, that is to the left of the left in the spiritual quest."* [34]

From here, the road to black magic is short. Paulo Coelho comes into contact with a sect (which is not explicitly named) whose teacher offers him "three or four books" by

34   *I Maestri Invisibili del Nuovo Ordine Mondiale, Ibid.,* p. 126-127.

Aleister Crowley. The thought of the magician fascinates him—the same Coelho admits that one of the reasons why he had approached the Left Hand (and to red tantric magic,) was sex, and his desire to "seduce women." Indeed, about this inspiration on the Thelemic sect he says: *"Everyone could join. I remember that there was a total sexual freedom, of thought, of everything, even of oppression. It was to bring the experience of power to its fullest extent."* The sect in question is said to be more dangerous than any other magical movement or Satanic sect, including the Church of Satan, as they *"had a more philosophical sect, more structured, more dangerous in its roots. In it they celebrated conventional rites of magic, but that was the realm of pure power. Sometimes we call evil with very concrete results, but nothing has ever been like that black that has invaded my home."* [35]

Aside from the obvious clues that may lead to speculation that the sect in question is the O.T.O., the same Paolo Coelho confirmed it in the summer of 2012 in an interview with the German newspaper *Sueddeutsche Zeitung Magazine*, where he admitted that he entered in 1972, the Brazilian section of the O.T.O. with the initiatory name *Luz Eterna:* [36]

SZ: *The most bizarre phase in your life began in 1969. You became engaged in occultism, sorcery and satanism and devoured huge tomes on UFOs, vampires, pentagrams and astrological systems. You wrote in your diary: "Immersing myself into black magic is the only way out from desperation and depression for me."*

PC: *I remember writing this but I am not the same person that wrote it. The reasons that led me to black magic are encapsulated in my past.*

SZ: *In 1972, you became the member named Luz Eterna of the Satanic sect of the O.T.O., the order of the Oriental Templars, of which British Aleister Crowley was the chief theorist. One of the followers of the "Great Beast," as Crowley called himself, was Charles Manson, who ordered the killing by gunfire, knifing and clubbing of four people in movie director Roman Polanski's house.*

PC: *The dictums of this organization are bordering on spiritual fascism. It's all about the experience of power to the most extreme. When you are a member of the chosen few, you are freed of all ethical codes and can do whatever you want—even if you want to be a monster. When I realized that the O.T.O. will lead me into the abyss, I quit and severed every contact. I was nearly dead spiritually, but I had understood that one needs to have an ethical code to live.*

SZ: *You say that the O.T.O. is "worse than Satanism." Can you attest any specific practices?*

PC: *I do not like the word Satanism. It sounds like a cheap Hollywood horror movie to me. In the O.T.O. there were no babies sacrificed, but we practiced black magic and worked with powers that I will not disclose. I have no interest to excite curiosity for this organization because this could be mistaken for promotion. That's why I declined to speak of the O.T.O. by its official name publicly for so many years, and have always referred to it as "the Society for the advent of the Apocalypse."*

SZ: *You told your biographer Fernando Morais that four days after you joined the O.T.O. you encountered Satan. Morais writes: "Coelho noticed the smell of death in his apartment and dark fog, as if the sun had suddenly gone."*

PC: *Stop it! I do not wanna talk about this any longer.*

35 *Ibid.*, p. 127.
36 *Ibid.*, p. 132.

SZ: Is it true that you have written a 600-page manuscript about your experiences?

PC: This is true, but my present wife advised me to destroy it, and I have done so.

Here Coelho refuses to repeat to the German newspaper what he had confessed to Arias, about the most tragic moment within the Illuminati sect, where he lived among the real presence of evil. It was after two years of membership that one day in 1974, while he was home alone, Coelho began to see only darkness around him: *"It was very early, and as I told you, I began to see all black; I had the feeling that I would be dead. It was a very real black, physical, visible. It was not my imagination, it was something tangible. Like I said, my first impression is that I was going to die. ... It was as if suddenly this candle began to make smoke, and the smoke began to invade the house, it was like a very black smoke densification that prevented me to see for a moment, but above all I sank into a panic ... Perhaps the worst part was a series of noises that I can not describe accompanying the formation of the black smoke."* The reaction was devastating. darkness enveloped Coelho who believed he was about to die: *"I collapsed in panic, because that phenomenon testified to the presence of evil."* Coelho understood that any technique or subterfuge to escape the darkness did not work, Coelho decided to go to a church but *"some sort of force prevented me from leaving the house and I felt very powerful feelings of impending doom. At that moment came the woman I knew then, who belonged to the sect. She had just lived through the black experience. And, little by little, we learned that all the followers were experiencing the same thing ... The presence of evil was something visible and tangible. It was as if the evil said, **you called me, here I am**."* [37]

Later, Coelho relived those two years in the O.T.O in a manuscript of six hundred pages, however, his wife Cristina advised him not to publish it and to destroy it. The autobiography also reported of musical activities with the late **Raul Seixas** Brazilian rock composer, singer, and songwriter who, like Coelho, was introduced to the O.T.O. He writes, *"The two friends decided to put their music 'to the service of the secret society' ... The verses of the songs contained in principle the sect statements, perceptible in a very subliminal way. There where totally technical mantras, precise, perfect. Because evil is really something true."* [38] Later, in the Netherlands, Paolo Coelho came into contact with a person, the "J" character in the books *The Pilgrimage,The Valkyries* and *Aleph,* mentioned in the dedication of *The Alchemist.* *"A. J. the alchemist, who knows and uses the secrets of the Great Work"* mentioned in the online version of *Warrior of Light* that has changed his life and brought him back to Christianity. In *The Pilgrimage* he says he became a member of a Catholic Masonic group called RAM (*Regnus Agnus Mundi*), [39] with J. as his Master. The problem is that this Latin acronym (i.e. RAM) makes no sense literally as "Regnus" for example does not exist as a word, it should be "Regnum" and no groups or spiritual movements seem to have ever used this denomination. In addition to this anomaly, which does not necessarily imply the non-existence of the group (the author could have made use of a pseudonym to maintain secrecy about the real Order), the characteristics described by the same Coelho are a hodgepodge of New Age and pseudo-Masonic beliefs, that confuse rather than clarify the ideas on the origin of RAM and its possible actions. It was further proposed in an interpretation of RAM that R stands for "Rigor," A for "Amor" (that means love), and M for "Mercy." In the Catholic Church, however, there is no order or movement like that. The popular Catholic site *www.cattoliciromani.com* specified that: "During the trip [to Santiago] Paolo Coelho faces sever-

37   *Sueddeutsche Zeitung Magazin*, 17th of August, 2012.
38   Arias Juan, *Ibid.*, p. 130.
39   *Ibid.*, p. 131.

al trials, and to overcome them, a certain Petrus presents him with exercises that are part of the rituals of the Tradition. Some rituals are shocking, because it is pure spiritualism. In the book we find some dangerous and absurd teachings on the devil and evil spirits." [40]

Coelho's "Rituals of the Tradition" are presented in the wake of counter-initiation and spiritism. In the interview with Arias, Coelho said that *"after having completed the Camino de Santiago starting in France (the most powerful experience of my life), I decided to follow the RAM tradition—a very ancient spiritual tradition, born five hundred years ago within the Catholic Church that I belong to with another four disciples— it is known as the 'feminine way.' Some call this the 'path of Rome' its purpose is to reveal the feminine side of our personality. ... The book contains numerous references to Neo-Spiritualism and occultism and is therefore more close to the New Age genre than traditional Christian literature."* [41] The novel begins with the ceremony where the Master of the Order of RAM is crowned, resulting in the delivery of a new sword, replacing the old woman who had accompanied him to overcome all the trials that had brought him here. The ceremony is interrupted abruptly when Coelho holds his hands out to receive the sword from the Master. The Master makes it clear to him that his experience should have taught him that during the ceremony he should have actually refused the sword. That gesture, in fact, indicates the presence of "impurities" in the heart and mind of the apprentice. To achieve the sword he is ordered to resume the path of tradition, following the Camino de Santiago, also known by the English name Way of St. James. Along that path, among the simple and overcoming of obstacles difficult for people (which correspond to the sins of greed, pride and fascination, found in the wonders with which Coelho has sinned during the ceremony), he should have found the Sword waiting for him at a certain point, at a certain date and time, which has been in the meantime handed over to his wife, that he could not touch without the Master's order. During the trip Coelho is joined by a guide, **Petrus,** a character who has already completed the walk with the same mission. During the trip Paulo Coelho will face *The Dog,* that is, the incarnation of the devil, and will have to defeat it. To help him in this quest there will be some exercises taught by the guide, which is part of the rituals of the Tradition. Among these teachings given to him by Petrus we find, as we advance, some occult practices: among them the evocation of the Messenger, or *Daimon* or "personal demon" that everyone has by his side, opposite to the Guardian Angel. We will see later how the *Daimon* has nothing in common with the Socratic/Platonic expressed in **the myth of Er.** Finally, you can not even compare it to the *Daimon* widely described by Jungian analyst James Hillman or the fictional one and esoteric one presented by Philip Pullman, that we find in the trilogy **His Dark Materials.**

Although the description of the Messenger appears to refer to the philosophical concept of Daimon, the Camino de Santiago description should cause us to compare it, if anything, to the angel Uriel evoked by the Elizabetan Era alchemist and Illuminati **John Dee (1527 – 1608),** a key figure in the occult world of the Illuminati that I have widely described in Volume 1 of my *Confessions.* Even the summoning system that Petrus teaches Coelho fits into typical practice of ceremonial magic of the *Golden Dawn,* which resumed the Enochian magical system developed by Edward Dee and Kelley. Before teaching the traveling companion the practice of evocation, Petrus explains the need for an initiate to come to terms with this "demon" that paves the way for an interpretation far from Christian teachings contained in the novel. It seems Coelho has never abandoned magical practices and the occult, despite the fact he left the O.T.O. So Petrus says: *"To fight the good*

40   *Ibid.,* p. 128.
41   See Paolo Coelho, *Il cammino di Santiago,* (Milan,IT: Bombiani, 2001, original title: *O Diario de Um Mago,* 1987), p. 68.

fight we need help. We need friends and, when they are not close, we must transform the loneliness to our revised main weapon. Everything around us has to help us take those steps which bring us closer to our goal. Everything has to be a personal manifestation of our will to win the Good Fight. Without this—without understanding that we need everyone and everything we will be only arrogant warriors. And, finally, our arrogance will lead us to defeat, because being so confident with ourselves we do not see the traps on the battlefield path." He introduced the need to ally with **"everything that surrounds us."** Petrus continued: *"In addition to the physical forces that surround us and help us, next to us exist in spiritual form two main spiritual forces, an angel and a devil. The angel always protects us—and it is a divine gift and is not necessary to invoke it. ... Even the devil is an angel: but it is a free force, rebellious. I prefer to call it 'Messenger,' since it is the main connecting link between you and the world. In ancient times it was represented by Mercury, as Hermes, the messenger of the gods. Its implementation is limited to the material plane. It is present in the gold of the Church, because gold comes from the earth, and this is His domain. It is present in our work and in our relationship with money. When we let him free, it tends to disperse. When we exorcise, we lose all its profitable teachings, since he knows a lot of the world and of men. When we are fascinated by its power, he possesses us, away from the Good Fight."* [42] These words are part of his first book, *O diário de um mago* (1987), which was published in English as *The Diary of a Magus* in 1992 and was reissued as *The Pilgrimage* in 1995. I translated it myself from the Italian version so I hope Coelho will be satisfied, but of course I invite the interested parties to check the official English translation for a more in-depth look at his work.

Petrus then explains to Coelho, the apprentice, that *"the only way to cope with the Messenger is to accept him as a friend. Listening to his advice, asking for his help when needed, but never allowing him to dictate the rules."* [43]

Petrus distinguishes five fundamental points:

1) The Guardian Angel should not be evoked because there is no need. From here the evidence that the author has awareness that whatever evoked entity is not angelic but rather "demonic."

2) It is accredited by the fact that the Messenger is actually a "personal demon" whose jurisdiction is limited to the material plane. No coincidence that Satan is called the "prince of this world," i.e. the material sphere.

3) It follows that Petrus Coelho teaches how to evoke the devil to ask some practical help or advice and teachings that can help him realize the material plane. To transpose this is the typical "pact with the devil:" the initiate must in fact compromise with his personal demon king to receive tips and benefits on the material plane. The demon / dragon / shadow, in fact, is not "tamed" but is evoked to become a "permanent presence" alongside the initiate in order to advise him in practical life choices.

4) Petrus compares the messenger to Hermes. As we have seen, however, Hermes also embodies the characteristics of the Divine Trickster, and as such is a trickster, a Deceiver. As such mind manipulates and systematically deceived men. Coelho definitely knows the characteristics of the trickster as he quotes from his initial note on the book from the works of Castaneda.

· ·

42   *Ibid.,* p. 69.
43   *Ibid.*

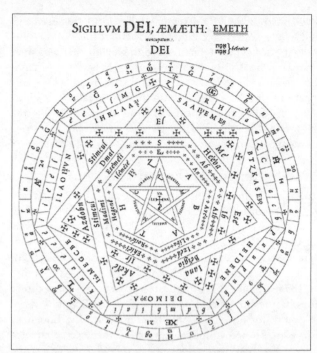

FIG. 126 – Reproduction of Sigillum Emeth, the legendary "Hand of Glory" made by the alchemist John Dee, which would be lost immediately after his death. An object with the same name belonged to Edward Kelley, and is now preserved in the British Museum. Kelley claimed to have received it from the hands of the angel Uriel in person and thanks to it, found it was possible to communicate with the spirits.

5) The vision and "philosophical" teachings of Petrus partly correspond to the arcane figure of the Chariot in the Tarot, a charioteer inspired by the myth of Plato's Phaedrus content. The tarot blade represents a definite stage of apprenticeship: the initiate has come to know and to distinguish the Good (white horse) from Male (black horse) and to drive his chariot he does not even need to hold the reins. The mystery in question, however, refers to an explicitly ethical level. The initiate in the Camino de Santiago, however, distinguishes between good and evil, angel and devil, decides for practical interest, economic and social, to come to terms with the second, conscious of the dangers that can arise from this relationship. [44]

The question, however, refers to an explicitly ethical level. The initiate in the *Camino de Santiago* distinguishes between good and evil, angel and devil, and eventually decides for practical, economic and social interest, to come to terms with the second—conscious of the dangers that can arise from this dangerous relationship. Independent of the "moral" teaching that can be attributed to Coelho, it is clear that you are not within the Christian tradition, but, on the contrary, in a **magical-occult arena that draws from the Enochian magical system** deviced and practiced by Illuminati sects like the O.T.O. Finally, in the *Camino de Santiago* we also find a profound contradiction, because Petrus claims that all these occult teachings may simply be learned by any ordinary person, in their every day life: *"The extraordinary lies in the Way of the common people."* However in the book the members of RAM need these occult rituals for their "illuminations" just like in any other Illuminati sect, and these indications are supplied indirectly to the readers so they can practice them with no proper intiation. It definitely seems like a dead end road dictated by the usual sect of Illuminati or pseudo ones manipulating every side of contemporary culture.

People became interested in Enochian Magic in 1912, when Aleister Crowley published the highly successful book called *The Equinox*. The **Enochian system** was codified in the Renaissance by John Dee and his aide and medium Edward Kelley, (FIG. 126) reworked in a systematic way by Samuel Liddell MacGregor Mathers, and then used and abused by Crowley, who wanted so desperately to contact the **Secret Chiefs** of the Illuminati. 1582 was the year that saw the key event in the life of John Dee: the meeting with Edward Kelley, a seer with a dark past, who Aleister Crowley claimed to be the reincarnation. It was said that Kelley was accustomed to black magic, and thus began a long collaboration that was the cause of the misfortunes of Dee, who then progressively fell into the hell of necromancy. Dee took on Kelley as a full-time psychic, and *charged* a fee of 50 pounds a year, an enormous amount for its time. These two key figures in the history of occultism are detailed in various aspects in Chapter 6 of Volume I of my *Confessions*.

From Zecharia Sitchin to Satanism in the Vatican

The task of Kelley was to gaze into the stone that he said the angel Uriel had given to Dee, describing what he saw inside. Sometimes a spirit came out of the stone, speaking or issuing prophecies. The angels had taught him their alphabet, Kelley said was called Enochian (corresponding to the language that was spoken by Adam in the Garden of Eden, before the Fall, a language with its own grammar and syntax of "alien" origin, or at least extradimensional). There are a total of nineteen "Call" or "keys"—the "calls" were also dictated upside down. The reason for this complicated procedure is that a direct communication with the entities in question would be too powerful and would evoke forces that the two magicians would not have been able to command. The Enochian magic used by the two, derives its name from the biblical patriarch Enoch. This character derived from two important apocryphal books: *the Book of Enoch* and *The Book of the Secrets of Enoch*. The Jewish Kabbalah is also associated with the superimposed complex figure of the Archangel Metatron. Taken up into heaven by God's will, Enoch became an extraordinary angel called Metatron, inaugurating his ascent to the sky. The figure of Enoch undoubtedly hides many mysteries, and like every mystery has been variously studied and interpreted not only by religious historians, philologists, hermeneutics, but also by kabbalists, occultists, and in recent decades by lovers of ufology. Erich Von Daniken is seen as the first man "astronaut" led by the angels/extraterrestrials in the universe, and in the fall of vigilant angels told in the *Book of Enoch*. In this version "God" would then lead Enoch to heaven aboard a chariot of fire which, as in the case of Ezekiel's vision, would be nothing but an alien spacecraft.

As shown by Jean-Bruno Renard, sociologist at the University of Montpellier, this thesis, later reworked by **Zecharia Sitchin (1920 – 2010)**, and in Italy to a lesser extent by the translator Mauro Biglino, belongs to a UFO trend that intends to unveil the supposed "true" meaning of the ancient religious scriptures, whether Egyptian, Sumerian, Indian, or, more often, biblical, showing for example that the great civilizations have come from space, or that men were not created by God, but by extraterrestrials (in Hebrew *elohim, the gods*)—a view that, apart from its sci-fi charm, does often flatten the religious scope, supporting at times relativism and growing individualism.

I think these theories unfold on television thanks to what has become a kind of important sector of the media industry promoted by the elite, to install new elements in the collective conscious. They are used to somehow break down barriers of superstition and ignorance, in a manner certainly more immediate and direct than a book. You can also find sometimes in addition to the usual unfounded theories, the great truths of our Age, otherwise ignored by the official version of events perpetrated by academics. We now need to understand what these beings really are, these extra-dimensional entities, with a serious and more rigorous approach, involving as much as possible the different elements from the religious, scientific, Masonic, and occult sector. Unfortunately, today the prevailing approach in the media, appears to be the result of New Age brainwashing, in which there is not a very specific form of religion, nor a concept or objective of the transcendental deity, but a divine abstract, interior to the individual who lives it and experiences it, in different ways than other people. The individual is encouraged to implement especially the "temple" of the self, the crucial process of transformation of one's consciousness, one's self, corresponding with the ability to "create your own reality," while the saving process is a necessarily psychological process, an inner journey into the psyche. One of the constituent elements of **the New Age of the Illuminati** is a pantheism which results in the rejection of a creator God, personal, transcendental cosmos, in favor of an ultimate reality, called various things, that appears as Mind, Energy, Life.

New Age seemingly presents all religions as equally effective in the pursuit of happiness, but then, in practice, denies all judgments outdated, compared to its message and the advent of the so-called "New Age." Everyone thinks that thanks to their eventual "Gnosis" (the highest and perfect form of enlightened knowledge), that leads to the discovery of the Self, you can regain possession of your true nature, tuning in with your own kind, living in harmony with the cosmos, loving, etc., etc. This is the mantra of the New Agers, but at the same time they are willing slaves to the New World Order and a "religion," without God and the Church, a "religion" with no afterlife and without judgment. No one can be held responsible for the harm done to others, because evil, in fact, does not exist for them, but it coincides with the ignorance that surrounds the human mind as to its true nature of divine origin. It is the illusion of being able to make man god of himself, an idea that I also demonstrated in previous volumes, is one of the foundations of the high degrees of one of the darker para-Masonic Illuminati cults of today, the **Ordo Templi Orientis.** They gradually deleted the philosophical, religious and esoteric sense of Jewish mysticism and the moral teaching of some biblical passages, and what remains in the end is a cosmos without God, but inhabited by extraterrestrial creatures where these "gentlemen of the New Age " create the future of man in a test tube. But in reality a series of question arises, if the aliens have created man to serve and adore them, then who created these aliens? Other even more powerful aliens? This reasoning makes us understand that this theme is exploited beyond measure by the New Age, to thus give rise to an atheistic society without God.

Zecharia Sitchin was a brilliant author and researcher, but his *The Lost Book of Enki; Memories of an Extra-Terrestrial God*, unfortunately is quoted today as a source of inspiration by numerous Satanic sects, when in fact Sitchin, in the last period of his life, was in an intense relationship with Christianity and the Vatican through Father Corrado Balducci, (FIG. 127) a privileged relationship that also saw the direct involvement of his dear friend Gianmario Ferramonti, and people close to Count Licio Gelli and the famous P2 lodge. Years ago, I spoke publicly of the relationship between Sitchin and the Vatican, and the possibility something more deep or sinister was hidden. I also said in my famous interview to *Project Camelot,* I could not bring at that time any evidence to the public of my assertion and did not speak further. I have finally managed to materialize the evidence of what I said years ago, with an exceptional direct witness of those events. On the 2nd of December, 2015, I brought to the attention of documentary makers of *GenSix Productions,* **Gianmario Ferramonti,** which in turn has presented numerous photos to support his claims. Photos which I partly publish in this book (FIGS. 128, 129, 130) to show that he actually met with Sitchin on several occasions, giving a crucial and credible testimony to understand the link between Sitchin, Balducci and the Vatican. In December 2015, I was therefore able to convince Ferramonti to release this historic interview to documentary producer Steve Quayle, released later in June of 2016, under the appropriate title **The Unholy See,** conducted by Timothy Alberino. (FIG. 131) A journalistic scoop whose importance has perhaps been underestimated by *Gen-Six Productions*. Gianmario Ferramonti is a well-known Italian politician close to the Donald Trump staff, (FIG. 132) tied for years to the international world of Intelligence, and was in this case the messenger chosen by his old friend Zecharia Sitchin. And even if Sitchin remains for most academics a charlatan or at least a dubious source, the Vatican thought otherwise. Speculation

FIG. 127 – Zecharia Sitchin and Monsignor Corrado Balducci.

on Sitchin, based on his own interpretation of the Sumerian texts, are in fact considered pseudo-science and pseudo-history by the scientific community, rejected by ordinary scientists, historians and academics. I wonder, **why was the Vatican so interested in the work of Sitchin?** And why did they want to involve him in a secret project with Monsignor Corrado Balducci, even giving him, as admitted by Gianmario Ferramonti in front of the cameras of *GenSix Productions,* boxes fuelled with top secret material probably of an alien nature, hidden in the infamous underground vaults of the Vatican. These revelations and also the visit I made with the American TV crew and Alberino right into the heart of the Vatican, which included the headquarters of the Jesuits in Borgo Santo Spirito, but also the Piazza Vittorio Magical Door—known as an extradimensional portal, have contributed to a great documentary, but certainly have created a few problems to the documentarist in question on their return to the States. Let me begin at the beginning of this story.

One day the staff of *InfoWars* contacted me because of the interests of Christian documentary filmmakers **GenSix Productions** to my story and my books, which had just been released in the States. Strangely enough, I had never been invited to appear in this information network which portrays alternative flavor "Christian" gospel, so I was amazed by the fact they wanted to see me in Rome, with their team that had already been filming for a couple of weeks around Europe. This filming in various locations was part of a larger project that also included Malta and Sardinia, as well as Rome, where they wanted to meet me and some of my close contacts. The *True Legends Documentary series* is actually a series of documentaries created in the USA by Steve Quayle and conducted in the field, around the world by Timothy Alberino. However, the brief adventure in Rome with *GenSix Productions* and Timothy Alberino, originally part of a project focusing on certain mysteries hidden by the Vatican as part of a supposed research on the giant bones, turned instead to something more ambitious entitled "Unholy See." In this documentary they for the first time, filmed the place where the Vatican holds their Black Masses, which is the church of **San Lorenzo in Piscibus,** a mysterious place located in the Borgo area near St. Peter's Square. It's inconspicuous as to not attract attention, between two buildings of the twentieth century, on the southern side of Via della Conciliazione, and Piazza Pio XII, with the apse seen from Borgo Santo Spirito and of course a stone's throw from the General of the Jesuits, the infamous "Black Pope," where the occult power of the Vatican resides. Even Pietro Orlandi, brother of Emanuela Orlandi whom I mentioned earlier, during his own research on his missing sister,

FIG. 128 – The well-known researcher and author Zecharia Sitchin and the Italian politician and entrepreneur Gianmario Ferramonti.

heard from various representatives of the Vatican hierarchy that this was the place where the Vatican conducts secret Black Masses under the cover of the night.

Where is the link between the Black Masses and the supposed alien power? Well, this topic I will cover in more detail in my next book *Invisible Master*, but in the meantime we return to my strange adventure with *GenSix Productions* around Rome. Definitely being able to film inside the headquarters of the Jesuits was a great example of how, with a little strategy, you can safely bypass the tight security of the most powerful Intelligence service in the world—The Jesuits! However, another place that surprised the crew of *True Legends* was the The Alchemical Door, also known as the Alchemy Gate or Magic Portal of Piazza Vittorio, which is in effect a kind of "Alchemical Stargate," an extradimensional portal created by the Illuminati of the Golden Rosicrucian tradition and their secret controllers, the Jesuits. The erudite Jesuit Athanasius Kircher, the creator of the first imaginary map of Atlantis published in his *Mundus Subterraneus* in Amsterdam in 1665, was active in the creation of this extradimensional portal with Italian sculptor and architect Gian Lorenzo Bernini, also known as Gianlorenzo or Giovanni Lorenzo (1598 – 1680). Strangely enough, Kircher designed the map where he oriented North down, an interesting fact, even in relation to a possible polar shift as a further reason for the disappearance of Atlantis. Kircher created this map of the mythical Atlantis after a visit to Mentorella, a place near Rome where years ago I went with a camera crew for a documentary transmitted by English web television *Enigma TV*.

All this brings us to speak again of Plato, the great philosopher who I have already spoken in the introduction of this book in relation to the myth of the Cave. Plato was actually the first to speak of the lost civilization of Atlantis in one of his works. Plato writes, *"Before that narrow passage called the Pillars of Hercules, there was an island. And this island was larger than Libya and Asia together, and from it you could move on to other islands, and from these to the mainland opposite. ... In later times, ... earthquakes and extraordinary cataclysms followed, in the space of one day and a bad night ... all in mass sank beneath the earth, and the island of Atlantis similarly swallowed by the sea disappeared."*

We hope we do not end up the same way, disappearing from the face of the earth, swallowed by the seas for tampering with the mood of our creators. Recall that the Atlantean civilization had become a rich and powerful monarchy, it was an island divided into ten zones, each was governed by the son of Poseidon and his descendants. Basically a civilization once again dominated in all respects by the usual demigod aliens, who were however not hiding in disguise as they do today, amongst the earth's aristocratic bloodlines, but ruled this planet openly and at times ruthlessly. This still happened at the time of the pharaohs in Ancient Egypt, until the arrival of the Roman Empire, with the **Caesar-Cleopatra alliance** and the result of this union called **Caesarion** that ended this tradition. This almost forgotten figure (i.e. Cesarion) was the last Pharaoh of Egypt, and the final member of the Ptolemaic dynasty of Egypt. He reigned jointly with his mother Cleopatra VII of Egypt, and he held the position of sole ruler between the death of Cleopatra and the time when his death was ordered by Octavian, who then became the Roman emperor Augustus.

FIG. 129 – Zecharia Sitchin and Gianmario Ferramonti photographed while having dinner.

Going back to Atlantis, initially, the demigods of Atlantis set up a wise and just government, but unfortunately living with mortals corrupted them to the point that Zeus was forced to intervene, sinking the island, and at that point a handful of survivors found themselves having to rebuild past civilizations hoping it will work out better. It never happened and every time terrestrial empires reach the pinnacle of their success, somehow they inevitably plunge, even if only metaphorically, as our present society is on the brink of the end. Since its supposed elite, while descending from the gods (as the tradition of the Illuminati mystery schools teach) has become corrupted to the point of not respecting the criteria and laws of the cosmos, which will lead inevitably to self-destruction over and over again. Let us remember that what Plato describes in *Timaeus* as the island of Atlantis, which was a little larger than Libya (North Africa) and Asia (Anatolia) put together. It's like the possible disappearance one day of the entire state of California, or the entire eastern coast of the United States. Remember that if, for example, the super volcano Yellowstone, a subject of numerous and extensive studies in recent years pointing in this direction, ever erupted, it would implement the same massive change and destruction that happened in Atlantis. According to scientists, volcanoes of this power are real time bombs ready to explode at any time, with all the dramatic consequences that they leave behind. However when I speak of "gods" some "Christian" readers will be turning up their nose for sure, but remember that the gods are nothing more than the angels and demons of Judeo-Christian Tradition seen from a different viewpoint, maybe at times a more human one, which is good, as we are bound to them. Or by an invisible link, and unknown to most people, but still present as an imprint in the DNA of the ruling elite that descend from them. We are basically talking about higher or lower beings who were created before us, good and evil manifestations of the one God of which we ourselves are living images in this dimensional space, which is why, for example, according to the *Zohar: The Book of Splendor,* one of the most cryptic texts of Jewish mysticism, the Kabbalists have identified as many as **72 names of God,** reflected constantly in their secret tradition in the **72 Elders of the synagogue,** which thus reflect the many aspects of God as they are also 72 chosen Illuminati in the Rosicrucian tradition. For Muslims, however, and their mystical brotherhoods names and emanations of God are ninety-nine and 99 Names of Allah, whose mystery of all mysteries rotates around emantion number 100. The particularly sacred values of most religions are hidden to the majority of people, known only to the highest level intiates particularly aware of their

FIG. 130 – Zecharia Sitchin and Gianmario Ferramonti during one of their many meetings for the delivery of top secret "alien" material to take to the Vatican.

long and arduous journey of learning. In the *Quran* it says: *"The most beautiful names belong to Allah. so call on him by them; but shun such men that use profanity in his names: for what they do, they will soon be requitted."* (*Quran*, 7: 180).

This is the End

The Papacy is at the center of a prophecy that mysteriously stops at the dawn of the third millennium of our era. The best-known of the prophecies concerns the Irish Bishop Malachi, who prophecied all the Roman pontiffs who would have succeeded on the throne by his time (twelfth century) to the last. Well after John Paul II (marked by the motto *de Labore Solis*), only two popes remain, that is what is referred to as *Gloria Olivae* (possibly Ratzinger) and *Petrus Romanus* (possibly Pope Francis). For many, including the author of this book, Pope Francis is the last Pope. It would be the end of the world as we have known it, and a new era will be born from the ashes of the old Civilization. I tend to emphasize that with Peter II, that there will not be the end of Christianity, but rather the papal monarchy, and that at the summit of the Church, there will no longer be just a man but a meeting of Illuminati, not necessarily all Christian, as the coming "One World Religion" will change all this.

The Messiah, or Savior of the nations, is the One expected to overcome all this. *"Therefore, stay awake, for you do not know on what day your Lord is coming. But know this, that if the master of the house had known in what part of the night the thief was coming, he would have stayed awake and would not have let his house be broken into. Therefore you also must be ready, for the Son of Man is coming at an hour you do not expect."* (Matthew 24:42-44 English Standard Version). **But who will recognize this "Lord," this authentic "Messiah?"** I doubt that the current members of world religions, led by a Jesuit and relativistic Pope, truly want the return of a character like that, an uncomfortable enemy of the great evil that prevails and dominates in today's society, a spiritual desert without end. However the same people, including the Jesuit Pope, are always quite ready to support the Antichrist on duty, and his minions including the United Nations and so on. The Messiah could risk His immediate end and obviously the persecution of His followers, as well as his family if detected before His time.

Jesus will then come like a thief in the night? Yes, probably, but not for saints but for sinners; not for the children of God but for the children of the devil; not for those in the light, but for those who are in darkness still in search of him. For this it is what the apostle Paul explains when he said to the Saints in Thessalonica: *"Now, brothers and sisters, about times and dates we do not need to write to you, for you know very well that the day of the Lord will come like a thief in the night."* (1 Thessalonians 5:1-2 New International Version).

And although I am convinced that the return of the ultimate messianic figure will happen in our lifetime, the terms and manner of His return will be known only to God and to a limited circle of his initiates, who are the same ones who were with him 2,000 years ago, and as a matter of affinity prodigiously manifest themselves in this incarnation with Him, but that's another story that I hope one day to be able to tell. Remember, also that even if we all belong to different Christian denominations, American Christianity needs to be united in their understanding of these unprecedented times.

A few months ago, in February of 2016, I received a strange email by the aforementioned Timothy Alberino which frankly left me puzzled when I initially read it:

Timothy Alberino <timothyalberino@...........> Feb 28 at 6:12 PM

To

leoyoung1999@yahoo.com

Message body

Leo,

It looks like someone may have attempted to murder my family and I last week by poisoning us while we were sleeping. I suspect it was related to the work we are doing on the Vatican. Have you heard my name or Steve Quayle's name brought up in the Vatican circles in Rome? I believe they are concerned about the content of our upcoming film ... especially the Jesuits. Let me know if you hear anything. Thanks.

Tim Alberino

So what happened to Alberino? Was it revenge by the Vatican mafia for revealing too much to the outside world? The Jesuits certainly did not appreciate my revelations to *GenSix Productions*, but threatening Alberino's life, and that of his family, is certainly something very serious. The day after receiving the mail above, on February 29, 2016, Timothy Alberino and his boss, Steve Quayle, were guests of a program called *The Hagmann & Hagmann Report* where they made some shocking revelations that confirm the contents of the email sent to me one day earlier. This is the description of the interview to **Steve Quayle & Timothy Alberino—Perilous Times are Here on The Hagmann Report 02.29.16** Posted on Youtube by *The Official Hagmann & Hagmann Report:*

In the darkness of last Monday night into early Tuesday morning, Timothy Alberino, his wife and children nearly lost their lives as a result of an incident that remains under investigation. The specific details of this incident, until now, have been kept under wraps as the investigation by law enforcement continued. What occurred in the cold darkness of that night would not only have taken the life of a leading researcher of matters of vital importance to current happenings, but the lives of his wife and children. For a time, their lives hung perilously in the balance, except for the saving intervention of God. Anyone daring to be at the tip of the investigative spear that exposes an agenda of evil and darkness is aware of the perils of such activities, and accepts those perils. Many have come before and met their fates as casualties in a battle between good and evil, light and darkness. It is becoming more obvious today than ever before that the enemies of truth care nothing about the collateral damage of the physical and spiritual war in which we fight. It is no longer the soldiers of truth who are at risk, but their families as well. When evil is about to be exposed, the purveyors of darkness will stop at nothing to keep their evil deeds hidden. A child, a wife, a mother, or anyone in the way are considered expendable. The only recourse for the safety of the truth warrior is to expose the evil deeds with as

FIG. 131 – Cover of True Legends video **The Unholy See** released in June, 2016.

much detail as permissible, but not so much as to compromise the official investigation as well as a concurrent independent investigation. It is through this narrow valley that Timothy Alberino and Steve Quayle will walk, providing details of the incident that nearly took the life of Mr. Alberino and his family. Steve Quayle and Timothy Alberino will discuss not just the incident of last week, but the key investigations that could well be considered as motives behind such nefarious acts—including other events that appeared to culminate early last week. Following the coverage of that incident (from the remainder of the first hour through the third hour), Timothy Alberino will provide new information about his findings from his various trips to South America that includes evidence of a race of giants consistent with Biblical accounts. ... Steve Quayle will also discuss in greater depth the rise of Nazi influence that is serving as a major part of the infrastructure for the globalists in the formation of the new World Order. Both will discuss how each topic intersects to form an ideological foundation for current events. Join Steve Quayle and Tim Alberino as they explain the strange occurrences over the last few weeks that culminated in the near death of Mr. Alberino and his entire family last week—tonight on The Hagmann & Hagmann Report, 7:00-10:00 PM ET. [45]

Something present in what became the documentary called *The Unholy See* must have truly bothered the Vatican elite, to attempt to murder poor Timothy Alberino and his family. Certainly having shown the supposed place where the Vatican has their Black Masses, which is the church of San Lorenzo in Piscibus, a little-known place a stone's throw away from Piazza San Pietro, provoked strong retaliation by the Satanic lobby in the Vatican. We should try to figure out if there are other elements in the documentary that could have led to such a bad reaction by the controllers of the New World Order. We focused also on the previously mentioned "Alchemical Door" or "Magical Door" present in Rome in the gardens of Piazza Vittorio. This little-known place where I went with Alberino and his film crew in December, 2016, is considered of great importance by the Rosicrucians and the Jesuits, and appears to be one of the leading extradimensional portals in the city of Rome. Imagine that even today, often in the middle of the night, hidden from prying eyes, prominent politicians and Church representatives gather at this place where the access is usually restricted by a gate (whose keys are always in the hands of a controller from the municipality of Rome), to perform occult rituals, at times drawing pentagrams on the grassy ground and then removing them in the early hours of the following morning. One night, a dear friend and brother of the *Ordo Illuminatorum Universalis*, found himself reluctantly brought there by a well-known Italian politician for a ritual devised for his re-election, attended by several personalities in the political and military world. Strangely enough, on the same day I went to the "Magical Door" to film with Timothy Alberino, I was actually featured in the Italian newspapers in connection to the *Vatileaks 2* scandal.[46] (FIG. 133)

Finally I hope that for those people who still believe that I am a "fake" or a charlatan, that the first three volumes of my *Confessions*, and all the work done in recent years with documentarists like Alberino or Alex Jones have been able to prove the genuinity of my persona with the evidence that I have brought forth since the start of my online *Confessions* in 2006.

FIG. 132 – Count Alfredo Esposito and **Trump** *Tower resident* **George Lombardi,** *a close collaborator with President Donald J. Trump and Gianmario Ferramonti.*

Arcanissima

Before leaving my dear readers, I want to dig a little deeper into one of the biggest secrets of the Illuminati called the **Arcana Arcanorum**. For this reason I have found a clear and essential explanation of its mysteries and secrets, in a brief essay written by a high level French initiate named **Denis LABOURE**.

From Cagliostro to the ARCANA ARCANORUM

By Denis LABOURE

For years, several authors have referred to the existence of the Arcana Arcanorum. Some have done so with full reason of personal acquaintance, such as **Jean Mallinger, Jean Pierre Giudicelli de Cressac-Bachelerie and Michel Monereau**. Others speak without having the least idea of what it was about. In order that the apprentice mason separate the wheat from the chaff, so that he understands that the Order to which he belongs, that is really a Path, I wish to write the following overview.

In 1614, the doctor and **alchemist Michael Maier (1568-1622)** titled his first book *Arcana Arcanissima*. This work was dedicated to the English doctor William Paddy, friend of Robert Fludd. Up to the 18th century, the expression "Arcana Arcanorum" is found in Rosicrucian literature, for example in "The Secret Symbols of Altona," published in 1785 and 1788. 'Til the end of 18th century, the expression

---

46   http://www.dagospia.com/rubrica-29/cronache/vatileaks-caciara-che-cosa-cercavano-corvi-benotti-lanino-114286.htm ✝ Archived 11th January, 2017.

FIG. 133 – Article by Giacomo Amadori published by the Italian newspaper Libero on the 2nd of December, 2016 about the involvement of the author in the Vatileaks 2 affair.

Arcana Arcanorum designates materials (teachings and rituals) from which Cagliostro would draw in the course of his numerous journeys amongst the initiatic Orders of Europe. His teaching do not evoke the **Arcana Arcanorum**, but the **Secreto Secretorum** (the Secret of Secrets), to which it is similar. Taking into account the secrecy which surrounds these practices, examination of the teachings of Cagliostro constitutes the best possible approach to the study of the contents of the Arcana Arcanorum such as they were in this era. teachings and rituals descended from these materials are revealed at the summit of several Orders, under diverse forms, more or less complete. Remitted on October 8, 1816 to the Grand Orient of France, an abridgement of the last four degrees of the rite of Misraim are presented November 20 1816 to the five members of an examination committee. Written in Italian, it is entitled "Arcana Arcanorum." These Arcana Arcanorum returned to Italy, about 1816, by the Joly brothers, Gabboria and Garcia who had received them in 1813. They were introduced in the Rite of Misraim, in parallel to the last four degrees, of 87e to the 90e, which didn't until then present any operative aspect.

More recently, practices descended from the Arcana Arcanorum were integrated in the fourth and last degree of the Order of Hermes Tres-Megistus (O.H.T.M.), founded in 1927 by Emile Dantinne (1884-1969), Jean Mallinger (1904-1982) and Francois Soetewey.

Up to the 18th century, the adepts meet and worked on similar concluding paths. Let us cite two circles of this type:

* the German Order of the Golden Rosy Cross of the Ancient System and above all the Order of the Initiated Brothers of Asia, on distictly kabbalistic foundations. Cagliostro crossed Germany in 1779 where he participated in various alchemical and theurgical works in the Masonic milieu.

* the School of Naples—a city where Cagliostro stayed in 1783—heiress to Chaldean, Egyptian and Pythagorean currents. Its materials appear to have been Hebraic << Kabalistics>> 'til the 18th century.

These circles of adepts involved themselves in the study of three distinct domains, but in permanent interrelation, for each contributes to the realization of the other two:

A theurgic system of invocation of the Holy Guardian Angel or of a plurality of angels. The invocations of the eon guide and those of four, seven, nine angels come down to us from this time.

Practice of metallic alchemy in the laboratory. The texts that were given to me to consult, work with antimony.

Practice of internal alchemies, using the processes and substantial qualities of the physical body considered as an athanor, this "oven of constant temperature of the alchemists." Every element, every stage of metallic alchemy finds its correspondences in the body of the adept. This affects a permanent way of Return between the exterior Work and the interior Work.

The Arcana Arcanorum insists on theurgy, considered as a key opening for the initiate in the way to the practice of metallic and internal alchemies to which they are only an introduction. They suggest a technique of making contact with the eon guides who relay to him the unveiled secrets of internal alchemy.

And now let's talk about THE EVOCATION OF ANGELS:

The seventy two returned all happy, saying: "Lord, as the demons we are submitted in your name!" He said to them: "Now that I have given you the power of trampling underfoot snakes, scorpions, and all the power of the Enemy, nothing will harm you. However don't rejoice at this, that the spirits are submitted to you; but rejoice that your names are written in the heavens." Luke 9, 20.

That which is named the "first quarantine" is described in the catechism of Master of the the Egyptian Rite. There, Cagliostro reveals the means which culminates in the retirement of forty days "in order to succeed in regenerating the degenerate man." At the end of this confinement, **"I Am Who I Am,"** words which, according to the Bible, are those of God to Moses, from the burning bush. Retiring in a three-storied pavilion called Sion, constructed according to architecturally precise prescriptions, he will deliver himself to long hours of meditation, to works having for their goal preparation of the sacred pentagon, and from the thirty third to the fortieth day will communicate with the Angels. He will have at this time acquired infinite knowledge embracing the past, the present and the future and "his power will be immense." After thirty three days, he begins to receive the favor of visible communications with the seven primordial angels and to know the seals and the numbers of these immortal Entities. "After the fortieth day, he receives the first pentagon, which is the virgin paper on which the primordial angels placed their numbers and their seals" thus that seven "secondary pentagons" on whom "only seven angels have placed its seal." By the pentagons, he "orders the immortals in the name of God" with the "effect of obliging or ordering the aerial spirits, and of doing many marvels and of miracles." This constitutes the theurgic ritual. According to Cagliostro, its goal is "obtaining the Pentagon and becoming morally perfect."

We again find the origin of such a path in the Masonic system of the Flaming Star of Tschoudi and in the rituals of the Golden Rosy Cross. The Golden Rosy Cross itself received the evocation of seven primordial angels or Holy Guardian Angel, from more ancient sources. For the evocation of the Holy Guardian Angel, the sacred magic, better known under the name of the *Book of Abramelin the Mage,* is an important antecedent. The books which compose the "forbidden work of Cornelius Agrippa"—explicitly cited by Cagliostro in the first quarantine—is also of the **15th century**. However, the origins of the theurgy and the evocations of the angels are more ancient. They go back also to the XV century, with the works of Pelagius, the hermit of Majorca whose Anacrise was republished by Robert Amadou; to the XIVe century with Pierre of Abano; to the first centuries of the Christian era with the Chaldean Oracles, assigned to a certain Julien called "the chaldean" and to his son Julien named "the theurgist." A text such as the Anacrise contains many similar rites to those of Cagliostro. This remark is equally true for a grand number of rituals of the Renaissance. The expression "do many marvels and miracles" is deceptive. It appears useful that the theurgy (as the title of the first quarantine of Cagliostro specifies) serves over all to "become morally perfect." This path rests on the classic pattern of death and of rebirth. It implies a process by which the initiate dies to the darkness in which humanity fell in order to be born again to a superior life. This "perfection" could be obtained by the performance of rites where the symbolism is present from the beginning, but is not explained and illustrated other than progressively and in sections as the candidate progresses. It is the model for the ceremonies of the Egyptian Masonry of Cagliostro which caused the birth of many so-called "Egyptian" Masonic rites. All these rites owe a good share of their rituals and doctrines to Cagliostro. For Cagliostro, a continuity existed between "Egyptian Masonry" and the theurgic rites. The first was only a preparation and a symbolic representation second. The initiate of the Egyptian rite, prepared by his Masonic work, could pass to the theurgic techniques with the feeling of natural continuity.

The relationship between the Arcana Arcanorum and the the Egyptian Rites are ambiguous. A rite such as Misraim was born under the form of a purely kabbalistic system, without the Arcana Arcanorum which were grafted in parallel to its last degrees years later, after their arrival from Italy. So, the 89th degree of the Rite of Misraim suggests the following program: In this degree that one could call the last of the Masonic Rite of Misraim, one is given a developed explanation of the relationships of man with divinity, by the mediation of the celestial spirits. This degree, the most astonishing of all, requires the greatest strength of mind, the greatest purity of morals and the most absolute faith. **The password is Uriel**, the name of one of the chiefs of the celestial legions, who communicates "more easily with man." Later, they were newly lost. Some parties reinstated the Egyptian Rites through other orders. In the first meaning of the term, the Arcana Arcanorum is therefore the theurgical evocation of one or several angels by talismens, seals, pentagons or other techniques. The Arcana Arcanorum revealed in the highest degrees of the initiatic Orders quoted at the beginning of this exposition call attention to this definition, if the same elements of the second quarantine of Cagliostro show through at times. Far from being an end in itself, this evocation marks the beginning of a path. Benefiting from the aid of the Guardian Angel or evoked angels, the initiate undertakes the process of transmutation. This evocation permits the initiate to enter into possession of the key. It remains for him to penetrate the part of being able to use it in the proper way. *"And it came to pass, as he prayed, that the aspect of his face became changed, and his garment, a shining and glistening white."* (Luke 9, 29).

"My little children, of whom I travail in birth again until Christ be formed in you." (Galatians 4, 19).

In descending Sinai, Moses had a rejuvenated face, vivid with light. Cagliostro suggests that after moral (that is to say psychic) regeneration, during which he would have increased his faculties, an initiate is ready to regenerate physically. The final objective of the two quarantines are evoked subtly in the catechism of *Companion in the Egyptian Rite* that he dictated to Saint Saint-Costard; "D. What is the use of and why do I always wear a talare? R. Man being regenerate morally and physically, he regains the great power that the deprivation of his innocence had made him lose. This power procures for him spiritual visions and at first, he recognizes that the physical garment of all mortal consecrated to the Eternal must be the clothes [talare]. A similar one was worn, in all the religions and in all the times, by the those who sacrificed, priests or men devoted to God. It is in the catechism of Mistress of the Egyptian Rite of Adoption that this program of forty days retirement figures, inspired by the one that Moses made on the Sinai on leaving Egypt, for regeneration and physical immortality. During this second quarantine which had to be repeated every fifty years, the adept attempts to become physically and no longer only morally perfect. Accompanied by a friend, the candidate will shut himself up in a house in the countryside having a room whose windows are to the south. The operation must begin in the full moon of May; during the first sixteen days the food will consist only of light soups and tender plants and the patient will always leave the table a little hungry. The initiate will drink the May dew, collected from sprouting wheat on pure and white linen. He will begin the meal with a large glass of dew and will finish it with a biscuit or a simple crust of bread. The seventeenth day, at sunrise, the candidate for regeneration must extract a palette of blood, that is to say a light blood-letting. Starting from this day, he will take some white drops of balm of azoth, six in the morning and six in the evening, and increasing the dose two drops by day until the thirty second. The thirty-third day, after the same regime, he will remain in bed until the end of the quarantine. He will take a grain of Materia Prima. On first wakening, after bleeding himself, he will absorb a first grain of universal medicine, he will repeat this the following days. After an unconsciousness of three hours, then convulsions, perspirations and considerable evacuations, he will change the bed linen. He will then eat some beef consomme which has had the fat removed, seasoned with refreshing and laxative plants. The following day he takes the second grain of universal medicine. The day after, he will take a tepid bath. The thirty sixth day, the third and last grain of universal medicine. A deep sleep will follow. The hair, teeth, the nails and skin will blacken and be renewed. The thirty-eighth day, bath with the above mentioned aromatic herbs. The thirty ninth day, he will swallow, in two spoonfuls of red wine, ten drops of the elixir of Acharat. The fortieth day, he will return home rejuvenated and perfectly recreated. Thanks to the strengths thus acquired, the regenerated man will be able to propagate the truth, annihilate vice, destroy idolatry and spread the glory of the Eternal."

What does this apparent dark text teach us? In springtime, during the full moon of May, the initiate isolates himself physically and psychologically for the purpose of undertaking its operation, the first arcana of internal alchemies. He submits to a regime whose object is the purification of his organism by the means then known: a particular food diet; bleeding; pure water; pure baths; and sweatings. Then he begins the absorption of the Materia Prima which is here, neither cinnabar nor potash! It is perhaps the Materia Prima about which Cyliani speaks centuries later, in *Hermes Unveiled*. The absorbed substance is dissolved by this oven, this source of continuous fire that is the body. Just as the body of Hiram was in an advanced state of putrefaction when he was revived, the materials of the Great Work must be dissolved (solve), decomposed in order to liberate their power. So that the substance delivers its essence, beginning from the seventeenth day when the initiate ingests drops of balm of azoth, a mixture of sulfur and of mercury (neither common sulfur or mercury), intimately and inseparably united, which comprise philosophical mercury. Thus rid of its coarse envelope, the obtained essence is assimilated by the blood. From that moment, it weaves and nourishes the construction (Coagula) of a particular incorruptible body, the soma psychikon, the golden wedding garment which replaces the tunic of slavery that Adam was clothed since the fall. This type of path will appear completely incongruous to the contemporary Freemason cut off from the hermetic sources of his Order. He knows that his lodge is a society in miniature, a picture of the outside society. But who has told him that it was also the reproduction of human microcosm? Like in a manner to Egyptian or Hindu temples, or cathedrals, it reproduces the head, arms, legs and all the organs of body. The entrance and the departure of the initiates, the position and the movements of the officers teach us the procedures of internal alchemy.

A method of rejuvenation which preceded Cagliostro is contained in the *Thesauro-rum thesaurus*, a complex manual used by the Golden Rosy Cross, dated 1580, but certainly created more recently. Under the title *How one uses Magic in order to change their nature and become young again*, one reads very similar prescriptions to those of Cagliostro, often almost identical. The two rituals describe a magic retirement of forty days in very similar terms. The German text requires taking the **Lapis Medicilanis Macrocosmi**, obtained by laboratory alchemy which formulated the use of earth and drops of rain, but suggests that one uses rainwater more easily. According to the German Thesaurus, it is necessary to add a "stone of the philosophers" obtained at the start by the distillation of his own blood—we found a similar reference to blood with Cagliostro. Cagliostro and Thesaurus refer to **"grains of Materia Prima."** These formulas are used in order to recover lost youth, but appear very perilous. They testify that the medical aspect is inalienable of this action, to the benfit of oneself and of others. The ancient Rose Cross practiced hermetic medicine. The people defended Cagliostro by recognizing his devotion towards the sick. The objective of the Hermetic and Magic Fraternity of Myriam was the application of powers that the pupil could acquire for the recovery of others. The evocation of angels glimpsed in the first chapter raises an "external way" and the conquest of immortality in the second chapter suggests an "internal way." The evocation of angels is a procedure of calling on and making contact with outside Intelligences when the conquest of the immortality opens to the interior of the operator. The calling of angels without internal prolongation will satisfy the curiosity of the apprentice mage, but it will lead to an embittered agnosticism. To convince oneself it is sufficient to keep intimately close to those occultists at the end of their career who thought that Magic was sufficient in itself.

Inversely, too many scholarly alchemists have collected the most sophisticated procedures without arriving at how to make them work, then the light emanates from more ignorant apprentices whose heart is opened. The Spirit blows where it will, and it is neither secular magic nor alchemy. The natural exercises of the arcanas are practiced in a religious setting, within an operating myth—in the most noble sense of term. By this myth, the candidate is focused toward his ideal and quiets his mind, which H. P. Blavatsky called "the great murderer of the Real." Take the example of Christianity, where prayer and liturgy teach the neophyte to control his capricious and lunatic mood. "The faithful is sad, throttled by worries of money, a sick person: he comes to Easter and it is necessary for him to sing the Resurrection. He is happy to be alive, the heart full of joy: it is Good Friday and it is necessary for him to sing hymns before God crucified by men. Entering in the liturgical rhythm, he is to get used to no longer living one's own small myth evolving according to its impressions, but to live as the Unique Man—the Second Adam—to rejoice and to cry with humanity. When the mind is quiet, the heart opens. The myth, in the midst of which the alchemist operates, has for its object the encouragement of this opening, this breathing of the heart. The alchemists knew how to be Christian, Muslims or Hindu while not identifying with the myth amidst which they operated. The adept knows how to recognize that a myth functions, but he is not conceited enough to imagine that only his myth functions. **The distinctions such as the "internal way," or the "external way" are convenient, but are too rigid**. On one hand, no result in the evocation of the angels can be obtained without the acquisition of a particular interior attitude. On the other hand, the conquest of immortality will conduct the neophyte to disaster if the angel neither remains nor guides. Let us simply say that, in this work, and at the core of

those of the same charac-
ter, one comes and goes
unceasingly operating be-
tween Mage—or priest—
and alchemist. [47]

Explaining the Magical Door

I nvolved in the
creation of the Al-
chemical/Magical door
(FIG. 134) was one Atha-
nasius Kircher, a close
collaborator and mentor
to Queen Christina of
Sweden (1626 – 1689),
who along with him was
a key figure of the Illuminati in the mid-17th cen-

FIG. 134 – The "Alchemical Door" in Rome's Piazza Vittorio is considered an important extradimensional portal by the Illuminati sectarian network.

tury. Queen Christina was a person of great charisma and intelligence, that was more influential than any other female figure in the history of the occult. It is worth dwelling for
a moment on her figure, given her importance for subsequent periods. Christina was also
a generous spendthrift, and lived apparently in debt, but managed nevertheless to leave a
legacy to the Church with her priceless art collections. But in secret the Queen was linked
to a hidden chain of Illuminati and alchemists that united the greatest figures of the time
devoted to the *Great Work*. Among those Illuminati close to the Queen was Massimiliano Palombara, Marquis of Pietraforte (1614 – 1685), esteemed creator of the famous
Magical Door of Rome, now present in Piazza Vittorio. Some say the aforementioned
Athanasius Kircher secretly worked on it with artist Gian Lorenzo Bernini, with whom
Kircher also worked in the construction and design of the much wider known **Fountain
of the Four Rivers** in Piazza Navona. Bernini was, therefore, beyond the romance and
fictional ties to the Illuminati told in Dan Brown's novel *Angels and Demons* (where
we find him mentioned several times), a character with a real link to the Illuminati, i.e.
Kircher and the Golden Rosicrucians of the nobility and their philosophy imbued in
ancient Egyptian and Chaldean wisdom.

This story becomes incredibly dark and mysterious on November 28, 1680, nine years
before the death of Queen Christina of Sweden, when one night in Rome, on the same
day, Massimiliano Palombara, Athanasius Kircher and Bernini died, all three are said to
have became the victims of an alchemical experiment that went badly wrong. But some
say that in reality all three of them were punished for having shown too much of their
secrets in the inscription we find still today on the mysterious door. According to legend,
the same Alchemical/Magical Door was built in 1680 as a celebration of a successful
transmutation that occurred in the alchemical laboratory of Riario palace. (FIG. 135)
It's a shame that the experiment in question seems to have necessitated a triple human
sacrifice from its creators, that brings us to the importance of the number three carved
into the Magical door:

47   See. Denis Labouré, *Les rites maçonniques Égyptiens: de Cagliostro aux arcana arcanorum* (Paris,
FR: CIRER, 2001).

FIG. 135 – Ex-Riario Palace of Christina, Queen of Sweden, today Palazzo Corsini in Rome, Trastevere.

TRIA SUNT MIRABILIA DEUS ET HOMO MATER ET VIRGO TRINUS ET UNUS

There are three wonderful things: God and man, mother and virgin, three and one.

CENTRUM IN TRIGONO CENTRI

The center (is) in the center of the trine.

The experiments were supposedly divided into three operations, each of which generated a particular entity, but the first result was then poured out in the second and the product of this outpouring was then poured out into the third. So the sentence inscribed on the door seems to have a deep initiatory value, tied to the astral plane, and the secrets of this operation that might have eventually opened this extradimensional door to the willing trio. In one of his writings, the Illuminati Ciro Fomisano aka Kremmerz, illustrates the Major Arcana of the Tarot, mentioning the initiatic paths that correspond to the Kabalistic forms, which he relates to the Magical Door and what he defines as "Piromagia," namely that state of fire (**in greek *Pira* means fire**) **as a pyramid,** which is exalted to the pure love that opens the perception of a super-sensible world described so well by the Marquis of Palombara who commissioned the Alchemical/Magical Door, and was a member of the Rosicrucians, which in the Western tradition perhaps reflect the pure intentions of privileged contact with the Invisible Masters. Timothy Alberino ended his documentary filming my speech at the Magical Door in Piazza Vittorio, the "Stargate" of my beloved city Rome. The city where I was born in 1970, and where back in 1993, I started my fantastic adventure of discovery and awareness of the Kingdom of God, that brought me for fifteen years around the world before my return to Rome in the middle of 2008, conscious of my new mission, to write this trilogy. In fact, it took me three years to put together the basis of this work, and three more years to translate them into English, with the help of my wife Christy. I feel fully satisfied and ready to introduce to you my next work, *The Invisible Master*, where I will face the theme of the relationship between alien entities, secret societies, and the Vatican-led New World Order.

In this scenario a prime figure has always been Aleister Crowley, who I first encountered on the physical plane at the age of 11, in the form of an edition of *The Book of Thoth*, a volume he wrote on the Tarot, that my grandmother Felicity Mason gave to me at this young age, knowing my early interest for magic and the occult. It included pictures of a 78-card set inspired by his designs and strikingly painted by Lady Frieda Harris. I have included her version of the Masonic Tracing Boards at the start of each volume of my *Confessions*. (FIG. 136) Whilst her work on Aleister Crowley's Thoth tarot deck is well-known, it is not generally realized that Frieda Lady Harris was an active co-mason. This is the branch of masonry which was founded by Madame Blavatsky, Leadbeater and others associated with the

Theosophical Society, that as I have shown you in my Trilogy, was instrumental for the spreading of the New Age virus that deeply permeates our age.

From Straw Man to the New Cornerstone

Today in 2017, three hundred years after the official foundation of Speculative Freemasonry, we are living in a period of absolute distress, due to demonic pacts, and the terrible compromises made by our leaders and their institutions, whether political, military or religious, but we will pray and we will

FIG. 136 – Posters of the Masonic Tracing Boards by Lady Frieda Harris. These posters have their own history. The original paintings were acquired by British Occultists in the 1970's. Around 1976 a few hundred sets of these now very rare posters were printed but unfortunately only a few survive today as posters and are not collected by libraries, and their existence is not recorded in catalogues and bibliographies.

defend ourselves mentally as I taught you earlier. Those of you who are not ready, who tend to remain in the vestibule, who are unable to look beyond the veil of Isis, will perhaps find fun and excitement from my trilogy, but nothing more. Those instead who are lucky enough to interpret it in an initiatic way, will discover in it during the course of time, a true and solid foundation to be passed on to the next generations. My brothers and sisters, at this critical time in the future of the human species, remember that all of you are the Salt of the Earth, the Light of the World and the Fire of the Universe, but you need to understand this and act upon it before it is too late. There are only two realms upon this world, one of God in a Natural State of spiritual Life and Self-Existence, and one of the legal state of fiction in a spiritual **death**, also called a *civil life*. What is civil is always artificial. What is artificial must be recreated and renamed into what is legal. And what is legal is that which is opposed to Reality, to Nature, to God, and to Life. This legal state of the pretended death of the spirit in false persona is also called legally *citizenship*, which is why United States citizenships are called "natural persons" in law, and not spiritual persons. When the word nature or natural is recreated and renamed into its legal equivalent, as that which is opposed to the real thing, then that which is legally called "natural" can only ever be that which is an artificial representation thereof. This is the way of fictional things, of a civil, legal, artificial existence, the evidence of which being more than conclusively shown herein to satisfy even the most ardent skeptic, if he or she should dare to challenge the power of the ego so as to finish this work and discover the nature of this false, devilish *id*-entity, also known as the strawman.

The spirit is of life, not death. It is not an after-life, except to say that every human may rise from the dead persona (artificial status) of a legal *existence*. It may surprise the reader to discover that the word "after-life" or any variation thereof, is not written anywhere in the Bible. It may also be a surprise that the only actual concept of a "life after death" comes not from the notion of a physical death of the human body at all, but as the end of Natural

Life itself, and that such an attainment of a Natural, spiritual *Life after Death* is only accomplished by those that wake up from the big lie that is legal fiction. A citizen or member of any fictional thing is a dead form of *existence*. It is the state and status (personification) of a Godless and spiritually-void life. Belief in lies, in artificial persons, places, and things (nouns) and the artificial (legal) laws that control them, is a state of being (entity) that *exists* only in spiritual death, while a spiritual life lives eternally (at all times) and is the only cure for such a legal disease as this. Life only exists in Nature, and can be found nowhere in fiction. Fiction is always temporary, never eternal, for that which is eternal is Self-evident and Self-Existent. Reality needs no proof of man for its ambiguity of eternal (unchangeable) existence. That which is legal is that which is opposed to the essence, force, and Soul of Life. Thus a legal *existence* can only be lived in the realm of "hell;" in the realm of the spiritually dead. Only through the overcoming of any perceived validity and authority of the many artfully "created" marks and signs of fictional person-hood, of Being thus figuratively "born again" from a civil, artificial *life* (false *existence*) into the innocence of our Natural and Original state of Conscious Being (as we are Originally born into God's Nature). **May we break free of the bonds and surety of this legal matrix code which controls every fictional strawman id-entity.** The loss of all fiction, in other words, is the gaining of eternal Life. There is no life after death in this regard, for the death spoken of in the Bible is exclusively referential to the legal fiction, and eternal Life can only be found through the abandonment of all legal marks that cause us to live in the spiritual death of legal fiction. The Word of God is simply the Purest and most harmonious Life possible in Nature (Jehovah) that any human may lead without obstruction, as the Law of Nature personified into the story of Christ in scripture. It is nothing more and nothing less than this—an instruction manual for the untainted (eternal) spiritual Life of every human.[48]

And now, aware of this, some of you may become the living Cornerstones of a New Civilization that is being born out of the ashes of this old one, no longer built on the evil and the lies of this age. I recommend to everyone *The Kingdom of God Is Within You,* by Leo Tolstoy published for the first time in 1893, where he explains all this, and surely it is no coincidence that the Russian side of my family, which was acquired by the second husband of my great-grandmother, was linked by a deep friendship to this great author. He wrote: *"No honest and serious-minded man of our day can help seeing the incompatibility of true Christianity—the doctrine of meekness, forgiveness of injuries, and love—with government, with its pomp, acts of violence, executions, and wars."* His **"love as law of life"** and principles of non-violence, that is based on love for humankind, were deeply embedded in the writings of Tolstoy and influenced people like Ghandi, another great friend of my family, who was even guested in London on one occasion. I know some of these assertions might create wonder, and even disbelief in my story, but if you are serious about knowing the vast history of my family, no problem, I have all the evidence in my family archives, and serious historians will be able to find such evidence if they wish to do so. However I hope in my small way to contribute to the greatness of my family history with my work, and this trilogy in particular, It was written to help humanity change for the better. Because as Jesus unmasked the false religious leaders of his time waging war against hypocrisy and evil, today the mission does not change, and what He said is still our main source of inspiration: *Then you will know the truth, and the truth will set you free.* So what is the secret of Freemasonry? Knowing it, will actually set you free? Well, this is what Aleister Crowley wrote in *The Secret of Freemasonry.* In the instructions he wrote directly to the high degree members of his Order:

48   See. Clint Richardson, *STRAWMAN The real Story of Your Artificial Person*, availble at http://www. strawmanstory.info/

*Now of Him is our Lord the Sun Father, Creator, Preserver and Destroyer, One, Exalted, Perfect, Giver of Life and Death, Vicegerent and Viceregent of Heaven; and upon Earth is His representative the Sacred Eidolon within the Ark of the Covenant of whom even in this place we speak not but in hidden terms, for that He is sacred and secret beyond all that are or may be, the Rod wherein Prometheus brought down Fire from heaven. And either Image and Son of the All-Father undergoeth Death and Resurrection; and the symbols are cognate; and the Feasts of one and the other have been celebrated throughout all recorded time by the initiates of all faiths. And the vulgar, ignorant of this, have mingled the two worships, appointing the times of one and the seasons of the other, the observances of the second and the ordinances of the first in the same ritual; wherefore have minds been darkened and understandings confounded. Thus at Easter is the Crucifixion or Copulation, and nine months later is **the Birth of the Child, which liveth 33 years, being a generation of mankind, and is crucified.** Yet is this coming led with the descent of the Sun below the Equator and His resurrection, and again with the daily agony of the Sun. Now then our Brethren, having the true Keys of all religion; namely that all cults typify either the Mysteries of Lingam and Yoni or of Sol, Luna, and Terra, can for themselves interpret all rites, create new faiths and new feasts, ruling the world in justice and righteousness under the Supreme and Most Holy King X° that is to them Father and God. For this is the arcanum of the Hierophants of old, that in this cult of the Sun in Heaven and of the Phallus on Earth all men can unite, for that these mysteries are reasonable and true, and no man can deny them. This is that which is written "Peace on Earth, Goodwill toward men!" And this is the true and final secret of Freemasonry; this Sun, is it not the Great Architect of the Universe, the Father of the System, the Eidolon of the Macrocosm? And this Phallus, is it not the Great Architect of this other Universe of Man, the Father of the Race, the Eidolon of the Microcosm? Is not this that Truth which is established in the mouth of two witnesses? Wherefore be ye vigilant, **preserving that Kingdom of God which is within you from defilement,** chaste unto your Lord that is Light, Life, Love and Liberty indeed. Also, remember well that in all this instruction no word is wasted; and that by deep and continuous study of the text may ye enlighten your souls. Now then at last are ye indeed initiates of Freemasonry; now at last are ye worthy to rule and govern the Rite in the law of Righteousness and Truth, giving Light, Life, Liberty and Love to all men of full age, free and of good report, that solicit admission to the Lodge.*

The truth is there, and there is no great mystery in the Masonic symbols. They are simple working tools endued with moral teaching, but Crowley's interpretation of the mysteries of the Craft are different, and involve the teachings of the various mystery schools of the Illuminati in the various ages. For this reason, I suggest you study with care the words above, as some of you will learn a lot from them. For three centuries, maybe longer, men have been "exposing" the secrets and mysteries of the Freemasons, and they continue to do so today, but the truth is that the true secret of Freemasonry can not be described in the interpretation of the Masonic teachings, but ultimately in your heart. I hope those "Conspiracy Theorists" out there will finally accept this and move on to a more constructive and intelligent form of criticism towards Freemasonry and the Illuminati, as I tried to do for over a decade now with my work over the internet, and now with my books. Often, unfortunatey, I have become the subject of ridicule and even smear campaigns against my person, but that's part of the game, as only time will tell if I was right in doing all this, as the fundamental truth is that we are all slaves of this system, not only because of our ignorance or incompetence but because of our lack of true will in wanting to turn things around. We should now meditate on the words given as instructions in the first chamber of the ***Mysteries Class*** of the Illuminati:

If everyone, right from the outset, were what sensible men should be, if one could disclose and explain to them the holiness of the cause and the greatness of the plan during their initiation, then many things would be possible. But since everyone hopes, everyone wants to receive, and no one wants to give, since the allure of the hidden is almost the only means of attracting men who would otherwise turn their backs on us after having satisfied their curiosity, or who might even use their knowledge for evil, since we are primarily concerned with the moral education of these often still raw men, and yet everyone hurries, keeps complaining, and becomes impatient about any delays, it is easy to see that effort, patience, persistence, and an overwhelming love of the cause are required here; that the Superiors must be convinced that the cause is a noble one, since otherwise they would not apply their wealth, all their powers, their whole existence, for which they are neither reimbursed nor recognised, but for which they are often repaid with ingratitude. ... I say an overwhelming love of the cause is required so that one does not give up in the middle of the work and turns one's back forever on the endeavour to make people better. To prevent all this, to help where aid is often difficult to give, to accomplish all of this, is what we call the secret art of governing. [49]

I hope within my books you have begun to grasp "the secret art of governing," which is not only the perverse way of todays' rulers, but also something very different based on the true concern of the good side of the Illuminati. Originally even Adam Weishaupt's order was born on good intentions for his Brothers and for the world. Weishaupt advised:

To observe others day and night, to educate them, to come to their aid, to care for them, to instill courage in the fearful, and to incite zeal and activity in the luke warm and the listless, to preach to the unknowing, and to teach them, to raise up the fallen, to strengthen the wavering and the weak, to restrain heated tempers, to forestall disputes or to settle them, to conceal flaws and weaknesses, to be on your guard against the intrusion of the curious and of meddlers, to prevent carelessness, to foster in your men respect towards the Superiors, love and sympathy towards one another, and tolerance towards outsiders—these and more tasks and duties are awaiting you! If you still have the courage to overcome all this, then listen on! Do you know at all what secret alliances are, what their place is in the great chain of events in the world? Do you think they are just an inconsequential, transitory phenomenon? O, my Brother! God and nature, who have arranged all things in the world, great and small, in their proper time and place, use these as means to cause tremendous effects which could otherwise not be achieved. Listen and marvel! All morality is oriented according to this perspective, and the very notions of right and wrong receive their necessary correction from it alone. Here you stand, at the juncture of the past and the future world. One glance into times gone by, and immediately ten thousand locks fall away, opening the gates to the future—prepare yourself to make a fleeting yet bold glance inside. You will behold the unspeakable wealth of God and nature, the humiliation and dignity of man, and the human race in its adolescence if not its childhood, where you believed you would find it in its grey, decrepit age, close to its downfall and disparagement. [50]

The problem is that today's Illuminati elite are completely out of touch with the problems of ordinary people or the proper understanding of God and nature, and their duties towards humankind. Just think of **Meryl Streep**, one of Hollywood's most decorated and

49   Joseph Wages, Reinhard Markner, Jeva Singh-Anand, *The Secret School of Wisdom* (Surrey, England: Lewis Masonic, 2015), pp. 254.
50   *Ibid.*, p.255.

revered actresses with three Oscar awards, that while she was accepting the Cecile B DeMille award for lifetime achievement in January 2017, started a nonsense attack against President Donald J. Trump, demonstrating once again the loyalty of Hollywood's elite towards mondialism and the depopulation campaign sponsored by the inbred Illuminati bankers. The Club of Rome, the Bilderberg and even the *New York Times* are all advocating for extreme depopulation. The only remaining question is how far are the global elite willing to go to carry out their depopulation goals? Will they go as far as to kill Donald J. Trump? Prominent Russian TV host and journalist Dmitry Kisiliov warned that the elite "may kill" Donald Trump because of his desire to build better relations with Moscow. [51] Let's remember that George Soros and other rich liberals who spent tens of millions of dollars trying to elect Hillary Clinton, gathered in Washington for a three-day, closed door meeting to retool the big-money left to fight back against

FIG. 137 – The author next to Lucifer in St. Benedict's Cave (Sacro Speco) in Subiaco near Rome (Italy), the place where the Vatican Illuminati worship this alien entity, but whom the Illuminati consider different from Satan.

Donald Trump in November, 2016. These evil doers from the elite of the New World Order will stop at nothing to get back in power. So We the People, have to be very careful of their sabotage projects during Trump's presidency, that as we all know will bring us all the way to **2020.** The year when a full on war will problably erupt worldwide between the two factions of the New World Order for world domination. The one close to God, with Christian and Jewish values at the core represented by Trump, the other instead, the progressive and liberal one, slaves of Satan and secretly in bed with their supposed Islamic enemies, who are their sponsors. In all this, former President Barack Obama will not disappear, unfortunately, and will actually gather even more influence in liberal circles in the upcoming years, before eventually reappearing on the world stage thanks to that dangerous club of criminals from the elite called the United Nations. I have described for you in Volume II of my *Confessions* the corruption of the UN, which is linked since its origins to the **Rockefeller family.**

In this context, one of the most dangerous figures of today is **Dave Spencer, fifth-generation Rockefeller,** who was raised on the practical standards of what used to be known as Rockefeller Republicanism, founded in recent years. *Practically Republican* is a forum where George Soros can promote his evil agenda in the Republican field. Spencer promotes what he defined as "a national college program that brings together diverse groups of socially minded Republicans, Democrats and Independents, to converse, brainstorm and resolve

51   See. http://www.infowars.com/putin-appointed-tv-host-they-may-kill-donald-trump/ ‡ Archived 11th January, 2017.

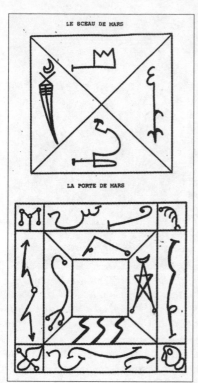

FIG. 138 – Magical seal used to open extradimensional gates for beings from the planet Mars, allegedly drawn by Remi Boyer and Jean-Pierre Giudicelli de Cressac Bachelerie.

problems based on issues, rather than affiliations." [52] However, beware of this seemingly innocent bipartisan project that is born to sabotage and manipulate the democratic structure of the USA, and undermine once again the will of the American people, who have decided to vote for President Trump. This person, who some of you for a number of reasons may dislike, is actually, believe it or not, the last opportunity we have to fight the current mafia heading the New World Order, so please give him a chance.

Trilogy Conclusion

I began this volume with the allegory of Plato's Cave, and I return to it in closing. In this ancient myth we learn the faults of the human story, and the limits of humankind. In it, Plato wishes to represent the history of man that is freed from the bondage of darkness and ignorance. The human mind develops a speculative process that is strongly influenced by the shadows, which are in reality our human experience. Only in the next step, by going beyond this stage, can we contemplate the highest and most sublime reality outside the cave; the sun, which represents the "Truth." Well, there are many ways to interpret the concept of "TRUTH," But at the close of this book I propose only two interpretations of what I mean by **"Truth"** as follows:

1) **Before interpretation** truth is regarded as the property of Being, for example God is eternal; and this truth is eternal and immutable for us. And it is a truth that continues to be interpreted this way, though no one knows for sure. It is an objective truth that remains so beyond what we can perceive with our senses, so we simply accept it as dogma. This knowledge of the truth, we'll call it, hereinafter, in our discourse, **knowledge of the Absolute**. And this kind of interpretation, by going back to my faded high school memories, was called ONTOLOGICAL INTERPRETATION. For those who don't know what ontology is, it's the philosophical study of the nature of being, becoming, existence or reality, as well as the understanding of the basic categories of being and their relations.

2) **A second aspect** of truth allows us to know things as they are, with an adjustment of our mind to it. It is a subjective sense that expresses OUR TRUTH as we see it through our senses and our experience. And this is a fact always relative, because it is linked to our particular interpretation. This interpretation we call EPISTEMOLOGICAL INTERPRETATION.

Today, we live in a world of shadows, and often we are inclined to take "Truth" from the shadows, so we can make judgments and determine behavior. However, the Masonic initiation opens a road, but not the only one, to exit our cave and leave the shadows, that

FIG. 139 – Masonic Warrant for the reawakening of the Strict Templar Observance issued by the Supreme Council of the Ordo Illuminatorum Universalis—in the photo with Bishop Monsignor Irenaeus (Vitaly Kuzhelnyy), proudly displayed after the Mass for the reawakening of the Rite on March 5, 2016, e.v. Year Ordinis 898.

are our false dogmas, to achieve what man since his inception has always sought, and that is the *truth*. That said, what kind of truth do we seek? It's not something what we can acquire from most modern religions like Scientology or any New Age crap promoted by the New World Order. As we seek ultimately an answer to the great questions that have always haunted man: **"Who am I, where do I come from, where am I going, why life, death, and suffering?"** We seek an answer to the questions that we ask ourselves on the knowledge of the Absolute. The term Absolute denotes unconditioned and/or independence in the strongest sense. It can include or overlap with meanings implied by other concepts such as the infinite, totality, and perfection. In Christian theology, the Absolute is conceived as being synonymous with or an essential attribute of God, and it characterizes other natures of God such as His love, truth, wisdom, existence (omnipresence), knowledge (omniscience), power (omnipotence), and others. Absolute love, for example, denotes an unconditional love as opposed to conditional, limited love. Likewise, the absolute can also be understood as the Ultimate Being, or a characteristic of it, in other religious traditions. [53]

To attain knowledge of the Absolute, man must finally understand the essence of life, the essence of man, the essence of God. However, for us, this knowledge is mostly unattainable during our human existence. Knowledge of the Absolute is, perhaps, the ultimate goal of humanity, however we still live in Plato's Cave. It is today, a technological cave, just watch your average human playing with their smartphone. We live in a civilization that bombards us with images, and sounds. Our life in the average modern city, in reality, is life in a technological cave.

However, in this complex, and at times apocalyptic scenario, the esoteric principles are regaining their value, as, for example, the principles of **freedom, equality, brotherhood, tolerance**. These concepts are in fact, **HUMAN CONCEPTS**, i.e. concepts that help us create a physical world and a more just human society, but at the same time, they are concepts whose exercise helps us on our way towards perfection. To us, the Masonic

FIG. 140 – Image featuring the secret motto of the Christian Rosicrucian Illuminati: **ad rosam per crucem ad crucem per rosam** *"To the rose through the cross. To the cross through the rose."*

initiation has given us the ability to undertake and make this journey, like a man who, suddenly out of the darkness, acquires the ability to see the light. Remember the words: ***Visit the interior of the earth, and purifying it, you will find the hidden stone,*** represented by the acronym **V.I.T.R.I.O.L.**, usually found in the **Chamber of Reflection**; this a small darkened room adjoining the Lodge room, traditionally present in the Ancient and Accepted Scottish Rite, the French Rite, and related jurisdictions, including Co-Masonry. Before the ceremony of initiation, the candidate is placed for a time in the Chamber of Reflection, in order to meditate and consider how Freemasonry is about to change his life. He is given a series of questions to answer. Typically, he is asked his duties to God, his fellow men, and himself. In some lodges he is also asked to make a Will. At the end of this time, he is led to the Temple for initiation. [54]

This is the basic first step for many Freemasons in order to leave the **CAVE WORLD**, a beautiful cave, but still a cave, although now it's a seemingly comfortable technological cave for most people. Brothers and Sisters (Masons and non-Masons), as I consider you as such after reading and understanding my trilogy of truth, be happy and rejoice because after this period of tribulation, the final liberation will be reached after the critical turning point of 2020, and a full on World War. Following all this, for the survivors, we will have the re-birth of a new civilization and a period of prosperity, and awareness for humanity, a period that will last for a thousand years. The thousand years concept appears nowhere in the sixty-six books, 1,189 chapters, 31,173 verses of the Bible, except in one particular passage of great importance where it occurs six times in six consecutive verses. This is the crucial passage to be found in ***Revelation 20:1-6*** (**New International Version**):

And I saw an angel coming down out of heaven, having the key to the Abyss and holding in his hand a great chain. He seized the dragon, that ancient serpent, who is the devil, or Satan, and bound him for a thousand years. He threw him into the Abyss, and locked and sealed it over him, to keep him from deceiving the nations anymore until the thousand years were ended. After that, he must be set free for a short time. I saw thrones on which were seated those who had been given authority to judge. And I saw the souls of those who had been beheaded because of their testimony about Jesus and because of the word of God. They[a] had not worshiped the beast or its image and had not received its mark on their foreheads or their hands. They came to life and reigned with Christ a thousand years. (The rest of the dead did not come to life until the thousand years were ended.) This is the first resurrection. Blessed and holy are those who share in the first res-

FIG. 141 – The author and the most influential and respected Italian Masonic author Aldo A. Mola, member of the Supreme Council of Ancient and Accepted Scottish Rite for Romania, presided by General Bartolomeu Constantin Săvoiu at the Convent (Annual General Meeting) of the Romanian National Grand Lodge – 1880 on the 17th of December, 2016.

urrection. The second death has no power over them, but they will be priests of God and of Christ and will reign with him for a thousand years.

Of course, the famous motto **Know Thyself**, will also help Masons and non-Masons in our introspective journey to rectify ourselves in these critical times. Outside of our personal achievements with our own soul, are we really ready for the sea of change that will take place around us in the coming years? I invite you to prepare, and to inform yourself with this book, and other publications. Knowledge is the greatest weapon we can use against the elite of the New World Order. Is this human "reality" intrinsic to the physical form of the universe, or just a perception, a socially reinforced mass delusion? Ultimately it comes down to what you choose to believe, and your awareness that it is a choice. [55] In the film *Matrix Revolutions* (2003) there is a brilliant conversation between Agent Smith and Neo:

> Agent Smith: *Why, Mr. Anderson? Why do you do it? Why get up? Why keep fighting? Do you believe you're fighting for something? For more than your survival? Can you tell me what it is? Do you even know? Is it freedom? Or truth? Perhaps peace? Yes? No? Could it be for love? Illusions, Mr. Anderson. Vagaries of perception. The temporary constructs of a feeble human intellect trying desperately to justify an existence that is without meaning or purpose. And all of them as artificial as the Matrix itself, although only a human mind could invent something as insipid as love. You must be able to see it, Mr. Anderson. You must know it by now. You can't win. It's pointless to keep fighting. Why, Mr. Anderson? Why? Why do you persist?*
>
> Neo: *Because I choose to.* [56]

55   https://dissention.wordpress.com/2010/01/01/agent-smith-why-do-you-persist/ ‡ Archived 11th January, 2017.

56   http://www.imdb.com/title/tt0242653/quotes ‡ Archived 11th January, 2017.

FIG. 142 – General Bartolomeu Constantin Săvoiu and the author as Sovereign Grand Master The Rite of Strict Observance intervening at the Convent (Annual General Meeting) of the Romanian National Grand Lodge – 1880 on the 17th of December 2016.

At the entrance of **St. Benedict's Cave (Sacro Speco) in Subiaco,** (FIG. 137) where I am writing these last pages, we find the image of Lucifer, the head of the rebel angels, the eternal prisoner of the cave for his sin of pride towards God. Lucifer has another function in Gnostic vision, which is a vision embraced by most Illuminati sects and occult Freemasonry. This is a view of Lucifer as a sort of Prometheus, a hero, who gives us the divine light at the cost of being punished himself. In the end, the gnostics or others, decide to embrace the lost cause of Lucifer for convenience, because he is the dispenser of divine light in a increasingly dark cave. The reliance on Lucifer, unfortunately, facilitates a fall into the clutches of Satan, the enemy and the oppressor overlooking the Satanists and pseudo-Gnostics of today's elite. A group of individuals basically made up of willing puppets of the alien world that manipulate them consciously or unconsciously. This is the big mistake of the caveman of today, believing that Lucifer can be an ally that can facilitate escape from the cave, made impossible by the alien watchers, our Guardians since the beginning of time. Having said that, some Illuminati Grandmasters like **Remi Boyer,** actively work with these alien forces, opening doors in our dimension still to this day. (FIG. 138) This is a subject of great interest that I will write about in detail in my next book, entitled *The Invisible Master*. However, this trilogy concludes with a firm condemnation of Satanism and occultism in general, as in the best tradition of the Strict Templar Observance, the Christian Masonic Rite I have the honor and responsibiltiy to preside over since 2016, (FIG. 139) and the only one to have risked extinction for this unique position in the Masonic world. The Strict Observance was in fact particularly devoted to the reform of Masonry in the 18th century, with special reference to the **elimination of the occult sciences which at the time were widely practiced in many lodges,** and the establishment of cohesion and homogeneity in Masonry through the enforcement of strict discipline, the regulation of functions, etc. [57]

Keep in mind, that the only real guide to find the exit of this **prison planet/cave** for true Freemasons and real initiates (who are obviously not on the dark side), remains always the **Messiah Jesus Christ, our only true Masonic cornerstone.** (FIG. 140) That's why Christian Freemasonry should be in control of this idiotic and dangerous Masonic Network running the New World Order. Today's Craft is in the hands of brainwashed Illuminati sects like the O.T.O., or Scientology, Satanists, New Agers, and Jesuits. For this reason we need to return to our Christian roots, ridding ourselves of this liberal and malig-

57   René le Forestier, *Les Illuminés de Bavière et la franc-maçonnerie allemande*, Paris, 1914, Book 4 Chapter 1, pp. 343-388.

nant Communist cancer that is present at the core of Free-masonry, both in the Grand Orient of France Network, as in the United Grand Lodge of England Network. Especially now that we are celebrating 300 years from the first meeting of the Grand Lodge of London and Westminster, the first Grand lodge in the world. To celebrate this momentous occasion the United Grand Lodge of England is coordinating a series of special events. Instead the World Masonic Christian Alliance will meet in Bucarest, Romania, in June 2017, with another two thousand Masons under the direction of Grand Master **General Bartolomeu Constantin Săvoiu,** (FIGS. 141 and 142) who is not

FIG. 143 – General Grand Hierophant of the Ancient and Primitive Rite of Memphis and Misraim of the Grand Orient of Italy, Giancarlo Seri 33:. 90:.97:.. and the author in Perugia (Italy).

part of a group of "abusive Masons" like Dan TROFIN 33 (Grand Chancellor on Foreign Affairs of the main Romanian Masonic Obbedience working under the patronage of the UGLE). [58] These are Masonic "Brothers" who are losing control of True Freemasonry, in favor of a mild and faded version of the once great Masonic Institution, so let me tell these pompeous idiots that both General Bartolomeu Constantin Săvoiu, and Giancarlo Seri (FIG. 143) cited by Trofin, even if apparently divided in the Masonic world, are both members of the *Ordo Illuminatorum Universalis.* An Opinion by R.W. Bro. Michael A. Delgado, Sr., FPSH Grand CCFC, MWPHGL of Georgia states:

> *Masonic recognition is as complex a study as one can imagine when looking at the overall structure of freemasonry. Even the most ardent student of the Craft will find it difficult at times to fathom the many intricate workings of the recognition process. One would be amazed and probably overwhelmed by the numerous facets of recognition which must be observed by sovereign grand obediences as they relate to treaties of recognition between each other. Recognition may range in scope from full, to partial, to limited in its application; it may include inter-visitation, and even dual membership. The ground rules may differ somewhat from jurisdiction to jurisdiction, but basic to most is: an unfaltering belief in God; the Volume of the Sacred Law (VSL) as an essential part of the furniture of the lodge; prohibition of the discussion of religion and politics in lodge; initiation of only men; and an adherence to the Twenty-five Landmarks of Freemasonry. The list is somewhat more extensive, but it is evident that all of these elements must be satisfied before the recognition process is to take place. I am informed that in many instances the protocol is that the younger of the*

FIG. 144 – Masonic Warrant at the origin of the Ancient Accepted Scottish Rite issued in 1769, by the Grande Loge de France, for The Sovereign Council of Emperors of the East and of the West.

two grand bodies must initiate the recognition request. [59]

In regards to my own mission and my work, I have been at war with the "Regular" Masonic Network headed by the United Grand Lodge of England, for over a decade now, but fraternally, I hope my criticism towards these troubled Brothers has helped them in some way to move from their old dinosaur positions. Pushing them to support a new traditional approach, that is Masonically speaking, in line with the times, and more realistic. Their way of misleading and manipulating history and tradition must end after 300 years of what is basically a colonial British imposition, because it's full of lies, and the UGLE can't pretend they are the Vatican of Freemasonry forcing the U.S. obediences to neglect their recognition to otherwise "Regular" Obediences like the current **Grande Loge de France.** The Grande Loge de France, although never recognized by the United Grand Lodge of England (UGLE), was (briefly) recognized by a few of the Grand Lodges in the United States around the time of the First World War (UGLE and most of the American Grand Lodges currently recognize the Grande Loge Nationale Française instead). How can this be possible if this old Masonic body gave birth to **The Sovereign Council of Emperors of the East and of the West**, Sublime Scottish Mother Lodge of the world, (FIG. 144) of what became later the Ancient and Accepted Scottish Rite? Basically U.S. Freemasons, who as we know have a preference for this Masonic Rite, are forced to neglect part of their history and their links in order to continue the pathetic show directed by the Hannoverians (renamed in 1917 the House of Windsor). Maybe the *God and my right* motto of the Thirty-third Degree of the Ancient and Accepted Scottish Rite, and hence adopted as that also by the Supreme Council of the Rite described in detail in Volume I, should give us a clue.

What more can I say at this point, if not that I am still happy to be part of this Masonic World, even if in a different Family or Network from the majority of mainstream Freemasons, unfortunately compromised by ignorance and Masonic politics. A question however arises, now that Pope Francis will begin his war against Freemasonry because of

59   http://www.thephylaxissociety.com/images/clipart/Lux/Delgadorecognition.pdf ✝ Archived 11th January, 2017.

Messaggio del Santo Padre

The Honorable Donald Trump
President of the United States of America
The White House
Washington, DC

Upon your inauguration as the forty-fifth President of the United States of America, I offer you my cordial good wishes and the assurance of my prayers that Almighty God will grant you wisdom and strength in the exercise of your high office. At a time when our human family is beset by grave humanitarian crises demanding far-sighted and united political responses, I pray that your decisions will be guided by the rich spiritual and ethical values that have shaped the history of the American people and your nation's commitment to the advancement of human dignity and freedom worldwide. Under your leadership, may America's stature continue to be measured above all by its concern for the poor, the outcast and those in need who, like Lazarus, stand before our door. With these sentiments, I ask the Lord to grant you and your family, and all the beloved American people, his blessings of peace, concord and every material and spiritual prosperity.

FRANCISCUS P.P.

FIG. 145 – Pope Francis' message on the day of his inauguration as the 45th President of the United States of America to President Donald J. Trump: "I pray that your decisions will be guided by the rich spiritual and ethical values that have shaped the history of the American people."

President Trump, a war directed to the rebel Freemasons of the Knights of Malta and the Knights of Columbus: ***Will the Knights in question respect their Masonic oath or will their Catholic Faith be hijacked by a Jesuit mondialist Pope?*** U.S. Freemasons are on the verge of an unprecedented crisis that requires another War of Independence, this time against the Vatican, possibly headed by Brother Donald J. Trump. Let's remember what Pope Francis stated to the press as Donald Trump was being sworn in as the 45th President of the United States on the 20th of January 2017, warning against populist leaders, saying to the Spanish newspaper *El Pais,* that Germany came to elect one in 1933, and ended up with Adolf Hitler as its dictator. Pope Francis, who later wrote a friendlier message to President Trump, (FIG. 145) should explain why Himmler used the Jesuits as the model for the SS, since the latter found they had the core elements of absolute obedience. [60]

I would like to thank two figures, even if they are long dead, for their constant inspiration in my literary journey: **Rene Guenon (1886 – 1951) and Julius Evola (1898 – 1974).** And this final quote from **Nikola Tesla:**

Of all the frictional resistances, the one that most retards human movement is ignorance, what Buddha called "The greatest evil in the world." The friction which results from ignorance can reduced only by the spread of knowledge and the unification of the heterogeneous elements of humanity. No effort could be better spent.

Ad maiora, **"Towards greater things"**

Leo Lyon Zagami

60   https://en.wikipedia.org/wiki/Ideology_of_the_SS ‡ Archived 11th January, 2017.

FIG. 146 – John Johnston (c. 1753-1818) watercolor sketch with the Square and Compass the most identifiable symbol of Freemasonry, n.d. Original at American Antiquarian Society, 185 Salisbury St, Worcester, MA 01609-1634.

FIG. 147 – Domenico Macrì Master of Ceremonies of the Grand Orient of Italy, the author, and 33rd degree Elio Sacchetto Intelligence expert and ex P2 leading member during a lodge meeting at the castle of Sorci near Arezzo.

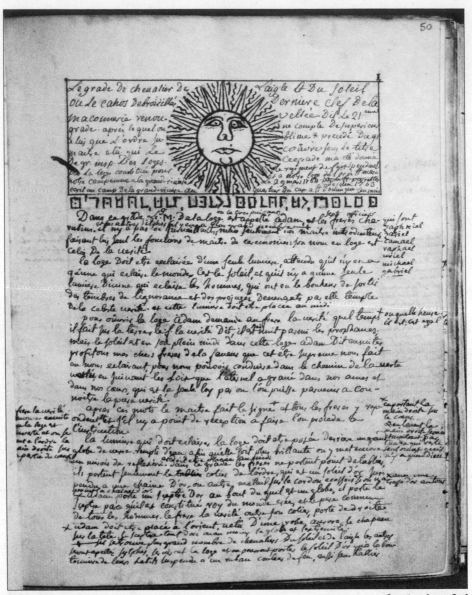

FIG. 148 – *Page extracted from the Santo Domingo Masonic Manuscript of 1764 identified as a major source for Scottish Rite Freemasonry.*

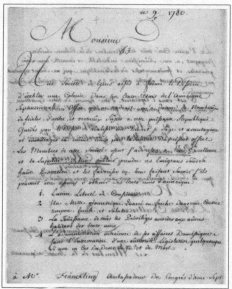

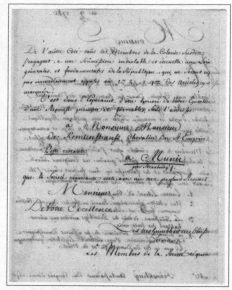

FIG. 149 – A Letter that was sent to Benjamin Franklin on May 9, 1780 from professor Baader, head of the Munich lodge of the Illuminati.

FIG. 150 – Letter that was sent to Benjamin Franklin on May 9, 1780 from professor Baader, head of the Munich lodge of the Illuminati.

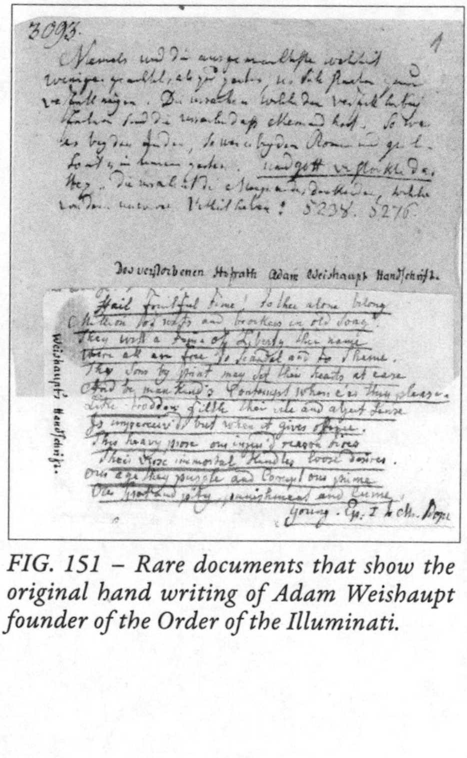

FIG. 151 – Rare documents that show the original hand writing of Adam Weishaupt founder of the Order of the Illuminati.

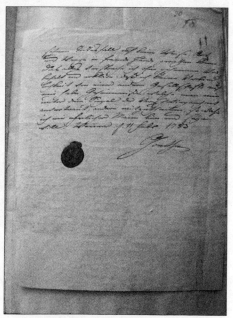

FIG. 152 – Original document showing the oath in the Illuminati signed by Johann Wolfang (von) Goethe while joining the order in February 1783 with the alias "Abaris".

FIG. 153 Alphabet of the Freemasons and Knights Templar Secret Societies.

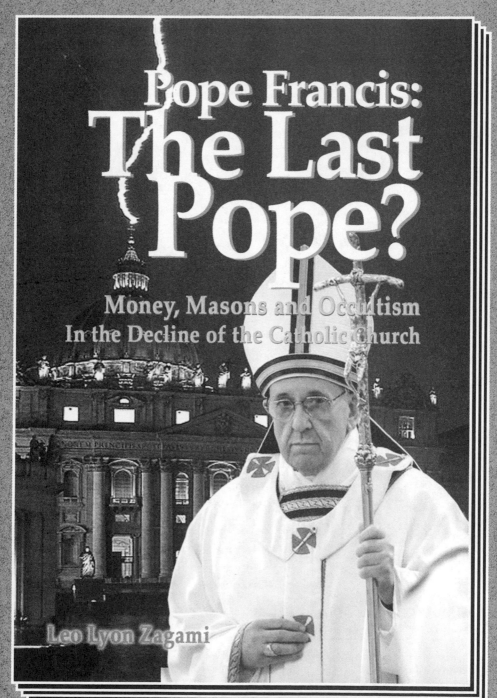

ANOTHER IMPORTANT BOOK BY:
Leo Lyon Zagami

Pope Francis:
The Last
Pope?

Money, Masons and Occultism
In the Decline of the Catholic Church

Leo Lyon Zagami

ISBN: 978-1888729542 • paperback • $16.95

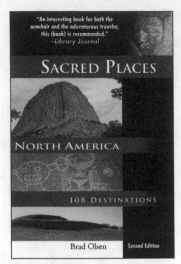
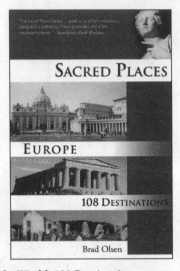
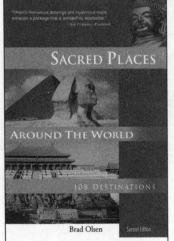
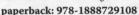

ESOTERIC BOOKS BY CCC PUBLISHING

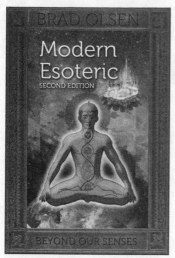

Modern Esoteric: Beyond our Senses

– 2nd EDITION; by Brad Olsen

Organized into three sections (Lifeology, Control and Thrive), *Modern Esoteric: Beyond Our Senses* author Brad Olsen examines the flaws in ancient and modern history, plus explains how esoteric knowledge, conspiracy theories and fringe subjects can be used to help change the dead-end course we humans seem to be blindly running into.

$17.95 :: 480 pages   **paperback: 978-1888729825**

all Ebooks priced at $9.99

Kindle: 978-1888729856
PDF: 978-1888729832
ePub: 978-1888729849

Future Esoteric: The Unseen Realms

– 2nd EDITION

by Brad Olsen

Organized into three sections (Secrets, Cosmos and Utopia), *Future Esoteric: The Unseen Realms* examines the nature of the national security state; looks forward as we enter the promise of a Golden Age; and, explains how esoteric knowledge, the extraterrestrial question, and discovering our true human abilities will lead us into the great awakening of humanity.

$17.95 :: 416 pages   **paperback: 978-1888729788**

all Ebooks priced at $9.99

Kindle: 978-1888729801
PDF: 978-1888729795
ePub: 978-1888729818

The Tribes of Burning Man: How an Experimental City in the Desert is Shaping the New American Counterculture

by Steven T. Jones

The Burning Man Festival has taken on a new character in recent years, with the frontier finally becoming a real city and the many tribes of the event—the fire artists, circus freaks, music lovers, do-gooders, sexual adventurers, grungy builders, and a myriad of other burner collectives—developing an impactful perennial presence in sister cities all over the world.

$17.95 :: 312 pages   **paperback: 978-1888729290**

all Ebooks priced at $9.99

Kindle: 978-1888729443
PDF: 978-1888729450
ePub: 978-1888729436

The Key to Solomon's Key: Is This the Lost Symbol of Masonry?

– 2nd EDITION

by Lon Milo DuQuette

Is King Solomon's story true? Is his account in the Bible to be considered historical fact? Or do myth and tradition hold the key that unlocks mysteries of human consciousness infinitely more astounding than history?

$16.95 :: 256 pages   **paperback: 978-1888729283**

all Ebooks priced at $9.99

Kindle: 978-1888729412
PDF: 978-1888729368
ePub: 978-1888729375

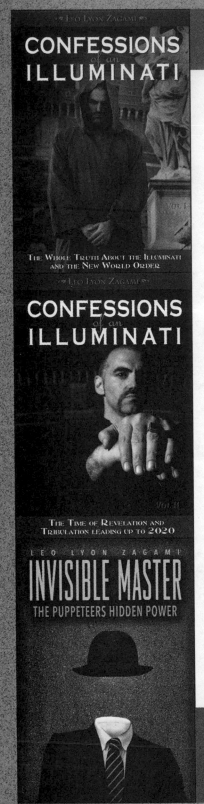